D1365258

Perceptual Development in Children

Perceptual Development in Children

Edited by

ALINE H. KIDD *and* JEANNE L. RIVOIRE

INTERNATIONAL UNIVERSITIES PRESS, INC.

NEW YORK

To Our Children:
Geoff, Liz, Karen, and Kathy

Contributors

LOUISE B. AMES, Ph.D. Director of Research, Gesell Institute of Child Development

R. EBERT Instructor, Pennsylvania State University

DAVID ELKIND, Ph.D. Associate Professor and Director of the Child Study Center, University of Denver

GEORGE ELLMAN, Ph.D. Chief Research Biochemist, The Langley Porter Neuropsychiatric Institute

ROBERT L. FANTZ, Ph.D. Assistant Clinical Professor in Psychology, Western Reserve University

JOHN H. FLAVELL, Ph.D. Associate Professor, University of Rochester

LAWRENCE K. FRANK Lecturer, Massachusetts Institute of Technology

JOSEF E. GARAI, Ph.D. Assistant Professor, Pratt Institute

JOYCE L. GOLDFARB, M.Ed. Research Assistant and Instructor, Houston State Psychiatric Institution

SANFORD GOLDSTONE, Ph.D. Associate Professor, Department of Psychiatry, Baylor University College of Medicine

G. GREENBERG, Ph.D. Psychology Department, Wichita State University

WARD C. HALSTEAD, Ph.D. Professor, University of Chicago College of Medicine

EDNA HEIDBREDER, Ph.D. Professor Emeritus, Wellesley College

JEROME KAGAN, Ph.D. Chairman, Department of Psychology, The Fels Research Institute

ALINE H. KIDD, Ph.D. Assistant Professor, California State College, Los Angeles

R. M. KIDD, B.D. Instructor, La Verne College, California

KENNETH LOVELL, Ph.D. The Institute of Education, The University, Leeds, England

DOROTHEA A. MCCARTHY, Ph.D. Professor, Fordham University; Research Consultant in Differential Diagnosis of Retarded Children, Rutgers University

GARDNER MURPHY, Ph.D. Director of Research, Menninger Foundation

N. H. PRONKO, Ph.D. Professor and Chairman of the Department, Wichita State University

P. M. RENNICK, Ph.D. Neuropsychologist, Menninger Foundation

JEANNE L. RIVOIRE, Ph.D. Director of the Extended Education Department, Pepperdine College.

CHARLES M. SOLLEY, Ph.D. Associate Professor, Wayne State University

M. D. VERNON, Ph.D. Professor, The University, Reading, England

Acknowledgments

We wish to thank the following publishers and individuals:

The American Psychological Association and the authors, R. L. Fantz, J. M. Ordy, and M. S. Udef, for permission to reprint Table 1 (on p. 151 of this volume) from "Maturation of Pattern Vision in Infants during the First Six Months," which appeared in *The Journal of Comparative and Physiological Psychology* (1962, 55, p. 914).

The American Psychological Association and the authors, W. W. Lambert, R. L. Solomon, and P. D. Watson, for permission to reprint Figure 2 (on p. 292 of this volume) from "Reinforcement and Extinction as Factors in Size Estimation," which appeared in *The Journal of Experimental Psychology* (1949, 39, pp. 637-641).

Basic Books, its president Arthur Rosenthal, and the authors, C. M. Solley and G. Murphy, for permission to reprint Table 1 (on pp. 299-300 of this volume) from *Development of the Perceptual World* (New York: Basic Books, 1960).

Contents

Preface

EDNA HEIDBREDER

This is not a definitive book on perceptual development in children. That no such book is to be expected at present is one of the impressions a reader is most likely to receive as he follows the contributors to this volume through the very different paths by which they approach the notoriously difficult problem of perception.

Of late new complexities have appeared in the problem. During the last few decades experiments have been reported as indicating determinants of perception not traditionally regarded as such—affective, motivational, and cultural determinants, to mention a few examples. Partly because of these experiments, and largely because of long-accumulating evidence from clinical and developmental research, many psychologists have become convinced that perception cannot be adequately understood unless it is studied as part of a complex of processes which, though not themselves primarily perceptual in function, may nevertheless significantly affect the course and content of perceptual processes and achievements.

It is from this point of view that the contributions to this book have been assembled. Taken together, they present perceptual development as one of many currents in a stream of interdependent processes, among which are affective, social, and conceptual activities, and the acquisition of such important skills as speech and other forms of social communica-

xiii

tion and participation. The reader's attention is in fact invited to a wide variety of topics, ranging from the physiological conditions of perception to the enculturation of the individual; from the kinds of visual stimuli upon which an infant is most likely to fix his gaze, to the development of religious, scientific, and philosophical concepts.

The editors make no attempt to present these contributions as falling into a single, coherent pattern, though they do sometimes guide the reader from one to another part of the forest. Neither do they try to minimize the complexities and obscurities of the situation in which a student of perceptual development finds himself. Instead they plunge him into the uncertainties and intricacies of ongoing research. That they do so is greatly to the reader's advantage, for they thereby enable him to see the central problem of the book as it looks to different investigators who are actively at work on it from their different points of view, and who see the research on it, including their own, as still far from complete. Essentially the book presents a picture of research now in progress.

Foreword

Historically, perception was the only problem subsumed under experimental psychology. Although the field has expanded tremendously, the organization of information about the environment received through the sense organs and the meanings attached by human beings to such data remains a major problem for behavioral scientists. It has been demonstrated that perception involves symbolic and emotional processes as well as receptor processes, that what is perceived depends upon needs and motivations, upon learned ways of behaving and thinking, and upon selection from the environment of details which are to be perceived. Any consideration of the topic of perception must include the developmental aspects as well as adult responses to perceptual stimuli and theoretical formulations regarding the causation of developmental changes in addition to hypotheses relating to adult perceptual behavior.

In preparation for teaching courses in the experimental psychology of perception and in developmental psychology, we located several excellent collections of readings in adult perception. We found many texts devoted to child development. However, the sections of these books relating to perception tended to be brief and, often, incomplete. The present volume represents an attempt to bring together material relating to the developmental aspects of perception. In planning this book, we have defined perception broadly in order to include as many of the important and influential variables as possible. Perception, we believe, cannot be totally separated from physiology, cognition, personality, and the social framework in which percepts arise, because such a separation reduces the concept of perception to mere sensation and fails to explain in any way sensitivity and responsiveness to the environment.

This book has been divided into six major sections: Physiological Factors in the Development of Perception, Theories of Perception, Visual and Auditory Perception, Social Aspects of Perception, Affective Aspects of Perception, and Cognitive Aspects of Perception. Each section contains at least one review of the literature. Such reviews serve a triple purpose. They indicate what observation or research has been done in the past and, more importantly, they outline the areas in which further work is urgently needed. Occasionally, also, a review of the literature can suggest to a reader a new theoretical framework.

In each of the areas, some indications have been given of research in progress. In the physiological and affective sections, these have been included in the reviews by the researchers themselves. In the other four parts of the book, separate chapters have been devoted to research. Such reports have always proved to be stimulating to both students and other researchers in the field, suggesting new research designs, additional theoretical implications, effective techniques of studying phenomena, and, occasionally, demonstrating the excitement inherent, for so many of us, in research.

Finally, wherever possible, theoretical formulations are given. In the area of developmental psychology, the research literature has long concentrated on the developmental-descriptive approach, indicating a variety of different kinds of changes with age in performance on assigned tasks. That such changes do occur cannot be doubted. However, at present it appears more important for research to be centered on hypothetical mechanisms and theoretical problems relating to why the developmental changes occur as they do than to describe the changes as a function of increasing chronological age. Ideally, then, this book should emphasize theoretical formulations, but theory in this area is still limited in scope, in predictiveness, and in validity. An attempt has been made to include present theory, but a cohesive, predictive theory of the development of perception is a future ideal rather than a present reality.

We have made as few changes in the writing styles of the contributors as possible. The book is intended as a supplement to developmental and experimental texts rather than as a text itself. It therefore does not require the uniformity of such a text. Additionally, we believe that differences in style and phrasing increase the freshness and interest of the book. It has been our experience that students are stimulated and excited by "knowing" an author and that the feeling of acquaintance with a contributor is increased by allowing his style to remain his own.

We want to acknowledge our debts to the many people without whom this book could not have been completed. We are particularly grateful to John McKee, Ph.D. for his critical reading of some of the chapters, to W. L. Faust, Ph.D., Mary Schneidler, Ph.D., and P. C. Vitz, Ph. D. for their helpful suggestions at different stages in the preparation of the manuscript. We wish to thank Robert M. Kidd, B. D., who, as editorial assistant, gave unstintingly of his time. His suggestions added immeasurably to this book. Finally, we are grateful to all of our students on whom the chapters have been "class tested" for their suggestions and help in clarifying some parts of the total book.

Aline H. Kidd
Jeanne L. Rivoire

Introduction

There are at least three things that will strongly commend this book to progressive teachers of child psychology, and to those who venture, as students, into this challenging field:

1. One can find here the world of the child, the world in which the child grows, perceives, thinks, feels, and strives. The data are selected in terms of their appeal to sober and cautious scientists; yet they are not desiccated and flattened down into movements executed in space and time; they help the reader to apprehend what it *means,* what it *feels like,* to be a child. The area sampled is immense, all the way from auditory threshold determinations to the child's struggle toward apprehension of the world's religious and moral implications. There is a moving searchlight turned upon the commanding place of perceptual-cognitive development in the course of childhood experience.

2. The editors and the authors try to see the world of perception and cognition as an aspect of a larger world comprising the whole existence of the child in the wholeness of his personality and in the wholeness of his place in the world. "How can one separate perception sharply from the rest of experience?" The answer is that one does not try to.

3. The investigators cited, and those who evaluate their investigations, are first-class psychologists who have themselves trodden the difficult road into this new region, and for this reason they know how little is really

known, how much remains to be done. What we have before us here today is only a tiny fragment of a systematic child psychology. Because their cautious presentations constantly draw our attention to gaps, contradictions, and obscurities, they show how great the task will be to bring it all into order. This is one reason why the tone of the book is progressive; it looks forward to the knowledge of childhood which will follow when the present tentative efforts move toward completion.

PART I

Physiological Factors in the Development of Perception

Because we perceive only what our sense organs, nervous system, and chemical activities permit us to experience, it becomes obvious that neurological and biochemical factors underlie all perception. Anatomical details or physiological descriptions of structural factors in perception are readily available in the perceptual, anatomical, and physiological texts; therefore acquaintance with such literature is assumed by the authors of the two chapters in this section.

Halstead reports an experiment which points to the interactions among neurological deficits, environmental handicaps, and perceptual-cognitive development. The experimental evidence raises more questions than it answers, but nowhere in this book is the need for future research more dramatically demonstrated nor the directions which future research can take more clearly pointed out.

Chapter 2 presents the biochemistry at the synapses as a potential substratum for perception. Because terms common to biochemistry are employed without clear definition by Dr. Ellman, a glossary designed for psychologists is presented here.

The editors are particularly grateful to Thomas F. Sherman, Ph.D., Zoology Department, Pomona College, who provided this glossary.

1

GLOSSARY OF BIOCHEMICAL TERMS

Acetylcholine. A compound considered to be of great importance in synaptic transmission in the central nervous system. It can be formed from acetic acid (activated) and choline.

Acetylcholinesterase. An enzyme capable of destroying the activity of acetylcholine by catalyzing its hydrolysis to acetic acid and choline.

Adenosinediphosphate (ADP). A coenzyme of importance in many biological reactions. See adenosinetriphosphate below.

Adenosinetriphosphate (ATP). A coenzyme of importance in many reactions involving the transfer from one molecule to another of a chemical group of high potential energy. This group is the high energy phosphate bond, which may be transferred from ATP to another molecule, leaving ADP and a phosphorylated molecule of higher potential energy than the previous substance.

Adrenergic. A term applied to any nerve ending at which, during activity, noradrenalin (norepinephrine) is liberated.

Catecholamine. A compound such as epinephrine or norepinephrine which contains an orthodihydroxybenzyl group and an amino group.

Choline. A compound from which acetylcholine can be formed by reaction with an activated acetyl group.

Choline acetylase. An enzyme capable of catalyzing the formation of acetylcholine from acetic acid (activated) and choline.

Cholinergic. A term applied to any nerve ending at which, during activity, acetylcholine is liberated.

CoA (Coenzyme A). A coenzyme of importance in enzyme reactions involving the transfer of acetyl groups from one molecule to another. CoA is a necessary cofactor in the formation of acetylcholine from choline.

Coenzyme. A compound of relatively small molecular weight which is essential for a particular enzyme-catalyzed reaction. For example, coenzyme A is a necessary cofactor for the enzyme choline acetylase.

Dihydroxyphenylalanine. A compound formed by the oxidation of tyrosine. Dihydroxyphenylalanine can be modified to form norepinephrine and epinephrine.

Histone. A protein found in close association with nucleic acid. Histones contain relatively large amounts of the basic amino acids, and are particularly prevalent in glandular tissue.

Isozymes. Two or more enzymes which are identical or almost identical in catalytic activity (including substrate specificity), but which can nevertheless be distinguished by physicochemical methods, such as by chromatographic or electrophoretic behavior.

Methionine. One of the eight amino acids which are essential for adult human nutrition.

Norepinephrine (Noradrenalin). A substance liberated by adrenergic nerve endings as well as by the adrenal gland. Its physiological action is essentially the same as that of epinephrine (adrenalin).

Peptide. A compound made up of several amino acids.

Phenylalanine. One of the essential amino acids.

Puromycin. An antibiotic which inhibits the synthesis of protein in many tissues.

Ribosome. A small organelle within a cell. Ribosomes contain ribonucleic acid and protein, and are thought to be active centers of protein synthesis.

RNA (Ribonucleic acid). An acidic compound containing D-ribose, phosphate, and guanine, adenine, cytosine, and uracil. It is found in the nucleus; in mitochondria; as a soluble constituent of the cytoplasm (S-RNA), and especially in the ribosomes. It plays an important role in protein synthesis.

Tryptophane. One of the essential amino acids.

Tyrosine. An amino acid. Also known as hydroxyphenylalanine, it can be a precursor of dihydroxyphenylalanine, and of norepinephrine and epinephrine.

Valine. One of the essential amino acids.

CHAPTER 1

Perceptual–Cognitive Disorders in Children

WARD C. HALSTEAD

PHILLIP M. RENNICK

In the last few decades (Chapman and Wolff, 1959; Shure and Halstead, 1958; Reitan, 1955a; Halstead, 1938, 1939, 1940, 1947) it has been possible to develop neuropsychological tests that have proved to be valid, reliable, and reasonably sensitive in detecting in adults the presence of various types of brain dysfunction or impairment. Such tests are essentially nonverbal, and have given considerable promise of being culture-fair. An assessment method has been evolved which exploits for a variety of scientific purposes the objective and quantitative data yielded by these instruments.

An important use of these tests is in the development of a unique class of information about the central nervous system, independent of such other classes as may be found (1) in the medical chart or history, and (2) by a kind of clinical evaluation which tends to arise spontaneously in the testing situation. To this end, the method characteristically involves the interpretation by one person of data obtained from neuropsychological tests administered by another person.

We are indebted to Mrs. Cleo Wallace and the trustees of Wallace Village for their cooperation in making our studies possible. Individuals at the University of Colorado Medical Center who aided us are acknowledged in the body of the manuscript.

This research was supported in part from funds granted to the senior author by the National Institutes of Health, United States Public Health Service, Grant HD-00206, and by the National Society for Crippled Children and Adults.

Another essential characteristic of our test method is the nature of the testing situation. The tasks chosen for the subject to attempt are such that the usual requirement for rigorously standardized verbal instructions is not present. Rather, the subject and the examiner work in an atmosphere of cooperative exploration of the subject's capacities to perceive, manipulate, and/or make judgments about a variety of stimulus objects. No test is begun until the subject indicates verbally or by actual performance on a sample that he is ready to attempt the task required of him. It is permissible for the examiner to use several exploratory methods and a variety of motivational techniques.

Extension of this method to increasingly younger age groups, including children, constitutes a legitimate scientific goal. We can expect difficulties in reaching this goal, because of the widely recognized fact that the poorer testability of children presents many problems encountered much less frequently, if at all, in working with adult populations. Often, the examiner's ability to establish test rapport may become the limiting factor in determining the ultimate utility of any so-called quantitative test.

There are equally formidable obstacles in the formulation of adequate criteria for validation in populations of children with cerebral dysfunction (Reitan, 1962). The practical need for dependable behavioral tools for assessing central nervous system functioning in children is acknowledged both within and outside medical disciplines. This need is felt by pediatric neurologists in their efforts to establish a sound diagnosis. But it is felt equally by other specialists as well, particularly where predictions must be made concerning the implications of diagnosis for future development. With at least some awareness of the methodological complexities involved, the present studies, aimed at an intermediate age group of children, 9 through 14, were undertaken.

In concrete terms, a minimum criterion for such a battery of tests, appropriate for any age group, would be that it yield a minimum of so-called "false negative" information concerning subjects who can otherwise be shown in fact to have focal or diffuse brain damage. Once this point is reached, it is apparent that many second- and third-order levels of questions can be raised about the integrity of higher brain functioning. For example, a battery of such tests might be used to help identify the commonly encountered adaptive disorders of children, particularly the associated states that often obscure the role of brain damage per se. Among these might be mentioned emotional disturbance, mental retardation with or without associated emotional disturbance, the state resulting when a child has been so deprived of challenge and opportunities for learning in his environment that his intellectual growth and emotional maturing are submarginal (cf. Norris, Spaulding, and Brodie, 1957), and other types of handicaps ranging from spasticity and atonias to more peripheral types of sensory and motor abnormalities. "Brain damage" is obviously an umbrella term commonly employed to cover a causal influence upon adaptation which can arise prenatally, perinatally, and at any subsequent point during the life span.

We have addressed ourselves to preliminary study of 8 subgroups of children. These populations were selected to permit early estimation of the range and magnitude of the problems likely to be encountered in any definitive validation study.

SUBJECTS

Our populations include normal children, cerebrally impaired children, and slow-learning children. None of these children was so defective intellectually, emotionally, or physically as to be off-scale on the measures chosen. Forty-two children, aged 9 through 14—of whom we expected a large percentage to be cerebrally impaired—were found at the Wallace Village for Children, Broomfield, Colorado. (The Wallace Village is a private school specializing in active therapy for brain-damaged children. Admission standards now include: [1] evidence of cerebral dysfunction, and [2] no profound motor, emotional, or intellectual disorders.) Roughly concurrent with the time of testing, neurological examinations were given these children by either of two pediatric neurologists, Dr. Frederick Horner or Dr. Barbara Thulin, both of whom were University of Colorado Medical Center staff members. We did not, owing to the recency of inclusion of the neurological criterion for admission, find in all of them medical evidence of cerebral dysfunction. All of them had had educational or developmental difficulties, however.

Before all of the neurological examinations had been completed, a control group was selected to match in age and sex the 42 Wallace Village children. This control group was selected by screening the cumulative school records of approximately 500 children aged 9 through 15.2 years enrolled in a Chicago public school. Besides the age and sex criteria, the children selected had to have a recorded Kuhlman-Anderson IQ of between 90 and 105, and had to be making normal school progress. It was felt that adaptive difficulties of the Wallace Village children would be particularly well brought out in comparison with such a control group, while the intellectual differences would not be extreme.

After the neurological examinations were completed, showing that 24 of the tested Wallace Village children presented evidence of congenital or infantile diffuse cerebral dysfunction, while 18 did not, the control group was subdivided into two smaller groups by matching with the appropriate Wallace Village children. Altogether 8 groups were formed for this study:

Group I_A: All of the tested Wallace Village children, a group considered to have prima facie evidence of adaptive disorder. N = 42.

Group II_A: The Wallace Village children with diagnosed congenital or infantile diffuse cerebral dysfunction. N = 24. Nineteen of these presented signs, such as spasticity, weakness, increased deep tendon reflexes, etc., in one or more limbs, which resulted in their being classified in such categories as mild to moderate cerebral diplegias, hemiplegias, hemipareses, and quadripareses. Three presented developmental anomalies affecting cerebral function, one had an infantile head trauma, and one had a lifelong history of idiopathic seizures, poor coordination, and intellectual retardation.

Group III_A; The Wallace Village children with normal neurological examinations or with noncerebral neuromuscular disorders. N = 18.

Group I_B: All of the tested control children. N = 42.

Group II_B: The control children matched in age and sex with Group II_A. N = 24.

Group III_B: The control children matched in age and sex with Group III_A. N = 18.

The mean ages of all these groups were roughly the same, approximately 12 years, with a more or less rectangular distribution in the range tested, from 9.2 years to 14.9 years.

Groups IV & V: Fifteen children each from the two Wallace Village groups, II_A and III_A, matched in age in pairs.

PROCEDURES (see Figure 1)

All the Wallace Village children were tested with a modification, made by Reitan, of the Halstead Battery of Neuropsychological Tests. Besides these

FIGURE 1

Examples of neuropsychological instruments employed in testing children. (A—Upper) Category Test. (B) Color-Naming Test combined with test for delayed auditory speech feedback.

tests and the neurological examinations, the children were given electro-encephalographic examinations by Dr. David Metcalf of the University of Colorado Medical Center, and were rated on a 3-point scale of "basic adaptive capacity" by their therapists as described below.

The modified Halstead Battery used in this study consisted of the following tests:

1. *The Halstead Category Test* (modified by Reitan for this age group). *Scored for errors.*

2. *The Tactual Performance Test* (modified by Reitan for this age group.) *Scored for Total Time for 3 trials.* Two additional scores are obtained, Memory and Localization, from a drawing made by the subject. Then two similar scores are obtained objectively from the subject's selection and arrangement of a variety of drawn figures on cards.

3. *The Rhythm Test. Scored for errors.*

4. *The Speech Perception Test* (modified by Reitan for this age group). *Scored for errors.*

5. *The Finger Oscillation Test. Scored for average taps per 10-second interval.*

6. *The Auditory Flutter Fusion Test. Scored for errors.*

7. *The Visual Flicker Fusion Test. Scored for average threshold in cps.*

8. *The Time-Sense (Memory) Test. Scored for errors.*

9. *The Time-Sense (Visual) Test. Scored for errors.*

In addition, the following tests were administered to each subject:

10. *The Wechsler-Bellevue (Form I) Intelligence Test* (ages 10 through 14).

11. *The Wechsler Intelligence Scale for Children* (age 9).

12. *The Trail-Making Tests. Scored for time.*

13. *The Halstead-Rennick Color-Naming Tests. Scored as described below, for time or errors.*

Most of these tests have been described previously in the literature (Reitan, 1955a; Symmes, Chapman, and Halstead, 1955; Halstead, 1947). Only the modifications and the new Halstead-Rennick Color-Naming Tests will be described here.

The Category Test. The original test as used in adult testing contained 208 items in 7 groups. The modification for this age level consisted of simplifying and shortening the test to 168 items in 6 groups. Otherwise no changes were made.

Modification of the Tactual Performance Test. Two of the 10 forms have been removed from the board, leaving the cross, square, rectangle, circle, oval, diamond, hexagon, and semicircle. The board is presented to the blindfolded subject as in the adult version with three separate trials, the drawing from memory, etc. After the subject has drawn the picture of the board, he is presented with a stack of cards upon which are drawn figures representing with various degrees of accuracy the blocks on the board. He is asked to select those that he thinks were on the board. When this selection is completed, he is presented with a masonite sheet similar in shape to the board, and is asked to arrange his selected cards on the sheet in the same positions they held on the board. The selection of cards is scored by a weighted, objective system, and the arrangement is scored by placing a transparent template over the masonite sheet, giving credit for accurately located figures.

Modification of the Speech Perception Test. The only change made here was in the number of alternatives to be scanned for each item. Three instead of 4 were used. The one eliminated from each item was the alternative that had incorrect both beginning and end consonants.

The Color-Naming Tests. The basic task in all of these tests was the naming of 1-inch colored lights presented in a horizontal row of 4 at a distance of about 3 feet from the eye.

More details on the construction, scoring, and rationale of the naming tests are available elsewhere (Rennick, 1961). For the purpose of this study, only two of the scores generated were used, as the scores most likely to be representative of future, simpler tests using the same basic task. One of these is a summary score showing all the errors made in the automatically presented tasks which were given with instantaneous speech feedback; the other is a summary score showing the total number of seconds required for the performance of all the self-timed tasks that were given with the instantaneous speech feedback. A simplified version of the color-naming test, using only a time score for the self-timed test, without microphone or tape recorder, is now in standard use in the Chicago laboratory.

In both the naming tests and the Halstead tests, subjects were instructed until the examiner felt the subject understood what to do and was ready to do it, as explained above. The Halstead tests were then administered in a standard manner. (Deviations from rigid procedure consisted of encouragement given to anxious subjects, often coupled with admonitions to the effect of, "Keep trying," or "Try to think how to do it," or "You're not through yet.") The Wechsler tests were given in the standard manner with standard verbal instructions and scored in the standard manner. The naming tests, once started, permitted no nonstandard procedures except the occasional restarting of a test when a child displaced a headset.

The examiner was in the test environment with the child throughout.

EEG EXAMINATIONS

These were administered to all but two of the Wallace Village children. Children whose EEGs were interpreted by Dr. Metcalf as "normal" were assigned the score of 1, children with "suspected" abnormalities in their EEGs were assigned the score of 2, and children with "clearly abnormal" EEGs were assigned a score of 3. These classifications were made by the authors on the basis of written reports of the interpretation of the record, which in every case included the interpreter's clinical impression. This impression served as the basis for the classification, which was quite easy to make in every case.

THERAPISTS' RATINGS

In an attempt to judge the Wallace Village children in the wide range of life situations offered them, we asked the therapists there to furnish a rating of their impressions of the basic intelligence of each child: Good, fair, or poor, discounting any physical handicaps. Each therapist was very well acquainted with each of the children he worked with, having the child for individual therapy for an hour a day or as a part of a group of 5 or 6 for several hours each day. As a check on reliability, these same therapists were also asked to rank-order each child on the same criterion, within reasonably small-sized appropriate groups. When we received these double ratings, a 3 x 3 matrix was set up for each child as follows:

		Rating		
		Good	Fair	Poor
	1	1	4	7
Rank	2	2	5	8
	3	3	6	9

The rank order of children ranked in groups of more than 3 was determined to be in the upper, middle, or lower 33 1/3%, and assigned a 1, 2, or 3 rank accordingly. Then a score was assigned on the basis of the combined rank order and basic rating by the use of the above matrix. Notice in the matrix that the rank order is secondary to the basic rating for each child by the same therapist. Being in the middle third in a class of children with "fair" intelligence is rated with a matrix score of 5, while being in the middle third in a class of children with "good" intelligence is rated with a matrix score of 2.

The matrix scores for each child from each therapist were averaged—in some cases this meant averaging as many as 8 or 9 scores for children who were seen regularly by as many therapists—and then were assigned a final 1, 2, or 3 score as follows:

$$\text{Matrix average } 1 - 2.99 = \text{Score } 1$$
$$\text{Matrix average } 3 - 4.99 = \text{Score } 2$$
$$\text{Matrix average } 5 - 9 \quad = \text{Score } 3$$

RESULTS

In a pilot study, a first step is to check one's instruments on a realistic criterion. Table 1 represents such an effort. The test results for the children with diagnosed cerebral dysfunction are compared with those of their matched controls. Twenty scores are presented, including verbal, performance, and full-scale IQ scores. The T-ratios for this and all other such tables in this report are based upon differences between matched pairs. Of the 17 pairs of mean scores from the Battery, 11 were significantly different from one another at the .001 level of confidence or better, 3 at the .005 level, and 3 were not significantly different from one another. Both the virtues and faults visible in Table 1 are due, perhaps, to the fact that the Battery is a modification of our adult Battery. Our feeling is that the last three, non-discriminating, tests may be insufficiently modified for this age group, but pending further study no changes in them have been made. On the whole, the comparisons in Table 1 are encouraging to us. The children in both groups were generally on-scale on the measures, and the Battery is apparently capable of making a real discrimination between such groups of children.

Comparing the Battery scores with the IQ scores obtained by the two groups, it may be seen that the latter, particularly FSIQ and PIQ, would serve to discriminate the two groups as well as or better than many of the Battery scores. In view of the known facts that IQ scores may remain at high levels in adults with serious brain damage (Halstead, 1938, 1947; Hebb, 1942), and that the tests in this Battery are more sensitive than the

TABLE 1

Means, Standard Deviations, and Significance of Differences in Means in 24 Cerebral-Dysfunction Children and 24 Matched Control Children

	Public School Control Children		Wallace Village Cerebral Dysf'n Children			
	Mean	SD	Mean	SD	T	P
Full Scale IQ	101.95	14.04	70.04	12.46	7.94	<.001
Tactual Performance— Time	10.03	3.46	21.60	7.54	7.40	<.001
Speech Discrimination	10.08	5.88	26.30	8.77	7.37	<.001
Performance IQ	108.21	12.57	78.00	17.61	6.35	<.001
Category	33.50	13.75	65.50	24.72	6.04	<.001
Color Naming—Errors	82.63	23.85	157.90	57.32	5.88	<.001
Color Naming—Time	104.63	18.81	203.60	86.61	5.87	<.001
Verbal IQ	95.17	17.06	68.6	9.58	5.99	<.001
Rhythm	5.00	3.74	11.7	4.24	5.68	<.001
Time Sense—Visual	78.04	46.49	311.40	201.20	5.42	<.001
Tactual Performance— Local'n (Cards)	3.25	1.67	1.17	1.70	5.47	<.001
Trails B—Time	57.00	31.83	113.5	51.67	4.47	<.001
Tactual Performance— Local'n (Drawing)	2.83	1.68	1.20	1.81	3.68	<.001
Trails A—Time	28.96	13.90	58.17	36.21	3.61	<.001
Tapping—Dom. Hand	38.04	5.47	30.90	8.53	3.37	<.005
CFF	24.71	3.52	20.50	4.54	3.32	<.005
Tactual Performance— Memory (Drawing)	4.83	1.53	3.58	1.94	3.47	<.005
AFF	38.58	7.87	42.70	7.13	1.86	<.100
Time Sense—Memory	391.50	235.5	346.00	220.30	.57	<.600
Tactual Performance— Memory (Cards)	48.50	14.80	47.63	14.86	.31	<.800

W-B-I tests (Reitan, 1956, 1959) to cerebral dysfunction factors in adults, this finding requires analysis.

Table 2 presents the comparison between the same two groups on the subtests of the IQ tests. (Two pairs of subjects in the 9-year age group were given WISCs rather than the W-B-I. Their weighted scores were adjusted for the purpose of this table to compare with W-B-I scores for equivalent IQ.) All of the subtest comparisons showed differences between means significant at better than the .001 level of confidence. With this size sample it would be premature to assign a significance to the order of discriminat-

TABLE 2

Mean Wechsler Scores, Standard Deviations, and P-Values for Cerebral-Dysfunction Population and Matched Controls

	Cerebral Dysfunction (Wal. Vil.)		Matched Controls (Pub. Sch.)			
	Mean	SD	Mean	SD	T	P
Digit Symbol	3.79	1.59	8.38	2.10	8.90	<.001
Arithmetic	.54	1.26	7.00	4.74	7.22	<.001
Picture Completion	5.00	3.26	9.87	2.39	6.82	<.001
Picture Arrangement	4.62	2.11	9.62	3.54	5.98	<.001
Block Design	4.83	2.57	8.29	2.58	5.37	<.001
Comprehension	3.25	1.94	7.62	3.11	4.84	<.001
Digit Span	2.88	2.50	6.08	2.34	4.84	<.001
Vocabulary	3.92	1.52	6.46	2.91	4.28	<.001
Information	3.67	2.11	6.67	3.41	3.80	<.001
Object Assembly	5.79	3.68	9.58	2.63	3.74	<.001
Similarities	4.71	2.09	8.42	3.86	3.54	<.001
Verbal Wted. Scale	15.96	4.92	33.33	14.91	5.30	<.001
Performance Wted. Scale	24.09	10.09	43.37	12.83	5.50	<.001
Total Wted. Scale	40.04	13.10	76.70	25.20	6.21	<.001

ing power, particularly since there is such a high rank-order correlation, .74, between the means of the two groups. However, it is worth noting that the digit symbol subtest is also the most likely to reflect impairment in adults (Reitan, 1959), and that the arithmetic subtest was very poorly performed by the children with cerebral dysfunction. Table 2 and Table 1 show that a combined Battery might be expected to satisfy one requirement for tests in this area, that of identification of children with cerebral dysfunction, with a minimum of false negatives.

Tables 3 and 4 present the other side of the picture, with comparisons between the Wallace Village children who were free from neurological signs of cerebral dysfunction and their matched normal school controls. These tables show that there is an obvious possibility that the use of scattered measures of adaptive capacity can result in an excess of false positives for the presence of cerebral dysfunction in children. This can be deduced from the presence of a variety of indicators generating significantly different mean scores for the two groups. Since, however, so many of the differences are less striking between these two groups than they were be-

TABLE 3

Means, Standard Deviations, and Significance of Differences in Means in
18 Wallace Village Normal Children and 18 Matched Control Children

	Public School Control Children		Wallace Village Normal Children			
	Mean	SD	Mean	SD	T	P
Verbal IQ	98.05	11.93	72.16	11.42	8.27	<.001
Full Scale IQ	101.33	11.22	77.77	15.33	7.06	<.001
Category	27.72	10.79	49.94	13.54	5.34	<.001
Tactual Performance— Local'n (Cards)	3.78	1.54	1.78	1.39	3.91	<.001
Performance IQ	105.38	10.70	88.32	19.50	3.79	<.001
Color Naming—Errors	78.38	18.94	115.15	41.12	3.37	<.005
Rhythm	6.00	3.80	9.83	3.25	3.09	<.005
Color Naming—Time	100.71	11.30	144.21	58.82	3.08	<.005
Tactual Performance— Time	10.71	4.38	15.87	7.70	2.21	<.05
Time Sense—Memory	516.45	325.50	367.85	216.70	2.08	<.05
Speech	13.61	7.69	17.89	8.80	1.70	<.10
Trails B—Time	62.05	31.10	75.49	13.35	1.56	<.20
Tactual Performance— Memory (Cards)	49.00	14.41	54.00	14.18	1.47	<.20
Time Sense—Visual	81.44	51.83	131.15	154.00	1.25	<.25
Tapping—Dom. Hand	39.94	5.80	38.05	9.41	1.09	<.30
Trails A—Time	29.44	9.90	35.89	27.81	1.04	<.40
CFF	23.80	3.30	22.38	3.65	1.00	<.40
Tactual Performance— Memory (Drawing)	5.11	1.10	4.72	1.70	.84	<.50
AFF	37.00	8.52	35.83	9.04	.39	<.30
Tactual Performance— (Local'n Drawing)	2.77	1.76	2.55	1.65	.36	<.80

tween the first two groups considered, it may be that there are particular combinations of behavioral indicators which will separate adaptively impaired children with cerebral dysfunction from those without
medical evidence for it.

From our data we were able to find two groups, of 15 children each,
within the Wallace Village populations formed on the neurological criterion, who could be matched in pairs within a few months of age. We thus
had two roughly comparable groups of adaptively impaired children from
the same institution, receiving the same treatment, who were different

TABLE 4

Mean Wechsler Scores, Standard Deviations, and P-Values for Wallace Village Normals and Public-School Controls

	Normals (Wal. Vil.)		Normals (Pub. Sch.)			
	Mean	SD	Mean	SD	T	P
Comprehension	3.88	3.28	9.11	2.83	6.17	<.001
Picture Arrangement	6.82	3.37	9.89	2.30	4.67	<.001
Arithmetic	2.35	2.38	6.94	3.60	4.41	<.001
Digit Symbol	6.23	2.41	3.44	1.97	3.54	<.005
Similarities	6.00	3.57	8.78	3.14	3.13	<.005
Information	5.17	2.40	7.22	2.73	2.48	<.02
Block Design	7.82	3.12	9.44	2.58	2.28	<.05
Digit Span	4.41	2.88	6.94	2.79	2.18	<.05
Object Assembly	8.51	3.56	9.70	1.52	1.39	<.20
Vocabulary	6.23	2.48	6.89	2.26	.93	<.30
Picture Completion	7.94	4.10	8.67	2.64	.59	<.70
Verbal Wted. Scale	23.41	9.59	38.61	11.08	4.23	<.001
Performance Wted. Scale	37.29	13.70	46.28	7.82	5.88	<.001
Total Wted. Scale	60.70	24.20	84.90	17.20	3.60	<.005

from each other in that the children in one group presented neurological signs of diffuse infantile or congenital cerebral dysfunction, while the other was free from them. In spite of the small Ns, Tables 5 and 6, which present the comparisons between these groups, are worthy of attention. (The Ns vary in some of the comparisons because of the elimination from these tables of those cases for whom no realistic score was assignable on one of the tests, because of poor performance. In Tables 1-4, on the other hand, the cases falling in this category were assigned low-quartile scores for the groups in which they fell.) Perhaps the most striking finding is that in spite of the appearance of the arithmetic subtest at the top of Table 6, the verbal IQ seems very nearly equal in the two groups, with only a 10% level of significance for the difference. Yet the verbal IQ is lower than performance IQ in both groups. Also striking is the fact that a variety of the Battery tests, which measure a variety of abilities, do show differences in means obtained from the two groups. We shall return to the consideration of these tables after presenting Tables 7 and 8.

Table 7 shows the intercorrelations among all the Wallace Village children's scores. Table 8 shows the intercorrelations among all the public-

TABLE 5

Means, Standard Deviations, and P-Values for Cerebral-Dysfunction Population and Matched Controls (Wallace Village)

	Cerebral Dysf'n		Normals				
	Mean	SD	Mean	SD	N	T	P
Time Sense—Visual	330.35	208.81	132.61	167.33	15	3.14	<.005
Performance IQ	73.93	19.32	91.64	17.32	14	3.08	<.005
Full Scale IQ	66.29	12.25	79.50	14.87	14	3.01	<.005
Trails B—Time	106.00	48.48	65.00	34.79	13	2.91	<.01
Simultan. Feedback— Total Errors	154.10	41.90	112.30	42.31	15	2.60	<.01
Category	64.50	23.45	48.36	12.72	14	2.50	<.015
Speech Discrimination	25.80	9.73	17.87	8.53	15	2.26	<.025
Tapping—Dom. Hand	31.87	9.01	36.74	8.94	15	1.86	<.05
Simultan. Feedback— Total Time	176.14	50.10	140.47	62.45	15	1.67	<.05
Tactual Performance— Local'n (Drawing)	1.71	2.12	2.79	1.65	14	1.61	<.07
Verbal IQ	65.57	7.26	72.22	11.64	14	1.48	<.10
AFF	40.46	6.09	35.84	9.59	13	1.29	<.10
Tactual Performance— Local'n (Cards)	1.54	1.78	2.15	1.11	13	1.22	<.15
Trails A—Time	45.40	24.47	34.40	28.98	15	1.04	<.15
Time Sense—Memory	338.02	192.61	425.29	331.66	15	1.03	<.15
Tactual Performance— Memory (Drawing)	4.14	2.16	4.79	1.56	14	.99	<.20
CFF	20.94	4.93	23.53	8.40	15	.90	<.20
Tactual Performance— Time	19.42	9.69	16.40	8.17	12	.68	<.25
Rhythm	11.21	5.04	10.36	3.21	14	.67	<.25
Tactual Performance— Memory (Cards)	53.84	14.39	54.61	13.82	13	.145	<.90

school children's scores. It is obvious that the correlation coefficients are higher in the adaptively impaired group than in the normal group. This is a reversal of typical findings in adult populations (Reitan, 1959). This probably reflects the fact that ability levels in the impaired child tend to be down generally, with only scattered abilities, varying amongst individual children, retained at higher levels. In contrast, the normal children tend to have more variability within their individual ability patterns.

The abilities that seem to be particularly impaired in those children with diffuse cerebral dysfunction, that is, those measured by the 10 best-

TABLE 6

Mean Wechsler Scores, Standard Deviations, and P-Values for Cerebral-Dysfunction Population (Wallace Village) and Normal Controls (Wallace Village)

	Cerebral Dysfunction (Wal. Vil.)		Normals (Wal. Vil.)			
	Mean	SD	Mean	SD	T	P
Arithmetic	·93	1.53	2.21	7.40	3.15	<.005
Block Design	5.71	2.41	8.07	2.66	2.82	<.01
Digit Symbol	4.21	1.58	6.07	2.50	2.68	<.01
Picture Arrangement	4.50	2.29	6.93	3.17	2.61	<.01
Object Assembly	5.93	3.49	9.00	3.58	2.55	<.01
Vocabulary	4.07	1.95	5.93	1.98	2.05	<.025
Picture Completion	5.00	3.72	7.57	4.02	2.02	<.025
Digit Span	3.07	2.71	4.00	2.59	1.10	<.15
Similarities	4.57	1.92	5.50	2.82	1.01	<.15
Comprehension	3.64	2.06	4.50	3.27	.85	<.2
Information	4.43	2.22	4.86	2.47	.40	<.3
Verbal Wted. Scale	17.43	4.63	22.57	9.79	1.69	<.06
Performance Wted. Scale	25.36	11.58	37.64	13.19	3.18	<.005
Total Wted. Scale	42.79	12.53	60.22	21.33	3.34	<.005

discriminating tests, excluding IQ, of Table 5, are quite highly correlated in the Wallace Village children. These 10 tests provide a 10 x 10 intercorrelation matrix whose average coefficient is 0.38, with a standard deviation of 0.16, while the 10 x 10 matrix formed by the other 10 tests in the same children has an average coefficient of 0.19, with a standard deviation of 0.16. This difference appears highly significant.

Thus the 10 tests with the most significant difference in means in Table 5 obviously measure some things in common with one another. Yet the correlations are not so high that one would feel that they all measure essentially the same thing with different types and degrees of error variance. A brief characterization of the "discriminating" tests may add weight at this point. One of the tests, the tapping or finger oscillation test, was designed as a relatively pure measure of effector function. This test is often used by neurologists in a less precise form. Two of the tests, the auditory flutter fusion test and the speech perception test, were designed as relatively pure measures of perceptual function, although rather different from the perceptual tasks used by neurologists. The Time-Sense Visual

TABLE 7

Intercorrelations Between Measures within the Wallace Village Population

	Color Naming Time	PIQ	VIQ	FSIQ	Trails B	Trails A	TS Visual	TS Memory	Tapping	Speech	Rhythm	Color Naming Errors	CFF	TPT Loc. Cards	TPT Loc. Draw.	TPT Mem. Cards	TPT Mem. Draw.	TPT Tot.	Cat.
Performance IQ	-.21																		
Verbal IQ	.00	.49																	
Full Scale IQ	-.16	-.93	.76																
Trails B—Time	-.33	-.47	-.20	-.42															
Trails A—Time	-.49	-.43	-.09	-.35	.64														
Time Sense—Visual	-.37	-.42	-.25	-.41	.24	.38													
Time Sense—Memory	-.66	-.06	.14	.02	.14	-.04	.09												
Tapping	-.53	-.34	.02	.35	-.19	-.40	-.50	.09											
Speech Discrim.	-.37	-.10	-.13	-.19	-.45	-.31	-.45	-.07	.36										
Rhythm	.26	-.24	.01	-.12	.25	.28	.00	.28	-.34	.35									
Color Naming—Errors	.76	-.51	-.24	-.49	.58	.63	-.51	.00	-.62	.48	.01								
CFF	.04	.14	.21	.17	-.19	.09	-.10	-.11	-.34	.21	.12	.35							
TPT—Location (Cards)	-.19	.42	-.03	.30	-.30	-.37	-.27	-.25	.29	-.20	-.22	-.43	.10						
TPT—Location (Drawing)	-.30	-.55	.03	.42	-.45	-.46	-.28	-.23	.47	-.28	-.35	-.51	.18	.76					
TPT—Memory (Cards)	-.30	.24	.00	.18	-.30	-.22	-.27	-.39	.57	-.24	-.20	-.40	.19	.60	.46				
TPT—Memory (Drawing)	-.30	.56	.16	.48	-.40	-.38	-.25	-.23	.57	-.34	-.30	-.54	.12	.51	.70	.77			
TPT—Total	.10	-.59	-.25	-.53	-.40	-.28	-.34	-.20	.30	-.17	-.28	-.40	.15	.28	.40	.33	.31		
Category	-.49	-.57	-.28	-.54	-.55	-.53	-.34	-.44	.62	-.30	-.45	-.51	-.30	-.33	-.52	-.23	-.53	.66	
AFF	.24	-.30	-.12	-.28	-.49	-.49	.12	.06	-.14	-.05	.09	.08	.06	-.02	-.18	-.31	-.27	-.34	-.33

TABLE 8

Intercorrelations Between Measures within the Public-School Population

	Performance IQ	Verbal IQ	Full Scale IQ	Trails B	Trails A	Time Sense—Visual	Time Sense—Memory	Tapping	Speech Discrim.	Rhythm	Color Naming—Errors	CFF	TPT—Location (Cards)	TPT—Location (Drawing)	TPT—Memory (Cards)	TPT—Memory (Drawing)	TPT—Total	Category	AFF
Color Naming Time	-.06	-.16	-.15	-.51	.21	.14	.29	-.24	.28	.31	.48	.04	-.31	-.15	-.42	-.24	.12	.08	.17
PIQ		.36	.78	-.13	-.32	-.04	-.03	.06	-.19	.19	-.34	.12	.10	.35	.09	.33	-.20	-.22	-.23
VIQ			.87	-.35	-.12	-.07	.08	.17	-.30	-.14	-.26	.09	.21	.21	.10	-.09	.99	-.17	-.31
FSIQ				-.31	-.26	-.03	.03	.15	-.19	-.19	-.36	.13	.20	.29	.12	-.38	-.18	-.35	-.33
Trails B					.39	.30	.15	-.38	.37	.15	-.44	-.03	-.15	-.14	-.35	-.24	.09	.26	.07
Trails A						.19	.16	-.12	.44	.13	-.35	.13	-.40	-.30	-.47	-.32	-.34	.36	.01
TS Visual							.19	.02	-.52	.14	-.14	.27	-.14	-.33	-.28	-.26	-.40	.21	.14
TS Memory								-.38	.09	.16	.16	-.13	-.13	-.39	-.15	.40	.03	-.23	-.18
Tapping									-.24	-.10	.31	.08	-.14	-.04	.04	-.03	.21	.09	.26
Speech										.24	.14	-.13	-.39	-.37	-.40	-.26	-.34	-.33	.14
Rhythm											.16	.27	.08	.18	.20	.03	.01	.21	.10
Color Naming Errors												-.10	.01	-.18	-.12	-.20	.09	-.33	.14
CFF													.21	-.19	-.20	-.23	-.13	-.32	-.01
TPT Loc. Cards														.69	.75	.59	-.49	.42	-.24
TPT Loc. Draw.															.80	.67	-.35	-.45	-.19
TPT Mem. Cards																.72	-.45	-.32	-.17
TPT Mem. Draw.																	-.42	-.33	-.16
TPT Tot.																		.17	.09
Cat.																			.24

Test is a relatively pure measure of visuomotor coordination. The two trail-making tests and the tactual performance test require good control of hand movements and the ability to organize a "search" in visual or tactile space. The two color-naming tasks were designed as "nonverbal" verbal tasks, which is to say they test the speed and accuracy of the basic, overtrained, verbal skills involved in the art of naming discrete, familiar stimuli. The category test was designed as a test of abstraction capacity (defined as the ability to find communalities in diverse stimuli and differences in related stimuli), but is undoubtedly a test requiring a very complex mixture of perceptual organization, decision-making, "working" memory, and concern with appropriateness of response, in addition to abstraction capacity.

In all of the above tests the culture-impressed skills required are minimal. The one such skill obviously required in a minimum amount is the ability to cooperate with a trained tester. Cooperativeness is also, of course, definitely required for the nondiscriminating tests, although the entire battery of tests was designed, in the tradition of most tests for children's abilities, to elicit this cooperative attitude in sufficient degree through variety and interest. A more important ability they require in common is the capacity for selective, appropriate, concentrated attention to the task. This ability, which also appeared in adults as the *power factor* in Halstead's (1947) factor analysis of the performance of neurosurgical patients, is the most likely candidate for a "general" factor in the impairment of these children. Note that a deficit in this ability would tend to compress the range of expression of the abilities that depend upon it, whereas normal levels of this ability would allow the expression of the variance in other abilities.

In an effort to make tentative norms for discrimination of the child with cerebral dysfunction from his peers, the best cutoff score for each of the 10 best discriminating tests, excluding IQ, on the comparison in Table 5 was computed and applied in a manner similar to the Halstead Impairment Index for the adult Battery. A summary score for each child was computed on the basis of one point per each performance poorer than the cutoff score, giving an ordinal scale, from 0 to 10, as a rough estimate of degree of resemblance to the child with diffuse infantile or congenital cerebral dysfunction. This scale was applied in the three comparisons of Tables 1, 3, and 5, discussed above, with the results presented in Table 9. It was also applied to the three major groups of this study, groups II_A, III_A, and I_B, with the results graphed in Figure 2.

TABLE 9

Comparison of Impairment Scores Between Three Different Populations

Population$_1$	Population$_2$	Mean$_1$	SD	Mean$_2$	SD	N	T	P
Public School Controls	Wallace Village— with Cerebral Dysfunction	1.79	1.58	7.58	2.12	24	10.53	<.001
Public School Controls	Wallace Village— without Cerebral Dysfunction	1.78	1.78	4.17	2.21	18	5.20	<.001
Wallace Village— without Cerebral Dysfunction	Wallace Village— with Cerebral Dysfunction	3.73	2.51	7.13	2.52	15	5.62	<.001

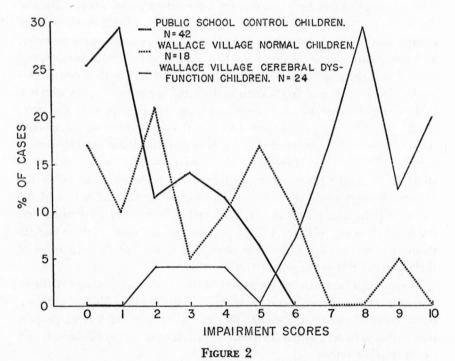

FIGURE 2

Distribution of Impairment Scores in Three Populations

As can be seen, this method of analysis results in an interesting discrimination amongst these groups. There is almost no overlap between the children with diagnosed cerebral dysfunction and the public-school normal controls. In no case did one of the normal children achieve a poorer score than his matched peer with cerebral dysfunction. There was more overlap in other group comparisons. The "slow learners," or Wallace Village children without cerebral dysfunction signs, for example, did in some ways resemble the children with cerebral dysfunction in this study, and they also resembled in some ways the normal public-school controls. As a whole, the increase in the significance of the difference between the mean "impairment score" over that of the IQ score shows that the Battery and the IQ tests assess different aspects of impairment in children. We are currently using the impairment score for further analyses and comparisons, though we do not feel that the cutoff points or the tests used will necessarily represent our ultimate norms.

In an effort to test the conservatism inherent in cutoff scores chosen to discriminate "slow learners" from "slow learners with diffuse cerebral dysfunction," as these were, we applied all but the two color-naming scores and the auditory flutter fusion score to a population of children examined with almost the same battery in the laboratory of Ralph M. Reitan. This population consisted of 50 children in the same age group as ours who had known cerebral dysfunctions of various types and degrees with the onset in the postinfantile period, and 50 normal school children (Reed and Reitan, 1963). We predicted that we would, using these cutoffs, classify many of the impaired children as false negatives, i.e., more like normal children than like the children with cerebral dysfunction tested at the Wallace Village. Only 18 of the 50 impaired children, and only 2 of the 50 control children tested in the Reed and Reitan study were much less impaired than the Wallace Village population, for none of them was institutionalized. We felt this might be related to the fact that the onset of their disorder was in the postinfantile period.

The multiple correlation coefficient of the 20 tests against the trichotomous therapist's ratings was 0.82, with 40 of the Wallace Village children being rated. However, the verbal IQ score accounted for a large proportion of this variance, with a correlation coefficient of —0.47 between it and the therapist's rating.

How well the therapist's ratings and the neurological diagnosis agree

TABLE 10

Agreement Between Therapist Ratings and Neurological Findings

		Therapist Ratings		
		3	2	1
Neurological Findings	Wallace Village Cerebral Dysfunction Children	16	5	3
	Wallace Village Normal Children	5	3	6

may be examined from two viewpoints. (The therapists at the Wallace Village were not informed, at the time their judgments were made, of either the test findings or the neurological diagnoses.) A 2 x 3 contingency table relating the neurological findings to the therapist's ratings is presented in Table 10. The agreement between them is significant, with a chi square of 5.03, at the .08 level of confidence. Another approach uses the measures in this study most predictive of the neurological criterion. The 2 x 3 contingency table relating the psychological test dichotomy and the therapist's ratings is presented in Table 11. The agreement between them is significant, with a chi square of 9.30, at the .01 level of confidence. These results suggest a fair amount of agreement between adaptive impairment, as assessed by therapists, and neurologic findings, in spite of the apparent bias of the therapists in favor of verbal abilities. They are particularly interesting in view of the fact that these children were all adaptively impaired to some degree, while in almost all cases the neurological status was obvious only to the expert diagnostician. On first acquaintance most of these children seemed remarkably intact.

TABLE 11

Agreement Between Therapist Ratings and Psychological Findings

		Therapist Ratings		
		3	2	1
Impairment Score	6 and Over	17	4	2
	5 and Less	4	4	7

The EEGs in this study provided data which were completely unrelated to the psychological testing, the neurological diagnoses, and the therapists' ratings. A correlational analysis provided no significant r's against the threefold EEG criterion for any of the data. Further analysis by Dr. Metcalf of the EEGs is in process, and it may be that some of the variables generated by this analysis (Metcalf et al., 1960) will be more fruitful from the neuropsychological point of view than the normal-suspicious-abnormal trichotomy.

DISCUSSION

Neurologists have long known, and Hebb (1942) in an early study using psychological tests has indicated, that while diffuse static cerebral dysfunction such as that often resulting from head injury is quite compatible with excellent retention of basic verbal abilities if it occurs in adulthood, it is very likely incompatible with the development of basic verbal abilities if it occurs in infancy. It may be, as Hebb suggested, that more intactness of the system is required to acquire a complex function than to retain it.

We now suggest, further, an interaction of disturbed brain physiology in children with some related environmental situations. This may explain the general finding that acquired skills, such as those tested by the more verbally oriented psychometric tests, are likely to be severely impaired in cases of dysfunction beginning in infancy, while in cases of damage to the otherwise normally developed brains of adults they may recover or be retained. On the one hand, the children's disturbance in function acts to reduce the effectiveness of learning situations by impairing the perceptual systems that organize the environmental inputs, and by impairing the effector systems that produce rewarded behavior. On the other hand, these impaired children are not likely to be given as enriching an environment as normal children, either emotionally or intellectually, because of the inappropriate responses they produce. There is a body of clinical observation to suggest this. For instance, there is the case of the newly born impaired child for whom an intimate and developmentally necessary symbiotic mother-child relationship does not get established because of his inappropriate affective responses. Later in life, the impaired child is taken from school because of his inability to learn, and allowed to vegetate at home or in a custodial institution. In both cases the child's impairment has acted to alter his environment in a developmentally harmful way, resulting in an exaggerated impairment of learned skills. Much of the modern therapy for these children is an effort to break the positive feedback cycle, by selective enrichment of their environment.

In testing children with congenital or infancy-acquired cerebral dysfunction, the psychologist may expect to find, on the basis of this interaction, not only basic weaknesses in adaptive capacity but also severe impairment of culturally acquired skills. In testing adults who late in life have acquired a mild, static dysfunction, he may expect to find many of the highly overlearned, basic, culturally acquired skills rather resistant to impairment, in contrast to those abilities required for problem solving in new situations.

The analysis of our test findings presented above was based on chi-square and T-ratio tests for significance of differences between mean scores of populations. We felt somewhat justified in our use of these procedures because we had evidence that our populations differed mainly on certain variables: adaptive adjustment (enrollment in the Wallace Village vs. enrollment in an ordinary public school) and cerebral dysfunction. Our findings in this analysis were surprisingly clear-cut, in view of a risky statistical assumption. The assumption was that adaptive adjustment or cerebral dysfunction are unitary quantities with known distributions. The fact is that even within the limitations on these variables that we used, such as the restriction of the type and age of onset of cerebral dysfunction, or of the type of adaptive disorder which resulted in placement at the Wallace Village rather than in other types of institutions, there are many qualitatively different categories. For example, there are the differences in pathology underlying a symptom of hemiparesis due to congenital vascular abnormality and that due to infantile head injury. We also feel that there are neuropsychologically detectable differences in higher brain function attributable to the physiological differences. In this study more effort was made than in previous child studies to narrow the range of the variables of cerebral dysfunction. It is a commentary on the present understanding of cerebral dysfunction in children that in spite of relatively sophisticated neurological and psychological techniques, we had to settle for the general category we used, admitting that we could not localize or characterize the underlying lesions in our population of children with "congenital or infantile diffuse cerebral dysfunction."

How far does this limit our conclusions? Our best guess is that it should limit our rejection of some of the negative results produced by the analysis involving the comparison of mean levels of performance. The tests we used have an appealing face validity, and we feel that under properly controlled conditions the differences between well-delimited populations of cerebrally dysfunctional children would appear.

We do not feel that the routine statistical analysis of our data has provided us with all we can get from it. We would like to show, perhaps through a "pattern analysis," the relevance of type and extent of dysfunction within our general category, or equally important, to show the relevance of type and extent of therapeutic efforts made for each child. The difficulty is that we do not have even a few clear-cut cases of any particular dysfunction, or any particular training effort.

Even the statistical study has shown us the value of the Battery as a whole, however. With its systematic application to the special cases that accumulate, more penetrating analysis will be possible.

One possible hypothesis from our analysis warrants presentation. It is well known that some children classified into diagnostic categories such as infantile spastic diplegia or mild hemiparesis do not seem to suffer adaptive impairment. The importance of having a reasonable prediction of the degree of adaptive impairment in these cases is itself obvious. More important, it may be possible through long-term study to discover the relationship of brain pathology type and extent to a measured degree of adaptive disorder defined by these tests. Our hypothesis, based upon analogy with our results in adults, is that those children so diagnosed who do not show adaptive impairment in our tests will not have a primary cortical lesion underlying their neurologic signs.

The converse possibility, that the children with severe adaptive impairment as measured by these tests may have neurologically undetectable cerebral dysfunction, represents a trap for the overeager psychologist. We do not feel that we are able, from these tests, to state that all the "false positives" have an identifiable "organic" pattern of performance deficits. Until further external criteria are forthcoming, it is, of course, impossible to carry the discussion further.

A recurrent problem in the study of the "brain-damaged child" is that of composing groups for the assessment of therapeutic techniques. A multivariable battery of this kind offers a tool for this purpose. It is so difficult to control the physiological variables included within diagnostic categories that a resort to ability measures as a first step toward physiological measures may allow the only progress possible in this area. But it is necessary, of course, to have some evidence that the psychological measures are in some way related to possible physiological measures. We believe that the present study has provided such evidence.

Finally, it may be that the ability profiles generated by such a battery as this may have useful applications in the planning of therapy for individual children. Those few abilities that remain high in individual children provide the opening wedge in their training. Those tasks to which the child brings too little aptitude, on the other hand, are sources of frustrating failures which often slow the entire training program. The discovery of the good points in a given child need not be a hit-or-miss procedure if tests specifically designed to measure in the lower ranges of a wide variety of abilities are used. To this end, the tests used here are useful, but are some distance from a complete inventory. They may also measure functions that are likely to be resistant to change through currently conceived therapeutic efforts. However, the possibility exists that therapeutically induced improvement in some particular functions may be associated with a rise in some of the more general higher brain functions tested in this study. Descriptive measurements are not the only key to advances in this field. Invention and validation of successful therapeutic techniques may provide a more far-reaching class of experiments for which good measurements are only necessary, not sufficient.

SUMMARY

Eighty-four children, aged 9 to 14, were tested with a modification of the Halstead Battery of Neuropsychological Tests. Half of the children were enrolled in a special school for adaptively handicapped children. The other half, matched in age and sex with the first half, were chosen from 500 students making normal progress in a regular public school, and limited in recorded Kuhlman-Anderson IQ to the range 90-105. Of the children in the special school, a subgroup of 24 children was identified through systematic neurological assessment as a "congenital or infantile diffuse cerebral dysfunction" group, with the remaining 18 forming a group in which no neurological evidence for cerebral dysfunction was uncovered. The children in the special school were also assessed by their therapists on a 3-point scale of "basic adaptive capacity," and were given EEGs.

The functions measured by the tests of the modified Halstead Battery are those which apparently depend least for their expression upon environmental background. Some basic perceptual and effector skills, the capacity to focus a high level of attention to tasks, a good working memory, and abstraction capacity seem to be particularly impaired in children as they are in adults. The important difference, verified in this study, between children's cerebral dysfunction and that of adults is that impairment in these functions from infancy seems to be associated with severe impairment of culturally acquired skills as well, in contrast to impairment in adults, in whom acquired skills may be retained when a chronic mild cerebral dysfunction is imposed upon a normally developed brain.

BIBLIOGRAPHY

Chapman, L. F. & Wolff, H. G. (1959), The Cerebral Hemispheres and the Highest Integrative Functions of Man. *American Medical Association Archives of Neurology and Psychiatry*, 1:357-424.

Halstead, W. C. (1938), A Method for the Quantitative Recording of Eye Movements. *Journal of Psychology*, 6:177-180.

——(1939), Behavioral Effects of Lesions of the Frontal Lobe in Man. *Archives of Neurology and Psychiatry*, 42:780-783.

——(1940), Preliminary Analysis of Grouping Behavior in Patients with Cerebral Injury by the Method of Equivalent and Non-equivalent Stimuli. *American Journal of Psychiatry*, 96:1263-1294.

——(1947), *Brain and Intelligence*. Chicago: University of Chicago Press.

Hebb, D. O. (1942), The Effect of Early and Late Brain Injury Upon Test Scores, and the Nature of Normal Adult Intelligence. *Proceedings of the American Philosophical Society*, 85:275-292.

Metcalf, D. R., Locketz, H. D. & Turrell, E. S. (1960), A Flexible International Business Machine System for Collating Electroencephalographic and Clinical Data. *Electroencephalography and Clinical Neurophysiology Journal*, 12:202-208.

Norris, M., Spaulding, P. & Brodie, F. (1957), *Blindness in Children*. Chicago: University of Chicago Press.

Reed, H. B. C., Jr. & Reitan, R. M. (1963), Personal communication.

Reitan, R. M. (1955a), Investigation of the Validity of Halstead's Measures of Biological Intelligence. *American Medical Association Archives of Neurology and Psychiatry*, 73:28-35.

——(1955b), The Relation of the Trail Making Test to Organic Brain Damage. *Journal of Consulting Psychology*, 19:393-394.

——(1956), Investigation of Relationships Between "Psychometric" and "Biological" Intelligence. *Journal of Nervous and Mental Disease*, 123:536-591.

——(1959), The Comparative Effects of Brain Damage on the Halstead Impairment Index and the Wechsler-Bellevue Scale. *Journal of Clinical Psychology*, 15:281-285.

——(1962), Psychological Deficit. *Annual Review of Psychology*, 13:415-444.

Rennick, P. M. (1961), *Analysis of an Elementary Speech Function*. Unpublished doctoral dissertation, University of Chicago.
Shure, G. H. & Halstead, W. C. (1958), Cerebral Localization of Intellectual Processes. *Psychological Monographs: General and Applied,* 72 (12).
Symmes, D., Chapman, L. F. & Halstead, W. C. (1955), The Fusion of Intermittent White Noise. *Journal of Acoustical Society of America,* 27:470-473.

CHAPTER 2

Molecular Events
in Learning and Perceiving

GEORGE L. ELLMAN

We recognize intelligence, learning, memory, and perception a posteriori. They are usually described in terms of the behavior of an individual—generally ascribing a positive value to increased learning, new memories, and perceptions. We say that an intelligent organism is one that can learn and that, of two organisms, the one which learns fastest is the more intelligent. Probably the most certain statement that can be made about intelligence is that superior intelligence is well correlated with survival value both to individuals and to groups that have it. In a complex organism, such as the higher mammalia, behavioral responses to environmental changes can take a wide variety of forms, i.e., they are usually regarded as flexible. It is a truism that this flexibility of response to environmental changes is the result of the extent and use of intelligence. The physiologist or biochemist who becomes involved in these considerations needs, perforce, the aid of psychologists in outlining precise molecular theories that are testable. In a gross way, memory, learning, responses, and perception are also the province of newer disciplines—i.e., information theory—cybernetics—systems analysis, etc. It is proposed, in this chapter, to make use of some deductions from this field, and to develop ideas about molecular events in learning and memory.

The basic concepts of information theory are relatively simple, although the mathematics may be difficult. For purposes of formulating the subject of this chapter, the pertinent conclusion from this theory that will be used is this: The responses of an organism depend on its decision-making rate, which depends on its total storage of information available at that moment, and on the maximum rate at which decision-making "equipment" can operate. To be adaptive—i.e., to survive changes in its environment— the individual must continually retest his present behavior against the results of his past behavior. This, too, becomes a part of the individual's storage of information. In each of these points, it is implicitly understood that the mechanisms for storage of information, decision-making, and information reception are operative. In the central nervous system, such systems very probably operate as networks of interconnecting "channels" with "switches" at the interconnecting joints. The interconnections are more usually called synapses.

What is meant by interconnections in this context? In basic information theory, little discussion of this point has been made, since it is assumed that switches and buss-bars are acting as they usually do. In respect to the functional organ of the mind, no such simple interpretation is possible. We know that there are several types of interconnections, both anatomically and biochemically speaking (Bullock, 1959; Crossland, 1960). In a computer, switches are generally regarded as having an off and an on position. In a nerve network, a nerve may be regarded as part of the circuit (i.e., acting as a conductor) for only the few milliseconds during which it "fires." Thus, the over-all on-time of part of the network depends on frequency of firing of the nerve. The activity of a given neuron is conditioned by the immediate environment, so that minor changes in concentrations of metabolites, hormones, pH, CO_2, pressure, etc., can act to change the firing characteristics of whole regions of the brain. In addition, it may be well to suppose that there exist presynaptic regions, i.e., not functional, but capable of being converted to connections by minor chemical changes. In recent years, protein chemists have shown in great detail how the immediate environment in which a protein exists establishes its shape, the orientation of its various groups, and how these conformations are changed by changes in the environment (Klotz, 1960a, b; Tanford et al., 1961, 1962; Featherstone et al., 1961; Pauling, 1961). These changes can be brought about by salt ions, polar organic molecules, etc. In addition, seemingly minor but functionally important changes in structure are brought about by absorption, e.g., of substrates on enzymes (Koshland, 1958).

There is, in the central nervous system, only one fairly well-established transmitter agent: acetylcholine (ACh) (Crossland, 1960; Feldberg, 1957; Hebb, 1962). There is evidence that other transmitters exist; exactly how many is unknown. From the previous discussion of the importance of synaptic interconnections, it would seem reasonable to conclude that intelligence is positively correlated with the number of such interconnections. Such a conclusion is extremely difficult to test for two reasons: the difficulty in measuring intelligence and the difficulty in measuring the number of synaptic connections. The former is the job of educators, psychologists, etc., the latter of physiologists, biochemists, and anatomists. Attempts have been made to investigate this correlation, but discussion of this work will be postponed until after the section on the nature of synapses.

In summary, it would seem that many years of research will be necessary to establish the nature and types of interconnections in the central nervous system (CNS). Even now, however, it is clear that these interconnections, with multiple feedback inhibitions, can adequately explain *many* of the "higher functions" of the CNS. There remains an enormous amount of work for the investigator of CNS function at the many levels of its activity. The formation and mode of functioning of synapses is probably the central problem facing the biochemist and biophysicist, and may remain so for some time.

NATURE OF SYNAPTIC INTERCONNECTIONS

A.   GENERAL

Present ideas about the operation of the CNS are strongly influenced by computer technology logic. Many of the operations of these "machines" are entirely analogous to certain thought processes (Paxson and Smith, 1962; Eccles, 1953; George, 1961; Bell, 1962). The elements which either switch off or on are comparable to the frequency modulated circuitry of the brain. Clearly, the on-time of a given CNS "channel" is directly proportional to the frequency of firing. The simplest nerve nets have formally analogous "states" as do "flip-flop" circuits. In these and many other ways (Chapman, 1959) the involved neural connections resemble a modern computer rather more than the older "switchboard" ideas; i.e., the circuitry is automated. In fact, studies of "neural nets" indicate that it is probable that much of the relatively *simple* animal behavior can often be explained with fewer than 20 interconnected neurons (Wiener, 1948; Shannon and Weaver, 1949; Attneave, 1959).

However, the basic difference between such computers and the brain is that the interconnections in the brain are not functionally the same from second to second nor from day to day. By this is meant that although a synapse may exist between two neurons, the interference of external agents (drugs, hormones, cofactors, etc.) is variable so that at one time the synapse may conduct a circuit; yet seconds later, it may be nonfunctional, and some minutes later, restored. This variability of function is one of the most difficult problems to deal with, both theoretically and in practice.

The accomplishments of workers in the electronic fields who have developed logical networks cannot, however, be ignored, and in fact do support the idea that multiply interconnected networks of time-delayed, sequentially operated switching circuits can perform many of the operations which the brain performs. We have no reason to reject the idea that, in fact, the neurons do indeed represent such time-delayed switching circuits as exist in these networks.

What then are we to make of the nonneural constituents of the central nervous system? The brain is made up of a relatively small percentage of neurons, and it is richly endowed with blood vessels and several types of glial cells. Glia may represent (in certain regions of the mammalian brain) approximately 90% of the cellular constituents thereof (Freide, 1953). Traditional biochemical thinking about these cells suggests that they are metabolic in function and nutritional in character. They provide glucose and other essential constituents for the neurons which are "busy at their job." Recent observations suggest that although this may well describe their role, some specific details of their function are now becoming known. For example, it is likely that some at least of the oligodendroglia have as their function the formation of certain hormonelike secretory products. Other of the glial cells act as scavengers, removing cellular debris from the region of the central nervous system. For example, Pomerat (1958) suggests that considerable numbers of the glial cells of the central nervous system are actively in motion not only as regards portions of the cell but also as regards actual translation of the whole cell in relation to the more fixed constituents of the brain. The pulsating movements functioning in

the "stirring up" of the media in which the brain finds itself, are participated in by very many cells of the central nervous system and may not
represent any significant functional aspect except as a by-product of some
other activity. Certainly the stirring activity does not seem physiologically
significant in view of the tremendous vascularity of the central nervous
system. Another function which the glial cells seemingly serve is the protection of the neural tissue from the direct administration of components
found in the circulating blood system. It is likely that most of the constituents which arrive at nerve cells have passed through a glial cell (Bairat,
1958).

B.   DETAILS OF SYNAPTIC CONNECTIONS

In considering the functional synaptic ending we must study the cholinergic synapse, since it is the only synapse about which we know in any detail. Even here, the actual state of the synapse is known best as part of a
theory since some (at least) of the evidence for the nature of the cholinergic synapse is not yet available. This theory is predominately that which
Nachmansohn (1959) has promulgated for many years. The theory includes at least four elements: acetylcholine (a) is formed in the neuron
and stored at the synaptic endings; (b) is released by the impulse arriving at the nerve ending; (c) interacts on the adjacent neuron and initiates the permeability changes of the membrane at the synaptic region
followed by sodium influx and potassium efflux from the subsynaptic neuron; (d) is removed by the enzyme acetylcholinesterase, and subsequently
the subsynaptic membrane re-forms into its original relatively impermeable
state.

More is known about the synthesis of acetylcholine and its subsequent
inclusion in bound particulate state than when Nachmansohn first proposed this theory. It is now well established that the acetylcholine exists
at synaptic nerve endings in small particulate forms (Arniaz and DeRobertis, 1962; Whittaker, 1959); these particles have been isolated and many
of their properties studied, and they do indeed contain the acetylcholine
of the nerve endings which can be released by a variety of stimuli. It is
also known that the particulate material which stores acetylcholine also
contains the enzymes necessary for the synthesis of acetylcholine. In addition, there is some evidence which suggests that the formation of acetylcholine takes place as the particle is traversing the distance from the neu-

ral cell body to the extremities of the synapse. Thus, one can picture the formation of acetylcholine in the following way: the enzymes and structural elements for making bound acetylcholine are probably made in the nerve cell bodies from protein by the same sort of mechanism that is responsible for the production of protein in other cell systems; that is, the ribosomal-messenger RNA complex (see below). These particulate bodies are then transported down the axon, and, providing substrates and energy are available, synthesize and bind acetylcholine during their journey. The movement of materials down the axon is now well established (Weiss, 1959) and is known to exist in all axons that have been studied. The particles are then stored at the presynaptic endings.

The nature of the release phenomenon is much less well understood. It is known that a number of conditions can cause the acetylcholine to be released from the particulate bound form: organic solvents, e.g., chloroform, ether; snake venom, freezing and thawing, hypotonic solutions, pH below 4.5, and temperatures over about $25°$ (Whittaker, 1959). These agents seem then to be acting on the protein matrix to change its conformation so that it is no longer able to bind acetylcholine. Whether, in fact, any of these operate *in vivo* seems somewhat unlikely at the present time. The release of the acetylcholine by means of the "impulse" that arrives from the nerve body represents a properly vague description of the events at the synapse. Perhaps it is no more than the passage of an electropotential field somewhat different from that pre-existing in the region. No chemically defined mechanisms are yet available to describe the release phenomenon. A plausible mechanism might involve something analogous to the ion exchange mechanism which explains the release of histamine from its binding sites (Paton, 1957), perhaps involving acetylcholine as the displacing agent (Koelle, 1962).

Perhaps the most mysterious and certainly the most important aspect of the action of acetylcholine is its combination with the receptor in the subsynaptic region. Here, acetylcholine probably combines with a macromolecular membrane substance in such a way that the conformation of this substance is drastically changed, so that the net permeability of the membrane increases several hundredfold (Nachmansohn, 1959, pp. 4-6). Clearly this change involves some sort of trigger activity on the part of the acetylcholine and must be such that the events can happen extremely rapidly and the change of permeability can be entirely reversible. Unfortunately, no detailed suggestions of the mechanism of the acetylcholine effect on nerve-ending permeability changes have been made by Nachmansohn. A possibility which occurred to the author is that the synaptic region may contain contractile elements, similar to muscle, which contract reversibly in the presence of acetylcholine. Such a hypothesis could be tested by a combination of electron microscopic, physiological, and biochemical procedures.

Finally, the acetylcholine is hydrolyzed by a specific enzyme: acetylcholinesterase. This enzyme is localized in the synaptic membrane and is ideally situated for the absorption of free acetylcholine. It has an extremely rapid action; the products of acetylcholine hydrolysis are essentially without activity. The amount of acetylcholinesterase at most cholinergic synapses appears to be many thousands of times more than what would be needed were even a large amount of acetylcholine released at the nerve ending. Nachmansohn originally proposed that the function of the acetylcholinesterase was to destroy rapidly the acetylcholine in the region so that the length of time during which the synaptic membrane was depolarized, that is, permeable to ions, would be short. More recently, Koelle (1962) has suggested that the function of acetylcholinesterase may not be solely that of limiting the action of acetylcholine in time but that it may also limit the spatial distribution of acetylcholine activity. For example, not only would the release of acetylcholine in the central nervous system at a synaptic ending in the absence of any acetylcholinesterase cause firing of the subsynaptic nerve, but the diffusion of the molecules might cause many nerves in the surrounding region to be fired. Hence, the cholinesterase may serve to limit the activity of acetylcholine in space as well as in time.

This model of a cholinergic synapse, while it may be incomplete and inadequate in some respects, is the functional connection about which we know the most; it includes the least number of elements that are likely to be found at other synapses. First, the enzymes and structures necessary to make and store transmitter agents are essential. Second, a release at some specified time and by some specific agent such as the impulse is essential. Third, some specific receptor substance which changes permeability when combined with the active transmitter is essential. Finally, the necessity for an enzyme to hydrolyze or in some way inactivate the transmitter substance is perhaps not as well established as the other three points. Certainly, as

Koelle (1962) has pointed out, the activity of acetylcholine at a nerve ending may disappear simply by the diffusion of acetylcholine away from the site of its release. Nerves would then become repolarized in the complete absence of acetylcholinesterase. Nevertheless, an inactivating agent for any hypothetical transmitter substance seems a logical possibility at this time.

We can therefore summarize the necessary components of a synaptic region as requiring at least the following: (a) the transmitter substance, probably in a bound form, and therefore (b) the enzymes needed for the synthesis of the transmitter as well as (c) the protein(s) necessary for the binding of the transmitter. We would also expect to find (d) nonspecific membrane components in the synaptic region in which exists the (e) specific protein receptor for the transmitter. This latter protein should have the primary property of changing its structure in such a way that the permeability of the membrane is drastically changed when the transmitter molecule is released in its presence; finally, (f) the enzyme or enzymes necessary for inactivating the transmitter. All of these materials are suggested by analogy with the acetylcholine system. It is conceivable that considerable modifications of this scheme are possible. For example, it may not be essential that the receptor substances be solely responsive to a single specific transmitter. Or alternately, the synaptic regions of certain neurons may have more than one specific receptor substance. For example, if we consider two probable transmitters, acetylcholine and norepinephrine, a neural cell can have at least three types of response to each of these agents: stimulation or firing (+), no response (o), or inhibition (−). In examining cells of the brain stem, Bradley and Wolstencroft (1963) found the distribution of cell responses shown in Table 1. The numbers in the Table are percentages of

TABLE 1

		Norepinephrine			
		+	0	−	
Acetylcholine	+	14	5	5	24
	o	13	47	10	70
	−	4	0	1	5
		31	52	16	99

the 95 cells that were studied: e.g., 13% responded to norepinephrine by firing but did not respond to acetylcholine at all. Such cells might be considered as the "classic" adrenergic cells. By the same logic, 5% are "pure" cholinergic cells. The importance of these data are then: (1) The relative sparsity of "pure" cells of either transmitter and (2) the large number (47%) which seem to be unresponsive to either transmitter.

If one extrapolates to, say, 6 possible CNS transmitters, one can devise a 6-dimensional table with $3^6=1029$ "cubicals" if we allow for only three types of response. Thus, it is to be expected that as our knowledge of neural transmitters increases, the number of cell "types" may increase explosively, possibly approaching several hundred. The fact that 47% of the cells, although electrically stimulable, were not responsive to acetylcholine or norepinephrine, suggests that other transmitter substances are still to be discovered (Crossland, 1960).

Let us consider now the problem of determining the number of synapses in a given region of the CNS. The size of such interconnections is such that they are barely discernible in the light microscope. If they were somewhat larger, it might be possible to count them. The small size and large numbers of such connections makes this approach extremely difficult. The synaptic regions are fairly readily observed with the electron microscope, however. With this instrument no very large section of tissue can be examined. Consequently, with this technique one can count synapses in a very limited region of tissue.

An alternate approach is to measure some component of the synapse. Preferably it should be one which (a) is present in constant amount per synapse, (b) can be assayed easily, and (c) is present at all synapses. No single currently known cellular component fulfills these requirements. From the description of the cholinergic synapse just given, the bound acetylcholine might seem to qualify as a proper component. One would need to prove at least two points—that one can quantitatively remove and assay this material from a section of the brain, and that rapid fluctuations in amounts per synapse do not occur. The measurement of acetylcholinesterase as an estimate of synapses in a given region fulfills the second requirement—that is, it can be easily assayed. At present, there are no data which would allow us to say how much is present at any synapse. In fact, the information that is available (Koelle and Friedenwald, 1949) suggests that this enzyme is not uniformly located in all cholinergic synapses, nor is the amount per synapse likely to be even reasonably constant. Finally, it is not to be expected that cholinesterase will be found at noncholinergic synapses. Therefore, measurement of this enzyme at best can be regarded as an estimate of the cholinergic synapses in a given tissue; more likely, no such simple interpretation is possible. It is evident that further studies of synaptic transmission depend very heavily on the identification of the natural transmitters.

C. SYNTHESIS OF SYNAPTIC COMPONENTS

Let us consider each of the components in the order in which they were previously presented; first, the transmitter substance and its bound form. Here, again, we must rely on the information known about acetylcholine. In this instance it is known that this transmitter is retained in the synaptic region in the form of small granules. These granules are probably formed in the cell body and migrate down the axon to the synaptic regions where they are stored until the impulse to release acetylcholine arrives. These granules contain not only the acetylcholine but the enzyme choline acetylase (Whittaker, 1959), as well as the protein or other component to which the acetylcholine is bound, and possibly another protein which may cover the granule. The biosynthesis of acetylcholine has been studied extensively and is outlined below.

Acetate + ATP + Coenzyme A → Acetyl-CoA + ADP   (A)

Acetyl-CoA + Choline → Acetylcholine + CoA   (B)

Acetylcholine + Protein X → Bound Acetylcholine   (C)

It should be noted that this series of reactions requires the components of acetylcholine, namely acetate and choline, but in addition it requires ATP, Coenzyme A, and at least three and possibly four enzymes. The enzymatic components are found in the storage granules mentioned previously. However, the substrates are not synthesized by the granules but arrive from cytoplasmic areas outside these granules. As indicated above, the nature of the substance to which acetylcholine is bound (Protein X) has not been elucidated, nor have the details of the process in reaction C been studied. This is most certainly a problem for biochemists to examine.

It may be desirable to present in brief summary form here the present status of our knowledge of protein synthesis, for we have mentioned that certain protein materials are to be expected as parts of synaptic regions.

Where we have detailed information it is now becoming clear that the nuclear deoxyribonucleic acid molecule (DNA) is a primary source of the specification of amino-acid sequence in the protein chain. This material (DNA) is the material of inheritance, i.e., the primary nuclear genetic material. The DNA transmits this information regarding sequence of amino acids to a closely related material, ribose nucleic acid (RNA), a substance which ultimately ends up in the cytoplasm of the cell. This material is now usually referred to as messenger RNA (m-RNA) since there exist several other types of cytoplasmic RNA. This other type of RNA, referred to as soluble RNA (s-RNA), is also involved in the synthesis of the proteins. The apparent sequence of events for proteins that have been studied is as follows (Campbell, 1960):

Amino acid + ATP → Adenyl-Amino acid	(D)
Adenyl-amino acid + s-RNA → s-RNA-Amino-acid ester	(E)
s-RNA-Amino-acid ester + m-RNA → Complex	(F)
Complex + GTP → m-RNA-Amino acid-Phosphate + s-RNA + GDP	(G)
m-RNA-Amino acid-Phosphate + s-RNA-Amino-acid ester →	
m-RNA-Amino acid-Amino acid-s-RNA + Phosphate	(H)

The reaction (D) above involves a specific enzyme as well as the amino acid and ATP; an activated amino acid is formed attached to the enzyme. This complex, then, reacts with one of many different types of soluble RNA to form a soluble-RNA amino-acid ester which is essentially a specific amino-acid carrier (reaction E). The specificity for the particular sequence of amino acids in a protein appears to reside in the proper placement of each of these s-RNA-amino-acid ester complexes on its specialized position on the messenger RNA as illustrated in the reaction (F). Each of the specific soluble-RNA-amino-acid ester complexes apparently can complex with messenger RNA in only certain selective sites. In this way the precise sequence in which the amino acids can be ordered on the surface of the messenger RNA is determined. The major components of cells for carrying out these reactions are small bodies called ribosomes. Recent electron micrographs have shown that ribosomes are somewhat smaller than messenger RNA units and seem to complex with the messenger RNA so that several ribosomes actually "read off" the code message to be found on a single m-RNA at one time. Since each ribosome is capable of making an amino-acid sequence as specified by the messenger RNA, several protein molecules can be made sequentially from a single strand of m-RNA. The exact nature of the final steps (G, H) in which the complex of soluble RNA amino-acid esters and messenger RNA are converted into the peptide is not as yet known in detail. These suggested reactions from a recent paper (Noll et al., 1963) explain the requirement for guanosine triphosphate, an aspect of protein syntheses that has long been puzzling. Nevertheless, over-all, this sequence of events is very probably the type of reaction sequence which forms the peptide bonds of most proteins. It should be noted, how-ever, that proteins have, in addition to the main peptide backbone struc-ture which would be accounted for by the above sequence, auxiliary bonds, such as ionic bonds between positively charged nitrogens and negatively charged carboxylate ions, disulfide bonds which are formed by oxidation of sulfhydryl groups on adjacent peptide chains, and numerable hydrogen bonds introduced by the proper placement of donor and receptor atoms. It is now generally believed that the specific secondary and tertiary structure of proteins, that is, their spatial conformation, is determined primarily by the amino-acid sequence: for when specific amino acids are introduced into a peptide sequence in a specific order, a high probability is introduced that certain specific conformations will be predominant owing to subse-quent folding and bending to achieve maximum stability under the ex-isting conditions. These processes would presumably apply to each of the several protein components required for the formation of a synapse, (a) for synthesizing acetylcholine or other transmitter, and (b) for binding-site-protein, the membrane and other structural proteins, cholinesterase, etc.

Detailed information about the nature of the nonspecific membrane components in a synaptic region in which the specific receptor protein might be expected to be found is not now available. The nature of cell-wall material has been studied extensively, especially in plant materials. But animal membranes are especially difficult to study. Most of the work in this field is primarily histochemical in nature and often fails to specify pre-cise chemical compounds. Nevertheless, it is probably true that a consid-erable amount of neutral lipid and phospholipid is to be found in cell membranes. However, continuing reports of protein, proteolipid, lipo-protein, and carbohydrate materials to be found in the cell membranes of most cells suggest merely that all kinds of materials are to be expected there and have been found. As regards the specific receptor, for example of acetylcholine, even less can be said. Ehrenpreis (1960), working in Nachmansohn's laboratory, felt some years ago that they had isolated a protein which did have the requisite properties for being the specific receptor. In recent years, however, Ehrenpreis has rejected this possibility. This material was originally isolated by means of its precipitability with curare; since curare is known to be a strong inhibitor of cholinergic synapses, it seemed a logical possibility that the protein precipitated by curare might well have been the cholinergic receptors. However, careful work has indicated that the affinity for acetylcholine by this particular protein is rather low for what would be expected if this were the receptor (Ehrenpreis, 1962). It seems, in fact, to have less affinity for acetylcholine than acetylcholinesterase, a situation which seems somewhat improbable since we would expect the cholinergic receptors to have a greater affinity for the agent than the enzyme which destroyed it. Otherwise, no firing of cholinergic nerves would be expected since the preponderant amount of acetylcholine released at any receptor would go immediately to the acetylcholinesterase and not to the receptor protein. This, too, is a field which biochemists and molecular biologists will no doubt exploit extensively in the next decade. In addition, the primary property of this receptor protein will require extensive study. This property essentially is that the protein changes its conformation drastically in the presence of acetylcholine. Physiologists have known for a long time that when the nerve synapse is stimulated with acetylcholine the permeability of the membrane to sodium ions drastically changes, increasing some several hundredfold in magnitude. Such a change in permeability could only be accounted for by some conformational change.

It may well be worth mentioning that the adrenergic synapse (if such there be) may well be a modification of a cholinergic synapse. Burn and Rand (1959) have suggested that the adrenergic synapse is, in fact, a cholinergic synapse at which granules containing norepinephrine or epinephrine are to be found and that these granules are themselves sensitive to acetylcholine released in their presence. The existence of chromaffin (catecholamine-containing) granules in the nervous tissue is well established (DeRobertis et al., 1958). However, the specific relationship that Burn and Rand have suggested is not well established as yet. Nonetheless, the idea has great heuristic value and much research remains to be done to establish or deny the validity of the concept.

The synthesis of chromaffin granules may well be similar to that of the acetylcholine granules. The pathway of synthesis of epinephrine and norepinephrine is now well worked out. Catecholamines derive primarily from the amino acid tyrosine or possibly from phenylalanine. In a series of steps, tyrosine is oxidized to dihydroxyphenylalanine which is decarboxylated to dopamine. The dopamine is oxidized in the position adjacent to the ring to form norepinephrine. Norepinephrine may or may not be methylated on the nitrogen to produce epinephrine. This sequence of reactions, like those discussed previously for the synthesis of acetylcholine, requires a specific enzyme at each step and these enzymes are in turn determined by the information contained in the DNA code. Again, then, we must rely on genetic information for the appropriate determination of pathways of synthesis.

In the discussion of the synthesis of proteins it was implicitly assumed that the specific components necessary for the synthesis of the protein are all available. Obviously, many pathological conditions may ensue if this is not so. For example, it is now well known that the accumulation of phenylalanine in the young organism which has phenylketonuria is the result of a specific genetic defect whose result is to cause the absence of an enzyme which synthesizes tyrosine from phenylalanine (Wright and Tarjan, 1957). Studies of such individuals indicate that most of the other enzymes for the metabolism of tyrosine and phenylalanine are present in normal amounts. The predominant influence of this defect is to cause the accumulation of dietary phenylalanine to such an extent that the normal concentration of phenylalanine in the blood and in the tissues becomes much elevated. The effect of this elevated phenylalanine level on the uptake of other amino acids was studied by McKean et al. (1962), who found that levels of phenylalanine comparable to those in phenylketonurics are capable of almost completely preventing the cells of the central nervous system from taking certain other amino acids into the organ. In other words, the uptake of these amino acids (tyrosine, tryptophane, methionine, and valine) is competitively inhibited by phenylalanine. The result of this is obvious; the cells of the central nervous system which are actively growing and maturing after birth are deprived of a significant portion of the amino acids which they cannot make, and the consequent synthesis of necessary proteins, enzymatic and structural, is either delayed or completely abolished. In any event, the over-all delay of the growth of the axonal elements and the subsequent delay in the laying down of functional synapses could account for the generally recognized slower learning behavior of such individuals. This phenomenon, that is, the selective slowing of neural growth patterns, has been studied by Hicks and D'Amato (1961) who radiated rats at various stages of their development with moderate doses of X rays; they showed that even small doses of radiation could cause definite impairment of the rate of development of the axonal elements in young animals and that histological consequences of this slower development were numerous.

Another instance of the effects of amino acid deficiencies is the condition called kwashiorkor (DeToni, 1960), which is found in many places where protein foods are extremely difficult to obtain. Individuals with this condition very frequently suffer from gross neurological developmental deficiencies. Such a conclusion about intelligence would also follow logically from the arguments that we have presented previously regarding the number of synaptic connections that an individual may complete.

In addition to the necessity for an adequate supply of amino acids, the cells require an efficient and adequate mechanism for the formation of adenosinetriphosphate, the "high-energy" currency of the cell. The importance of high-energy compounds is evidenced by the reactions (A), (D), and (G) illustrated previously; practically every molecule synthesized by the cell requires the participation of ATP at some stage. The enzymes for synthesizing ATP are found in the cell's mitochondria. There are at present no indications that nerve cells are deficient in mitochondria; however, such a mechanism of brain dysfunction might be worth further consideration.

The entry of the sodium ion into nerve cells when they are fired requires further investigation. For example, in a cell that is fired repeatedly, does the average internal sodium and/or potassium ion concentration change appreciably? If so, it is conceivable that any of the processes concerned with protein synthesis (reactions D-G) may be inhibited or stimulated. In this way, the pattern of cell firing could affect the internal workings of the protein synthesizing systems, which, in turn, could affect the pattern of cell firing.

At present, our knowledge of mechanisms of control of protein synthesis is very limited; the most extensive studies of this problem have been in bacterial systems. The present ideas of Jacob and Monod (1961) are somewhat as follows: (a) A series of *structural* genes on the nuclear DNA is known to supply the information of amino-acid sequence for the synthesis of certain enzymes. (b) Elsewhere on the DNA (not necessarily on the same chromosome) there exists a gene whose product [possibly (Huang and Bonner, 1962) a histone] inhibits the activity of (c) the *operator* gene. This gene, either directly or through some protein product, controls the activity of the "structural" genes. There is evidence (Gerhart and Pardee, 1962) that rates of synthesis of products of enzyme action in the cell cytoplasm can interfere with the gene products in combination with the "operator" gene. Recent observation may help to identify the precise cellular component (s) which "turn off" the DNA information transfer. Huang and Bonner (1962) have shown that nuclear histones prevent the formation of m-RNA. Since these basic proteins (the histones) are probably also synthesized in a manner similar to other proteins, some sort of cyclic control system in which environmental effects may be important can be visualized.

These components may well be part of most mammalian cell "control systems" also. However, rates of enzyme synthesis in mammalian organisms are not so easily studied; the problem of distinguishing enzyme activity from enzyme concentration is, in general, not solved. Furthermore, the problem of distinguishing a measurable enzymic activity from the specific function of that (those) protein(s) requires further work. For example, recent electrophoretic methods allow the separation of an enzyme activity into many protein components called isozymes (Markert, 1961). It is not obvious, however, that the method used to identify a given protein on a gel electrophorogram provides evidence that that is its *in vivo* function. This is most obvious in the situation where a wholly synthetic substrate is used to localize the "isozyme." An example of this situation is the separation of several pseudocholinesterases in serum (Bernsohn et al., 1961). These problems in higher organisms make the study of control mechanisms much more difficult than it is in bacterial systems. There, at minimum, the gross nutritional state of the organism is known, and very often close control of the genetic background is possible.

There are now several fairly direct studies of the relationship of protein synthesis in the CNS and memory. The studies of Brattgard and Hyden (1952) suggested that protein synthesis is markedly stimulated in nerve cells that have been fired extensively. Flexner et al. (1963) used

Puromycin in conjunction with Y-maze learning to study protein synthesis during learning. Puromycin causes an almost immediate inhibition of protein synthesis in many tissues. If it was injected intraventricularly into rats within two days after they had learned the Y maze, the learned behavior was not retained. On the other hand, injections after two days did not impair the "fixation" of memory. Furthermore, if rats were first trained to turn, say, right in the maze, and then retaught to go left, then given an injection of Puromycin one day after learning the new trait, the new task was not retained, but the rats would then go to the right: i.e., newly learned behavior could be prevented from being fixed, but once fixed, Puromycin did not interfere with recall and utilization of memories. As the authors point out, this effect of Puromycin may not have anything to do with its ability to prevent protein synthesis, but it would seem to be the simplest interpretation of the data. Thus it suggests that learning requires the formation of some protein constituents (which can be prevented by Puromycin) and that the process of "fixation" of a learned trait such as maze learning, in a rat, requires something like two days for completion.

The problem of localizing and identifying specific proteins of the brain that have to do with memory and/or learning is extremely difficult. The separation and examination of tissue proteins, especially of the brain, has not been as systematic as, e.g., that of the serum. Furthermore, about two-thirds of the proteins of the CNS are insoluble in aqueous media (Ellman, 1962); it is in this portion that one might expect to find those cellular or synaptic components having to do with transmission-learning memory and other functions.

The processes of cell growth and development at the molecular level are poorly understood at the present time. The details of the fertilization of the ovum have been studied extensively and the initial sequence of events occurring after the first few cell divisions have been well studied at the histological level (Boell, 1955). The intimate biochemical details of these processes, however, are not known. The necessary sequence of biochemical events must involve many hundreds or thousands of reactions which must be started and perhaps stopped in the proper sequence, so that ultimately the primary zygote can produce a replicate set of the nuclear components and form a daughter cell. This process, of course, repeats several times before differentiation is noticeable. An illustrative hypothetical example of the importance of the timing sequence in the development of the organism may be given as follows. One of the problems in understanding development is the specificity of nerve innervation of end organs. How does the growing axonal tip know with which muscle or other end organ to form a synapse? Axons grow from the CNS along somewhat defined paths, but when does a specific nerve stop growing and form an end plate? And with which muscle or nerve? If one hypothesizes that a cholinergic nerve, in growing toward the muscle or other end organ which it is going to inervate, releases in front of its growing tip a small cloud of acetylcholine, then the growing tip of the nerve ending is always growing into a finite concentration of acetylcholine. Suppose, however, that the end organ which it approaches already has acetylcholinesterase present as the neuron is approaching it. In these circumstances the acetylcholine being released from the growing nerve tip will be hydrolyzed, and the concentration of the acetylcholine in the region between the growing tip and the end organ will diminish markedly. As a consequence, a concentration gradient will form between the growing tip and the end organ; it is conceivable that a number of processes which depend on the existence of such a concentration gradient may ultimately lead the growing tip to attach firmly to the end organ. This hypothetical example is given mainly to illustrate the importance of the prior existence of the enzyme acetylcholinesterase. If, before the formation of the synaptic interconnection between the growing nerve and the end organ, some seemingly minor event occurs which would slow down the rate of formation of acetylcholinesterase in the end organ, it is conceivable that the nerve ending approaching its end organ and not encountering the concentration gradient (which in the normal organism it would have) would as a consequence not make the proper synaptic connection. Throughout this chapter stress has been placed on the importance of the synaptic interconnection between cells for the proper development and existence of the organism.

Another conclusion which might be derived from the importance of synaptic interconnections to the mammalian organism concerns the appearance of the adult EEG pattern in the growth of the organism. It is well known that in most species the electroencephalographic pattern of the newborn is unlike the adult pattern; in fact, it may be nonexistent. This is not true, however, of the guinea pig, which is born with the adult EEG pattern; the EEG pattern has developed fully by the forty-fifth day of gestation, which is some two weeks before birth. If the cholinergic interconnections can be taken as an example of one of the functional components involved in synapses, then one would expect that the cholinesterase levels would have reached adult levels, or almost so, before the appearance of the adult EEG pattern, but not afterwards. Such a correlation is in general found for the guinea pig, rabbit, cat, dog, and human but not for the rat, which appears to have developed its adult EEG pattern somewhat before the adult cholinergic cholinesterase level is reached (Himwich, 1962). Unfortunately, the data available at present for making these correlations is not detailed enough so that one can be entirely certain of this conclusion. Yet, over-all, it does seem that the cholinesterase levels in developing organisms appear either before or simultaneously with the development of the EEG pattern. Other enzymes which have been studied, such as those involved in myelination of nerve fibers, appear much before the adult EEG levels or much afterwards. Certainly enzymes such as lactic dehydrogenase and the oxidative enzymes involved in mitochondrial metabolism are present long before the electrical activities of the cell are developed, since these are necessary to supply the energy requirements for the building and maintenance of the cell prior to any functional activities. This and much related material, especially behavioral development, has been adequately covered in the recent review by Himwich (1962).

In this light it might also be reasonable to consider again the possibility that the observed anatomical connections in the central nervous system may not, in fact, be functional connections. Our knowledge of the shape and structure of these regions is primarily the result of the development of the electron microscope. Such photographs indicate that there is, between certain regions of nerve cells, a synaptic cleft of between 150 and 300 Angstrom units in width; usually on one side of this cleft is to be found an accumulation of small granules absorbing electrons intensely and appearing then as dark bodies in these photographs. These bodies are about the right size to be the granules of transmitter substance that have been isolated by several workers. Hence the electron microscopist takes as evidence of the existence of synapses those regions of the nervous tissue wherein a single size of intensely absorbing granules is to be found on one side of a cell boundary. As has been pointed out previously, however, a functional synapse could have several other components: a mechanism involving the release of the transmitter substance with the subsynaptic membrane and possibly an enzyme or enzymes for the destruction of the transmitter. These substances, these additional features of a functional synapse, are at present not identifiable by electromicroscopy primarily because of ignorance about the nature of the transmitter substance. One would expect within the next decade to know that a certain synaptic connection belongs to certain kinds of transmitters, and, by the use of histochemical methods, we will no doubt know that all of the necessary components are present to form a functional connection. That this type of definition will be satisfactory to physiologists is unlikely. However, the correlations between the microelectrode work that is being done in physiology and micro- and histochemical work will undoubtedly establish the necessary requirements for calling a given synapse a functional synapse. For these reasons it seems reasonable at present to be somewhat cautious about describing observed synaptic regions in electromicrographs as functional synapses. Rather, it seems reasonable to think of them as potential synapses. Indeed, the formation of all functional synapses in higher organisms depends on the continued interaction between the environment and the organism, which suggests that functional synapses may well be formed throughout the life of the organism. Were this not so, it is hard to understand how one could learn anything.

We believe that the amount of information that an individual receives via the genetic route is enormous. Certainly the synaptic pathways for all the inborn behavior are present at birth or shortly thereafter. In higher organisms that learn after birth, new information is stored and utilized. This must come mainly from the environment. In considering an adult animal one must expect, then, that any newly learned information and/or behavior is to be added to a large storehouse already pre-existing; i.e., new material probably represents only a very small percentage of the total already present. Hence, were one to look for the "new protein" synthesized during a learning experience, one would be looking for an extremely small increment in pre-existing components. An alternate approach is to examine the proteins of organisms raised in various levels of stimulation and attempt to compare the content and type of proteins with those of "normal" animals. For example, many animals can be raised in the dark (Riesen, 1961); they display a type of behavior that can be described as a deficit in visual form or shape discrimination. Furthermore, such animals can eventually learn the shape discriminations known by their litter mates who have been raised in the light. Their behavior is analogous to that of humans who have had cataracts from birth and at the age of 20 undergo surgery, whereupon they describe the difficulties of "acclimating" to a world in which they have always existed. Clearly, these phenomena are related to the concept of perception. All that they suggest, however, is that the necessary concept—i.e., information, memory, "connections"—must be in existence for new information to be able to be processed. Such ideas are, no doubt, quite old to psychologists and learning theorists. However, the possibility of translating them to synaptic connections is relatively new. Precisely what this can lead to is hard to predict. However, a better knowledge of the molecular events in the formation of synapses might produce techniques for alleviating genetically caused mental deficits; the detailed knowledge of the functioning of such synapses might permit a better control of specific types of conditions. At present, much work along these lines is being pursued in an empirical fashion. Given the relative degrees of sophistication of chemistry, physics, and theories of CNS function, the empirical approach does not seem unreasonable. Perhaps future generations of pharmacologists, physicists, biochemists, psychologists, and information theorists can lead us to better theories than those we now utilize.

BIBLIOGRAPHY

Arniaz, G. R. deL. & DeRobertis, E. D. P. (1962), Cholinergic and Non-Cholinergic Nerve Endings in the Rat Brain. *Journal of Neurochemistry,* 9:503.

Attneave, F. (1959), *Applications of Information Theory to Psychology.* New York: Henry Holt and Company.

Bairat, A. (1958), Perivascular Relationship of the Neuroglia Cells. *Biology of Neuroglia,* Windle, C. (Ed.), p. 85. Springfield, Illinois: C. C Thomas.

Bell, D. A. (1962), *Intelligent Machines.* London: Pitman.

Bernsohn, J., Barron, K. D. & Hess, A. R. (1961), Multiple Nature of Acetyl-Cholinesterase in Serum. *Proceedings for the Society of Experimental Biology and Medicine,* 108:71.

Boell, E. J. (1955), *Analysis of Development,* Willier et al. (Eds.), p. 520. Philadelphia: W. B. Saunders and Company.

Bradley, P. B. & Wolstencroft, S. H. (1963), Excitation and Inhibition of Brain Stem Neurones by Noradrenaline and Acetylcholine. *Nature,* 196:840.

Brattgard, S. O. & Hyden, H. (1952), Lipid, Pentose Nucleoproteins and Proteins Determined in Nerve Cells by X-Ray Microradiography. *Acta Radiological Supplements,* 94. Stockholm.

Bullock, T. H. (1959), Neuron Doctrine in Electrophysiology. *Science,* 192:997.

Burn, J. H. & Rand, M. J. (1959), Sympathetic Postganglionic Mechanism. *Nature*, 184:163.

Campbell, P. N. (1960), The Synthesis of Proteins by the Cytoplasmic Components of Animal Cells. *Biological Review*, 35:413.

Chapman, B. L. M. (1959), A Self Organizing Classifying System. *Cybernetica*, 2:15.

Crossland, J. (1960), Chemical Transmission in the Central Nervous System. *Journal of Pharmacy and Pharmacology*, 12:1.

DeRobertis, E. D. P., Nowinski, W. W. & Salz, F. A. (1958), *General Cytology*. Philadelphia: W. B. Saunders and Company.

DeToni, E. Jr. (1960), Kwashiorkor. *Ann. Paediat.*, 195:286.

Eccles, J. C. (1953), *The Neurophysiological Basis of the Mind*. New York: Oxford University Press.

Ehrenpreis, S. (1960), Isolation and Identification of the Acetylcholine Receptor Protein of Electric Tissue. *Biochem. Biophys. Acta*, 44:561.

——(1962), Exchange of Letters with Nachmansohn. *Science*, 136:175-181.

Ellman, G. L. (1962), Problems of Cholinesterase Solubility. *Proceedings of the Western Pharmacological Society*, 5:18.

Featherstone, R. M., Muehlbaecher, C., DeBon, F. & Forsaith, J. (1961), Interactions of Inert Anesthetic Cases with Proteins. *Anesthesiology*, 22:997.

Feldberg, W. (1957), *Acetylcholine in Metabolism of the Nervous System*, Richter (Ed.), p. 493. New York: Pergamon Press.

Flexner, J. B., Flexner, L. B. & Stellar, E. (1963), Memory in Mice Affected as by Intracerebral Puromycin. *Science*, 141:57.

Freide, R. (1953), Gliaindex und Hirnstoffwechsel. *Wien. Zschr. Nervenh.*, 7:143.

George, F. H. (1961), *The Brain as a Computor*. New York: Pergamon Press.

Gerhart, J. C. & Pardee, A. B. (1962), The Enzymology of Control by Feedback Inhibition. *Journal of Biological Chemistry*, 234:891.

Hebb, D. O. (1962), Cholinergic Neurons in Vertebrates. *Nature*, 1192:527.

Hicks, S. P. & D'Amato, C. J. (1961), *Disorders of the Developing Nervous System*. Springfield, Ill.: C. C Thomas.

Himwich, W. E. (1962), *International Review of Neurobiology*. New York: Academic Press.

Huang, R. C. & Bonner, J. (1962), A Suppressor of Chromosomal RNA Synthesis. *Proceedings of the National Academy of Science, United States*, 48:1216.

Jacob, F. & Monod, J. (1961), Genetic Regulating Mechanisms in the Synthesis of Proteins. *Journal of Molecular Biology*, 3:318.

Klotz, I. M. (1960a), Non-covalent Bonds in Protein Structure. *Brookhaven Symposia in Biology*, 13:25-48.

——(1960b), Protein Molecules in Solution. *Circulation*, 21:828.

Koelle, G. B. (1962), Functions of Acetylcholine. *Journal of Pharmacy and Pharmacology*, 14:65.

—— & Friedenwald, J. S. (1949). A Histochemical Method for Localizing Cholinesterase in Tissue Sections. *Proceedings for the Society of Experimental Biology and Medicine*, 70:617.

Koshland, D. E. (1958), Application of a Theory of Enzyme Specificity to Protein Synthesis. *Proceedings of the National Academy of Science, United States*, 44:98.

Markert, C. (1961), Physiochemical Nature of Isozymes. *Annals of the New York Academy of Sciences*, 94:678.

McKean, C. M., Schanberg, S. M. & Giarman, N. J. (1962), A Mechanism of the Indole Defect in Experimental Phenylketonuria. *Science*, 137:604.

Nachmansohn, D. (1959), *Chemical and Molecular Basis of Nerve Activity*. New York: Academic Press.

Noll, H., Staehelin, T. & Wettstein, F. C. (1963), Ribosomal Aggregates in Protein Synthesis. *Nature*, 198:632.

Paton, W. D. M. (1957), Histamine Release. *Pharmacological Review*, 9:269.

Pauling, L. (1961), A Molecular Theory of General Anesthesia. *Science*, 134:15.

Paxson, E. W. & Smith, J. W. (1962), A General Neural Net. *ASTIA Document*, 291-806.

Pomerat, C. M. (1958), Functional Concepts Based on Tissue Culture Studies of Neuroglia Cells. *The Biology of Neuroglia*, Windle, C. (Ed.), p. 162. Springfield, Illinois: C. C Thomas.

Riesen, A. (1961), Studying Perceptual Development Using the Technique of Sensory Deprivation. *Journal of Nervous and Mental Disease*, 132:21.

Shannon, C. E. & Weaver, W. (1949), *The Mathematical Theory of Communication*. Urbana, Illinois: University of Illinois Press.

Tanford, C., Buckley, C. E., Paritosh, K.De & Lively, E. P. (1962), Effects of Ethylene Glycol on the Conformation of Gamma-Globulin and Beta-Lactoglobulin. *Journal of Biological Chemistry*, 237:1168.

—— & Paritosh, K.De (1961), The Unfolding of Beta-Lactoglobulin at Ph 3 by Urea, Formamide and Other Organic Substances. *Journal of Biological Chemistry*, 236:1711.

Weiss, P. (1959), Evidence of Replacement of Nerve Fibers from Their Cell Bodies. *Science*, 129:1290.

Whittaker, V. P. (1959), The Isolation and Characterization of Acetylcholine Containing Particles from Brain. *Biochemical Journal*, 72:694.

Wiener, N. (1948), *Cybernetics*. New York: Wiley; second edition, 1961.

Wright, S. W. & Tarjan, G. (1957), Phenylketonuria. *Journal of Diseases of Children*, 93:405-419.

PART II

Theories of Perception

Pronko, Ebert, and Greenberg present a view of all the traditional theories of perception and a suggested solution to the problems inherent in these formulations. Their conclusions differ from those which Fantz presents in Chapter 6. Until psychology can produce one theory to explain all of the perceptual data, a multiplicity of theories leading to clarification of the issues in the development of perception is desirable because theoretical disagreements do stimulate further research and increase the interest of both students and experimenters in a field.

CHAPTER 3

A Critical Review
of Theories of Perception

N. H. PRONKO

R. EBERT

G. GREENBERG

The pervasiveness of perception is attested throughout every chapter of the present volume. Each of the individual's reactions is preceded by perception. No one can fear, hate, love, learn, or recognize anything or anybody unless he first involves himself in seeing, hearing, touching, tasting, or smelling. Perception is the *sine qua non* of psychological adaptiveness of organisms to their life circumstances. It is the warp and woof in which all the rich variety of responses are embedded. Surely the abundance of perceptual data is comparable to the prevalence of oxygen in chemical inquiry.

The ubiquity of the data of perception has not guaranteed an adequate theory of perception. The statement credited to Leucippus that "where ignorance exists, theories abound" is as pertinent in the present century as it was in his times; the only difference lies in the accumulation of theories over the years.

In their recent volume, *Development of the Perceptual World,* Solley and Murphy (1960) are of the opinion that "our scientific knowledge can only grow through research, and a great deal more is needed in this neglected area of psychology" (p. xi). The present writers disagree; they question whether a mere increase in the number of experiments and field ob-

---

Space limitations prevent the coverage of experimental support for the variety of theories to be examined, but we should indicate that all theorists have generated research to prove their points.

servations will of itself beget valid theory. In fact, a search of *Psychological Abstracts* shows a prodigious labor carried out in behalf of perception.

After all, experiments themselves are not free of the experimenter's silent or explicitly stated assumptions in his approach to the data that he collects even in the laboratory.

At any rate, the present chapter focuses attention upon perceptual theory rather than perceptual research. We shall examine what psychologists say about perception. How do they understand or interpret perception? We intend to study and compare perceptual constructions much as if we were entomologists examining various bugs under our magnifying lens.

The psychological literature is replete with the idea that perceptual theory has evolved from conceptions of a passive action of the mind to conceptions of active processes of mind to the more recent scientific interaction conceptions. It has even been suggested that there has been a revolution in perceptual theorizing (Chaplin and Krawiec, 1960): "The traditional approaches are being abandoned" (p. 139), making room for more tangible formulations. But is this chain of events, this so-called evolution of theory, indeed a reality? Have the older mentalistic views been replaced by scientific views? Perhaps a brief examination of the "development" of perceptual theorizing will answer these questions. Only by means of studying the past of science can we come to appreciate its present.

THE EMPIRICISTS

We need go back no further than the last three centuries and the empiricists, who held that all knowledge is gained through experience. At birth the mind is a tabula rasa, a blank slate, upon which experience will leave its mark in the form of vibrations, engravings, or traces. All learning, then, is a result of perceiving. But what does the perceptual process involve? Each primary exposure to a stimulus is occasioned by the quiet and unnoticed recording of the event by the mind. Subsequent exposures to the stimuli are followed by the again unnoticed (and instantaneous) reference by the mind to the original image, which has been stored in some (as yet undiscovered) vault in the brain.

The key to the empiricists' approach is *passivity*. Perception, a primary function of the mind, is a passive activity, automatic and unaccompanied by any strain or fatigue. It seems as if the empiricists, impressed by the scientific developments of their times, tried to "reduce man and his thoughts to nothing more than a part of the mechanical universe, with all his apparently creative and spontaneous activity simply explained as *passive* mechanical response to his environment" (Hochberg, 1962, pp. 257-258).

An exponent of such a view was Berkeley, who suggested that everything we know comes through our senses; it was Berkeley who stated that nothing can be said to exist if we do not perceive it; and it was Berkeley who implied that we cannot directly sense the characteristics of the physical world. All that is available to us as knowledge and as truth is what our senses reveal, what our minds perceive. According to Kantor (1959), Berkeley truly "reduced all reality to sensational appearance, that is to properties of mind" (p. 27).

UNIFIED MIND THEORISTS

It comes as no great surprise, then, to find the conception of a "unified mind" that is passive in action prevalent in the perceptual theorizing of John Locke. It was Locke who suggested that perception is accomplished by virtue of powers possessed by objects—powers which instigate ideas in the mind. Again, the mind is considered passive in the perceptual process. Small wonder, then, that associated with the Lockean and the entire empirical view is the attempt to create a "picture of the mind."

THE NATIVISTIC SCHOOL

Another "older" idea of perception comes from the nativistic school of thought. Where the empiricists placed great emphasis on experience in the perceptual process, the nativists were of the opinion that the mechanisms and the "how" of perception were innate; they existed prior to experience. When we realize that this train of thought coexisted with the early sensory psychologists and was bred in the physiological tradition, we can see that the problem becomes increasingly complex and confused. Great stress was put on the function of the brain and nervous system by this tradition, by both the strict nativists and the physiological school. The brain then became something like a modern telephone switchboard and the theoretical job was one of identifying the receptors and the end organs responsible for each sensation experienced. Thus we find ideas of specific energies of nerves abundant in the teachings of this era.

Woodworth and Schlosberg (1960) appear to be correct in suggesting that "the more we study the sense organs, the more we seem compelled to emphasize the role of the higher centers" (p. 296). But one might here argue that the nativists (and all those of the Kantian approach) were not speaking of brains or of higher centers, but rather of mental processes, of mind. The two ideas appear to be quite different. But appearances can indeed be deceiving if Kantor's (1959) evaluation of the situation is correct. He states that, "As far as psychologists are concerned, Kantian epistemology, reinforced by Johannes Müller's and Helmholtz's neurological adaptations, is the basic model for handling perceptual problems. The only difference is that the absolute and *a priori* properties of *mind* have been made into attributes of the *brain*" (p. 28).

PSYCHOPHYSIOLOGY

We find great activity among the physiologists in the areas of perceptual and mental processes during this period. In fact, this is the time of the creation of psychophysiology—an attempt to avoid the difficulties of handling inscrutable mental states and processes by turning to the more concrete bodily substrates. Consequently, we find a shift from concepts of *mind* to concepts of *brain*. In both cases, perception is the function of these entities and occurs inside the organism.

The conceptions of perception arising from this school of thought are quite similar to the earlier empiricist ones, except for a change in terminology. Hence, Müller suggests that in perception, the brain perceives only the states and the conditions of the nerves; "not of external bodies, but of the nerves of sense themselves" (Dennis, 1948, p. 162), a conception much like that of Berkeley. Helmholtz too holds similar views. The Young-Helmholtz color-vision theory holds that color is merely the physiological state of the particular photoreceptor stimulated and color, therefore, is in the brain, not in the object perceived.

Throughout its long history, perception theory reveals conceptions of the perceptual process as involving the mind's passive recording, storing, and comparing of mental images to active processes of the brain and nervous system. The point is this: In the empiricist approach as well as here, the function of the mind in the perceptual process is to compare and interpret mental images, and by so doing, perceive. There is, then, no perception unless the mind in some way interprets the sensory data that impinges on it. Helmholtz develops this idea to its fullest by proposing that the mind makes "unconscious inferences" when confronted with stimuli.

In all of the foregoing approaches to perception, there appears to be general agreement that we never perceive objects directly. What do we perceive? The answer most acceptable to perception theorists is best put by Hochberg (1962): "We do not directly see things, people or the space in which they move. An object reflects light to the retina of our eye, this light stimulates the receptor cells upon which it falls, and it is always the aggregate of specific nerve energies thus aroused, *not the object, nor the light from it,* that causes the group of sensations we experience" (p. 276; italics added).

The view that perception is an active process of mind was espoused by Harvey Carr, the Chicago functionalist. We find Carr defining perception as "a form of mental activity in which the meaning of present situations, objects, and events is determined, in part, by past learning" (Chaplin and Krawiec, 1960, p. 128). Notice that here, as above, mind is endowed with the power to select and interpret sensory data. The idea is the same, the terms identical to the older transcendental approaches.

Returning to more current thinking, we find E. G. Boring employing similar concepts and constructs. Boring (1933) suggests that "perception depends upon the functioning of a fairly well localized region of the cortex" (p. 105). Furthermore, Boring goes on to develop ideas first posed by Müller 100 years earlier. He suggests, as Müller did before him, that within the brain there is a perceiving mind that can become directly aware of the state of the nerves which end in the brain.

But Boring is perhaps better known as a proponent of Titchener's core-context theory of perception, the core being the basic sensory excitation that identifies the perception and connects it with the objects perceived. The context implies that other sensory data "modify or correct the data of the core as it forms the perception" (Boring, 1946, p. 100). Boring proposes that the brain corrects the upside-down retinal image, and furthermore, "the brain can do an excellent job in this kind of correction" (p. 99). This is undoubtedly a psychophysiological conception, one that Müller or Helmholtz would not have rejected.

The foregoing hasty sketch has made "spot checks" of the fundamentals of perception theory as it has evolved during the past several hundred years down to contemporary times. There appears to be an essential sameness in these *apparently* diverse constructions. Nor have the theories examined so far shown a willingness to "abandon older approaches." If this first quick glance is a preview of things to come, we should not entertain hopes of a sudden "breakthrough" to a radically novel theory of perception. But before we attempt to examine and evaluate the most recent constructions, we intend to benefit from Floyd Allport's keen analysis of certain historical developments that have strait-jacketed efforts at formulating contemporary theories of perception.

Among the endless series of tomes on perception, surely Floyd Allport's (1955) *Theories of Perception and the Concept of Structure* will long hold a respected place. His scholarly contribution is important here for two main reasons: (1) his incisive analysis of past and current theories of perception, and (2) his own contribution. We shall, at this point, discuss both of these aspects of his work in turn.

CLASSICAL VIEWS OF PERCEPTION

Allport first traces the following seven historical strands of development of perception theory which still effect contemporary attempts at theory construction.

1. *The mind-body problem.* The relation of the mental to the physical with such attendant problems as psychophysical parallelism, interactionism, the doctrine of specific nerve energies, and the psychophysical movement constitute one strand of this evolution.

2. *Mental elements and their attributes.* Down through the ages, sensory qualities and their attributes have held the attention of philosophers and psychologists. Structuralism and introspectionism under Wundt and Titchener were attempts to reduce sensations to their fundamental components. Analysis appeared as the most hopeful mode of attack for finding the basic constituents of mind. We shall encounter this approach in the latest theories.

3. *The need for a synthesizing agent.* Reduction of mental contents into their basic elements at once demands some way of combining them into the unity that is theirs prior to analysis. Therefore, from the Greeks on down some sort of integrating process had to be conceptualized. Crea-

tive synthesis, association of ideas, and Titchener's core-context theory of meaning are several answers to the problem.

4. *Agency and unconscious inference.* The idea that various organs have specific functions in the total adjustment of the organism is a hoary one. An alternative to the associationistic theories of how perceptual elements get combined is Helmholtz's idea of unconscious inference. But, as Allport points out, "can a neuron or a group of synapses in the brain make an inference?" (p. 83), for if "inferring" goes on, there must be an "inferrer."

> It is one of the riddles of the history of psychology that a doctrine so unsatisfactory as unconscious inference should keep reappearing through successive generations. The answer probably lies in the fact that this sort of thinking is not readily escapable for those perceptionists who lean toward functionalism. Helmholtz was merely the classical example of this tendency. The theme appears again in the constancy theory of Brunswik, though it is there worked out in much greater detail, and with new concepts and experimental interpretations. Something resembling unconscious inference, in the sense of assumptions, purposive selection, and appraisal, is seen in the work of such men as Ittelson and Cantril and in the writings of Ames. From another angle manikin tautology crept into the work of theorists who tried to show that motivation influences the perceptual process. In the course of these endeavors a "pre-perceiver" reared its head and had to promptly be exorcized. When the system was revised as an "hypothesis-theory" it was found that until the matter could be restated in more physiological terms it still had a resurrected odor of unconscious-inference. Cybernetics, the latest word in "teleological mechanisms," is unable to fully harmonize purpose with objective description. The legacy bequeathed by Helmholtz is still in our hands [pp. 83-84].

5. *Attitude, set, and determining tendency.* In their introspective analyses of perception, the Würzburg school came across the importance of the "task attitude" (*Einstellung*) and "determining tendency" in influencing perceptions in ways that linking or association of elements could not account for. We shall encounter a modern counterpart of this strand later in the present chapter.

6. *Nativism versus empiricism.* Is space perception inherited or acquired? Perception has been bedeviled by this conundrum as much as has "the IQ" and mathematical and musical talent and capacity. The concep-

tion of local signs as put forth by Lotze was in opposition to the nativistic theory of the innate nature of perception. The gestaltists still support the latter conception while the behaviorists favor "the environmentalistic" version. Much of the experimental literature reviewed elsewhere in this volume was carried out in an attempt to support or refute one or the other of these opposed theories. On this point, Allport entertains the possibility that the preservation of the nativist-empiricist controversy may be merely a reflection of "temperamental differences among scientists" (p. 89). It seems to the writers that a resolution of this perplexing problem should have a firmer basis than an *ad hominem* argument. Further on, we shall suggest another possible basis.

7. *Gestalt theory.* The last classical strand that Allport deals with comes to fruition with the development of the gestalt school of psychology which was preceded by the Kantian idealistic trend. A quick sketch would point to the phenomenological nature of experience culminating in the work of Husserl, Brentano's act psychology, Mach and von Ehrenfels' "form-qualities," and finally, the unitary nature of perception as denoted by the very term, gestalt.

The above seven themes which appeared at different points in history both separately and severally, infiltrated the evolution of theories of perception, but their greatest significance lies in the fact that they influence contemporary theories for good or ill. To quote Allport: "Though most of the classical theories contributed something of value, they also bequeathed to later generations a legacy of problems and perplexities" (p. 95). To understand these theoretical difficulties, we now turn to a consideration of eleven contemporary approaches of thirteen possible ones to the data of perception. Space prevents more than a thumbnail sketch of each theory. The more persistent reader will find Allport's elaborate discussion of all thirteen theories informative and stimulating.

MODERN THEORIES OF PERCEPTION

1. *Gestalt theory's configurational approach.* If one were to free associate to gestalt psychology, one would undoubtedly include the following items: phenomenological in outlook and taking immediate experience as its subject matter, it explains perception in terms of wholes that are more than the sum of their parts, dynamic configurations, and field forces. Forms exist in nature as well as in psychological phenomena and the two

gestalten (one from the physical and the other from the mental realm) are linked together via the principle of isomorphism which posits a brain or nervous-system configuration to correspond with the other two gestalten. Gestalten are never assemblages of parts but have a "whole character" about them which defies their analysis into elements. The wholeness or unitariness of experience is guaranteed by a field force that keeps the phenomenological as well as the physical and physiological gestalt in equilibrium or organization. There is free speculation about how the nervous system effects isomorphism and gives rise to a percept which departs in form from a one-to-one correspondence with both the neural substrate and the physical configuration.

2. *Topological field theory*. As an offshoot of gestalt theory and a development of Lewin's, topological theory departs from orthodox gestalt theory in its indifference to the intervening link furnished by the nervous system. Isomorphism becomes an unnecessary fixture in a system which employs a topological (i.e., nonmetric) phenomenological space organized through psychic forces and a "life space" in which the individual is acting at the moment. Barriers, vectors, and goals that have positive or negative valences are other Lewinian appurtenances. While topological theory seems to merge perception with cognition and to reduce it to merely "a sudden reorganization of the cognitive field," it is nevertheless important for its reinforcement of gestalt perceptionists who did apply field theory.

3. *Cell-assembly and phase-sequence theory*. Association theory does not exist in its original form today, but Allport (Chapter 7) makes a case for its influence on contemporary theory as exemplified in the work of Hebb. While Hebb is not ready to throw the entire gestalt theory overboard, he introduces elements into the physiological bases of percepts in the form of units that get connected in an additive way. This is provided by reverberating circuits that make possible a connection between neurons long enough to allow a lasting association to be built up. Functional associations between groups of cortical neurons or cell assemblies provide the substrate for percepts. More complex perceptions are built up by the linking of cell assemblies through facilitation conduction and consolidation in timing. An assembly of unitary assemblies involves the phase sequence which, with motor components (as, for example, eye movements), provides the basis for the perception of a complex. Essentially, Hebb has evolved

an association or aggregate of neurons in place of the historical association of ideas and in place of the gestaltist's *cortical fields*.

4. *Sensory-tonic field theory*. The gestaltists ignored motor components of response in their theory of isomorphism. While Hebb gives some place to muscle movements in perception, it is Werner and Wapner (Allport, Chapter 8) who unite the motor and sensory aspects of response in their "sensory-tonic theory of perception." The term "sensory" covers both the physiological and the phenomenological systems and is therefore ambiguous. Tonus refers both to muscle tensions and to the grosser contractions in the form of movements. Motor changes within the organism form a part of the total perceptual process by giving rise to one form of sensory element (kinesthetic components) to combine with the truly sensory. Thus, perception has an entirely sensory foundation. However, the interaction of the two traditionally different components gives their contribution in a dynamic equivalence. The gestaltlike concept of sensory and tonic as a "whole" is apparent.

5. *Set and motor adjustments*. While not a full-fledged theory, motor aspects of perception as utilized in Hebb's theory and more so in that of Werner and Wapner are (Allport, Chapter 9) developed to their fullest significance and are illustrated by the work of a single theorist in this area, Freeman. Allport is of the opinion that a consideration of muscle and set will be an important task for theories of the future.

Some of the main effects of motor factors and set on contemporary theories of perception are revealed in the following list of propositions derived from psychological experiments:

(a) Set prepares and facilitates perception; it sustains or enhances it, at the same time constituting a perceptual background that precedes, accompanies, and even outlasts overt performances or the perceptual acts themselves.

(b) Set is a selective process; it excludes certain reactions as well as making possible certain others.

(c) Set is a factor localizable in the organism rather than in the stimulus object and therefore makes possible two different percepts from the same stimulus pattern. (Ambiguous figures are pertinent examples.)

(d) Sets can have the character of intention or expectancy.

(e) Sets can be voluntary or involuntary, they can involve or be involved in learning, and they can be conscious or unconscious. According to Freeman (Allport, Chapter 9), his "dynamotor" theory requires both central and peripheral factors. A tension in any muscle has a backlash action that affects the brain in such a way that it, in turn, lowers the response threshold of the motor pathways involved.

6. *Adaptation level, perceptual norm, and frame of reference theories.* Spatial or other perceptual magnitudes as ends in themselves have been investigated in a movement that may be considered a derivative of psychophysics. While psychophysics is stimulus-bound with presentation of stimuli of controlled magnitude, it is possible, in a relativistic fashion, for the subject to specify how low a tone must be in order to be perceived as low. The scale or frame of response involved in such investigations is specified by the subject rather than by the experimenter. According to Helson's (Allport, Chapter 10) theory, the individual establishes an "average" for himself in ordering a class of stimuli in a dimensional or quantitative order. This average becomes a standard of reference by which other stimuli are judged as of a specific higher or lower magnitude in that frame of reference. Quantification of data is possible in Helson's approach.

The study of attitudes has been furthered by Sherif and Cantril in an approach similar to Helson's. "Social norms" within a "framework of the group's activities" become the focus of interest here.

7. *Functional and molar theories.* How objects retain their constancy under varying conditions of illumination, distance, perspective, etc., is the central question of "probabilistic functionalism," a theory espoused by Brunswik (Allport, Chapter 11). Essentially, Brunswik works with the environment and the organism as a whole, eschewing physiological analyses. His approach is not in search of absolutistic and rigorous laws but correlational and statistical propositions which is probabilistic functionalism.

A viewpoint about perception closely related to Brunswik's is represented by Ames, Kilpatrick, and Ittelson's transactional view. These investigators have worked out ingenious demonstrations such as the rotating trapezoidal window and the distorted rooms. Their underlying philosophy is a distortion of Dewey and Bentley's transactional approach which takes the perceived object into account in a manner similar to that of Brunswik. Both theories represent perception as "a function of some sort of weighted average of our past experiences" (Kilpatrick, 1952, p. 10). These processes that are brought into operation following impingements from sensory

receptors are unconscious. They are presumably cerebral and bear a
strong resemblance to Helmholtz's unconscious inference. These unconscious assumptions derived from past experience form our "assumptive
world" (Kilpatrick, 1952, p. 89); they function upon each response occasion and constitute our perceptions of a world which can be known in
no other way.

8. *Directive-state theory.* A contribution of Bruner and Postman, this
theory operates with two fundamentally opposed factors: the structural
or autochthonous and the behavioral. The first set (the formal factors)
includes the stimulus, the receptors, and the nervous-system components
as a perceiving mechanism. The second set, including the person's needs,
values, tensions, defenses, and his past experience, constitutes a central
directive state through "higher level" processes. Together they make up
the functional or behavioral factors in perception. It is apparent that the
organismic factors dominate stimulus factors in Bruner and Postman's
theory.

9. *Hypothesis theory.* A subsequent evolution of Bruner and Postman's
theory led to their hypothesis or expectancy theory in which sets were elaborated into hypotheses. Perception was seen in the light of the other cognitive processes (such as thinking or recalling). A process of hypothesis
confirmation or rejection guides the individual's adjustment to his environment. When the hypotheses, largely unconscious, are confirmed, percepts, memories, or ideas arise in consciousness from interaction with information provided by the sense organs. Essentially, Bruner and Postman's
later theory is not a radical revision of the central directive state which
now employs hypotheses and expectancies instead of vague "higher processes."

10. *Learning theory.* Behavioral theories of perception, of which there
are two types, lean heavily upon learning as an explanatory principle.
The first group, associationist theories, are S-R forms of theoretical construction, and the second are S-S or field theories. While abjuring cognitive and phenomenological factors, learning theory does permit explanation in terms of stimulus traces and excitatory potentials. Hull is an outstanding exponent of S-R theory.

As a representative of the S-S theory, Tolman puts forth a "sign-gestalt
expectancy" construction in terms of a goal achieved or a field coming to
equilibrium through the organism's action. Gestalt psychology and Lewin's

topology provide a model for Tolman. He does accept cognition terminology even in explaining the behavior of rats. Rats do carry "cognitive maps" around with them in their brains and they also have hypotheses. Though incompatible, Hull's and Tolman's learning theories have been applied to perception. Hull's theory does the job in terms of habit strengths and reaction potentials of discriminatory responses. Tolman's account has obvious direct connections with older gestalt formulations of perception.

11. *The cybernetic or system theory.* A new trend has come into psychology from mathematicians, physiologists, and engineers. It derives not from living things but from machines. From constructing marvelous electronic computers that carry out complex analytic functions, the men who built them apply knowledge of the structure and operation of these machines to understanding how man can construct such machines. "A curious reversal this. First the product is created by its designer; then the designer is explained in terms of his product" (Allport, 1955, p. 468).

Machines are open systems and, like organisms, they have a continual input. In fact, the computer "feeds on" "information," and "retains" or "stores" that "information" as "memory." There are many other terms that derive from analogy with organismic structures and functions. Organisms, in turn, are credited with a scanning device such as the alpha rhythm of the brain. There is an invariant relationship between a brain condition and a brain's having a certain percept or idea, although it need not be isomorphic as in the gestalt system. In other words, there are stable relationships under constantly changing stimulus patterns. As a final comment on this latest of mechanical theoretical systems of perception, Allport's perceptive query is especially pertinent.

> In this whole notion we find another instance of our old problem of the *inside* and the *outside*. What is it that computes? Is it the organism or just the organism's brain? Cybernetic theory stresses, and quite naturally, the latter. This way, however, lies "encapsulation" and some very confusing issues. The brain now becomes the "inside" system; and the rest of the body becomes the "outside," a region under the control of the central cerebral agency. But does this not give us two levels of operation, the brain and the organism as a whole? It is bewildering to contemplate that our brains, in using calculus for solving spatial perceptions, have been employing practically from birth

an advanced mathematical strategy that *"we"* have had to acquire a college education to learn [p. 517].

ALLPORT'S EVALUATION OF PSYCHOLOGY'S PERCEPTION THEORIES

Physics may be embarrassed by the necessity to conceptualize light sometimes as a particle and sometimes as a wave. Consider the discomfiture which has been generated in psychology by a theoretical affluence that has bequeathed it thirteen theories! And yet, how has such an opulent heritage advanced our understanding of perceptual data? Again, the hard labor of analyzing, weighing, comparing, and evaluating the series of theories has been done for us by Allport (1955), whose help we enlist at this point.

By using a hypothetical, homely perceptual occurrence as a test, Allport (1955) measures the adequacy of each of the series of perception theories in turn and specifies the particulars in which he finds it wanting. He finds that his review "has brought to light many shrewd observations and suggestive findings. It has revealed some important generalizations. But out of it all there has not yet come a theory that promises to be fully explanatory and general" (p. 574). Indeed, "all the problems that were interwoven in the strands of classical thinking . . . reappear within the gamut of the modern theories" (p. 95). So much labor for such meager progress!

In answer to the above theoretical quandary, Allport proposes another theory which is not a synthesis of the others but an attempt "to synthesize their major contributions" (p. 611). "Structure" forms the foundation for Allport's theory of the perceptual act which is conceived to be a "dynamically operating *structure* that presents the very picture of a self-delimited and self-contained structuring of ongoings and events" (p. 612). "Events" of stimulation are generated when energy impinges upon a receptor, which, in turn, initiates an "ongoing process" in the receptor. The resulting excitation in an afferent neuron sets off another event. Another ongoing process leads to an event at a synapse in the brain as a succeeding central neuron is excited. Ongoing contractions of muscles, afferent neural backlash, and a multiplicity of other "ongoings" all feed into the brain while the brain itself is conceived as a source of other ongoings and events such as filling in of the gaps, the whole complex constituting a structure of ongoings and events (p. 616).

Events are not describable in quantitative terms because they are "all-or-none" affairs rather than continuous functions; they either occur or do not occur, for which reason mechanical and quantifiable laws cannot account for structure. This structure which underlies and accounts for perception is not yet known nor can it be invented; it must be discovered. Allport therefore adopts the concept of structure as a working hypothesis for integrating the heretofore separate aggregates of perception with the hope that quantitative laws may be discovered within the structural setting. The principle of "structural probability" is added as a related principle which accounts for the probability of occurrence of the structure at all. This qualitative principle permits the correlative statement of quantitative laws that pertain to the structure. Allport then proposes an abstract kinetic (not static) model for structure, involving the principle of circularity in imitation of circular feedback systems and reverberatory circuits, which he expands to a theory of "structural kinematics" (p. 635). Higher orders of structures are built up into a "cycle of cycles of ongoings and events" (p. 636).

It would take us too far afield to give an exhaustive account of Allport's theory, but the main principles of it have been outlined. We need only add that he considers perception as occurring at two levels, i.e., in the physiological and the phenomenological realms (p. 51). He favors working at the physiological level because "even though our knowledge here is limited, the very fact that receptors, neurons, and muscle fibers are denotable and that their processes are often capable of experimental detection and study helps us to see that, in a particular instance of perceiving, some broad physiologically or physically expressed principle underlying the phenomenology may be illustrated. For this reason a satisfactory theory of perception must carry on a large part of its work of explanation in the physiological rather than the phenomenological realm" (pp. 50-51).

All perception theories from the oldest to the most recent (cf. e.g., Bartley, 1958, or Solley and Murphy, 1960) appear to have a built-in obstacle to theoretical adequacy and acceptability. Sometimes these creations are criticized even by their own creators as well as by other theorists. They all deal with perceptual facts in terms of "outside" and "inside." Differences among them may be analogized as a theme with variations.

A FINAL COMMENT ON TRADITIONAL THEORIES OF PERCEPTION

Elsewhere, one of the writers (Pronko, 1961) has analyzed some of the problems inherent in the traditional constructions of perceptual data. These comments are quoted below *in extenso*.

The writer believes that one factor underlying the psychologist's sense of uneasiness with the facts of perception is what might be labeled a "start-from-scratch" or "all-or-nothing" attitude. With this orientation, the psychologist seems to feel that he must give a complete and exhaustive account of perceptual data. Is such an attitude really justifiable? Does the physicist do a similar total job for magnetism, cosmic rays, or oxygen? To take the last item, oxygen, is this datum really not an altogether evanescent and subtle phenomenon? After all, can the physicist say much more than that this gas is without odor, smell, and taste, and that it has a certain property of supporting combustion and a certain weight? And yet, he attacks this problem as he does his others, positivistically and vigorously, and makes headway in understanding them all. But suppose one had never in his life observed oxygen, magnetism, gravitation, or electricity. Would any amount of description duplicate the experience of these data or substitute for such an experience? Obviously, one would have to observe such events before their theoretical description could have any significance.

Why then do psychologists seem to set up double standards and make excessive demands on their own statements about perception? After all, are not the facts of perception as ubiquitous and abundant as oxygen? Their pervasiveness and shared nature actually give them an advantage over the less intimate and personal conditions in our surroundings. Through social checks we can enter into and compare our perceptions, however subtle they may be, much more intimately than we can ever share or enter into magnetism *qua* magnetism. A realization of this fact should dispel forever our sense of embarrassment over perceptual data and our unnecessary compulsion to describe them exhaustively. After all, they, as much as oxygen and the rest, are the proper starting point for theoretical construction.

Another stumbling block in the development of a valid theory of perception has a semantic origin. In this writer's view, we are too much bound by our everyday language, which distorts and gives a determining direction to theory development. Take the simple situation expressed in the phrasing of the man in the street, "I see a tree."

This statement formulates (nay, strait-jackets) the working basis of current theories of perception. Immediately, an entity, "I," over here, and another, "a tree," over there, are brought into juxtaposition. So far only two disparate entities have been related as if they were puppets on a stage, but trouble appears when we try to introduce them to the verb, "see." Convention has shied away from imputing "seeingness" to the tree. For that reason, no one has verbally created entities within the tree to carry the theoretical ball. Instead, tradition has always moved over to the organism's side of the fence and attributed the "seeingness" to a pseudo localization *within* the organism. From here on, we have double talk in terms of an "outside," "the tree," and an "inside," the perception of the tree.

Several points need to be made concerning the semantic disorder which we have created even before our theory has gotten off the ground. First of all, there is the easily overlooked differential status of the terms "inside" and "outside." The arbitrary carving up of the space referred to can be avoided. Nevertheless, we must acknowledge that even the bad start such a theory has taken should accord a different status to the terrestrial "outside" (i.e., the locus of the participating tree) than it can to the imputed but never designated "inside" the organism. How can we possibly work at establishing the interior location of "the perception"? After all, lens, retina, optic pathways, and visual cortex have already been gone over with a fine-tooth comb without ever establishing a position for "the percept." What a pity that the epidermis of the organism permitted erection of this artificial and arbitrary boundary. If we may speculate in science-fiction fashion, a more amorphous separation of organism-in-environment might have prevented the theoretical creation of an "inside" and "outside." At any rate, once these noncorrelative, nonanalogous "spaces" have been rent asunder, no amount of theoretical ingenuity can join them together again.

However, our troubles are not yet over. Another specter rises. This difficulty comes from our traditional predilection for the organism and the resultant need for creating perception *within it*. This preference for the organism creates a *deus ex machina* situation in which (theoretically, at least), I appear to generate "seeingness" even in advance of my confrontation with "tree." The tree appears only as a cue or a trigger for the "see-ing." Surely this is not a correct statement of the reality that we started with.

But it is not only spatial problems that bedevil us, for our "time" is also out of joint according to the manner in which it has been forced to do duty in the construction of perceptual theory. The conventional temporal framework in conventional theories of perception employs *instant* time. And yet no one ever saw tree, or anything else for that matter, in the same kind of time as is occupied by an explosion. We acknowledge the fact that perceptions *develop over time,* but we do not treat them that way. The writer would venture to predict that our difficulties with perception will not be surmounted until we adopt a framework similar to the one employed by the embryologist or the historical geologist. Their time marches on and is an integral feature of their theoretical description. Per-ception theory has hobbled along with a cramping, crippling instantaneous temporal framework.

The deleterious side effects of our ages-old perceptual theory have by no means been exhausted. Consider the looseness and vagueness of per-ceptual semantics. The term "perception" refers to (a) the thing perceived (b) the perceiving of the thing (c) the perception projected back out from the organism's inside to the place where the thing *really* is, and (d) the mysterious goings-on within the organism. Consider also the obscuring of the undisputed fact and existence of perceptual data by the traditional "eye-as-a-camera" approach implicit in perceptual theory. How the living eye could ever project an image of the tree (even though upside down) on to a transparent retina appears next to impossible with all the imperfections inherent in the visual system. And how the alleged "picture" could be trans-mitted intact through the optic pathway is a deeper mystery still. But over-look all the preceding and imagine that somehow the tree is imaged on the occipital lobe. How do we get the organism back into the impersonal chain reaction? With what mind's eye could the "image" be seen and what is really being seen—the tree out there, the picture in the eye, the one on the visual cortex? That theoretical confusion is rampant is rather obvious by this time (Pronko, 1961, pp. 313-314).

AN ALTERNATIVE APPROACH TO PERCEPTUAL DATA

If the above criticisms of conventional theories of perception are justified, then radical remedies are called for. As the writers view it, the essential sameness (with humor variations) of past and present theories that we have scrutinized reflects a basic identity of approach to all the data of psychology, including perception. The viewpoint implicit in all the theories is one that might be categorized as a "one-variable" or "self-actional" orientation. Kantor (1946) has traced the history of science as well as that of psychology through the following three stages: (1) substance-property stage (2) statistical-correlation stage, and (3) integrated-field stage. The first stage may be illustrated by faculties, abilities, capacities, instincts, drives, "the IQ," etc., conceived as mental properties *of* the organism. The statistical-correlation stage took in a larger territory when statistical formulae were derived to express the relationship between the mental world and the magnitude of the stimulus or physiological excitation. Psychophysics is the best representative of this stage.

The vast bulk of theories have not advanced to the third stage as yet. All hover over and close to the organism with a grudging acknowledgment of the need for a stimulus, which is often reduced to a mere "cue" or "trigger" for a perceptual or other act. All theories stress the "interior" of the organism as a quasilocation for perception. This is true even of the transactional approach with its "internalized assumptive world." All alike, from cybernetics to gestalt theory, shift the perceptual drama to hypothetical spots within the organism. The result has been the erection of an elaborate but abstruse intraorganismic theater. For the most part, the brain has played the heaviest role in the alleged goings-on. Skinner (1938) long ago berated psychologists for carrying on traffic with a "C.N.S., a conceptual nervous system" (p. 421). It seems that perceptual theory has got itself out on a limb in this respect with its attainment of highly hypothetical and obscure alleged events. Yet, despite a unanimous and ready admission of ignorance about the "neural substrate" of perception, theorists persist in constructing highly inferential theories in such a framework. Even after his prodigious and highly commendable labor in behalf of perception theory, and as a preview of the shape of things to come, Allport (1955) declares that "we must now have better theories of what is going on 'inside' "[1] (p. 467)! But how else can one proceed if he forces the organism to carry the entire theoretical burden of the perceptual act?

---

[1] The quotes around the term "inside" call for some heavy thinking.

With such an approach, perception inevitably becomes an intraorganismic creation or psychic epiphenomenon, presumably of the brain.

AN INTEGRATED-FIELD APPROACH TO PSYCHOLOGICAL DATA

Ever since 1924, Kantor (1924, 1933, 1947, 1953, 1959) has been developing a theory that is *event*-oriented. For him an event is constituted by an organism on the one hand *and* a stimulus object on the other. A stimulus object can be another person, a thing, or a situation. These two factors are really peripheral to the reciprocal or mutual *interaction* or *interbehavior* that occurs when the two variables confront each other. Kantor's view is, thus, *action*- or *process*- rather than *thing*-oriented. While the interaction is of central importance, setting or surrounding factors are also taken into account in so far as they condition the event.

Kantor's treatment of the organism departs from traditional views in his treatment of it as a unit variable. While the "hollow-organism" concept is appropriate in one respect, Kantor, at the same time, recognizes the organism as a cluster of biological variables that, at best, *participate in,* but do not *cause*, psychological events. Therefore, no attempt is made to (theoretically) invade the organism for explanatory concepts. The brain is acknowledged to have physiological functions only; it is no more and no less important than the other organismic structures or systems.

Kantor's interest is not in what goes on in the organism but what is transpiring in the total integrated field or event. Cause-effect thinking is ruled out and analysis is in terms of *functions* of all the factors concerned. Both in the observation of the data and in theory construction, all the variables are held together in their joint and reciprocal activity. Thus, thinking, learning, and perceiving are not *functions of an organism* nor are they said to occur *in the organism*. They are located in the total field because all the variables in a given field are necessary for their occurrence. Strictly speaking, one does not study persons but interbehaviors.

With focus on the event, Kantor proceeds to analyze how, centrally, the organism and the stimulus object act in relation to one another. The term "stimulus function" refers to the action of the stimulus object. The organism's action is the response function. The role of the other factors is also assessed in this situational approach. Kantor's uniqueness also lies in his use of a historical dimension to unify or relate and interpret the succession of behavior segments that others unify by hypothetical brain or mind states or conditions. All the behaviors pertaining to a given individual come into being during his lifetime through his psychological history or reactional biography. It is obvious that in Kantor's system there are no psychological givens at birth, and heredity is viewed as explaining only the anatomical and physiological characteristics of individuals.

Within such a framework, perception is viewed as a discriminatory response that originates out of purely biological organismic functions such as light sensitivity. These biological actions are all that are present at birth, but they constitute the raw materials for the evolution of genuine psychological interbehaviors. One way Kantor has of avoiding theories in terms of hypothetical brain functions is to demarcate behavioral from physiological events (cf. Kantor, 1933, Chapter 1), a distinction lacking in all the theories under review here, absence of which has facilitated looking into the organism for interpretations. Certainly, nerves, brain, retinae, etc., participate in visual perception (i.e., they are an aspect of the visual event) but so do light conditions (medium of contact), setting factors (as in the simultaneous-contrast situation), and an object-to-be-seen.

The advantage in Kantor's system is the absence of a need to create the perceptual act (however it is conceived inside the organism). The theoretical job, thus, becomes immeasurably simple because it is *factually given*. It becomes a datum in its own right with the same status as air or light which are also factually guaranteed. Perception does not have to be explained as an intraorganismic emergent or epiphenomenon any more than gravitational phenomena require transformation. All the variables share the explanatory burden and the organism is freed from its crushing and perplexing job of doing a theoretical solo. The job becomes one of determining how, what, when, and where (i.e., in *terrestrial* space) perceptual interactions arise and change.

The above brief sketch of Kantor's interbehavioral framework brings our critical review of theories to a close. As a parting remark, we cannot help suggesting that theorists put a stop to the compulsive rephrasing of perceptual constructions carried out from an ages-old approach. If and when they are ready to try a new posture, a trial from Kantor's interbehavioral framework might permit a fresh attack upon the puzzling problems that past theoretical developments have dumped on our doorstep.

BIBLIOGRAPHY

Allport, F. H. (1955), *Theories of Perception and the Concept of Structure*. New York: Wiley.

Bartley, S. H. (1958), *Principles of Perception*. New York: Harper and Brothers.

Boring, E. G. (1933), *The Physical Dimensions of Consciousness*. New York: The Century Company.

——(1946), The Perception of Objects. *American Journal of Physics*, 14:99-107.

Chaplin, J. P. & Krawiec, T. S. (1960), *Systems and Theories of Psychology*. New York: Holt, Rinehart and Winston.

Dennis, W. (1948), *Readings in the History of Psychology*. New York: Appleton-Century-Crofts.

Hochberg, J. E. (1962), Nativism and Empiricism in Perception. *Psychology in the Making*, Postman, L. (Ed.). New York: Alfred A. Knopf.

Kantor, J. R. (1924), *Principles of Psychology*. New York: Alfred A. Knopf.

——(1933), *A Survey of the Science of Psychology*. Bloomington, Indiana: The Principia Press.

——(1946), The Aim and Progress of Psychology. *American Scientist*, 34:251-263.

——(1947), *Problems of Physiological Psychology*. Bloomington, Indiana: The Principia Press.

——(1953), *The Logic of Modern Science*. Bloomington, Indiana: The Principia Press.

——(1959), *Interbehavioral Psychology*. Bloomington, Indiana: The Principia Press.

Kilpatrick, F. P. (1952), *Human Behavior from the Transactional Point of View*. Washington, D. C.: Office Naval Research Publication.

Pronko, N. H. (1961), Perspectives in Psychology: XVIII. Some Reflections on Perception. *Psychological Record*, 11:311-314.

Skinner, B. F. (1938), *The Behavior of Organisms*. New York: D. Appleton-Century Company.

Solley, C. M. & Murphy, G. (1960), *Development of the Perceptual World*. New York: Basic Books.

Woodworth, R. S. & Schlosberg, H. (1960), *Experimental Psychology*. New York: Henry Holt and Company.

PART III

Visual and Auditory Perception

Research in the area of perception has been concentrated upon visual and auditory perception. Subjective impressions of the environment have been assumed to be based primarily upon these modalities. Because visual and auditory stimuli are relatively easier to present than are chemical or haptic stimuli, because these stimuli are seldom confused with one another as are the chemical or haptic stimuli, and because these senses adapt less readily than do the other senses, vision and audition have presented less complex experimental design problems for the researcher than have the other senses.

Chapter 4 is a review of the literature relating to the development of color, space, and movement perception, and Chapter 5 reviews the literature relevant to the development of auditory perception in children. Together these chapters present a comprehensive outline of the research which has been done and suggest the areas in which further research is needed. By their omissions both chapters indicate the lack of a developmental theory of perception based upon experimentation and yielding testable hypotheses.

Chapter 6 presents a theory of the development of form perception which is solidly based upon research findings and from which predictive hypotheses can be derived.

Chapter 7 serves a dual role. It presents the design and results of a new experiment. More importantly, perhaps, it strongly indicates that perception does not progress from infancy to a maximal or optimal level in adulthood and remain static and unchanged for the remainder of the life span. Perception of the environment continues to change. Any theory of perceptual development must explain changes from birth to death and not merely changes from infancy to adulthood.

CHAPTER 4

The Development of Perception of Color, Space, and Movement in Children

JEANNE L. RIVOIRE

ALINE H. KIDD

Freud emphasized infant behavioral processes. Piaget continued the thought with an interesting semiclinical approach to investigating the development of the whole child. The study of perception as a learning process has recently led all psychological research. While there have been reviews of studies of the perception of form and movement (Gibson and Olum, 1960; Wohlwill, 1960), though apparently none of color, a review of the literature, bringing together the separate studies of the perception concepts of color, space, and movement, could help point to needed future research concerning their interrelationships.

DEVELOPMENT OF HUE, BRIGHTNESS, AND SATURATION PERCEPTION

HUE DISCRIMINATION IN INFANTS

Most of the early studies of developmental responses to color were mere observations of what one child, or a very few children, would do in terms of the stimuli presented.

Preyer's (1888) study of the development of color discrimination in his own child used ovals of the primary colors presented with the question "Where is a color?" By the 112th week, the child apparently was able to grasp the idea of "color" and connect the "name" with the proper primary color, yellow being the first and most easily distinguished. The question was then changed to "What is that color?" as Preyer pointed to one of the ovals. Yellow was correctly named, but blue was confused with green through the 146th week. Blue was often called "gray" in the dusky morning light even into the fourth year, while the right naming of gray did not occur before the end of the third year. Apparently a child learns yellow first and blue last. However, Preyer reported that a boy aged 2-8 was attracted by dark violet, yellow, red, blue, and green, the violet singled out apparently because it was dark, while a 4-year-old boy who had received no prior color instruction named decisively: red, yellow, green, and blue, when asked to name the rainbow's colors, and that some 3-year-old children were perfectly sure in naming colors, though uncertain at age 2.

Shinn's (1893-1899) rather thorough observations of her niece revealed that chromatic rather than achromatic objects attracted far more attention up to the third month; that, except for daffodils, hard, bright-surfaced, cold color objects were preferred to soft, dull-surfaced, warm-colored objects; and that for the first year, color liking had little part in color interest, though the small number of observations seemed to indicate that yellow, orange, red, and pink attracted notice, while blue, violet, and green hardly attracted the child at all. During the second year, using colors of medium brightness only, and having withdrawn any colors that caused confusion, Shinn found a fairly complete grasp of the primary colors, though blue and green were still troublesome and often confused. Her observations would seem to indicate that her 2-year-old subject had as much color understanding as Preyer's 3-year-old subject.

However, there were few indications that Shinn controlled for saturation and brightness, lighting, or indeed any of the dependent variables, so it is impossible to be certain that color discrimination was actually involved. Individual differences and differences in observation techniques could explain Preyer's and Shinn's "findings," but, while age differences in level of achievement seem indicated, the development of color perception appears similar in that both subjects developed perception of the long wave end of the spectrum before the short end.

This, in part, seems to be supported by other, later, observations using multiple subjects. Holden and Bosse (1900) investigated the color preferences of 30 infants under 12 months of age and obtained no definite reactions before age 6 months, but found prompt reactions in precocious 6-

month-olds and average 7- and 8-month-olds to red, orange, and yellow, in 9-month-olds to red, orange, and yellow but sluggish reaction to green, blue, and violet. The 10- to 12-month-olds usually reacted promptly to all colors, while 12- to 24-month-olds preferred red, this preference slowly changing toward blue after age 2. However, they found that the achromatic colors were preferred before any chromatic colors. Segers (1936) observed Decroly's film showing a 6-month-old choosing a bottle containing a white liquid over bottles containing red and blue liquids and concluded that children below age 12 months could recognize "white." However, the filmed infant was bottle fed and may have been responding to some variable other than color.

Marsden (1903), McDougall (1906-1908), and Valentine (1913-1914) observed fixation, reaching, and grasping responses and concluded that infants do discriminate color within an age range of 6 weeks to 8 months, while Malrieu (1955) contented himself with suggesting that differential color reactions probably could be evoked at the third month. Brown (1951) reported the same developmental color order found by other observers, but noted in passing that Garbini (see Brown, 1951) had reported a white, black, red, green, yellow, blue order, while Winch, as well as Neuman (see Brown, 1951), had reported a black, white, red, blue, green, yellow, orange developmental order. Staples (1932) relied on these same responses, but used over 250 infants ranging from age 69 days to 24 months and responding to red, yellow, blue, green, and gray paper squares of equal brightness. She reported that chromatic, as distinct from achromatic, sensations were experienced as early as the end of the third month, that four colors were probably distinguished at 12 months, and that infants between 6 and 24 months were unequally responsive to red, yellow, blue, and green in that order of effectiveness.

While Canestrini, in 1913, used fontanelle pulsations and respiration responses to measure differential color response in infants 1 to 14 days old and reported that no distinct reactions to different colors could be found, even using colored electric lamps under conditions "entirely similar to using white electric lamps," it was not until the 1930s that investigators really began using color stimuli which would yield data produced by responses other than fixation, reaching, and grasping. Pratt, Nelson, and Sun (1930) used the stabilimeter to study general body responses to colored lamp stimuli in infants under 2 weeks old, and reported that the number of specific movements decreased to the order of white, yellow, green, red, blue. However, because the transmission of the colored lights was only in that same order, it is possible that an artifact may have been operating and their results are somewhat questionable.

Chase (1937) tested wave-length discrimination in 24 infants, 15 to 70 days old, by projecting a small circle of one color within a larger surrounding circle of another color onto a screen above the infant's field of vision so that the small center color, when moved, appeared to move within the field of the other color. If an infant detected that movement, discrimination between the two colors was assumed. Recorded observation of eye pursuit showed discrimination between red and yellow-green, between red and green, and between red and blue-green. These results are probably quite valid, because Chase controlled for brightness and mechanical aspects.

BRIGHTNESS DISCRIMINATION IN INFANTS

Peiper (1937) tested premature subjects in order to determine the brightness of gray, red, green, blue, and yellow needed to produce an eye-neck reflex, and found that premature infants responded to the same brightness values as did adults. He felt that his findings established that the Purkinje phenomenon occurs in, and therefore that the cones are functional in, the premature. Duke-Elder (1933), however, found that the cones in the fovea of the newborn infant were short, ill-defined, and probably nonfunctional.

Smith (1936) tested 20 infants, 7 to 9 days old, for relative brightness values with blue, green, and red lights of the same physical energy. After a five-minute dark adaptation, the subject was exposed to five minutes of color illumination. Using percentage of inhibition of activity, she found that activity was greatest in darkness, 23% for red, 30% for green, and 50% for blue, and that the boys were far less sensitive to light and color than were the girls. In fact, the values for the boys corresponded very closely to those of the adult deuteranope, and the values for the girls were similar to the adult protanope. Smith concluded that because the long wave end appeared as bright as the short wave end, even after dark adaptation, the Purkinje shift had not been demonstrated and therefore Peiper's (1926) finding was not confirmed. Peiper (1937) replied that the relative brightness value of colors in the Purkinje phenomenon meant the relative brightness value of colors to one another and not, as Smith's criticism seemed to imply, the relative brightness value of colors with respect to white light. He also suggested that Smith's short adaptation period might account for her contradictory results in regard to color blindness in the infant, and that the differences between her means did not warrant one sex being classed as deuteranopic and the other protanopic. Smith (1937) replied that the crux of the disagreement was obviously in the conflicting definitions of the Purkinje phenomenon. However, the present authors doubt the validity of Smith's findings, because the infants responded identically whether their eyes were open or closed.

Stirnimann (1944) recorded the number of seconds that each of more than 350 neonates continued to stare at cards which had patches of saturated colors, unsaturated colors, and a colored cross or circle on a background of another color, used as stationary and as moving stimuli. Blue, green, red, and white stimulated the longest, black and yellow the shortest responses during the first two weeks. Duration of staring increased for red and blue, decreased for black and white during the first two weeks, increased for green and yellow the first week, decreased the second week. Duration of response was longer for saturated than for unsaturated colors, and saturation rather than brightness was related to the duration of the response. It was also determined that perception of contrast and movement was well developed the first day of life.

Trincker and Trincker (1955) also used the eye-neck reflex to investigate relative sensitivity of the newborn to different areas of the spectrum, and to study increasing sensitivity with age. Thresholds were determined by using narrow wave-band filters for light-adapted as compared with dark-adapted conditions and for numerous regions of the spectrum. Under light adaptation, the maximum sensitivity of prematures and newborns was found to be similar to adult sensitivity. At one month of age the relative sensitivity under dark adaptation shifted to give the usual scotopic curve.

Thus, one might find here partial confirmation of Peiper's findings that prematures and infants responded to the same brightness values as adults. If the Trinckers' finding that the typical scotopic curve under dark adaptation does not occur until the age of one month is valid, it is, therefore, probable that Smith's subjects were too young to be tested for this variable. Munn (1938), however, felt that Smith's criticism of the inadequacy of Peiper's data which equates brightness values for infants and adults is valid, though he states that Smith's findings of sex differences and brightness values for the different colors are not statistically reliable. On the whole, however, these studies of brightness discrimination in infants were an improvement over the earlier observations which were structured and standardized assessment situations at best, while the brightness studies show more rigor and the responses were more clear-cut.

COLOR DISCRIMINATION IN PRESCHOOL AND SCHOOL CHILDREN

An exploratory study of color discrimination in children was carried out by Synolds and Pronko (1949) on 74 boys and girls ranging in age from 3 to 8 years. The 3-year-olds could not name correctly the colors of the rotating color discs used, and the preschoolers were inferior to the school groups. However, tracing the digits on the Dvorine Color Perception Testing charts was accomplished with 78 to 100% accuracy by all the subjects, and no significant sex differences were found.

Brown's (1951) study to determine whether school children had the same color vision pattern as adults showed no significant differences. He also asked 5- to 15-year-old boys and girls to name colored spots of light and noted the confusion of blue and green, although there was no marked increase of the confusion with decreasing age. Although his sample was too small to determine significance, it should be noted that more boys than girls confused these colors.

Malrieu (1955) pointed out that the development of color concepts parallels other areas of cognitive development. At a preverbal stage, a child will learn the value of a color associated with a need reduction. In the early verbal stage, a single color may be learned correctly because it is a part of an object of particular significance to the child, while any other colors will be confused. Once color naming has been acquired, there will be manipulations of colors not connected with significant objects, and this play manipulation usually leads to the development of the system of nomenclature.

Clifford and Calvin (1958) reported that 120 kindergarten through fifth-grade children found learning color discrimination more difficult than brightness discrimination. However, no differences in performance among the children of different age levels and no sex differences were recorded, which is in accord with Koffka's (1925, p. 285) report:

The Sterns report of their daughter that "at the age of 3 years 2 months, Hilda called bright and dark things white and black; otherwise she named correctly only the color *red*." As Winch has noted, it often happens that variegated colors are distinguished from neutral tones by giving them all the same name, which indicates that all variegated colors have a common characteristic in contrast to the achromatic tones, and that this common factor must therefore be much more influential than any difference seen between the variegated colors themselves.

COLOR MATCHING

Cook (1931) asked 110 children, aged 17 months to 6 years, to match red, green, yellow, and blue squares of paper mounted on gray cards on the basis of color, brightness, and saturation. By the age of 2 years, the subjects matched specimens differing in color with 45% accuracy, and named the four primary colors with 25% accuracy, a finding which would seem to indicate color naming at the chance level. By the age of 6, matching ability had increased to 97%, but color discrimination by name appears to develop later than matching discrimination since only 62% accuracy was found in the 6-year-olds. Children at all age levels discriminated more accurately for color than for brightness or saturation, apparently, because no significant differences in the age levels were found for these qualities.

Heider and Heider (1940) studied how children sort colors and found that younger children selected color matches from a wider range than did older children, while Smith (1943) observed color-matching development beginning with 6-year-olds, and noted that scores improved rapidly with age, although he attributed his findings to "attitudinal factors" rather than to "receptor physiology."

COLOR PREFERENCE

A number of studies of color preference have been made within the past half century, and although, again, a general looseness of controls, of definitions of terms, of structured observations, and of standardized assessments leaves one wondering what the results really indicate about the development of the perceptocognitive processes in humans, a consideration of the techniques and results might at least point to some realistic possibilities for the creative designing of an experiment which would result in meaningful, useful data.

Winch (1909) wrote the names red, yellow, green, blue, black, and white on a chalkboard and asked 2000 school children to list these colors in order of preference from memory. Girls preferred blue over red, boys preferred red over blue. Yellow decreased in popularity as age increased, while green increased in popularity. Dashiell (1917) asked 212 kindergartners and 126 college sophomores to choose from simultaneously presented colors. The kindergartners preferred blue, red, and yellow; the college students preferred blue, red, and green.

Reavis (1920) showed colors singly and recorded red and blue as the first and second choices of the first through fourth grades, and blue as first choice with fifth-graders. Polson (1924) presented a series of colors against a gray background to elementary school children and found more spontaneity of color reaction in the lower grades, found that all highly saturated colors were preferred, and that orange, blue, and red were preferred in that order. Garth (1924) had 1000 school children arrange colored discs in order of preference and recorded that 498 children preferred blue, red, green, violet, orange, yellow, and white, that the first-graders preferred red to blue, but that blue took first place in all other grades. Ricker (1925) studied the preference for saturated colors, tints, and shades in 821 children of the first, third, and fifth grades and found they preferred saturated red, saturated blue, and a red tint, in that order, with saturated yellow in tenth place of preference. Dorcus (1926) used paired color comparisons with 8-, 9-, and 10-year-olds and found that blue was preferred to all other colors, and that the order of preference for saturated colors was blue, purple, green, red, orange, and yellow.

Gale (1933) studied 7- to 16-year-olds and found a preference for orange, red-violet, and blue, while blue-green, violet, and yellow were least preferred. Warm colors were preferred by all the children, and the near—rather than the exact—complementary color combinations were desired. Apparently experience did not affect preferences after the third grade. It should also be noted, however, that this was the first study to use more than seven colors to test color preferences in children. Garth and Porter's (1934) study of 1032 young children showed that the feeling for colors increased with age and was more precise in boys than in girls. Red was preferred by all the age groups, yellow was at the bottom of the list, and blue was more esteemed as age increased.

Imada (1938) studied 700 Japanese 5- and 6-year-olds and found that although differentiation of color preferences apparently had not yet developed, their choices were not completely haphazard nor by chance, nor were there significant sex or age differences. He also required some of his subjects to color an outline drawing and found an apparent preference for red and yellow, while black and brown were least preferred. Ekhaus (1958-1959) also found red preferred over blue and yellow by 976 Israeli children.

Subes (1959) presented art works, and found a preference for contrasts and for bright colors whether he employed paired comparisons or a modified rank-order procedure. This preference was found to be less clear with abstract than with representative art, and interindividual differences were found to be highly important.

Ames and Ilg (1962) studied 2- through 16-year-old American children's mosaic patterns as an expression of color preference, since a child does not ordinarily use a color unless he actually has some type of affinity for it. Most of the girls except for the 9-, 13-, 14-, and 16-year-olds used blue most frequently. Black was used most often by the 9- and 13-year-olds, white by the 14-year-olds, and black and white equally by the 16-year-olds. Yellow was used least by the 2-, 3-, 8-, 9-, 11-, 12-, 14-, and 16-year-olds, yellow and white were used least by the 4- and 5-year-olds white was used least by the 6-, 7-, 10-, and 13-year-olds, while green was used least by the 15-year-olds.

A majority of the boys used blue most frequently, except for the 2-year-olds who used black most often. Yellow was used least by the 2-, 5-, 12-, 14-, and 16-year-olds, white was used least by the 3-, 4-, 6-, and 8-year-olds, white and green were used least by the 7-year-olds, and green was used least by the 5-, 9-, 10-, 11-, 13-, and 15-year-olds.

SATURATION AND BRIGHTNESS DISCRIMINATION IN PRESCHOOL AND SCHOOL CHILDREN

Gilbert (1894) presented 10 pieces of red cloth of different saturations to 6- through 17-year-old school children. The least saturated item was used as the standard, and 57% of the 6-year-olds did not discriminate at all. The other 6-year-olds selected 9.6 saturations as identical with the standard, while only 3.9 saturations were selected to be the same as the standard by the 17-year-olds.

Peters (1927) reported a study by Jones, who used the method of limits, a sector of a gray disc on a color wheel being increased constantly until the color was named correctly by a group of children, from 4 to 14 years old, and a group of adults. It was found that sensitivity to color increased markedly with age, and that the adults were 118% more sensitive than the 6-year-olds.

When Burzlaff (1931) presented a group of comparison shades of gray simultaneously, he found no developmental curve whatever. However, when he used a color wheel with a method of adjustment, he found a very distinct developmental curve. This would seem to indicate that the method or technique used by an investigator is highly influential in producing meaningful, useful data about the nature of the development of color perception in humans. Brunswik (1956) used a method of single comparisons with a graded series of black and white papers and the standard presented at different distances from a light source. He found a developmental curve which increased up to age 10, but which showed a decrease later at about age 16.

COLOR AND FORM

By far the most extensive developmental research concerning color has been with relation to form or space. Brian and Goodenough (1929) demonstrated the relative potency of color and form perception at different ages by showing two objects that differed from a third in either form or color, and asking the subjects to place the third object with the one just like it. The children tended to match by color rather than by form until the sixth year of age, after which the dominant response was to form. Ritter (1930) found that when his group of adolescents sorted a group of objects according to color or form, they divided into two definite groups. Those who used color for sorting were characterized by a sharpness of perception, memory, imagination, and sensitivity. Those who used form for sorting were better adapted to the external world and to a practical way of life. However, he noted no correlation between these two groups.

Rabello (1933) investigated 3- to 11-year-olds and found that color preferences decreased with age, while form perceptions, especially for common form, increased. Engel (1935) studied proportionate interest in 800 2- to 11-year-olds and found that children under 3-6 showed an almost exclusive interest in form, after which age there was a stronger preference for color. In the lower grades, 19.5% of the pupils chose by form and 70%

by color. The highest percentage of form reactors were of high IQs and the highest percentage of color reactors had relatively lower IQs. Lindberg's (1938) 2446 elementary students showed that color responses decreased with increasing age, and color sorters tended to have low IQs. Later, however, Honkavaara (1958), who allowed children to display emotions toward colors in a color-form preference test, reported that low IQs preferred form while high IQs did not, an apparent reversal of the earlier observations.

Blasius (1943) used a Kretschmer type of questionnaire to investigate personality characteristics of older adolescents who chose to paint carpets by either form- or color-dominant patterns. Good spatial perception was encountered almost exclusively in form-predominant and in schizothymic (leptosomes, dysplastics, athletics) types, while poor spatial perception was found in color-predominant and in cyclothymic types.

Kindergarten children were asked by Huang (1945) to indicate which of two objects was like a third referent object in respect to color or form. Where plane and solid geometrical figures and plane figures of real objects were used, the choice was predominantly based on form. On the whole, where large color differences were used, the choice was based on color, but where large form differences were used, the choice was based on form.

Baley and Witwicki (1948) had preschoolers choose between size and form, and between size and color. In the size-form choice, the children chose form at all ages, although the younger the child, the greater the percentage of size-based choices. With the size-color choice, color was predominant with the younger, while size was predominant with the older children. The authors proposed that as a child develops, form elements in perception dominate over such material elements as color. This is supported in part by Kagan and Lemkin's (1961) study of 69 children, 3 to 9 years old, who were asked to group geometric stimuli which differed in form, color, or size, into similar pairs. The results indicated that form was distinctly preferred, as was color over size as a basis of similarity, and that older girls were less likely than younger girls to use color as a basis of choice, although no age differences appeared for the boys.

From such studies, it is an easy transition to research into space perception.

DEVELOPMENT OF SPACE PERCEPTION

DEVELOPMENT IN INFANTS

Visual Acuity

A few investigators have reported developmental trends in visual acuity processes. Peckham (1933) stated that visual acuity in children of 28 months and older is as great as that of the adult, and Gorman, Cogan, and Gellis (1957), using an apparatus for measuring visual acuity in infants by the opticokinetic response, found perception of a pattern which when viewed at 6 inches corresponds to the Snellen notation of 20/670 in 93 of 100 newborns 1½ hours to 5 days of age. This finding is roughly equivalent to 1/16th inch at 6 inches, but, because the investigators did not use a full range of patterns, it is possible that this index may be lower. However, Fantz (1958), having shown that infants prefer patterned to plain objects, tested for infant visual acuity and determined that the width of stripes that could be distinguished by an infant decreased rapidly during the first half year of life. Infants under a month old could perceive 1/8-inch stripes at 10 feet, while by 6 months, infants could see 1/64-inch stripes at 10 feet. It is possible, of course, that the results differ because the Fantz study concerned preference, while the Gorman, Cogan, and Gellis study concerned a more concrete response. Watson and Lowrey (1962), however, have stated that visual acuity is approximately 20/70 by 2 years, 20/30 by 5 years, and 20/20 by 7 years of age, and that lack of better acuity in infants is probably affected greatly by hyperopia which is usually present during the infancy period.

Object and Pattern Perception

Rabinow and Frankl (1934) found 5 graded reactions of recognition in the feeding situation in infants 4 to 10 months old. These reactions depended on a sudden approach of an object, of a pointed object, of a nipple, of a nipple with a white fluid, and of a white fluid, and the authors observed that development was not based on trial and error but upon the infant's maturation.

Stirnimann (1940) found that infants younger than 14 days were more interested in patterned cards than in plain color cards. Ling (1942) found that subjects aged 6 through 15 months could discriminate among blocks shaped as triangles, cubes, spheres, and curves, although her subjects were little affected by orientation changes, and Berlyne (1958) found that infants preferred contoured patterns.

Fantz (1961a) tried various patterned visual materials and found a differential response to pattern at all ages. This he interpreted as some degree of form perception being innate, with further development of visual behavior being a complex interplay of innate ability, learning, and maturation. He then (1961b) presented to 1- to 6-month-old infants a sphere and a circle for 20-second periods in order to determine the preference. He recorded a preference for the sphere when both objects were textured and exposed to direct light under both monocular and binocular conditions, and found, interestingly enough, that these preferences showed no correlation with age. Watson and Lowrey (1962) reported that associations between sight and higher centers were developed to the extent that an infant 3 months old could recognize such familiar objects as his bottle, and that, by 5 or 6 months, the visual images were retained so that increased recognition of familiar objects appeared.

DEVELOPMENT IN PRESCHOOL AND SCHOOL CHILDREN
Orientation

That younger children tend to ignore spatial orientation in their response to form was first reported by Stern (1909), and Gellerman (1933) found form discrimination in 2-year-olds with a choice situation and food reward, although little attention was paid to orientation and the responses were transposable. Rice (1930) and Newhall (1937) used drawing, recognition, and matching to study the ability of 3- to 5-year-olds to identify plane figures through a series of changing orientations and found that their subjects could identify the transposed figures. However, Burkhardt (1925) found a sharp decrease in the number of orientation changes in reproductions of primitive drawings by children 6 through 8 years of age, while Lord (1941) studied fifth- through eighth-graders concerning the development of spatial orientation and found no well-generalized idea of cardinal directions present even in eighth-graders.

Somewhat different developmental trends were found by Hanfmann (1933) when 4- to 7-year-olds were asked to copy triangles in varying orientations. A predominance of vertical and horizontal orientations was found to be already strong at 4 years, and the children made shifts and reversals in copying apparently because they needed to change the figure to a "natural position," an occurrence which suggests that these children had developed some rudimentary concept of transposability. However, when she used the Schumann-square illusion which involves the overestimation of a square tilted 45 degrees compared with a square resting along a horizontal-vertical referent, she found an increase in the percentage of subjects responding between ages 3 and 6 years, and a decrease in the number of subjects responding positively to this illusion after age 6.

Children also have great difficulty discriminating mirror-image and up-down reversal forms, as Davidson (1935) demonstrated by using a matching technique with the letters b, d, p, and q on preschool and first-grade children. The developmental stages progressed from a confusion of all four letters, to the d and b, and p and q identified as the same letter in different orientations, to identification as four different letters. Newson (see Vernon, 1957) found that 5-year-olds could detect up-down reversals with fewer difficulties than mirror-image reversals after instruction, and Rudel (1959) confirmed this result with 3- to 5-year-olds. It should be noted that these last three studies dealt with simple geometrical figures. When Hunton (1955) showed complex meaningful pictures to 22-month-olds through 14-year-olds, he found that when these stimuli were inverted, the perception of the relationships between objects was disturbed.

A comparison of two similarly staggered vertical lines was studied by Piaget and Morf (1956) who found that the top lines became increasingly overestimated by 5- to 8-year-olds, but that, if two vertical lines were superimposed so that the spatial reference systems could not play an important role, the top line overestimation decreased with age. Piaget and Taponier (1956) also found similar results with a comparison of the two horizontal lines of a parallelogram. However, Piaget and Lambercier (1956) concluded that age differences are less consistent as the separation of the lines is increased.

Walters (1942) studied the horizontal-vertical illusion directly and tentatively concluded that if the two lines of the figure intersect, the effect will decrease with age increase. Wörsten (1947) found that with a comparison of noncontiguous segments the horizontal-vertical illusion increased to its greatest extent up to age 10 and decreased thereafter to adulthood. Fraisse and Vautrey (1956) found an increase in this misperception up to age 10 so long as the figure was made up of two spatially separated lines.

Figure-Ground

Meili (1931) found that attention to the whole or to the part by young children depended on the degree of structure of the figure. If the whole was a strong structure, the whole was perceived, but if the stimulus was either a weak or a very complex structure, the children concentrated on the parts. Schroff (see Meili, 1931) used line drawings of rows of cups or teapots and the children reported seeing form that corresponded to the intervals between the figures. It would appear that the figure-ground relationship had been reversed by this group.

Munn and Steining (1931) investigated the 15-month- to 2-year-olds' concepts of triangularity and found that this concept developed most readily in children who discriminated figure and ground readily. Meister (1949) compared the figure-ground perception of preschoolers with that of adults and reported that adults chose a figure either slightly smaller or slightly larger than a test card whereas the children chose only a larger figure. Adults, however, chose denser grounds than did the children, and Meister concluded simply that children and adults do not perceive figure and ground in the same way.

Solley and Sommer (1957) and Solley and Engel (1960) investigated how figure is determined and reported that 5- through 8-year-olds organized the figure significantly better if rewarded than if punished, while 9- through 12-year-olds showed little effect from either reward or punishment. However, Jackson (1954), using a reward-punishment of receiving or losing money, determined that young adults seemed to organize figure significantly better if punished.

There is little evidence in the literature that perception of details or parts appears before perception of the whole. Cramaussel (1924) obtained positive results from young children who were able to match pictures which included very fine details and also found that the attention of young children goes from one object to another in a picture, but that the relation between them is not seen. He concluded that children do not have syncretic perception. Segers (1926) asked 4- to 10-year-olds to match 16 small houses with 16 large houses which differed from each other only in very small details. The youngest group had the greatest difficulty matching, and the percentage of correct matching increased with age. Binet (see Meili, 1931) believed that a child points out details before he matures enough to describe the total picture.

The ease of perceiving symmetrical or asymmetrical embedded figures was studied by Crudden (1941) in five 6-, and six 6-year-olds. She reported that the children found symmetrical figures more easily than they found asymmetrical figures. Ghent (1956) studied recognition of Gottschaldt-type embedded forms by 4- through 13-year-olds and found that the younger the child, the more difficult the perception of figures which shared contours, although there was a marked improvement with increased age. Heiss (1930) had found similar results when studying the ability to detect an angular shape forming a part of a continuous line, while Meister (1949) had concluded that the preschooler's ability to discriminate figure from ground was nearer the adult level than was his perception of geometrical forms per se.

The development of the perception of wholes was studied by Ames, Learned, Metraux, and Walker (1953) who used Rorschach cards as stimuli and found that early childhood responses were highly global with a high percentage of white responses, that in middle childhood and adolescence more attention was paid to both large and small details, and that adults showed an integrated perception of the whole. Dworetski's (1939) and Hemmendinger's (1953) studies tended to confirm these results, and Wohlwill (1960) concluded that the question of children viewing the whole at the expense of the part or vice versa was closely connected with the degree of embeddedness.

Gestalt Factors in Perceptual Organization

Rush (1937) investigated the development of such classical gestalt laws of visual organization as proximity, similarity, continuation, and common fate in 6- to 21-year-olds. Simple dot patterns which could be organized in one or more ways were presented in order to determine which method of organization was dominant. Results indicated that use of continuation increased up to about 14 years of age and then dropped to a lower usage level, that use of similarity and proximity increased steadily with age, but that there was a shift from seeing equally spaced dot patterns as horizontal rows to seeing them as vertical columns, a shift from horizontal to vertical emphasis in visual organization which increased with age.

Closure

Studies of closure, on the whole, have indicated that the adult is much more capable of recognizing an incomplete form. Street (1931) devised a Gestalt Completion Test but failed to find significant differences in his elementary and high-school children, possibly because he did not use a sufficient number of stimuli. Line (1930-1931) investigated the growth of visual perception and found that 4- and 5-year-olds could differentiate a square from a rectangle and a circle, but could not distinguish between open and closed figures of the same shape. Siegel and Ozkaplan (1953) cut geometrical figures into two parts and asked 4- through 7-year-olds and adults to make whatever they liked from the pieces. While results showed a higher percentage of "correct" responses from the adults, the authors concluded that it was largely due to familiarity and previous conditioning. In their study of closure ability, Piaget and Albertini (1954) found that children did not achieve even 75% success until the age of 7. However, the fact that the child had to achieve his goal by tracing with a finger or drawing in the missing part may have influenced the results. Otherwise, very young children apparently perceived the stimuli as wholes and it was not until the age of 9 that all the figures were recognized and seen as incomplete. On the other hand, Mooney (1957) found a significant correlation between age and closure ability, though his results are questionable because he did not control for such other variables as categorization and discrimination.

Size and Area Perception

Some relation between size and area discrimination and the shape of the particular form presented has been noted. Peters (1927) found that stars, ellipses, and triangles were judged larger than squares, rectangles, and circles of equal area by kindergarten and school-age subjects, and concluded that the sharp angles and greater linear distance between corner points of the stars, ellipses, and triangles tended to enhance the apparent size. Welch (1939a) found that practice and increasing age helped improve his 16-month- through 40-month-olds' ability to discriminate size. His results, however, were limited by the concepts of big and little, and the subjects were unable to judge a middle figure. Hicks and Stewart (1930), Thrum (1935), and Welch (1938, 1939a, b, c, 1940) found that the concept of middleness developed later than the concepts of big and little. Meyer (1940) found that his 5-year-olds could select middle-sized objects, while Graham, Jackson, and Long (1944) and Vinacke (1951) found that the middleness concept developed at approximately 9 years of age. The difference in these findings, however, can probably be explained by the magnitude of the size differences to be discriminated.

Ten children, 4 to 9 years old, learned to discriminate large from small stimuli of the same shape and form (Long, 1941). Although there were large differences in the amount of training needed, these children also learned to discriminate between other pairs of forms of the same size but with smaller intrasize differences than in the original training pairs. When two different shapes were used to be size-discriminated, there was a significantly lower percentage of success than when same-shape forms were used.

That affective factors may have some influence on perceived size was shown by Bruner and Goodman (1947). However, Blum (1957) studied the value factor in size perception and found that highly valued objects were not viewed as larger than neutral or low-value objects. Botha (1959), who investigated effect of preference on size perception, found that an object was likely to be perceived as smaller than life-size if the general response evoked was Approach, and larger than life-size if the response was Avoidance.

Piaget, Inhelder, and Szeminska's (1960) general results concerning area are especially noteworthy. They found that the development of conservation and measurement runs parallel whether objects are lengths or areas; that conservation is always the outcome of two groupings, additive subdivisions and ordered positions or changes in positions being complementary; that the operations required for subdividing an area are identical with those which are used in subdividing classes or discontinuous collections; and that children could not double an area until they understood the multiplicative relation between length and area. With these major findings, they then used a semiclinical method and found a series of developmental stages generally similar for all concepts: an elementary stage of no understanding of the problem, an intermediate stage of intuitive problem solving, and a final stage of established internal operations for problem solving.

Updegraff (1930) found that by 4 years of age a child's perception of distance was similar to an adult's, Johnson and Beck (1941) found that 2-year-olds had well-developed stereoscopic vision, while Garrison (1952) reported that his 6-year-olds had poor ability to see three dimensions. It would thus appear that the ability to judge distance may develop more rapidly than the ability to judge depth. However, Walk and Gibson (1959) used their "visual cliff" technique to test depth discrimination and found that by the time a child was ready for locomotion, he could discriminate depth. Thus, although there are many depth cues such as monocular focus, binocular convergence, and texture gradients available to a child, the one necessary and sufficient cue, according to these studies, is movement-produced parallax. This is critical in relating the development of depth perception to the haptic exploration of objects in three dimensions and is compatible with Piaget's emphasis on active exploration.

Developmental Experience with Space

Lowenfeld (1957) traced the development of the 4- through 17-year-olds' perception of space by analyzing children's drawings, clay models, linoleum figures, wooden models, and papier-mâché forms. Defining everything outside of the body as "space," he found that in the youngest children the interrelations of things in space were subject to no discoverable laws, that the stage was primarily characterized by no orderly space relation except for an emotional type of relationship such as "this is my doll" which occurred in 4- to 7-year-olds.

The next stage of development occurred in the 7- to 9-year-olds, and was called the *schematic stage* because the most important and basic experience of the child's spatial development was the discovery of order in space relationships. In other words, whenever the child related himself to others, saw himself as a part of the environment, his first common experience of space had occurred, and was expressed by the drawing of everything on a common base line.

In 9- to 11-year-olds, Lowenfeld saw a stage of *dawning realism,* a stage characterized by the formation of gangs, lack of cooperation with adults, a greater awareness of self with regard to sex, and the drawing of more than simple geometric figures or schematic representations. At this stage the child becomes aware of the concept of overlapping—that a tree growing from the ground will partly cover an area of the sky—but has difficulties in spatial correlations because of his egocentric attitude and lack of cooperation. Such a child has not fully developed a visual percept of depth, but certainly has taken a first step toward such a concept.

In the 11- to 13-year-old a *pseudorealistic* stage occurs and another psychologically important development enters the picture. As Lowenfeld (1957, p. 217) put it:

> ... the closer we study adolescence, the more we see a distinction in the sensory reactions of the children toward creative experiences. We see clearly a preference by some children for visual stimuli while others may be more concerned with the interpretation of subjective experiences.

It is with approaching adolescence that these preferences crystallize; in this stage of development, perception of perspective begins to form. For the visually oriented, a horizon line becomes meaningful, while frequently the nonvisually oriented will revert to the base-line type of response. In this stage, however, the recognition of distance moves into the focal point of interest in the visually oriented child, although Lowenfeld believed that such a concept of distance was almost entirely intuitive. In the nonvisually oriented child the distance concept appears later, frequently not occurring until the next developmental stage.

Lowenfeld's final stage occurred in the 13- to 17-year-olds and, in the visually oriented, was characterized by a perceptive space representation with knowledge of the size and detail of distant objects. Children who had a preference for subjective experiences evolved into children having preferences for tactile and kinesthetic experiences of space. There was a placing of emphasis on feelings as contrasted with outside appearance, and perspective was of value only in relation to the self.

Topological to Euclidian Perceptoconceptual Development

The work of Piaget and Inhelder (1956) suggests that a child's concept of space develops or evolves from simple nonmetrical concepts to complex metrical concepts. In the preschool years, the child is considered to have ideas which are primarily topological in regard to space, a category which includes the relationships of proximity, separation, order, enclosure, and continuity. These relationships are built up empirically between the various parts of figures or patterns which they organize, but are independent of any contraction or expansion of the figures. Piaget, therefore, believed that it is impossible for relationships of this type to lead to comprehensive systems linking different figures together by means of perspective or axial coordinates, and that these relationships are bound to remain psychologically primitive. Thus, *topological space* furnishes the basis for the type of analysis which operates from the standpoint of each figural object considered in isolation, rather than from a comprehensive system capable of coordinating all figures within a whole and organized in terms of a common spatial structure.

In this view, the next stage of development begins at about school age and ends during adolescence. It is marked by the development of the ability to locate objects and their configurations relative to one another in accordance with a general perspective system as well as by the ability to locate objects according to coordinate axes. This general perspective system was termed *projective space,* and it begins psychologically at the point where the object or pattern is no longer viewed in isolation but is considered in relation to a point of view, and therefore a child comes to comprehend such concepts as Above, Below, Left, Right, Before, and Behind. By age 11, a child can coordinate the various perspectives of the same scene, and by 13 or 14 can coordinate various perspectives of different scenes.

An apparently intuitive stage of development which is concerned with affine geometrical relationships occurs about age 7 and ends about age 11. This stage is characterized by similarities conserving parallels, angles, and distances. It would thus appear that this type of development is similar to development of concepts of projective and Euclidian space.

The final stage is the development of *Euclidian space.* Piaget and Inhelder (1956), and Piaget, Inhelder, and Szeminska (1960) noted that a child learns to conserve straight lines, angles, curves, distances, volumes, areas, and lengths, and these investigators distinguished several levels of achievement. At the beginning the child was capable of carrying on such operations as partitioning and reuniting, placing and displacing, and measuring. Then qualitative operations, length and distance, began to evolve and the majority of these were elaborated before the age of 11 or 12. At 11 the child could perform simple metrical operations such as the measurement of length in one, two, or three dimensions, could construct a metric coordinate system, and demonstrated the beginning of measurement of angles and area. The final level was reached about age 13 or 14 when areas, volumes, and proportions were calculated.

Developmental Trends in Field Dependence

Witkin et al. (1954) demonstrated several broad developmental trends in perception by setting 8-year-olds through adolescents such tasks as the Rod and Frame Test, Tilting Rod and Tilting Chair Tests, and the Embedded Figures Test. They found that in part-of-a-field perceptual situations, the developmental sequence followed a definite order. In 8- to 10-year-olds, the perception of an item was greatly influenced by the structure of the surrounding field, in the 10- to 13-year-olds there was a dramatic decrease in the extent of this influence, in the 13- to 17-year-olds there were slight changes toward independence from the field, but after age 17 there was a reversal of this trend so that the adults showed a greater average susceptibility to field influence than did the 17-year-olds.

These investigators found no such developmental trends with field-as-a-whole perceptual tasks, however. Children of 8 to 10 were somewhat less prone to "go along with" the field than were adults, and, although the young children were on the average influenced more compellingly by the field in perceiving an item within a field, they were at least as able as adults to evaluate the position of the field as a whole.

These investigators also found that at each age level there was a wide range of individual differences in performance. Even in the youngest groups the range of scores and the extremes of the range were quite similar to those of the adults. It would therefore seem that individual differences in perception appear early in life. It was also found that for all ages tested, people tended to be self-consistent in their perceptions under different conditions, and that at all ages the females tended to be more influenced by the field than were the males.

DEVELOPMENT OF MOVEMENT PERCEPTION

Perhaps movement, the most primitive of all visual perceptions, may be thought of as favoring detail perception provided the movement is not too fast or too slow. It is, therefore, the development of perception of detail in movement that is of special interest to psychology. Research on this type of perception, however, is highly scattered, cross-sectional, unorganized, and still in a very elementary stage, and far less research has been done in this area compared to research into other visual processes. What variables there are to be studied in tracing this development are still relatively undetermined; they have not even been identified by preliminary research. Indeed, a refined longitudinal study of this process is greatly needed.

DEVELOPMENT IN INFANTS

Probably the earliest, most primitive perception available to a child is that of movement. It had been noted that premature babies pursued a slowly moving light with their eyes (Kussmaul, 1859; Kroner, 1881). Preyer (1882, 1888) noticed that at about the third week eyes could follow slowly moving objects, while Peterson and Rainey (1910) recorded that in the first eight days a baby would follow a light. Jones (1926) made a study of visual pursuit in an infant and found that horizontal pursuit movements were first consistently present at about one month, the median age being 58 days; that consistent vertical and circular pursuit occurred about the 51st day, median ages for these types of pursuit being 68 and 75 days respectively. Shirley (1931), using moving steel tape, confirmed these findings, as did Beasley (1933), while, in general, Gesell and Thompson (1934) also found such developments. Morgan and Morgan (1944) studied the general order of object pursuit and recorded the occurrence sequence as being Fixation, Horizontal following, Vertical following, and Circular following. Stirnimann (1944) found glancing at moving objects well developed in neonates on the first day.

DEVELOPMENT IN PRESCHOOL AND SCHOOL CHILDREN
Velocity
Fraisse and Vautrey (1952), using two toy cyclists moving along parallel tracks at different speeds, found that 5-year-olds were capable of comparing the speeds of the two moving objects, and that they could make the comparison even when a passing of one cyclist by the other did not correspond to a greater speed. It was concluded that perception of speed seems to involve a reasoning ability which places in relation the spatio-temporal givens of an experience.

Edgren (1953) investigated the relative speed of two moving objects under a number of conditions similar to those studied by J. F. Brown (1931) and found that age differences were very irregular or even nonexistent. It is, however, possible that his method of analysis may have been too gross to detect developmental differences or that with meaningless stimuli, developmental responses were not elicited, since Wapner and Werner (1957) found that with meaningful stimuli, age differences could be discovered. Using stationary and seemingly moving stimuli with both being pulled along simultaneously by moving belts, it was found that adults could adjust these quite accurately for relative speed, although children overestimated the speed of the seemingly moving stimuli, a characteristic which progressively decreased with age.

Stroboscopic Movement

It has been demonstrated that stroboscopic movement thresholds are lower for children than for adults. Meili and Tobler (1931) used 5- to 12-year-olds and adults to investigate the development of perceptual processes operating in the viewing of stroboscopic (apparent) movement. They found that children perceived movement under similar conditions to the adults but with greater time intervals, and thus the children saw movement while the adults saw succession. They also found, in general, a decrease in perceiving stroboscopic movement with an increase in age.

Gantenbein (1952) investigated the development of perceived movement by varying the stimulus exposure, the distance, temporal interval, exposure time, and intensity, using the same age range as Meili and Tobler. She found that as age increased, so did the threshold between succession and movement, and that age differences were less pronounced for movement and simultaneity. Brenner (1957), however, found just the opposite result for movement and succession, i.e., age differences were greater for the movement-succession threshold.

Botwinick and Brinley (1963) recently studied another area of stroboscopic movement, the relation of critical flicker frequency and stroboscopic movement in adolescents, young adults, and older people. They found that critical flicker frequency and transit types of motion have statistically significant correlations for the adolescents and young adults, whereas critical flicker frequency and any motion were highly correlated for the older group.

Michotte (1946), Olum (1958), and Piaget and Lambercier (1958), studying children's ideas of the forces producing movement, demonstrated the greater sensitivity of young children to apparent movement, according to Wohlwill (1960).

DISCUSSION

The preceding studies represent efforts to determine the development of the perception of color, space, and movement in children. Many of them, particularly the early studies, were technically inadequate in design, number of subjects, and analysis of the data. Much of the later research is merely a report of observations and experimental results with no attempt to explain the phenomena recorded. It is obvious that further research is essential in these areas.

Perhaps the most important problem is the lack of agreement on operational definitions of terms. For example, psychologists should attempt to define the colors used as stimuli in terms of wave length, brightness, and saturation. Space and form should be clearly distinguished from one another, again in terms of the physical properties of the stimuli. Apparent movement must also be clearly defined operationally. At present, responses to physically motionless Rorschach cards and to stroboscopic motion are considered to represent similar phenomena despite the extreme differences in physical stimuli. Additionally, experimenters must consider the differences between absolute stimulus qualities, defined in terms of physical properties, and the perceived stimulus qualities. This becomes clear, for example, when one considers the central lines of the two Müller-Lyer figures. The lines are identical in terms of absolute qualities but are perceived as nonidentical. Thus, although operational definitions of terms based upon both absolute and perceived stimulus properties represent a real problem for the experimenter in the area of visual perception, such precise statements about the stimuli do appear to be very necessary for further progress in our knowledge of this development.

Studies in this area have concentrated on the developmental-descriptive approach, and although such studies do indicate changes in visual perception with increasing age, they explain only when developmental changes occur. They do not indicate the theoretical problems and the hypothetical mechanisms relating to why development occurs as it does. In this area, as in so many others, a theoretical approach with experimentation rigorously designed to clarify the critical problems appears to be a necessity. For such an approach to produce meaningful and valuable results, however, all of the pertinent variables must be considered, including such facts as: (1) various types of methodology may, of themselves, produce differential results; (2) subject selection is of critical importance in an area in which individual differences appear to be so significant; (3) selected statistical techniques must be able to deal with the possibility of nonlinearity or discreteness in visual perceptual development; and (4) although experimentation must be rigorous, it must permit the discovery of influential variables which in the past have not been considered pertinent to the development of visual perception.

Thus the complexity and scope of these problems in the area of the development of visual perception indicates at least two definite steps: further research to clarify and amplify the problems of the studies cited, and then research into the actual development of visual perception.

BIBLIOGRAPHIES

INTRODUCTION AND DEVELOPMENT OF COLOR PERCEPTION

Ames, L. B. & Ilg, F. L. (1962), *Mosaic Patterns in American Children*. New York: Harper and Brothers.

Baley, S. & Witwicki, T. (1948), Barwa, Ksztalt i Wielkosc in Spostrzezeniu Dzieci. *Psychol. Wzchow.*, 13:1-23.

Blasius, W. (1943), Das Raumsehvermögen bei Formund Farbbeachtern. *Zeitschrift Sinnesphysiol.*, 70:52-74.

Brian, C. R. & Goodenough, F. L. (1929), The Relative Potency of Color and Form Perception at Different Ages. *Journal of Experimental Psychology*, 12:197-213.

Brown, R. (1951), An Investigation into the Color Vision of School Children. *British Journal of Educational Psychology*, 21:150-153.

Brunswik, E. (1956), *Perception and the Representative Design of Psychological Experiments*. Berkeley: University of California Press.

Burzlaff, W. (1931), Methodologische Beiträge. Zum Problem der Farbenconstanz. *Zeitschrift Psychol.*, 119:177-235.

Canestrini, S. (1913), *Über das Sinnesleben des Neugeborenen (Nach Physiologischen Experimenten)*. Berlin: J. Springer.

Chase, W. P. (1937), Color Vision in Infants. *Journal of Experimental Psychology*, 20:203-222.

Clifford, L. T. & Calvin, A. (1958), Effect of Age on the Discriminative Learning of Color and Brightness by Children. *American Journal of Psychology*, 71:766-767.

Cook, W. M. (1931), Ability of Children in Color Discriminations. *Child Development*, 2:303-320.

Dashiell, J. F. (1917), Children's Sense of Harmonies in Colors and Tones. *Journal of Experimental Psychology*, 2:466-475.

Dorcus, R. M. (1926), Color Preferences and Color Associations. *Pedagogical Seminary*, 33:399-434.

Duke-Elder, W. S. (1933), *Textbook of Ophthalmology: Volume I. The Development, Form, and Function of the Visual Apparatus*. St. Louis, Missouri: C. V. Mosby.

Ekhaus, D. (1958-1959), Hatseva Betsiyurey Hayeladim. *Hahinukh*, 31:183-188.

Engel, P. (1935), Über die Teilinhaltliche Beachtung von Farbe und Form; Untersuchung an 800 Schulkindern. *Zeitschrift Pädagog. Psychol.*, 36:202-214, 241-251.

Gale, A. V. (1933), Children's Preferences for Colors, Color Combinations, and Color Arrangements. Chicago, Illinois: University of Chicago Press.

Garth, T. R. (1924), A Color Preference Scale for 1,000 White School Children. Journal of Experimental Psychology, 7:233-241.

—— & Porter, E. P. (1934), The Color Preferences of 1,032 Young Children. American Journal of Psychology, 46:448-451.

Gibson, E. J. & Olum, V. (1960), Experimental Methods of Studying Perception in Children. Handbook of Research Methods in Child Development, Mussen, P. H. (Ed.). New York: John Wiley and Sons.

Gilbert, J. A. (1894), Researches on the Mental and Physical Development of School Children. Studies of the Yale Psychology Laboratories, 2:40-100.

Heider, F. & Heider, G. M. (1940), A Comparison of Color Sorting Behavior of Deaf and Hearing Children. Psychological Monographs: General and Applied, 52 (2).

Holden, W. A. & Bosse, K. K. (1900), The Order of Development of Color Perception and of Color Preference in the Child. Archives of Ophthalmology, 29:261-277.

Honkavaara, S. (1958), A Critical Reevaluation of the Color and Form Reaction, and Disproving of the Hypotheses Connected with It. Journal of Psychology, 45:25-36.

Huang, I. (1945), Abstraction of Form and Color in Children as a Function of the Stimulus Object. Journal of Genetic Psychology, 66:59-62.

Imada, M. (1938), Preference in the Appreciation and Use of Colors and Color Combinations by Young Children. Japanese Journal of Psychology, 13:133-146.

Kagan, J. & Lemkin, J. (1961), Form, Color and Size in Children's Conceptual Behavior. Child Development, 32:25-28.

Koffka, K. (1925), The Growth of the Mind. New York: Harcourt, Brace.

Lindberg, B. J. (1938), Experimental Studies of Color and Non-Color Attitude in School Children and Adults. Acta Psychiat., Kbh., Suppl. 16:165.

Malrieu, P. (1955), Quelques Problèmes de la Vision des Couleurs chez l'Enfant. J. Psychol. Norm. Path., 52:222-231.

Marsden, R. E. (1903), A Study of the Early Color Sense. Psychological Review, 10:37-47.

McDougall, W. (1906-1908), An Investigation of the Color Sense of Two Infants. British Journal of Psychology, 2:338-352.

Munn, N. L. (1938), Psychological Development: An Introduction to Genetic Psychology. Boston: Houghton-Mifflin.

Peiper, A. (1926), Über die Helligkeits-und Farbenempfindungen der Frühgeburten. Arch. Kinderheilk., 80:1-20.

——(1937), Comments upon J. M. Smith's Work, "The Relative Brightness Values of Three Hues for Newborn Infants." Child Development, 8:299-300.

Peters, W. (1927), Die Entwicklung von Wahrnehmungsleistungen beim Kind. Zeitschrift Psychol. Physiol. Sinnesorg., 103:129-184.

Polson, M. E. (1924), Color Reactions of School Children. Journal of Home Economics, 18:299-302.

Pratt, K. C., Nelson, A. K. & Sun, K. H. (1930), The Behavior of the Newborn Infant. Columbus, Ohio: Ohio State University Press.

Preyer, W. (1888), The Mind of the Child: Part II: The Development of the Intellect, Brown, H. W. (Trans.). New York: Appleton. Reprinted edition, 1901.

Rabello, S. (1933), A Percepcao das Cores e das Formes Entre as Criancas de 3 a 11 Annos. Bol. Educ., Pernambreco, 3, 16-45.

Reavis, W. C. (1920), The Interests of Children of the Primary and Intermediate Grades in the Use of Color. *School Arts*, 16:575-579.
Ricker, O. (1925), Color Preferences of Elementary School Children. *National Education Association*, Department of Superintendence, Third Yearbook, 349-350.
Ritter, E. (1930), Die Teilinhaltliche Beachtung von Form und Farbe bei Jugendlichen in ihrer Beziehung zur Strukturpsychologischen Typenlehre. *Zsch. Psychol.*, 117:307-338.
Segers, J. E. (1936), Nouvelles Observations Relatives à la Perception des Couleurs chez l'Enfant. *Arch. Belges Sci. Educ.*, 2:52-56.
Shinn, M. W. (1893-1899), *Notes on the Development of a Child*. University of California Publications in Education, 1:iv-424.
Smith, H. C. (1943), Age Differences in Color Discrimination. *Journal of Genetic Psychology*, 29:191-226.
Smith, J. M. (1936), The Relative Brightness Values of Three Hues for Newborn Infants. *University of Iowa Studies in Child Welfare*, 12 (1):91-140.
——(1937), Reply to Peiper. *Child Development*, 8:301-304.
Staples, R. (1932), The Responsiveness of Infants to Color. *Journal of Experimental Psychology*, 15:119-141.
Stirnimann, F. (1944), Über das Farbempfinden Neugeborener. *Ann. Paediat.*, 163:1-25.
Subes, J. (1959), Des Goûts des Enfants pour les Couleurs, *Enfance*, 2:117-142.
Synolds, D. L. & Pronko, N. H. (1949), An Exploratory Study of Color Discrimination of Children. *Journal of Genetic Psychology*, 74:17-21.
Trincker, D. & Trincker, I. (1955), Die Ontogenetische Entwicklung des Helligkeits-und Farbenehens beim Menschen. I. Die Entwicklung des Helligkeitssehens. *Albr. v. Graefes Arch. Ophthal.*, 156:519-534.
Valentine, C. W. (1913-1914), The Color Perception and Color Preference of an Infant During its Fourth and Eighth Months. *British Journal of Psychology*, 6:363-386.
Winch, W. H. (1909), Color Preferences of School Children. *British Journal of Psychology*, 3:42-65.
Wohlwill, J. F. (1960), Developmental Studies of Perception. *Psychological Bulletin*, 57:219-290.

DEVELOPMENT OF SPACE PERCEPTION

Ames, L. B., Learned, J., Metraux, R. & Walker, D. (1953), Development of Perception in the Young Child as Observed in Responses to the Rorschach Test Blots. *Journal of Genetic Psychology*, 82:183-204.
Berlyne, D. E. (1958), The Influence of the Albedo and Complexity of Stimuli on Visual Fixation in the Human Infant. *British Journal of Psychology*, 49:315-318.
Blum, A. (1957), The Value Factor in Children's Size Perception. *Child Development*, 28:3-14.
Botha, E. (1959), Effect of Preference on Perception of Size. *Perceptual and Motor Skills*, 9:325.
Bruner, J. & Goodman, C. C. (1947), Value and Need as Organizing Factors in Perception. *Journal of Abnormal and Social Psychology*, 47:33-44.
Burkhardt, H. (1925), Veränderungen der Raumlage Kinderzeichnungen. *Zeitschrift Pädagog. Psychol.*, 26:352-371.
Cramaussel, E. (1924), Ce que Voient les Yeux d'Enfants. *Journal de Psychologie*, 21:161-170.

Crudden, C. H. (1941), Form Abstraction by Children. *Journal of Genetic Psychology,* 58:327-351.

Davidson, H. P. (1935), A Study of the Confusing Letters b, d, p, and q. *Journal of Genetic Psychology,* 47:458-468.

Dworetski, G. (1939), Le Test de Rorschach et l'Evolution de la Perception. *Arch. Psychol., Genève,* 27:233-396.

Fantz, R. L. (1958), Pattern Vision in Young Infants. *Psychological Review,* 8:43-47.

——(1961a), A Method for Studying Depth Perception in Infants Under Six Months of Age. *Psychological Record,* 11:27-32.

——(1961b), The Origin of Form Perception. *Scientific American,* 204(5):66-72.

Fraisse, P. & Vautrey, P. (1956), The Influence of Age, Sex, and Specialized Training on the Vertical-Horizontal Illusion. *Quarterly Journal of Experimental Psychology,* 8:114-120.

Garrison, K. C. (1952), *Growth and Development.* New York: Longmans.

Gellerman, L. W. (1933), Form Discrimination in Chimpanzees and Two-Year-Old Children. *Journal of Genetic Psychology,* 42:1-50.

Ghent, L. (1956), Perception of Overlapping and Embedded Figures by Children of Different Ages. *American Journal of Psychology,* 69:575-587.

Gorman, J. J., Cogan, D. G. & Gellis, S. S. (1957), An Apparatus for Grading the Visual Acuity of Infants on the Basis of Opticokinetic Nystagmus. *Pediatrics,* 19:1088-1092.

Graham, V., Jackson, T. A. & Long, L. (1944), Generalization of the Concept of Middleness. *Journal of Genetic Psychology,* 65:227-237.

Hanfmann, E. (1933), Some Experiments on Spatial Position as a Factor in Children's Perception and Reproduction of Simple Figures. *Psychol. Forschung,* 17:319-329.

Heiss, A. (1930), Zum Problem der Isolierenden Abstraktion. *Neue Psychol. Stud.,* 4:285-318.

Hemmendinger, L. (1953), Perceptual Organization and Development as Reflected in the Structure of Rorschach Test Responses. *Journal of Projective Techniques,* 17:162-170.

Hicks, H. & Stewart, F. D. (1930), The Learning of Abstract Concepts of Size. *Child Development,* 1:195-203.

Hunton, V. D. (1955), The Recognition of Inverted Pictures by Children. *Journal of Genetic Psychology,* 86:281-288.

Jackson, D. N. (1954), A Further Examination of the Role of Autism in a Visual Figure-Ground Relationship. *Journal of Psychology,* 38:339-357.

Johnson, B. & Beck, F. L. (1941), The Development of Space Perception: I. Stereoscopic Vision in Preschool Children. *Journal of Genetic Psychology,* 58:247-254.

Line, W. (1930-1931), The Growth of Visual Perception in Children. *British Journal of Psychology,* Suppl. 5(15).

Ling, B.-C. (1942), Form Discrimination as a Learning Cue in Infants. *Comparative Psychology Monographs,* 17(2).

Long, L. (1941), Size Discrimination in Children. *Child Development,* 12:247-254.

Lord, F. E. (1941), A Study of Spatial Orientation of Children. *Journal of Educational Research,* 34:481-505.

Lowenfeld, V. (1957), *Creative and Mental Growth.* New York: The Macmillan Book Company, third edition.

Meili, R. (1931), Les Perceptions des Enfants et la Psychologie de la Gestalt. *Arch. Psychol., Genève,* 23:25-45.

Meister, D. (1949), A Comparative Study of Figure-Ground Discrimination in Preschool Children and Adults. *Journal of Genetic Psychology*, 74:311-323.

Meyer, E. (1940), Comprehension of Spatial Relations in Preschool Children. *Journal of Genetic Psychology*, 57:119-151.

Mooney, C. M. (1957), Age in the Development of Closure Ability in Children. *Canadian Journal of Psychology*, 11:219-226.

Munn, N. L. & Steining, B. R. (1931), The Relative Efficacy of Form and Background in a Child's Discrimination of Visual Patterns. *Journal of Genetic Psychology*, 39:73-88.

Newhall, S. M. (1937), Identification by Young Children of Differently Oriented Visual Forms. *Child Development*, 8:105-111.

Peckham, R. H. (1933), Visual Discrimination in Preschool Children. *Child Development*, 4:292-297.

Peters, W. (1927), Die Entwicklung von Wahrnehmungsleistungen beim Kind. *Zeitschrift Psychol. Physiol. Sinnesorg.*, 103:129-184.

Piaget, J. & Albertini, B. (1954), Recherches sur le Développement des Perceptions. XIX. Observations sur la Perception des Bonnes Formes chez l'Enfant par Actualization des lignes Virtuelles. *Arch. Psychol., Genève*, 34:203-243.

—— & Inhelder, B. (1956), *The Child's Conception of Space.* London: Routledge and Kegan Paul.

——, —— & Szeminska, A. (1960), *The Child's Conception of Geometry.* New York: Basic Books.

—— & Lambercier, M. (1956), Recherches sur le Développement des Perceptions: XXXI. Les Comparaisons Verticales à Intervalles Croissants. *Arch. Psychol., Genève*, 35:321-367.

—— & Morf, A. (1956), Recherches sur le Développement des Perceptions: XXX. Les Comparaisons Verticales à Faible Intervalle. *Arch. Psychol., Genève*, 35:289-319.

—— & Taponier, S. (1956), Recherches sur le Développement des Perceptions: XXXII. L'Estimation des Longueurs de deux Droites Horizontales et Paralleles à Extremités Décalies. *Arch. Psychol., Genève*, 35:369-400.

Rabinow, O. & Frankl, L. (1934), Die erste Dingauffassung beim Säugling. *Zsch. Psychol.*, 133:1-71.

Rice, C. (1930), The Orientation of Plane Figures as a Factor in Their Perception by Children. *Child Development*, 1:111-143.

Rudel, R. G. (1959), *Discrimination of Direction of Line in Children.* Paper read at Eastern Psychological Association, April.

Rush, G. P. (1937), Visual Grouping in Relation to Age. *Archives of Psychology*, 31, (217).

Segers, J. E. (1926), La Perception Visuelle et la Fonction de Globalisation chez les Enfants. *Documents Pedotechniques, 5me Année, # 2.* Bruxelles.

Siegel, A. I. & Ozkaplan, H. (1953), Manipulative Completion of Bisected Geometrical Forms by Nursery School Children. *American Journal of Psychology*, 66:626-628.

Solley, C. M. & Engel, M. (1960), Perceptual Autism in Children: The Effects of Reward, Punishment, and Neutral Conditions upon Perceptual Learning. *Journal of Genetic Psychology*, 97:77-91.

—— & Sommer, R. (1957), Perceptual Autism in Children. *Journal of Genetic Psychology*, 56:3-11.

Stern, W. (1909), *Psychology of Early Childhood.* New York: Holt.

Stirnimann, F. (1940), *Psychologie des Neugeborenen Kindes.* Zurich: Rascher.

Street, R. F. (1931), *A Gestalt Completion Test.* New York: Bureau of Publications of Teachers College.

Thrum, M. E. (1935), The Development of the Concept of Magnitude. *Child Development,* 6:120-140.

Updegraff, R. (1930), The Visual Perception of Distance in Our Children and Adults: A Comparative Study. *University of Iowa Studies in Child Welfare,* 4(4).

Vernon, M. D. (1957), *Backwardness in Reading.* Cambridge: Cambridge University Press.

Vinacke, W. E. (1951), The Investigation of Concept Formation. *Psychological Bulletin,* 48:1-31.

Walk, R. D. & Gibson, E. (1959), *A Study of Visual Depth Perception in the Human Infant with a Visual Cliff.* Paper read at Eastern Psychological Association, April.

Walters, Sister Annette (1942), A Genetic Study of Geometrical-Optical Illusions. *Genetic Psychology Monographs,* 25:101-155.

Watson, E. H. & Lowrey, G. H. (1962), *Growth and Development of Children.* Chicago: Medical Year Book Publishers, fourth edition.

Welch, L. (1938), A Preliminary Study of the Interaction of Conflicting Concepts of Children Between the Ages of Three and Five Years. *Psychological Record,* 2:439-459.

——(1939a), The Development of Size Discrimination Between the Ages of 12 and 40 Months. *Journal of Genetic Psychology,* 55:243-268.

——(1939b), The Span of Generalization Below the Two Year Age Level. *Journal of Genetic Psychology,* 58:269-297.

——(1939c), The Development of Discrimination of Form and Area. *Journal of Psychology,* 7:37-54.

—— (1940), A Preliminary Investigation of Some Aspects of the Hierarchical Development of Concepts. *Journal of Genetic Psychology,* 22:359-378.

Witkin, H. A., Lewis, H. B., Hertzman, M., Machover, K., Meissner, P. B. & Wapner, S. (1954), *Personality Through Perception.* New York: Harper.

Wohlwill, J. F. (1960), Developmental Studies of Perception. *Psychological Bulletin,* 57:249-290.

Wörsten, H. (1947), Recherches sur le Développement des Perceptions: IX. L'évolution des Comparaisons de Longueurs de l'Enfant à l'Adulte avec Variation d'Angle entre la Verticale et l'Horizontale. *Arch. Psychol., Genève,* 32:1-144.

DEVELOPMENT OF MOVEMENT PERCEPTION

Beasley, W. C. (1933), Visual Pursuit in 109 White and 142 Negro Newborn Infants. *Child Development,* 4:106-120.

Botwinick, J. & Brinley, J. F. (1963), Age Differences in Relations between CFF and Apparent Motion. *Journal of Genetic Psychology,* 102:189-194.

Brenner, M. W. (1957), The Developmental Study of Apparent Movement. *Quarterly Journal of Experimental Psychology,* 9:169-174.

Brown, J. F. (1931), The Visual Perception of Velocity. *Psychol. Forschung,* 14:199-232.

Edgren, R. D. (1953), *A Developmental Study of Motion Perception, Size Constancy, Recognition Speed and Judgment of Verticality.* Unpublished doctoral dissertation, Stanford University.

Fraisse, P. & Vautrey, P. (1952), La Perception de l'Espace, de la Vitesse, et du Temps chez l'Enfant de Cinq Ans. *Enfance,* 5:1-20, 102-119.

Gantenbein, M. (1952), Recherches sur le Développement de la Perception du Mouvement avec l'Age (Mouvement Apparent, dit Stroboscopique). *Arch. Psychol., Genève,* 33:197-294.

Gesell, A. & Thompson, H. (1934), *Infant Behavior, Its Genesis and Growth.* New York: McGraw-Hill.

Jones, M. C. (1926), The Development of Early Behavior Patterns in Young Children. *Journal of Genetic Psychology,* 33:537-585.

Kroner, T. (1881), *Über die Sinnesempfindungen der Neugeborenen.* Breslau: Grass, Barth. (Abstracted in Preyer, 1882.)

Kussmaul, A. (1859), *Untersuchungen über das Seelenleben des Neugeborenen Menschen.* Tübingen: Moser. (Abstracted in Preyer, 1882.)

Meili, R. & Tobler, E. (1931), Les Mouvements Stroboscopiques chez les Enfants. *Arch. Psychol. Genève,* 23:131-157.

Michotte, A. (1946), *La Perception de la Causalité.* Louvain: Vrin.

Morgan, S. S. & Morgan, J. J. B. (1944), An Examination of the Development of Certain Adaptive Behavior Patterns in Infants. *Journal of Pediatrics,* 25:168-177.

Olum, V. (1958), Developmental Differences in the Perception of Causality. *American Journal of Psychology,* 69:417-423.

Peterson, F. & Rainey, L. H. (1910), The Beginnings of Mind in the Newborn. *Bulletin of the Lying-in Hospital, City of New York,* 7:99-122.

Piaget, J. & Lambercier, M. (1958), Recherches sur le Développement des Perceptions: XXXIII. La Causalité Perceptive Visuelle chez l'Enfant et chez l'Adulte. *Arch. Psychol., Genève,* 36:77-201.

Preyer, W. (1882), *The Mind of the Child.* Part I: The Senses and the Will, Brown, H. W. (Trans.). New York: Appleton. Reprinted edition, 1901.

——(1888), *The Mind of the Child.* Part II: The Development of the Intellect, Brown, H. W. (Trans.). New York: Appleton. Reprinted edition, 1901.

Shirley, M. M. (1931), The Sequential Method for the Study of Maturing Behavior Patterns. *Psychological Review,* 38:507-528.

Stirnimann, F. (1944), Über das Farbempfinden Neugeborener. *Ann. Paediat.,* 163:1-25.

Wapner, S. & Werner, H. (1957), *Perceptual Development: An Investigation Within the Sensory-Tonic Field Theory.* Worcester: Clark University Press.

Wohlwill, J. (1960), Developmental Studies of Perception. *Psychological Bulletin,* 57:249-288.

CHAPTER 5

The Development of Auditory Perception in Children

ALINE H. KIDD

ROBERT M. KIDD

The development of auditory perception has recently interested Russian psychologists but has been largely ignored by Americans for several reasons. Historically, Barber (1950) noted that child psychology held a limited interest for the profession during the '30s and '40s, while Koch (1954) observed that much of the exploring of the area was in inexperienced hands because the psychology of children was of greater interest to educators and parents than to psychologists. Lack of interest in perception in children was still noted by Radke-Yarrow and Yarrow in 1955, and Pollock, in 1961, commented on the unfortunate isolation of psychoacoustics from psychology.

Instrumentation for production of stimuli has been a major drawback to carrying out controlled research in auditory perception. From 1873 to the present, toys and noisemakers, clackers and bells, Urbantschitsch whistles and Galton whistles, tuning forks and myriad other devices were utilized to give a constant if unmeasured stimulus to elicit responses in infants and children. But these instruments produced broad-band, rather than pure-tone, stimuli of variable and varying loudness and timbre differences which made it difficult or impossible for experimenters to compare their results. However, instrumentation has been improved since World War II, and it is now possible to produce controlled auditory stimuli of any specific nature the experimenter desires.

A meaningful response has been a third area of research difficulty. Such diversified responses as the orienting reflex, the auropalpebral (eyeblink) reflex, the acoustic muscle (defined as either Moro or startle) reflex, the auditory oculogyric (movement of eyes) reflex, the heart rate, the respiration rate, the Féré effect, the Tarchanoff effect, conditioned foot withdrawal, increase or decrease in general movement, gross movement, head movement, conditioned sucking, and waking from sleep have been used to determine the presence of auditory sensitivity in infants and young children. Some of these same responses plus verbal responses, pointing responses, button pushing, and EEG changes have been attempted with older children. The results have not been comparable because of attentional and adaptational factors and because individual differences in neuromuscular responsiveness have been demonstrated to be so great that lack of response to auditory stimuli cannot be considered as specific evidence that the infant or young child cannot hear (Myklebust, 1954).

Finally, because the deaf or severely hard-of-hearing child has been found to be extremely limited in his ability to communicate with others, in his personality development, and, therefore, in his educational achievement, researchers have tended to concentrate on the need for research in detection of auditory handicaps and the improvement of the communication skills of such children rather than on research in the development of auditory perception in general.

There is a considerable body of research on the neurological development of the auditory mechanism, but in order to delimit the area, only research concerned with prenatal, infant, and child auditory development, and adult auditory research which suggests developmental problems, will be reviewed.

Research methods seem to have interfered most with genuine developmental studies. Because the studies reviewed suggest a tremendous range of individual variations, cross-sectional or longitudinal sampling techniques must use large numbers of subjects so that the variations will be statistically manageable. A broad age range of subjects must be divided into narrow-span age groups because perceptual development has been shown to be frequently discontinuous or nonlinear (Wohlwill, 1960). For infants, the length of pregnancy may influence the physiological development of the auditory mechanism, and so that variable must be controlled. For children, mental age, cultural differences, parental socioeconomic status, and specific or general auditory training are factors which must be controlled or comparable from age group to age group. The many variables influencing a child's verbal and speech development, such as the amount and warmth of verbal interaction between the child and other people, along with his physical and emotional health, should be taken into consideration as influences on his auditory perceptual development. All in all, the wide variety of possible influential variables makes subject selection a difficult and important problem.

Instrumentation and required response techniques, which must be comparable from age group to age group and experimenter to experimenter, pose another set of problems. The sound source must emit either a constant or a continuing sound or a series of sounds of specific measurable characteristics. Selected responses should be applicable to as great a chronological age span as possible. The Moro reflex response of the neonatal period cannot be demanded after 6 months when it has been replaced by the startle response. Infants cannot be expected to perform button pushing as adequately as can children. Thus the results obtained from infants and from children may not give a consistent developmental picture. At present, the conditioning techniques seem to be the most promising for giving a more consistent picture of auditory perceptual development.

Few of the studies reviewed concerned themselves with statistical techniques or significance. Age groups are reported merely as having or not having perception of a specific auditory dimension, a procedure which makes impossible the determination of age trends and the range of individual differences, both variables which could be clarified through curve-fitting techniques, through trend analysis of curves (Grant, 1956), and through nonparametric statistics (Siegal, 1956).

The assumptions that discriminatory ability among all auditory dimensions is inherent and therefore appears as a result of maturation (Seashore, 1934), and that those aspects of auditory perception dependent upon learning are learned in very early childhood, have interfered with genuine developmental studies and have produced, instead, research based on the ages at which children respond to specific auditory dimensions. It seems more probable that perception in each auditory dimension develops with the interaction of auditory experience and maturity. Although Piaget and his collaborators have been criticized for unsystematic and imprecise psychophysical methods and experimental designs producing results of dubious significance (Wohlwill, 1960), it has been just such techniques and the significant developmental concepts resulting from their research which suggest future methodologies for meaningful developmental research. Indeed, refinement of Piagetlike manipulation of pertinent stimulus variables in combination with a modern statistical technique such as curve fitting or trend analysis (Grant, 1956) might lead to a genuine understanding of the development of auditory perception.

Although all the studies reviewed are subject to methodological criticism and the reviewer's conclusions are tenuous, a review of the studies of the development of auditory perception is of great value to indicate the problems and theoretical issues which might be and perhaps will be resolved by future experimentation.

EXPERIMENTAL STUDIES

PRENATAL RESEARCH

Whether a fetus hears or not is still an open question. After preparing 6 pregnant women not to respond to the stimulus, Peiper (1924) sounded an automobile horn when the fetuses were motionless. Definite fetal reactions were observed, but there were individual differences in response and responses varied from day to day for the individual fetuses. He also noted that after one reaction the fetuses did not respond again to the stimulus for several minutes.

Forbes and Forbes (1927) record a pregnant woman who, approximately a month before delivery, was in a metal bathtub which her 2-year-old struck with a glass. The fetus was reported to have jumped and, 8 days later when the tub was again struck, the movement was repeated. Two weeks later, fetal movement at the sound of a board clattering to the floor beside the mother was reported. Eight days after birth, the infant responded to a sound by flattening his ears against his head. Forbes and Forbes believed that this confirmed Peiper's (1924) findings concerning prenatal hearing.

Further confirmation of Peiper was made by Ray (1932) and Sontag and Wallace (1934). The latter tried 214 experiments with 7 pregnant women. A sound frequency of 120 cps produced a reliable increase in detectable fetal movements in the first minute following the application. The fetal response was noticeable from the start of the 31st week of intrauterine life and increased in magnitude as the fetuses neared term.

Bernard (1946) amplified and delivered through a loud-speaker the pure tones of an audio-frequency oscillator, using as criterion of response a change in fetal heart rate. After 73 stimulations of 4 subjects, he concluded that the human fetus responds to tonal stimulation throughout a range of pure tones from 20 to 5000 cps.

Bernard and Sontag (1947) reported fetuses in utero reacting to vibratory stimuli.

Spelt (1948) recorded fetal movement by means of a tambour placed on the mother's abdomen. Using a vibrotactile conditioned stimulus and a loud noise as the unconditioned response he was able to establish a conditioned response in the fetus during the last two months of gestation. He reported the extinction and spontaneous recovery of the response.

Munn (1955) concluded that fetuses respond to loud sounds and that such responses can be conditioned. However, Forbes and Forbes (1927) had already questioned whether such responses arise from auditory or from tactile stimulation, or from both. Peterson and Rainey (1910) believed that a fetus can hear before birth because they found evidence of an auditory response in a premature infant soon after its breathing, crying, and yawning had permitted drainage of the fetal middle-ear fluid. Additional support for such hearing is noted in Polikanina and Probatova's (1955) records of a diffuse reaction to sound in prematurely delivered infants during the first postnatal month.

There have been no studies concerning prenatal discrimination of pitch or timbre, but because the prenatal movement response to sound can be conditioned, it is possible that future research could determine quantitatively whether fetuses respond differently to differing pitches and timbres.

INFANT RESEARCH

Although hearing apparently occurs during the prenatal period, there has been much controversy over whether it is functional at birth or not. Kussmaul (1859) found the neonate insensitive to sound, as did Shinn (1893-1899) who attributed this to imperfect auditory nerve development. Compayre (1896) attributed the newborn's auditory insensitivity to a fixity of the auditory ossicle, while Feldman (1920) said it was due either to an occlusion of the external auditory meatus or to failure of the tympanic membrane to be in the condition required for an easy response to air vibrations. Lowenfeld (1927) and Bryan (1930) reported relative auditory insensitivity in newborns, and Haller (1932), utilizing an audiometer as sound source, found infants to be relatively insensitive to auditory stimuli during early postnatal life.

Kröner (1881), however, reported some newborn infants sensitive to sound but found early auditory sensitivity extremely variable. Sachs (1893) considered the palpebral reflex to sound as evidence of early auditory sensitivity and reported as a "fear reaction" a gross muscular response to relatively intense auditory stimuli. Poli (1893) also considered the palpebral reflex as indicative of auditory sensitivity.

One of the few efforts to build up a developmental sequence for auditory perception was Preyer's (1893) report of the auditory development of a child from birth to 36 months. He found the child "deaf" for the first 3 days but that such sounds as hand clapping were heard on the 4th. The child quieted upon hearing his father's voice and responded to whispering on the 11th and 12th days, blinked at the sound of a quiet voice on the 26th day, and showed fear at a loud voice on the 30th. During the 5th and 6th weeks the baby did not sleep if people walked or talked near him, and he showed a startle response to noises. During the 7th and 8th weeks he began to show pleasure at musical sounds such as the playing of a piano, and he attended to a watch's ticking during the 9th. He oriented his head toward a sound at 11 weeks, turned his head toward a sound with the certainty of a reflex at 16 weeks, and enjoyed the sound he made when he himself crumpled paper during the 19th week. By the 11th month he responded to a whispered "shhh," and on the 319th day he distinguished between the sound of a spoon on a plate held by a hand and the sound when the plate was not held by hand. By the 15th month the child laughed at new sounds, and at the 16th held a watch to his ear to hear the ticking. At 30 months the baby covered his ear with his hand while a kettle of water boiled beside him and he noticed the decrease in sound. At 36 months the child was unable to name the notes "C," "D," and "E" despite teaching by his parents. The significance of Preyer's reporting is limited by the fact that he reported on only one child, that his stimuli were not calibrated, and that he was not precise in defining the child's responses to auditory stimuli.

In 1907, Koellreutter confirmed auditory sensitivity in the neonate, as did Peterson and Rainey (1910), Blanton (1917), and Walton (1921), who used whistles and tuning forks to test auditory acuity.

Muzio (1933) reported a more rapid response to auditory stimulation by newborn girls than boys, but he did not use instrumentation to record responses or reaction times and his conclusion is open to question.

Pratt (1934) also reported auditory sensitivity in the newborn and noted that repeated auditory stimulation produced a lessening of the cochlear-palpebral reflex.

Using Urbantschitsch whistles and tuning forks, Froeschels and Beebe (1946) investigated the hearing of 33 infants ranging in age from 12 hours to 9 days. They recorded eye blinking to intense whistles, grimacing, blinking, body withdrawal, turning toward the sound source, and expression of pleasure or pain responses to whistles, but found no response to tuning forks. They concluded that they had demonstrated "the presence of hearing in a great majority of newborn infants."

The review supports Carmichael's (1946, p. 136) conclusion:

> . . . it may be said that the auditory mechanism seems to be well developed structurally during later fetal life but in general, possibly because of the closure of the external ear or because of the gelatinous liquid which fills the middle ear, the fetus is probably deaf to sounds of normal intensity before birth and during a short period immediately after birth. Strong sounds, however, especially those which can directly pass through the mechanical block, seem to be able to bring about auditory stimulation.

STUDIES USING GENERAL OR SPECIFIC MOVEMENTS AS THE MEASURED RESPONSES

Utilizing a toy giving a loud, brief, disagreeable sound and discordant high overtones, which could be continued identically in trial after trial, and with this sound source brought very close to the ear without involving other nonauditory stimuli, Moldenhauer and Von Tröttsch (1880) experimented with 50 newborns, 10 of whom were less than 12 hours old, 7 of whom were from 12 to 24 hours old, and the rest a little older. The weakest reaction noted was a quiver of the eyelids without interruption of sleep. A stronger reaction was a wrinkling of the forehead. Considered as a still stronger response was a series of head movements involving single, short thrustings of the head. The strongest reaction was a quivering of the head, arms, and upper torso accompanied by sleep interruption and crying or screaming. The responses at the end of the second day were significantly stronger than those of the first and early part of the second day.

When stimulations were in quick succession, the amount of reaction notably diminished and there might finally be a complete absence of reaction. It was also noted that the babies tended to turn their heads toward sound by the 9th day and that in general responses were more intense to high-pitched than to low-pitched sounds.

Sachs (1893) used tuning forks and Galton whistles but did not instrumentally record responses to these sound sources. He reported that easily observed responses were more likely to occur with high-pitched than with low-pitched sounds, that overt responses were greater with stimuli of short duration, and that inhibition of activity or complete lack of response might result with stimuli of long duration.

Pratt, Nelson and Sun (1930), in confirming newborn auditory sensitivity, noted that the amount of measurable and observable activity did not seem to correspond with adults' ratings of intensity or loudness of experimental stimuli, but indicated that their incomplete control of stimulus variables made questionable the validity of their results.

Haller (1932) used amplifier and loud-speaker-controlled audiometer tones sounded at four different intensity levels and eight pitches at octave intervals to test 11 boy and 8 girl infants from 3 to 5 weeks of age. Infant responses showed more positive and varied indications of discomfort than of comfort. All noted reactions were of a reflex character related to stimulus intensity and did not persist after stimulus removal. Tones of greater intensity and higher vibration rate were more disturbing than less intense tones of lower pitch. When tone duration was lengthened, it was harder for the infants to adapt to pure tones of high intensity and high vibration rate than to pure tones of high intensity and low vibration rate.

Weiss (1934) investigated the effects of two intensities (50 ± 5 dbs and 75 ± 5 dbs) of a tone with a frequency of 470 cps for 5-minute durations. Activity was measured by stabilimeter oscillation, and the results showed that the infants exhibited a significant tendency toward lessened activity with increased sound intensity under sound-dark conditions.

Riesen (1960), in concluding that pure tones produce little or no response in neonates but that high intensity noise produces a startle and/or increase in general body activity, recapitulated the assumption that newborn hearing is impaired by external and middle-ear blockage, especially the amniotic fluid blockage in the middle ear which results in limitation of movement of the ossicles.

STUDIES UTILIZING BODILY PROCESSES AS RESPONSES

Canestrini (1913) noted that when infants are asleep, such auditory stimulation as musical tones makes breathing slower, shallower, and decreases the pulse rate, that utilization of stimuli intense enough to waken the baby increases respiration and pulse rates, and that such intense short-duration stimuli as pistol shots evoke an immediate increase in amplitude of respiration, followed by irregular breathing.

Bridger (1961) experimented with 50 1- to 5-year-old normal full-term infants at a set time after feedings. He used a pure tone of constant intensity and varied the intervals between and the durations of the stimuli, the intensity being sufficiently intense to produce a response whether the baby was asleep or crying loudly. Three observers independently recorded the behavior. Because some of the infants failed to respond to auditory stimuli whether they were asleep or crying, the stimuli were varied to make certain that the lack of response was caused by adaptation rather than by a shift in the arousal state. It was found that when stimuli are applied in less than 5-second intervals, the baby adapts first with a cessation of a marked response and then with a cessation of all responses. All the infants utilized in the study showed the first stage of adaptation, but few showed the second.

Bridger then experimented with discrimination of pitch, or auditory frequency, and used an intense tone with controlled loudness because the degree to which loudness depends on frequency decreases as the intensity rises. After habituating the babies' responses to one pure tone, he substituted another tone. He found pitch discrimination in 15 of his 50 infants, and one baby had such fine discrimination that he responded differentially to 200 and to 250 cps.

REFLEXIVE RESPONSE STUDIES

Genzmer (1882) stressed individual differences and insisted that not only does the newborn possess auditory sensitivity on the first or second day but in all probability the fetus receives auditory stimuli from the heartbeats, aortic pulse, and activity of the digestive tract of the maternal organism. He was the first experimenter to measure responses to auditory stimuli and used as criterion the greatest distances at which 15 infants' eyelids quivered when a small bell was struck with a small iron rod. He found that early reactions were variable but that hearing grew more acute during the first day, and that infants sometimes responded on the first day but always responded on the second day. He studied the relationship between the distance from the bell to the babies and their responses, and noted that a very active baby responded on the first day when the bell was 8 inches away, on the 6th day when it was 18 inches away, and on the 24th day when it was 24 inches away. With a phlegmatic baby, the auditory response was very irregular on the first day, was regular on the 8th and 24th days when the bell was 5 inches and 11 inches away, respectively. He also noted that infants of more than two days sometimes turned their heads toward the sound of the bell struck softly, but responded with restlessness when the bell was struck hard, and that all of the babies tended to ignore a softly struck bell if they were nursing.

Cemach (1920) found that the cochlear-palpebral reflex to sound continues beyond the neonatal period, and Irwin (1932) confirmed auditory sensitivity in the newborn when he used auditory stimuli of 581 cps with a duration of 0.07 seconds and a constant unmeasured intensity, finding that the mean startle reaction time of 12 infants measured by stabilimeter polygraph record was 0.18 ± 0.03 seconds.

Stubbs (1934) used an audiometer and oscillator to produce stimulus intensities of 30 to 50 and 70 to 85 sensation units and stimulus durations of 1, 3, 5, and 10 seconds. The obtained percentage of responses showed that eyelid opening and decrease in body activity occurred more often at low than at high frequencies, that louder stimuli produced more body movement, more eyelid closing, more respiratory action, and a greater decrease in crying than did softer stimuli, and that the percentage of responses to stimuli of the longest duration was significantly greater than to stimuli of the shortest duration. Stimuli lasting 10 seconds elicited the most body activity, an increase in respiratory rate, and a decrease in the amplitude of the respiratory response.

Stubbs and Irwin (1934) noted that startle responses to loud tones occurred with only 70% of the stimulations whereas respiratory responses occurred 100% of the time. The average reaction time of the respiratory response was 0.09 seconds with a standard error of 0.025 seconds; the average reaction time of the startle response was 0.19 seconds.

Hunt, Clarke, and Hunt (1938) reported that because infants started at a sound, a light, and at puffs of air the startle response was not ideal for the determination of hearing. The startle pattern could not, therefore, be considered to be merely an auditory reflex, but must be considered a general response to sudden intense stimuli. Clarke (1939) then studied motion pictures of newborn to 20-week-old infants' responses to the sound of a 2-pound iron weight dropped 3 feet onto a hardwood surface and noted that, during the early weeks, the response was a Moro reflex. As the chronological age increased, extensor movements were replaced by flexor movements and, at 16 to 20 weeks, the Moro had been replaced with the startle reflex.

Landis and Hunt (1939) used a click of .35 milliseconds with frequencies around 1000 cps predominating, and an oscilloscope to record eyeblinks. They found that in normal infants eyeblinks started at 50 decibels above threshold, increased in number as the click's intensity was raised, and that the infants blinked at each stimulation when the intensity of the clicks was 130 decibels above threshold. Infants with hearing losses responded like normal infants, but greater intensity was required to elicit responses. They concluded that the palpebral reflex was the most stable component of the startle pattern to intense sounds. Ewing and Ewing (1944) showed that sound localization was developed by one year, as indicated by a turning of the head to sound. Hardy, Dougherty, and Hardy (1959) studied all of the responses to the sound of noisemakers to determine the best auditory responses for the screening of infants and children with hearing losses. They indicated that while the Moro reflex was an efficient indicator of a neonate's responsiveness to sound, it disappeared at about 4 months, being replaced by the startle reflex. From 7 to 24 months, the orienting, or turning of the head to sound, reflex was felt to be the most efficient indicator. They believed that after 2 years, audiometry was possible for the identification of hearing losses.

Riesen (1960) indicated that the startle response was the usual test of infant auditory sensitivity and that pure tones produced little or no response in neonates while high intensity noise produced startle and/or an increase in general bodily activity. However, the use of sound-induced reflexes makes it difficult to determine the nature of infant hearing, because the auditory stimuli must be of at least moderate intensity to produce startle responses. It is, therefore, impossible to use reflexes to ascertain the thresholds of infant sensitivity.

Using the sound of a gong, Fröding (1960) elicited the eyewink reflex one-half hour after birth, and Wertheimer (1961), having noted that his own child had turned his eyes toward a soft click beside one ear or the other a half hour after natural birth, used clicks from a cricket placed next to the right or the left ear in a predetermined order with another infant from 3 to 10 minutes after natural birth. Two observers determined, independently, whether the infant's eyes moved and the direction of movement. There were 52 trials before the infant no longer responded, and the observers agreed on 45 of the trials. Twenty-three of the trials yielded no response. Of the 22 responsive trials, the baby's eyes moved toward the click 18 times and away from the click 4 times, a difference significant beyond the 1% level. Wertheimer concluded that at 10 minutes after birth the baby showed a rudimentary directional oculomotor response with a rough coordination of auditory and visual space.

Chun, Pawsat, and Forster (1960) studied 26 2- to 49-week-old infants, placing the babies on their backs with buzzers of identical pitch and intensity at the mid-line anterior, the mid-line inferior, the mid-line superior, and at the two ears. Twenty-five of the infants showed a startle response. Twenty-two showed a horizontal roving eye movement. The 11 babies under 26 weeks old looked neither toward nor away from the sound. All 15 over 26 weeks old could localize sound at one ear or the other. Twelve of these 15 could localize sound at both ears, and 10 of the 15 could localize at the mid-line anterior. In 9 infants, the auropalpebral (eyeblink) reflex was the most common response to auditory stimuli for the first 5 months.

Hardy et al. (1962) found that the orienting reflex to sounds selected to interest infants is a relatively good indication of hearing at 8 months, and that approximately 61 of every 100 infants who fail to pass the auditory test will later be shown to have other psychological abnormalities.

STUDIES USING CONDITIONING

Marquis (1931) was able to condition sucking to auditory stimuli during the first 10 days after birth. Kasatkin and Levikova (1935) used 3 children from 11 to 30 days old at the beginning of experimentation and reported that conditioned alimentary reflexes in response to auditory stimuli appeared in the first half of the second month of life. They noted developmental stages of indifference, movement inhibition, and the appearance of the first signs of conditioned reactions, and finally clear conditioned reactions, and that the child's age seemed more important than the number of stimulations in the formation of conditioned auditory reflexes. At 2½ to 3½ months, the child could differentiate as small a difference as 11½ tones and, at 4 months, 5½ tones. There were great individual variations in the formation of even the most simple auditory discrimination and, before the auditory differentiation was complete, it passed through the three stages of no differentiation, unstable differentiation, and stable differentiation.

Wickens and Wickens (1940) conditioned 12 infants under 10 days old using shock to the foot as the unconditioned stimulus and the sound of a buzzer as the conditioned stimulus. The experimental and control groups' responses were sufficiently similar so that conditioning under 12 days was not conclusively demonstrated, but the results indicated that pseudoconditioning could be used as an indication of sensitivity to sound.

Levikova and Nevymakova (1948) used nursing and food-seeking as unconditioned stimuli and the tone B^{iv} sounded on an organ as the conditioned stimulus. The baby was able to discriminate between the B^{iv} and a B^{v}, and between the B^{iv} and the sound of an electric bell with the discrimination achieved between 110 and 122 days of age.

Hardy and Bordley (1951) used a Pavlovian conditioning technique with the Féré effect as the conditioned response, shock of sufficient magnitude to annoy but not to harm as the unconditioned stimulus, and tones as the conditioned stimuli. Eight to 12 trials of a tone followed by a mild shock produced a conditioned reflex. Conditioning at 3 weeks of age was achieved in some infants, but great individual variability was noted.

Mirzoiants (1954) noted that a conditioned orienting reflex to sound could be developed in 4- to 5½-month-old children, some of them being able to differentiate 5 tones higher and 2 tones lower than the basic musical tone. Differentiation formation, however, proceeded differently in different children.

Nechaeva (1954) reported that with Pavlovian techniques, a differentiation of 17 musical tones apart could be established in 4-month-olds, and of 2/3 to 1½ musical tones apart in 6- to 7-month-olds.

Simmons and Lipsitt (1961) reported that auditory stimuli served as satisfactory reinforcers of differential reactions in infants to different colors. However, Grings, Lowell, and Rushford (1960) concluded that the criteria of conditioning need investigation also because they noted that a child can only be conditioned to a tone he can hear, therefore the intensity must be well above the child's threshold, that the conditioned response must differ from responses produced by sensitization or fatigue, and that children tend to give spontaneous GSRs because meprobromate does not reduce these in children as it does in adults.

Additional conditioning problems occur because, as Combs (1938) pointed out, repeated stimulation with tones produces adaptation and eventually the GSRs disappear, and, as Prokasy, Grant, and Myers (1958) showed, some individuals cannot be conditioned.

The work on audition in infancy indicates that, if the auditory-neurological mechanism is normally developed, children respond to auditory stimuli after the first few days of life, that pitch discrimination can be conditioned within the first year, with localization of sound direction usually established by or during the last 6 months, and that some localization of the distance away of the sound source seems to occur within the first year.

However, all of the research indicates a tremendous range of individual variability of infant responsiveness to auditory stimulation. No method of ascertaining the development of auditory perception in the child can determine absolutely whether the unresponsive baby does or does not hear a stimulus. Conditioning techniques may fail because the infant does not become conditioned or because random responses are interpreted as conditioned responses. Affective factors, too, may influence responsiveness to auditory stimuli. Solley (Chapter 11) has shown that some infants respond with fear to the stimulus of a human face which usually evokes a pleasure response in the infant. Therefore it is possible that sound stimuli may evoke fear and withdrawal in some infants. Certainly there are differences in the amounts of time mothers spend singing and talking to their infants, in the warmth of their maternal verbalizations, and in the types of infant-mother interactions in which such verbalizations occur. These and similar unstudied and uncontrolled variables may and probably do play an extremely important role in the development of the auditory perception of the infant.

CHILD RESEARCH

INTENSITY STUDIES

Much of the research on intensity is based on an attempt to screen audition and locate defective hearing; therefore only a few of these studies will be reviewed because the purpose of this chapter is to discuss studies of the development of normal auditory perception.

Bryant (1907) insisted that auditory acuity reached its maximum at adolescence. Lauer (1928) tested 5000 grade- and high-school children with standard audiometric techniques and found better auditory acuity in children over 12 years of age than under. Chayer (1929) noted a steady decrease in the percentage of pupils with poor hearing from third grade to the end of junior high school. Sterling and Bell (1930) tested 710 8- to 17-year-old children and reported that auditory acuity increased with age. Below age 11 or 12, the boys had greater auditory acuity, and above those ages, the acuity of the girls was superior.

In 1931, Jarvis, studying the durations and types of responses to optical and acoustical stimuli, reported that receptiveness in audition and in vision tended to develop through defined stages. He did not, however, find an ascending scale of receptiveness in either modality, but instead noted stages of high receptiveness at some ages and low receptiveness at others.

To 4- to 8-year-olds, with 14 to 18 subjects in each age group, Black (1939) gave standard audiometer tests at one-year intervals. He did not find differences in acuity from age to age but found greater acuity than was found in adults.

Williams (1932) investigated the responses of 3- to 7-year-olds by asking the children to repeat prerecorded numbers they heard through a telephone receiver. He defined "threshold" as the point in the decreasing intensity at which the children could no longer report the numbers accurately, and concluded that acuity increases with age.

Weinberg and Fischgold (1932) tested 387 6- to 13-year-old children with a Western Electric Audiometer and reported an increase in auditory acuity from 6 to 10 years of age. Reymert and Rotman (1946) studied 173 10- to 18-year-old children, with 9 or 10 boys and 9 or 10 girls at each age level, and reported that acuity for the middle tones of 1024 to 8192 cps was greater than for the other tones, while the greatest acuity occurred at 2040 and 4096 cps. They found that in girls the only change in acuity between 10 and 18 years of age is a slight loss in the ability to hear low tones. After puberty, the boys showed an increase in ability to hear low tones and a decrease in ability to hear high tones. In general, boys hear low tones better and high tones more poorly than do girls.

Wishik and Kramm (1953) reported that 3.3% of first and second graders, 4.0% of third and fourth graders, and 2.2% of fifth and sixth graders failed standard hearing tests. These figures suggest little change in the percentage of grade-schoolers with very poor acuity.

Eagles and Wishik (1961) tested over 3000 children and concluded that audiometric testing requires a good acoustic environment, such as their Acoustic Room or the isolation cabinet of Dockeray and Valentine (1939). They further maintained that an audiometer calibrated to the standard American Audiometric Zero is not adequate because normal children tended to show acuity greater than this Zero. In general, their range of thresholds was from −16.0 to 0 decibels for the right, and from −14.8 to 0 decibels for the left ear. The mean and median results for different frequencies are shown in Table 1.

TABLE 1

Frequency	Mean (in decibels)		Median (in decibels)	
	Rt ear	L ear	Rt ear	L ear
250 cps	−8.3	−9.1	−10.4	−10.5
500 cps	−5.6	−5.9	−6.4	−6.3
1000 cps	−3.8	−3.7	−5.8	−5.4
2000 cps	−3.1	−3.2	−4.5	−5.0
4000 cps	−1.9	−1.7	−3.8	−3.6
6000 cps	−0.1	0.0	−2.4	−2.3
8000 cps	−1.2	−1.2	−3.4	−3.5

Obtaining the child's interest so that consistent trends in the development can be obtained is a major problem in studying auditory acuity. Audiometry technique results usually show increasing acuity with age. However, because, it is difficult to say whether these results indicate auditory acuity improvement or merely improvement in cooperation and ability to follow directions, other methods of studying auditory acuity have been attempted.

Dix and Hallpike (1947) taught children to turn and push a button under a window as soon as they heard a tone. The button-pushing illuminated a picture of interest to a child. During silent periods the button was inoperative. The experimenters believed that acuity could be most easily studied in this way because the child was not required to describe his sensations or give reports. O'Neill, Oyer, and Hillis (1961) used a variant of this procedure in which the reward was a view of one of 7 interesting figures, and reported more success in determining acuity with play techniques than with standard audiometric procedure.

Bloomer (1942) utilized pictures along with sounds, and asked the child to point to the correct picture when he heard "the train's whistle" or "the bird's song."

Keaster (1947) made a list of nouns which had been spontaneously elicited from children by pictures. Directions, e.g. "put the *baby* on the floor," were then given through a radio while the children held the pictures. These directions were given in 2-decibel steps over an 85-decibel range. Auditory threshold was considered to be the lowest number of decibels at which instructions were followed.

Although play techniques do offer a method of interest to young children, it is difficult to compare results with those obtained from standard audiometric techniques because they do not yield evidence on differing acuity at different frequencies and may present broad-band rather than pure-tone stimuli.

Beebe (1951) used an audiometer with leads to both ears and asked the child to put a peg into a pegboard whenever he heard a tone and found that children responded easily to this task.

Ewing and Ewing (1944) first determined what sounds are ignored by children, what sounds children attended to best, and how children responded to sounds which interested them, and then constructed a test with percussive, with pitch-pipe, and with voiced meaningful sounds such as "own name," commands, vowels, consonants, and conversation. Their test detects deafness reliably, but yields little evidence about the development of normal auditory acuity.

While standard conditioning techniques have been employed in various experimentations, Nober (1958) stated that even with recent standardization of apparatus and techniques, GSR audiometry is not completely reliable and no absolute estimation of a subject's auditory threshold is really possible. However, Grings, Lowell, and Honnard (1961) used GSR conditioning to determine auditory thresholds in children, and Chaiklin, Ventry, and Barrett (1961) found GSR audiometry to be reliable with adults but unreliable with children who are active and produce a number of random GSRs.

Atkinson (1959), using both normal and retarded children, taught them to blink at the sound of a tone to avoid a puff of air to the cornea, and determined the threshold by a descending method of limits. He defined threshold as the intensity of a tone which did not produce a blink.

EEG techniques have been utilized by Derbyshire, et al. (1956), who compared subjectively obtained and EEG-obtained thresholds for 22 4- to 13-year-old children and obtained differences between the two thresholds of 4 to 40 decibels. They also reported a large sample study in which they found no change in EEG thresholds from 3 to 27 years of age. Perl, Galambos, and Glorig (1953) also reported that EEG thresholds for auditory acuity were significantly higher than subjectively determined thresholds. EEG thresholds, therefore, are not comparable with thresholds obtained by other methods. In general, auditory thresholds have been found to be extremely dependent upon the methods used to obtain them.

PITCH STUDIES

The meager present knowledge about the development of pitch discrimination leaves much room for investigation. Gilbert (1893), using the method of limits plus a same-different judgment, found that pitch sensitivity increased from age 6 to age 10 and attributed the change to practice, attention improvement, maturation, comprehension improvement, or to a combination of these; Peters (1927) also showed that, when the differences between tones to be compared are small, pitch discrimination improves with age.

Ivanshiva (1930) studied the generalization of auditory conditioned responses in 19 5- to 10-year-olds, using food grasping as the unconditioned response. A conditioned response was formed to the sound of e^i, and then sounds from g^i to d^{iv} were tested. Twelve children generalized to d^{iv}, 5 to e^{iii}, and the remaining 2 only to g^i.

Hattwick (1935) constructed a pitch test and found an increasing number of differential reactions to small pitch differences as the children's ages increased, and Wyatt (1945) showed that improvement of pitch discrimination in children could be achieved through training.

Jeffrey (1958) taught children to press a button on the left in response to a low tone of 128 cps, and a button on the right to a high tone of 1152 cps, and then to discriminate between 256 and 384 cps. He utilized 3 groups of 7 kindergarten children each. The first group did the criterion task, the second group had pretraining in singing the test tones, and the third group was shown a piano with the two test tones marked on it and each child played the test tones. One of 7 in the first group, 5 of 7 in the second group, and 7 of 7 in the third group of children learned to discriminate between the test tones. Endovitskaya (1959) performed two similar experiments. In the first, 40 4- to 7-year-olds were conditioned to discriminate between two pitches. Discrimination was established in all the children over 4-6 years old, while those below this age were believed to be pitch deaf. However, in the second experiment, two subjects younger than 4-6 were trained to react with different hand movements to 11 sounds of pitches ranging from 500 to 1000 cps and then retested with the first experiment. Pitch discrimination was better than it had been for the older subjects. Endovitskaya concluded that pitch discrimination in children could be taught and was not inherent.

Repina (1961a) used 42 3- to 7-year-olds and presented a tone of 2-second duration and 15-decibel loudness intensity. The task was to discriminate the standard tone from a tone 30 cps higher and a tone 30 cps lower. Children under 5-0 were unable to learn this discrimination, although older children learned it easily. Then (1961b) 20 3- to 5-year-olds were trained that a 250 cps tone represented a "bear's voice," a 400 cps tone was a "dog's voice," and a 1500 cps tone was a "chicken's voice." The younger children were able to discriminate between the extreme tones and the older to discriminate among the 3 tones, although all 20 children had been considered "pitch deaf" in Repina's earlier (1961a) experimentation.

TIMBRE STUDIES

Timbre differences have also been largely overlooked in experimentation with children. Gebhardt (1929) reported on a single child who could, at 2 years of age, discriminate between a tone of the same pitch played on a piano and on a violin and could, at 3, recognize the difference between the sounds made by old and new streetcars. Repina (1961c) taught 3- to 7-year-olds to discriminate among 7 tones of identical pitch and different timbres by making each tone the specific voice of one of 7 teddy bears. At the present time, however, little can be hypothesized about the development of timbre discrimination, especially in children.

RESEARCH ON OTHER AUDITORY VARIABLES

Orsini (1958) noted that, before training, his group of 30 adults, ranging in age from 35 to 45, could estimate the duration of a sound far better than could his group of 30 7-year-old children. After training, the children reached the level of estimation of sound duration which the adult group had shown during the original testing.

Templin (1943) investigated the influence of the position of a sound in a word on the child's ability to discriminate the sound from other sounds and found that grade-school children made significantly more errors when a sound was in the final position than when it was in the initial position in a word.

Provost and Dumbleton (1953) asked first graders to point to the correct picture when given the name. He paired such similar words as cat-bat, pen-pin, and vase-face and found that 10% of his first graders were deficient in this type of sound discrimination.

Winitz and Bellerose (1962) studied the ability of 72 fourth graders to learn to discriminate between two speech sounds as a function of types of pretraining. They found that incorrect reinforcement did not make this type of discrimination learning impossible for the children, and that the type of pretraining was less important than was the number of trials.

Liebert and Rudel (1959) investigated the performance of 72 children ranging in age from 5-7 to 17-6, in a test situation involving auditory localization and body tilt. The children were blindfolded and seated in a tiltable chair which had an attached PDR -10 phone emitting 10-millisecond clicks, one per second, at 10° and at 30° tilt to the left and to the right of the mid-line. When the children were in the upright position there was no significant displacement of the subjective mid-line, but with a 28° tilt or greater to the left, there was a progressive displacement of the subjective mid-line to the right. The older the child, the greater was the error in subjective judgment. Further experimentation with the same subjects indicated that the child's orientation in space is less determinate and more labile than the orientation of the adult because the child accepts a very tilted position as being an erect position and will accept more deviation from the erect position than will the adolescent.

Costa (1950) investigated the child's ability to arrange musical tones in a mathematical series and found this development to be similar to the development of the ability to order other quantities, such as weights.

Omwake (1940) studied 555 children and concluded that auditory stimuli suggested specific visual pattern to children. Lindquist (1945) reported that visual memory develops before the auditory memory which becomes obvious at about 18 months.

Frymier (1958) studied the relationship of aural perceptions to cultural situations and noted that subjects from different milieus perceive identical sounds differently. Sixty-four northern urban children displayed a greater number and accuracy of auditory perceptions than did 91 southern rural children. The northern children had more auditory perceptions relating to people and inanimate objects, while the southern children had a greater number of perceptions relating to animals and mechanical objects.

Bugg and Thompson (1952) suggested that the combinations of sounds which are heard as consonant or dissonant, as pleasant or unpleasant, depend upon the culture in which the child is raised and upon individual past experience.

Reed (1961) noted that the auditory thresholds for high tones in children diagnosed as "hysteric" and as "anxious" were more variable than were the thresholds for other children.

Vernon (1955) has shown that percepts are organized in terms of cognitions and past experiences as well as in terms of immediate needs, and that immediate needs tend to achieve importance when past experience is not valid for a specific, ambiguous, or transitory stimulus.

Leeper (1935) showed that some sensory organizations of visually presented materials were more easily retained than others. However, if some organizations of auditory stimuli are more easily retained because of past experience, thresholds for differing types of stimuli may be widely divergent.

All these studies suggest the presence of a number of little studied variables which may be influential. However, a great amount of research would be required in order to determine the interactions among all these variables in the development of auditory perception in children and infants.

ADDITIONAL QUESTIONS RAISED BY ADULT AUDITORY RESEARCH

In the adult, there are such interactions among auditory dimensions as a logarithmic relationship between stimulus intensity and perceived loudness (Stevens and Davis, 1938; Wever, 1949). Perceived loudness, however, depends upon the frequency or pitch of the stimulating sound (Fletcher and Munson, 1933) and the duration of the stimulus (Wever, 1949). Pitch sensitivity depends upon the intensity and duration of the stimulating tone, according to Irwin (1937), but Morgan, Garner, and Galambos (1951) have indicated that the pitch-intensity relationship is not a constant, but is a specific function and a matter of individual differences. Further research into the development of the interactions of auditory dimensions and into the nature of early interrelationships among variables is, therefore, needed.

Wallach, Newman, and Rosenzweig (1949) showed that binaural fusion, following rules similar to those for binocular fusion, occurs in the adult. Two brief sounds reaching the ears at different times from different directions will be heard as one sound if the sounds are discontinuous, of equal intensity, and if the interval between them does not exceed 5 milliseconds for a single sound and 40 milliseconds for a complex sound. If binaural fusion occurs, the individual localizes the fused sound as coming from the direction of the first sound.

Illusions of hearing, similar to geometrical optical illusions, have also been demonstrated. Identical tones may be heard as higher or lower than their actual frequency because of the subject's expectation that a scale will terminate on a specific note, while quarter and half tones may give the illusion of whole tones (Orlow, 1930), and intervals which are nonmusical may be heard as major sixths or sevenths (Meyer, 1959).

Aftereffects similar to those obtained in visual research have been found in studying the auditory perception of adults. If one ear is stimulated by a tone of 1000 cps for a prolonged time, the difference limen for the other ear is significantly lowered (Deutsch, 1951), and if both ears are stimulated by a high-intensity buzzing sound for a time, the timbre of such complex sounds as a handclap, a typewriter, or the human voice seems altered to a metallic sound, and this aftereffect lasts for several seconds (Rosenblith et al., 1947).

Köhler and Adams (1958) have shown that thresholds for intentional perception are significantly lower than for incidental perception, but attention may also accelerate satiation and thereby intensify aftereffects.

In sum, while attentional factors in audition have been used to explain the lack of response of some children to auditory stimuli, the effects of attention on audition have not been carefully studied, nor have binaural fusion, auditory illusions, and aftereffects been adequately investigated in children or adults, and, although there may be auditory constancies which are analogous to visual constancies, there is no research indicating the presence of invariants. However, because auditory stimuli are organized, meaningful, and related to past experience, the presence of auditory constancies may be hypothesized.

DISCUSSION

As the preceding studies indicate, research is needed to determine the developmental stages of acuity, pitch and timbre discrimination, the relationship of intensity to loudness, sound localization, sound fusion, sound aftereffects, sound illusions, the importance of personality and cultural factors, and the interactions among these variables in the development of auditory perception. Further experimentation may also reveal other variables which influence this development.

The studies also point to problems of theory, the first being that of the relative importance of heredity, training, and maturation. Such genetic research as Rife's (1960) on pitch discrimination, Kalmus' (1949) on "tune deafness," and Ashman's (1952) suggest that inheritance may be influential. However, in some families and some milieux, the child may also receive unusual auditory stimulation and training, and several of the studies (Repina, 1961b, c; Jeffrey, 1958; Orsini, 1958) especially indicate the importance of training. The trend toward greater auditory acuity and pitch discrimination with increasing age suggests that maturation also may be an important factor in auditory development. However, it is impossible at present to determine whether maturation influences the perception per se or whether it changes only such factors as the child's ability to attend, to follow directions, and willingness to cooperate.

The theoretical question whether there are critical periods in the development of auditory perception as there are in visual perception development (Riesen, 1950) is also of importance. An occasional case study (Burton, 1961) has pointed toward reduced audition in children raised by two deaf-mute parents. However, these children may have an inadequate development of the auditory mechanism which is not obvious to external examination or may simply have learned to emphasize other means of communication, such as hand movements, and to ignore auditory cues.

Total perceptual development is another theoretical issue. Although the importance of such research has been emphasized (Gibson, 1963), there have been no studies of the interrelationships existing among auditory, visual, haptic, and kinaesthetic perceptions. It seems probable that a perception arising in any modality is strengthened or weakened by perceptions arising from all of the sensory modalities. A cohesive theory of perception demands knowledge of the relationships and of their development during the life span of the individual.

The nature of perceptual development, whether the development proceeds in a relatively orderly manner from an autistic, nonveridical view of the environment to a realistic perception, or involves a change in the importance of some cues and so is merely a change in psychological forces, has already been discussed in the literature (Wohlwill, 1960; Piaget, 1950; Gibson and Gibson, 1955) but remains an important problem.

A final theoretical issue is the influence of audition on other psychological aspects of the individual. It is obvious that audition is directly related to speech. In addition, the placing of labels on objects affects the recall of objects and the perceptual organization of stimuli (Leeper, 1935; Vernon, 1955), so it may be hypothesized that auditory cues have a significant relationship to cognitive development as well as to speech development. The reported social and emotional problems of deaf children (DiCarlo and Dolphin, 1952) suggest a close relationship between auditory development and the socialization and emotional development of the child.

If the present review has emphasized questions about auditory development, it is because auditory perceptual development has received less attention than other kinds of development. While interest in this subject now exists, problems of instrumentation and response selection also still exist. This review may stimulate research which may find answers to some of the questions posed.

BIBLIOGRAPHY

Ashman, R. A. (1952), The Inheritance of Simple Musical Memory. *Journal of Heredity*, 43:51-52.
Atkinson, C. J. (1959), The Use of the Eyelid Reflex as an Operant in Audiometric Testing. *Journal of Experimental Analysis of Behavior*, 2:212.

Barber, A. (1950), Child Psychology. *Annual Review of Psychology*. Washington, D. C.: American Psychological Association.

Beebe, H. (1951), Testing the Hearing of Young Children. *Nervous Children*, 9:8-14.

Bernard, J. (1946), Human Fetal Reactivity to Tonal Stimulation. *American Psychologist*, 1:256.

—— & Sontag, C. W. (1947), Fetal Reactivity to Tonal Stimulation: A Preliminary Report. *Journal of Genetic Psychology*, 70:205-210.

Black, M. C. (1939), 2-A Audiometer Norms for Determining Hypacusia in Children Between the Ages of Four and Eight. *Journal of Speech Disorders*, 4:3-14.

Blanton, M. G. (1917), The Behavior of the Human Infant During the First Thirty Days of Life. *Psychological Review*, 24:456-483.

Bloomer, H. (1942), A Simple Method for Testing the Hearing of Small Children. *Journal of Speech and Hearing Disorders*, 7:311-312.

Bridger, W. H. (1961), Sensory Habituation and Discrimination in the Human Neonate. *American Journal of Psychiatry*, 117:991-996.

Bryan, E. S. (1930), Variations in the Responses of Infants during the First Ten Days of Postnatal Life. *Child Development*, 1:56-77.

Bryant, E. (1907), The Importance of Aural Inspections and Functional Tests in Healthy Individuals. *Annals of Otolaryngology, Rhinology and Laryngology*, 26:347-379.

Bugg, E. G. & Thompson, A. S. (1952), An Experimental Test of the Genetic Theory of Consonance. *Journal of Genetic Psychology*, 47:71-90.

Burton, A. (1961), Personal communication.

Canestrini, S. (1913), Über das Sinnesleben des Neugeborenen. *Monogr. Gesamtgeb. Neurol. Psychiat.*, #5. Berlin: Springer.

Carmichael, L. (1946), The Onset and Early Development of Behavior. *Manual of Child Psychology*, Carmichael, L. (Ed.). New York: Wiley.

Cemach, A. I. (1920), Beiträge zur Kenntnis der Kochlearen Reflexe. *Beitr. Anat. Physiol. Pathol. Therap. Ohres, Nase, Halses*, 14:1-82.

Chaiklin, J. B., Ventry, I. M. & Barrett, L. S. (1961), Reliability of Conditioned Galvanic Skin Response Pure Tone Audiometry with Adult Males Using a Test-Retest. *Journal of Speech and Hearing Research*, 4:269-279.

Chayer, M. E. (1929), Experiments with 4-A Audiometer. *Public Health Nurse*, 21:602-603.

Chun, R. W. M., Pawsat, R. & Forster, F. M. (1960), Sound Localization in Infancy. *Journal of Nervous and Mental Disease*, 130:472-476.

Clarke, F. M. (1939), A Developmental Study of the Bodily Reaction of Infants to an Auditory Startle Stimulus. *Journal of Genetic Psychology*, 55:415-427.

Combs, C. H. (1938), Adaptation of the Galvanic Response to Auditory Stimuli. *Journal of Experimental Psychology*, 22:244-268.

Compayre, G. (1896), *The Intellectual and Moral Development of the Child*. New York: Appleton.

Costa, A. M. (1950), L'evoluzione Operatoria nella Seriazone dei Suoni. *Riv. Psicol.*, 46:156-165.

Derbyshire, A. I., Fraser, A. A., McDermott, M. & Bridge, A. (1956), Audiometric Measurements by Electroencephalograph. *Electroencephalography and Clinical Neurophysiology*, 8:476-478.

Deutsch, J. A. (1951), A Preliminary Report on a New Auditory After-Effect. *Quarterly Journal of Experimental Psychology*, 3:43-46.

138   ALINE H. KIDD AND ROBERT M. KIDD

DiCarlo, L. M. & Dolphin, J. E. (1952), Social Adjustment and Personality Development of Deaf Children: A Review of the Literature. *Exceptional Child*, 8:111-118.

Dix, M. R. & Hallpike, C. S. (1947), The Peep-Show: A New Technique for Pure Tone Audiometry in Young Children. *British Medical Journal*, 2:719-731.

Dockeray, F. C. & Valentine, W. L. (1939), A New Isolation Cabinet for Infant Research. *Journal of Experimental Psychology*, 24:211-214.

Eagles, E. L. & Wishik, S. M. (1961), A Study of Hearing in Children. *American Academy of Ophthalmology, Otolaryngology Transactions and Directory*, 65:261-296.

Endovitskaya, T. V. (1959), Ozvukysotnoi Razlichitei'noi Chuvstvitel' nosti u detei Doskolnogo Vozrasts. *Dokl. Akademie Pedagogy Nauk. RSFSR.*, 5:75-80.

Ewing, I. R. & Ewing, A. W. G. (1944), The Ascertainment of Deafness in Infancy and Early Childhood. *Journal of Laryngology*, 59:309-333.

Feldman, W. M. (1920), *The Principles of Antenatal and Postnatal Child Physiology, Pure and Applied*. London: Longmans, Green.

Fletcher, F. M. & Munson, W. A. (1933), Loudness, its Definition, Measurement, and Calculation. *Journal of the Acoustic Society of America*, 5:82-108.

Forbes, H. S. & Forbes, H. B. (1927), Fetal Sense Reaction: Hearing. *Journal of Comparative Psychology*, 7:353-355.

Fröding, C. A. (1960), Acoustic Investigation of Newborn Infants. *Acta, Otolaryngology*, 52:31-40.

Froeschels, E. & Beebe, H. (1946), Testing the Hearing of Newborn Infants. *Archives Otolaryngology*, 44:710-714.

Frymier, J. R. (1958), Relationship of Aural Perceptions to Cultural Situations. *Perceptual and Motor Skills*, 8:67-70.

Gebhardt, M. (1929), Beitrag zur Erforschung des absolutes Gehörs im Vorschulpflichtigen Kindesalter. *Arch. gesamte Psychol.*, 68:273-294.

Genzmer, A. (1882), *Untersuchungen über die Sinneswahrnehmungen des Neugeborenen Menschen*. Halle: Niemeyer.

Gibson, J. J. (1963), The Useful Dimensions of Sensitivity. *American Psychologist*, 18:1-15.

—— & Gibson, E. J. (1955), Perceptual Learning: Differentiation or Enrichment? *Psychological Review*, 62:32-41.

Gilbert, J. A. (1893), Experiments on the Musical Sensitiveness of School Children. *Studies of the Yale Psychology Laboratories*, 1:80-87.

Grant, D. A. (1956), Analysis-of-Variance Tests in the Analysis and Comparison of Curves. *Psychological Bulletin*, 63:141-154.

Grings, W. W., Lowell, E. L. & Honnard, R. R. (1961), Galvanic Skin Response Conditioning in Preschool Deaf Children. *Journal of Comparative and Physiological Psychology*, 54:143-148.

——, —— & Rushford, G. M. (1960), The Role of Conditioning in Galvanic Skin Response Audiometry with Children. *Journal of Speech and Hearing Research*, 3:120-129.

Haller, M. W. (1932), The Reactions of Infants to Changes in the Intensity and Pitch of Pure Tone. *Journal of Genetic Psychology*, 40:162-180.

Hardy, J. B., Dougherty, A. & Hardy, W. G. (1959), Hearing Responses and Audiologic Screening in Infants. *Journal of Pediatrics*, 55:382-390.

Hardy, W. G. & Bordley, J. E. (1951), Special Techniques in Testing the Hearing of Children. *Journal of Speech and Hearing Disorders*, 16:122-131.

——, Hardy, J. B., Brinker, C. H., Frazier, T. M. & Dougherty, A. (1962), Auditory Screening of Infants. *Ann. Oto. Rhin. Laryng.*, 71:1-8.

Hattwick, M. S. (1935), A Genetic Study of Differential Pitch Sensitivity. *University of Iowa Studies of Child Welfare*, 11(2):7-68.

Hunt, W. A., Clarke, F. M. & Hunt, E. B. (1938), The Startle Pattern in Infants in Response to Non-Auditory Stimuli. *Journal of Genetic Psychology*, 52:443-446.

Irwin, O. C. (1932), The Latent Time of the Body Startle in Infants. *Child Development*, 3:104-107.

———(1937), A Study of Differential Pitch Sensitivity Relative to Auditory Theory. *Journal of Experimental Psychology*, 21:642-652.

Ivanshiva, E. A. (1930), Isslyedovaniye Staticheskoy Irradiatzii Razdrazhitel'nogo i Tormoznogo Protzesa v Zvukovom Analizatora u dyety. *Trudy Laboratorii Fiziologii Vysshey Nervnoy Deyatel'nosti Rebyonka pri Leningradskom Pedagogicheskom Institute Gertzina*, 2:157-176.

Jarvis, J. L. (1931), Akustische Rezeption im Zweiten Lebensjahr. *Zsch. Psychol.*, 123:193-258.

Jeffrey, W. E. (1958), Variables in Early Discrimination Learning. II. Mode of Response and Stimulus Differentiation in the Discrimination of Tonal Frequencies. *Child Development*, 29:531-538.

Kalmus, H. (1949), Tone Deafness and Its Inheritance. *Proceedings of the International Congress of Genetics*, 605. Stockholm.

Kasatkin, M. L. & Levikova, A. M. (1935), On the Development of Early Conditioned Reflexes and Differentiations of Auditory Stimuli in Infants. *Journal of Experimental Psychology*, 18:1-19.

Keaster, J. (1947), A Quantitative Method of Testing the Hearing of Young Children. *Journal of Speech Disorders*, 12:159-160.

Koch, H. (1954), Child Psychology. *Annual Review of Psychology*. Washington, D. C.: American Psychological Association.

Koellreutter, W. (1907), Schwerhörigkeit der Neugeborenen als Reine Störung im Schallzuleitenden Teile des Ohres. *Zeitschrift Ohrenheilk. Krankh. Luftwege*, 53:123-138.

Köhler, W. & Adams, P. A. (1958), Perception and Attention. *American Journal of Psychology*, 71:489-503.

Kröner, T. (1881), *Über die Sinnesempfindungen der Neugeborenen*. Breslau: Grass, Barth.

Kussmaul, A. (1859), *Untersuchungen über das Seelenleben des Neugeborenen Menschen*. Tübingen: Moser.

Landis, C. & Hunt, W. A. (1939), *The Startle Pattern*. New York: Farrar and Rinehart.

Lauer, F. H. (1928), Hearing Survey Among a Group of Public Schools in Syracuse. *American Journal of Public Health*, 18:1353-1360.

Leeper, R. (1935), A Study of a Neglected Portion of the Field of Learning: The Development of Sensory Organization. *Journal of Genetic Psychology*, 46:41-75.

Levikova & Nevymakova (1948), Abstracted in Razran, G. H. S. Conditioned Responses in Children. *Arch. Psychol.*, 23:1933.

Liebert, R. S. & Rudel, R. G. (1959), Auditory Localization and Adaptation to Body Tilt: A Developmental Study. *Child Development*, 30:81-90.

Lindquist, N. (1945), Some Notes on the Development of Memory During the First Years of Life. *Acta. Paediatr.*, 32:592-598.

Lowenfeld, B. (1927), Systematisches Studium der Reaktionen der Säuglinge auf Klänge und Geräusche. *Zeitschrift Psychol.*, 104:62-96.

Marquis, D. P. (1931), Can Conditioned Responses Be Established in the Newborn Infant? *Journal of Genetic Psychology,* 39:479-492.
Meyer, M. (1959), New Illusions of Pitch. *Perceptual and Motor Skills,* 10:323-324.
Mirzoiants, N. S. (1954), Uslovnyi Orientirovochnyi Refleks i ego Differentsirovki u Rebenko. *Zhurnal Vyssh. Nervn. Deiatel.,* 4:616-619.
Moldenhauer & Von Tröttsch (1880), *The Mind of the Child,* Preyer, M. (Ed.). New York: Appleton, 1882.
Morgan, C. T., Garner, W. R. & Galambos, R. (1951), Pitch and Intensity. *Journal of the Acoustical Society of America,* 23:658-663.
Munn, N. L. (1955), *The Evolution and Growth of Human Behavior.* Boston: Houghton-Mifflin.
Muzio, O. (1933), Sulla Audizione die Neonate. *Ann. Laring Ecc.,* 33:105-110.
Myklebust, H. R. (1954), *Auditory Disorders in Children.* New York: Grune & Stratton.
Nechaeva, I. P. (1954), K. Funktsional'noi Kharakteristike Slukhovogo Analizatora Rebënka Ranego Vozrasta. *Zhurnal Vyssh. Nervn. Deiatel.,* 4:610-615.
Nober, E. H. (1958), Galvanic Skin Response Magnitudes for Different Intensities of Shock, Conditioned Tone, and Extinction Tone. *Journal of Speech and Hearing Research,* 1:316-324.
Omwake, L. (1940), Visual Responses to Auditory Stimuli. *Journal of Applied Psychology,* 24:468-481.
O'Neill, J. J., Oyer, H. J. & Hillis, J. W. (1961), Audiometric Procedures Used with Children. *Journal of Speech and Hearing Disorders,* 26:61-66.
Orlow, J. E. (1930), Über Täuschungen des Gehörs. *Arch. Gesamte Psychol.,* 74:391-400.
Orsini, F. (1958), Etude Experimentale des Conduites Temporelles. Effet de l'Apprentissage sur la Reproduction d'une Durée chez l'Enfant et chez l'Adulte. *Année Psychologie,* 58:345-399.
Peiper, A. (1924), Sinnesempfindungen des Kindes vor seiner Geburt. *Monatsschrift Kinderheilk.,* 29:236-241.
Perl, R. E., Galambos, R. & Glorig, A. (1953), The Estimation of Hearing Threshold by Electroencephalography. *Electroencephalography and Clinical Neurophysiology,* 5:501-512.
Peters, W. (1927), Die Entwicklung von Wahrnehmungsleistungen beim Kind. *Zeitschrift Psychol. Physiol. Sinnesorg.,* 103:129-184.
Peterson, F. & Rainey, L. H. (1910), The Beginnings of Mind in the Newborn. *Bulletin of the Lying-In Hospital, City of New York,* 7:99-122.
Piaget, J. (1950), *The Psychology of Intelligence.* New York: Harcourt, Brace.
Poli, C. (1893), L'audito nei Neonati. *Arch. Ital. Otol.,* 1:353-364.
Polikanina, P. I. & Probatova, L. E. (1955), Razvitie Orientirovoch noi Reakskii na Zvukovoe Razdrazhenie u Nedonoshennykh Detei. *Zhurnal Vyssh. Nerv. Deiatel.,* 5:226-236.
Pollock, I. (1961), Hearing. *Annual Review of Psychology.* Washington, D. C.: American Psychological Association.
Pratt, K. C. (1934), The Effects of Repeated Auditory Stimulation upon the General Activity of Newborn Infants. *Journal of Genetic Psychology,* 44:96-116.
——, Nelson, A. K. & Sun, K. H. (1930), The Behavior of the Newborn Infant. *Ohio State University Studies: Contributions in Psychology, #10.*
Preyer, W. (1893), *The Senses and the Will.* New York: Appleton.
Prokasy, W. F., Grant, D. A. & Myers, N. A. (1958), Eyelid Conditioning as a Function of

Unconditioned Stimulus Intensity and Intertrial Interval. *Journal of Experimental Psychology*, 55:242-246.

Provost, W. & Dumbleton, C. (1953), A Picture-Type Speech Sound Discrimination Test. *Journal of Speech and Hearing Disorders*, 18:258-266.

Radke-Yarrow, M. & Yarrow, L. J. (1955), Child Psychology. *Annual Review of Psychology*. Washington, D. C.: American Psychological Association.

Ray, W. S. (1932), A Preliminary Report on a Study of Fetal Conditioning. *Child Development*, 3:175-177.

Reed, G. F. (1961), Audiometric Response Consistency, Auditory Fatigue, and Personality. *Perceptual and Motor Skills*, 12:126.

Repina, T. A. (1961a), O Nekotorykh Methodikakh Izucheniia Zvukovystnoi Chuvstvitel-'nosti u detei Doshkol'nogo Vozrasta: Soobshchenie I. Differentsirovannoe Razlichenie doshkol'nikami Ehistykh tonov. pri ikh. slovesnoi Otsenkie. *Dokl. Akademie Pedagogy Nauk. RSFSR.*, 4:101-105.

——(1961b), O Nekotorykh Methodikakh Izucheniia Zvukovystnoi Chuvstvitel'nosti u detei Doshkol'nogo Vozrasta: Soobshchenie II. Differentsirovka Christykh tonov v Usloviiakh Opredmechivaniia. *Dokl. Akademie Pedagogy Nauk. RSFSR.*, 5:69-72.

——(1961c), O Nekotorykh Methodikakh Izucheniia Zvukovystnoi Chuvstvitel'nosti u detei Doshkol'nogo Vozrasta: Soobshchenie III. Opyt Razrabotki Methodiki Sposobstvuiushchei Formirovaniiu u detei Differentsirovannogo Zvukovysotnogo Razlichiia Tembral'no Okrashennykh Tonov. *Dokl. Akademie Pedagogy Nauk. RSFSR.*, 6:55-60.

Reymert, M. L. & Rotman, M. (1946), Auditory Changes in Children from Ages Ten to Eighteen. *Journal of Genetic Psychology*, 68:181-187.

Riesen, A. H. (1950), Arrested Vision. *Scientific American*, 183:16-19.

——(1960), Receptor Functions. *Handbook of Research Methods in Child Development*, Mussen, P. (Ed.). New York: Wiley.

Rife, D. C. (1960), Personal communication. *Behavior Genetics*, Fuller, J. L. & Thompson, W. R. New York: Wiley.

Rosenblith, W. A., Miller, G. A., Egan, J. P., Hitsch, I. J. & Thomas, G. J. (1947), An Auditory After-Image. *Science*, 106:333-355.

Sachs, R. (1893), Beobachtungen über das Physiologische Verhalten des Gehörorgans Neugeborener. *Arch. Ohrenheilk.*, 35:28-38.

Seashore, C. E. (1934), The Discovery and Guidance of Musical Talent. *Thirty-Fourth Yearbook of the National Society for the Study of Education*. Bloomington, Illinois: Public School Publishing Company.

Shinn, M. W. (1893-1899), Notes on the Development of a Child. *University of California Publication*, 1.

Siegal, S. (1956), *Nonparametric Statistics*. New York: McGraw-Hill.

Simmons, M. W. & Lipsitt, L. P. (1961), An Operant-Discrimination Apparatus for Infants. *Journal of Experimental Analysis of Behavior*, 4:233-235.

Sontag, L. W. & Wallace, R. F. (1934), The Movement Response of the Human Fetus to Sound Stimuli. *Child Development*, 6:253-258.

Spelt, D. K. (1948), The Conditioning of the Human Fetus in Utera. *Journal of Experimental Psychology*, 38:338-346.

Sterling, E. B. & Bell, E. (1930), The Hearing of School Children as Measured by the Audiometer and as Related to School Work. *Public Health Report*, 145:1117-1130.

Stevens, S. S. & Davis, H. (1938), *Hearing: Its Psychology and Physiology*. New York: Wiley.

Stubbs, E. M. (1934), The Effect of the Factors of Duration, Intensity, and Pitch of Sound

142   ALINE H. KIDD AND ROBERT M. KIDD

Stimuli on Responses of Newborn Infants. *University of Iowa Studies of Child Welfare*, 9(4):75-135.
——— Stubbs, E. M. & Irwin, O. C. (1934), A Note on Reaction Times in Infants. *Child Development*, 5:291-292.
Templin, M. (1943), A Study of Sound Discrimination Ability of Elementary School Pupils. *Journal of Speech Disorders*, 8:127-132.
Vernon, M. D. (1955), The Functions of Schemata in Perceiving. *Psychol. Rev.*, 62:180-192.
Wallach, H., Newman, E. B. & Rosenzweig, M. R. (1949), The Precedence Effect in Sound Localization. *American Journal of Psychology*, 62:315-336.
Walton, O. (1921), L'Audizone neu Neonate. *Il Policlinico*, 28:1010-1011.
Weinberg, D. & Fischgold, F. (1932), Recherches sur l'Acuite Auditive chez les Ecoliers. *Année Psychologique*, 33:120-145.
Weiss, L. A. (1934), Differential Variations in the Amount of Activity of Newborn Infants under Continuous Light and Sound Stimulation. *University of Iowa Studies of Child Welfare*, 9:1-74.
Wertheimer, M. (1961), Psychomotor Coordination of Auditory and Visual Space at Birth. *Science*, 134:1692.
Wever, E. G. (1949), *Theory of Hearing*. New York: Wiley.
Wickens, D. D. & Wickens, C. (1940), A Study of Conditioning in the Neonate. *Journal of Experimental Psychology*, 26:94-102.
Williams, H. M. (1932), An Audiometric Test for Young Children. *Child Development*, 2:237-241.
Winitz, H. & Bellrose, B. (1962), Sound Discrimination as a Function of Pretraining Conditions. *Journal of Speech and Hearing Disorders*, 5:340-348.
Wishik, S. M. & Kramm, E. R. (1953), Audiometric Testing of the Hearing of School Children. *Journal of Speech and Hearing Disorders*, 18:360-365.
Wohlwill, J. F. (1960), Developmental Studies of Perception. *Psychological Bulletin*, 57:249-288.
Wyatt, R. F. (1945), Improvability of Pitch Discrimination. *Psychological Monographs: General and Applied*, 58(2).

Pattern Discrimination and Selective Attention as Determinants of Perceptual Development from Birth

ROBERT L. FANTZ

The human infant starts life as a helpless, uncoordinated, very immature organism. The only adaptive behaviors in the early weeks are alimentary and respiratory activities. The neonate has neither the ability nor the need to use vision to direct behavior. During the succeeding months and years he becomes spatially oriented, exploratory, playful, socially responsive, and purposive in his behavior, largely through the use of vision. How does this change come about? This is the basic problem of perceptual development.

PERCEPTION VS. ACTION IN DEVELOPMENT

Development is clearly a complex process involving both perceptual and motor aspects. But different theorists have given different priority to perception and to action in the development process. Some, especially the gestalt psychologists (e.g., Koffka, 1928), have in the past emphasized the early role of perception in a general way, but failed to provide sufficient explication and empirical support. The currently dominant view, held by both nativists and empiricists, is that action precedes perception and

Based on a paper read at a symposium on "The Development of Perception During the First Six Months of Life" at the American Association for the Advancement of Science meeting at Cleveland on December 30, 1963. The previously unpublished research reported was supported by Grants M-5284 and HD-00314 from the National Institutes of Health, United States Public Health Service.

143

brings about perceptual development. In this view, perception is absent before the perfection and repeated use of oculomotor coordination, hand-eye coordination, and locomotion. A considerable variety of specific means has been proposed for the derivation of perception from action. For Mc-Graw (1943), postnatal neuromuscular growth is required for object vision; for Gesell et al. (1949), maturation and practice in the use of various action systems are the primary agents for visual development; for Hebb (1949), associative learning based on repeated sequences of eye movements underlies form perception; for Held and associates (Held, 1961; Held and Hein, in press), previous exposure to the changes in stimulation accompanying active movements of limbs or body is critical for perceptual development; for Piaget (1952), action is transformed to perception and cognition through a complex series of stages in which experience plays a major role; while for most behaviorists and students of learning, reinforcement or other consequences of past responses are of most importance, and in an extreme view (Taylor, 1962) are necessary for all sensory processes.

A directly opposing viewpoint will be presented here: that perception *precedes* action and that early perceptual experience is necessary for the development of coordinated and visually directed behavior. The perfection of sensorimotor coordination will in turn increase the efficiency of the perceptual process, learning through past responses will change what is attended to and how it is responded to, but these are secondary influences which do not create perception or fundamentally alter it. What is perceived, on the other hand, is crucial for determining behavior and for determining what is learned from experience at all stages of development, including the early months when sensorimotor coordination is developing.

Underlying this viewpoint is a distinction between two aspects of perception: *localization* and *discrimination*. In spatial orientation this distinction is not clear-cut, but in object perception it is crucial for understanding perceptual development. The information received and utilized by the perceiver might be described in terms of the answers to two questions: "Where is it?" or object localization, and "What is it?" or object discrimination and recognition. The answer to one does not imply the other, even though for the adult perceiver both are often answered by a single look or reach. For the adult under natural conditions, object localization is achieved automatically and with high accuracy; perhaps for this reason the discriminative aspect of perception is most often studied in the adult. For the infant the situation is reversed: object localization is initially poor and develops gradually; probably for this reason the accuracy of localization has been studied almost exclusively. We are faced with an anomalous situation in which perception in the infant is operationally defined as skill in oculomotor and hand-eye coordination, while at later ages it is operationally defined as the ability to discriminate between objects or to recognize a particular object. This shift in what perceptual achievements are studied prevents continuity and consistency in theories of perceptual development. It provides no source of data on the origin and early influence of discriminative perception, and it has contributed to the common belief that perception is initially lacking and develops only through action.

This state of affairs can be illustrated by the work of Piaget and Gesell. Piaget's theory of perceptual and cognitive development (see Flavell, 1963) is based on the progressive appearance of sensorimotor coordinations and on actions made possible by these; vision is presumed to be reflexive, passive, and receptive only of light intensity—brightness—until the development of "vision schemas" through repetitive actions. But his method of inquiry during the early stages of development—informal observation—is not capable of testing these assumptions or of revealing the possible prior influence of what might be seen in addition to brightness. Gesell approaches the field from a more applied and clinical viewpoint —setting performance standards for skill in fixating, following, and reaching for objects at successive ages. These are presumably used to assess the development of perception and intelligence, but they give little information on discrimination abilities, which are more important in the measurement of perception and intelligence in the adult. The ability of an infant to follow a dangling ring with his eyes (as a sample test item of Gesell) does not imply the ability to distinguish the ring from another object; conversely, the lack of sufficient skill to maintain fixation of the ring to the tester's satisfaction does not imply that the infant is unable to perceive discriminable qualities of the ring whenever his gaze is on it.

In the attempt to counterbalance such approaches, in this paper I will stress the early development of the discriminative aspect of perception and will ignore the localization aspect. The ability to locate accurately and respond to an object with no ability to distinguish it from any other object is an empty skill with little adaptive value, while the demonstration of visual discrimination, at least pattern discrimination, is sufficient to indicate differential experience with parts of the environment and thus evidence of useful perception. The main argument, then, is that pattern discrimination is present at birth, that it is not dependent upon prior actions, and that it provides visual experiences which influence further perceptual and behavioral development.

This position needs considerable empirical support in view of its opposition to prevailing beliefs. The experiments to be presented here will be grouped according to their bearing upon, first, the presence of basic pattern-vision capacities in the infant; second, the use of these capacities in visual exploration and selective attention to parts of the environment; and third, the effects of early visual experience. The experiments all use modifications of the same method—the visual preference test. Since this is a new method for studying perceptual development, and since the findings are dependent on the nature of the method, a discussion of method is in order.

TESTING PERCEPTION IN THE INFANT

As a practical matter, perception cannot be tested independently of all action. Some differential response to visual stimulation is necessary to demonstrate visual discrimination. The only response with sufficient coordination during the early weeks of life to be directed at specific parts of the environment is visual orientation or the looking response. If the direction of gaze and the maintenance of the gaze are related to the visual characteristics of what is being fixated, then we know these characteristics can be seen. More specifically, the consistent differential fixation of different targets on repeated exposures with position varied indicates a *visual preference* and is evidence for the discrimination of some difference between the targets. This method has been used in the past to study color vision in infants by varying the color of the target (e.g., Staples, 1932; Stirnimann, 1944). The same principle applies to the study of pattern vision and form perception: discrimination of these aspects can be shown by a consistent visual preference among targets differing only in form or pattern. The absence of a preference among particular targets, of course, does not prove anything; as with other discrimination tests, stimuli and conditions are sought which will give consistently positive results.

Any test of discrimination, whether it is discrimination training in animals, perceptual judgments in adults, or visual preference in infants, must meet certain requirements. The stimulus targets must be presented in a controlled situation with a minimum of distractions and with equal opportunity for responding to each. Whatever the response, it must be directed unambiguously toward a particular target and it must occur more frequently to some targets than to others, either initially or after training. These requirements have seldom been met in previous studies of infants.

One frequent procedure for testing the vision of an infant is to observe his visual response to an object held or moved in front of him. This can indicate in a gross way whether vision is present or absent and may to an experienced observer suggest the degree of visuomotor coordination, but it can give no information on discrimination. Other descriptions of visual behavior in the infant are based on the observed tendency to look at particular objects in the natural environment. Assuming that this gives reliable evidence for visual preference, it cannot indicate what stimulus aspect was discriminated and preferred. Looking responses reported to occur in the infant have almost invariably been attributed to attraction of the brightness, color, or movement of an object such as the head of a person (Gesell et al., 1949; McGraw, 1943; Piaget, 1952; Shirley, 1933); other possibilities, such as form, solidity, texture, or figure-ground contrast, are not considered. Finally, many statements about the vision, or rather the lack of vision, of the very young infant seem to be based on nothing more than the impression of a blank stare—on the absence of the ocular, facial, and postural adjustments characteristic of the fixations of older infants. But these motor accompaniments may not be necessary for discrimination; they may develop only after early discriminative experiences.

The same looking response can be used to test discrimination simply by comparison of the amount of fixation of different targets exposed in a systematic way in a test chamber. The present technique was originally developed for chimpanzee infant subjects (Fantz, 1958a). In subsequent studies of human infants, involving several thousand tests, the apparatus and procedures have been varied somewhat from study to study. In general, the infant is placed face-up in a comfortable hammock type of crib inside a "looking chamber" which covers his visual field. The inside is as homogeneous as possible so that the infant will concentrate his attention on stimulus targets overhead. These targets are exposed either in pairs or singly for a series of test periods.

The infant's eyes are observed through a ¼-inch hole in the center of the chamber ceiling. To provide an objective criterion of fixation, the stimulus and lighting conditions are adjusted so that tiny images of the targets are clearly visible to the observer, mirrored from the surface of the infant's eyes. The location of these corneal reflexes in relation to the pupil indicates whether a target is fixated (Figure 1). When the left reflection, for example, is over the center of the pupil, the infant is looking at the target on the left. The left of two finger switches is then pressed to

CHECKERBOARD TARGET REFLECTION, SHOWING ONE CORNER FIXATED

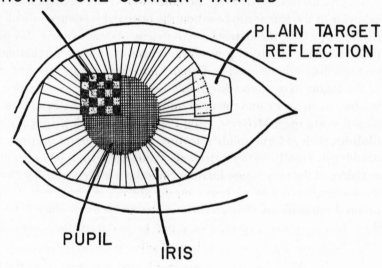

FIGURE 1

Schematic drawing of infant's eye as seen in the test chamber by the experimenter, when checked and plain squares are exposed. This illustrates the limiting condition for satisfying the criterion of fixation; more generally the target reflection would overlap the pupil to a greater degree.

record on a timer the duration of fixation. The right eye is observed unless it is not easily visible or unless the left appears to be better coordinated for a given infant. This response measure was found to be reliable in repeated tests of the same infants, each recorded by two observers (Fantz et al., 1962).

PATTERN DISCRIMINATION

The apparatus used in the first study (Figure 2) was simple and light so that it could be carried to the home of each subject for weekly tests. A hole in the middle of two cardboard shields tended to attract the infant's gaze to the center at the start so as to equalize the chance of his looking at the two targets. The targets were exposed by raising the center edges of the shields. This action started a 30-second timer. At the end of the period the shields were lowered and the targets reversed in position for a sec-

FIGURE 2

The first visual preference apparatus for infants, used in weekly tests at their own homes. The form-fitting crib was attached to the bottom of the "looking chamber" in which targets were exposed by pulling cords attached to the intervening shields. A tiny observation hole between the cross and circle targets is not visible here. The timers were manually operated by telegraph key switches on top.

ond 30-second period. Time scores for the two periods were combined to cancel out any effect of position preference. A partial restriction of head movements also helped to prevent position effects.

Thirty infants, starting at ages ranging from 1 to 15 weeks, were tested with 4 pairs of targets in random order. The main data analysis was based on 22 infants who completed 10 weekly tests. Average results for all infants at all ages (Fantz, 1961a) showed longest fixation of the most complex pair of patterns—horizontal stripes vs. bull's-eye; least response to a control pair of identical triangles; and intermediate response to the two pairs of intermediate complexity of pattern or outline—checks vs. square and cross vs. circle. This ranking of the pairs was consistent among the subjects; even the first tests of those infants under 2 months of age showed a significant difference.

Differences within the pairs gave still clearer evidence of pattern discrimination (Fantz, 1958b). Cross vs. circle elicited no consistent preference from the group, although several of the subjects showed a preference for one or the other target which was stable in repeated tests. Each of the pairs equated in outline form, area, and brightness, however, gave quite consistent over-all results, with a definite change shown at about 2 months. The mean percentage of fixation time for checks over plain square increased from 60% under 2 months to 72% over 2 months of age; in an analysis of the consistency among subjects in direction of preference, 8 out of 12 infants under 2 months preferred checks while 21 out of 22 over that age did so. For the other pair there was a reversal from 66% of fixation time for stripes under 2 months to 72% for bull's-eye over that age; under 2 months all but one preferred stripes while over 2 months all but one preferred bull's-eye. The latter change was not due to repeated testing experience since it was evident in the comparison of the first test scores of infants of varying ages. A similar age change was shown with another sample of infants, raised in an institution.

The changes at 2 months may have been due to maturation, oculomotor practice, or general visual experiences. They cannot be attributed to the sudden appearance of pattern vision or of interest in pattern complexity since before 2 months a consistent differential was shown between 2 relatively complex patterns but not between patterned and plain surfaces. Apparently infants are responsive to the form of contours as well as to the presence of contours.

These patterns were fairly gross, consisting of ½-inch lines or 1-inch squares seen at 12 inches. To determine the acuteness of pattern vision, the visual-preference method was modified. A card containing vertical black-and-white stripes had been found to be preferred to a gray card of the same over-all light reflectance. By using a graded series of striped patterns and finding the smallest pattern differentiated from gray, visual acuity could be estimated. The results from several studies of a total of 83 infants (Table 1) showed improvement with age, as would be expected. The finest stripes discriminated during the first 2 months subtended 40 minutes of arc; this decreased to 20 minutes for the next 2 months; then to 10 minutes over 4 months. The standard for adults is 1 minute for comparison.

TABLE 1

Combined Results for Two Studies of Visual Acuity in Infants Based on Selective Attention to Patterns

Age in Months	Total No. Infants	No. infants showing longer fixation of stripes (minutes of visual angle) vs. no. for gray (G)								
		5′	G	10′	G	20′	G	40′	G	80′	G
0–2	30	7 – 7		10 – 11		18 – 12		28 – 2**		12 – 1*
2–4	31	11 – 10		18 – 12		28 – 3**		28 – 3**		6 – 1
4–6	22	14 – 8		19 – 3**		22 – 0**		22 – 0**		—
Total	83	32 – 25		47 – 26*		68 – 15**		78 – 5**		18 – 2**

* Significant at .01 level (sign test).
** Significant at .001 level (sign test).

Table After Fantz, Ordy, and Udelf (1962, p. 914).

These results are restricted to the specific testing conditions, as is true of any measure of a sensory threshold. To determine the absolute limits of pattern vision it would be necessary to know the optimal conditions for infants. One of the conditions affecting visual acuity is illumination. The preceding tests were made under fairly dim illumination. In a study comparing 4 levels of illumination (1, 5, 20, and 80 foot-candles), the moderately bright condition of about 20 foot-candles gave the best performance, with discrimination of 3.5-min. stripes, the finest presented. This means that 1/64-inch stripes were seen at a distance of 15 inches by infants around 3 months old. This is comparable to 20/70 vision in the Snellen notation used in clinical testing. That the preference technique is sufficiently sensitive for threshold measurement is indicated by the fact that better acuity was shown than by any previous technique used for infants up to 1 year of age (Eichorn, 1963; Fantz et al., 1962).

Some preliminary acuity tests have been made with newborn infants. Eighteen out of 19 have discriminated 50-min. stripes; this included all 7 of those less than 24 hours old. For those 1 week of age, still better acuity was suggested. This means that hours after birth infants can see and respond selectively to 1/8-inch stripes at 9 inches. While this is poor vision by adult standards, it is far from an absence of pattern vision. Further maturation of the eye and brain, along with improvement in oculomotor coordination, allow the resolution of finer patterns during the first 6 months but do not cause the sudden appearance of a new "form sense."

It may be concluded that the various parts of the visual system are functional to some degree soon after birth. This includes in particular the visual cortex of the brain, which is known to be essential for pattern vision in animals from rats to man (Morgan and Stellar, 1950). Some functioning of the cerebral cortex was suggested also by an analysis of the acuity data into two component measures—first the number of separate fixations of each target, and second the average length of each fixation (Fantz et al., 1962). The first gave a less consistent and less sensitive measure of pattern discrimination than the second, especially during the early months; the second gave very similar results to those based on the resultant fixation time. Thus responsiveness to fine patterns was due mainly to the tendency to maintain fixation of a localized, stationary, patterned object; this is similar to the use of vision in later voluntary behavior. The discrimination was not dependent upon reflex eye movements toward a peripherally seen pattern. Neither was it based on optokinetic nystagmus —that is, reflex pursuit of a large moving striped field. The latter response, which has been used to test acuity in infants and animals, is completely involuntary and is based largely on peripheral vision and subcortical visual centers, and therefore has an uncertain relevance to form perception.

PATTERN SELECTIVENESS AND DIFFERENTIAL EXPERIENCE

The pattern-preference acuity results indicate that the pattern-vision capacities underlying form perception are present to a fair degree even in the newborn infant. But *perception* means more than the presence of sensory capacities; it implies that the capacity is used in directing behavior or in making contact with the environment. In this meaning it could be that the infant does not perceive the environment until the development of eye-hand coordination and locomotion or until learning occurs through action. Thus to answer the initial question—whether perception precedes and leads to action—it is not sufficient to prove that infants can discriminate patterns. Do they discriminate parts of the environment in a way which has consequences for behavior development, and does this occur without the influence of previous actions? These are large questions which cannot be fully answered without further research; however, experiments to date indicate that infants starting soon after birth have differential or selective experiences with parts of the environment which *may* influence subsequent perceptual development.

A clue to the possible use of pattern discrimination in the infant is given in the above results, which show a strong tendency for a pattern with some complexity, such as stripes or checks, to be fixated more than a plain square. Since most of the information conveyed through visual stimulation is given by patterns or configurational aspects, selective attention to these aspects would seem to increase the usefulness of vision; the opposite tendency, to look only at homogeneous surfaces or empty space, would prevent effective use of vision.

An early visual interest in patterns was shown dramatically by preferences among three patterned and three plain targets. They were presented one at a time, randomly and repeatedly, and exposed only for the duration of the initial fixation—that is, until the infant looked elsewhere or closed its eyes. This successive presentation technique allowed more targets to be compared than was possible with paired comparisons. It had the further advantage of not requiring head movements for fixation in neonates with poor control over head position, thus eliminating any effect of position preferences.

Figure 3 shows the results from 18 infants ranging from 10 hours to 5 days old (Fantz, 1963) as well as results from 25 infants ranging from 2 to 6 months old (Fantz, 1961a). Fixation times were converted to percentages because of wide variations in response time among subjects, and then averaged for each target. Tabulations of the longest-fixated target for each infant bring out the visual selectiveness even more strikingly: more than half of each group showed highest preference for the schematic

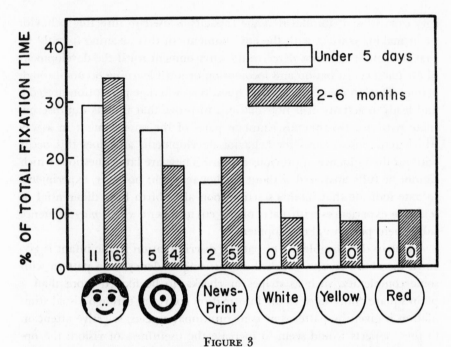

FIGURE 3

Visual preferences of newborn and older infants for black-and-white patterned discs over plain and colored 6-inch discs, presented randomly and repeatedly for the length of the first fixation. At the bottom of the bar is given the number of infants showing longest fixation of that target.

face pattern, while none of either group looked longest at white, fluorescent yellow, or red.

Another variable which might be expected to increase the attention value of a target is size. However, there was little difference in response to ovals measuring 4, 6, and 9 inches across but containing similar face patterns, by infants up to 6 months of age. The only consistent differential was a low response to the smallest pattern by infants under 1 month.

It has long been common knowledge that color, brightness, and size are primary sense qualities of high attention value, while form and pattern are secondary and acquired. But infants have not yet learned this; they act as if patterns are innately perceivable and are intrinsically interesting, while color and brightness without patterning offer little to attract their attention. What must be learned is not pattern discrimination and interest in patterns, for it is a mistaken belief that such learning is necessary!

This evidence for the high unlearned attention value of patterning in comparison to other visual dimensions is surprising in view of past beliefs, but it is in good agreement with facts about the structure and functioning of the visual system. Various parts of the visual system are designed for precise pattern vision—the optical system of the eye, the fine grain of the retina, the point-to-point projection of neural fibers to the brain. The receptors are more readily activated by the stimulus change produced by a pattern moving across the retinal mosaic than by the constant input from a homogeneous area of any color, brightness, or size. Furthermore, it has recently been discovered by Hubel and Weisel (1962) that individual cells in the visual cortex of the brain are maximally stimulated by a specific type of pattern falling on the retina—typically by a line or edge in a particular orientation. The optimal pattern varies from cell to cell, but diffuse light is a generally ineffective stimulus. This neural basis for form perception was evidenced not only in mature cats and monkeys, but also in newborn kittens with no opportunity for visual learning. Since the visual system seems to be constructed specially for seeing patterns, and since patterns are highly "stimulating" in the direct sense of activating the nervous system, it is understandable that patterns receive selective attention from birth.

The early pattern selectiveness is somewhat restricted by the degree of maturity of the visual system. Less acute vision prevents the seeing of fine patterns, especially if they are at a distance. Early distance vision is further hindered by the poor development of accommodation, according to recent findings. Haynes (1962) found that alert infants in the early weeks have a fixed point of clearest vision at 8 or 9 inches and that objects either closer or further away cannot be brought into sharp focus. Haynes' finding clears up much confusion about this matter. It is known that infants are hyperopic ("farsighted") and that their muscles of accommodation are not well developed, which would seem to imply better vision at a distance; this now appears to be true only when the eyes are relaxed by drugs or by sleep, while at other times a fixed power of accommodation is in effect. This fact explains the frequent reports of better near-vision and more interest in looking at objects at close range (Gesell et al., 1949; Ling, 1942), although the subsequent development now appears to be in both directions from initial accommodation at a moderately close distance.

A consequence for perceptual development is that the infant during the first month or two will have more experience with objects and patterns which happen to be at a particular close distance; distant objects may be seen if large enough, but perhaps not with sufficient clarity to distinguish patterning. While this represents a restriction on the infant's experiences, it may have the adaptive value of simplifying his visual world in the beginning and allowing concentration of attention on the few objects and patterns present at close range. These will often include objects of potential importance for behavior. For example, the infant's environment is such that a patterned object of particular importance—his mother's face—is frequently exposed at about the optimal distance of 8 or 9 inches under natural conditions of feeding, fondling, and care. The infant will have multiple opportunities for visually experiencing social objects, and for the development of social responsiveness based on purely perceptual contact instead of, or in addition to, physical contact or need reduction (Rheingold, 1959).

These opportunities for social learning can be utilized only if the social objects are of sufficient interest to hold the infant's gaze and elicit visual examination. The literature is full of references to the tendency of infants to look at human faces from an early age (Bühler, 1933; Koffka, 1928; McGraw, 1943; Piaget, 1952; Shirley, 1933). These are mostly casual observations, incidental to other aims; for example, Kestenbaum (1930) used his own face as a test object for studying the development of visual fixation and pursuit in infants during the first month because it seemed to attract their gaze better than any other object. The human face and head have a number of visual characteristics of potentially high attention value. It is often assumed without empirical support that the characteristics of initial interest are limited to brightness or shininess, figure-ground contrast, and movement. But various configurational aspects are also prominent and may be of equal or greater importance. The preference for a schematic face pattern over 5 other targets, including bright and contrasting ones (Figure 3), suggests that this is the case but does not specify the pertinent configurational aspects.

One study (Fantz, 1961a) showed a strong and consistent preference throughout the first 6 months for a schematic face pattern over a simple control pattern of the same brightness; it also showed a less pronounced preference for the correct arrangement of the schematic features over a "scrambled face." A number of further studies using these and similar targets have given varying degrees of confirmation. The results of studies of two stimulus dimensions—pattern complexity and pattern arrangement —are presented in Tables 2 and 3.

Table 2 gives the results of two studies—the first using facelike patterns of 3 levels of complexity for infants under 3 months of age, the second using 4 levels of complexity for older infants. All patterns contained black

TABLE 2

Relative Visual Fixation of Facelike Patterns of Varying Number and Complexity of Features

Age in Weeks	Realistic Features	Schematic Features[b]	Eye Spots	Plain Ovals	p of Dif.[c]
			% of Response Time followed by number Infants Preferring[a]		
		First Study			
0–1	—	45% (12)	36% (3)	19% (0)	.01
1–7	—	45% (5)	40% (6)	15% (0)	.001
8–12	—	54% (9)	33% (2)	13% (0)	.001
		Second Study			
10–12	39% (7)	25% (2)	26% (2)	10% (0)	.001
13–27	31% (6)	30% (6)	19% (2)	14% (1)	.001

[a] Each complexity level gives total for two patterns with correct and scrambled arrangements, or different brightnesses for plain ones.
[b] In first study these were the moderately complex patterns used previously (Fantz, 1961a), more complex than schematic features of second study, but less so than the realistic ones.
[c] Based on chi square analysis of variance by ranks.

TABLE 3

Number of Infants Visually Preferring Facelike Patterns with Different Arrangements of Features

Age	Schematic Features: Correct vs. Scrambled	Eye Spots: Correct vs. Uncentered
Under 1 wk.	6 – 8	5 – 8
1 wk–1 mo.	15 – 14	10 – 4
1–2 mo.	17 – 12	6 – 4
2–3 mo.	31 – 15	21 – 9
3–4 mo.	15 – 8	11 – 6
4–6 mo.	33 – 20	13 – 6

features painted on 6 x 9-inch white ovals; each level included correct and scrambled arrangements. One of the 2 plain ovals was white (similar in brightness to the eye-spot patterns); the other was gray in the first study (similar in average brightness to the most complex patterns), black in the second study. For the newborn infants the 6 targets were exposed successively and repeatedly in varied order for 30-second periods, during each of which the fixation times were cumulated; for older infants, who tended to fixate any pattern steadily for more than 30 seconds, the length of the first fixation was timed to give a better chance for differential response. The targets were exposed at a distance of 12 inches and in "upright" orientation in relation to the infant.

The preference for facelike patterns of greater complexity and number of features was strong in both studies and at all ages including newborn infants. The plain ovals were rarely chosen over any of the patterns even though lesser preferences were shown between the two brightnesses—generally white was favored over gray in the first study and black over white in the second.

Data on the relative choices within each pair of patterns in these studies were combined with similar data at the several ages from other studies, using one or the other pair of patterns, presented either simultaneously or successively (Table 3). There was an increasing selection of "face" over "scrambled face" until the third month, followed by a decrease. Results for eye spots over uncentered spots (either placed together at one edge or at opposite ends of the oval), from smaller numbers of subjects, were more variable but also indicated maximum differentiation between 2 and 3 months. At this age the discrimination was significant (sign test) for each pair of patterns.

These findings have several possible interpretations. It is clear that two configurational characteristics of the human face can be perceived and are selectively attended to—the complexity of the patterning of the face starting from birth, and the particular arrangement of the features at least by the third month. There are several interpretations of these findings which are *not* warranted. First, even if the correct arrangement of features were preferred from birth, this would not imply "instinctive recognition" of the human face, since a visual preference carries no commitment to a particular kind of further response such as approach or avoidance; it is a component of exploratory behavior rather than instinctive or consummatory behavior. Second, a preference for a particular pattern does not mean it is of highest attention value since it is only relative to the comparison patterns; it is assumed that there are other patterns which would be preferred over a face pattern. Third, the results with the particular facelike patterns used do not necessarily accurately reflect the development of responsiveness to actual faces, since faces have many further and varied visual aspects; thus lack of preference for the schematic face might mean not lack of discrimination but the ability to distinguish between a real and simulated face. Finally, these results, from institutional infants, are not necessarily representative of infants raised in private homes, even though the infants in this particular institution receive a relatively high level of social and other stimulation. These findings do suggest, however, that configurational aspects of social stimuli are prepotent for young infants, and thus increase the opportunity for the early development of social recognition and social responsiveness.

The human head also has distinctive three-dimensional aspects—solidity, curvature, and the pattern produced by the contours and shadows of features. The attention value of these aspects was tested by comparing a life-size model of a head with a flat form of the same outline, both painted white. Infants were exposed to the pair of objects for 4 25-second periods with alternating left and right positions, either with one eye covered or with both open; the test was then repeated with the other eye condition.

The relative responsiveness to the head model at successive months of age is shown in Figure 4. Infants less than 2 months old preferred the flat form under both conditions. At 2 months a sharp reversal occurred to a significant preference for the solid and contoured head. The differential was greater when the infants used both eyes, but was consistent with monocular vision as well. While the early preference for the flat form may have resulted from the higher light reflectance caused by the absence of shadows, the later preference for the solid model, with or without binocular cues, indicates the importance of the patterning that results from the facial contours and the curvature of the head.

Similar results were obtained from a sphere and a flat disc. No differential was shown unless both objects were visibly textured and were illuminated from one side rather than diffusely. Under these conditions the sphere, patterned by texture and brightness gradients, was consistently

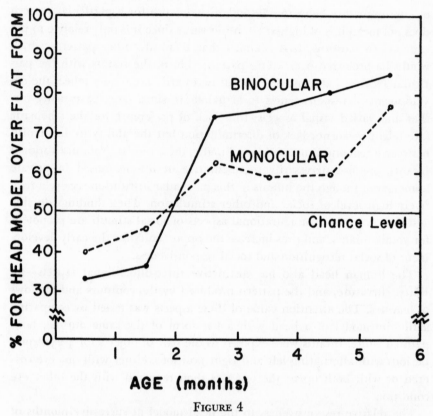

FIGURE 4

The development of visual interest in a solid, contoured model of a female human head, painted white, over a similar flat form, when seen either with both eyes open or with left eye covered. Different infants were tested at each age level, including 10, 9, 9, 7, 2, and 3 subjects at successive months of age.

preferred to the circle by 52 infants ranging from 1 to 6 months old, whether using one or both eyes. In the original data analysis (Fantz, 1961b) the total group was divided at 3 months; under this age a consistent sphere preference was shown only in the monocular condition. When divided at 2 months, the response was highly variable under this age and showed a clear increase in fixation of the sphere after 2 months under both eye conditions.

These results indicate both depth discrimination and solidity preference. Regarding the first, infants can differentiate between solid and flat forms by 2 months of age. Binocular cues were not essential for this but may have been of supplementary value. Surface patterning produced by light and texture gradients and contours was essential, but it is not known whether this was because of the difference in pattern complexity of solid and flat objects, cues from movement parallax or accommodation which require some patterning, or even the difference in brightness produced by the patterning of solid objects. It is possible that a number of the stimulus variables associated with solid objects and utilized by adults for depth perception can also be discriminated by the infant as a beginning stage of depth perception.

That the discrimination favored the solid object over the flat is also of interest since solid objects—as distinct from patterned or colored surfaces or two-dimensional forms—are of particular significance in active interactions with the environment. They support manipulation and play, provide tactile and kinesthetic feedback, and are often reinforcing or useful. The child and adult selectively attend and respond to solid objects; as if in preparation for this the infant shows a visual preference for solid objects. At first this is of little practical value, but it may have developmental value by facilitating visual exploration and familiarization with these important parts of the environment. It may also lead to manual, oral, and locomotor exploration of objects as soon as the necessary motor skills have developed.

To summarize this section, the use of pattern discrimination capacities by infants was indicated by selective attention to patterned over plain surfaces; by a particular visual selectiveness for the patterning of social objects; by preferential fixation of solid objects, also based on patterning; and more generally, by the tendency to look differentially at objects differing in pattern, but not those differing only in color, brightness, size, outline form, or binocular depth.

A probable significance of this early pattern selectiveness for the later use of vision can be seen by analysis of the visual aspects underlying object recognition (Fantz, 1961a). Recognizing objects requires attention to visual aspects which remain constant regardless of the varied conditions in which they are seen and regardless of differences among specific objects of a particular class. The color and brightness of objects are often of little identification value alone since they change with illumination and vary widely within a class of objects—for example, the different coloring among different food objects, trees, books, dogs, people, and so forth. The size of the retinal image of an object is of no help by itself since it depends on distance and varies within a class of objects. Outline form has limited value for recognition purposes since it changes with the observer's viewpoint and with orientation and movement of the object or its parts. Three-dimensional shape as given by binocular vision is useful only at short range.

On the other hand, aspects of pattern such as surface texture, shading, arrangement of details, and the general shape and complexity of contours are relatively constant under varying viewing conditions and for the various objects of a class. This is illustrated in particular by social perception. The general configuration of the face and head is the best means of distinguishing another human being either for the infant or the adult. More precise perception of facial pattern is an aid in recognizing a particular person, while details of facial expression are indicative of emotional state and give a basis for predicting the person's behavior.

EFFECTS OF EARLY VISUAL EXPERIENCES

Given that the infant tends to look at patterned surfaces and that the child and adult perceive and recognize objects largely through differences in patterning, what is the developmental connection between these two facts? For adaptive responses to particular patterned objects to develop out of an initial general tendency to look at patterns, learning or some effect of past experiences must occur.

The question of the degree of influence of learning on early visual behavior has not been emphasized above since it is secondary to the question whether visual discrimination and selective attention are present at all. If they are present, further effects of experience are possible; but without discrimination and selection there is no visual experience and no opportunity for visual learning. For the infant to learn from experience he must have experience to learn from. Without the capacity to see differences between objects, particular objects could not be remembered, while without selective attention to the multifarious visual input there could be no orderly association between parts of it or between certain stimuli and certain responses. In such circumstances, learning would be chaotic and nonadaptive if it could occur at all.

Having sufficient evidence for visual discrimination and selection in the infant as prerequisites for perceptual learning, from what age and through what process does this learning occur? Of particular concern from the present viewpoint is whether incidental learning occurs in the course of the infant's visual explorations. If it does not occur, if all the time the infant spends during the early months in looking at his surroundings has no effect other than to aid in the perfection of sensorimotor skills, if more active explorations and reinforcement are required to gain any useful knowledge of the environment, then the argument for the priority of perception over action is refuted.

The limited response capabilities of the infant place the same restrictions on the study of the effects of experience as on the study of discrimination. The visual preference method again provides one solution, simply by finding changes in preferences which can be attributed to experience. Some changes were noted in the results already given: the reversal from stripes to bull's-eye preference, the increased checkerboard preference, the discrimination of the correct facial arrangement, and the preference for solid over flat objects. But these changes may have been due to maturation or to oculomotor practice rather than to previous visual experiences.

In the attempt to determine the general effects of visual experience on early perceptual development, rhesus monkey infants were reared in a laboratory nursery and kept in darkness for varying periods starting at birth (Fantz, 1964). Animal subjects are, of course, necessary for this severe restriction of visual experience. Monkeys are ideal for this purpose, since they combine similarities to human vision and behavior with rapid motor development and wide response capabilities soon after birth.

The visual preferences of animals who had been deprived for varying lengths of time were compared during the early months of unrestricted visual experience. Those kept in darkness for 6 weeks or less all subsequently showed strong preferences for various patterns over plain or colored surfaces; they showed less strong but consistent preferences for solid over flat objects; and they showed low and inconsistent preferences for a particular color, brightness, or size of target. This is similar to the results from human infants.

On the other hand, those kept in darkness 2 months or longer showed little or no preference for patterned or solid objects but generally showed consistent differential responses to the nonconfigurational variations. It would seem that the supposed high initial attention value of color, brightness, and size over form and pattern is true only for dark-reared monkey infants! This failure to attend selectively to patterns and solid objects may have been responsible for the fact that these animals showed generally poor visual performance and were very slow in learning to use visual cues to direct locomotion and recognize objects; many months later they were inferior in discrimination-training performance.

This study indicates the deteriorating effect of prolonged and complete lack of visual experience but does not show how maturation and experience enter into the normal development of pattern selectiveness. Maturation alone had some effect, as shown in the preferences during the first 5 weeks of life of animals kept in darkness except for the short test exposures. Fixation of a patterned target increased during the first 3 or 4 weeks, whether it was initially preferred to the plain or colored target or not. For example, the fixation of checks was initially equal to plain square but subsequently increased, suggesting that the similar increase in human infants may have been primarily maturational. After this increase a downward trend for each pattern revealed the beginnings of the effects of prolonged dark-rearing. Solid and flat objects were fixated about equally during this period.

If the monkeys were moved to a lighted nursery by 6 weeks of age the maturational increase in pattern selectiveness was maintained and furthered during the following several months of opportunity for visual learning. These less deprived animals also gradually developed a consistent preference for solid objects through some effect of unrestricted visual experience, suggesting that the similar appearance of a solidity preference in human infants was experiential in origin.

These results suggest a complex interaction of innate, maturational, and experiential influences on the development of pattern selectiveness. The specific nature of the effects of experience is not known since the animals had opportunity for manual and locomotor exploration as well as visual exploration. Some pattern selectiveness was present from the first as a determinant of the early experiences and of their effects on subsequent selective responses. When this unlearned pattern selectiveness was absent—that is, in the animals kept 2 months or longer in darkness—visual experience no longer had the same developmental effects.

The final 2 experiments took the opposite approach of varying visual experience in a very limited way, by giving human infants successive exposures to the same patterns during testing. The first experiment used 2 different black-and-white patterns of high attention value—bull's-eye and a section of newsprint. They were presented one at a time for the duration of the first fixation. One pattern was presented for 5 successive exposures, then the other for 5, and so on for a total of 30 exposures. It was expected that decreasing responses would be shown for each pattern followed by longer fixation of the relatively novel pattern. But this did not happen with a group of 14 infants between 2 and 6 months old. The first fixation in a series was just as often shorter as longer than the last of

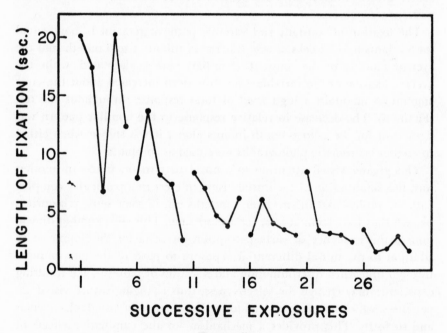

FIGURE 5

Mean length of fixation, by 14 infants 2 to 6 months old, on successive exposures of 2 patterns, presented in alternating series of 5 exposures. Half of the subjects started with each pattern. The changes with a relatively novel pattern were not consistent; the over-all response decrement was.

the preceding series. However, there was a marked drop in fixation time throughout the whole test (Figure 5), indicating some nonspecific effect of the successive exposures, such as fatigue, sensory adaptation, decreased arousal, or a general habituation of response.

Very different results were obtained when a particular pattern was exposed repeatedly for constant periods, paired with a new pattern each time (Fantz, in press). The patterns were 11 complex photographs cut from magazines, selected to give maximal variation in pattern (for 6 of them color also varied). One of these, varying among the subjects, was used as a constant pattern. It was exposed for 10 consecutive periods of 1 minute, paired with each of the remaining 10 photographs in random order. Midway in each exposure the positions of the constant and variable patterns were reversed.

The fixation of constant and variable patterns remained about equal for 6 infants 6 to 8 weeks of age. But for 22 infants 2 to 6 months old the average fixation of the constant (familiar) pattern decreased, while the average fixation of the variable (novel) pattern increased about the same amount to maintain a high level of total response throughout the test (Figure 6). The decrease in relative response to the familiar pattern was significant for the 2- to 3-month infants alone; it was shown when either colored or achromatic photographs were used as constants.

This greater visual attention to a novel pattern or, stated in another way, this habituation of the initial visual interest in a particular complex pattern, implies that infants over 2 months can in some sense recognize a pattern they have seen, at least for a short time. This adds another dimension to the influence of early perception on behavior development; in addition to the initial differential exposure to parts of the environment through unlearned discrimination and selection of patterns, the resulting experience may change the selectiveness, thus changing future visual experiences, which may in turn lead to further changes in visual selectiveness and so forth. This provides a mechanism for the cumulative effects of experience.

It is likely that much of what is termed perceptual learning is nothing more than such experiential changes in selective attention. This recalls the differentiation or specificity theory of perceptual learning proposed by Gibson and Gibson (1955): One process by which increasing stimulus differentiation along with increasing veridicality can occur is through

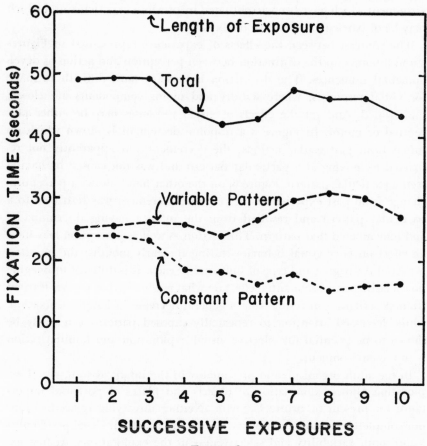

FIGURE 6

Mean fixation time during successive 1-minute exposures of paired magazine photographs—one of them different on each exposure, the other repeatedly exposed but in varied position. Data are from 22 infants ranging from 2 to 6 months.

gradual changes in what objects or patterns tend to be looked at and in what stimulus variables of these are attended to. This process might tend toward increasing selection of novel objects (or old ones seen from new angles or in new situations), toward attention to increasingly finer or subtler stimulus variations, and toward selection of those aspects of the environment which have been accentuated by previous experience and which may be of particular relevance for behavior.

The contrast between the effects of experience represented in Figures 5 and 6 points up the distinction between perception and action as developmental influences. The distinction is perhaps most difficult to make for visual responses, where sensory and motor components are closely intertwined. And yet the effects of visual responses may be either perceptual or motor. In Figure 5 a response decrement is shown which resulted from past ocular actions; the decrement was apparently not restricted to looking at a particular pattern and was not caused by having seen a particular pattern. Figure 6, on the other hand, shows a perceptual change from past experience; the response decrement was restricted to a particular pattern and resulted from the infant's having discriminated and remembered that pattern. Thus action as well as perception may have an effect on later visual behavior during the early months; the question is that of the degree and type of influence of each. It is difficult to imagine how a lasting or consequential effect on what is perceived or what is learned from experience can result from a general decrease in length of fixation, while decreased attention to repeatedly exposed patterns can easily be shown to be essential for effective visual exploration and familiarization with the environment.

In the adult organism, and presumably in the infant as well, visual exploration allows examination of objects and places of potential importance for present or future behavior. Neither unvarying reflex fixations nor completely random fixations will serve this function; visual preferences assure both variability and selectiveness in the explorations. At first exploration is facilitated by the unlearned pattern selectiveness. Eventually, perhaps starting around 2 months of age, the explorations are made more efficient by less looking at objects already explored, leaving more time to examine unknown objects. The unlearned selectiveness remains useful in the selection among novel objects and for preventing complete habituation to objects of potential importance for behavior.

This is, of course, a very incomplete account of the role of visual experience in perceptual development. For example, it leaves out the question of how increased responsiveness to particular familiar but consequential objects, such as social objects, can occur in spite of the general stimulus satiation effect of repeated exposure. Increased attention to certain objects might occur because of the accentuating effect of movement, high figure-ground contrast, or reinforcements. A familiar object seen from a new angle or in a new situation may have heightened interest, or a long-term increase in attention to a familiar object may follow a short-term satiation of interest. It is also possible that decreasing length of fixation may mean only the ability to recognize more quickly, without prolonged visual examination, a particular object to which the infant is nevertheless *more* responsive in other ways, such as smiling or approach, or under other environmental or motivational conditions. However, such possibilities are speculative in view of the very limited knowledge of the conditions necessary for various effects of experience during the early months of life. It is certain only that among the effects are changes in visual preferences and among the conditions are repeated visual exposure to particular patterns.

There have been several visual preference studies by other investigators which support some of the findings given above. In studying the color preferences of newborn infants, Stirnimann (1944) incidentally found that a simple figure on a color card greatly increased the fixation time, and that a horizontal line was a more effective figure than a circle. Berlyne (1958) found a greater number of first fixations given to a checked pattern and to a fine random pattern than to less complex patterns by infants 3 to 9 months old; white, gray, and black targets elicited no preference. More recently Spears (1962) found various pattern preferences in 4-month-old infants, especially for a bull's-eye, while the same patterns in different colors brought out little difference in response; the pattern preference was dominant over the color preference as shown by choice of a black-and-white bull's-eye over a colored but less preferred pattern. Selective attention to a facelike pattern over a simpler pattern and over a plain target was shown in newborn infants by Stechler (1964). Pictures of faces received more attention from 6-month-old infants than pictures of a nursing bottle or geometric patterns in a study by Lewis and associates (1963). Using a variant of the visual preference method Graefe (1963) found that infants 10 to 13 weeks old tended to follow one of two cards, displaying various plywood forms, which were moved apart from an initial adjacent position; the most consistent preferences were for 5 circles over a single circle or ring, bent over straight line, large over small circle, and linear over irregular trio of circles; no significant individual differences were found. Finally, a study of the effects of familiarity and novelty by Saayman, Wardwell, and Moffett (in press) showed decreased attention by infants around 3 months old to a circle or to a cross, whichever was initially preferred, after a 4½-minute exposure to that form; when the form differed in color as well, increased fixating of the novel form-color was shown as well as decreased fixation of the familiar one.

There is no known study which has failed to give some evidence for selective attention to form or pattern in early infancy. The least clear-cut results have been obtained by Hershenson (1964), who incidentally verified the reliability of the visual-preference technique with precise photographic recordings, and found a surprising degree of binocular fixation of a target by newborn infants. He found more consistent preferences among targets differing in brightness (favoring an intermediate level) than among those differing in pattern. However, the brightness differences—in amount of light transmitted from a projection bulb to a milk-screen—were extreme, while the pattern differences—in number of units in a checked pattern or in arrangement of facial features—were less marked and had, in the studies reported early in this article, failed to elicit consistent preferences during the early months.

At this early stage in the study of perceptual development through visual preferences the choice of stimulus variables is necessarily trial and error or guesswork; visual characteristics known to be important for the child and adult may or may not be discriminated and selected by the infant. Much more research is necessary to give a solid basis for describing the visual world of the infant, for predicting the responsiveness to particular aspects of patterning at particular ages, and for determining the relation of these early visual preferences to the development of later selective perceptions.

CONCLUSIONS

1. Human infants from birth can see and discriminate patterns as the basis for form perception. While this capacity is limited by less acute vision than that of adults, by imperfect oculomotor coordination, and by inability to accommodate for varying distances, much visual experience is possible within these limits.

2. Visual patterning is intrinsically stimulating or interesting; it elicits

much more visual attention from birth than do color and brightness alone. The selectiveness among patterns is more variable, depending on the pattern differences and the age of the subjects, but in general favors more complex patterns.

3. Pattern discrimination and pattern selectiveness allow the infant to explore his environment visually and to have increased experience with parts of it, including faces and solid objects, which have potential importance for later behavior.

4. At some point in development, at least by the third month, the unlearned visual selectiveness begins to be modified by past visual experiences. One of the changes is decreased attention to familiar patterns and consequent increased attention to novel ones. This and other possible effects of early visual experiences give a means for perceptual learning and familiarization with the environment; they prepare the infant for more active exploration and manipulation of the environment.

5. These findings give evidence that in development visual perception precedes action rather than the reverse as is often assumed. A primitive type of perception is present from birth; the only visually directed response present this early is the looking response itself, and this is initiated and maintained by the characteristics of what is perceived. Further improvement of oculomotor coordination gives more efficient use of the visual apparatus; the development of other forms of sensorimotor coordination allows perception to direct more active forms of behavior, while feedback and reinforcement from past responses may change what is attended to and perceived or what response is made to what is perceived. But at all ages, starting from birth, what is attended to and perceived has a direct influence on action and on what is learned from past actions. These points sum up the present argument for the priority of perception over action in development.

6. The visual-preference method has proved to be a powerful tool for determining what the infant perceives and what effects his visual experiences have. While it may not be true that the eyes are a window to the soul, it is true that the direction of gaze as reflected in the eyes of the infant can be a window to his perceptual and mental processes if one is patient enough to wait until the window is open, and if adequate conditions of observation are obtained. It has not been possible to see inside clearly enough to know whether there is a manikin looking out at the observer;

but the findings to date have tended to destroy other myths—that the world of the neonate is a big blooming confusion, that his visual field is a formless blur, that his mind is a blank slate, that his brain is decorticate, and that his behavior is limited to reflexes and undirected mass movements. The infant sees a patterned and organized world which he explores discriminatingly with the limited means at his command. When and under what conditions this visual contact with the environment makes a lasting impression on behavior are very good questions for further research.

BIBLIOGRAPHY

Berlyne, D. E. (1958), The Influence of the Albedo and Complexity of Stimuli on Visual Fixation in the Human Infant. British Journal of Psychology, 49:315-318.

Bühler, C. (1933), The Social Behavior of Children. A Handbook of Child Psychology, Revised Edition, Murcheson, C. (Ed.). Worcester, Massachusetts: Clark University Press.

Eichorn, D. H. (1963), Biological Correlates of Behavior. Child Psychology, Stevenson, H. W. (Ed.). Chicago: The National Society for the Study of Education.

Fantz, R. L. (1958a), Visual Discrimination in a Neonate Chimpanzee. Perceptual and Motor Skills, 8:47-50.

——(1958b), Pattern Vision in Young Infants. Psychological Record, 8:43-48.

——(1961a), The Origin of Form Perception. Scientific American, 204(5):66-72.

——(1961b), A Method for Studying Depth Perception in Infants Under Six Months of Age. Psychological Record, 11:27-32.

——(1963), Pattern Vision in Newborn Infants. Science, 140:296-297.

——(1964), Ontogeny of Perception. Behavior of Non-Human Primates: Modern Research Trends, Schrier, A. M. & Harlow, H. F. (Eds.). New York: Academic Press.

——(in press), Visual Experience Effects in Early Infancy: Decreasing Attention to Specific Repeatedly-Exposed Patterns. Science.

——, Ordy, J. M. & Udelf, M. S. (1962), Maturation of Pattern Vision in Infants During the First Six Months. Journal of Comparative and Physiological Psychology, 55:907-917.

Flavell, J. H. (1963), The Developmental Psychology of Jean Piaget. Princeton, New Jersey: Von Nostrand.

Gesell, A., Ilg, F. L. & Bullis, G. E. (1949), Vision: Its Development in Infant and Child. New York: Harper and Brothers.

Gibson, J. J. & Gibson, E. J. (1955), Perceptual Learning: Differentiation or Enrichment Psychological Review, 62:32-41.

Graefe, O. (1963), Versuche über Visuelle Formwahrnehmung im Sauglingsalter. Psychologishe Forschung, 27:177-224.

Haynes, H. M. (1962), Development of Accommodative Behavior in Infants. Paper read at Conference on Theoretical Optometry and Visual Training at St. Louis, January.

Hebb, D. O. (1949), The Organization of Behavior. New York: Wiley.

Held, R. (1961), Exposure-History as a Factor in Maintaining Stability of Perception and Coordination. Journal of Nervous and Mental Disease, 132:26-32.

ATTERN DISCRIMINATION AND SELECTIVE ATTENTION 173

—— & Hein, A. (in press), Movement-Produced Stimulation in the Development of Visually-Guided Behavior. *Journal of Comparative and Physiological Psychology.*

Hershenson, M. (1964), *The Visual Preference Behavior of Newborn Infants.* Unpublished doctoral dissertation, Yale University.

Hubel, D. H. & Weisel, T. N. (1962), Receptive Fields, Binocular Interaction and Functional Architecture in the Cat's Visual Cortex. *Journal of Physiology*, 160:106-154.

Kestenbaum, A. (1930), Zur Entwicklung der Augenbewegungen und des Optischen Nystagmus. *Arch. Opthalmol.*, 124:115.

Koffka, K. (1928), *The Growth of the Mind.* New York: Harcourt, Brace.

Lewis, M., Meyers, W. J., Kagan, J. & Grossberg, R. (1963), *Studies of Attention in Infants.* Paper read at Symposium at American Psychological Association Meeting, Philadelphia.

Ling, B.-C. (1942), A Genetic Study of Sustained Visual Fixation and Associated Behavior in the Human Infant from Birth to Six Months. *Journal of Genetic Psychology*, 61:227-277.

McGraw, M. B. (1943), *The Neuromuscular Maturation of the Human Infant.* New York: Columbia University Press.

Morgan, C. T. & Stellar, E. (1950), *Physiological Psychology.* New York: McGraw-Hill.

Piaget, J. (1952), *The Origins of Intelligence in Children.* New York: International Universities Press.

Rheingold, H. (1959), The Effect of Environmental Stimulation upon Social and Exploratory Behaviour in the Human Infant. *Determinants of Infant Behaviour*, Foss, B. M. (Ed.), p. 143. London: Methuen.

Saayman, G., Wardwell, E. & Moffett, A. (in press), Response to Novelty in the Human Infant. *Journal of Experimental Child Psychology.*

Shirley, M. M. (1933), *The First Two Years.* Minneapolis: University of Minnesota Press.

Spears, W. C. (1962), *The Assessment of Visual Discrimination and Preference in the Human Infant.* Unpublished doctoral dissertation, Brown University.

Staples, R. (1932), The Response of Infants to Color. *Journal of Experimental Psychology*, 15:119-141.

Stechler, G. (1964), Newborn Attention as Affected by Medication during Labor. *Science*, 144:315-317.

Stirnimann, F. (1944), Über das Farbenempfinden Neugeborener. *Ann. Paediat.*, 163:1-25.

Taylor, J. G. (1962), *The Behavioral Basis of Perception.* New Haven: Yale University Press.

CHAPTER 7

Verbal and Motor Responses to Perceptual Stimuli throughout the Life Span

LOUISE BATES AMES

Psychology has long recognized that perception is considerably more than a simple stimulus-response phenomenon. It is generally accepted that the age and individuality of the subject stimulated strongly influence the response to any perceptual stimulus. It is also recognized that the response to any given stimulus tends to become more complex and more discriminating with increasing age of the subject, and that many perceptual responses tend to diminish or to become less discriminating in old age. However, literature is lacking on the specific patterning of responses to any one specific visual stimulus in human subjects throughout the entire life span. Ideally, data for such a study would consist of observations of the response of individuals studied throughout their entire lifetimes. No such data are at present available. Instead we have only mean scores or typical responses for groups of individuals at different ages.

The present study reports what may be considered typical responses to a group of behavior tests given in childhood, adulthood, and old age. The following tests have been used: (1) The Rorschach—a highly visual test requiring a verbal response. (2) Monroe Visual I, Monroe Visual III, Gesell Copy Forms, Gesell Incomplete Man—visual tests to which visual and motor responses are required. (3) Lowenfeld's Mosaic test and the Gesell Cube tests which require a primarily motor response.

No one of these tests is a purely perceptual test to the extent that the

174

kinds of visual-response tests given by the visual specialist may be considered tests of pure perception. Certainly the most clear-cut measure of what the child perceives can be made by the visual specialist when he directly measures stereopsis or depth perception. Such measures really begin to allow us to see how the child understands parts in relation to larger wholes.

For the psychologist, the view is less clear. He must for the most part be content to measure the child's response, either motor or verbal, in some more general situation, as a clue to what that child is perceiving. However, the subject's initial response in each of the tests used here may be called perceptual. That is, each of these tests, except perhaps the Mosaic, requires a perceptual evaluation of a stimulus before the necessary verbal or motor response can be made.

The Rorschach in particular is considered, by Rorschach, to be clearly a test of perception. He states (1942):

> The interpretation of the chance forms falls in the field of perception and apperception rather than imagination. Perceptions arise from the fact that sensations, or groups of sensations, ecphorize memory pictures of former groups of sensations within us. This produces in us a complex of memories of sensations, the elements of which, by virtue of their simultaneous occurrence in former experiences, have a particularly fine coherence and are differentiated from other groups of sensations.
>
> This identification of a homogeneous group of sensations with previously acquired analogous complexes, together with all their connections, we designate as apperception. It also embraces the narrower term of perception.
>
> If perception can also be called an associative integration of available engrams (memory pictures) with recent complexes of sensations, then the interpretation of chance forms can be called a perception in which the effort of integration is so great that it is realized consciously as an effort. This intrapsychic realization that the complex of sensations and the engrams are not perfectly identical gives the perception the character of an interpretation [pp. 16-18].

Responses to all tests, for subjects aged 2 through 16 years of age, are considered in terms of chronological age levels. Thus we customarily speak of the typical 3-year-old, 4-year-old, 5-year-old (etc.) response. This holds whether we are discussing responses to a primarily developmental type of test such as the simple Cube or Copy Form tests, or to a more subjective, so-called projective test like the Rorschach which is intended primarily to measure individuality rather than developmental factors. That is, such tests as the Cubes and Copy Forms were constructed primarily as tests to measure how far a subject had developed in terms of his behavior response. Was any given subject, for instance, responding like a 3-year-old, a 4-year-old, a 5-year-old, or what? The Rorschach test, on the other hand, was constructed as a measure of individuality factors, but it has been demonstrated (Ames, 1960; Ames et al., 1952, 1959) that even here it is possible to assess developmental levels.

Norms for cube responses, copy forms, Visual I and Visual III have been determined through the first 10 years of life. For each of these tests a correct score is normative by or before 10 years of age. Thus it may be assumed that a normal adult should be able to perform on all of these tests with a score of 100% correct.

Presumably typical responses to the Rorschach and Mosaic have been defined through 16 years of age (Ames and Ilg, 1962; Ames et al., 1952, 1959). For the Rorschach (though not for the Mosaic), in spite of tremendous individual differences, investigators have assumed or defined what might be considered the typical adult response (Ames et al., 1952).

Thus up to and including "normal" adulthood, responses have been identified in terms of chronological age. When we come to old age, however, a different kind of determination has been found necessary.

ELDERLY SUBJECTS CLASSIFIED BY DEVELOPMENTAL STAGE RATHER THAN BY AGE

This new type of classification was first worked out on the basis of the Rorschach response. The way in which we hit upon this classification will be described in detail since it is in this age range only that we depart from a simple classification by chronological age alone.

Our first approach, in investigating the process of aging as reflected in the Rorschach test, was a straightforward consideration of the records of subjects classified into age groups: the 70-year-olds, 80-year-olds, and 90-year-olds. Examination of this material gave results which were meager and inconsistent. Age-group means for most Rorschach scoring categories did not increase or decrease steadily from one decade to the next, and overall age trends tended to differ unpredictably at different socioeconomic levels of our sample.

Furthermore, in giving the Rorschach to elderly subjects, we observed that the records of some subjects differed in no appreciable way from those of any normal adult, and that this normality of response did not appear to be directly related to the age of the subject. Not only did we not find consistent differences between the different age groups, but individually, some 80-year-olds and even some 90-year-olds gave more adequate responses than did some of the 70-year-olds.

These results were at first disappointing, in view of our clinical impression that Rorschach data gave a good deal of information about the aging process. We felt strongly that the developmental continuum was there, but our method appeared inadequate to delineate it. We concluded, then, that some division of subjects into groups other than by age might be more fruitful than the more conventional age approach.

The most obvious division appeared to be into a "normal" group and a "senile" group. In a number of our subjects, the extremely high animal or anatomy percent, the high form percent, the low correct form percent, and in some cases complete or virtually complete "static perservation" (repetition of a concept on several cards regardless of its adequacy as a response), made a diagnosis of senility obvious.

However, the majority of cases seemed in our judgment to occupy a position somewhere between "normal" and "senile." By no means yet senile, these subjects still differed conspicuously, in their responses, from the normal person. Such subjects we designated as presenile. (This term corresponds to "senescent" as used by some investigators who thereby imply a definite, but relatively benign, state of decline.) We used the term as the term preadolescent is customarily used; not to designate *any* age or behavior period preceding adolescence (or senility), but rather to indicate the age or behavior period *just preceding*—in this case—senility.

Subjects were thus classified as *normal* when the total patterning of their records was about as rich and varied as one would expect to find in any normal adult sample, and when they showed none of the qualitative signs of presenility (Ames et al., 1954), or when just one or two such signs appeared in an otherwise full and normal record.

Classification in the *presenile* group was determined by clinical judgment of the over-all adequacy of the record and by the presence of several of the specific qualitative signs which we associate with beginning deterioration of performance.

Subjects were classified as *senile* when the animal percent or the anatomy percent or a combination of the two was close to 100% and when at the same time there was a very high F% and a very low F+%. Complete or virtually complete static perseveration was also a basis for classification in the senile cases.

The presenile group of subjects—the largest group—was later divided into normal preseniles, medium preseniles, and deteriorated preseniles depending on whether the Rorschach was nearer to the normal or nearer to the senile category.

The present chapter aims to present typical or normative changes in the responses of the human organism throughout the life span to a group of stimulus situations primarily perceptual in character. The purpose of this chapter is to present evidence that as the human subject responds to any given stimulus at increasing ages, the response increases, improves, elaborates, and changes in a somewhat predictable manner until adulthood or early middle age. This elaborated response presumably then holds somewhat constant until old age, when it then becomes less active, effective, and elaborate, narrowing down or decreasing or deteriorating in a manner which is to a large extent the exact reverse of the manner in which it developed or elaborated to begin with.

Thus the pattern of response to any single test throughout the life span may be considered to take the form of a somewhat flattened-out diamond:

FIGURE 1

Or the reader may get a clearer picture by thinking of the increasing and then decreasing responses in the schema presented in Tables 3-8.

SUBJECTS AND TESTS

SUBJECTS

Child subjects were all chosen from among research subjects tested at the

Gesell Institute. Slightly different groups were used for the different tests as follows:[1]

Cube and Copy Form tests (3 to 6 years) were standardized on a presumably normative group of 107 children, a selected and homogeneous group whose parents were of middle socioeconomic status with respect to occupation, schooling, avocational interests, and home equipment. Fathers' occupations fell in the 4.98 to 11.74 range of values listed on the Barr Scale of Occupational Intelligence (1934). The parents were born in the United States and the grandparents were of Northern European extraction. All subjects lived in New Haven, Connecticut (Gesell and Thompson, 1938; Gesell et al., 1940).

Incomplete Man test (5 to 10 years); *Visual I* (5 to 5 1/2 years); *Visual III* (5 to 10 years). Norms for these tests were determined on students attending two public schools in North Haven, Connecticut. Fifty girls and 50 boys were examined at 5, 5 1/2, 6, 7, 8, 9 and 10 years. Mean IQ for these subjects on the WISC scale (Wechsler, 1949) was 104.8 for girls, 106 for boys. Occupational status of parents on the Minnesota Scale (Institute of Child Welfare, n.d.) was 27% in Groups I and II, 43% in Groups III and IV, 30% in Groups VI and VII.

For both the Incomplete Man and Visual I tests, subjects under 5 years of age were children in attendance at the Gesell Guidance Nursery School in New Haven. These children were on the average (Gesell Developmental Scale; Gesell et al., 1940) of superior intelligence with fathers in occupational class I on the Minnesota Scale.

Rorschach (2 to 16 years). Subjects were for the most part from New Haven, 50 girls and 50 boys at each age. Mean and modal ratings on the Gesell Developmental Scale for younger subjects were superior; rating for three fourths of subjects was above the average category. Mean IQ on the Wechsler-Bellevue Scale for older subjects was 116.

As to parents' occupations, more than half the parents were in the professional group and three quarters were in either the professional or managerial groups (Minnesota Scale) (Ames et al., 1952, 1959).

Mosaic (2 to 16 years). Fifty boys and 50 girls at each yearly age level.

---

[1] Ideally all tests used would be standardized on some one group of subjects as they matured from age to age. This was not practical in the present instance. Not only were different subjects used at different periods of the life span, but also several different groups of subjects were used in the early years.

Two- to 10-year-olds, rated on a developmental scale, were, for the majority, of high average, superior, or very superior intelligence. For older subjects, mean IQ on the Wechsler-Bellevue Scale was 118.04 (S.D. 14.25) for girls, 117.58 (S.D. 11.62) for boys (Ames and Ilg, 1962).

SES, for both sexes. With only a few exceptions, fathers' occupations fell in either the professional or semiprofessional category.

Older subjects (over 70 years old) were a group of 100 inmates of the Masonic Home in Wallingford, Connecticut (Pelz et al., 1961; United States Bureau of the Census, 1963). This initial group of subjects was chosen largely on the basis of willingness to be tested, and of being well enough both physically and mentally to cooperate in taking the battery of psychological tests which we proposed. Of this initial group, 9 were classed by us, on the basis of their responses to the Rorschach test, as "normal," 30 as "intact presenile," 39 as "medium presenile," and 22 as "deteriorated presenile."

From this initial group of 100 subjects, 60 were chosen for further testing. This selection was made not on the basis of degree of psychological intactness or deterioration, but rather on the grounds of willingness, cooperativeness, and enough visual and auditory acuity to make further participation in the study practical.

Age and Sex. Of the 60 subjects thus selected, 35 were female, 25 male. Ages ranged from 69 to 92, with a mean age for women of 80, for men of 83. Median ages were 80 for women, 85 for men. Table 1 gives data for age and sex of subjects.

Socioeconomic Status. For this group of old people we have little information about socioeconomic status. However, we do have information on own or spouse's occupational level. For purposes of comparison we in-

TABLE 1

Age and Sex of Elderly Subjects

Age in years	Females	Males	Total
65–69	2	0	2
70–79	11	7	18
80–89	20	17	37
90–	2	1	3
Totals	35	25	60

TABLE 2

Men's Own and Women's Own or Husband's Occupations on the
Minnesota Scale

		Percentage	
Class	Type of Occupation	Wallingford Sample	Census
I	Professional	5%	3%
II	Semiprofessional, managerial	13	5
III	Clerical, skilled, retail business	26.6	14
IV	Farmers	5	19
V	Semiskilled, minor business	30	27
VI	Slightly skilled	6.6	13
VII	Day laborers	5	19
	Unclassified	8	0

Compared with the 1920 U.S. Census data when current population was
aged 29 to 52.

clude a tabulation (Table 2) of the same data for the total U.S. population in this age range and geographic area, computed from the U.S. Census
data (United States Bureau of the Census, 1963). Occupation is classified on
the Minnesota Scale of Paternal Occupations.

As this table shows, subjects of all levels of social status and ability were
included in our sample, but those of higher levels were overrepresented
in comparison with the total U.S. population.

TESTS

Tests used included a selection from the Gesell Developmental Battery,
notably Cube tests (tower of 10, bridge, gate, steps), Copy Forms (circle,
cross, square, triangle, rectangle with diagonals, diamond), and the Incomplete Man test. We also used the Monroe Visual I and Visual III, and
two projective tests—the Rorschach and the Lowenfeld Mosaic. Descriptions of these tests, directions for administration, and school-age norms
are given in full in *School Readiness Tests* (Ilg and Ames, in press) and
elsewhere (Gesell and Thompson, 1938; Gesell et al., 1940; Gesell and
Amatruda, 1947).

FINDINGS

Findings are presented in tabular form in Tables 3-8 which indicate, for
Cubes, Copy Forms, Mosaic, Visual I, Visual III, Incomplete Man, and

TABLE 3

Cubes

3 Years: Tower of 10
  3½ Years: Imitates bridge, builds tower of 10
    4½ Years: Imitates gate and bridge, builds tower of 10
      5 Years: Six cube steps, gate, bridge, tower
        Normal Adult: Ten cube steps, gate, bridge, tower
        Normal Elderly Person: Ten cube steps, gate, bridge, tower
      Intact Presenile: Six cube steps, gate, bridge, tower
    Medium Presenile: Gate, bridge, tower of 10
Deteriorated Presenile: Tower of 10 only

Copy Forms *

3 Years: Copies circle
  4 Years: Copies cross, circle
    4½ Years: Copies square, cross, circle
      5 Years: Copies triangle, square, cross, circle
        5½ Years: Copies divided rectangle, triangle, square, cross, circle
          6 Years: Copies diamond, divided rectangle, triangle, square, cross, circle
        Normal Adult, Normal Elderly, Intact Presenile, and Medium Presenile: Copies diamond, divided rectangle, triangle, square, cross, circle
      Deteriorated Presenile: Copies triangle, square, cross, circle

* Copying forms appears to be the last of the abilities considered in the present study to disappear. Thus even the deteriorated presenile adult still responds, on this test, at a 5-year-old level.

Rorschach, the degree of improvement and elaboration of the responses at increasing ages till maturity, then the stages of deteriorated responses. For each test it is shown that as the subject grows older (past normal maturity) the response resembles that of increasingly young subjects.

DIFFERENTIAL DIAGNOSIS

The perceptual response of the human organism thus appears to develop, and then decline, in a highly patterned manner during its lifetime. It is, therefore, obviously possible to use this perceptual response to determine the developmental level of any given individual at any given time.

TABLE 4

Mosaic

3 Years:

Class A—Nonrepresentational without pattern   56%
Class B—Nonrepresentational with pattern   21%
Class C—Representational   23%

4 Years:

Class A	28%
Class B	28%
Class C	41%
Mixed	2%

5 Years:

Class A	11%
Class B	28%
Class C	59%
Mixed	2%

16 Years:

Class A	5%
Class B	46%
Class C	48%

Normal Elderly:

Class A	0%
Class B	28%
Class C	57%
Refused	14%

Intact Presenile:

Class A	20%
Class B	62%
Class C	17%

Medium Presenile:

Class A	40%
Class B	46%
Class C	7%
Refused	7%

Deteriorated Presenile:

Class A	53%
Class B	38%
Class C	0%
Refused	8%

TABLE 5

Visual I

Below 4 Years: Less than 5 responses correct
4 Years: 7.6 correct
5 Years: 10 or more correct
5½ Years: 12 correct
Adult: 12 correct
Normal Elderly: 12 correct
Intact Presenile: 10.96 correct
Medium Presenile: 10.20 correct
Deteriorated Presenile: 4.69 correct

TABLE 6

Visual III

4 Years: 0–2 correct
5 Years: 3.43 correct
5½ Years: 4.55 correct
6 Years: 5.7 correct
7 Years: 7.68 correct
8 Years: 8.85 correct
9 Years: 10.4 correct
10 Years: 11.2 correct
Adult: 12 correct
Normal Elderly: 8.93 correct
Intact Presenile: 2.77 correct
Medium Presenile: .83 correct
Deteriorated Presenile: .92 correct

This type of differential diagnosis has long been used to evaluate the developmental level of infants and young children (Ames et al., 1952; Gesell and Thompson, 1934, 1938; Gesell et al., 1940; Gesell and Amatruda, 1947; Ilg and Ames, in press). However, it is only recently that the perceptual response has been used in this manner to yield a differential diagnosis of the behavior level of the older person (Ames et al., 1954; Pelz et al., 1961, 1962).

Since the literature on differential diagnosis in the older age range is so sparse, we shall emphasize the older ages here. Since, as discussed earlier, age in years is not a good clue to the behavior level of elderly subjects, present subjects have been differentiated on the basis of the degree of intactness of their Rorschach responses.

TABLE 7

Incomplete Man

4 Years: 3 parts:
Arm, leg, eyes

4½ Years: 6 parts:
Leg, arm, eyes, foot, ear, fingers

5 Years: 9 parts:
Arm, fingers, leg, foot, eyes, ear, hair, body line, and one other part

10 Years: 10.34 parts:
Arm, fingers, leg, foot, eyes, pupil, hair, ear, neck, bow

Normal Adult: 10 parts:
Arm, fingers, leg, foot, hair, eyes, eyebrow, ear, neck, bow

Normal Elderly: 8.57 parts:
Arm, fingers, leg, foot, eyes, ear, hair, body line, and one other part

Intact Presenile: 7.87 parts:
Arm, fingers, leg, hair, eyes, ear, neck, and one other part

Medium Presenile: 6.31 parts:
Arm, fingers, leg, hair, ear, neck

Deteriorated Presenile: 3.39 parts:
Leg, arm, and one other part

When subjects are thus grouped on the basis of the level of their Rorschach responses, these different groups (normal elderly, intact presenile, medium presenile, and deteriorated presenile) show clear-cut and obvious differences in perceptual responses to the other tests here considered, as follows:

(a) *Normal elderly subjects* respond on all tests in this battery about as would normal adults of any age—succeeding on all Cube, Copy Form, and Visual tests as well as making adequate responses to the Incomplete Man and Mosaic tests.

(b) *Intact presenile elderly subjects* respond almost as well, especially on the Cube and Copy Form tests. The foot tends to drop out on the Incomplete Man, but otherwise the response to this test is at a 4½-year-old level or better. There may be an occasional error on Visual I. On the Mosaic, objects are less likely to appear than with the normal adult subjects, and there is the possibility of nonrepresentational designs without pattern (5-year-old level or better). However, the significant clue which distinguishes normal from intact presenile subjects is that the latter can make

TABLE 8

Rorschach

Number of Responses

2 Years: 9.6
  2½ Years: 10.8
    3 Years: 13
      6 Years: 16
        Normal Adult: 20–50
      Normal Elderly: 15
     Intact Presenile: 13
   Medium Presenile: 11
Deteriorated Presenile: 7

Experience Balance

3 Years: .2M: .77sC
  4 Years: .4M: .97sC
    6 Years: 1M: 2sC
      10 Years: 1.7M: 1.5sC
        Normal Adult: 2–3M: 2½sC
      Normal Elderly: 1.85M: 1.14sC
    Intact Presenile: 1.37M: .56sC
  Medium Presenile: .54M: .72sC
Deteriorated Presenile: .46M: .46sC

F%/ F+%

3 Years: 84%F/ 60%F+
  5½ Years: 62%F/ 84%F+
    7 Years: 52%F/ 82%F+
      8 Years: 58%F/ 87%F+
        16 Years: 56%F/ 92%F+
          Normal Adult: 50%F/ 80–90%F+
        Normal Elderly: 64%F/ 85%F+
      Intact Presenile: 58%F/ 85%F+
    Medium Presenile: 64%F/ 80%F+
Deteriorated Presenile: 76%F/ 60%F+

Number of Content Categories

2 Years: 2.6 categories
  3 Years: 3.6 categories
    4½ Years: 4.6 categories
      16 Years: 5.6 categories
      Normal Adult: 5–6 categories
    Normal Elderly: 4.4 categories
   Intact Presenile: 3.6 categories
  Medium Presenile: 3.6 categories
Deteriorated Presenile: 1.9 categories

only the most limited response to Visual III (somewhere below a 5-year-old level), whereas the former respond adequately.

(c) *Medium preseniles.* Though these subjects can respond adequately to all Copy Form tests, and make only an occasional error on Visual I (5-year level), they fail on the 10 cube steps and perform on other cube tests at approximately a 4-year-old level. They are unable to respond adequately to Visual III, add neither eyes nor foot to the Incomplete Man (4-year-old level), and are much more likely to make nonrepresentational designs without pattern or 4-year-old patterned designs on the Mosaic test than they are to make recognizable objects.

(d) *Deteriorated preseniles.* Deterioration shows itself very clearly on the present battery of preschool and school-age tests. Deteriorated subjects can build a tower of 10 cubes, but fail the bridge, gate, and steps (3-year-old level of response). They can copy correctly a circle, cross, square, and triangle but not the rectangle with diagonals or the diamond (about a 6-year-old level of response). They fail signally on both Visual I and Visual III, responding somewhere below a 5-year-old level on both. They make only a meager response to the Incomplete Man test, adding on the average, a leg, arm, and one other part (about a 3-year-old level). On the Lowenfeld Mosaic test they are most likely to make nonrepresentational designs without pattern (about a 3-year-old level).

Thus, in general, normal elderly subjects respond on the present group of tests from a 5 + to an 8- to 9-year-old level. Intact preseniles respond from 4½ to 6 years +. Medium preseniles respond from 4 years to 6 years; deteriorated preseniles from a 3-year-old to a 5-year-old level.

SUMMARY

The process of perception, so far as it is measured by the individual's response to the battery of tests used here, which include also motor and verbal responses, not only reverses itself, but as it declines in old age shows stages of behavior almost identical to those expressed as the response "improves" as the individual approaches maturity. This fact presents some of the strongest evidence to date to suggest that human perception, like other aspects of human behavior, does develop through the patterned unfolding of predictable stages of behavior. Thus, present results support the thesis that behavior is a function of structure.

Individual differences are large. The effect of environmental variables, such as emotional condition, motivation, such mechanical factors as lens help, must at all times be considered.

Beneath individual differences and environmental factors, however, it appears that a highly structured and to a substantial extent predictable pattern of response is unfolding and then diminishing as the individual matures into adulthood and then goes on into old age.

It is suggested that this fact should be clearly kept in mind whenever the perceptual responses of any given individual are being measured. Obviously any given perceptual response has a different meaning as it is given at different stages in the life span.

BIBLIOGRAPHY

Ames, L. B. (1943), The Gesell Incomplete Man Test. *Journal of Genetic Psychology*, 62:217-270.

—— (1960), Age Changes in the Rorschach Responses of Individual Elderly Subjects. *Journal of Genetic Psychology*, 97:287-315.

—— & Ilg, F. L. (1962), *Mosaic Patterns of American Children*. New York: Hoeber.

—— (in press), The Gesell Incomplete Man Test as a Measure of Developmental Status. *Genetic Psychology Monographs*.

——, Learned, J., Metraux, R. W. & Walker, R. N. (1952), *Child Rorschach Responses*. New York: Hoeber-Harper.

——, ——, —— & —— (1959), *Adolescent Rorschach Responses*. New York: Hoeber-Harper.

——, Metraux, R. W. & Walker, R. N. (1954), *Rorschach Responses in Old Age*. New York: Hoeber-Harper.

Barr Scale of Occupational Intelligence (1934), *Genetic Studies of Genius*, Terman, L. M. (Ed.). Stanford, California: Stanford University Press.

Gesell, A. et al. (1940), *The First Five Years of Life*. New York: Harper.

—— & Amatruda, C. S. (1947), *Developmental Diagnosis*. New York: Hoeber-Harper.

—— & Thompson, H. (1934), *Infant Behavior*. New York: McGraw-Hill.

—— & —— (1938), *Psychology of Early Growth*. New York: Macmillan.

Ilg, F. & Ames, L. B. (in press), *School Readiness Tests*. New York: Harper and Row.

Institute of Child Welfare, University of Minnesota (Minneapolis) (no date), *The Minnesota Scale for Paternal Occupations* (Pamphlet).

Monroe, M. (1935), *Primary Form Reading Aptitude Tests*. Chicago: Houghton Mifflin Company (Pamphlet).

Pelz, K., Pike, F. & Ames, L. B. (1961), Measurement of Psychologic Function in Geriatric Patients. *Journal of the American Geriatric Society*, 14:740-754.

—— (1962), A Proposed Battery of Childhood Tests for Discriminating between Different Levels of Intactness of Function in Elderly Subjects. *Journal of Genetic Psychology*, 100:23-40.

Rorschach, H. (1942), *Psychodiagnostics*. Berne, Switzerland: Hans Huber.

United States Bureau of the Census (1963), Sixteenth Census of the United States, 1940, Population. 1, Characteristics by Age, Part 1, United States Summary. Washington, D. C.: Government Printing Office.

Wechsler, D. (1949), *Wechsler Intelligence Scale for Children*. New York: The Psychological Corporation.

PART IV

Social Aspects of Perception

Anthropologists and sociologists have demonstrated the influence of cultural and social factors on perception. Where the culture expects its members to "have visions," most of the individuals in that society will perceive as "real" entities which have no tangible existence. When the taboos of a society prohibit certain members from "seeing" persons with specified kinship relationships to them, the tabooed kin will not be seen.

The social aspects of perception are less clear in our Western society, although such cultural factors as religious and philosophical systems probably influence members of Western cultures in much the same way as they do individuals in less complex societies. In Chapters 8 and 9 Elkind and Frank review the development of religious and philosophical concepts and suggest a relationship between such concepts and the child's perception of his world. As is indicated clearly, both areas are characterized by inadequate definitions of terms, by inadequately designed and reported research, and by a complete lack of theoretical formulations beyond those of Freud and Jung. It is to be hoped that these chapters will help stimulate further clarifying research.

However, anthropologists long ago carefully defined many of the social-structure aspects in terms of the duties and expectations attached to the possible roles in any given society. Chapter 10 indicates a type of study that is possible for the total area of the social aspects of perception. Dr.

Flavell's research strongly points to some of the determinants of social roles taken. Thus, future research may clearly demonstrate that perception of the environment depends upon the roles available to an individual in a given culture and upon the determinants of those roles to a far greater extent than has formerly been believed.

CHAPTER 8

The Developmental
Psychology of Religion

DAVID ELKIND

Over the past 70 years there has been a slow but steady trickle of research contributions dealing with the religious development of children and with the factors which condition and are conditioned by this development. Although the accumulated body of work is not large, it is sufficiently varied to warrant presentation as an established developmental psychology. The present essay will attempt to provide a broad view of this field of development including a look at its theoretical issues, its methodology, its empirical findings, and its most promising areas for future research.

THEORETICAL ISSUES

While the developmental psychology of religion cannot boast of any comprehensive explanations of religious development, it can lay claim to a number of theoretical issues, i.e., opposing explanations for particular religious phenomena. Three such issues will be summarized and evaluated in the present section.

THE PROBLEM OF DEFINITION

One of the major issues in the developmental psychology of religion, as in the psychology of adult religion, is the question of how "religion" is to be defined. A wide array of possible answers has been given to this question, and religion has been defined as a dominating purpose in life (Chaplin, 1948); a response to the supernatural (Koons, 1903); a need for security, achievement, and social consciousness (Manwell and Fahs, 1948); and as a habitual attitude toward society and toward the mysteries of life (Smith, 1936). Many more such definitions could be cited, but these will suffice to show the diversity of opinion among those attempting to describe the religion of childhood. The difficulty with all such definitions, from the operational point of view, is that they give no criteria for distinguishing between religious and nonreligious behavior. Without such criteria the labeling of certain needs, attitudes, or purposes as religious is purely arbitrary and gratuitous.

To make some headway on the problem of definition it is first of all necessary to step back and see religion as a whole before proceeding to those of its regions which are the special province of psychology. From this broader perspective, religion appears to have at least three more or less distinct areas, which might be called institutional, personal, and prepersonal religion. *Institutional religion* refers to all the formal aspects of religion including such things as theology, dogma, ritual, and church organization. *Personal religion,* on the other hand, includes the cognitive, affective, and motor responses which the components of institutional religion elicit in the individual. Finally, *prepersonal religion* includes all those responses which resemble those found in personal religion except that they appear prior to any contact with institutional religion. The faith and trust shown by the infant, for example, resemble affects experienced in connection with the deity but are originally experienced only in relation to the parents. So long as the responses are made to the parents and not to a deity they should, according to the terminology proposed here, be called prereligious.

From the point of view of these definitions, the developmental psychology of religion is concerned only with personal and prepersonal religion. It should be noted, however, that personal religion is defined in relation to institutional religion and is thus not independent of it. Said differently, it seems to the writer that it is impossible to classify any particular psychological attitude, need, or purpose as religious in and of itself and that it can be called religious only in so far as it becomes associated with elements of institutional religion. While this definition of personal religion may not satisfy everyone, it has the advantage of providing clear-cut criteria for deciding whether or not a response is to be called religious. In this connection it should be noted that the introduction of the term prepersonal religion enables us to talk about the religionlike responses that appear in very young children without at the same time putting us in the position of ascribing an awareness of theology or dogma to the newborn and toddler.

Although the phenomena of prereligion have been described and talked about in the pedagogical literature, most if not all the actual studies dealing with religious development have been exclusively concerned with personal religion. Adequately to describe these studies, however, it is necessary further to subdivide personal religion into its acquired and spontaneous components. *Acquired (personal) religion* refers to all those responses elicited by institutional religion that have been derived from religious instruction or example. A child's rote knowledge of certain prayers or his ability to recite the standard definition of religious terms would be instances of acquired religion. In addition to these acquired responses, however, there are others which arise out of the child's limited ability to grasp some of the abstract institutional terms and practices to which he is exposed either casually or through instruction. An example of spontaneous religion would be the response of the young boy who, having heard that God was everywhere, refused to occupy his favorite chair for fear of "sitting on God and hurting him."

To make these various relations among religious phenomena concrete, they are presented below in graphic form:

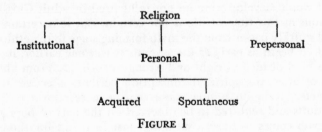

FIGURE 1

In the remainder of this paper the term "religion" will be used to refer to personal religion and the terms "acquired" and "spontaneous" religion will be used in the sense in which they have been defined in the preceding paragraphs.

DEVELOPMENTAL CHANGES IN SPONTANEOUS RELIGION

It is a common observation that the spontaneous responses elicited by institutional religion change with age in a more or less predictable sequence of stages. Young children, for example, tend to accept religious teaching uncritically and clothe it with anthropomorphic garments of their own design. Adolescents, on the other hand, tend to doubt a great deal of what they passively accepted as children. One explanation of this developmental sequence was put forth by G. Stanley Hall (1908), who argued that the spontaneous religion of the child recapitulated the religious development of mankind. Hall borrowed this recapitulation theory from the 19th century artist-biologist Ernst Haeckel who, on the basis of Fritz Muller's embryological studies, contended that ontogeny was the epitome of phylogeny. For Hall this meant that each stage of religious development could be explained as a manifestation of the child's racial inheritance.

A student of Hall's (Haslett, 1903) put the recapitulation theory of religious development in a much less embellished form than was possible for his exceedingly erudite mentor. Haslett described the theory as follows:

> In the earlier years of the child's life, he is in the animistic, fetishistic stage of religious development. He is then a nature worshipper. At about the fourth or fifth year he has passed into the mythopoeic or myth forming stage which he soon outgrows. The polytheistic stage is not clearly marked in the child's religious development and seems to be recapitulated very quickly. Just what condition religiously the child would develop were he not influenced by adult Christian conceptions at this time of life is not certain. But it is certain that the child quickly passes from the myth-forming stage to the ethical. Many children begin as early as the seventh year, some earlier, to manifest some kind of idea of right and wrong as such. . . . From about fourteen or after, the spiritual conception becomes effective in shaping character. Religion is now more than a mere ethical code formed by adults and *required* to be observed on the part of boys and girls. Religion comes to have a meaning, just as it did for those nations which developed a spiritual-ethical religion [1903, pp. 222-223].

Recapitulation theory never attained wide acceptance in psychology, just as the embryological recapitulation theory was never generally respectable in biology. According to Werner (1948):

1. There exist certain similarities between developmental series. These similarities, for instance, between the child's mentality and that of primitive man, cannot be reduced to conform with any law of recapitulation. *It is the very fact of development itself, in so far as it implies a change from generalized to more specialized forms, which gives the false impression of a recapitulation* and occasions certain parallel phenomena in two related genetic series.

2. For all practical purposes one may speak of a principle of parallelism: development in mental life follows certain general and formal rules whether it concerns the individual or the species. Such a principle implies that apart from general and formal similarities there do exist specific material differences in the comparable phenomena [pp. 25-26; italics added].

An example of what Werner calls "material differences" between the child's mind and the primitive mind is the case of animistic thinking. Anthropologists, following Tylor (1924), have concluded that animism involves the belief in spirits or in a soul. Piaget (1929), on the other hand, found that animism in children results from just the opposite, namely, the absence of a differentiation between self and world and hence the absence of a soul or spirit concept. It would be presumptuous to assume that Tylor was wrong and that primitive animism is the same as child animism or vice versa. Although less parsimonious, it seems more in line with the facts to assume that the animisms of the primitive and of the child are parallel rather than identical phenomena in the sense that both involve attributing life to things, but for different reasons.

In general, the bulk of present-day opinion seems to be that the spontaneous religion of the child follows a course determined by general principles of growth rather than by any law of recapitulation.

MECHANISMS OF TRANSITION FROM PRERELIGION TO PERSONAL RELIGION

A number of writers have attempted to derive personal religion from the responses originally made toward the parents. As Jones (1944) put it, "The religious life represents on a cosmic plane the emotions, fears and longings which arose in the child's relations to its parents." Such a position raises the question why the child should transfer these "emotions, fears and longings" from parent to deity. Two different accounts have been given, one by Bovet and the other by Freud.

Bovet (1928) contended that the child's first gods were his parents and that the conceptions and sentiments felt toward the deity were initially experienced in connection with his mother and father. To support the thesis of the relation between the filial and religious sentiments, Bovet cited a number of personal documents in which this identification was clearly expressed. Bovet, however, did not stop with demonstrating the isomorphism between the filial and religious sentiments. He also took up the question of how the transition between the two came about. According to Bovet, the growing child's increasing experience eventually discloses to him that the perfections he attributed to his parents are illusory, and this realization often comes suddenly and dramatically as it did to Edmund Gosse.

> My mother always deferred to my father and in his absence spoke of him to me as if he were all wise. I confused him in some sense with God; at all events I believed that my father knew everything and saw everything. One morning in my sixth year, my mother and I were alone in the morning room, when my father came in and announced some fact to us. I was standing on the rug gazing at him, and when he made his statement I remember turning quickly in embarrassment and looking into the fire. The shock to me was that of a thunderbolt, for what my father had said *was not true.* ... Here was the appalling discovery, never suspected before, that my father was not as God, and did not know everything. The shock was not caused by my suspicion that he was not telling the truth as it appeared to him but by the awful proof that he was not, as I had supposed, omniscient [cited by Bovet, 1928, pp. 33-34].

Bovet argued that the discovery by the young child that his parents were less than perfect was a moral and an intellectual *crisis* comparable to the commonly observed crisis of religious doubt in adolescence. The crisis of adolescence (in which the adolescent, through his exposure to science and history, comes to doubt the absolute affirmations he previously accepted from religion) was, according to Bovet, simply a repetition of the crisis in early childhood caused by the discrepancy between observed fact and the unquestioned belief in the perfection of the parent. This crisis in early childhood established the model for all later transfers of thought and feeling from one ideal figure to another. Bovet also held that the transfer of filial thoughts and sentiments to a deity could occur in steps and involve intermediaries such as ministers, priests, or political or military heroes who came to be believed in as God or perfection. Such intermediary beliefs also fall, one by one, in the face of experience and knowledge, until the child attributes perfection to God alone.

A somewhat different interpretation of the transformation of filial into religious behavior was given by Freud (1927). In Freud's view, the mother is the child's first love object who, through her ministrations, protects the child from frustration and anxiety. Later, in the first year of life, the father comes to play an increasingly prominent role in the child's life. The role is, however, an ambivalent one, for the father is an object of both love and fear. These ambivalent feelings toward the father are the ones which are later transferred to the God image. For Freud the precipitating crisis which causes man to transfer filial feelings to the gods is the discovery that he is "destined to remain a child forever, and that he can never do without protection against unknown and mighty powers: he creates for himself the gods, of whom he is afraid, whom he seeks to propitiate and to whom he nevertheless entrusts the task of protecting him" (p. 42).

In Freud's view, man is destined to remain a child in three connections: his continued helplessness in the face of nature, in the face of fate (as exemplified by death), and in the face of endless suffering arising from the instinctual renunciations required by culture. When man realizes that he will never be free of anxieties and dangers from nature, fate, and his own impulses, he reverts to the infantile prototype and seeks protection from the overwhelming anxiety of this discovery in an all-powerful father figure who will safeguard him as his real father did when he was a child.

If one compares the Freudian view with that of Bovet, the similarities lie in the fact that both derive the religious sentiments from the filial. On the other hand, Bovet assumes that the transfer of filial attitudes to the Deity comes about as a result of the *child's* discovery that his *parents* are not perfect and that he must seek perfection elsewhere. For Freud the transfer comes about because the *adult* discovers *his own helplessness* in the face of nature, fate, and his own instincts.

The only experimental evidence bearing directly on these hypotheses comes from two recent studies which have attempted to test the view that the conceptions of God and of parents are similar. Using the Q Technique, Nelson and Jones (1957) found that Deity conceptions were more closely related to the conception of the mother than they were to the conception of the father. Strunk (1959), using the same technique as Nelson and

Jones, obtained roughly similar results with the exception that the Father-Jesus conceptions were the most highly correlated of all. In general, both studies suggest that there is a positive correlation between conceptions of God and conceptions of the parents in agreement with the positions of both Freud and Bovet.

METHODS

The methods used to study religious development have varied according to whether the investigator was primarily interested in acquired or spontaneous religion. In general, the early investigators were concerned with acquired religion and used relatively structured tests whereas, on the whole, contemporary workers have been concerned with spontaneous religion and have employed more open-ended techniques.

ANECDOTAL OBSERVATIONS

The spontaneous remarks made by children with respect to religion have been collected by a number of investigators. Barnes (1892) was perhaps the most systematic in that he collected such remarks from children at successive age levels. Similar types of remarks have been collected and described by Sully (1895) and by the Scupins (cited by Werner, 1948). In recent years anecdotal observations have been employed by the Research Committee of the National Council of Churches of Christ, which requested parents to collect their children's unsolicited questions about religious matters. While collections of anecdotes are important as a starting point for more systematic forms of investigation, they cannot provide the facts on which the developmental psychology of religion must ultimately rest.

PERSONAL DOCUMENTS

A number of investigators (including James, 1902, and Bovet, 1928) have used excerpts from letters, autobiographies, and personal documents to reveal some aspects of religion in childhood. Bovet cited the autobiography of Edmund Gosse, the art critic, because Gosse so clearly described the religious convictions and disillusionments he experienced as a young child. James (1892, 1902) used to excellent advantage the deaf-mute D'Estrella's description of his spontaneously constructed religion in which he regarded the moon as a deity. Personal documents, like anecdotal remarks, are useful starting points for more systematic research but cannot substitute for such research.

QUESTIONNAIRE METHODS

The questionnaire has been the most frequently used method for studying the development of religious behavior and experience. In terms of structure, the most highly directive tests include yes or no items such as this one: "Do you think religion means obeying God's laws?" (Franzblau, 1934). Almost equally high in structure are the multiple-choice tests containing items such as: "The book of Romans was written by: Peter, Paul, James, John" (Hightower, 1930). Somewhat less structured are openended tests that include items like the following from Ross (1950): "What would you say is irreligious about your own ideas and conduct?" Least structured of all are composition tests that contain items such as the following: "When do you feel closest to God?" (Elkind and Elkind, 1962). The difficulties with all types of questionnaires are, however, legion, and future work with these instruments must take into account the current recognition of such factors as social desirability and response set.

SEMICLINICAL INTERVIEW

This method was introduced by Piaget (1929), who adapted psychiatric interview techniques to the questioning of children. The aim of these interviews is to obtain what Piaget calls the child's *spontaneous or liberated convictions* as opposed to *answers at random, suggested answers,* and *romancing* (spoofing) *answers.* To attain this end the child is seen in a familiar setting in which there are few distractions. The adult tries not to suggest to the child and, at the same time, tries to get him to follow his own train of thought. Thus the adult attempts to be directive and nondirective at the same time. If an answer is suspect, the examiner questions all around it and offers countersuggestions to test its strength and fixedness in the child's thought. Further checks on the spontaneity of the child's thought are made by means of group comparisons. Piaget (1929) suggested three criteria for inferring the genuineness of a spontaneous developmental sequence: (a) uniformity of response among children of the same level, (b) transition with age from a global to a more adultlike conception, (c) the presence of adherences (ideas from an earlier age level) embedded in the generally global thought of the young child. The semiclinical interview thus provides a method by which suggestion, social desirability, and response set can be, if not overcome, at least identified and dealt with.

GRAPHIC AND PICTORIAL METHODS

In the more recent studies of religious development there has been a trend away from the traditional questionnaire and an increasing use of graphic and pictorial techniques. Although several early investigators included drawings of the Deity in their studies, the first major use of this technique was made by Harms (1944), who analyzed the drawings of God made by several thousand children and adolescents. Other investigators have tried to combine the advantages of the verbal and graphic methods and have devised what amounts to religious projective techniques. Godin and Coupex (1957), for example, published a set of "Religious Projective Pictures" and tables of normative responses to the pictures. Likewise, Malhoit (1947) has devised a religious equivalent of "The Children's Apperception Test." In America a similar tack has been taken by Graebner (1960), who devised a set of captioned pictures for investigating children's God conceptions. These graphic and pictorial methods appear to have considerable promise for eliciting types of material not previously encountered in studies of religious development.

While this catalogue of methods does not exhaust those which have been used to investigate religious development, they will suffice as a general introduction to the studies presented in the next section.

EMPIRICAL FINDINGS

Studies dealing with the religious development of children are widely scattered in time, uncommonly varied in method, and quite often pedagogical in aim. To introduce some order into this array of investigations it is useful to divide them into three broad classes. In the first group of studies, which might be called *descriptive,* the aim is to observe and classify hitherto unexplored religious responses. The classic example of such an investigation is James' (1902) *The Varieties of Religious Experience.* The second group of studies, which might be called *developmental,* aims at delineating the content and/or form of religious behavior at successive age levels. An example of such an investigation is the work of Harms (1944), which dealt with developmental changes in the child's manner of portraying the Deity. A final group of studies, which might be called *cor-*

relational, seems to be directed at discovering the relationships between religious behavior and other variables which are either religious or secular in nature. An example of such a study is the work of Mathias (1943), who attempted to relate conservative and liberal God conceptions to moral and ethical behaviors.

Like so many neat classificatory schemes, the one described here does not adequately represent what has actually been done. For the most part, the studies in the field are of a mixed breed and contain various combinations of descriptive, developmental, and correlational approaches. Yet, for purposes of clarity, the threefold classification will be adhered to and the studies will be arbitrarily picked apart and the pieces placed within their appropriate categories. In this way, all the correlational work dealing with the relation of sex to religiosity, for example, can be brought together in one place even though the individual studies in which the results were obtained were otherwise classed as developmental or descriptive. It is not the best solution, but it makes heuristic sense.

DESCRIPTIVE STUDIES

Religious Conversion. Of all religious phenomena studied by psychology, conversion is by far the most popular. McKeefry (1949), for example, reviewed 32 studies of this topic carried out since the beginning of this century. More recently, Argyle (1958) summarized much of the statistical work on conversion experiences. Since the broad summary approach has been taken both by McKeefry and Argyle, only a single, representative study will be presented here. For this purpose, the work of Starbuck (1900), which, after 65 years, still retains its prominent position in the field, is a logical choice.

Starbuck's general orientation to the study of religion was that it could be investigated scientifically with profit both to psychology and to religion. He was convinced that psychology could analyze and organize the facts of religious consciousness and that it could ascertain the laws which underlie its growth and character. Starbuck used the word *growth* in the literal sense and was concerned with the question of how individuals become religious. It was Starbuck's concern with religious growth that led him to the study of religious conversion, which he defined as "characterized by more or less sudden changes of character from evil to goodness, from sinfulness to righteousness and from indifference to spiritual insight and activity" (1900, p. 21). Thus, for Starbuck, conversion was a growth process and he wished to study all the psychological manifestations which preceded, accompanied, and followed this experience.

For his method, Starbuck used a modification of the question list first introduced by Darwin and Galton. He composed 11 questions which required his subjects to introspect about their religious growth and describe it in the manner of an autobiography. The 11 questions were administered to young adults. About 200 subjects were used for the major analyses, although a much larger number was used for some statistical tabulations, such as the age of conversion.

Although there is no space to summarize all of Starbuck's findings and conclusions, a few will be presented to convey the general tenor and outcome of his work. With respect to the age of conversion, Starbuck found empirical confirmation for Hall's dictum that conversion was a phenomenon of adolescence. While the curve for age of conversion began at about age 7 or 8, it did not begin to ascend rapidly until adolescence, where it reached a peak at about age 15-16 after which it rapidly declined, becoming asymptotic at about age 25. Conversion generally appeared earlier in girls than it did in boys, although there was not a very close relation between age of conversion and age of puberty.

In looking at the motives for conversion, Starbuck found at least 8 different forces to be of importance. The most frequently mentioned among these were: fear of death and hell; remorse or conviction for sin; following a moral ideal; imitation; and social pressure. With regard to the experiences which preceded conversion, Starbuck found that while the sense of sin was always present, different individuals reacted to this sense of sin in different ways. One group reacted positively and envisaged the ideal life, a second group reacted negatively and envisaged the sinful life, while a third group was intermediate. In a sense, Starbuck made a distinction between individuals who used conversion to move away from something bad and those who used it to move toward something good, a dichotomy which has both an ancient and a modern ring.

Starbuck had much more to say about conversion and religious development, but this capsule presentation of his findings and conclusions may suffice to indicate why his book has remained the classic work on conversion.

Varieties of Religious Experience. In his discussion of religious experience, James (1902) explicitly chose extreme cases because of his belief "that we learn most about a thing when we view it under a microscope, as it were, or in its most exaggerated form" (p. 39). There is also value, however, in cataloguing the more ordinary forms of religious experience common to the average man and child. Two recent investigations have dealt with this subject.

Klingberg (1959) had 630 Swedish children aged 9 to 13 write compositions completing the statement, "Once when I thought about God." When Klingberg analyzed these compositions, she found 4 types of situations described by her subjects. In order of frequency these were: (1) situations of distress; (2) experiences in nature; (3) moral experiences; (4) formal worship experiences. Klingberg also analyzed her data with respect to the depth of experience reflected in the compositions and found that prayer experiences seemed to involve the deepest emotional reactions.

The writer and his wife (Elkind and Elkind, 1962) recently undertook a similar investigation. We assumed that religious experiences could be defined in terms of the situations that occasioned them. Two types of situations were distinguished. *Recurrent situations* were those which were habitual and to some extent consciously chosen, such as church attendance. *Acute situations*, on the other hand, were those which were unusual and unexpected, such as an accident or a sudden death in the family.

To determine whether this distinction had meaning for young people and to obtain some idea of the range of recurrent and acute situations, 144 ninth-grade students were asked by their English teacher to compose two paragraphs in answer to the following questions: (1) When do you feel closest to God? (2) Have you ever had a particular experience when you felt especially close to God?

The questions did elicit two quite different types of situations with very little overlapping. The 6 different recurrent situations in their order of frequency were: church situations, solitary situations, anxiety and fear situations, worry situations, prayer situations, and moral action situations. The 5 different acute situations in order of frequency were: appreciation situations (thanking God for something), meditation situations, initiation situations, lamentation situations (in connection with a death), and revelation situations. Apparently there is a wide variety of commonplace religious experiences in addition to the extreme types described by James (1902).

Of less direct relevance to the issue of varieties of religious experience is the Pixley and Beekman (1944) work dealing with faith among high-school seniors. These investigators queried almost 3700 students regarding their attitudes toward church attendance, prayer, and the role of religion in their everyday lives. For present purposes only the responses to the prayer question are of immediate interest. In order of frequency the reasons for prayer were: to derive personal benefits, to express thanks, to talk to God, to ask for guidance, to comply with habit, to seek comfort, to ask for help for others, and to ask for forgiveness. According to Pixley and Beekman, these prayer experiences derived from the adolescent's feelings of loneliness, guilt, and insecurity.

DEVELOPMENTAL STUDIES

The Child's Conception of God. By far the majority of studies in religious development have dealt with the meanings that the term "God" has for children. The evidence regarding the child's conception of God is, however, conflicting, probably because of what was discussed earlier about the structure present in tests of religious development. By and large, those studies which have used the most structured tests have found only slight age differences, whereas those which have employed relatively unstructured tests have revealed fairly definite stages in the attainment of the God conception. In reviewing these investigations the studies using structured tests will be taken up first.

One of the earliest studies of the God conception was made by Barnes (1892) as part of a larger investigation which will be described later. Barnes had mothers and teachers carry out conversations with children starting from such questions as, "God, where is He? What does He do? Why cannot we see Him?" Some 27 children were interviewed in this way. Barnes found that the mental images of God tended to be "misty and indistinct" but that more than half the children thought of Him as a great and good man. "He is generally an old man with a long white beard and flowing white garments." God's omnipotence, in the sense of His being able to do anything, was generally grasped by the children, but few were able to conceptualize His omnipresence. Although Barnes did not deal with age changes as such, his findings are typical for young children.

More than 10 years later Tanner (1906) used Barnes' questions with 315 children aged 3 to 15. Tanner's subjects were of Pennsylvania Dutch origin and with two exceptions had United Brethren, Lutheran, Methodist, and Presbyterian affiliations. When she examined her results, Tanner found that the character of the answers was not apparently affected by the sect to which the child belonged or by his age. With respect to the God concept, Tanner found that in answering the question, "God, where is He?" 85% of the children said that He was in heaven; 8% said He was everywhere, and 5% admitted ignorance. Answers to the question dealing with what God does were much vaguer, 21% saying that God helped them, 12% saying that He taught them to be good, and 41% confessing that they did not know.

The next major study dealing with the God concept was most probably Bose's (1929) investigation of religious concepts of children. Bose was familiar with the work of Barnes and Tanner and tried to improve on their techniques. He first gave some 500 children a free-association test on which they were to write whatever came to mind in response to a clue religious word. The clue words were culled from religious education materials and were the words most commonly presented in these materials. Bose tabulated the 5 most frequent associations to each clue word and built a multiple-choice test incorporating them. The great innovation in Bose's multiple-choice test was the fact that all of the alternatives were spontaneous associations given by children and were not arbitrarily chosen by an examiner. Bose administered his test—containing 100 concepts—to 2500 young people between the ages of 8 and 18 who were attending a variety of church schools. His findings regarding the God conception were that 67.2% thought of Him as the Heavenly Father, 12.0% viewed Him as the Holy Spirit, and 2.2% conceived Him as a good man. With respect to the age factor, Bose concluded that in general the junior children seemed to understand religious terms as well as senior students, but that there was some slight tendency for older subjects to conceive the Deity in terms comparable to the adult conception. Like Tanner, Bose was inclined to dismiss age changes as relatively insignificant.

In a study related to religious education, MacLean (1930) devised interviews (for children under 9) and several questionnaires (for children from 9 to 14) to test children's agreement or disagreement with the many thoughts about the Deity presented in Sunday-school literature. On the basis of his results MacLean concluded that young people manifested an astonishing lack of discriminative thought with respect to the Deity. "Ideas with little similarity and sometimes ideas which are flatly contradictory are all frequently accepted by the same children as true" (p. 113). He also observed, "that children's responses show that their ideas are strikingly similar to ideas found in Sunday school literature" (p. 117). Although MacLean did note some age differences, his method of scoring was such as to obscure them.

Still another approach to measuring the God conception was taken by Mathias (1943), who, in his attempt to relate the idea of God to conduct, was forced to construct an "Idea of God Scale." Like Bose, Mathias tried to get at children's spontaneous thought before making up his questionnaire. For his study proper Mathias employed 270 subjects ranging in age from 10 to 13. Results showed a tendency for ideas of God as All-Powerful, as Dependence, as Love, and as Nonexistent to increase with age, while ideas of God as Fear, as Impersonal, and as Mystery showed a tendency to decrease with age. Mathias was cautious in evaluating the consistent though slight age differences, and concluded: "Evidently grade in school is of significance, but there is no sure prediction that children of an advanced grade will have a better average score than those of an earlier grade" (p. 54). As in the previous studies, evidence for age changes in conceptualization appeared but so timorously that they could be easily dismissed.

In a more recent study Graebner (1960), in cooperation with the Lutheran Education Association, devised an "Ideas About God Inventory." Thirty-eight captioned pictures were drawn up to provide the child with an opportunity to answer questions about the relationship of God to the depicted persons. For example, one drawing portrayed a boy in his pajamas clutching a teddy bear and standing in night shadows. Under the drawing the caption read, "What would God tell this boy who is alone in the dark?" None of the pictures contained any direct religious content or symbolism. Graebner administered this test to 977 children who were attending Lutheran Parish Schools and enrolled in grades 1 to 8. The test was administered individually to young children and as a group test to the older children. With respect to age changes in God conception, Graebner concluded: "When the answers for most of the questions in the study were reviewed along a grade continuum, it was found that similarity of answers at all grade levels was the rule rather than the exception. Many tests of significance were applied to pairs of percentages of answers by children of higher and lower grade levels on the same question (s) with no significance found" (p. 75). On the other hand, Graebner did note age trends occurring in the responses to one or two of his pictures.

In all of the studies reviewed so far, the tests have been more or less structured despite preliminary work to get at the spontaneous thoughts of the child. In the studies reviewed below, less structured tests were used and more evidence of marked age differences in the conceptualization of the Deity was obtained.

The most compelling evidence for age changes in the God conception comes from the work of Harms (1944). Harms was critical of the verbal question approach to the study of religious development and felt that it tapped only the rational and intellectual part of personal religion. He recalled Wundt's question about why man should have created the language of music, of fine arts, and of poetry if he could say everything with prosaic words. Harms acknowledged his indebtedness to Lévy-Bruhl and to C. G. Jung for the views that the most powerful religious meanings lie in that region of consciousness (or of the collective unconscious) which the average person is unable to verbalize. Thus to Harms the verbal approach to the study of religious consciousness missed the most significant aspect of personal religion.

To get at these affective and nonverbal religious meanings, Harms had his subjects draw pictures of how they imagined God looked. The subjects were entire classes of children from public and private schools, chosen without regard to their religious affiliation, and ranging in age from 3 to 18. The instructions for young children were first to imagine how God would look to them if they were to picture Him in their minds or to imagine the highest being they thought to exist. Older children, who apparently objected to imagining God as such, were given the option of drawing what to them represented religion or the highest ideal expressed in religion.

Although he did not describe his method of analysis, Harms arrived at three broad classes of drawings which were related to age and reflected what he took to be universal developmental stages in the growth of religious experience.

At the first stage, ages 3 to 6, children drew God as a king, or as a daddy of all children, or as someone living in a golden house above the clouds. Harms called this the *fairy-tale stage*.

Children of elementary-school age (6 to 11) were classed by Harms as being in the *realistic stage* with respect to their drawings of the Deity. According to Harms, children at this stage were willing to accept the teachings and concepts of institutional religion. Conventional symbols such as the crucifix and the Jewish star were the most frequently chosen representations of God. Somewhat less often these children drew priests or priestlike persons serving as mediators of God. Even when persons such as the God father, angels, or saints were portrayed, they were depicted as human figures who were helping, assisting, influencing, and supervising people on earth. As Harms used the term, realism seemed to refer to a personalization of deitic conceptions.

Among adolescents, of whom he tested 4000, Harms found a great diversity of religious expression and therefore termed this age period the *individualistic stage*. Harms was, however, able to divide his adolescent subjects into three more or less distinct groups. One group of adolescents was inclined to express their religious imaginations in a conventional way and drew such things as a crucifix, a madonna, gates of heaven, conventional angels, synagogue scenes, Moses and the burning bush, etc. A second group of adolescents expressed their religious imaginations in highly original and unique drawings. Among these young people Harms found abstract or semiabstract drawings and symbolic drawings in which the symbolism was unconventional, such as a sunrise or light breaking through a dark sky. The third group of adolescents expressed their religious imaginations in a rather surprising way. Among these young people Harms found what he regarded as religious and cult motifs which were never directly experienced by the persons who drew them and which were quite foreign to the milieu of their upbringing.

Of relevance to Harms' stages is the work of Smith (1941), who described the 4 stages in the development of religious emotion as: "(1) emotional, imaginative enthusiasm that has little basis in fact, (2) the opposite extreme of hard realism with little emphasis on imagination, (3) preadolescent doubt or fluctuation between idealism and realism, and (4) a more steady and practical idealism" (p. 280). It is not clear from Smith's presentation, however, whether these stages—which closely parallel those of Harms—are based upon experimentation or upon general observations of children. In another study carried out in India, Loomba (1944) also found similar stages of religious development, although he did not use drawings. Of direct relevance to Harms' stages is a recent investigation by McCann (1955), who reported intensive interview studies of persons "in process religiously." He found that 82% of his subjects (college students) had as children a pictorial, anthropomorphic deity conception. Later a majority arrived at a deconcretized, spiritualized (abstract) conception.

Considering the work on the God conception as a whole, it is perhaps justified to conclude that in so far as acquired or Sunday-school meanings are concerned, there appears to be relatively little change with age in the way God is conceived. On the other hand, when the child's spontaneous thoughts about the Deity are explored, one finds what appear to be definite, age-related changes in the child's conceptualization of God.

Other Traditional Religious Concepts. Concepts such as heaven and hell, the Devil, angels, the Trinity, and other religious concepts have received far less experimental attention than has the God concept. The work that has been done suggests that such terms elicit a rich store of spontaneous responses in addition to their acquired definitions.

Although he collected only anecdotal remarks, the work of Brown (1892) deserves mention here. One of the categories into which these remarks fell was "Thoughts and Reasonings about God, Christ, and Heaven." Examples of such remarks are given below.

> Obs. 95 (7 years): S's little twin sister had just died two days before. When told that he had lost his little sister, he replied, "Well, I suppose she has got to Heaven by this time."
> Obs. 100 (9 years): "I guess Jack won't go to Heaven when he dies if he runs away much more."
> Obs. 102 (8 or 9 years): There was a picture, in a book, of Christ walking on the sea. E saw it. E: "Didn't He sink?" (said with great eagerness). I: "No." E: "Well, He was pretty light, wasn't He?"

Many more such anecdotes could be given but these are sufficient to convey the concrete way in which children tended to interpret standard theological conceptions.

In the same year and in the same journal that Brown presented his anecdotal records, Barnes (1892) published his questionnaire study on the

"Theological Life of a California Child" which was mentioned earlier in connection with the God concept. In addition to the interview material mentioned above, Barnes collected close to 1100 compositions written by young people from 6 to 20 on the subjects of heaven and hell. Barnes found that heaven was most commonly described as a beautiful place but that it was also frequently described as a city, a mansion, a palace, a fine house, a garden or park. It was usually described as having streets, gates, plants, flowers, birds, and trees. The one thing which was most associated with heaven was gold, and it was thought to have gold streets and walks.

Angels were found by Barnes to be most often described as having wings and looking like people dressed in white. Many young people thought of angels as women and a few regarded them as fairies, ghosts, birds, or as little babies. Barnes noted that his subjects had great difficulty when it came to describing what angels did. Most of the children said the angels flew around, played on harps, and helped God. A few children mentioned the monotony of angel life in heaven. To other children the freedom from work enjoyed by the angels was heaven's chief attraction. Thus Barnes found two types of heaven, "one severe and restrained and the other like a free day in the open countryside" (p. 445).

With respect to the Devil and his abode, Barnes found that these were described less frequently and in less detail than were the angels and heaven. What the children did describe, however, was more uniform than what they had said about heaven and its inhabitants. As a typical portrayal of the Devil, Barnes cited one boy's description: "I thought the Devil had a man's head with a long hooked nose and a pointed chin with an ox's ears and horns. He had a tail with a ball of three points at the end. He carried a spear with three prongs the same as his tail. He could spit fire and had a tongue like a snake" (p. 445). Hell was described as a fire and sometimes as a furnace. In general, however, Barnes found that hell and heaven were infrequently mentioned in the compositions and tended to disappear entirely from the replies written by children over 10 years of age.

By and large, the results of studies dealing with the conceptions of heaven, hell, soul, etc. seem to show that these are conceived in conventional form with considerable spontaneous elaboration. A definitive developmental study of these conceptions remains to be carried out.

Development of Religious Identity. Religious identity can be defined in terms of the spontaneous meanings children attach to their religious denomination. A developmental study of these meanings was undertaken by the writer, who investigated the growth of religious identity among Jewish (Elkind, 1961), Catholic (Elkind, 1962), and Congregational Protestant (Elkind, in press) children.

In these studies the method was a somewhat standardized version of Piaget's semiclinical interview. Each of the children was individually interviewed and asked 6 questions which were the starting point of the discussion. The questions were, with the appropriate denominational term inserted: (a) Is your family ...? Are you ...? (b) Are all boys and girls in the world ...? (c) Can a dog or cat be ...? (d) How do you become a ...? (e) How can you tell a person is ...? (f) Can you be ... and American at the same time? In order to clarify the meaning of the child's responses and to insure that these were firmly rooted in his thought, additional questions, following no set pattern, were asked. More than 700 children were examined and Piaget's (1929) criteria for justifying a developmental stage classification of data were applied to the interview materials. The results met all three criteria and it was possible to distinguish three fairly distinct stages in the attainment of religious identity which held true for Jewish, Protestant, and Catholic children.

At the first stage (usually ages 5 to 7) the child had only a global, undifferentiated conception of his denomination as a kind of proper name. Although he acknowledged being a Jew, Protestant, or Catholic, he confused these names with the terms for race and nationality, for example:

Sid (6.3): What is a Jew? "A person." How is a Jewish person different from a Catholic? "Cause some people have black hair and some people have blond."

Mel (5.9): How is a Jewish person different from a Catholic? "He comes from a different country." Which one? "Israel."

Furthermore, at this stage the child regarded having a denominational name as incompatible with possessing a racial or national designation. For example, it was common for the child at this stage to reply, in answer to the question about being an American and a Jew (Protestant, Catholic) at the same time that, "You can't have two." That is to say, because you can't have two names.

Children at the second stage (usually ages 7 to 9) had a concretely differentiated conception of their denomination. Their conception was concrete in the sense that they used observable features or actions to define their denomination and their conception was differentiated because they used these same observable features to distinguish among persons belonging to different denominations. For example:

Mar. (7.9): What is a Jew? "A person who goes to Temple or Hebrew school."

Bill (8.0): What is a Catholic? "He goes to mass every Sunday and goes to Catholic school."

Ron (7.9): Can you be a Catholic and a Protestant at the same time? "No." Why not? "Cause you couldn't go to two churches."

Unlike the first-stage children, young people at the second stage said they could be an American and their denomination at the same time. The reasons given in explanation were concrete and personal, to the effect that "You can live in America and go to church" or "I'm an American and I'm a Protestant."

Third-stage children (usually ages 10 to 12) demonstrated an abstract, differentiated conception of their denomination. It was an abstract conception in the sense that these children no longer defined their denomination by mentioning names or observable activities but rather by mentioning nonobservable mental attributes such as belief and understanding. For example:

Bi (12.0): What is a Catholic? "A person who believes in the truths of the Roman Catholic Church." Can a dog or a cat be Catholic? "No, because they don't have a brain or intellect."

Sed (11.10): What is a Jew? "A person who believes in one God and doesn't believe in the New Testament."

When third-stage children were asked the question whether they could be American and their denomination at the same time, they replied that one was a nationality and the other was a religion and that they were two different things.

As in the Harms (1944) study, the use of an unstructured technique revealed what appeared to be fairly distinct stages in the development of spontaneous religious conceptions.

CORRELATIONAL STUDIES

Studies aimed at exploring the relations between religious and nonreligious variables can be divided into two types depending upon whether the religious or the secular variable is the focus of study. In the *religiocentric* studies, the religious variable is on stage, but in the *seculocentric* studies, the secular variable upstages the religious factor. Both types of study have contributed considerably to the knowledge about the variables which condition, and are conditioned by, religious development.

RELIGIOCENTRIC STUDIES

Religious Development and Sunday-School Attendance. Although apparently no investigator has made the effect of Sunday-school attendance on religious understanding a major focus of study, many persons exploring religious development considered the relationship in their investigations.

In Bose's (1929) study (described earlier), concerned with the religious concepts of children, he found that church-school attendance had no measurable effect on children's understanding of religious terms. Children who attended church school for only a brief period did as well as those who attended it for quite long periods. Bose also administered his test to a group of boys who attended a boys' club but who did not attend a church school. Boys who had no church-school experience performed only slightly below those who had considerable religious education.

Results obtained by Mathias (1943) are in general agreement with those attained by Bose. Using his own measure of the God concept, Mathias related it to regularity of Sunday-school attendance and to length of time attended. The correlation between regularity of Sunday-school attendance and the traditional God conception was +.0161 while for years of Sunday-school attendance and traditional God conception it was a slightly higher value, +.1018. Apparently neither regularity nor length of Sunday-school attendance had any significant effect upon the child's conception of the deity. In accord with the results of Bose and Mathias, Graebner (1960) found that children who did not attend Sunday school gave the same answers to the "Idea of God Inventory" as did children who had attended Sunday school for varying lengths of time.

In a recent study Hyde (1961) examined some 2000 English young people between the ages of 11 and 18. He used three types of tests, including a questionnaire, a concept test wherein subjects agreed or disagreed with certain statements, and a multiple-choice concept test. Hyde found that there was little change in positive attitudes toward the church among churchgoing adolescents, while a sharp decline in such attitudes was apparent in nonchurchgoing groups. The same relationship held true for adolescent conceptions of God, with no change among churchgoers and deterioration of the conception among nonchurchgoers. Hyde concluded that in general, religious growth continued during adolescence among those youths who maintained their church affiliation but that no further religious growth occurred among adolescents who broke away from the church.

The results of Hyde's study, which show that church attendance has an effect on religious conceptions, does not really contradict the findings of Bose, Mathias, and Graebner. The reason is that the latter investigations were dealing with children and the formation of conceptions, whereas Hyde was dealing with adolescents and the deterioration of religious ideas. It is not contradictory to argue that Sunday-school or church attendance has no differential effect on concept formation but may prevent religious concept deterioration.

Of indirect relevance to the question of church-school attendance and religiosity are the studies of Woodward (1932) and Symington (1935) dealing with the effects of Sunday-school attendance on the religious conservatism or liberalism of adults. In the Woodward study 384 adults, including theological students, members of an interdenominational conference, members of a philosophy of education class, and an atheist forum were given a complex 88-item questionnaire. Included in the questionnaire were questions about Sunday-school attendance as well as liberal vs. conservative religious views. Woodward found a correlation of .43 between religious conservatism and church-school attendance.

Symington (1935) gave the "YMCA Test of Religious Thinking" to 612 young adults from various communities and colleges, and from both conservative and liberal religious backgrounds. One of Symington's many findings about the groups was related to reports of their years of attendance at Sunday school. The results indicated that the more years a person had attended a conservative type of Sunday school, the more conservative was his religious thinking, and that the same relationship obtained between years of attendance at a liberal Sunday school and liberal religious thinking. Symington concluded that years spent at Sunday school had a positive effect upon the adult's liberal or conservative religious thinking.

Results obtained by Woodward and Symington seem to contradict the findings of the earlier studies mentioned which found no relation between

Sunday-school attendance and quality of religious thought. It may be, however, that the Sunday-school influence has a delayed effect which does not appear until young adulthood. This does not necessarily mean that the teachings of the Sunday school are given renewed credence in young adulthood, only that at this time there seems to be, in a majority of young people, a felt need for a religious orientation in their lives (Allport, 1950). It would not be surprising if such an orientation should follow in the direction given it in childhood.

Religious Development and Sex. Studies of adult religious experience and behavior have consistently shown women to be more religious than men on every criterion of religiosity that has been employed. Argyle (1958), for example, has collated a large number of such studies and brought their findings, with respect to sex differences, together in tables which show that women consistently attend church and say private prayers more often than do men. They are also consistently more conservative in their beliefs. From the developmental point of view the question is at what age do these sex differences in religiosity begin to appear?

As far as children are concerned, sex differences appear to play little or no role in the attainment of religious conceptions. In MacLean's study (1930) of the God concept in Protestant children, for example, he found only slight sex differences and these were inconsistent. Of the 50 children displaying the most liberal conceptions 58% were girls, while of the 50 children displaying the most conservative conceptions 68% were girls. Graebner (1960) also found no differences between 6- to 13-year-old boys and girls in their performance on the "Concept of God Inventory." Likewise, Elkind (1961, 1962) found no sex differences in level of denominational concept attainment among children of elementary-school age.

In contrast to this work with children, the work with adolescents has revealed some apparent sex differences. Franzblau (1934), in his study of Jewish adolescents, found that girls tended to accept more traditional beliefs than did boys. Although the mean difference in traditional beliefs was not great, it was statistically significant. The study by Elkind and Elkind (1962) also reported sex differences in the frequency with which young adolescents reported particular types of recurrent religious experience. More girls than boys reported religious experience in solitude whereas the reverse held true for moral-action experience.

As a whole, then, the evidence regarding sex differences in religious development suggests that they do not play a significant role until adolescence.

Religious Development and IQ. Studies of religious development in children have shown that brighter children have a better understanding of religious conceptions and that brighter adolescents tend to be more liberal in their thinking about religious dogmas.

With respect to children's understanding of religious conceptions, Bose (1929) found a low but positive correlation (.20) between intelligence as measured by the Binet test and the understanding of the 100 religious terms on his (Bose's) test of religious concepts. Mathias (1943) obtained results similar to those of Bose. Using the CAVD achievement tests, he found a correlation of +.26 between composite (complexity of conception) idea-of-God scores and intelligence quotients obtained from the CAVD. More recently, Graebner (1960) obtained a like result when he examined God concepts from the point of view of mental levels.

Other studies have shown that IQ tends to be related to liberalism in religious thinking among adolescents. Franzblau (1934) found that IQ was negatively related to acceptance of traditional religious dogmas. He also found, however, that mental age showed an even higher negative correlation with acceptance of traditional beliefs than did IQ. He concluded that mental maturity, rather than rate of mental growth, was the most significant factor in the acceptance or rejection of venerable religious ideas.

Of less direct bearing on the issue of IQ and religious conservatism in young people is the same relation observed in young adults, namely college students. Sinclair (1930) presented his subjects with a "Point Scale Self-Rating" test to differentiate between those who did and those who did not profess the experience of the Divine Presence. He then compared those who did and did not profess such an experience on a variety of tests, including some of mental ability. As a result of this comparison Sinclair concluded: "In mental traits the negative (those who did not profess the experience) is decidedly superior. This appears not only in the intelligence tests, where the advantage is most apparent, but also in those tests which measure such auxiliary capacities as observation, memory, and association and ideation" (p. 38).

In another study, Howells (1928) adapted the "Self-Rating Scale" devised by Sinclair and Starbuck to discriminate between religious radicals and conservatives among 542 students of elementary psychology. Fifty of the most extreme radicals and 50 of the most extreme conservatives were chosen for study. Howells compared the two groups on such things as reproductive imagination, memory for objects, reconstructive imagination, association of objects, maze problems, rational judgment, etc. After reviewing the results of these tests he commented:

> In all the tests of intellectual ability the typical conservative always made the poorer score. The facts (1) that in most of the tests the differences are large enough practically to guarantee that similar tests of a large number of similarly selected sample groups would show differences of the same kind, and (2) that the different bits of evidence are mutually supporting, would seem to constitute fairly convincing evidence that the students who accept conservative statements in the criterion [test] are, in general, relatively inferior in intellectual ability [p. 47].

The results for adolescents and young adults are straightforward as far as IQ and religious conservatism are concerned. Whether or not the same holds true for elementary-school children remains to be determined.

SECULOCENTRIC STUDIES

Religious Behavior, Character, and Conduct. Quite a number of investigations have been concerned with the relation of religious instruction, Biblical knowledge, and religious conservatism or liberalism, to character as it is manifested in conduct. By and large the results have been negative.

One of the earliest of these studies was carried out as part of the Character Education Inquiry under the direction of Hartshorne and May (1928). As part of their larger investigation Hartshorne and May compared the deceptiveness of children receiving religious education with those children not receiving such instruction. There is no space to describe all the ingenious tests used to measure deception; a typical one will have to suffice. The "Information Test" consisted of 28 multiple-choice items. The child was required to circle his choice in ink and was not allowed to hand in his paper until he had at least attempted every question. To cheat on this test the child had to erase the ink mark when he was correcting his own paper.

Tests of deception were administered to public-school children whose enrollment or lack of enrollment in Sunday schools was known. For one school system including 945 children, 38% of the Sunday-school population cheated at school as opposed to 43% of the non-Sunday-school children. On the other hand, 38% of the Sunday-school population cheated on work taken home in comparison to only 34% of the non-Sunday-school population. Hartshorne and May also correlated regularity of Sunday-school attendance with deceptiveness and found it to be zero. Summarizing their findings, these investigators concluded: "Yet so far as the facts go, we may say that neither the length of time that children are associated with Sunday school nor the regularity of their attendance seems to be at all associated with their tendency to deceive either at school or on work taken home" (p. 360).

In a study similar to that of Hartshorne and May, Hightower (1930) explored the relation of Biblical information to character and conduct. Hightower tested 485 children both for knowledge of the Bible and for their tendencies toward cheating and lying as well as for their tendencies toward loyalty and service. After presenting his results, Hightower concluded: "Within the limits of this study, there appears to be no relationship of any consequence between Biblical information and the different phases of conduct studied" (p. 33).

The work of Franzblau (1934) has already been mentioned in other connections. The major purpose of his study was, however, to relate religious belief to character measures. Using a carefully constructed "Idea of God Test"—which measured the conservative dimension of religious belief—he related scores obtained on it with various character measures such as "The Good Citizenship Test," "The Ethical Judgment Test," and "The Cooperation and Persistence Tests." Franzblau found no relation between acceptance of traditional beliefs and cooperativeness, persistence, or readiness to confess to socially undesirable conduct, to justify such conduct, or to report other children who were guilty of it.

Perhaps the most comprehensive study yet made of religious conceptions and conduct was carried out by Mathias (1943). The "Idea of God Test" constructed by Mathias has already been described. The test was administered to 135 boys and 135 girls who were also given tests of suggestibility, emotional stability, cooperation, honesty, high motives, social functioning, and school deportment. Mathias found that scores representing a mature God concept had a low but positive correlation with character measures. Mature God ideas were most highly correlated with high motives in conduct, self-functioning, and suggestibility. Correlations between mature God-concept scores and various measures of honesty were all positive but below +.10.

Although the Franzblau and Mathias studies seem to be contradictory —since one found correlations between God concepts and character and the other did not—the conflict is only apparent. Franzblau was concerned with the effects of acceptance of traditional (conservative) beliefs on conduct and found that there were none. Mathias, on the other hand, dealt with the relation of mature (liberal) God concepts and found low but positive correlations between a measure of a mature God concept and measures of conduct. In short, what evidence there is suggests that liberal but not conservative religious ideas are associated with the conduct aspects of character in children.

RELIGIOUS ORTHODOXY AND CAUSAL THOUGHT

The question whether religious training affects the form of thought is an intriguing one and seems related to Whorf's (1956) doctrine of linguistic determinism which says that in any given person the structures of his perception and thought are determined by the structure of the language he speaks. Thus to the degree that religious training involves learning a special vocabulary, to that degree will such training affect perception and thought.

A recent study by Ezer (1961) provides evidence which could be interpreted as favoring the Whorfian hypothesis. Although Ezer did not mention Whorf, the way in which he phrased his problem certainly suggests a linguistic determinism position. Ezer hypothesized that since all three major religious denominations (Protestantism, Catholicism, and Judaism) contain both animistic and anthropomorphic concepts, the child receiving formal religious training would be more likely than the child not receiving such training to manifest animistic and anthropomorphic ideas in connection with nonreligious thought.

Ezer used 153 boys between the ages of 6 and 8 of whom 47 were Protestant, 54 were Jewish, and 52 were Catholic. Approximately half of the boys in each group were enrolled in a parochial school while the other half were enrolled in a public school. Four measures of physical causality concepts involving story completion and multiple-choice items were administered by Ezer to all of his subjects. In addition, he also administered a questionnaire to the parents of his subjects designed to reveal their position on the liberal-conservative continuum with regard to traditional religious beliefs. When he examined the results, Ezer found that children who came from more devout homes (as measured by the parental questionnaires) or who had more formal religious training (as measured by attendance at a parochial school) gave significantly more anthropomorphic and animistic responses than did the less devout children who attended public school. Apparently, orthodox religious training does affect the form of nonreligious thought. The results appear, therefore, to support a Whorfian hypothesis and seem to demand further exploration from that point of view.

CONCLUSION

In concluding this survey of the developmental psychology of religion, it is perhaps appropriate to close by pointing out some of the work that remains to be done.

First of all, there are a number of descriptive studies that would be of great interest and would broaden our knowledge of religious experience. For instance, the varieties of religious experience reported by children brought up in one of the extreme religious sects such as the Holy Rollers would be of great comparative interest. Descriptive studies of the religious experience of Indian children would further round out our knowledge of religious growth. Only when the religious experiences of these minority groups have been explored will we be able to state with some assurance which aspects of religious experience are attributable to culture and which to the general principles of growth.

In addition to such descriptive studies, a great many developmental investigations are needed. As yet there are no definitive studies dealing with the development of prayer, belief, and faith, and the meanings which these have for children at successive age levels. It would also be interesting to explore, developmentally, Bovet's (1928) contention about the transfer of filial sentiments to the Deity. This could be done by determining whether the child begins to attribute omniscience and omnipotence to a deity or heroic figure just at the time when he withdraws these qualities from his parents.

Numerous correlational studies are also waiting to be done. One of the most important is the correlation of various personality measures, other than those related to character, with degree of religious conviction or conservatism. The work of Ezer (1961) suggests that it might also be fruitful to correlate cognitive and perceptual styles with religious training and background. In addition, the correlation of religious values with measures of the political, social, and economic influences on children of different social classes is almost totally unexplored territory.

Many more areas of research could be described, but those mentioned should suffice to show that even after 70 years, the developmental psychology of religion is still young in promise for those who wish to explore it.

BIBLIOGRAPHY

Allport, G. W. (1950), The Individual and His Religion. New York: Macmillan.
Argyle, M. (1958), Religious Behavior. London: Routledge and Kegan Paul.
Barnes, E. (1892), Theological Life of a California Child. Pedagogical Seminary, 2:442-448.
Bose, R. G. (1929), Religious Concepts of Children. Religious Education, 24:831-837.
Bovet, P. (1928), The Child's Religion. New York: Dutton.
Brown, A. W. (1892), Some Records of the Thoughts and Reasonings of Children. Pedagogical Seminary, 2:358-396.
Chaplin, D. P. (1948), Children and Religion. New York: Scribner's.
Elkind, D. (1961), The Child's Conception of His Religious Denomination I: The Jewish Child. Journal of Genetic Psychology, 99:209-225.
—— (1962), The Child's Conception of His Religious Denomination II: The Catholic Child. Journal of Genetic Psychology, 101:185-193.
—— (in press), The Child's Conception of His Religious Denomination III: The Protesant Child. Journal of Genetic Psychology.
—— & Elkind, S. (1962), Varieties of Religious Experience in Young Adolescents. Journal for the Scientific Study of Religion, 2:102-112.
Ezer, M. (1961), The Effect of Religion upon Children's Responses to Questions Involving Physical Causality. The Causes of Behavior, Rosenblith, J. & Allensmith, W. (Eds.), pp. 481-487. Boston: Allyn & Bacon.
Franzblau, A. N. (1934), Religious Belief and Character Among Jewish Adolescents. New York: Bureau of Publications, Teachers College, Columbia University.
Freud, S. (1927), The Future of an Illusion. London: Hogarth, 1928.
Godin, A. & Coupex, A. (1957), Religious Projective Pictures, A Technique of Assessment of Religious Psychism. Lumen Vitae, 12:260-274.
Graebner, O. E. (1960), Child Concepts of God. Illinois: Lutheran Education Association.
Hall, G. S. (1908), Adolescence II. New York: Appleton.
Harms, E. (1944), The Development of Religious Experience in Children. American Journal of Sociology, 50:112-122.
Hartshorne, H. S. & May, M. A. (1928), Studies in Deceit. Chicago: Macmillan.
Haslett, S. B. (1903), The Pedagogical Bible School. New York: Revell.

224 DAVID ELKIND

Hightower, P. R. (1930), Biblical Information in Relation to Character and Conduct. *University of Iowa Studies in Character*, 2:186.
Howells, T. H. (1928), A Comparative Study of Those Who Accept as Against Those Who Reject Religious Authority. *University of Iowa Studies in Character*, 2:167.
Hyde, K. E. (1961), The Religious Concepts of Adolescents. *Religious Education*, 56:329-333.
James, W. (1892), Thought Before Language: A Deaf Mute's Recollections. *Philosophical Review*, 1:613-624.
——(1902), *The Varieties of Religious Experience*. New York: Longmans.
Jones, E. (1944), The Psychology of Religion. *Psychoanalysis Today*, Lorand, S. (Ed.). New York: International Universities Press.
Klingberg, G. (1959), A Study of Religious Experience in Children from Nine to Thirteen Years of Age. *Religious Education*, 54:211-216.
Koons, W. G. (1903), *The Child's Religious Life*. New York: Eaton and Mains.
Loomba, R. M. (1944), The Religious Development of the Child. *Indian Journal of Psychology*, 14: 161-167.
MacLean, A. H. (1930), *The Idea of God in Protestant Religious Education*. New York: Teachers College, Columbia University Press.
Malhoit, B. (1957), Et Dieu se fit Enfant: Réactions d'Enfants et de Groupes d'Enfants a l'Age Préscolaire. *Lumen Vitae*, 22:37-42.
Manwell, E. & Fahs, S. L. (1948), *Consider the Children—How They Grow*. Boston: Beacon Press.
Mathias, W. D. (1943), *Ideas of God and Conduct*. New York: Teachers College, Columbia University Press.
McCann, R. V. (1955), Developmental Factors in the Growth of a Mature Faith. *Religious Education*, 50:147-155.
McKeefry, W. J. (1949), A Critical Analysis of Quantitative Studies of Religious Awakening. Unpublished doctoral dissertation, Union Theological Seminary and Teachers College.
Nelson, M. D. & Jones, E. M. (1957), An Application of the Q Technique to the Study of Religious Concepts. *Psychological Reports*, 3:293-297.
Piaget, J. (1929), *The Child's Conception of the World*. London: Routledge and Kegan Paul.
Pixley, E. & Beekman, E. (1944), The Faith of Youth as Shown by a Survey in Public Schools of Los Angeles. *Religious Education*, 44:336-342.
Ross, M. G. (1950), *Religious Beliefs of Youth*. New York: Association Press.
Sinclair, R. D. (1930), A Comparative Study of Those Who Report the Experience of the Divine Presence and Those Who Do Not. *University of Iowa Studies in Character*, 3.
Smith, J. J. (1941), The Religious Development of Children. *Child Psychology*, Skinner, C. E. & Harriman, P. L. (Eds.), pp. 273-298. New York: Prentice-Hall.
Smith, J. W. D. (1936), *Psychology and Religion in Early Childhood*. London: Christian Movement Press.
Starbuck, E. D. (1900), *The Psychology of Religion*. New York: Scribner's.
Strunk, O., Jr. (1959), Perceived Relationships Between Parental and Deity Concepts. *Psychological Newsletter*, 10:222-226.
Sully, J. (1895), *Studies of Childhood*. New York: Appleton.
Symington, T. A. (1935), *Religious Liberals and Conservatives*. New York: Teachers College, Columbia University Press.

Tanner, A. E. (1906), Children's Religious Ideas. *Pedagogical Seminary*, 13:511-513.
Tylor, E. B. (1924), *Religion in Primitive Culture*. New York: Brentano.
Werner, H. (1948), *Comparative Psychology of Mental Development*. New York: International Universities Press, revised edition.
Whorf, B. L. (1956), *Language, Thought and Reality*. New York: Wiley.
Woodward, L. E. (1932), *Relations of Religious Training and Life Patterns to Adult Religious Life*. New York: Teachers College, Columbia University Press.

CHAPTER 9

The Development of
Philosophical and Moral Concepts

LAWRENCE K. FRANK

Every cultural group attempts to transform the infant, who arrives as an immature mammal with all the inherited wisdom of the body, into a human personality who can live in its symbolic cultural world of meanings and goal values and participate in its social order.

To trace this process of transformation in detail would call for a careful inventory of the many complicated steps and stages through which the child moves on his way to adult status. It would begin with the child's initial experiences at birth, the various practices to which the newborn is exposed, his continuing close contact with the mother or his separation from her, his freedom to move his arms and legs or his subjection to swaddling or a cradle board—the amazing variety of ways by which a newborn is treated in each culture in accordance with its basic beliefs about what is necessary or desirable.

In this discussion we will focus on some of the more generalized patterns of child care and rearing which have a direct impact upon the child and are clearly related to his progressive orientation to group living. We find that with greater or less insistence and with different timing and pressures for conformity, each cultural group is concerned with the regulation of eating, eliminating, sleeping, and emotional reactions. In many cultures, there is a concern with the child's early search for pleasurable experiences in his own body and, at adolescence, there is an expectation that the boy and girl will conform to the prescribed patterns for expression and regulation of human sexuality.

These practices of early child care and rearing compel the child to surrender much of his own physiological autonomy and learn to function according to parental directions and control. The parentally established feeding intervals gradually establish the timing for his hunger and thirst, and for sleeping, as he learns to expect food and drink and to rest or sleep at the intervals they have set; he is also expected to regulate his eliminations in accordance with parental requirements; and he is permitted to express emotions freely, or with constraint, as required or imposed by parental patterns. Through these initial experiences the child's physiological functioning becomes progressively responsive to family and social regulations and patterning. These lessons are the first steps in learning to live in a symbolic cultural world and in the social order of his family, and they operate to impose some orderliness and regularity upon indispensable physiological functionings of all members of his cultural group.

When the child begins to move about and explore the world, he may be blocked, diverted, and often physically punished when he attempts to handle, take, push or pull, strike, put in his mouth or bite, or enter into restricted areas. After innumerable frustrations, in what may be called the "Don't Stage," he begins to refrain from forbidden actions. The psychoanalytic version of this learning is that the child "internalizes" the parental authority which has forbidden his activities; it would be equally appropriate to say that in this stage the child is pressed to view the world, things, animals, persons, and places as inviolable, or untouchable, except when and as specifically permitted. This may be explained by considering the child as learning to alter his naïve perception of the world, which no longer appears to invite his approach but presents itself as inviolable, not to be touched, taken, eaten, hit, or entered upon. This is not dissimilar to what happens when a child learns to avoid painful objects, as in the old saying that "The burnt child avoids the fires," but, in this socially patterned learning, the child learns to avoid what has been defined and clearly established, by scolding and often physical punishment, as that which must be avoided.

In what may be called the "Do Stage," the child is expected to perform a variety of prescribed activities, none of which are natural antecedents or requirements, but are imposed by parental authority, for instance, grooming, cleansing, manners, and etiquette, and similar conventionalized performances. Here again the child's perception of the world is altered as he learns to perceive situations and events as occasions for these prescribed performances.

Both the "Dont's" and the "Do's" are steps in the process of humanizing the child and making him learn to deal, not with the actual situation or event, but with its meaning and social significance, and also to meet the expectations of others. The naïve impulsive behavior of a child is slowly transformed into the orderly, patterned conduct required by his social order as he becomes responsive to this perceptually patterned world, as it is defined by more experienced persons.

Obviously this parental teaching is not completely effective, since parents differ in the emphasis which they put on various lessons. Parents, assuming they are observing the requirements of tradition and social order, may place a greater or lesser emphasis upon one or more of these lessons, and thus communicate an idiomatic version of what they are attempting to indoctrinate. The child being thus instructed brings to the lessons his unique heredity, his body build and modes of functioning, his temperamental make-up, and his accumulating life experiences, especially his feelings toward the world and toward the parent instructing or punishing him. Of necessity, therefore, he will interpret all prescriptions in his own idiosyncratic ways and will develop his own idiomatic patterns of compliance or of evasion and resistance, and he may also develop chronic feelings of anxiety, guilt, shame, and resentful hostility, engendered by these interpersonal encounters.

What the child experiences as an organism, how he is treated or mistreated, loved, or neglected and coerced, in his bodily functioning, what pain has been inflicted and what deprivations imposed, give rise to his image of his own body, an image that usually persists for life and is accompanied by a feeling of confidence in his own organism or a lack of organic security and self-confidence. Basic trust, to use Erikson's (1950) phrase, is developed or fails to develop through these early experiences.

He also develops an image of the self. This image of the self is a symbol of his individual personality and, like many other symbols, is verbalized as "I," "myself," "me," "mine," by which the person represents himself to and communicates with others while he also uses these same verbal symbols in all his imaging, his fantasying, his reflective thinking, and his inner speech as he communicates with himself. This image of the self emerges and becomes established in accordance with the ways the child is treated by others, with the way his appearance, his conduct, and his communications are evaluated by others in the day-by-day interpersonal relations in which he is engaged. Through verbalized admonitions and scoldings, he hears that he is bad, troublesome, disobedient, hateful, disliked, and incapable; or through occasional admiration and praise, he is told that he is good and lovable. From these verbalized judgments to which he is continuously exposed, he builds up an image of the self primarily in terms of what others tell him he is and frequently in terms of his deficiencies, shortcomings, and failures, infused by feelings.

This image of the self is not simple, nor unrelated to the child's growing awareness and perceptions of the world and of other people; since obviously much of what he says and does is considered wrong and inappropriate, his own individualized ways of perceiving and evaluating and feeling about the world are frequently rejected or sternly corrected. Moreover, he is expected to perform all the required and increasingly complicated patterns of conduct, and to relate differentially to a variety of persons—his parents of both sexes, his siblings of both sexes, his grandparents of both sexes, his aunts and uncles, and his cousins of different degrees of kinship, to each of whom he is required and expected to exhibit the prescribed roles of child, of brother or sister, of grandchild, nephew or niece, cousin, etc., but with recognition of the status of each individual personality involved.

Beginning almost at birth the child is addressed and treated as a boy or a girl, and is expected to learn and display the prescribed masculine or feminine roles in all his or her varied performances and interpersonal relationships. Thus, the image of the self is many-dimensional, and because of the varied and often conflicting performances that are expected, if not demanded, the individual must develop some central core or image of the self which persists despite changing outward activities, and provides a stance for facing the world and enabling him to achieve some kind of resolution among conflicting demands and his enlarging opportunities and privileges for entering into new relationships.

It seems clear that the individual child is confronted with many discrepancies and conflicts which he must somehow resolve or reconcile by rationalizing not only his own conduct and feelings, but also the social and cultural world in which he must live. This rationalization operates through a process of "relativizing" all that he is taught and learns about the cultural and social worlds as he perceives them and feels toward them. He strives to live and carry on his varied life activities in the public world with other people and he accepts and relies upon the socially sanctioned theories and explanations for that world, but he makes these more or less abstract, impersonal explanations individually meaningful and acceptable, and by various and sundry devices he reconciles them with his own idiomatic, often highly idiosyncratic and deviant beliefs and overt conduct. If and when he deviates too far from the social norms he may be judged to be criminal or mentally disordered and be subjected to whatever treatment has been established for such deviance.

Only in his own private world can he maintain any beliefs and fantasies, and rehearse actions, however criminal or psychotic they might be judged if overtly expressed, without risking social intervention.

The infant, at birth, is capable of all the linguistic sounds used in all the languages of the world, but he gradually loses this capacity and becomes limited to those phonemes which are consonant with what he hears; his ear becomes tuned to the language of his family and he progressively practices the sounds which he hears. Gradually he begins to recognize the patterned sounds of articulate speech and responds to them before he masters speech of his own. The capacity for speech is uniquely human and emerges as the child learns to regulate and pattern his breathing and his vocalizations into articulated sounds for communication.

With the mastery of speech the child begins *learning to learn*. At first he may learn the verbalized names of objects, animals, situations, and events, and especially identifiable persons. He continually rehearses these names and labels everything he can recognize and identify, finding endless satisfaction in repetition; along with the naming and identifying of what he recognizes, he increasingly exhibits the patterned conduct appropriate thereto (Schachtel, 1959).

The significance of the learning of language is seen when we recognize it as the first in a series of steps for transforming the geographical world of actual events into the symbolic cultural world in which, as a human personality, along with others, he must live, dealing with the surrounding world in terms of the symbolic meanings that have been defined for him by tradition and by the personal interpretation and explanation he receives from other persons.

As Benjamin Whorf (1940) has remarked: "The categories and types that we isolate from the world of phenomena we do not find there because they stare every observer in the face; on the contrary, the world is presented to us in a kaleidoscopic flux of impressions which has to be organized by our minds. . . . We cut nature up, organize it into concepts, ascribe significances as we do, largely because we are parties to an agreement to do it in this way."

It cannot be too strongly emphasized that the humanization of the child takes place through a series of interpersonal relations and communications, a more experienced person defining the world for the child, instructing him, and enforcing his compliance in the performance of what is required and imposing upon him an often rigid "thought control."

With his growing mastery of language the child enters upon the "Why-Because Stage," when, if not handicapped or retarded, he continually asks "Why, Mama?" to which his mother or other persons reply, "Because . . ." In this way more experienced persons convey the meaning of and give explanations for whatever the child inquires about, plus what they believe is necessary and desirable for his development. In this way they interpret the world in terms of their folklore and traditions, their religion, their moral and legal beliefs and convictions, communicating in terms of more or less specific instances and situations the conceptual framework by which they order experience, and relate to and communicate with the larger universe, surrounding nature, other people, and, of major importance, the self.

Every cultural group has developed a selective awareness and a highly patterned perception of its environment, ignoring as much if not more than it pays attention to, utilizing the available natural resources only in so far as their use is congruent with its traditional beliefs and its permissible activities. Likewise, each cultural group has selectively recognized, cultivated, and rewarded some, but only some, of the human potentialities of its members, disclaiming, rejecting, and often severely suppressing other potentialities believed not to be desirable or consonant with its cultural and social world.

Accordingly, we may say that each cultural group has created an "as if" world, a "virtual world" as Suzanne Langer (1955) has described artistic creations, a symbolic cultural world in which the group strives to live, imposing its beliefs and assumptions upon that actual world in which it exists and finding order and meaning, significance and fulfillment of its values and aspirations and, not the least important, a rationale and sanction for this way of life.

One may say that every culture is an attempt to rationalize the nonrational, to regulate and pattern man's organic functioning and impulsive behavior and also to embellish, elaborate, and enhance this functioning to provide increased enjoyment and fulfillment, as in eating, defecating, sleeping, sexual relations, and the variety of esthetic experiences and emotional provocations. Man, with his creative imagination and skillful hands, has been bored with nature unadorned and with his own physiological processes, and so has lavished his time and energy upon the arts whereby human living becomes more than organic existence.

Every child born into the group is enculturated and socialized, expected, and if necessary compelled, to learn the appropriate modes of bodily functioning and of overt conduct and interpersonal relations required for living in his social order. He is also under continuous pressure and constraint to learn to perceive the world in terms of the basic conceptions and assumptions of his group with its religious, moral, legal, and other beliefs and expectations, and to accept the sanctions that are invoked to maintain this design for living.

By learning to perceive the world according to the prevailing concepts and assumptions of his people, the individual member of the group becomes an active participant, who may carry on varied activities and relationships, assuming the prescribed roles and offices for his life career. For his orientation and for his interpretation of how the group carries on its varied economic, political, social, and religious affairs, seeks esthetic experiences and whatever personal fulfillment is permitted, he relies upon the oral and written language of his culture. To this we may add a statement by Dorothy Lee (1959) who writes: "A discussion of language as a system through which the individual transforms physical reality into experienced reality will clarify what I mean. I do not mean only oral or written expression, but the entire system of codification underlying all verbal expression."

Since this conceptual framework of a culture is a human creation, although often believed to be of supernatural origin or "revealed truth," these basic beliefs and assumptions are expressed in the three major symbol systems of each culture, namely: its theology, its arts, including language, and its science or protoscience. In cultures that have long persisted with little or no intrusions or internal upheavals, each of these three symbol systems gives support to and finds support from the others; but today many cultures, including the so-called great civilizations, exhibit many conflicts and incongruities in their symbol systems, especially in so far as scientific thinking has given rise to questioning of many traditional theological beliefs and expectations.

Apparently, long before there was any theology, religious experiences were sought and expressed nonverbally in dance, chorales, and dramatic performances, in which individuals participated in rituals with others and enjoyed a feeling of belongingness and shared experience while they engaged in important performances, such as fertility rites. Apparently the arts began with these early religious experiences and continued for ages to be religiously oriented and expressive of the beliefs and convictions and the feelings of the groups. Human cultures, with their three pervasive symbol systems, have been the products of the creative imagination of the poets, the prophets, and the artists who have provided the images, the symbols, and the symbolic performances through which human aspirations and purposive goal-seeking have been oriented.

What we call science apparently began with the systematic observation of the orderliness and regularity of events which enable man to cope with his many and difficult life tasks in a precarious world, tasks for which he invented tools, techniques, and weapons. The development of a scientific symbol system, with its reliance upon mathematical methods and symbolic interpretations, has only lately occurred in the history of mankind, but today has become ever more valid and reliable as an orientation to the world.

While religion, art, and science employ many nonverbal modes of communication, such as graphic symbols, they have been developed largely through language, both in reflective thinking and in shared communication and interpretation. Thus language provides a highly fluid and plastic symbol system which permits its idiomatic use in communicating with others and with the self. But, as indicated earlier, the vocabulary and syntax of a language operate through symbols of the actual world and its operations and therefore imply a cosmology, an epistomology, a psychology, a biology, indeed a rationale for whatever exists and happens. Consequently, as Benjamin Whorf (1956) and Dorothy Lee (1959) have pointed out, a people can think and discuss and communicate only in language, and the implicit assumptions and expectations of its syntax and vocabulary cannot be avoided. As he learns to use language, the child is gradually oriented to the world as his culture has conceived it. He is more or less compelled to create, and continually to recreate, his symbolic cultural world in accordance with the language through which it has been interpreted to him and by which he carries on his *inner speech,* his reflective thinking, and actively participates in reiterating these linguistic assumptions in all his overt verbal communications (Vigotsky, 1962).

The names of things, events, and persons operate as symbolic feedbacks to direct behavior toward that which is named in accordance with whatever that name means to the individual because of his life experience. Thus he learns to deal with meanings, not with actual things, except as he may be trained to manipulate and to develop specific skills for that purpose.

Theology emerged, apparently, as a method of reflective and creative thinking for the exploring, interpreting, and, above all, ordering and rationalizing of the religious experience of the individual who, without group-imposed constraints and formal channeling, may deviate and seek his own idiosyncratic religious experience and ways of communication with the larger universe, as exhibited by the mystics. Theologians have been alert to the appearance of these deviant patterns as threats to the unanimity of the group, to be suppressed as heresies or "deviationism."

When critical reflective thinking begins to focus on theological teachings and seeks to rationalize what was once unquestioned and unquestionable, then philosophical exploration and critical inquiry arise, looking for a more secularized interpretation and sanction for what is to be believed and expected. While "divine philosophy" is often regarded as a highly specialized, often esoteric, concern of a few, everyone is a philosopher in the sense of having his own, often not critically examined, highly individualized set of beliefs and assumptions about nature and man, his own personal way of explaining and interpreting and rationalizing the world and his own life experience. Indeed it seems clear that the normal person will build up a set of philosophical beliefs and expectations which are derived from the traditions of his people and reflect the artistic and sometimes scientific symbol systems, but are formulated by and express his own personal, individualized orientation to the world. The function of tradition is to keep alive the values and aspirations of our predecessors so that we can pay our debt to them by doing for our day what they did for theirs, but reformulating their assumptions and expectations in the light of contemporary knowledge and understanding and, above all, new sensibilities and human concerns.

We may go further and say that the individual personality develops an image of the self and rationalizes his place and status in the world by constructing a personal philosophy of living in which every dimension he recognizes will be relative to his own individual stance in that world. It is as if each person has to relativize the world and modify and revise all the official socially sanctioned explanations and interpretations so that they will be congruent with, and supportive of, his own central concern, his private world and his image of the self.

When and as critical thinking and creative imagination are focused upon nature in the search for an understanding of the order of events, how and when things happen, then what we call "science" emerges. It arises as a symbol system for interpreting and exploring events, for disclosing the orderliness and regularity of events, and for creating, like art, an "as if" or "virtual" world of postulates, concepts, and assumptions, with criteria of credibility which undergo cumulative change on further study and reflection.

The significance of the three symbol systems—theology, art, and science —may be better understood when we recognize that we can *know* only that which is symbolized. Obviously we directly experience the many impacts of the world upon our organisms through the input to our sensory apparatus of pressure, movement, heat and cold, light and dark, pain and pleasure, and all the other direct organic and esthetic stimuli of the world. But we can *know* only through cognitive experiences involving recognition of and response to symbols such as language, mathematics, symbolic logic, graphic symbols, by which the world becomes re-cognizable. These cognitive experiences are essentially transactional; they do not occur as cause and effect or stimulus and response events, nor do they take place in terms of physical action—reaction and interaction. Rather, personalities learn to recognize symbols onto which they impute or project the meanings they have learned; then they respond to that meaning which they themselves have invested in the symbol, with the actions and also the feelings that were developed in learning it and which continue to be evoked by it.

This view is what Dewey and Bentley (1949) offered some years ago in *Knowing and the Known,* in which they proposed relinquishing the traditional concept of knowledge as a substance to be acquired, stored, or imparted, and replacing that mysterious entity, or rarified abstraction, *knowledge* with the concept of *knowing*—substituting a verb for a noun in accordance with the increasing scientific practice of focusing upon processes and dynamic events rather than upon static things.

Through *knowing* we enter into a cognitive relation to the world; we engage in the process of *knowing* by using symbols, thereby what we observe becomes cognitively meaningful. As indicated, this is a transactional process by which every cultural group has established its own symbolic cultural world, transforming the natural world into a world of meanings and human significance, by learning to perceive the world and interpreting events in terms of the symbols provided by theology, art (including language), and now science.

Contemporary science explicitly accepts this viewpoint and disclaims any possession of a superior knowledge of the world or discovery of the truth. This has been clearly stated by Heisenberg (1958):

> The conception of the objective reality of the elementary particles has thus evaporated in a curious way, not into the fog of some new, obscure, or not yet understood reality concept, but into the transparent clarity of a mathematics that represents no longer the behavior of the elementary particles but rather our knowledge of this behavior. The atomic physicist has had to come to terms with the fact that his science is only a link in the endless chain of discussions of man with nature, but that it cannot simply talk of nature "as such." Natural science always presupposes man, and we must become aware of the fact that, as Bohr has expressed it, we are not only spectators but also always participants on the stage of life. . . .

Lanczos (1959) also has said that quantum physics is "comparable to a language whose words we do not understand, but whose syntactic rules we possess to such an extent that we can construct flawless sentences in that incomprehensible language."

In its advanced theoretical formulations science is transactional, engaged in developing a conceptual framework that is internally coherent and noncontradictory, in terms of which it formulates its problems, selects the methods and techniques for investigation of those problems, observes, records, and measures what it perceives, oriented by those assumptions which, in turn, govern its interpretation of its observations. Scientific "facts" are observations that have been made meaningful, by interpretation—decoding them—according to the conceptual framework that guided the study, while scientific generalizations at the conclusion of an investigation are explications of those initial assumptions that may be modified by the investigation.

We can see, therefore, that contemporary science has confirmed and further extended the transactional approach, whereby the human organism with its capacity for creative imagination, its ability to learn and also to *unlearn*, expresses its need for ordering the flux of experience and for making human living meaningful, by creating a symbolic cultural world, the product of the three great symbol systems we call theology, art, and science.

When these symbol systems lose their internal coherence, their intersystem consistency and interdependence, the cultural world which they have sustained becomes unstable and disturbed, no longer providing the guiding concepts and directing patterns for social order and depriving the individual personality of a stable stance for coping with the world. The individual's personality, his private world, his life space (Lewin), his idioverse (Rosenzweig), are threatened when he can no longer orient himself idiomatically by what seems dependable and consensually validated. The individual's image of the self which is both a reflection of, and a response to, that outside culturally patterned world, is likely to become impaired, especially, as Erikson (1959) has emphasized, when his social order also becomes confused and conflicting and prevents him from establishing his identity.

Existentialism may be viewed as the recognition of the breakdown of tradition and the loss of long-established patterns of conduct and interpersonal relations. We face an "existential vacuum," as it is called, and an "alienation of the self" since we can no longer confidently assume a stable and meaningful stance in the universe nor orient our personalities to a firmly established symbolic world. Those who assert a need for a radical alteration in human conduct have not recognized the basic requirement of a new, more credible and coherent conceptual framework for developing stable and self-fulfilling personalities with private worlds that are consonant with the emerging new climate of opinion.

Children today are growing up to face cultural disintegration, as the "unseen hand" of tradition no longer provides a sure and dependable guide. Children, and especially youth, are seeking some kind of personal philosophy and ethics for living, to replace the traditional moral codes which can no longer be accepted as the only sanctioned patterns of conduct; hence young people are indeed perplexed, unable to find any dependable and credible answers to the persistent questions which mankind has been raising from the beginning of reflective thinking. This perplexity is being steadily increased by the great prestige and truly amazing contributions from science and the immense reorientation of our ways of living coming from engineering and technology. The philosophical implications of contemporary science are not yet fully recognized and are far from being clarified. Much current thinking is concerned with attempts to reconcile the traditional concerns and assumptions of theology and philosophy with contemporary scientific thinking and reliance upon new criteria of credibility.

Children growing up are being indoctrinated by families with traditional concepts and assumptions that are becoming progressively anachronistic, because they reflect the theological and philosophical beliefs of "genteel tradition." When they go to school they are often given equally anachronistic and internally conflicting concepts and discrepant "facts" which increase their confusion and often fixate their misunderstandings. Confronted with an emerging climate of opinion, the schools, which have been instruments primarily for perpetuating tradition, now find themselves unable to revise their customary programs and practices because their teachers are unable or unwilling to change and new materials are not available, except for the recently developed new programs in physical science, mathematics, and biology which are only slowly being adopted and then chiefly in high schools.

Most elementary-school children continue for eight years to practice ways of thinking and learning "facts" that are out of date and increasingly in conflict with the newer ways of thinking, the novel assumptions and changing practices, in the social world in which they will soon be expected to participate. Moreover, many children continue to rely upon the frame of reference, the concepts and assumptions, they learned from their parents, assumptions which have been largely replaced in the new science programs and curricula for high-school students; when they enter high schools they must attempt to revise and reorient their thinking in order to benefit from these new programs. An exigent task for the schools today, as the writer has proposed (Frank, 1959), is to free the child from his anachronistic assumptions and ways of thinking, his reliance upon traditional concepts, which means that the schools should undertake systematically to help the child to *unlearn,* to give up and replace the orientation he has developed before entering school.

Faced with this situation the schools, both elementary and secondary, and also the colleges, should orient students to the world as revealed by science and also by the arts, by providing a conceptual reorientation and helping students to replace obsolete concepts with those that are more credible and operationally useful for "knowing" the world. Thus, instead of expecting students to master this enlarging body of "facts," the schools can provide ways for students to learn to use the concepts which have produced those facts and by which those "facts" have been disclosed and made meaningful. Examples are to be found in physics and chemistry and biology, which operate with concepts of time and space, quantity and sets, matter and energy, velocity and momenta, chemical bonds and molecular configurations, organic functions and processes, of which the quantified facts and generalizations are explicit expressions. Concepts, we may say, are essentially analogues, the models or patterns for selectively perceiving and for cognitively understanding and interpreting what we can observe in the world. The child's initial orientation to the world is through direct contact and experience of his organism and then through the learning of analogues which enable him to perceive the world, to recognize patterns and configurations that can be identified, named, and symbolically interpreted. This analogical approach has also been the historic way in which man, through theology and art, has attempted to understand the world and to guide and direct his relations with nature and other persons.

Since the 16th century, Western scientific study has been carried on primarily by analytic procedures seeking to fractionate and isolate and identify the many components, the variables and the mechanisms, which the investigator seeks to disclose, to measure, and to report as dependable "facts." Unlike the analogical process which seeks to discover patterns and configurations and to think in terms of the context and relations in which organisms, human institutions, and persons are disclosed, the analytic approach relies upon digital methods, step-by-step investigation, careful, logical, critical examination, and thinking, the truly marvelous and immensely productive procedures by which science has made its great contributions during the past 300 years. The assumption has been that for knowing the world, for establishing a cognitive, transactional relationship with the world, every individual must learn the many specific findings of empirical research, acquiring the tested "knowledge," memorizing and exhibiting a command of this knowledge in tests and examinations. It is also assumed that every student, under penalty of academic failure, must be competent in acquiring knowledge and skills in *all* the academic subjects prescribed for school children. The expectation is that through learning highly specific detailed knowledge in each subject a child will gain an understanding and will be able to travel along the academic sequence of courses of study in each field. For those who are preparing to work in the various fields of scholarship and science it is appropriate to expect that they will learn what each discipline has achieved in the way of understanding the field and contemporary problems with which it is concerned.

We should recognize that every individual needs a frame of reference, a set of concepts and assumptions, not only for orienting and guiding his knowing of a specific field in which he expects to become a scholar or scientist, but perhaps more importantly for developing his own conceptual framework and ways of relating to, and communicating with, nature; such a frame of reference is essential to his orientation, his participation as a personality in the social order, now being transformed by these new concepts, and, not the least important, for building up his own private world or idioverse and maintaining it in harmony with the emerging new climate of opinion.

Concepts as analogues provide what is necessary for knowing the world, since they enable individuals to impose or project upon the world the meanings which derive from these analogues, chiefly the linguistic symbols that each culture has developed for this purpose. The child's initial orientation to the world is analogical; he learns to perceive and to understand in terms of the patterns and configurations that he builds up through actual experiences of time, space, movement, and other physical dimensions, and then from the verbalized instruction and definitions given by more experienced persons. Only slowly and sometimes reluctantly do some children develop an analytic approach, learning to break down or fractionate the wholes of their naïve perception and slowly beginning to think digitally, with step-by-step, logical reflective thinking. Thus the child begins his *knowing* relationships, relying upon figures of speech, diagrams, pictures, models, charts—a variety of analogues—while he learns to use discursive speech, which, like mathematics, operates digitally, and syntactically, proceeding according to the logic of the user to a reasoned conclusion—a Q.E.D. since these digital processes are guided by prior and often implicit or unrecognized analogues such as the concepts and assumptions and the syntax of the language he is using. If these concepts and assumptions are no longer valid, the most rigorous logic can produce only erroneous conclusions. Much of the child's conceptual framework, the analogues he has developed before going to school, is likely to be anachronistic; whatever he learns in school may also be invalid and misleading today.

Today there is a growing realization of the crucial role of analogues, of imaging, of creative imagination, and of what we have long called intuition, not only in the arts but in the sciences (Bruner, 1960); the poet and the artist, and also the scientist, begin with analogues and then proceed to revise, enlarge, and develop these analogues by digital practices which enable them to produce the final analogue in the form of a poem, a picture, or in science, an equation or a chart. Studies are showing that children have different cognitive styles, have their own individual ways of perceiving and understanding events, of conceptualizing the world, some visual, others auditory, while others are so-called haptic and prefer to deal with the world as it can be directly manipulated and felt.

Various studies today, including accumulating clinical evidence, are showing that once a perceptual set has been developed it resists modification or replacement (Solley and Murphy, 1960); likewise a conceptual framework, once firmly established and utilized by an individual for orienting not only his thinking but his conduct and relations to the world and other people, may be equally refractory and resistant to alteration (Kilpatrick, 1954). Accordingly we may say that if the schools undertake the increasingly important task of freeing children from obsolete concepts and helping them to replace such beliefs with contemporary assumptions and revised patterns of perception, they face a seemingly difficult task because we have no effective methods for fostering *unlearning*, apart from that which is practiced by psychotherapists and then with limited success, even with those who are greatly in need of such emancipation.

The need for reorientation, or more appropriately, revision of our traditional moral concepts arises in a similar context of strongly established convictions and impressive sanctions for beliefs and assumptions and patterns of conduct that are becoming increasingly incongruous with, and inapplicable to, the changing culture and social world in which children must learn to live. We are greatly disturbed and perplexed as we discover that an individual may be obedient to the established moral and legal codes, but in his personal relations may violate the integrity of others, inflicting injury and humiliation, while self-righteously defending his conduct as within the legal and moral code. We may see this in marriage and in politics and business practices.

While some believe it is possible to re-establish traditional moralistic teachings and to revive the sanctions by which they were maintained, a growing number of thoughtful persons, especially among the young, are asking for an ethic to replace this familiar moralizing. Such an ethic may be viewed in terms of the individual's awareness and concern for the probable consequences of his action, or failure to act, for others and for his society, and also for his own personal dignity and integrity. An ethical orientation, therefore, is to be sharply contrasted with the authoritarian and often rigid prescriptions imposed on individuals and enforced by sometimes ruthless action, since ethics seek to elicit autonomous and responsible conduct. Ethics imply that individuals can be trusted, considered both capable of and responsible for contributing to the maintenance of a free society if they are reared and educated with that orientation and develop an image of the self as responsible individuals. Clearly an ethical evaluation of our traditional teachings and practices will reveal the wide conflict between the ethical, altruistic concern for others exhibited in our traditions, especially in our literature and in our theology ("love thy neighbor as thyself"), exalting unselfishness and generosity, and the emphasis on the primary duty of individual salvation. As the old Salvation Army song expressed it, "The bells of Hell go ting-a-ling for you, but not for me," emphasizing the self-righteous, ego-centered teaching of a tradition that has permeated almost all of our ways of living and conducting our social affairs. The crucial question we face in the development of an urbanized technological society is how to develop personalities who can bear the burdens of freedom, who have learned to be responsible for, and responsive to, others, and who have had a childhood and an education conducive to ethical conduct.

This ethical orientation calls for a continued awareness of other persons, their individuality and integrity, their dignity and worth as unique personalities. Treating others ethically also involves being generous of one's time, energy, and concern, giving of oneself and aiding others. Through such generosity the ethical person gains strength, the strength that comes not from power or exercise of authority in the control of people, but from the realization of one's own capacity to give to others and by that giving becoming stronger. This has been the source of women's strength through the ages; they have given of themselves to their families, their children, their neighbors in need, and so, despite the burdens and deprivations and the frequent unhappiness they suffered, being women, they found renewed strength and courage by being generous.

In a world suffering from so many ills, human defeats, and deprivations of even the basic requirements for human well-being, nothing, probably, is more urgently needed than a commitment to an ethical orientation and a devotion to the generosity whereby both the giver and the recipient are enhanced.

While not yet clearly enunciated nor effectively explored, contemporary scientific thinking, with its new conceptions of nature and of man, gives promise of a firm and valid basis for the formulation of an ethic that explicitly recognizes the more recently formulated conceptions of the relation of the individual to the larger universe, and of social orders as generated and maintained by all those who are members of that social order. Thus we may foresee the development of a new image of man, no longer distorted by ancient theological beliefs and a malign image of the self but illuminated and infused by the new understanding of human potentialities and the discovery of methods for releasing these potentialities with less of the self-defeat and antisocial misconduct by which the human enterprise has been so long impeded (Murphy, 1958; Frank, 1963).

We may, today, begin to see the human condition or the human predicament as arising from man's dual obligations: as a mammalian organism he must continue to function throughout his life and bear exposure to the unceasing biological stimuli and the physiological impulses that continually arise within him. But, as a personality, who is expected to live in a symbolic cultural world and to participate in its social order, he is required to regulate and pattern all these organic functions, to resist these biological impacts and physiological impulses except as they may be permissible under certain specified conditions and sanctions. Thus man is by his biological nature and by his aspirations subject to dual requirements which often conflict, and he is expected to conform to cultural and social constraints and coercions. Furthermore, many of these may no longer be necessary or desirable, and some are clearly productive of personality problems and social disorders. A crucial question we face in the development of a technological society is the resolution of this conflict in the light of our growing insights and understanding, especially the recognition of how many suffer from an "overstrict conscience" and deprivation of experiences that are needed in childhood and youth for mentally healthy personality development. "Man is the being who can be conscious of, and therefore responsible for, his existence" (May, 1960), but only if his culture and his social order provide what is essential to his well-being as an organism and to the integrity of his personality. Responsibility for one's own existence is generated in children and youth when they, as growing, developing, organism-personalities, learn from responsible *and responsive*, generously inclined adults, parents, teachers, and other more experienced but benevolent persons, what it means to participate responsibly in a social order.

Since every culture is an attempt to rationalize the nonrational, a major task today is to examine critically the "traditionally expected," to search imaginatively for new patterns of conduct and alterations in interpersonal relations, and to provide more occasions for nonrational experience and fulfillment, especially esthetic, so that individuals can sustain the increasing demand for orderly conduct and skilled performance in our urban, industrialized civilization. But these advances in living will come only as we revise our basic philosophic and moral concepts, replacing obsolete symbols with new symbols in theology, art, and science. As Whitehead (1927) remarked years ago: "Those societies which cannot combine reverence for their symbols with freedom for revision, must ultimately decay, either from anarchy or from slow atrophy of a life stilled by useless shadows."

BIBLIOGRAPHY

Bruner, J. S. (1960), *The Processes of Education*. Cambridge, Massachusetts: Harvard University Press.

Dewey, J. & Bentley, A. (1949), *Knowing and the Known*. Boston: Beacon Press.

Erikson, E. (1950), *Childhood and Society*. New York: W. W. Norton.

——(1959), *Identity and the Life Cycle*. Psychological Issues, 1(1). New York: International Universities Press.

Frank, L. K. (1959), *The School as Agent for Cultural Renewal*. Cambridge, Massachusetts: Harvard University Press.

——(1963), Four Ways to Look at Potentialities. *New Insights and the Curriculum*. Washington, D. C.: American Society of Child Development, National Education Association.

Heisenberg, W. (1958), The Representation of Nature in Contemporary Physics. *Daedalus*, 87:100-108.

Kilpatrick, F. P. (1954), Recent Experiments in Perception. *Transactions of the New York Academy of Sciences*, series 11:16, 420-425.

Lanczos, C. (1959), Albert Einstein and the Role of Theory in Contemporary Physics. *American Scientist*, 4o(March):41-59.

Langer, S. (1955), *Form and Feeling*. New York: Scribner's.

Lee, D. (1959), *Freedom and Culture*. Englewood, New Jersey: Prentice-Hall, Spectrum Book.

May, R. (1960), *Existence*. New York: Basic Books.

Murphy, G. (1958), *Human Potentialities*. New York: Basic Books.

Schachtel, E. G. (1959), *Metamorphosis*. New York: Basic Books.

Solley, C. M. & Murphy, G. (1960), *Development of the Perceptual World*. New York: Basic Books.

Vigotsky, L. (1962), *Thought and Words*. Cambridge, Massachusetts: Harvard University Press.

Whitehead, A. N. (1927), *Symbolism, Its Meaning and Effect*. New York: Macmillan.

Whorf, B. L. (1940), Science and Linguistics. *The Technological Review*, 42 (April). Massachusetts Institute of Technology.

——(1956), *Language, Thought and Reality*. New York: Wiley.

CHAPTER 10

The Development of Two Related Forms of Social Cognition: Role-Taking and Verbal Communication

JOHN H. FLAVELL

In a recent review of children's thinking, Wallach (1963, p. 270) correctly points out that we know considerably more about their intellectual abilities concerning the physical, nonsocial milieu than about their capacities in the arena of social cognition. The experiments to be described here deal with this latter, relatively neglected area of investigation. Specifically, they are part of a larger body of research (Flavell, 1961) on the ontogenetic development of two related skills of a social-cognitive sort: (a) the general ability and disposition to understand the role of another person, that is, to take a "reading" of his response tendencies and capacities; (b) the more specific ability to utilize this understanding of the other's role as a cognitive instrument in communicating effectively with him. Mead (1947) and Sarbin (1954), among others, have theorized about the nature and development of role-taking, and Piaget (1926) has particularly emphasized its functional significance for verbal communication. There are several studies which provide empirical evidence for the development of role-taking per se or related abilities, such as empathy, sympathy, etc. (Burns and Cavey, 1957; Dymond, Hughes, and Raabe, 1952; Feffer and Gourevitch, 1960; Gates, 1923; Milgram and Goodglass, 1961;

The studies reported here were supported by Research Grant M-2268 from the National Institute of Mental Health, United States Public Health Service. The present account of them is based in part upon a paper read at the meetings of the Society for Research in Child Development, Berkeley, April, 1963.

Moore, 1958; Murphy, 1937; Piaget and Inhelder, 1956; Walton, 1936; and Wolfe, 1963), but apparently only one which documents its increasing importance, with age, as a tool for communicating with others (Piaget, 1926).

The theoretical conceptions which guided the present research are based principally on Piaget's writings (Piaget, 1926; Piaget and Inhelder, 1956; Flavell, 1963, Ch. 8) and can be summarized as follows. As children develop, they become increasingly skilled in, and disposed toward, discriminating the "role attributes" of another person, i.e., the person's dispositions, capabilities, limitations, and other characteristics. As Piaget has argued, children are initially *egocentric*, unwittingly caught up in their own perspective and viewpoint to the exclusion of the other person's. As development proceeds, however, they begin to become aware of, and start making inferences about, the other's point of view. To put it simply, they tend to become better and better "people readers" as they grow older.

This burgeoning role-taking capacity must make its influence felt in a wide variety of cognitive and interpersonal activities. But one of its most important uses has to do with verbal communication. To the extent that a child fails to take soundings about those role attributes of his listener which are relevant to the sort of message the child should send to the listener, to that extent is the message likely to be ill-adapted to the listener's informational needs and hence inadequately communicative. Conversely, to the extent that the child does take an accurate measure of "listener-role attributes," so to speak, and then actively uses this knowledge to shape and adapt his message to this particular listener, to that extent ought the communication be an effective, nonegocentric one. An important part of what is involved in effective communicating might be conceptualized as a coding and then recoding process, in which the recoding component is monitored by role-taking activity. An ineffective, egocentric communication, on the other hand, is essentially arrested at the initial, coding step of the process. The following is a tentative schematization—and no doubt a grossly oversimplified one—of the probable microdevelopment involved in each type of communication:

EGOCENTRIC COMMUNICATION

1. S (speaker) cognizes X (data) and covertly codes it so that it is meaningful and communicable to himself.

248   JOHN H. FLAVELL

2. S sends L (listener) a message about X. The message is in all important respects unrecoded, i.e., it is essentially a simple externalization without modification of his private coding and is hence an egocentric communication (see Figure 1).

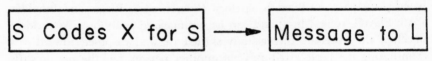

FIGURE 1

Schema of Egocentric Communication

NONEGOCENTRIC, EFFECTIVE COMMUNICATION

1. S. cognizes X and covertly codes it for himself, just as in step 1 above.

2. Prior to and/or during his communication to L (step 3 below), S attempts to discriminate those role attributes of L which appear to be pertinent to L's ability to decode communicative input regarding X.

3. S recodes X and externalizes it as a message to L about X. This recoding and externalization process occurs under the aegis of two concurrent (and related) activities: (a) S uses the information gained in step 2 to shape and fashion the message in such a way as to maximize the likelihood that it will meet L's communicative needs; (b) S actively suppresses the insistent and recurring tendency to allow his message to drift or "regress" toward the initial coding of step 1 (the egocentric error), a tendency which exists by virtue of the fact that this initial coding is both continuously and intrusively present in S's consciousness and, by definition, communicatively adequate for him, from his point of view (see Figure 2).

Our research project included two types of investigations, corresponding to the two sets of skills just described. On the one hand, there were studies of the development of role-taking skills in and of themselves, apart from their function as aids to effective communication. On the other hand, there were developmental studies of verbal communication performance in which the workings of role-taking activity could be inferred, i.e., studies using communicative tasks specially designed to assess the extent to which role-taking was brought into play in the construction of the communicative message. Two studies of each type are described below.

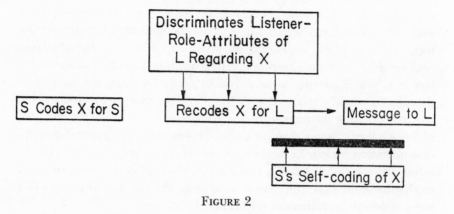

FIGURE 2

Schema of Nonegocentric Communication

ROLE-TAKING STUDIES

The two tasks described here and the first one described in the next section were individually administered within a single testing session to 160 children in a suburban public school:[1] 10 of each sex at each of grades 2, 3, 4, 5, 6, 7, 8, and 11. All grade groups, and the male-female subgroups within each grade, were closely matched on group intelligence test scores (the mean scores were a little above the population average). The experimenters were Charles L. Fry and John W. Wright. All subjects performed the two role-taking tasks in the order in which they are described here.

STUDY I

The child was shown two opaque plastic cups turned face down on the table. One cup had a nickel glued to its bottom side; the other, two nickels. The child was told that these coins indicated the amount of money that might be hidden under each cup, one nickel under the one and two nickels under the other, and that a game could be played with the cups. The two experimenters then played the game together twice through, as a demonstration. One experimenter (E1) closed his eyes and the other (E2) silently removed the money from under one of the cups. E1 then opened his

[1] The author is greatly indebted to District Principal John W. Parker and other members of his staff in the Rush-Henrietta school system for their splendid cooperation in providing subjects and facilities for this investigation.

eyes and, after deliberating, picked up one of the cups, thereby obtaining whatever money lay beneath it if he chose the nonempty cup (either one nickel or two nickels, depending on which cup it was), or else obtaining nothing if he chose the empty one. The game was structured as a competitive one, with E_2 trying to minimize E_1's gain by emptying the cup he thought E_1 would select, and with E_1 trying to maximize his own gain by correctly guessing the nonempty cup, whichever one it might be (e.g., one nickel is clearly better than an empty two-nickel cup). Throughout this demonstration period, E_1 kept up a running commentary on each player's action for the child's benefit, making sure that the child understood the mechanics of the play (for reasons soon to be obvious, he did *not* describe any game-strategic rationales for his and E_2's actions).

When the demonstration was over, E_2 left the room. The child was then told that he was to play the same game vis-à-vis E_2. The child was to remove the money from one of the cups and E_2 would try to guess the nonempty cup when he returned. The child was told to try to "fool" E_2, that E_2 *knew* the child would try to fool him and would act accordingly, and that the child should therefore "think hard" before selecting a cup to empty. The child then made his choice and was carefully questioned about his reasons for making that choice. The child's choice and its rationale in this single "trial" comprised the only experimental datum in this study; E_2's subsequent cup selection was actually an arbitrary one. Choice and rationale were tape recorded and subsequently converted to typescript for analysis purposes.

It was hypothesized that there would be a shift with age toward choices and rationales reflecting more complex and differentiated inferences about E_2's role attributes, *qua* opponent in this particular game. A logical analysis of the game had suggested a means of ordering choices and rationales in terms of role-taking complexity and differentiation, and the following category system was the outcome:

Strategy A. S states that E_2 will choose cup X for some reason, and thus S should remove the money from that cup. For most subjects adopting this strategy, the reason was a monetary one and the cup in question was the two-nickel one (E_2 chooses it because it potentially contains more money); in some cases, the imputed motive was a nonmonetary one, e.g., because E_2 remembers which cup paid off before (during the demonstration) and thinks it will pay off this time too. The following is an example of a monetary-type Strategy A protocol:

> Do you want me to tell you? *Umhum. Which one do you think he'll choose?* The dime. *You think he'll choose the dime cup. Why do you think he might choose that one?* He'll get more money—if the money is under there.

Strategy B. S begins with a prediction about E2's probable choice and associated motive (either monetary or nonmonetary), just as in Strategy A. But, unlike the Strategy A child, he goes on to recognize the likely possibility that E2 will guess that S is thinking along these lines, and will therefore change his choice (e.g., from the two-nickel to the one-nickel cup). Here is an example:

> [S chooses the one-nickel cup.] *Why do you think he'll take the one-nickel cup?* Well, I figured that, uh, if it was me I'd take this one [two-nickel cup] because of the money I'd get to keep. But he's gonna know we're gonna fool him—or try to fool him—and so he might think that we're gonna take the most money out so I took the small one [the one-nickel cup], I'd go for the small one.

Strategy C. This strategy is almost paranoid in the complexity of its inference structure. Having first reasoned according to Strategy B, the subject makes the further inference that E2 will suspect that S has so reasoned and will thus act accordingly (e.g., in the case of a monetary strategy, S suspects that E2 will end up choosing the two-nickel cup after all, through an "I-think-that-he-thinks-that-I-think, etc." chain of reasoning). We *thought* (but were not *sure*) that this interesting bit of reasoning was a case of nonmonetary Strategy C:

> Uh, when we were, he chose the dime cup the first time . . . and uh . . . well, let's see . . . I think uh that he would, I think that he would think that we would choose the opposite cup. *Opposite cup from what?* From the, in other words this cup, the nickel cup, but then might, he might, he might feel that we, that we know that he thinks that we're going to pick this cup so therefore I think we should pick the dime cup, because I think he thinks, he thinks that we're going to pick the nickel cup, but then I think he knows that we, that we'll assume that he knows that, so we should pick the opposite cup. *Okay, so we should pick the dime cup?* Yes.

Strategy O. This "wastebasket" category included all responses not scorable as Strategies A, B, or C. In most cases so scored, the child was either unable to make a choice or else, having chosen, could not offer any coherent rationale for the choice.

Two cautionary remarks should be made about this fourfold categorization. First, some protocols were difficult to score, especially if the strategy was nonmonetary and/or complex (see the Strategy C example cited above). One judge scored all the protocols and a second scored a random subset of them (the scoring was "blind" in both cases). The two judges agreed in their category assignments in the case of only 73% of the subjects—not bad, perhaps, but a far cry from unanimity. Second, whereas it certainly can be said that any child who exhibits Strategy B or C is capable of rather fancy role-taking behavior, it can hardly be stated with much assurance that a child who does not exhibit either of these two strategies is incapable of such behavior. In the first place, the task was a one-trial affair, scarcely an adequate test for a *capacity*. Moreover, a person with all manner of role-taking skills might nonetheless assume that E2 would in this situation simply act out of a direct and uncomplicated monetary motive (Strategy A), might just select at random (this would be scored Strategy O), etc. Despite instructions which hint otherwise, a given subject might simply have decided that E2 is probably not clever enough to warrant Strategy B or C treatment, even though the possibility crossed his mind.

It seems clear, then, that our measure almost certainly underestimates the role-taking capabilities of the sample. However, there was no reason to anticipate that such underestimation would act as a variable rather than constant error to obscure the predicted developmental trends, and indeed, it appears not to have. Table 1 shows the number of children in each grade who fall into each of the 4 strategic categories. It can be seen that Strategies A and B show the most clear-cut developmental change, with the latter tending to replace the former ontogenetically. Strategy C is a rare occurrence at any age, as might be expected; Strategy O shows no apparent age trends, accounting for roughly one-fourth of the subjects at each grade level. An 8-cell chi square table was constructed from Table 1 by combining adjacent grades and adjacent strategies, e.g., one such cell would include the second and third-graders who show either Strategy O or A. This procedure yielded a chi square of 18.18 (df=3), p<.01. Chi

TABLE 1

Number of Subjects per Grade Scored for Each Strategy in the
Two-Cup Game

	Grade							
Strategy	2	3	4	5	6	7	8	11
O	2	4	4	6	4	3	6	6
A	17	14	13	10	8	8	4	7
B	1	2	3	4	6	9	10	5
C	0	0	0	0	2	0	0	2

square tables were also constructed for sex and IQ (above versus below median), again combining adjacent strategies (O-A versus B-C). There was a tendency ($p<10$) for the boys to show the higher level strategies. No differences due to IQ were apparent, but this negative finding should be viewed with some skepticism, since our IQ range was relatively narrow.

It was interesting to us to find that Strategies A and B accounted for most of the developmental variance in this study, because they also appear to be the most unequivocal ones from an interpretative standpoint. Strategy A may not appear to bespeak a very sophisticated cognitive process, but most instances of it in our data do look like genuine expressions of role-attribute discrimination. In the most clear-cut cases, the child stated that E2 would probably choose the two-nickel cup because "he wants more money," "he'd get more money, if there was money in there," etc. (the case where the child simply asserted "it's more money" is admittedly more equivocal). It seems likely that the underlying process here consists of first endowing E2 with a motive and relevant action vis-à-vis the game materials (undoubtedly the same ones the child would espouse if he were in E2's position) and then—stepping back into his own role as opponent to E2—making the appropriate countermove. Unless the child had imagined himself, however minimally and fleetingly, in the role position complementary to his own, it is difficult to see why he would have responded with this kind of rationalized choice—why he would not simply have stated that he had no way of anticipating E2's choice, let alone knowing the reasons for any given choice. The imputed motive is after all neither relevant to the child's own role (he can obtain no money for himself in this game) nor, obviously, is it something directly perceptible in

254 JOHN H. FLAVELL

the situation. It does not seem unparsimonious, therefore, to assume that it emerged out of some sort of imaginal, role-taking activity.

Strategy B also involves role-playing—even more unequivocally so than Strategy A—but role-playing of a clearly more advanced and elaborated sort. The difference lies in what is imputed to the opponent, i.e., in the inferred content of his role. In Strategy A, as argued above, this content comprises at most a motive and motive-derived action with respect to the game materials. In Strategy B, on the other hand, the content includes this plus an important additional component: the opponent's cognitions about one's *own* cognitions, motives, and derivative behaviors with respect to both game materials and opponent. What is new here seems to be a cognition which subtends not only the other's view of some X which is external and perceptible to both of you, but also his view of *your* view of both X and of himself vis-à-vis X. The model is no longer simply S→ (O → X), but S → [O → (S → X)] or even S →{O → [S → (O → X)]}, where S = self, O = other, X = e.g., the game materials, and → signifies "cognizes," broadly defined.

If we look again at Table 1 in the light of the preceding discussion, certain tentative conclusions emerge. First, it seems clear that even our youngest subjects (age 7-8 or so) are quite capable of the straightforward and elementary role-taking activity represented by Strategy A. This seems to be the kind of activity Piaget (Flavell, 1963, Ch. 8 and elsewhere) has in mind in describing how the egocentrism of the preschooler is gradually replaced, during the early school years, by a nascent capacity to distinguish the other's viewpoint from one's own with respect to some mutually perceived datum. It seems likely that this developing capacity plays a vital instrumental function in the important social learning which is thought to occur during this epoch, for instance, the acquisition of techniques of cooperation and compromise with peers (e.g., Sullivan, 1953).

On the other hand, thinking at the level of Strategy B or better does not seem to occur very frequently in our sample until about age 11-12 years (although its development is obviously a gradual rather than an abrupt affair). This finding closely parallels the results of an interesting study by Moore (1958). Teams of children were given a problem the successful mastery of which required that each team's members construct a private code, one which would permit them to communicate aloud to one another without at the same time informing the members of the opposing team. Moore found that teams of 12- to 14-year-old children were much more likely to see the necessity of constructing such codes than were 9- to 11-year-olds; like our older subjects, Moore's adolescents showed a greater sensitivity to the other's perception of their own behavior.

The ability to engage in B- or C-level role-taking can perhaps be understood as one concrete expression of a more general cognitive transformation which seems to occur around early adolescence. Inhelder and Piaget (1958; Flavell, 1963, Ch. 6) talk about the genesis of *formal operational* thinking during this period. There are at least three characteristics attributed to this kind of thinking which could also be attributed to the more complex role-taking strategies found in our study. First, it is abstract thinking, quite at home in manipulating cognitive as opposed to concrete, physical entities; thinking about O's thoughts about your thoughts certainly qualifies as abstract. Second, and related, it is a hypothetico-deductive, "if this, then that" kind of reasoning; again, Strategies B and C seem to involve the setting up of complex hypotheses about what O will think and do, and then drawing the necessary implications for one's own counter-moves. And finally, it involves the ability to deal with reciprocal relationships; correspondingly, our older subjects well demonstrate their understanding of the reciprocal roles of S and O in this two-person game.

The argument was made earlier that the social-cognitive skill represented by Strategy A probably plays an important instrumental role in helping the child of the early school years cope with the social learning problems indigenous to this era, e.g., in helping him learn to cooperate, to compromise, to keep track of his own and the other children's roles in group games, etc. A similar argument could be made for Strategy B with respect to the interpersonal accomplishments which we associate with preadolescence and early adolescence. Sullivan (1953) draws a graphic picture of the normal preadolescent's proclivity for developing intimate interpersonal relationships with a same-sex chum, relationships in which meticulous attention is paid to the business of carefully gauging the thoughts and feelings of the other (especially toward oneself), of comparing and contrasting his perceptions of the world with one's own, and the like. This interpersonal seismography certainly continues with a vengeance during adolescence, vis-à-vis others of both sexes; "What will she (he) think of me if I do X?" is a common adolescent refrain, and seems to reflect the achievement of cognitive abilities of the Strategy B type. The nub of what has been argued here is simply this: the type of social-interpersonal activity of which the child is capable and in which he will be likely to engage is in large measure dependent upon the possession of those cognitive tools necessary to support the activity; the present study purports to have discriminated two such tools in the area of role-taking, and it has been suggested that they act as cognitive supports for certain common social activities in middle childhood and preadolescence-adolescence, respectively.

STUDY II

Although it was also designed to be a measure of role-taking ability, this task differs from the preceding one in two major respects. First, it does not admit of a clear hierarchy of qualitatively different role-taking strategies, although degrees of task mastery could be discriminated. Second, it focuses on a particular component of the role-taking process which is not highlighted in the cup game: the necessity to suppress temporarily one's own pre-existing cognition of a given event in order to intuit the other person's (different) cognition of the same event (essentially, the kind of suppressing activity described in step 3b of our model of nonegocentric, effective communication).

The procedure was the following. The child was shown a series of seven pictures which tell a story, much like a comic strip without dialogue. The pictures are as follows: (1) a boy is walking along, whistling; (2) sees a vicious-looking dog behind him; (3) runs, with dog in hot pursuit; (4) runs toward an apple tree (dog not shown, but apparently behind him, just out of the picture); (5) climbs tree, with dog nipping at his heels; (6) sits in tree, eating an apple, with dog again out of the picture; (7) stands up in tree, idly watching the dog walk away. The child was asked to tell the story which the pictures suggest. If he failed to verbalize a significant element in the story (e.g., that the boy climbed the tree to escape the dog, that he is eating an apple in the sixth picture, etc.) he was queried about it and prompted if necessary. Actually very few subjects had any difficulty in inferring the correct train of events from the picture series. These seven pictures were so constructed that if three of them (the second, third, and fifth) are removed, the remaining sequence of four pictures also suggests a story, but a story markedly *different* from that of the seven-picture sequence: namely, a happy-looking boy who spies a tree laden with apples, climbs up to get one, eats it, and is finally shown standing up (preparing to descend?) with an innocent-looking dog in the distance, apparently just part of the background.

When the child had finished telling the seven-picture story, the critical three pictures were removed and the remaining four pushed together. The second experimenter then entered the room for the first time and the child was told that the newcomer had never seen any of these pictures before. The child was instructed to pretend that he were this man, looking at *just* these four pictures, and to tell the story which he thought the *newcomer* (emphasized) would tell from looking at them. If the child did not spontaneously indicate these things in his narration of the newcomer's story, he was specifically asked why *he* (E1 points at E2) thinks the boy climbed the tree and what *he* thinks about the dog there, what *he* thinks the dog is there for. (Prior to running the experiment proper, we did pilot work which satisfied us that most second- and third-graders who are shown only the four-picture sequence can readily tell the "correct" four-picture story.)

As with the cup game, the subjects' four-picture narratives were judged according to a fourfold category system (interjudge agreement was 85%):

1. A more or less straightforward presentation of the correct four-picture story in its full detail.

2. A more or less straightforward presentation of the original seven-picture story, including mention of the fear-of-dog motive.

3. Although the child does not mention the seven-picture story's fear-of-dog motive in his narrative proper (the narrative is usually skeletonized, with no mention of motives of any sort), when asked during the inquiry why E2 thinks the boy climbed the tree, he blandly asserts that "The dog was chasing him," that "The boy was afraid of the dog," etc. Thus, behavior scored here is regarded as a disguised and less blatant form of category (4) role-taking failure, with "regression" to the seven-picture story taking place under minimal questioning rather than spontaneously.

4. This category includes all the remaining protocols. In most such cases, the child is unable to refrain from introducing some sort of fear motive (either in narrative or in inquiry), but, unlike the category (3) subjects, also says something which indicates that he recognizes that E2 is operating from the four-picture sequence only—says something which indicates an awareness of the role-taking problem confronting him. The children

scored here were therefore thought to show more sensitivity to the role of the other than those scored (3) or (4), but less than those scored (1). The analysis of data proceeded along the same lines as in the previous study. Table 2 presents the grade by category matrix. Categories (2) and

TABLE 2

Number of Subjects per Grade Scored for Each Category in the Four- vs. Seven-Picture Story Task

	Grade							
Category	2	3	4	5	6	7	8	11
(1)	8	8	12	12	13	18	12	14
(2)	0	1	4	2	2	1	2	4
(3)	8	8	1	4	2	0	3	0
(4)	4	3	3	2	3	1	3	2

(4) show little if any developmental change, whereas categories (1) and (3) appear to increase and decrease with age, respectively—especially across grades 2 to 4. As in the previous analysis, an 8-cell chi square table was formed by combining adjacent categories and grades, yielding a chi square value of 22.10, p < .01. Analogous chi squares for sex and IQ as independent variables failed to reach statistical significance (although IQ showed a weak trend in the expected direction).

Although drawing inferences from the shape of developmental curves is perhaps a risky procedure, the writer ventures the hypothesis that whatever skills are tapped by this task are developmentally intermediate between Strategies A and B of the previous task. If one combines category frequencies in the manner (1)+ (2) and (3)+ (4), and then plots the changes in the two sums across grades, the curves diverge sharply at grade 4 and remain relatively flat thereafter. On the other hand, Strategy A is at peak frequency at grade 2 (at least) and Strategy B does not reach asymptote until grades 6 to 8. And yet, on the face of it, successful performance on this task ought to be much *easier* than the construction of Strategy A in the previous one. The latter, as we have argued, demands that the child step out of his own role into a manifestly different one, that of an opponent who, unlike the child, will seek money under a cup and get to keep it if there is any there. In the former task, not only does the activity in question appear to be of a more concrete, perceptual sort, requiring relatively little cognitive inference in comparison to the cup game, but, in addition, both the child's role and the other's role have literally the same job description, namely, to "read off" a simple story from a set of four pictures (the same pictures and the same story in both roles). In short, it would appear that all the child has to do to achieve a (1) score is to make minimal inferences from the visual evidence directly before him, without worrying about E2's role at all; surely a simpler task than the construction of Strategy A.

The problem, of course, must reside in the fact that the child has just previously constructed a quite different story from the same perceptual information (taken together with some other information that interacts with it). The child would obviously have little difficulty in telling the correct story if the previous one were not still present in his field of awareness, somehow interfering with the telling. The word "somehow" is an important qualifier here, since there appear to be at least two possible ways in which it might interfere. First, it could be that the child in his concreteness becomes fixated on the idea that the initial, seven-picture story is *the* correct story, the *real* story, and that the four-picture sequence is simply an incomplete, elliptical presentation of it, rather than something which possesses an alternative but bona fide story line in its own right. Although the task instructions clearly go counter to such an interpretation (they strongly emphasize that the child is to predict a naïve other's inference from the four pictures alone), the child might be so enamoured of it that all dissonant instructions fall on deaf ears. An alternative explanation would be that the child does indeed understand and accept the fact that a four-picture story is required, but is to a greater or lesser degree unable to unhook himself from his previous, seven-picture cognition. In particular, the picture of the boy making for the tree (no dog shown) has through his prior self-coding become a powerful cue for a fear-of-dog explanation of the climbing.

Although the first of these two interpretations may account for the behavior of a few of our younger subjects, the impression one gets from reading the protocols is that the second interpretation applies more pervasively. For some subjects it looks as if the aforementioned cue touches off its original response immediately and automatically; most instances of categories (3) and (4) give this impression. However, in other cases, usually scored under category (2), one can see what appear to be conflicts and compromises between the old and the new. One child will impute to E2 the belief that the boy climbed the tree *either* to get an apple *or* because the dog was chasing him. Another will state that *"Something* [sic] *might have been* [sic] chasing him" (our italics). These transitional cases illuminate particularly well a process which the writer believes occurred in a great many of our subjects: (a) a fairly clear understanding of the role-taking requirements of the task (attested to by statements like "He would think," "He would say," etc., in reference to E2), together with a basic capacity to initiate role-taking activity of roughly Strategy A type; (b) but an inability to take, or at least maintain, the role of an entirely fresh and unbiased perceiver of these four pictures, due to the insistent, unremitting, but largely unperceived presence of a pre-existing self-coding. It would appear that the following is a safe generalization about role-taking; whenever the task situation is so structured that one's own perspective regarding some event is kept alive and active through the very act of trying to predict another's (different) perspective regarding the same event, one's role-taking capabilities are put to a severe test indeed, since the one perspective has a continuous tendency to creep in and contaminate predictions about the other. The present task was structured this way, and so were the two communication tasks which will now be described.

VERBAL COMMUNICATION STUDIES
STUDY I
The procedure was as follows. The child was first taught to play a simple competitive game with E1. Although this game was our own invention, it was deliberately designed to be a familiar prototype which children would have little difficulty learning. There is a cube with different colored faces on it which is shaken in a cup and then thrown on the table. If a red face turns up, say, the player moves his "man" (which is a toy pig) along a board which has colored bands on it and stops at the first red band he comes to. Then the other player takes his turn with the cube and moves his "man" to the appropriate band. The two players continue to alternate in this way and the first player to get to the end of the board and back twice wins the game. Finally, there is one small "rule," more or less self-evident to the player: namely, if the cube turns up a black face, the player cannot

move his "man," since there is no black band on the board. The game was taught to each child *nonverbally*. That is, E1 and the child simply played the game through together, E1 using gestures where needed. As we had hoped, even the youngest subjects quickly learned to play it correctly.

E2 then entered the room and the child was told that this man did not know anything about the game and that the child was to tell him how to play it, to tell him just as well as he could so that the man could play it himself when he got the chance, perhaps tomorrow. The child was also told that there would be two "rules" in operation. First, he was not allowed to touch any of the game materials as he communicated; that is, he could not teach the game by actually playing it, as he himself had just learned it. Second, E2, the listener, would not be allowed to say anything during the child's communication—he would just sit and listen. (Actually, E2 sat nodding and smiling in a friendly fashion, and might thus be regarded as an indiscriminate reinforcer for anything the child said.)

For half the boys and girls of each grade level, the listener was *blindfolded* throughout the proceedings, a fact that was very carefully brought to the child's attention. E1 explained that the listener would not be able to see anything as the child talked, and in the case of some of the youngest subjects, we actually had the child try a blindfold on to see what it was like. For the other half of the subject group, the listener was a normal, *sighted* one. In the case of the second-grade and eighth-grade groups only, those subjects—10 per grade—who had communicated to the sighted listener were immediately thereafter introduced to a second, blindfolded listener in the person of E3 (the writer), and were instructed to tell him how to play the game, too (the instructions here were the standard, "blindfolded-listener" ones). To recapitulate this rather complex design: 80 of the 160 children communicated to a sighted listener and the other 80 to a blindfolded listener; of the 80 sighted-listener subjects, 20 (10 second-graders and 10 eighth-graders) gave a second communication, this time to a blindfolded listener. All communications were tape recorded.

There were two hypotheses in this study. First, and more trivial, it was of course expected that communicative effectiveness in general, to blindfolded and sighted listeners alike, would show an over-all increase with age. Second, and more important, our developmental conception about the relationship between role-taking and communication led us to expect that older children would be more likely to adapt and tailor their message to the specific input requirements of a specific kind of listener. In the present study, this implies an increasingly greater *difference*, with age, between what gets said to the sighted listener and what gets said to the blindfolded listener, the latter, of course, requiring the fuller, more detailed communication. In analysis of variance terms, the first hypothesis simply asserts a main effect for age as regards amount and quality of information communicated, while the second hypothesis predicts an interaction between age and type of listener.

There were three measures in particular which seemed to work out satisfactorily as potential indices of communicative fullness or adequacy. One was *Game Information*, which involved judgments about the number and quality of explanations and descriptions regarding game materials, procedures, and rules. The second, called *Different Words*, was simply the number of different words used in the message (the number of "types" versus "tokens"). The third measure, *Inadequate Information*, involved estimates of the number of communicative units in the message at which someone in the listener's role would *fail* to obtain a correct understanding of what the child meant from what he said. A high score on this measure therefore implied a message which would either confuse or mislead the listener on a number of points, hence an inadequate message. Altogether, these three measures showed good credentials for our purposes. They seemed to possess reasonable face validity as estimates of communicative adequacy in this kind of communicative problem. They were continuous measures with adequate ranges. The interjudge reliabilities were fair to very high: the correlations between two judges were .76 for Inadequate Information and .84 for Game Information; the Different Words measure required very little decision-making on the judge's part and so we did not bother to assess its interjudge reliability. All three measures showed moderate correlations with age, thus confirming the first, less important hypothesis: Game Information correlated .60 with age in months, Different Words .63, and Inadequate Information —.44. As for intercorrelations among themselves, with age partialed out, Different Words and Inadequate Information did not correlate at all, whereas the other two pairings showed low-moderate partial r's (.42 and .37).

The second and major hypothesis could be tested in two ways: intersubject and intrasubject. In the intersubject case, one would predict an age by listener-role interaction on each of the three measures. Figure 3

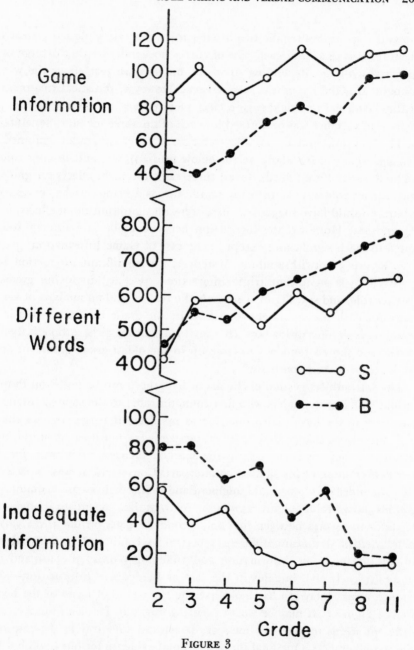

FIGURE 3
Communication to Sighted (S) vs. Blindfolded (B) Listener

shows the age curves for the two listener roles, separately plotted for each measure. It is clear that each pair of curves does indeed either diverge or converge with age, depending upon the measure, in just about the way it ought to if the hypothesis were correct. However, statistical treatment of these data did not yield such a clear picture. A 4 x 2 x 2 x 2 factorial analysis of variance was performed for each of the three measures separately. The four independent variables were: grade (adjacent grades combined, i.e., 2-3, 4-5, etc.), IQ (above versus below median), sex, and listener role (sighted versus blindfolded). In all three cases the main effects for grade and listener role were statistically significant, as a glance at the curves in Figure 3 would have suggested; there were no significant main effects for IQ and sex. However, the interaction between grade and listener role failed to reach significance except in the case of Game Information (p< .01), Figure 3 notwithstanding. Moreover, this significant interaction is qualified by a significant triple interaction (p < .05) involving grade, listener role, and sex. Figure 4 suggests the reason, and an analysis of variance for each sex separately confirmed it: the grade by listener-role interaction is significant for boys (p <.01); it is not for girls, although their curves also show a tendency to close up in the oldest grade group, in accordance with the hypothesis.

The intrasubject version of the major hypothesis can be tested on those second- and eighth-graders who first communicated to the sighted listener and then to the blindfolded one. It was predicted that the younger subjects would not change their original message very much in communicating to the new listener, despite the marked increase in informational needs over those of his sighted counterpart. Conversely, it was expected that the older children would augment and refine their second communications considerably. Figure 5 gives the relevant data. A statistical analysis of difference scores between first and second messages on our three variables yielded significant differences between second- and eighth-graders in the case of Game Information and Different Words (p < .01 and p < .05, respectively), but not in the case of Inadequate Information—although again, there is what looks like the right kind of trend at the bottom of Figure 5. It may be worth pointing out that the mean number of different words for the two messages is actually *identical* in the case of the second-graders. One final bit of anecdotal evidence for our hypothesis. Several of the younger subjects, but none of the older ones, showed what

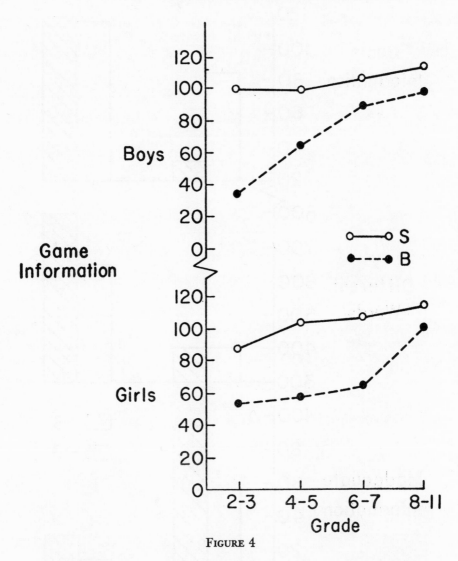

FIGURE 4

Game Information: Listener by Grade Interactions for Boys and Girls

we regarded as a most extreme failure to take account of the listener's role. They would sit there, facing the blindfolded experimenter, and blandly tell him that to play the game "You pick up *this*" (points to cube), "put it in *here*" (points to cup), and so forth.

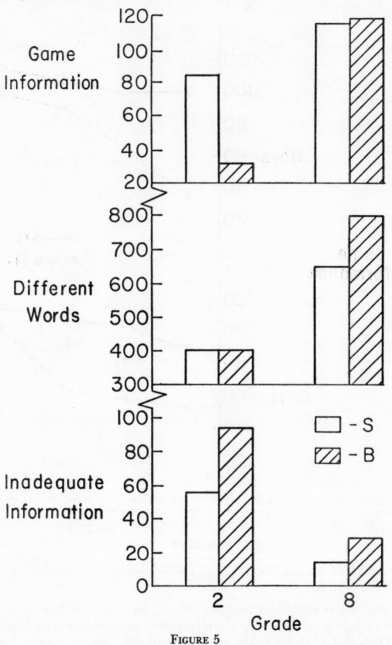

Communication to Two Listeners in Succession: Sighted (S) First and
Blindfolded (B) Second

Although the data from this experiment are not clear-cut enough to be entirely persuasive, the writer construes them as offering tentative support for the hypothesis that the development of role-taking abilities does play an important part in the genesis of communication skills. Needless to say, these abilities could scarcely be regarded as the *only* contributing factor, and no such extreme position is argued here. It is easy to think of other potential contributors, factors which doubtless interact both with each other and with the role-taking component. For instance, there is the child's growing ability to differentiate and organize conceptually the raw data from which the message is to be built (e.g., the game materials and procedure in this study). And intimately related to this is the matter of language skills, i.e., verbal fluency, available vocabulary, etc. Considering both factors jointly, it can simply be said that the speaker's ability to code effectively for the listener has to be dependent in large part upon his ability to cognize and code for himself.

The question then arises whether such factors might account for *all* developmental changes in communication in general and in this study in particular, i.e., whether it is necessary to assign any variance at all to the role-taking factor. For example, it might be argued that the following is a complete description of what happened in our experiment: the younger children quite rightly communicate as fully and informatively as they can (i.e., right up to the limit of their restricted cognizing and coding abilities) to the sighted listener and can therefore do no more for a blindfolded one, even though they are quite aware of his greater need for communicative input; the older children send a message which is adequate for the sighted listener but does not exhaust their cognizing and coding capabilities, and then approach their limit when confronted with the problem of communicating the game to a blindfolded listener. There are several reasons for thinking that this explanation does not catch the whole truth. First, the role-taking studies previously described—plus others not described here (Flavell, 1961)—do indicate that role-taking skills *are* age-dependent, with the implication that the older subjects in the present experiment may well have capitalized on these skills in organizing their messages to the blindfolded listener. Second, the cases of indefinite reference in the present study ("You pick up *this,*" etc.) certainly argue for the view that role-taking deficiencies in the younger subjects played some part in their communicative difficulties, above and beyond the contributions of cognitive immaturity, limited vocabulary, etc. And finally, we have also obtained similar results on communicative tasks where it is somewhat harder to see how these other factors alone could explain the developmental differences found (Flavell, 1961). In the present task, the blindfolded listener differs from the sighted one in that he requires a much more extended and complex message, one which gives full play to the speaker's cognitive and verbal abilities. In the task to be described below, the second listener also requires a different message than the first one does, but its construction more obviously presupposes role-taking as opposed to other intellectual skills than was perhaps the case in the present study.

STUDY II

The investigation of which this study is a part was of smaller scope than the one which included the preceding three experiments. The subjects were 60 girls, 20 from each of grades 3, 7, and 11 in the same school system from which the previous subjects were drawn. These three groups were matched on group-administered IQ test scores (mean score of about 108). The subjects were tested individually by one experimenter, Patricia T. Botkin. The subject was presented with the Aesop fable, "The Fox and the Grapes," set in extra large typescript. In the case of the seventh- and eleventh-graders, each subject was instructed to read the fable silently, to herself. The third-graders read it aloud one or more times, as needed, with the experimenter correcting reading errors, defining words which the child appeared not to understand, and generally trying to insure that the child thoroughly mastered it at both the reading and comprehension levels. All subjects were then shown a large photograph of a man, told to imagine it were a real man sitting there, and told to read the story to him. Following this reading, the child was shown a large photograph of a little boy, and given the following instructions:

> I want you to pretend he is a real four-year-old boy sitting there. Now tell *him* the story so he'll understand it just as well as you do. You can use this paper (the typed copy) or not, whichever you want —the important thing is for you to tell him the story so he understands everything, be sure he *understands* what everything in the story *means*. Go ahead.

The child's story was tape recorded and then transcribed for analysis purposes.

Each story was scored for the number of *simplifying recodings* it contained, defined as any alterations from the original story text which could reasonably be interpreted as a deliberate attempt to make the story easier for a 4-year-old to grasp. There were three categories of simplifying recodings: *substitutions*, e.g., "quoth he" replaced by the more familiar "he said"; *additions*, i.e., words or phrases added to clarify the story; *deletions*, i.e., the omission of unessential words or phrases which might not be understood by a young listener. Interjudge reliability has not yet been assessed for these scoring categories, but it will probably turn out to be adequately high. Simple analyses of variance were performed to test for significance of differences among the three grade groups for total simplifying recodings and for each of the above three component categories. F values were significant for total recodings and for substitutions (p < .02 and p < .001, respectively), but not for additions and deletions. Individual t-test comparisons between grades were then made for the former two measures. Table 3 presents the mean scores for all measures for each grade. For Total Simplifying Recodings, the grade 7 and grade 11 means are both significantly higher than the grade 3 means (p < .01 and p < .05, respectively), but are not significantly different from each other. In the case of Substitutions, all three possible comparisons yield statistically reliable differences: p < .01 for grade 3 versus grade 7; p < .05 for the other two mean differences. These data suggest an increase in over-all tend-

TABLE 3

Mean Scores for Total Simplifying Recodings and Component
Categories

Measure	Grade		
	3	7	11
Total Recodings	2.25	6.15	5.45
Substitutions	1.20	4.65	2.80
Additions	.60	.95	1.65
Deletions	.45	.55	1.00

ency to recode between grades 3 and 7, with little change thereafter; however, the preferred kind of recoding may change between grade 7 and
grade 11, with Additions and Deletions perhaps tending to replace Substitutions in the older group.

As in the previous study, maturation of cognitive-verbal skills apart
from role-taking ones no doubt plays a part in these group differences.
However, it is our suspicion that the third-graders actually had the basic
cognitive-verbal equipment to do considerably more recoding than they
did, if they had been more attuned to the need to do so. In this study, as
much or more than in any we have done, one gets the sense of actually
being able to "see" the presence or absence of a role-taking attitude in
many of the typed protocols. Since individual differences within age
groups are large (as they always are in developmental studies), one can
detect both its presence in younger children of limited verbal skills and
its absence in older children who may show considerable verbal fluency
and sophistication. Where it is absent, the child appears locked up in a
life space consisting of himself and the typed fable, and commonly reads
it verbatim, just as he did to the photograph of the man. Where it is present, you see the child pause at difficult or archaic phraseology, emit several "uhs" and "ums" while searching for a communicative solution, and
then come out with some sort of recoding, adequate or inadequate, which
you feel certain was her attempt to adapt the passage to the young listener's needs. The writer confesses to finding this sort of informal "evidence"
to be at least as persuasive as the statistical tables for the view that there
is an intimate connection between role-taking and good communication,
and that this connection is gradually formed during ontogenesis.

PRESCRIPTIONS FOR FUTURE RESEARCH

To show that role-taking skills and their utilization in communicative
situations develop with age is a proper research objective for a developmental psychologist, but it is obviously only a first-order, limited objective.
It is easy to summarize other types of researchable questions here (most
of them are interrelated), questions which the present experiments were
manifestly not designed to answer. First, there is the matter of ability structure, i.e., the number and kind of basic skills ("factors") which obtain
in this domain, the relationships between these and other types of intel-

lectual and perceptual abilities, etc. A beginning has been made by Feffer and Gourevitch (1960) and Wolfe (1963), who have found significant relationships between one role-taking measure (Feffer's) and several other cognitive measures. So far as the writer knows, however, no one has actually tried to factor analyze a whole set of different role-taking and communication tasks to tease out independent ability components in this area, but it clearly ought to be done. Likewise, there is the completely unexplored question of antecedents, correlates (especially of a noncognitive sort), and consequents of these skills: that is, what kinds of prior interpersonal and cognitive experiences with parents, peers, and others influence the acquisition of these abilities; what contemporaneous personality and other individual-difference variables correlate with them at any given age; and what other acquisitions does the attainment of these skills make possible or facilitate (a question broached earlier in this chapter). The question of possible antecedents of role-taking and communication skills is a particularly interesting one.

And finally, related to this last, there is the intriguing problem of how these behaviors are acquired in the child's everyday life, and especially, perhaps, how we might hasten or facilitate their acquisition through educational procedures. Two of the writer's research collaborators have been doing some pioneering work on this problem. Charles L. Fry (1961) had some limited success in improving the communicative performance of sixth-grade girls through a small-group "practicum course" in role-taking and communication, and has continued to explore the efficacy of this type of teaching procedure during the past several years at the University of Virginia. Patricia T. Botkin is currently engaged in a doctoral dissertation project (College of Education, University of Rochester) in which an attempt will be made to inculcate these skills by means of programmed instruction methods. Fry, Botkin, and the writer share the view that these abilities are important enough to deserve a niche in the elementary-school curriculum, provided that efficient and effective procedures for teaching them can be discovered.

BIBLIOGRAPHY

Burns, N. & Cavey, L. (1957), Age Differences in Empathic Ability Among Children. *Canadian Journal of Psychology*, 11:227-230.

Dymond, R. F., Hughes, A. S. & Raabe, V. L. (1952), Measurable Changes in Empathy with Age. *Journal of Consulting Psychology*, 16:202-206.

Feffer, M. H. & Gourevitch, V. (1960), Cognitive Aspects of Role-Taking in Children. *Journal of Personality*, 28:383-396.

Flavell, J. H. (1961), The Ontogenetic Development of Verbal Communication Skills. Final Progress Report (National Institute of Mental Health Grant M-2268).

——(1963), *The Developmental Psychology of Jean Piaget*. Princeton, New Jersey: Van Nostrand.

Fry, C. L. (1961), The Effects of Training in Communication and Role Perception on the Communicative Abilities of Children. Unpublished doctoral dissertation, University of Rochester.

Gates, G. S. (1923), An Experimental Study of the Growth of Social Perception. *Journal of Educational Psychology*, 14:449-462.

Inhelder, B. & Piaget, J. (1958), *The Growth of Logical Thinking from Childhood to Adolescence*. New York: Basic Books.

Mead, G. H. (1947), Language and the Development of the Self. *Readings in Social Psychology*, Newcomb, T. M. & Hartley, E. L. (Eds.), pp. 179-189. New York: Henry Holt.

Milgram, N. & Goodglass, H. (1961), Role Style Versus Cognitive Maturation in Word Associations of Adults and Children. *Journal of Personality*, 29:81-93.

Moore, O. K. (1958), Problem Solving and the Perception of Persons. *Person Perception and Interpersonal Behavior*, Tagiuri, R. & Petrullo, L. (Eds.), pp. 131-150. Stanford: Stanford University Press.

Murphy, L. B. (1937), *Social Behavior and Child Personality: An Exploratory Study of Some Roots of Sympathy*. New York: Columbia University Press.

Piaget, J. (1926), *The Language and Thought of the Child*. New York: Harcourt, Brace.

—— & Inhelder, B. (1956), *The Child's Conception of Space*. London: Routledge and Kegan Paul.

Sarbin, T. R. (1954), Role Theory. *Handbook of Social Psychology*, Lindzey, G. (Ed.), 1:223-258. Cambridge, Massachusetts: Addison-Wesley.

Sullivan, H. S. (1953), *The Interpersonal Theory of Psychiatry*. New York: Norton.

Wallach, M. A. (1963), Research on Children's Thinking. *Child Psychology: 62nd Yearbook of the National Society for the Study of Education*, Stevenson, H. W., et al. (Eds.), pp. 236-276. Chicago: University of Chicago Press.

Walton, W. E. (1936), Empathic Responses in Children. *Psychological Monographs: General and Applied*, 48(1).

Wolfe, R. (1963), The Role of Conceptual Systems in Cognitive Functioning at Varying Levels of Age and Intelligence. *Journal of Personality*, 31:108-123.

PART V

Affective Aspects of Perception

The affective aspects of perception have, during the last decade, been of immense interest to psychologists, who have produced a large quantity of research literature. Theoretical viewpoints have ranged from the hypothesis that affect is unquestionably the most important determinant of perception to the hypothesis that affect does not alter perception but rather produces response changes.

Solley in Chapter 11 and McCarthy in Chapter 12 review studies relating to the influence of affect upon perception per se and perception as represented in spoken and written language.

Garai's Chapter 13 is clinical in nature and indicates the emotional elements in the perception of the self. The majority of clinical studies seem to indicate that the affective elements in the development of the self-concept are important determinants of the perception of others in the environment.

All of the chapters in this section indicate a relationship between affect and perception, and all of them show that its exact nature and its precise developmental sequence are unknown. Perhaps if the current research, which is attempting to provide at least partial answers to these questions, includes new techniques for the separation of percepts and responses, and utilizes some of the clinical techniques for studying affect while controlling the influential variables, progress in this area can be anticipated in the near future.

CHAPTER 11

Affective Processes in Perceptual Development

CHARLES M. SOLLEY

An infant lies in its crib; it cries, thrashes around until its mother comes and changes its diaper and feeds it; and then it looks at its mother, smiles, and coos. On her first day at school, a small, prim girl is teased by a boy, has mud splashed on her pretty new dress, and breaks into tears. A 9-year-old boy gets angry when his father tells him he cannot go to the movies on Saturday. A young teen-ager blushes when the pretty girl in the next seat smiles at him. A high-school football team shouts with joy or cries with happiness as they win the championship game. Between the time of birth and the advent of adulthood there are many, many such bits and pieces of behavioral evidence that point to affective components in human functioning. There can be little doubt that these affective components influence how the child perceives the world about him, and that perceptual discriminations serve as cues for affect arousal. Indeed, the story of the perceptual development of the child is intimately intertwined with the story of how the child feels about things.

The word "development" implies change. It does not specify whether the change is brought about through maturation or through learning. Either maturation or learning can be responsible for the long-term changes that take place in the development of an individual. In addition, these changes rarely, if ever, occur as isolated events; they usually occur as parts of a dynamic system. For example, a child learns to walk at about one year of age. One week he cannot walk and the next he can. An important change has taken place, but it has taken place as part of a much larger system. His learning to walk represents important maturational changes in his nervous system, namely the motor cortex. It also represents an important biological achievement, in that the animal kingdom has survived by being able to locomote, to explore, in order to satisfy biological needs. Learning to walk changes the emotional, supportive, and communicative relationships between the child and the significant adults in his life. No longer is he completely dependent upon them for survival; no longer is his stimulus environment restricted. His stimulus habitat is enriched by virtue of the fact that, through walking, he can make contact with a wider variety of things. A wider spectrum of stimuli must be discriminated and organized perceptually. The act of learning to walk must be considered in terms of the role it plays in the over-all system of growth and achievement; it cannot be adequately viewed as a single, isolated event. This general principle holds for affective and perceptual events. Although we can and must examine bits and pieces of information in a meticulous manner, as we would examine a small specimen under a microscope, we must also step back from time to time and take a wider view in order to get a fuller perspective.

Looking at development from a close and a far view creates difficulties. But these are not the only problems. The development of children must be looked at in terms of the sweep of changes across years of growth and learning. Affective-perceptual development must be examined across years and not days. Unfortunately, many, many studies which use children as subjects simply use children as subjects. Properly speaking, these are not developmental studies. In the *Annual Reviews of Psychology* such studies are omitted from the sections on child development as not bearing directly upon developmental problems. Few indeed are studies which are genuinely developmental and which deal with the role of affective processes in perceptual development. Most studies which have examined affective-perceptual processes have used children of only one age or have indiscriminately pooled children of several ages. This means that a great deal of guessing and abstracting must be done in order to get a consolidated overview. This guessing and abstracting can only serve as a first approximation of a complete picture. Accordingly, what is presented in this chapter should be regarded as a hypothetical picture more than as an empirical establishment.

Let us begin by noting some of the functions of affective involvement with the world about the child. Affective involvement with the environment does several important things. A short list of such effects includes: (1) motivation to perceive and to act, (2) stimulation for growth, both physiological and psychological, and (3) alteration of the social environment in reaction or response to the affective implications of the behaviors of the child. The feelings and emotions of the infant and the young child are, indeed, not clearly differentiated from perception. How he perceives his mother, his older brother, his toys, his crib, is strongly embedded in the matrix of feelings he has about them. In turn, how he affectively acts toward the people in his little world determines to some degree how they act toward him. If the baby laughs and coos and wants to play with his mother, but also cries, frowns, and kicks at his father, the two parents will adopt different attitudes toward the infant. Similarly, if the mother holds the child gently and with ease while the father holds the baby awkwardly and without ease, the infant will begin to feel and to perceive the two as different. This does not mean we are faced with a chicken and egg problem about what comes first: it means we must recognize the transactions, the interactions, and the commerces between a child and his environment in the course of development if we are to grasp fully the role of affective processes in perception.

It is also essential that we understand that affective processes express themselves differently in perception and in behavior as the child grows. The child is indeed father to the man, but this does not mean that the child *is* a man. A child's means of expressing his likes and dislikes, his pleasures and his pains, his loves and his fears, are markedly different from an adult's. Whereas an adult uses language to express himself, the infant uses nonverbal behavior. Whereas an adult may conceal his feelings, a child is much less likely to do so. The child has a limited repertoire of behaviors for expressing his feelings and his perceptions as well as more limited means of controlling emotional and affective arousal. His feelings are more on the surface. This is one of the many reasons why children are so delightful to study. Perception and feelings are more visible and pliable.

All of the foregoing tells us that a careful examination of affective processes in perceptual development must focus upon several different aspects, that such an examination will not be an easy one, and that much profit can accrue to our understanding of child development through this undertaking.

EARLY AFFECTIVE-PERCEPTUAL DEVELOPMENT

In speaking of early "affective-perceptual" development, the hyphenating of the two terms is used to suggest that the affective system and the perceptual system do not exist as separate, distinguishable systems in the infant (Werner, 1957). As the course of development unfolds, affect and perception begin to function more and more independently, although there are still points of interconnection even in an adult. A description of the earliest observable aspects of perception automatically entails a description of affect, and vice versa.

The infant lying in his crib cannot speak, but his behavior "speaks" for him. Long periods of time are spent sleeping; shorter periods in eating; still shorter periods in looking, listening, and touching. At times he may smile and at times he may cry. By observing and noting *what* the infant smiles at, or cries about, or looks at, we can learn something about affective-perceptual development.

SMILING BEHAVIOR

It is always good to begin with a phenomenon that is fairly universal and clear. For this reason, let us look at smiling behavior in infants. A smile can mean many things. The smile of the Mona Lisa is not the same as the smile of the girl who wins the Miss America award, and that smile is not the same as that of a baby. In any case, a smile by and large signals pleasure and contentment. In addition, smiling is one of the earliest and most universal behaviors of a young child (Kaila, 1935). For these reasons the studies of smiling behaviors in infants, by Spitz and Wolf (1946), are especially instructive. Most textbooks which mention these studies state that the babies smiled at any human or humanlike face. This is only half true, and, besides, Spitz and Wolf ran several studies, not just one.

First of all, a trend was noted. Below 3 months of age the human infants seldom smiled. Between 3 and 6 months the infants smiled at *any* full-face view of a humanlike face. They would not smile at a profile view.

After 6 months, the babies stopped smiling at *all* human faces and began smiling, selectively, only to certain faces. During this brief period of time —between 3 and 6 months—a baby seems to enjoy contact with other humans. Apparently the child perceived the human face as a source of gratification or as connected with pleasure. He discriminated between human faces, *en face*, and human faces in profile as well as between full-view humanoid faces and inanimate objects such as toys. The smiling response reveals an affective attachment to a full-view human face as well as some of the dimensions which can be discriminated perceptually.

Second, these discriminatory affective-perceptual responses of smiling occurred in babies of different racial backgrounds. White, Negro, and Indian babies showed the same type of behavior. All of these infants had roughly the same type of cultural background, however, and more tests need to be run on children from radically different cultural milieus (Dennis, 1951).

Third, Spitz and Wolf also tested babies with a scarecrow setup. A dummy with a painted face which could bend its head toward the baby also was found to elicit smiles. This result may mean, however, that movement of a face *toward* a child is the adequate stimulus for smiling. After all, such movements accompany an adult's picking an infant up and giving it what Harlow (1959) calls contact-comfort. The real-face and masked-face tests also elicited smiles primarily when movement toward the baby was involved.

A fourth point brought out by Spitz and Wolf, which they discussed in some detail, is that a small percentage of children—roughly 1%—do not smile at a human face. In fact a few babies always cried. To these few babies the human face elicited fear rather than feelings of pleasure. Perhaps they had associated some kind of painful experience with human faces. Until a longitudinal study is made we will not know the answer to this puzzle.

No matter how one looks at the Spitz and Wolf studies, they are excellent examples of how one can use the most elementary procedures to study an affective-perceptual response. These studies leave little doubt that an infant perceives all adults as sources of pleasure, that his perception of people's faces is indelibly tied up with his feelings of happiness. They also tell us that infants are able to discriminate complex stimuli. A human face is a quite complex configuration, far more complex than a circle or a triangle. When the infant smiles at a full-view face but does not smile at a profile-view face, he is demonstrating that he can discriminate the two complex arrays of stimuli. Some psychologists would argue, however, that we do not know if the infant *really* perceives the human face as a form. This is a meaningless argument. For all nonverbal animals, including human infants, we can only use differential behavior toward two or more stimuli as evidence of discrimination. Even verbal behavior must be differential before we can use it as evidence of discrimination.

ATTENTIONAL BEHAVIOR

Inasmuch as the Spitz and Wolf study revealed a capacity on the part of the infant for discriminating complex stimuli, it is not surprising to discover that evidence of a quite different type supports such a conclusion. The reader will recall that the smiling response to human faces occurs at about 3 months of age. Earlier than that there is another natural form of behavior which we can use to study the affective-perceptual system. This behavior is that of attending.

Before an infant begins to smile at people he has already begun looking at some things while ignoring others. He has begun *selecting* from the environment; he is sampling from the environment those stimuli which satisfy his needs or which at least are biologically useful. Selective attending reveals a selective interest, a focalization of affect, or an investment of feeling in the world about the individual. As William James put it so beautifully: "Millions of items of the outward order are present to my senses which never properly enter into my experience. Why? Because they have no *interest* for me. *My experience is what I agree to attend to.* Only those items which I notice shape my mind—without selective interest, experience is an utter chaos" (1890, p. 402).

It is indeed quite apparent that certain stimuli can be dominant in experience at any given moment only to the exclusion of others. The kinds of stimuli which dominate attention in the infant can best be understood in terms of heredity and natural selection. Those organisms which were so constructed by heredity that they attended to dominant stimuli had the best chance for survival. Those who did not attend selectively to loud stimuli, movement, etc., were more likely to be exterminated. The infant who attends to significant stimuli is more likely to learn and to adapt.

One type of attentional behavior is the orienting-investigatory reflex which was called the "what is it?" reflex by Pavlov. It has been extensively investigated by several eminent Russians such as E. N. Sokolov (1954). Since this behavior is primarily elicited by new, novel, or sudden stimuli, it properly belongs to the field of attention. When the individual is not "ready" for a new or novel stimulus, he carries out a series of orienting and investigating responses, such as turning his head toward the stimulus, pricking up his ears, reaching and touching, and generally alerting himself to focus upon the unfamiliar or unexpected stimulus. By so doing he brings the object into a sharper salience by shutting out competing background stimuli.

The orienting-investigatory behavior consists of several responses. A short list of these includes the following: (1) gross body, head, and eye movements toward the new object, (2) dilation of blood vessels in the forehead and contraction of blood vessels in the fingers, (3) pupillary dilation, (4) an increase in the galvanic skin reflex (GSR), and (5) a blocking of the alpha rhythm in the electroencephalogram (EEG). If one or more of these behaviors occur, then the organism is said to be making an orienting-investigatory reflex.

Figurin and Denisova (1949) studied these behaviors during a child's first year of life. They found an orienting reflex to food (taste) at birth as well as an orienting reflex to changes in postural position (balance). The reflex emerged for sound (hearing) at about 2 weeks and the visual orienting reflex occurred at about 4 weeks. Biologically, orienting-investigatory behavior appears to be a primitive way of relating oneself to his environment. Indeed, without a visual orienting response we would not be able to see clearly at all. Gesell, Ilg, and Bullis (1949) have shown that an infant cannot focus both eyes upon a single stimulus until several weeks after birth. The infant will grossly orient his whole body toward a stimulus at first; then he will turn just his head; then he achieves the capacity to focus just his eyes on the object. At first the fixational response is predominantly to moving or bright objects. The infant attends to his toys and his hands, particularly if they are moving. While looking at the object, his hands open and close as if he were grasping it. Vision is integrated with the motor action of grasping: As Piaget (1954) would say, sensorimotor schemas of intelligence are achieved. Development proceeds from a gross to a fine form, from the massive to the particular (Gesell, 1946).

What do these studies on early attentional behavior tell us? They inform us that infants can perceive the *presence* of auditory, tactual, gustatory, and visual stimuli at an extremely early age. Out of literally millions of stimuli which are bombarding him, an infant can discriminate the presence of certain specific ones (Stirnimann, 1944; Ling, 1942). A perceptual world does exist for him—a world of tastes, sounds, pressures, and sights. This world is doubtless more poorly differentiated, in the Gibsons' sense (Gibson and Gibson, 1955), than the world of an adult, but it does exist and can be discriminated (Fantz, 1961).

The physiological basis of selectiveness, on the other hand, received a boost from the research by Hernández-Péon and his co-workers (Hernández-Péon, Guzman-Flores, Alcaraz, and Fernandez-Guardiola, 1956; Hernández-Péon, Scherrer, and Jouvet, 1956). Using cats as subjects, in one study they placed electrodes along the auditory pathway and in another they placed electrodes along the visual pathway. They found that the auditory nerve did not transmit impulses beyond the first ganglion when the cat was attending to two mice in a bottle in front of him. Attending to the visual stimulus (the mice) reduced or blocked energization of the auditory nerve. On the other hand, if the cat was focusing its attention upon sounds (mouse squeaks) or smells (food), then the visual pathway was partially or completely blocked. These studies tell us that attending to an object in one sense modality blocks the transmission of information from other sense modalities.

In all of these cases stimuli which would normally arouse strong affect block competing stimuli. If an infant attends strongly to a given stimulus, then it is not unreasonable to assume that that stimulus is affective for him. He is at least strongly motivated to attend differentially. Changes that take place in attentional behaviors as the child grows indicate either a change in affective involvement or a change in perceptual discrimination or both.

Some recent research by Fantz (1956, 1961) and Silbiger (1963) demonstrates some of the early changes in attentional behaviors. Fantz (1956) studied infants between 1 and 22 weeks old; Silbiger (1963) observed infants between 4 and 28 weeks old. Both investigators used similar pieces of apparatus. A boxlike crib with a bassinet type of chair was used. Stimuli were exposed in pairs above the infant. Left and right positions of stimuli were counterbalanced. The E looked at the infant's eyes to see the image reflected there. The amount of time the infant spent attending to each stimulus was recorded.

In Fantz's research the infants spent a great deal of time looking at the picture of a face, but they also spent an almost equal amount of time looking at a "scrambled" face. The preference for the real and the scrambled face over abstract designs increases up to a time between 2 and 3 months of age, and then decreases.

It is interesting that the age at which an infant shows discrimination of a human face is the age at which Spitz and Wolf first observed the smiling response to humanlike faces. The human face is indeed a complex stimulus, and Fantz and Silbiger have both shown that there is an attentional preference for complex stimuli. Is the human face attended to because it is complex or because it is a human face? Silbiger found that at 2 months the attentional preference is for the human face because of its complexity but at 6 months the human face is preferred to other equally complex stimuli.

These studies tell us that infants attend more to complex stimuli than to simple ones. They also prefer a picture of a human face to a simple form, but this is mostly due to their preference for complex forms. In Silbiger's studies (1963) the infants rarely smiled at any stimulus except for the three-dimensional face. One little boy, age 4 months, only paid attention to a male face, cooing and trying to touch it. His mother said, "He's Daddy's boy. I am just the diaper changer." The mother's remarks and the child's attentional behaviors indicate the child's strong affective attachment to his father.

The development of the smiling response, the orienting-investigatory reflex, and attentional behaviors occur at an extraordinarily early age. Whether these behaviors are learned or are innate is not known, but the consistency with which they occur in early infancy suggests they are not learned. Strong, new, or novel stimuli seem to elicit them automatically (see Berlyne, 1960). At later ages, such behaviors do become connected through learning to other stimuli. That is, attentional behaviors can become connected to stimuli which do not ordinarily elicit them (Luria and Vinagradova, 1959).

Such complex reactions on the part of infants to complex stimuli reminds one of the instinctual reactions reported by Lorenz (1937), Tinbergen (1948), Pastore (1956), Beach and Jaynes (1954), Jaynes (1956, 1957), and Gray (1958). Studies on imprinting deal with varied behaviors, and seem to depend upon the occurrence of specific, appropriate environmental conditions for their elicitation and growth. Birds, cats, chickens, ducklings, and human infants have been studied and indicate that there are critical periods in early development in which the parent or parent surrogate as well as things which are to be feared are imprinted.

In imprinting it is assumed that the young animal has an innate disposition or, to borrow MacDougall's term, "propensity," to learn to perceive what is its parent at certain critical stages in early development. If the young animal encounters a stimulus distribution which has the properties which "fit" this propensity, then that perceptual stimulus is imprinted as the parent. Imprinting takes place rapidly, often on the basis of a single encounter, and is very resistant to reversal. The imprinting itself can produce certain specific behaviors which release other stimuli from the "parent" who fixated the original imprinting. Imprinting may not occur, however, if there are no adequate stimuli present at the critical stage in development. Since imprinting denotes critical periods of development in which significant maturational and perceptual alterations take place, it is of special significance. In imprinting an affective-perceptual relationship is established, which tends to persist. This relationship may be one of fear, such as when a young gosling perceives the shadow of a hawk as a sign of danger. Or it may be such that the infant cathects positive feelings of love and delight in the object, as when a young child perceives his mother as a love object.

All of the foregoing tells us that an infant can perceive something before perceptual development and learning begin. A rough but grossly differentiated psychophysical relationship exists between the infant and his world of stimuli. This relationship is indelibly fused with affect. Through learning, the infant must come to differentiate one perceptual stimulus from another as well as perception from affect. He does not come to associate affect with perception: it is already associated. However, he can transfer affective relations from one percept to another or invest feelings in previously neutral events.

AFFECTIVE PROCESSES IN OLDER CHILDREN

AUTISM

Autistic perception in its extreme form is a withdrawal from the world of reality. It is living within a perceptual world generated by one's private needs, wishes, and motives. Bleuler (1912, 1922), of course, is the one whom we have to thank for the original description of autism as it appears in psychiatric patients. However, psychiatric patients are not the only people who mix the subjective with the objective, or fantasy with reality: children also confuse desire with reality, as any parent knows who has tried to reason with his children. A young child selectively hears and sees what he wants to hear and see, and can perceive, at times, the exact opposite of what did occur. It seems to be the very nature of man to introject wishes and motives into his perceptual interpretations to some degree. No one fully escapes from this trap, nor is it clear that complete freedom from autistic perception is desirable. Some degree of autism is effective during creative work: a scientist or an artist uses fantasy, imagination, and the not-yet-real to generate research and theory. He uses hunches based on feelings to guide his intellectual endeavors at some times and tough-minded logic at other times.

Whereas an adult can switch from an autistic mode of perception to a realistic one without much trouble, a child finds it more difficult to separate his feelings from his perceptual world. His perceptions are indeed drive representations, as Rapaport (1951) put it. The child's perceptual world is a mixture of wishes and reality. For these reasons, it is important to examine autistic perception and its fraternal twin, motivated perception, as the child grows.

Piaget,[1] among others, has provided us with some theory concerning autism in young children. He has outlined a theoretical sequence of mental development in *The Construction of Reality in the Child* (Piaget, 1954) in which autism appears early. First, there is a stage in which the infant cannot distinguish between himself and his experiences. Through development he comes gradually to discriminate between the "I" and the "not-I." However, even after this discrimination is made the child's concepts of causation are based on the principle of "When I intend an object in perception I cause it to happen." In this stage, primitive assimilatory schemata are formed based on simple circular chains of events: perception, then self-action, then object-action, new perception. The infant may see a rattle, strike it, see it move, and cognize the "cause" of the

[1] For an excellent summary and integration of Piaget's theories and research, see Flavell (1963).

rattle's action as his original perception of it. Then the infant comes to generalize the causation to the object itself, so that the object is perceived as alive. In later stages of development the child becomes more aware of his own actions and discriminates events caused by his actions from those caused by outside sources. This sequence is purely hypothetical at present, of course.

The development of awareness of self is crucial for outgrowing complete autism. For example, in *The Child's Conception of Physical Causality*, Piaget (1930) wrote:

> Let us examine these processes more closely. In order to be objective, one must have become conscious of one's "I." Objective knowledge can only be conceived in relation to subjective, and a mind that was ignorant of itself inevitably tended to put into things its own pre-notions and prejudices, whether in the domain of reasoning, of immediate judgment, or even of perception. An objective intelligence in no way escapes from this law, but, being conscious of its own "I," it will be able to say what, roughly, is fact and what is interpretation [pp. 241-242].

Writing more directly about autism, Piaget said:

> Autism . . . [is] thought in which truth is confused with desire. To every desire corresponds immediately an image or illusion which transforms this desire into reality, thanks to a sort of pseudo-hallucination or play. No objective observation or reasoning is possible: There is only a perceptual play which transforms perceptions and creates situations in accordance with subject's pleasure. From the ontological viewpoint, what corresponds to this manner of thinking is primitive *psychological causality*, probably in a form that implies *magic* proper: the belief that any desire whatsoever can influence objects, the belief in the obedience of external things. Magic and autism are therefore two different sides of one and the same phenomenon—that confusion between the self and the world which destroys both logical truth and objective existence [pp. 302-303].

Very similar ideas are expressed by Werner (1957). According to him, in an infant there is a fusion of the affective, perceptual, cognitive, sensory, and motor systems. It is almost impossible to study one of these processes without also studying the other. As Werner puts it: "It is characteristic of primitive mental life that it reveals a relatively limited differentiation of object and subject, of perception and pure feeling, of idea and action, etc." (1957, p. 59). Perception of one event is dependent upon the infant's perception of other events. "Things do not stand out there, discrete and fixed in meaning with respect to the cognitive subject. They are intrinsically formed by the psychophysical organization of which they constitute an integral part, by the whole vital motor-affective situation" (Werner, 1957, p. 59). Further, the infant's perceptual world is characterized by being vague, yet concrete, and extremely labile or susceptible to change. Constancies in perception which supply structure and articulation to the perceived world have not been developed, and the child often perceives in an "animistic" manner. As Werner says:

> The high degree of unity between subject and object mediated by the motor-affective reactivity of the organism results in a dynamic, rather than static, apprehension of things. Things as constituent elements of a dynamic event must necessarily be dynamic in nature [p. 57]. Such dynamization of things based on the fact that the objects are predominantly understood through the motor and affective attitude of the subject may lead to a particular type of perception. Things perceived in this way may appear "animate" and, even though actually lifeless, seem to express some inner form of life [p. 69].

Gradually the child separates the various psychological functions of feeling, perception, and activity. So long as affect is indelibly mixed with perception the child perceives autistically. In the course of development the pleasure-pain principle must be superseded by the reality principle. This is not accomplished easily. As Freud (1911) described it:

> There is a general tendency of our mental apparatus ... which seems to find expression in the tenacity with which we hold on to the sources of pleasure at our disposal, and in the difficulty with which we renounce them. . . . The supersession of the pleasure-principle by the reality-principle with all the mental consequences of this ... is not accomplished in reality all at once: nor does it take place simultaneously along the whole line [pp. 16-17].

Some aspect of feelings, wishes, and desires clings to our perceptual system, even when we have reached adult life. Our intelligence, our world of understanding, has bound-affect cathexes.

The theoretical ideas of Piaget and Werner make sense, but there is still virtually no solid research evidence concerning autism in infants. Nearly all the experimental evidence about autism stems from research on older children, research to which we now turn.

MOTIVATIONS, PERCEPTION, AND AGE

The impact of rewards, punishments, and other types of motivators changes with the individual's development. In order to understand the effects of a particular experiment, which might last an hour, on perceptual learning, we must look at years of development, not minutes or weeks. The particular effect of money, for example, as a reinforcer depends upon what other things a child has learned. A child of a year will try to put the money in his mouth; a child of 4 may prize a nickel more than a dime since it is larger; a child of 15 may think that a nickel is hardly worth having. To say the least, children perceive money and other reinforcers differently with age. The affective qualities of reinforcement stimuli change, are regulated or dampened, in so far as the child has developed ways and means of controlling affect discharge. We know very little, as yet, about how affect-control behaviors develop, but we can be reasonably sure that they do. A child who gets angry very quickly when young will get angry quickly when older, but he learns, as he matures, to control the discharge of his anger and to direct its energy into socially acceptable channels (Murphy, 1947). The development of affect-control behaviors implies that the relationships between motivating conditions and perception will change with age. It also implies that some of the most clear and direct relationships between motivations and perception can best be observed in younger children.

A strong relationship between motivation and perception can be seen in the way young children perceive mythical creatures. It may surprise some adults, but children do clap their hands to save Tinker Bell from Captain Hook's poison, and they do believe in the magic of Santa Claus, the Easter Bunny, and Halloween witches. A series of studies has been done on how children perceive Santa Claus, only one of which has been previously reported (Solley and Haigh, 1957). In that study 8 children between the ages of 5 and 7 were asked to draw a picture of Santa Claus once a week during the month before Christmas and twice afterwards. As Christmas drew near, the children became more and more excited (motivated?) about it, and about what Santa would bring. Their drawings of Santa became larger and larger; his costume became more elaborate; the bag with the toys and presents became more pronounced; and Santa was drawn as being near to a home. In short, with increased motivation there was a corresponding increase in perceived form. After Christmas, when the excitement, the hullabaloo, and the motivation diminished, Santa was perceived as shrunken in size, plainer, and less significant. Figure 1 gives some examples.

The changes noted in this early study could be interpreted as changes in fantasy and not in perception. Accordingly, other studies were designed. A student at Wayne State University (Farris, 1960) repeated the first study, using a larger sample of children and scoring the drawings according to the Goodenough Draw-a-Person Test criteria to get a single index of the many changes that were taking place. The Goodenough index increased rapidly during December but dropped off only slightly after Christmas. This score reflects goodness of organization and complexity, not size, however. A second repetition of the first study (Ballin, 1961) at Wayne State University used a version of the Harvard Size Estimation Apparatus. A spot of light on a milk-glass screen could be continuously varied in size, getting either bigger or smaller. Children between 5 and 7 years old were shown discs of white paper with either a Santa Claus or a house on them. The child made both ascending and descending estimates of the size of the discs. Estimations were taken once a week up to Christmas and one week afterwards. These size estimations—which were a "purer" perceptual measure than the drawing—showed an increase up to Christmas and then a decrease. Even estimations of the house disc increased, but significantly less than Santa. Perhaps the child's entire perceptual world increases with the excitement of Christmas.

The question then arose about the generality of these motivation-perceptual relationships. A study on how children perceive the Easter Bunny (Abram, 1960) was carried out on a group of first-graders (about 6 years old) and a group of fourth-graders (about 9 years old) in Washington School, Ferndale, Michigan. The art teacher, Miss Iona Altschuller, had the children draw a picture of the "Easter Bunny" once a week for a month before Easter and twice afterwards, in their regular art class. These protocols were collected, and the height of each bunny was measured. There was no significant change in the height of the bunny drawings. However, the number of eggs, the complexity of egg designs, and the size of the eggs increased up to Easter and then declined. It was concluded that the egg was the symbol of Easter, not the bunny, since everything happened to it that had happened to Santa. The fourth-graders showed less affect than did the first-graders, as one might expect.

FIGURE 1
Drawings of Santa Claus Before and After Christmas

The foregoing studies all involve situations in which pleasant affect is involved with the expectancies. What about unpleasant expectancies? Craddick (1962) has done a study which bears upon the problem. He had children draw pictures of witches before, on, and after Halloween. The size of the witches decreased on Halloween. It is almost as if there were a perceptual shove, an attempt to push frightening things away. The farther away an object is, the smaller it is. With pleasant events, there is an attempt to draw the pleasant object closer perceptually, and consequently it is perceived as larger.

This kind of relationship between affect and perception has been shown by several psychologists (e.g., Bruner and Goodman, 1947; Lambert, Solomon, and Watson, 1949; Lambert and Lambert, 1953; Dukes and Bevan, 1952). Bruner and Goodman (1947) had "rich" and "poor" children estimate the size of coins. The tendency was to overestimate the sizes, the poor children overestimating more than the rich ones. In addition, Dukes and Bevan (1952) found that children overestimated the weight of jars containing candy. In all of these experiments it was assumed that coins, or symbols, or "seeing" candy was rewarding.

The first *direct* attempt to build up the valence of a neutral stimulus, before assessing perception of its size, was made by Carter and Schooler (1949), but their procedures were too complex. A simpler procedure was used by Lambert, Solomon, and Watson (1949). Their procedure was ingenious but quite straightforward. Thirty-two children (ages 3 to 5) from the Harvard nursery school and 22 (of comparable ages) from a Salvation Army nursery school were divided into an experimental group (N = 37) and a control group (N = 17). Each S was tested individually. The experimental Ss were allowed to turn a crank 18 times, at which time they received a white poker chip, which could be put into a slot in another machine to produce a piece of candy. The control Ss turned the crank 18 times, received no poker chip, and then received candy. Size estimations were made by adjusting a circular patch of light until it was perceived to be the same size as the poker chip. Size estimations were taken before any candy rewards were given, after 10 days of getting candy, after extinction (on the 11th day), and after reinstatement of the reward (on the 12th day). Their results are shown in Figure 2.

There was no significant difference between the experimental and the control groups *before* the rewards began, but after 10 days the experimental group overestimated the size of the poker chip more than did the controls. After extinction (no candy) on the 11th day, there was no difference again, but on the 12th day following reinstatement of the candy reward for the poker chip, the chip was overestimated again. The authors concluded that "the estimation changes in the experimental group may be compatible with a generalized pattern of behavior which we could call the 'cookie effect.' That is, the effect may be peculiar to our culture where,

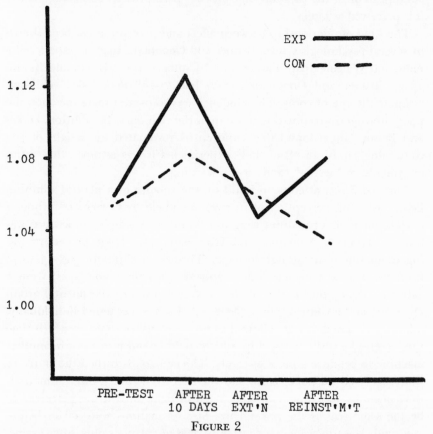

FIGURE 2

Size Estimation of Token Before Reinforcement, After 10 Days of
Reinforcement, After Extinction, and After Reinstatement of
Reinforcement

Figure after Lambert, Solomon, and Watson (1949, p. 638).

for example, a 'bigger cookie is *better* than a little one.' 'Bigness' and 'value' or 'bigness' and 'goodness' may be acquired equivalences for our children, particularly at the ages of the subjects used here" (1949, p. 640).

A repetition of this study (Lambert and Lambert, 1953) used a series of poker chips. A red chip was given after 9 turns of the crank; it was inserted in the slot and the machine was cranked for 9 more turns after which a white chip was received. The white chip became overestimated but the red chip, which was further away from the candy reward, was not.

PERCEPTION OF OTHERS

The research on the smiling response and on attentional behaviors clearly reveals that infants can discriminate human faces at an early age. Smiling and attending are certainly types of indicators of social responsiveness. But there are other indicators of how infants perceive others. Not all children react positively to other humans. Many infants who are raised in institutions, or who are hospitalized for long periods of time, or who are separated from their mothers often show apathy, emotional disturbance, mental retardation, excessive needs for attention, or an inability to form positive emotional relationships (Glaser and Eisenberg, 1956).

Institutions and homes are not alike, obviously. In a sense the term "institutionalization" is a meaningless catchall. Some institutions provide terribly restrictive and unstimulating environments while others provide active, challenging, and stimulating environments. The author recalls his first visit to the Sarah Fisher Home in Detroit. The infants there receive a great deal of love and attention, toys, opportunities to play with other infants, fondling, love, and stimulation. In fact, they may receive more opportunities to develop than most normal infants at home. Such casual observations of institutions are inadequate, of course. What is needed is a way of measuring the degree and quality of maternal care given in an institution or home. One reliable system for evaluation of maternal care has been developed by Rheingold (1960). This is neither the time nor the place to describe her system; the interested reader can look up those details. What is important here is that she found in applying her measuring procedure that:

> The home infant had many more contacts with a mother than the institution infant with a caretaker. Not only was more done for him but he was brought into contact with more things. He had a richer

life, a more complex environment. At the same time, one can speculate, his life was probably more the same from day to day. To the
extent that a mother gave care in her own way, his life would lack
the kind of complexity brought about by many different and frequently changing caretakers.

While the contrasts in care were noteworthy, so, too, were the similarities. The results showed, for example, that caretaking activities
were similar in kind and in order of frequency, whether in home or
in institution [1960, pp. 572-573].

Although the home infants received care 4.5 times more often, were
looked at 4.9 times more often, were held 6.2 times more often, were
talked to 9.5 times more often, were played with 14.8 times more often,
and were rocked 16.9 times more often, there were only negligible differences between home and institutional infants as to what activities the infants engaged in. In general, it might be said that home infants receive
much more social contact than do institutional babies. As a consequence,
they should develop stronger affective relations, both positive and negative, with other people. On the other hand, if institutional infants were
given as much care, handling, and contact by adults as normal home babies, then they should increase their social responsiveness.

This hypothesis was tested by Rheingold (1956). Sixteen infants who
lived in an institution for about the first 9 months of their lives were divided into two groups. Eight were in the experimental group and the
other 8 were controls. The experiment lasted from the sixth through the
eighth month of life. The control babies were given the ordinary institutional routine but the experimental infants received a great deal of attentional care by the experimenter for 7½ hours a day. The results of
this treatment revealed that the experimental babies had become more
responsive to the experimenter. In addition, in time they generalized this
social responsiveness to other adults. They did not do better on the Cat-
tell Infant Intelligence Scale or on tests of postural development and cube
manipulation. In general it appears that getting a great deal of attention
from a single adult increases social responsiveness. Such infants perceive
adults as potentially rewarding.

A question pertinent to experimental mothering arises here. What are
the long-term effects of just two months of treatment? Would such a brief
experience with a great deal of attention have any effect on the later development of these infants after they were adopted? Rheingold and Bay-

ley (1959) did follow up 14 of the 16 infants originally studied. When the children were about 18 months old, approximately one year after the original study, the 14 infants were re-examined. Some were back in their own homes, some were in adoptive homes, two were in boarding homes, and one was still in the institution. An examiner recorded the child's responses to the mother, to the experimenter (who had handled the experimental group originally), and to the examiner. The examiner did not know to which group the children had belonged. There were no significant differences between the experimental and control groups. All of the original differences in social responsiveness were gone. On only one measure was a difference found: the experimental group was more vocal. However, there are always large differences between children on almost all measures and the wide variation in homes would make such variation even greater. The effect would have had to be tremendous to show up with only 14 infants, 7 in one group and 7 in the other.

FIGURE-GROUND ORGANIZATION

One of the most elementary characteristics of the perceptual field is that it is organized. If the stimulus situation is chaotic, then the organism throws the net of its intelligence upon the disordered events to bring them into order, orchestrates, arranges, and makes the chaotic orderly. It is virtually impossible—yes, it is impossible—to perceive one event without its being related to at least one other event. A percept does not exist without a field, and a field is impossible without a percept. Furthermore, the perceptual field is always divided into that which is figure and that which is ground, that to which and in which we are investing energy and that which we are ignoring. We may in the course of development achieve some degree of field independence, that is, the ability to operate upon one small part at a time, but complete field independence does not exist.

As one might expect, children have more difficulty perceiving things out of their usual context than do adults. This is well illustrated by the research of Witkin and his fellow workers (Witkin et al., 1954). Two primary tasks were given to children between 8 and 21 years old. These were a Gottschaldt task and the Rod and Frame task. The Gottschaldt task required the child to extract a given figure from an embedding context. Here the child must extract one part from a dynamically interrelated field of stimuli. Children between 8 and 10 years old have difficulty dis-

296 CHARLES M. SOLLEY

connecting a figure from its context. However, there is a progressive improvement with age until at about 16 the child is as field independent as he will ever be. With adulthood there is some return to more dependence.

The effect of a context on perception, of ground upon figure, is also seen in certain illusions, such as the Delboeuf illusion. In the Delboeuf illusion a large circle contains a smaller one. The smaller one is seen as larger than an objectively equal circle on the outside. The effect decreases with age, as shown by Piaget, Lambercier, Boesch, and Albertini (1942-1943). In fact, nearly all of what Piaget calls "primary" illusions—those which decrease as the child grows older—are heavily dependent upon context effects for their distortions.

Perceptual field independence is not the only gain. Thresholds are lowered for certain types of stimuli (such as words) but not for others (such as objects) (Fraisse and MacMurray, 1960). The child becomes differentially sensitive to various stimuli, particularly those which surrounded him early in life (Gibson and Walk, 1956). In addition, the child organizes the perceptual field differently, using different strategies and methods to group and to structure stimuli (Rush, 1937).

What do these studies have to do with the role of affect in perception? We noted earlier in this chapter that affect is indisoluble from perception in the very young child and that it is ever-present in older children and adults. In brief, affect or how we feel about things is almost a perceptual ground for percepts. To the extent that ground influences or determines what is figural, the child's perceived world is structured about wishes, desires, feelings, and emotions.

Piaget (1953-1954, p. 146) discusses this last point. He says: "It is very evident that in perception affectivity intervenes constantly: Different subjects do not perceive the same elements in complex figures, and the choice is inspired by various interests; the child and the adult do not perceive the same details. But the laws of perception (which form the structure) rest upon the same nevertheless" (translated from the French by the present author). Affect does not destroy the basic laws of perception. It may alter what is perceived but it does not alter the fundamental ways in which what is perceived is organized.

A small number of studies on figure-ground organization in children support the contention that motives, rewards, and punishments influence what is figure and that this influence changes with age. The chief paradigm has been a simplified version of the Schafer-Murphy (1943) technique. In this procedure two profile faces are used, so that they can be joined together to form one profile line. During a training stage each profile was shown individually and was either rewarded (with money), punished (by taking money away), or had nothing done to it. Then, during a test stage, the double faces were shown, along with mirror images, and the child reported which face he saw—occasionally both faces were perceived.

A child was said to be perceiving autistically if the rewarded profile was figural in the reward-punishment or reward-neutral conditions or if the neutral profile was figural in the neutral-punishment condition. Children between 5 and 8 perceived more "autistically" than did older children. At 9 to 12 years of age the children are divided fairly evenly as to the strength of the pleasure-pain and the reality principles. On the other hand, young adults (Jackson, 1954) tend to emphasize the punished aspect in a punishment-neutral condition. In general there is a decrease in the "autistic" mode of perceptual organization and an increase in vigilance or alertness for mild punishers and rewards with age. The child gives up simply seeking pleasure and avoiding pain and becomes alert to mild punishers, particularly as he acquires behavioral means for dealing with punishment stimuli (Solley and Engel, 1960).

Younger children also show a great deal of fantasy connected with the profiles (Solley, Haigh, and Sommer, 1957). They nearly all consistently refused to call the profiles "faces" but referred to them as "moons" or "men in the moon." Unsolicited comments revealed that affect was cathected to the faces, especially the rewarded ones. One little boy commented: "Clem's a bright moon, like the man [laughs] in a full moon." With this boy Clem had been rewarded in the training phase. Another for whom Jake had been rewarded said, "Jake looks kind of happy. He's smiling, as if he's smiling. Here you look." (E looked.) "Don't you think he's happy?" Another: "Clem's a big fat moon." And another: "Both moons are there, only Jake has a line drawn around him with a heavy pencil." These spontaneous comments were corroborated by answers to "leading" types of questions in a second study. The children between 5 and 8 years old perceived the rewarded face, compared with the no-reward face, as happier, brighter, having a darker line drawn around it, and nearer to them. Solley and Engel also found similar results with children between 5 and 8 years old.

Children between 9 and 12, on the other hand, yield fewer spontaneous comments and less consistent results in answers to questions concerning the properties of what they perceive. They do, to a significant degree, perceive the rewarded profile as happier in a reward-neutral or reward-punishment condition, and a neutral profile as happier in a punishment-neutral condition. Although adults in the reward-punishment condition (Jackson, 1954) sometimes refer to the punished profile as a "goof" or an "idiot," it does seem that adults cathect far less affect to perceptual stimuli in experiments than do children. With children affect lies on the surface: with adults one must resort to projectionlike tests to probe deeper.

Indeed, the basic premise of the formation of autistic perceptions rests on the assumption that affect is cathected. An autistic perceptual organization is basically one in which cathected or immediate affect invades perception to such an extent that the person is swayed from perceiving veridically. From the evidence which exists, and it is indeed scanty, it seems that the major reason why children function more autistically than adults in their perceptions and cognitions lies in the lability of affect.

The trend which we have been describing seems complex, but is actually fairly simple. It can be summarized as follows: in young children, a simple pleasure-pain principle predicts what will be organized as "figure" in a figure-ground learning experiment; but with increase in age, mild punishers acquire "attention-getting" properties, particularly as the child develops affect-control behaviors. The development of behaviors which cope with, modulate, or regulate affect is of paramount significance in determining the extent and direction of cognitive development (Klein, 1954). At least this hypothesis is supported by experimental studies of perceptual learning in which figure-ground organization has been studied.

AN OVERVIEW

It is time to take an overview of the role of affective processes in perceptual development. What has already been covered will serve as a table of particulars for the schema we now have to construct, just as an over-all schema can serve to give fuller meaning to the experimental facts previously detailed. Several schemas have been suggested by various writers. In abbreviated fashion the over-all schemas of Piaget, Werner, Lewin,

Schilder, Bleuler, and Rapaport are presented in Table 1 (Solley and Murphy, 1960). In examining several writers' opinions at one time, a surprising and pleasing correspondence is noted in ideas. Indeed the general principles which underlie various stages of affective-perceptual development represent points of agreement.

TABLE 1

Some Major Point Made About Developmental Stages in Cognition

Author	Sequence of Stages
Piaget (1954)	(1) No distinction between self and experience. (2) Primitive, assimilatory schemata formed based on "I perceive—I move—Object moves—I perceive something different" circular reaction. (3) From second stage, magical beliefs arise that inanimate objects are alive, as well as superstitious behavior. (4) Child becomes aware of own actions, discriminates such from outside actions, and achieves more veridical perception.
Werner (1957)	(1) Perception is primitive and syncretic in infant. There is limited differentiation of object and subject, of perception and pure feeling, of idea and action. (2) Emotions (affects) become differentiated, and perceptual constancies arise to maintain drive satisfactions; actions as means and concepts arise as primitive meanings. (3) Synthetic modes of action, thought, and affect develop, i.e., action, thought, and affect can interact after each has been differentiated by the child.
Lewin (1946)	(1) Infant's discrimination is poor or nonexistent. "My own body" does not exist as an entity. Neither do future events or expectations. Child is ruled by immediate situation. (2) Cognitive areas acquire definite character, the first being centered around food and elimination needs. Needs are poorly distinguished. Child learns "my own body" which serves as reference point for learning immediate surrounds. Primitive social relationships develop; needs organize behavior; derived needs appear. There is intense need, high level of irreality, and fluid (loose) cognitive structure which permits easy movement from reality to fantasy and return. (3) As quasineeds develop, intentions (will) acquire status of quasineed and thoughts about future develop. Cognitive structures become more articulated and differentiated, which prevents full impact of needs on perception.
Schilder (1920)	(1) Indefinite percepts. (2) These are transformed into definite percepts, images, and ideas by drives (needs) and the associated affect. Ideas stem from drive-cathected percepts. (3) As percepts become more definite they lose some of the drive cathexis and more veridical perception is attained, but thinking and perception always vulnerable to pleasure-pain principle and to early affective ties.
Bleuler (1912, 1922)	(1) Affect (the subjective aspect of motivation and drive) is inseparable from percept. Percepts are fragmentary. (2) Child becomes aware of discrepancy between his percepts and reality. (3) Child becomes aware of relationship between his subjective experiences of affect and his perceptual experiences.

Author   *Sequence of Stages*
Rapaport (1951)   (1) Infant has certain givens: primitive perceptual apparatuses, tensions, and capacities for affect and affect discharge. The primary models of *action, thought*, and *affect* (see Rapaport for details of models)
operate simultaneously. This leads to close relationship between these
three, e.g., with increase in need infant will partially discharge need
through hallucination of need object. (2) Ideas are now drive representations; memories and ideas are organized around drives; and primary-
process thinking is evident. (3) As child learns more means to goals, a
connectedness along pathways in reality toward need-satisfying objects
forms basis for reorganization of ideas. Child partially acquires independence from original drives, and secondary-process thinking arises.

Most writers stress the vagueness, ambiguity, and lack of differentiation
in the perceptual world of the infant. However, experimental evidence
tells us that the infant is able to attend, to focus, to recognize, and to discriminate to some degree. He most certainly cannot discriminate as finely
as an adult, nor does he possess the means to attend to any and all stimuli, but his perceptual world is not a tabula rasa. Figure and ground are
differentiated even though what is figural may shift with increased experience. In short, an infant can perceive something at the beginning. Experience will increase the fineness of his discriminations, reduce his thresholds
for recognition, articulate meanings into larger wholes, and increase his
repertoire of perceptual behaviors (Hebb, 1949).

There is also good reason to believe that the primitive perceptual world
of the child is indelibly blended with his affective world. The earliest signs
of perceptual discrimination are affective indicators as well. Further, autism, or perception organized around wish fulfillment, appears most
strongly at an early age. It is only later that there is a substantial reduction in autism and an increase in veridical perception. The summaries
in Table 1 strongly suggest this trend, but the problem at hand is how and
why this particular sequence should occur in development. What is involved in early autistic perception and what leads to the development of
more veridical percepts? Why should the child give up perceiving autistically if such perception is genuinely gratifying his wishes and needs?
Let us examine these problems in several ways.

One way such changes could come about would be through a change
in the motivational hierarchy. We have already suggested that affect forms
the background for perceptual figures and that as motivation changes so
does perception. In the course of development the affective qualities of

many stimuli change. Parents, toys, pets, and home in general take on affective qualities which did not exist before. In addition, as the child achieves locomotion and moves about, his range of needs changes and social motives begin to express themselves more strongly. There is a change in the type, quality, and intensity of motivations. This diversification of motives may be sufficient to eliminate autistic perception in that the ground upon which the percept occurs is becoming more general and less specific.

It is also possible that, even though an autistic percept is related to need satisfaction, it never completely satisfies long-term needs. If these needs continue unabated over a long period of time, it is possible that the individual gives up autism in order to achieve fuller biological satisfaction. Cinderella might wish very strongly that the pumpkin be a coach and the mice be horses, but if they did not become such she might turn to other, more realistic means for getting transportation.

The differentiation and elaboration of motives implies that new motives lead to new goals, to new forms of experience, and also to greater conflicts in parent-child-environment relations. As conflict grows, new means for detouring the barriers must evolve and new behaviors must be developed for coping with the affects aroused by the newly encountered frustrating situations. Conflicts between wishes and reality, between needs and ability to control need-produced affect arousal, and between various segments of reality serve to produce motivation for change from autistic forms of perception to more veridical forms.

There is still another possible "explanation" of the dynamics of the developmental sequence of "primitive perceptual acts—autistically dominated state—veridical stage." It is thoroughly plausible that the basic ingredients of learning, namely contiguity (or time factors), reinforcement (positive and negative), motivation, and practice, carry different weights in influencing "literal" and "assumptive" perception. The principles of contiguity and practice may account for the achievement of veridical, "literal" perception whereas the principles of contiguity, motivation, and reinforcement may explain the development of autism. It is possible that both autistic and veridical development can go on independently, to a large degree, of one another. Autism and veridical perception can be reflected in exactly the same perceptual structure. The child may perceive his father as a powerful, friendly giant who takes care of him. From the

child's position, the planes, edges, surfaces, spots of light on a curved surface, etc. which constitute the complex stimulus source called "father"
are as if they were from a giant. However, the affective and meaning component—the "assumptive" aspect of "father"—may reach such proportions
of love or fear that the child perceives his father as a god capable of completely satisfying or denying his every wish.

There can be little doubt that affective processes play a role in perceptual development. The literature contains many studies which point to
this. The questions remain how affect and perception are interrelated,
what are the precise developmental sequences, and how affect-control behavior develops. The area is ripe for research and the future eagerly awaits
the answer.

BIBLIOGRAPHY

Abram, L. (1960), *How Children Perceive the Easter Bunny.* Unpublished study.
Ballin, J. (1961), *Size Estimations of Santa Claus and Neutral Figures.* Unpublished study.
Beach, F. A. & Jaynes, J. (1954), Effects of Early Experience upon the Behavior of Animals. *Psychological Bulletin,* 51:239-326.
Berlyne, D. E. (1960), *Conflict, Arousal, and Curiosity.* New York: McGraw-Hill.
Bleuler, E. (1912), Autistic Thinking. *Organization and Pathology of Thought,* Rapaport, D. (Ed. & Trans.). New York: Columbia University Press, 1951.
———(1922), Autistic-Undisciplined Thinking. *Organization and Pathology of Thought,* Rapaport, D. (Ed. & Trans.). New York: Columbia University Press, 1951.
Bruner, J. S. & Goodman, C. C. (1947), Value and Need as Organizing Factors in Percep-
tion. *Journal of Abnormal and Social Psychology,* 42:33-44.
Carter, L. F. & Schooler, K. (1949), Value, Need, and Other Factors in Perception. *Psycho-
logical Review,* 56:200-207.
Craddick, R. A. (1962), *Size of Witches Drawings as a Function of Time Before, On, and
After Halloween.* Talk given at APA meeting, St. Louis, Missouri.
Dennis, W. (1951), Cultural and Developmental Factors in Perception. *Perception: An
Approach to Personality,* Blake, R. R. & Ramsey, G. V. (Eds.). New York: Ronald
Press.
Dukes, W. F. & Bevan, W. (1952), Accentuation and Response Variability in the Percep-
tion of Personally Relevant Objects. *Journal of Personality,* 20:457-465.
Fantz, R. L. (1956), A Method for Studying Early Visual Development. *Perceptual and
Motor Skills,* 6:13-15.
———(1961), The Origin of Form Perception. *Scientific American,* 204(5):66-72.
Farris, J. (1960), *A Quantitative Study of Children's Perception of Santa Claus.* Unpub-
lished study.
Figurin, N. L. & Denisova, M. P. (1949), *Stages in the Development of Behavior in Chil-
dren From Birth to One Year.* Moscow: U.S.S.R.
Flavell, J. H. (1963), *The Developmental Psychology of Jean Piaget.* Princeton: Van
Nostrand.

Fraisse, P. & MacMurray, G. (1960), Etude Genétique du Sénile Visuel de Perception pour Quatre Catégories de Stimuli. *Année Psychologique*, 60:1-9.

Freud, S. (1911), Formulations Regarding the Two Principles in Mental Functioning. *Collected Papers*, 4:13-21. London: Hogarth Press, 1946.

Gesell, A. (1946), The Ontogenesis of Infant Behavior. *Manual of Child Psychology*, Carmichael, L. (Ed.). New York: Wiley.

——, Ilg, F. L. & Bullis, G. (1949), *Vision: Its Development in the Child*. New York: Harper.

Gibson, J. J. & Gibson, E. J. (1955), Perceptual Learning: Differentiation or Enrichment? *Psychological Review*, 62:33-40.

Gibson, E. J. & Walk, R. D. (1956), The Effect of Prolonged Exposures to Visually Presented Patterns on Learning to Discriminate Them. *Journal of Comparative and Physiological Psychology*, 49:239-242.

Glaser, K. & Eisenberg, L. (1956), Maternal Deprivation. *Pediatrics*, 18:626-642.

Gray, P. H. (1958), Theory and Evidence of Imprinting in Human Infants. *Journal of Psychology*, 46:155-156.

Harlow, H. (1959), Love in Infant Monkeys. *Scientific American*, 200(6):68-74.

Hebb, D. O. (1949), *The Organization of Behavior*. New York: Wiley.

Hernández-Péon, R., Guzman-Flores, C., Alcaraz, M. & Fernandez-Guardiola, A. (1956), Photic Potentials in the Visual Pathway During Attention in Unanesthetized Cats. *Federal Proceedings*, 15:91-92.

——, Scherrer, H. & Jouvet, M. (1956), Modification of Electrical Activity in Cochlear Nucleus During "Attention" in Unanesthetized Cats. *Science*, 123:331-332.

Jackson, D. N. (1954), A Further Examination of the Role of Autism in a Visual Figure-Ground Relationship. *Journal of Psychology*, 38:339-357.

James, W. (1890), *Principles of Psychology*. New York: Holt.

Jaynes, J. (1956), Imprinting: The Interaction of Learned and Innate Behavior: I. Development and Generalization. *Journal of Comparative and Physiological Psychology*, 49:201-206.

——(1957), Imprinting: The Interaction of Learned and Innate Behavior: II. The Critical Period. *Journal of Comparative and Physiological Psychology*, 50:6-10.

Kaila, E. (1935), Über die Reaktionen des Säuglings auf das menschliche Gesicht. *Zeit. Psychol.*, 135:156-163.

Klein, G. S. (1954), Need and Regulation. *Nebraska Symposium on Motivation*, Jones, M. R. (Ed.), pp. 224-274. Lincoln, Nebraska: University of Nebraska Press.

Lambert, W. W. & Lambert, E. C. (1953), Some Indirect Effects of Reward on Children's Size Estimations. *Journal of Abnormal and Social Psychology*, 48:507-510.

——, Solomon, R. L. & Watson, P. D. (1949), Reinforcement and Extinction as Factors in Size Estimation. *Journal of Experimental Psychology*, 39:637-641.

Lewin, K. (1946), Behavior and Development as a Function of the Total Situation. *Manual of Child Psychology*, Carmichael, L. (Ed.). New York: Wiley.

Ling, B. C. (1942), A Genetic Study of Sustained Visual Fixation and Associated Behavior in the Human Infant from Birth to Six Months. *Journal of Genetic Psychology*, 61:227-277.

Lorenz, K. Z. (1937), The Companion in the Bird's World. *Auk*, 54:245-273.

Luria, A. R. & Vinagradova, O. S. (December 1, 1959), An Objective Investigation of the Dynamics of Semantic Systems. *The Central Nervous System and Behavior*, selected

304 CHARLES M. SOLLEY

translations from the Russian literature. United States Department of Health, Education, and Welfare.

Murphy, G. (1947), *Personality: A Biosocial Approach to Origins and Structure*. New York: Harper.

Pastore, N. (1956), An Examination of One Aspect of the Thesis that Perceiving is Learned. *Psychological Review*, 63:309-316.

Piaget, J. (1930), *The Child's Conception of Physical Causality*. London: Kegan.

——(1953-1954), Les Relations entre l'Intelligence et l'Affectivité dans le Développement de l'Enfant. *Bull. Psychol.*, 7:143-150, 346-361, 522-535, 699-701.

——(1954), *The Construction of Reality in the Child*. New York: Basic Books.

——, Lambercier, M., Boesch, E. & Albertini, B. (1942-1943), Recherches sur le Développement des Perceptions. I. Introduction à l'Etude des Perceptions chez l'Enfant et Analyse d'une Illusion Relative à la Perception Visuelle de Circles Concentriques (Delboeuf). *Arch. Psychol., Genève*, 29:1-107.

Rapaport, D. (Ed. & Trans.) (1951), *Organization and Pathology of Thought*. New York: Columbia University Press.

Rheingold, H. L. (1956), The Modification of Social Responsiveness in Institutional Babies. *Monographs of the Society for Research in Child Development*, 21(2).

——(1960), The Measurement of Maternal Care. *Child Development*, 31:565-575.

—— & Bayley, N. (1959), The Later Effects of an Experimental Modification of Mothering. *Child Development*, 30:363-372.

Rush, G. P. (1937), Visual Grouping in Relation to Age. *Archives of Psychology*, # 217.

Schafer, R. & Murphy, G. (1943), The Role of Autism in a Visual Figure-Ground Relationship. *Journal of Experimental Psychology*, 32:335-343.

Schilder, P. (1920), On the Development of Thoughts. *Organization and Pathology of Thought*, Rapaport, D. (Ed. & Trans.). New York: Columbia University Press, 1951.

Silbiger, F. (1963), *Attention to Human Faces in Infants*. Unpublished doctoral dissertation, Wayne State University.

Sokolov, Y. N. (1954), The Orientation Reflex and the Problem of Reception. *Reports to the Congress on Problems of Psychology*, July 3-8, 1953. Academy of Pedagogical Sciences, RSFSR, Moscow.

Solley, C. M. & Engel, M. (1960), Perceptual Autism in Children: The Effects of Reward, Punishment, and Neutral Conditions upon Perceptual Learning. *Journal of Genetic Psychology*, 97:77-91.

—— & Haigh, G. (1957), A Note to Santa Claus. *T.P.R.*, The Menninger Foundation, 18(3):4-5.

—— & Murphy, G. (1960), *Development of the Perceptual World*. New York: Basic Books.

——, —— & Sommer, R. (1957), Perceptual Autism in Children. *Journal of Genetic Psychology*, 56:3-11.

Spitz, R. A. & Wolf, K. M. (1946), The Smiling Response: A Contribution to the Ontogenesis of Social Relations. *Genetic Psychology Monographs*, 34:57-125.

Stirnimann, F. (1944), Über das Farbempfinden Neugeborener. *Ann. Paediat.*, 163:1-25.

Tinbergen, N. (1948), Social Releasers and the Experimental Method Required for Their Study. *Wilson Bulletin*, 60:6-51.

Werner, H. (1957), *Comparative Psychology of Mental Development*. New York: International Universities Press, revised edition.

Witkin, H. A., Lewis, H. B., Hertzman, M., Machover, K., Meissner, P. B. & Wapner, S. (1954), *Personality Through Perception*. New York: Harper.

CHAPTER 12

Affective Aspects of Language Learning

DOROTHEA McCARTHY

In order to become a well-adjusted, well-integrated personality able to behave intelligently in our culture, a child must learn to communicate effectively with others. One of his major developmental tasks, therefore, in the preschool period, is to learn to understand the mother tongue and to speak it well. At school age, he must not only continue to grow in listening and speaking, but also develop skill in the other two language arts of reading and writing.

This chapter is concerned with language as the core or content that is being learned and with certain aspects of learning theory as they apply to language. A second major concern is how the child perceives reality, and what relationship exists between perceptual learning and language development. A third major concern is the significance of recent research on the affective aspects of both language and perception, and their implications for personality theory. Certain clinical data on language disorder syndromes are also examined for their implications for learning disabilities, distorted perceptions, and personality disturbances. Certainly no learning theory will be completely acceptable unless it adequately accounts for the major phenomena of human psychology involved in language and communication.

A revision and extension of the Presidential Address before the Division of Developmental Psychology, American Psychological Association, New York, N. Y., September 1, 1961.

THEORIES OF LANGUAGE LEARNING

The learning theory which most adequately accounts for the phenomenon of language learning appears to be Mowrer's (1958) so-called "autism" theory. The name of the theory is unfortunate, for while it derives from the emphasis on the child's *self*-stimulation with his own voice, it has many connotations from psychopathology. Mowrer considers that the usual explanation of the child's acquisition of speech in terms of conditioning accounts for his understanding of the words of others, but does not account for his ability to reproduce meaningful words. He points out that there are no unconditioned stimuli for conventional word responses, and even if there were, it would not be very useful if the child only learned to name things. This is the point at which most theories of language stop. They do not account for the learning of other parts of speech, or for the learning of grammar and syntax.

Previous theories, Mowrer claims, have leaned much too heavily on the child's initiation of sounds which are subsequently rewarded by parents with smiles, approval, and repetition. However, parents who are good language teachers usually do not wait for the child to make wordlike sounds in his babble, but talk to the child actively and expect him to imitate them. Hearing of words is a first step which is necessary before the child can reproduce them. Psychologists tend, however, to rely too heavily on imitation, which Mowrer claims yields a circular explanation. It is obvious that imitation is somehow important in the process because each child learns the language he hears spoken in his environment, but what is really needed is an explanation of *why* he imitates at all.

AFFECTIVE TONE OF EARLY LANGUAGE

Mowrer's "autism" theory originated in an effort to account for the languagelike behavior of talking birds. No birds have been taught to talk unless they have first become pets, but such birds are always eager to have their trainer appear, and certain good sounds associated with comfort and gratification become associated with the arrival of the trainer. Sounds associated with the trainer for the birds, or with the mother as language teacher for the child, offer reassurance that all is well. Because of her ministrations, her sounds become associated with comfort experiences. Her very presence, often indicated only by the sounds she makes, comes to have meaning for the child. They mean that the child will be fed, changed, and played with, and thus the child learns to *hope* according to Mowrer, although Dollard and Miller (1950) and Erikson (1950) call it learning to *wait* and to *trust*.

The talking birds were observed to become alert, hopeful, and happy on hearing themselves make sounds like those the trainer had made, so that they were acoustically rewarded for imitating the trainer in their own spontaneous rehearsal or *self*-stimulation. In the absence of the mother, the infant, too, can make utterances which sound like those which the mother makes, and which have come to be associated with the states of comfort which she induces. Here is *self*-stimulation with vocalizations which are *pleasantly toned emotionally*. Because this self-stimulation vocally is pleasant it becomes clear why the baby imitates adult vocalization in the first place. He tries to make sounds like the mother's because they are reassuring and make it seem as if the mother were there. According to Mowrer (1958), "Words are reproduced if and only if they are first made to sound good in the context of affectionate care and attention." Here then is an affective explanation of language learning.

Instances of negative experiences in which certain sounds come to seem bad or threatening also occur in the infant's experience, so that *fear* can become attached to certain sounds. One little girl was so hard of hearing that the only words which were spoken in loud enough tones of voice to get through to her were the harsh "No's" and the scoldings. Things said in a pleasant tone she could not hear, and she therefore did not develop a desire to communicate until she was fitted with a hearing aid which enabled her to hear the pleasant speech in her environment. There is abundant evidence in the literature that young children are sensitive to the manner of speech long before they speak themselves. It is clear then, that the general atmosphere of a home, whether it is harmonious and affectionate, or quarreling and bickering, will give children very different kinds of auditory stimulation, and very different affective tones associated with speech; hence they will acquire very different ideas of what speech is for and how to use it.

The child's first word is likely to be an interjection or an exclamation, if it is not a noun. Even if it is a name, it is likely to be uttered under strong emotional stress or excitement. In fact, the beginning stages of learning anything are likely to be highly emotional. The child utters sounds in calling into play his entire repertoire of behavior in his basic desire to communicate with others. Before a child speaks he has for some time been involved with the exploration of his environment on a pre-verbal level, pointing to objects that interest him, shaking his head in vigorous negations, bringing objects upon request, etc. All of these ges-tural and other nonverbal ways of communicating represent important stages in the child's developing personality. The child's involvement with the environment usually has to be emotionally charged before his efforts to communicate spill over into vocal responses which may subsequently become words.

In my 1930 monograph I reported that the responses of the youngest children, of 18 and 24 months, were often emotionally toned responses such as wishes, commands, threats, etc. These responses decreased in rela-tive number among the older children as they learned to express them-selves in more and more complex ways. Recent studies of the prelinguistic babblings of infants have served to bring into focus some of the reasons why these affective states of the infant are important in the development of language. Rheingold et al. (1959) have shown that an infant vocalizes more when an adult smiles at him. Lewis (1959) states that the conditions essential for vocal responses in infants are "contentment, attention [and] encouragement" (p. 55). When these conditions were present, he reported that a 10-week-old boy made a total of *only 4 sounds* in 3 minutes of ob-servation during which his father was silent. The same boy, however, dur-ing alternate minutes when the father said "hullo" every 10 seconds, made a *total of 18 sounds*. So hearing the speech of others is an essential condi-tion for the practice of vocalization in infancy. Good mothers *do* talk to their babies and treat them like human beings who will understand and reply some day.

LANGUAGE AND CONCEPT FORMATION

Nesbit (1955) in *Language, Meaning and Reality* stresses the important role of language in mental life, saying: "The creation and use of symbols is the method and foundation of all human thinking and, through it, of our increasing control of nature or reality and of ourselves and our so-ciety. It is the greatest human tool" (p. 167).

Church (1961) in a delightful book called *Language and the Discovery of Reality* describes a "cognitive developmental psychology." He attacks the assumption that "the material world . . . is given to us perceptually from the beginning [and that] ... language is in effect a set of labels to be attached to this pre-existing perceptual reality." It is his thesis that:

> ... the individual discovers the characteristics of reality as he goes along, that there are predictable regularities in the sequence of discoveries, and that language, including both what other people tell him and what he tells himself, plays an intimate part in this discovery and in enabling him to perceive the world as a coherent, stable place in which to live and act. ... Those objects, and those properties of objects, stand out which offer some relevance to the child himself, in terms of promise or threat or concrete action ... the child perceives only personally meaningful objects, and ... what he perceives is not so much the objects as their meanings. Developmentally ... meanings precede objects in perception ... it is this principle that enables us to understand "subliminal perception," the fact that we can react *affectively* to something without being able to identify the something to which we are reacting [pp. 4-5; italics added].

Hilgard (1951) also points out that "preference for one kind of stimulation over another places a motivational or affective component at the very beginning of perceptual discrimination" (p. 96).

Korzybski (1951) cites Cassirer's essay in which he discusses the "hunger for names" which every normal child shows at a certain age. "By learning to name things a child does not simply add a list of artificial signs to his previous knowledge of ready-made empirical objects. He learns rather to form the concepts of those objects. ... His vague, uncertain, fluctuating perceptions and his dim feelings begin to assume a new shape ... to crystallize around the name as a fixed center, a focus of thought" (p. 176).

Children in this naming stage often explore their environment thoroughly with constant questioning inflections in their voices, asking "What's this?" or "What's that?" until a long list of names has been acquired. As soon as these names are learned they serve as remarkably useful mental *handles* with which the child can *grasp* and *manipulate* the things in his environment, ask for them in their absence, recall their use on a previous occasion, and plan further play with them. The word thus facilitates the development of the concept and permits symbolic manipulation of ideas in place of the more primitive gestural language which always precedes the spoken word. Even as we attempt to describe the transition from gesture to speech it is amazing to note how dependent our language is on a vocabulary highly *manual* in character. We speak of "grasping" an idea, "manipulating" concepts in thinking, and the name as a symbolic "handle." The name is often used in isolation for some time with varying gestures and inflections of the voice to convey a variety of meanings before verbs, adjectives, and adverbs are acquired to express action and to express quality.

One little girl, after having been given names for all the people and objects in her Mother Goose book, pointed to the backgrounds of the pictures which were usually "sky." She then called a tablecloth "sky" in the background of a photograph of a table setting. Here is a good example of a child's overgeneralization in her efforts to find the limits of meaning of a new word.

The same child stooped down and pointed to the dining-room rug with her questioning inflection of "What's this?" She was told it was a "rug," and repeated the name after the adult. She was then told, "Show me another rug." She promptly walked over and pointed to a hall rug. When asked to find "another rug" she walked across a large wall-to-wall living-room rug to a sun room where she pointed to three more rugs whose borders she could see. On returning across the living-room rug, however, she stooped down and again used her questioning inflection with "Dis?" for reassurance that it too was a rug. This incident illustrates how a parent can help a child to generalize meaning as soon as words are learned. This kind of interaction between parent and child prevents fixation or limitation on too concrete or too specific meanings by immediately spreading the knowledge of the new word to every other object in the child's environment to which it can be applied.

Numerous studies have shown that learning verbal cues, names for objects, greatly facilitates learning and concept formation. For example, in the work of Pyles (1932), preschool subjects learned to find hidden toys under shapeless molds more quickly when the molds were given names than when the toys were under unnamed molds. Carey and Goss (1956) report that "prior strengthening of familiar word labels for blocks in height-size categories led to more rapid acquisition of placing the blocks by height-size." Goss and Moylan (1958) in a similar block-sorting experiment showed that the frequency of height-size placements was a function of degree of mastery of different nonsense syllables or familiar word responses for each of the four height-size categories into which the blocks could be sorted. These and many other studies of discrimination learning tasks, particularly those by the Kendlers (1961) and others, are adding much to our knowledge of how children form concepts.

LANGUAGE AND PERCEPTION

Woodworth (1947), one of psychology's grand elder statesmen, pointed out that theories of learning which emphasize the law of effect minimize the perceptual factor, and that those which stress the perceptual aspects of the process deny any direct importance of the factor of reinforcement. There is no obvious incompatability between the two, he maintained, and "both of them are essential to any process of learning." He elaborates his position by asking, "What is being reinforced in the early trials of conditioning experiments?" "Something present in the organism," he wrote, "from the first trial that is capable of reinforcement," and he believed that it belongs to the *receptive* and not the efferent side of the organism's total behavior. "Perception," he wrote, "is always driven by a direct, inherent motive which might be called the will to perceive." And further, "When a new percept is in the making . . . or when the meaning of a cue or sign is being discovered—an elementary two-phase process is observable. It is a trial and check . . . process."

Murphy (1956) agrees with Woodworth that what gets reinforced in learning experiments is the perception. To him this means that the work of Thorndike and his students, as well as the massive researches of Hull and Skinner, can also be interpreted as reinforcement of perception. He considers that it was probably the central process that was rewarded or punished, and not the peripheral act.

Murphy goes on to state that affect is not the only factor in perceptual learning, for it is also influenced by the learner's age and sex, by cultural factors, and by the affective and physical aspects of the situation. He suggests that perceptual structure changes in such fashion as to give *emphasis* to that which is pleasant in contrast to that which is unpleasant or affectively neutral, and that many such changes are *cumulative*, constituting a form of perceptual learning. "Objects that are at first devoid of great affect (words, gestures, coins, etc.)," says Murphy, "come to carry enormous affective freight and one's seeing and hearing may be influenced by the meaning of the symbol."

Gibson (1961), in a paper presented at Pennsylvania State College before the Society for Research in Child Development, stated: "Properties of natural objects are not always perceived to begin with although the potential stimulation is available. . . . The individual, during his development, *learns* to perceive these by abstracting the critical and invariant stimuli from the total complex. . . . When the dimension or quality has been differentiated, *words* may be learned for it, but they do not give the reference or the meaning. The meaning is achieved automatically as the observer differentiates the property—weight or density or whatever—from the mass of stimulation." She distinguished between "coded" and "uncoded" stimuli and then attempted to show the role of both differentiation and association in perceptual learning. She described the "natural" stimulation of thunderstorms or scenery where the meaning is in a sense contained in the stimulation. "The identification of coded stimuli is learned," Gibson stated, "and the learning probably involves an associative process. But the association with the code symbol or referent must be *preceded* by *differentiation* of the stimuli to be coded." Speech she cited as the perfect example of coded stimuli, but she points out that infants do not associate stimuli of given frequency and intensity with specific objects. She states:

> However this process may take place, we know that it must do so before . . . the word code can be learned. The name and the referent are undoubtedly experienced together, and presumably an associative connection made. But prior to this association of sound with object must be the discrimination of phonemic constituents of the sound.
>
> Probably learning the code of "meaning" of sounds begins as soon as a minimum of phonemic constituents have been discriminated. The two processes—that is, progressive differentiation and coding by association—may go on together . . . and in fact contribute to each other. *Production* of sounds . . . may play a role in perceptual differentiation; feedback from his own voice with a "zeroing in" corrective process to match a sound might help an infant to select out distinctive features. Likewise, association with a referent which is well differentiated and repeated fairly consistently may help sharpen . . . discrimination of the critical acoustic attributes [Gibson, 1961].

Dennis (1951) believes that if perception is studied in socially significant situations, of which reading is one, it will provide a focus for the understanding of personality, and Gibson (1961) does relate her theory of coded learning to the kind of perceptual learning which occurs in *reading*. "The letter forms themselves," she says, "must be differentiated, become discriminable, before any responses can be coded to them. This differentiation . . . is a process which continues up to 9 years of age in many children. . . . When the graphic forms can be to some extent discriminated, the child can proceed to the task of relating them to the spoken language." She raises the question of what are the optimal units to be decoded. Her answer is that they should not be single letters, for they have no invariant acoustic matches in our language.

Soffietti (1953) has shown, for example, that the 5 vowel letters of English stand for at least 5 to 7 different phonemes each, and the various phonemes of English are spelled in from 2 to at least 13 different ways each. He contrasts the situation with the almost completely phonetic spelling of Italian and suggests a new method of teaching children to read by beginning with all words which are strictly phonetic and adding nonphonetically spelled words in orderly and reasonable groups. The same problem has been approached in another way by Pitman (1963), who has developed the Initial Teaching Alphabet which employs 43 characters instead of the 26 letters of traditional orthography. It is claimed that children started with this completely phonetic system get a good start in reading and subsequently make a satisfactory transition to material written in "traditional orthography." Approximately 3000 children in Great Britain and the United States are participating in experimental programs employing this method.

According to Gibson (1961), whole-word reading has not been very successful for it creates poor spellers and does not encourage children to tackle new words. She claims that children need to discover a new high-order invariant, the *spelling-to-sound* correlation.

Since the child already knows the phoneme to morpheme code (that is, sound to meaning) when he begins to read, he has no problem of semantic learning in reading, and if the material being read is well within his speaking vocabulary, letter groups with a high spelling-to-sound correlation should be perceived more readily in fast tachistoscopic presentation than letter groups which are low in this respect (i.e., relatively unpronounceable). This hypothesis was confirmed in one of Gibson's (1961) experiments, where the letter groups "in strict correspondence with pronunciation were perceived as units thus facilitating the reading process."

SEMANTIC GENERALIZATION

Mention should be made of some articles which have important implications for methodology in research on children's language and should not be overlooked by the developmental psychologist. The interesting studies of Cofer and Foley (1942), Foley and Cofer (1943), and others, showed through conditioning experiments with adults that various kinds of generalization occur along semantic lines such as synonym, antonym, and homophone gradients. Subsequently Reiss (1946) performed developmental studies of mediated generalization with children 7, 10, 14, and 18 years of age. He found developmental trends in the amount of conditioning transfer which occurred at different ages. The greatest amount of transfer occurred in the youngest children on the homophones (words which sound alike), whereas the synonym type of relationship did not transfer until the age of 14 years. Probably closely related to these phenomena are the findings of Sayler (1949), Hockett (1950), and Spriestersbach and Curtis (1951) concerning articulatory defects of adolescents. After about 14 years of age certain speech sounds to which their ears have become attuned sound "right" to these older children and are more difficult to modify than at earlier ages when speech perception and articulation are more plastic and more amenable to training.

This point is of particular interest for it probably touches on the basic reason why children can learn a foreign language without an accent at early ages (7 to 10 years) and why it is so difficult to do so after adolescence. It would seem from these studies that at earlier ages children are more attuned to the acoustic aspects and feeling tone of language, and that as they approach adolescence their attention is directed more toward the cognitive and semantic aspects.

Closely related to this is the work of Flavell and Stedman (1961), who asked children in grades 2 to 9 which pair of words seemed more similar in meaning to a given pair of words. The pairs of words represented 11 different categories of semantic relationships such as synonyms, attributes, action of, action upon, etc. The youngest children, who were in second grade, did not show any definite ordering or similarity of meaning hierarchy among the 11 semantic relations studied. Such a hierarchy did begin to emerge, however, in the children in third to fifth grades, and the ordering of these relations, when it did appear, was similar to that found in adults. Brown and Berko (1960) have also used a word association technique which reveals changes with age as a consequence of the child's gradual organization of his vocabulary into parts of speech, and they conclude that "the formal change in word association and the ability to make correct grammatical use of new words are two manifestations of the child's developing appreciation of English syntax" (p. 13).

PSYCHOLINGUISTICS

Recent writings in the field of linguistics have posed some interesting challenges for the developmental psychologist. The core of the problem is Whorf's (1956) hypothesis which claims that the characteristics of a language, its structure, grammar, and syntax have a determining influence on the cognitive processes of the speakers of that language. As Heidbreder (1958) succinctly puts it, "A person's language, by setting the pattern to which his linguistic behavior conforms, determines deeply and strongly established ways in which he habitually perceives and thinks" (p. 89).

In her very thoughtful and incisive essay, Heidbreder contrasts Whorf's views with those of Woodworth. She says:

> Before a child begins to speak, or even to understand language he hears, the language of the *community* in which he develops, like the culture of which it is a part, has already begun to exert its influence through characteristic selections and emphases in determining those aspects of his world to which he responds. Yet this fact neither excludes nor nullifies the effects of his direct motor responses and of the direct stimulation of the receptors they involve, both in their execution and in their direct encounters with a non-linguistic environment. And it must not be forgotten that direct motor responses necessarily continue to operate throughout life [pp. 105-106].

This author concludes that "the chief difference in the treatment of thinking by Woodworth and Whorf is a difference in emphasis. Woodworth recognizes linguistic factors as among the important determinants of thinking, and Whorf, of course, does not rule out non-linguistic factors" [p. 107].

Roger Brown, author of *Words and Things* (1958), and Jean Berko have contributed an informative chapter to Mussen's *Handbook of Experimental Methods in Child Psychology* (1960) which should provoke a new series of studies in developmental psycholinguistics. The chief difficulties of research in this area are, first, that a whole new terminology must be mastered, and, second, the serious research worker really needs extensive training in phonetics also. This involves not just memorizing a set of symbols for speech sounds, but intensive auditory training in

316   DOROTHEA MCCARTHY

speech-sound discrimination. The linguistic approach gives the appearance of being extremely scientific, but the writings of linguists are replete with sweeping statements claiming to be based on scientific findings, yet supplying only anecdotal data for the most part. Lenneberg (1953), who has contributed a widely quoted study on color names in various cultures, states: "Demonstration that certain languages differ does not prove that the speakers of these languages differ from each other as a group in their psychological potentialities."

The great overconcern of linguists with the Eskimo's 20 words for snow does not mean that English-speaking people do not perceive many different kinds of snow. As a native of Minnesota, the writer can attest that English-speaking people living in northern climes do identify "fluffy" snow, "sparkling" snow, "wet" snow, "sticky" snow, "heavy" snow, "crunchy" snow, "driving" snow, "blinding" snow, "drifted" snow, and many other kinds. The fact that the English language uses adjectives to modify the single noun does not mean that differences are not perceived. It might be argued that the Eskimo's use of many nouns to describe many kinds of snow is evidence of immaturity and concreteness in his thinking, and of an inability to subsume many similar observations under the one class noun snow, which is further demonstrated by an inability to use a wide variety of qualifying words. Bastian (1959), in a critical review of Brown's book, says:

> In his examination of original language learning ... the author through his adroit employment of the notions of category theory, manages to glide the discussion smoothly over and away from most of the basic issues involved ... [the book] is for the most part concerned with problems related to the listener rather than the speaker ... [and] This listener orientation has determined the relatively small amount of space given to the most challenging topic in linguistic behavior, the problems of the syntactical organization of the speaker's behavior [p. 353].

Even Berko and Brown (1960) admit that although

> Jakobson and Halle [1956] are familiar with the international literature on speech acquisition and presumably derive their conclusions from this literature [their] ... report does not set down the detailed empirical support for the various generalizations that are made and does not give any explicit attention to methodological considerations. ... Necessarily, therefore, we must regard their generalizations as hypotheses rather than facts that have been established [pp. 528-529].

The Albrights (1958) of Stanford University published a helpful article on the application of descriptive linguistics to child language. They indicate that a child's language is not used by a community of speakers, and it is changing very rapidly in contrast to the slow rate of change in conventional language. They suggest special adaptations of linguistic techniques which should be helpful to future researchers in this field.

Irwin, one of the few child psychologists to become expert in phonetic transcription, has made some excellent contributions which linguists brush aside as "irrelevant." Although the linguists admit that most phonological learning occurs in the first 3 years of life, few if any of them have tried to secure the kind of data which Irwin (1947, 1960) has supplied. One troublesome problem concerns the matter of meaning. Berko and Brown (1960) say, for example: "The mere occurrence in child vocalization of a phone, which an adult observer would classify as belonging to a certain phoneme in the adult language, does not demonstrate that the phoneme [speech sound with meaning] exists as a cognitive construct for the child; neither does any particular frequency of such a phone provide this evidence." They state that phonemic conclusions cannot be based on babbling or echoic speech, for they claim that phonemic structure begins to develop only after the end of the babbling period. To straighten out some misunderstanding it would be better to say that Irwin's studies are of *infant phonology* rather than *infant speech,* and what he calls phonomes are more properly called phones or allophones. The Albrights (1958) even invented a new term, "infantemes," for the sounds uttered in infant babbling which seem to have no meaning.

A further analysis of Irwin's original data has been published recently by Winitz and Irwin (1958). The data were examined for the appearance of early words among children between 13 and 18 months of age. When total utterances were included in previous analyses of these data, Irwin (1947) reported that consonant development proceeded from back to front of the oral cavity, with the front consonants made with the lips appearing relatively late. When, however, *only words* are included, it appears that labial sounds / m/ p/ and / b/ are used *in words* more frequently than are other consonants. This is in harmony with many of the earlier biographical observations and cruder studies made without benefit of the International Phonetic Alphabet.

This apparent reversal of results, when only the early *words* are analyzed, rather than *all utterances* heard during the experimental period, seems to effect a reconciliation between Irwin's results and the older observational studies which undoubtedly were limited to words only; and it may be the basis on which a meeting of minds between developmental psychologists and linguists may occur. Empirical data are urgently needed based on the application of many of the techniques suggested by linguists.

A most pertinent research investigation is by Menyuk (1963), who attempted to use the linguistic model devised by Chomsky which gives a technique for describing the rules or categories from which the child may generate the sentences in his language. It is analogous to a categorizing theory of learning.

The speech of 48 nursery-school children and 48 first-graders of upper socioeconomic levels was tape recorded in three different situations. On the basis of the samples so recorded, a children's grammar was written. Menyuk concludes that, "The basic structures which generated all the sentences obtained could be described within the framework of the Chomsky model." The children's grammar included all the rules used at both age levels to generate structures consistent with adult usage, as well as those which were unique to children's usage.

All the basic structures used by adults to generate their sentences were found in the grammar of the nursery-school children. Most of the structures were used at an early age and used consistently, and structures not consistent with adult usage were rare. Those which were still in the process of being acquired by nursery-school children were not yet perfected by the first-graders.

In studies of the free associations of children and adults, it has long been known that the most frequent words given by children when asked to give the first word they think of, upon hearing a given stimulus word, differ from the most frequent word associations given by adults. It was not realized until recently, when it was pointed out by the linguists Brown and Berko (1960), that there is a definite linguistic principle which appears to differentiate the free associations of children and those of adults. Children usually give a different part of speech, whereas adults usually match on the basis of part of speech. For example, adults will respond "woman" most frequently to the stimulus word "man," whereas children respond most frequently with the word "work," a verb indicating what the man does. Likewise, in response to the stimulus word "table" adults most often give "chair," another noun, whereas the children's most frequent response is "eat," an action word associated with what one does at a table.

RECENT DEVELOPMENTAL FINDINGS

Linguists are asking questions such as how is it that a child who begins by merely parrot imitation of speech sounds without meaning can eventually write poetry and say things which have never been said or written before, but which are grammatical and meaningful in his speech community? This occurs because the rules of phonology, morphology, syntax, and reference are absorbed by the child from the speech of others in the community; especially first from his mother, his first language teacher. These rules, which are precious to the linguists and lexicographers, are, according to Berko and Brown (1960), "what naïve adult speakers of the language already know and what children born into the community will learn. They are not formulated by the naïve speaker [or mothers for that matter], but they are known in the sense that they are obeyed." Linguists seem strangely preoccupied with structure and form of language, and are most reluctant to admit that a child attaches *meaning* to his utterances, for they think he may be only parroting what he has heard others say. It is not until children make errors in their speech, which they are very unlikely to have heard, and which show that they are misapplying or stretching a rule or generalization, that they are credited with recognizing linguistic rules. Gibson (1961) agrees with Jakobson and Halle (1956) and other linguists that "perception of speech is based on the discrimination of *distinctive features* and *invariants* of speech sounds." The amazing thing is that children do learn to understand a word whether it is whispered, or shouted, whether it is spoken by a man, a woman, or a child who is present, or by an unseen radio commentator. The problem is therefore a perceptual one and is not determined only by the physical properties of speech sounds as recorded on a spectogram. Some of the techniques being used at the Haskins laboratories may be helpful here. Fischer-Jorgensen (1961) has pointed out especially how interdisciplinary cooperation between linguists and electronic engineers is essential to real research progress in this area. I submit that techniques such as those described by Liberman (1957) and by Miller and Nicely (1955) could well be applied by developmental psychologists to the language development of children with considerable profit to both psychology and linguistics.

Two contributions of Luria and his associates (Luria, 1959; Luria and Yudovich, 1959), available in English, indicate that the Russians are doing challenging work in the field of children's language development, although they do not report quantitative data, referring in the English version chiefly to the work of others which has not been translated. Luria and Yudovich (1959) state:

> The acquisition of a language system involves a reorganization of all the child's basic mental processes; the word thus becomes a tremendous factor which forms mental activity, perfecting the reflection of reality and creating new forms of attention, of memory and imagination, of thought and action. The word has a basic function not only because it indicates a corresponding object in the external world, but also because it abstracts, isolates, the necessary signal, generalizes perceived signals and relates them to certain categories; it is this systematization of direct experience that makes the role of the word in the formation of mental processes so exceptionally important [p. 12].

Observations are reported on a pair of retarded 5-year-old twins who were communicating at about the 18-month level. The children were able to respond to concrete situations and to select objects requested by the experimenter. Normal children, the authors state, when requested to point to an object which is not present become confused and do not point to anything, but these retarded twins pointed to erroneous objects which were present, thereby revealing the instability and diffuseness of their knowledge of the word. They could point correctly, for example, to a series of objects and a toy dog. When asked to point to an absent calf or a lamb, they pointed to the dog, revealing the generalized character of the verbal meaning of animals. They could supply the names of the objects they were asked to point out, and could understand and respond correctly to questions about the use or action of objects, and even to questions requiring descriptions of objects in gestures. They also were sensitive to the inflections of verbs which they did not use in their own speech. However, as soon as things not physically present in the immediate situation were asked about, their language comprehension deteriorated. Instead of responding to the whole sentence they would respond to a single word in the sentence. The behavior described was analogous to the behavior of the student who writes the answer to an examination question by putting down everything he knows on the topic, but not answering the question that was asked.

Speech was well understood by these children if it did not go beyond the bounds of the visual situation. As soon as it went beyond the immediate situation and became narrative, i.e., concerned something absent or abstract, it was beyond their comprehension. Nursery-school teachers are familiar with this phenomenon; some children do not listen to a story with the group if they have not attained the ability to follow narrative material in their understanding of spoken language.

Luria (1959) also reports that studies of the "directive function" of the speech of children 14 to 16 months of age indicate that when the child is asked for one of two toys (for both of which he knows the names) which are equidistant from him and equally attractive, he will hand it to the examiner. If, however, one toy is placed farther away from the other, and the examiner asks for the more distant one, the child will be distracted by the nearer object. Luria claims this shows that "the word loses its directive role if the immediate orientational reaction is evoked by the nearer, or the brighter, or more interesting object." By 16 to 18 months, however, the word is said to maintain its directive function, for these older children give requested objects in spite of distracting circumstances.

Further work along these lines has been reported by Fletcher (1962), who studied the effect of speech on reaction time in four groups of subjects aged 2, 3, 8, and young adults. For the youngest subjects the requirement of saying the word "Go" while pushing a buzzer disrupted the physical response, but the children of 3 and 8 years of age showed that the verbalization seemed to facilitate the motor response. Adults, however, were not aided by the verbal accompaniment. When decisions were imposed, such as deciding whether a light was on the right or left (disjunctive reaction time), the process was greatly slowed.

Meerloo (1952) considers that the "communicative act" is extremely important, since "talking to each other is loving each other," and "communication is the means whereby man fulfills his instinctive desire to reach other men's minds." The fact that lovers often develop a language of their own during a period of intense courtship coincides with this view, and when marriages begin to founder, the basic symptoms are usually misunderstandings and a breakdown in communication. Such couples have lost the ability they once had to communicate effectively with one another. Schizophrenic children often are mute and seem never to have learned to love or to communicate with anyone. Their mothers often complain that they were not "cuddly babies," and that they did not seem to want to be loved. Part of their characteristic withdrawal from life and from reality seems to be their lack of desire to communicate or to explore the environment.

In his delightful little book called *Becoming* Allport (1955) states: "In the course of learning ... we know that high intensities of emotional excitement tend to narrow the field of learning, to reduce the effectiveness of cues, and to diminish the range of similarity and transfer." He argues, however, that merely admitting the effect of emotional involvement is not sufficient, for he says:

> Propriate states are by no means always agitated states. A sense of worth-whileness, of importance, is not what we ordinarily call emotion. ... Propriate involvement ... increases the breadth of learning, of transfer effects, as well as the ability of the individual to perceive and organize all relevant information into the system as a whole. Thus, the experimental effects of emotionality and of propriate involvement may be precisely opposite. We cannot, therefore, permit the two conditions to be confused in our theory of becoming. ... An adequate psychology of becoming cannot be written exclusively in terms of stimulus, emotional excitement, association, and response. It requires subjective and inner principles of organization of the sort frequently designated by the terms self or ego [pp. 58-60].

Spitz (1959) in his essay on ego development postulates "organizers of the psyche" and points out that when a child has a normal environment there is great regularity with which the affective behavior patterns emerge, and that the road which leads to the integration of isolated functions is built by experiences of an affective nature.

LANGUAGE AND PERSONALITY THEORY

Personality theory is much in the forefront of psychology today, and some of the most helpful facts that these theorists use concern children whose psychological deprivation shows itself most strikingly in the various language disorders such as mutism, delayed onset of speech, stuttering, articulatory defects, and reading disabilities.

Of considerable interest, in connection with children's ability to form concepts, is Bowlby's (1951) analysis of data gathered by Goldfarb on children raised in an institution from 5 months to 3 years. Goldfarb (1955) states regarding Bowlby's analysis:

In brief, the institution children were more retarded intellectually. Of great importance also was the finding that they were distinctly impaired in conceptual ability. Indeed, they were inferior even to a group of known defective children in the Weigl Color-Form test while the foster home children were superior. It was felt that the institution children's impairment in categoric behavior and their characteristic "concrete attitude" was more than a reflection of low intelligence. There seemed to be a lack of differentiation and development of all aspects of personality. Most noteworthy was a generalized state of intellectual and emotional impoverishment and passivity. Along with the cognitive disability there were distinct emotional trends; chiefly, the absence of a normal capacity for inhibition. The institution group showed extremely difficult behavior with symptoms of hyperactivity, restlessness, inability to concentrate, and unmanageability. Further, although indiscriminatingly and insatiably demanding of affection, they had no genuine attachments.[Only 3 of the 15 institution children were considered to have reasonably normal speech.]

Goldfarb suggests that the individual's capacity to delay outward execution of impulse and to anticipate is the groundwork for conceptual thought which is based on a hierarchy starting with the psychosocial climate of the family which leads to the establishment of the social emotions of love, attachment, and sympathy, which in turn lead to the ability to delay immediate satisfaction, to inner control, planfulness, foresight, and finally conceptual thought.

These institutional children presented a syndrome strikingly similar to that described by Dr. Lauretta Bender (1947) as the syndrome of psychopathology in childhood. "There is an inability to love or feel guilty. There is no conscience. ... Their inability to enter into any relationship makes therapy or even *education* impossible. There is an inability to conceptualize, particularly significant in regard to time. They have no concept of time, so that they cannot recall past experience and cannot benefit from past experience or be motivated to future goals" (pp. 108-111; italics added). Recent studies by Brock and Del Giudice (1962) indicate a paucity of knowledge of time words among juvenile delinquents. Such observations seem to be in harmony with the emphasis of Dollard and Miller (1950) and Erikson (1950) on the infant's learning to wait, to trust, and to hope. It seems that in a well-ordered home, where children can trust parents whose behavior is reasonably predictable rather than erratic and inconsistent, children do acquire a kind of inner security which enables their language growth to thrive. This, in turn, enables them to achieve and, therefore, to receive further approval and acceptance which, in turn, enhance their feeling of security.

The important findings of Brodbeck and Irwin (1946) should be recalled here also, for children living in families were found to vocalize more, and to use more advanced forms of vocalization than children living in hospitals or institutions even in the first 6 months of life. The infant soon learns especially in a normal household that certain sounds mean that his bottle is being warmed, etc., or that his mother is preparing to nurse him, and thus he learns to wait, or to delay immediate satisfaction. This is the very beginning of trust in others and of the planfulness and foresight which Goldfarb (1955) claims lead directly to conceptual thought and even to the sense of time and to character formation. This it seems is closely related to Mowrer's (1958) "autism" theory of learning words which enable the child to learn to hope.

Rheingold and Bayley (1959) compared 8 infants who had a single mothering experience with 8 others who received physical nurturing care from 6 to 8 different mother surrogates. All of these children were subsequently placed in foster homes and retested at 19 months of age. Interestingly enough, the *only* variable in their research which yielded a significant difference in favor of the group having the single mother figure was vocalization.

I have indicated elsewhere (1954c) that there seems to be a gradient of normal language development related to the amount and kind of contact with the mother. Only children, especially only girls, who have the most intensive and most prolonged contact with the mother, are the most advanced in language learning. Singletons with siblings are next, but twins, who always have to share the mother from the very beginning, are usually quite retarded, as are other multiple birth children who have been studied. This ties in with the data of Spitz (1945), Spitz and Wolf (1946), Goldfarb (1955), Brodbeck and Irwin (1946), and others on the language retardation usually found in children who have suffered prolonged separation from the mother at a critical period in their development. These are the children who have no opportunity to identify with the mother or a mother substitute, so that the identification with the person who normally serves as the language model, and who mediates the structure of the mother tongue to the child, cannot occur.

Dr. Gertrud Wyatt (1958a,b), who is responsible for a developmental-crisis theory of stuttering, was working on a grant from NIMH to the Wellesley Public School System (1960). She and her staff presented a symposium at the 1962 meetings of the ASHA in New York, describing the therapy they are conducting with stutterers of various ages. The previous work, based on studies of the fantasies and feelings of stuttering children and their mothers, compared with a control group, led to three principles of therapy which are now being tried out. These are (1) that therapy should begin as soon as possible after the appearance of compulsive repetitive sounds and syllables; (2) that it should be specific for children of different ages and with different syndromes of language disorder; and (3) that the mothers should be included in the treatment process.

Preschool children are usually visited first in their homes where the therapist has an opportunity to observe the prevailing patterns of communication between mother and child, and often between the child and his siblings. After this, the mother is usually seen alone every second week either at home or at the therapist's office. Elementary-school children are seen individually at school once a week for individual therapy; conferences with the mothers are held every second week at school, and fathers are seen from time to time whenever possible. High-school students receive individual therapy once weekly and their parents together or singly every other week.

These investigators observe "speaking children" in their interaction with significant people, mother, father, teachers, brothers, and sisters. Speech in children is acquired in an interpersonal setting, and the vicissitudes of the child's early relationships with his mother and other members of the family have differential effects upon his language development and later command of language. Dr. Wyatt believes that the acquisition of language by a child, although dependent upon the normal maturation of a healthy organism, is essentially a process of learning through mutual imitation and reciprocal feedback between mother and child. A continuous, uninterrupted, and affectionate relationship between mother and child provides the optimum condition for such successful language learning in early childhood. The very young child needs a high degree of corrective feedback for the learning of auditory discrimination between speech sounds. Brown and Berko (1960) point out the importance of the new principle of learning through generalization which emerges as the child learns to handle grammar and syntax. Corrective feedback is needed as a constant monitoring process as the child experiments with building sentences, and this is done normally by affectionate adults. If the child is of normal mentality and has normal speech apparatus, his language development is dependent primarily on the *frequency* and the appropriateness of the corrective feedback provided by an affectionally significant adult. The manner and emotional tone with which this corrective feedback is supplied by the parent or other language teacher are also tremendously important. As Wyatt and Herzan (1962) point out, the adult must be ready to, and able to, attune her own patterns of communication to that of the child. She must become aware of the child's "linguistic code" which is changing rapidly as the child matures, and must be sufficiently sensitive to the child's growth in communication to "switch her code" as the child becomes capable of using more and more advanced language forms.

In our culture, the mother is, as we have said, the child's first language teacher, and increasing mastery of language patterns permits him to sustain the relationship with the mother at greater and greater distance in time and space. Once the child has internalized the basic language patterns, he is then able to reproduce them even if the mother is absent. As he gradually is able to remain away from the mother for longer periods in the psychological weaning process, the child's network of interpersonal communication changes, according to Wyatt, from a *dualistic* to a *pluralistic* one. The relationship of the child to the mother is particularly important, she claims, during the periods when the child is learning new patterns of a more complex nature, prior to the attainment of efficient performance. A disruption of the relationship between child and mother which occurs during a period of intensive language learning may be reflected in a language disorder. The symptom choice is determined by the particular aspect of language development which was in the period of ascendancy or rapid growth when the absence, separation, or other traumatic experience occurred, or when the emotional stress was most acute.

The term identification which is crucial in Wyatt's (1960) theory is a troublesome one, as Bronfenbrenner (1960) has indicated in his thoughtful critique of the concept. Because of the many ambiguous usages of the term identification, Bronfenbrenner says, "One could speak of the child's learning of parental behavior...without invoking the term identification

... one could employ some simple but noncommittal expression as such 'acquired similarity.' It would also be possible to examine the effects of parental aggression, withdrawal of love, or direct punishment and reward on the child's learning of parental characteristics." He also cites the interesting paper of Robert Sears (1957), who restated Freud's theory of anaclitic identification in learning theory terms, beginning with the child's psychological dependency on the mother and concluding that "the degree of identification of the child with his mother should bear a curvilinear relationship to the amount of affectionate nurture that mother gives. If she is universally present and always plays a part in the dyadic mother-child sequence, the child will never have occasion to perform mother acts, (i.e., make sounds like mother) to establish identification. On the other hand, if she is continuously punitive, and is rarely associated with the satisfying completion of the child's goal strivings, her acts will have no part in his action sequence, and there will be no initial instigation to act like her" (Bronfenbrenner, 1960, p. 28). Bronfenbrenner is concerned about the content of identification, and from some of the material we have been reviewing it would seem that much of it may be verbal.

The various forms of language disorders do not appear singly or in isolation (McCarthy, 1954a, b, c). Often a nonreader has been slow in learning to speak, or has had poor articulation, or has stuttered at one time or another. These problems tend to occur more often among boys than among girls, and tend to run in families. They seem to occur most often in families in which left-handedness and twinning occur. More than one language disorder is quite likely to be found in the same children (Yedinack, 1949). The tendency for such disorders to run in families does not mean that there is any tendency to inherit these problems in a genetic sense. Although there may be some inherited predisposition to develop language difficulties, most of the cases can be accounted for in environmental terms such as imitation of the defective speech of a relative, tension and anxiety about speech, and especially attitudes toward child-bearing, resulting in different patterns of child care which are passed along in families from mother to daughter.

There is a wealth of evidence from the clinical literature summarized elsewhere (McCarthy, 1947, 1949, 1952a, b, 1954a, b, c, 1956) which indicates that all children who manifest language disorders give evidence of emotional insecurity and poor family relationships. They have other problems of personality adjustment and their delayed speech, poor articulation, stuttering, or reading disability, is only one symptom shown by a rather disturbed personality adjustment. Beck (1950) found that fifth-grade poor readers had had six times as many problems as matched good readers even back in their nursery-school days, long before anyone expected them to learn to read.

Too often teachers make the mistake of assuming normal or ideal family relationships when they offer suggestions for these children. Usually, such is far from the case. It may not be possible to discover the real circumstances in a single interview with the mother, for many parents are skillful in covering up their real feelings. The mere presence of a language disorder in the child should be enough to alert the teacher, however, to the fact that probably all is not well at home (Kunst, 1949). Usually, complete clinical study of such children reveals a breakdown in family relations, immature, neurotic, and quarreling parents who have little understanding of the responsibilities of parenthood and even less strength of character to live up to them. Asking such parents to help their handicapped children at home with their reading, or with their speech, often only aggravates the problem, since it focuses the attention of the already rejecting parent on the child's worst shortcomings. A neutral tutor, who is not involved in the situation emotionally, is in a much better position to help and also usually has better techniques. The parents can help by paying more attention to the child, giving him more of themselves, looking for his successes, and trying to build up his emotional security while the technical matter of the teaching or remediation is left to the tutor or speech therapist. For such children, parents are often the worst people in the world to try to help directly in overcoming the specific deficiency, although Wyatt and Herzan (1962) try to retrain mothers of young children to be better language teachers.

Often the first few days at school are emotionally traumatic for the child, especially if he has recently acquired a baby brother or sister, or if the family has recently moved into a new home (Sheldon and Carrillo, 1952). He may rebel against being pushed out of the nest, as he sees it, and develop a resistance to reading as the all-important thing which is to blame for this separation from home and mother. As one little nonreader, who was very jealous of his little sister, put it, "I just can't wait to get home to see what they are doing behind my back," and he concluded by saying, "I just can't think with all these things on my mind."

Delayed onset of speech, articulatory defects, stuttering, and reading disability may all be thought of as language disorders or disturbances of the communicative process, each of which shows a distinctive syndrome associated with disturbed parent-child relationships making for emotional insecurity and symptom formation in the child. The language disorder appears to be but one symptom. Delayed speech in its most extreme form is the mutism and failure to communicate described by Despert (1938), and in many more recent reports of autistic behavior (see N. E. Wood, 1960). Peckarsky (1952) found that the mothers whose children were late in talking were worrisome, anxious, and neurotic women who were highly critical of their children. The mothers in her control group, however, whose children spoke at the normal age, were relaxed, calm, and used a great deal of common sense in handling their children.

Articulatory defects were found by K. S. Wood (1946) to improve much more rapidly if the mothers participated in group psychotherapy than if the children merely had speech therapy. The persistent lisper whose speech apparatus is normal almost always has an immature, babyish personality. Similar patterns occur with the child who has infantile "r" and "l" sounds. Speech therapists are becoming more and more aware of the functional aspects of these disorders and are using play therapy rather than the older speech correction techniques, often with great success.

The multiply handicapped child is quite likely to be overprotected because of his obvious physical disability; yet the brand of overprotection he gets is likely to be the disguised form due to guilt feelings because of his imperfections. Such a child is likely to respond to the mother's overprotectiveness in the same way a normal child would, and perhaps develop a speech problem, such as infantile speech superimposed on his organic involvement. In such cases the speech therapist may be working with the child, often with considerable success, on the speech patterns alone, yet the handicapped child may be quite unable emotionally to give up certain aspects of his symptom pattern because of a superimposed emotional problem. His dependence on his mother may make it all the more difficult for him to achieve emotional maturity.

Although highly critical of some of Wood's techniques, Andersland

(1961) found that kindergarten children profited greatly from certain speech-improvement methods, especially children whose mothers scored high on hostility-rejection keys of the PARI. Speech-improvement training seemed to counteract the negative effects on children's articulation associated with a maternal rejection and hostility syndrome. None of the 10 children who did not receive speech training, and whose mothers scored high on the rejection-hostility scale, had errorless speech; but, of 18 children whose mothers scored similarly high on this scale, 12 had errorless speech at the end of a training period. Kindergarteners of lower socioeconomic classes who were given speech lessons were brought up to the level of upper-class children at the end of the training period.

Evidence continues to accumulate which indicates that reading ability is a crucial aspect of the child's intellectual development. A child's failure to take on this secondary form of language growth at the normal age in spite of sufficient educational opportunity may be an important clue to his mental health.

There is one group of nonreaders who are shy, withdrawn, and immature. They show a whole syndrome of babyishness and submissiveness. Although they may be 8, 10, or 12 years old, or even older, they are still behaving like 3- or 4-year-old children in their severe dependence on their parents, inability to go places by themselves, inability to hold their own with their peers, and their generally emotionally infantile behavior. These submissive nonreaders are much like the stutterers described by Despert (1946) and by Moncur (1951) in personality adjustment, and similarly have considerable pent-up hostility. When they are helped to grow up in other ways, and their parents are helped to release them emotionally for independent growth, they often begin to read quite suddenly much above their former levels.

Another type of nonreader is the aggressive, bullying type who shows a pattern of predelinquency or actual delinquency which usually begins as truancy; for with continued failure in the language arts he comes to hate school and finally to break with it. These children often come from severely disturbed homes and are usually openly rejected by their parents, who often punish them severely, compare them unfavorably with a brother or sister, and in general give them no emotional support. Such a child has often given up trying to be good in order to ingratiate himself with his parents, who, in turn, have given up and always expect misbehavior from him. He may even be so hungry for parental attention that he comes to enjoy their attention even in the form of punishment. These children are difficult to help, because it is virtually impossible to find an adequate substitute for the parental love and affection which should be every child's birthright.

Ephron (1953) stresses that reading is one aspect of a child's life situation in which he may show how he feels about himself, and in which he may express both his conscious and unconscious needs. Remedial work, she considers, should attempt to correct the conditions which lowered the person's achievement and may still be holding him back. Tutorial opportunities can be, and often should become, a form of psychotherapy. Since psychotherapy is really a re-education in learning to know oneself, it can be brought into education, according to Ephron, and help one to learn more willingly and more pleasantly.

Walsh (1956) studied two groups of bright boys, one group achieving well academically, and the other not. A highly reliable technique, using the Driscoll Play Kit, was developed for classifying the play behavior of the boys. It was found that the low achievers less frequently than the adequate achievers depicted the boy doll as free to pursue his own interests and to express his feelings, and as adequately responding to the environment. Natchez (1959) also studied two groups of 30 boys each, one group being retarded in reading and the other not. Her results showed that the retarded readers were significantly more dependent, more aggressive, and more withdrawn than normal readers.

In an interesting study of first memories in fifth- and sixth-grade children, Wagenheim (1960) reported that more memories of physical accidents were reported by the children in the lowest quartile of reading. Especially among the boys, these early memories were of falling, tripping, and events that could be interpreted as indicative of personal failure and inadequacy.

Norman and Daley (1959), dealing with matched groups of approximately 40 superior and inferior readers, found poorer adjustment, greater rejection of self, and greater rejection by others among the poor readers. An analysis of variance showed clearly that personality adjustment of superior readers differs significantly from that of inferior readers. Sixty-seven items out of 144 were significantly different at the .05 level. They involved such things as self-reliance, sense of personal worth, feeling of belonging, withdrawing tendencies, nervous symptoms, skills, antisocial trends, as well as family, school, and community relations.

The two major reading disability syndromes, one of the aggressive pre-delinquent type with severely rejecting parents, and the other the shy, submissive, withdrawing children with severely overprotective parents, suggested by the writer in 1947, were subsequently verified by Spache (1957) who believes there are in addition several other patterns of behavior disorder associated with nonreading. The two types of mothers seen in the clinic whose children failed to learn to read are strikingly similar to the "universally present" (overprotective) and the "continuously punitive" (rejecting) mothers postulated by Sears (1957) in his restatement of Freud's anaclitic theory of identification. These data also fit in well with the gradient of language development previously discussed (McCarthy, 1954c) in regard to the amount and intensity of maternal contact with the child. Irving D. Harris, a Chicago psychoanalyst and on the staff of the Illinois Institute of Juvenile Research, devotes a chapter of his book on *Emotional Blocks to Learning* to "Aggression and Submission," and states, "Reading problems are associated with both extremes of aggressive tendencies—too little or too much—rather than with a simple lack of aggressivity. . .the main familial factor is concerned with how the mother handles her own critical, blaming, faultfinding tendencies" (1961, pp. 83-84), i.e., whether she turns them outward toward the world and makes a scapegoat of her son, or whether she turns her aggression or hostility inward toward herself. Thus, either extreme of maternal behavior seems to prevent healthy ego development and to lead to some form of language disorder. Much further research on symptom choice and overlapping of symptoms in the same cases is needed.

Generally, studies reported from schools rather than from clinical settings do not contain enough history information or sufficient evidence regarding the home situation to reveal the dynamics involved. Also, many studies which emerge with negative results in this area are designed to seek a single personality pattern for *all* nonreaders. Since contrasting types seem to exist, they often cancel each other out in such general studies when scores are averaged for an entire group without a preliminary separation on the basis of the type of syndrome shown. Still other studies yield results in apparent conflict with data of this sort, probably because they employ insensitive or unreliable psychological instruments in the field of personality measurement (Goodstein, 1958a, b).

Selective factors may operate in some investigations to give apparent negation to some of these findings. For example, one clinic which charged high fees for intensive remedial work with nonreaders never had any children with the aggressive syndrome and severely rejecting parents. Their clientele was composed almost entirely of the submissive overprotected children whose parents were sufficiently concerned to seek help. Certain cultural, religious, and ethnic groups may have attitudes toward child rearing which prevent confirmation of some of these findings, simply because these groups may not produce the extreme forms of language disorder usually found in clinical populations.

As mentioned above, lack of adequate language learning in the form of mutism is an outstanding symptom in the schizophrenic child. One of the greatest challenges for the therapist is to break through and establish contact with the schizophrenic child and to make him want to communicate. There is, in such cases, an inadequate development of the ego that Spitz (1959) and Allport (1955) referred to as a withdrawal from reality. Language has never been used by these children to come to grips with reality, as Church (1961) has so well described. Other schizophrenic children may learn to speak, but later on fail to learn to read.

Goldberg's (1952) report on the treatment of 12 schizophrenics with reading disabilities is of interest in this connection. These children reacted favorably to animal stories, but became quite disturbed with the "Happy Family" series. They spat on the pictures and tore them up and one boy said, "They have everything, and I have nothing." "No children ever get punished in your books," or "You have no stories with naughty boys."

These children regarded being able to read as being normal. They seemed to regard learning to read as being reborn, and the tutor was perceived as a new mother. The tutorial therapy they were given also seemed to help them with space and time orientation. The description of their progress from isolated concrete words and skipping around the page to continuity of approach and planning behavior is strikingly parallel to the stages described by Luria and Yudovich (1959) on the retarded Russian twins. Closely related to this is a psychoanalytically oriented report

on 35 poor readers by Silverman, Fite, and Mosher (1959), who conceive of "reading disability. . . as a disorder in ego-function—the inhibition
of learning and intelligence." Drawing an analogy between the early intake of food from the mother and the taking in of intellectual food from
the printed page, they point out that the child must be free from conflict
in the reading situation in order to permit himself active and passive use
of the eyes. He must be free to look openly and to see minute differences
clearly, if he is to satisfy his intellectual curiosity by reading. In their
group of 35 cases, two thirds showed anxiety, sibling rivalry, fears, depression, and distractability. Psychopathology in the family relationships was
present in half the cases, and half had unpleasant situational factors associated with early school experiences. Seventy-one per cent of these poor
readers were also having difficulty with arithmetic, and 43% were described as suffering from "intellectual inhibition in learning."

LANGUAGE AND SOCIOECONOMIC STATUS

In my early normative study on language development, I reported differences in language development associated with paternal occupation. The
dynamics of the observation were not at all evident at the time of publication. Many years later, however, the study by Milner (1951) which
compared children in the top and bottom third of the first-grade classes
in reading shed considerable light on the matter. Her study described in
detail the different way of life in the homes of the children who were the
good readers and those who were the poor readers. In the homes of children who read well, there were regular meal hours, and someone affectionally important to the child saw him off to school and was there to
talk to when he came home from school. In contrast, the children who
were poor readers were latchkey children whose mothers worked, or did
not get up for breakfast, and were not at home after school. Now, it can
readily be seen that these "under-the-roof conditions" which have an impact on the emotional life of the child can, and do, exist at all socioeconomic levels. The disorganized homes, however, are most likely to be
found in the lower occupational groups, and the better way of life is likely
to be found more frequently in the upper socioeconomic groups. The
gradient relating to socioeconomic status in regard to language development is quite similar to the one which has been reported for years in re-

gard to intelligence test results. In this connection it is well to remember that the best intelligence tests are highly verbal in nature and that such tests are still the best predictors of academic achievement.

Irwin (1960) has recently reported an ingenious experiment showing the environmental impact on children's language development. Twenty-four infants from lower socioeconomic status were visited in their homes regularly and phonemic records were made of their vocalizations from 13 to 30 months of age. The experimenter supplied appropriate, illustrated storybooks to the parents and urged them to read the stories to the children, and to talk to the children about the pictures. Ten other children of similarly low socioeconomic status were studied for language development without the provision of any supplementary educational materials, and without any special suggestion to the parents. They merely did whatever parents of that socioeconomic level would have done anyway. The differences in the mean number of phonemes used by the children at each age were in favor of the group which had the storybooks provided. They were not significant at the 13- to 16-month ages, but at all the higher ages, namely, 18 to 30 months, they were highly significant. Irwin concludes, therefore, that "Systematically increasing the speech sound stimulation of infants under 2 1/2 years of age in homes of lower socioeconomic status ... will lead to increase in the phonetic production of these infants over what might be expected without reading enrichment."

LANGUAGE AND ORGANIC FACTORS

Many kinds of language disorder, particularly the developmental aphasias described so well by Myklebust (1957) and by N. E. Wood (1959), quite obviously involve organic pathology. At this point it may well be asked how the findings of Kawi and Pasamanick (1959) fit into the functional theme presented here. These authors did a monumental piece of work on 372 white, male children with reading disorders born in Baltimore in a 10-year period, and compared them with the records of a similar matched control group of children who did not develop reading disorders. Comparisons were made on prenatal and paranatal factors, and the conclusion was reached that reading disorders probably constitute the mildest form of "a reproductive casualty continuum" ranging from abortions, stillbirths, and neonatal deaths, through cerebral palsy, epilepsy, and mental deficiency, to reading disorders, the implication being that some mild form of brain damage is involved. This is entirely possible, and indeed the histories of many clinical cases which are most resistant to treatment indicate that frequently a previous child in the family had died, or there had been a series of miscarriages, etc., or the child himself had had a difficult birth. De Hirsch (1952) considers that children with language disorders are suffering from developmental lags, usually of an organic origin. She has also made (1963) a very incisive interpretation of the poor reader's difficulties with sequential material in terms of gestalt theory.

Although many birth injuries are due to physical conditions, poor obstetrics, and other factors, it is also known that emotionally disturbed and poorly adjusted women are most likely to have problems in bearing children normally. The surviving children of mothers who have difficulties in bearing children are then brought up under the environmental pressures provided by severely maladjusted mothers who often do not afford good models with which to identify. In some cases there may be a strictly organic problem in the child; in others it may be purely functional; in still others there may be the combination of mild neurological involvement and the pressures of living with disturbed people in an abnormal environment.

Another monograph which also needs to be reckoned with in a discussion such as this is that of Smith and Carrigan (1959), which postulates a physiological imbalance of cholinesterase and acetylcholine which affects the passage of nerve impulses across the synapses. Their presentation is largely in the form of a theoretical model and it is not clear how many of their reading-disability cases actually conform to the model, or how many have been successfully treated along lines suggested by their hypotheses. The work has been severely criticized by A. Harris (1960), and few medical practitioners have so far accepted the theory or will treat cases on the basis of it at the present time.

When physiological findings are positive, for example, and the blood sugar analysis of stutterers is found to differ from that of nonstutterers, or when nonreaders are different from good readers in the presence or absence of certain hormones, it is tempting to conclude that *the* cause of a very complex syndrome has been found, since physiological data somehow take precedence in our culture and seem more primary than behavioral data. Because of the rapid strides in medicine in recent years, there seems to be a tendency to think that if a physiological aspect can be isolated, there is hope for a ready cure. If, however, it is realized that we are merely looking at the other side of the coin, merely completing the description of the syndrome by giving the physiological correlates, it is still possible to accept a psychogenic explanation of many of these phenomena.

Considerable evidence has been presented in this chapter that many children suffering from language disorders of various sorts have been living under conditions of chronic emotional stress for some time. Arnold (1960) in the second volume of her *Emotion and Personality* reports that "Fleetwood and Diethelm...found evidence for several kinds of cholinergic stimulation during the states of tension and anger. For instance, they found a cholinergic substance in human blood during emotional tension states (characterized by irritability, muscular tension, insomnia, inability to concentrate)." Arnold adds, "It is tempting to suggest that emotional tension might be a chronic form of anger or resentment." She cites another study by Funkenstein et al. (1954) in which young men were asked to solve difficult arithmetic problems without paper and pencil while being blamed for stupidity. Here is an experimental frustration situation very similar to the actual life situations experienced day in and day out by children with language disorders. Some of the young men in the experiment expressed their anger openly like the aggressive nonreaders; others blamed themselves, apologized, and kept their anger in, and still others showed anxiety like the submissive nonreaders and stutterers. Arnold (1960) says of this group: "Psychologically speaking, self-blame (anger in) is closer to fear than to anger, because the person appraises the situation as difficult and himself as inadequate in dealing with it. He feels helpless though he recognizes that the situation is not really threatening, and becomes impatient with his own reaction" (p. 224). This is reminiscent of the feelings of inadequacy of the nonreaders studied by Walsh (1956) and by Wagenheim (1960). Arnold's (1960) material is well documented with data from physiological studies, and she concludes: "We know that the most favorable condition for activity seems to be produced by mild cholinergic excitation as aroused by affection and interest. Both fear and anger are a spur to action but lose this effect if action does not overcome the obstacle or does not take us out of danger. Continuing fear and anger reduce the efficiency of action and disturb the economy of the organism" (p. 227).

I have chosen to focus this chapter on the affective aspects of language learning which seem so often to be overlooked in our concern for sensory, motor, and cognitive processes. It seems that there is considerable evidence stemming from experimental, developmental, and clinical studies that affective problems may arrest or completely override the influence of intellectual abilities. Nearly blind children can, and do, learn to read if sufficiently motivated (Dahl, 1949), as do severely hard-of-hearing children; yet minor disabilities may be used as reasons, conscious or unconscious, for learning failure in those whose motivation and/or emotional adjustment are precarious.

The neurological and physiological data, as well as the linguistic material, emphasize the necessity of the interdisciplinary approach to the problems of the whole child. The perfect experiment has not yet been made. Much of the clinical evidence, and even experimental studies using clinical syndromes to identify experimental subjects, often gives only partial answers. More adequate control groups of children who speak and read normally are needed, in order to find out how many of them read and speak normally in spite of stressful environments, and how many children develop language disorder syndromes without organic involvement, and without having experienced environmental stress. These data are difficult to get, for ethical considerations make it hard to secure the intimate details of family life from normal families whose children present no problems. As Shakow (1959) pointed out, more studies of children in their homes are needed, and this is hard to accomplish without invading the privacy of the home. It is just as necessary, however, to do large-scale studies using controls and placebos in the mental health field as it was in the development of the Salk vaccine for poliomyelitis. With public education in the need for research, the large-scale ideal studies need not be in the distant future. They can and should be undertaken now in communities which are more advanced in mental health orientation.

It is encouraging that psychologists, working in accordance with psychogenic explanations of language disorders, can and do change the attitudes of parents and of children. Several of the researchers cited show that the various aspects of language are susceptible to environmental manipulation. Psychologists are not neurosurgeons and cannot repair damaged tissues, nor are they permitted to prescribe drugs; but they can guide development, improve parental attitudes, release tensions, improve self-concepts, and help clients to a better way of life through the applications of knowledge gained by sound research.

BIBLIOGRAPHY

Albright, R. W. & Albright, J. B. (1958), Application of Descriptive Linguistics to Child Language. *Journal of Speech and Hearing Research*, 1:257-261.
Allport, G. W. (1955), *Becoming: Basic Considerations for a Psychology of Personality*. New Haven: Yale University Press.
Andersland, P. B. (1961), Maternal and Environmental Factors Relating to Success in Speech Improvement Training. *Journal of Speech and Hearing Research*, 4:79-90.
Arnold, M. B. (1960), Neurological and Physiological Aspects. *Emotion and Personality*, 2. New York: Columbia University Press.
Bastian, J. (1959), Review of *Words and Things* by Brown, R. *Word*, 15:353-356.
Beck, H. K. (1950), Relationship of Emotional Factors in Early Childhood to Subsequent Growth and to Achievement in Reading. Doctoral dissertation, University of Michigan (microfilm).
Bender, L. (1947), Psychopathic Behavior Disorders in Children. *Handbook of Correctional Psychology*, Lindner, R. M. & Seliger, R. V. (Eds.), pp. 360-377. New York: Philosophical Library.
Berko, J. & Brown, R. (1960), Psycholinguistic Research Methods. *Handbook of Research Methods in Child Development*, Mussen, P. H. (Ed.), pp. 517-557. New York: Wiley.
Bowlby, J. (1951), Maternal Care and Mental Health. *WHO Monograph*, 2.
Brock, T. C. & Del Giudice, C. (1962), Stealing and Temporal Orientation. *Journal of Abnormal and Social Psychology*, 66:91-94.
Brodbeck, A. J. & Irwin, O. C. (1946), The Speech Behavior of Infants Without Families. *Child Development*, 17:145-156.
Bronfenbrenner, U. (1960), Freudian Theories of Identification and Their Derivatives. *Child Development*, 31:15-40.
Brown, R. (1958), *Words and Things*. Glencoe, Illinois: Free Press.
—— & Berko, J. (1960), Word Association and the Acquisition of Grammar. *Child Development*, 31:1-14.
Carey, J. E. & Goss, A. E. (1956), The Role of Verbal Labeling in the Conceptual Sorting Behavior of Children. *Journal of Genetic Psychology*, 90:69-74.
Church, J. (1961), *Language and the Discovery of Reality*. New York: Random House.
Cofer, C. N. & Foley, J. P., Jr. (1942), Mediated Generalization and the Interpretation of Verbal Behavior. I. Prolegomena. *Psychological Review*, 49:513-549.
Dahl, B. (1949), *I Wanted to See*. New York: Macmillan.
De Hirsch, K. (1952), Specific Dyslexia or Strephosymbolia. *Folia Phoniatrika*, 4:231-248.
—— (1963), Concepts Related to Normal Reading Processes and Their Application to Reading Pathology. *Journal of Genetic Psychology*, 102:277-285.
Dennis, W. (1951), Cultural and Developmental Factors in Perception. *Perception: An Approach to Personality*, Blake, R. R. & Ramsey, G. V. (Eds.), pp. 148-169. New York: Ronald Press.

Despert, J. L. (1938), Schizophrenia in Children. *Psychiatric Quarterly*, 12:366-371.
——(1946), Psychosomatic Study of Fifty Stuttering Children. *American Journal of Orthopsychiatry*, 16:100-113.
Dollard, J. & Miller, N. E. (1950), *Personality and Psychotherapy*. New York: McGraw-Hill.
Ephron, B. K. (1953), *Emotional Difficulties in Reading*. New York: Julian Press.
Erikson, E. H. (1950), *Childhood and Society*. New York: Norton.
Fischer-Jorgensen, E. (1961), What Can the New Techniques of Acoustic Phonetics Contribute to Linguistics? *Psycholinguistics: A Book of Readings*, Saporta, S. (Ed.). New York: Holt, Rinehart and Winston.
Flavell, J. H. & Stedman, D. J. (1961), A Developmental Study of Judgments of Semantic Similarity. *Journal of Genetic Psychology*, 98:279-293.
Fletcher, S. G. (1962), Speech as an Element in Organization of a Motor Response. *Journal of Speech and Hearing Research*, 5:292-300.
Foley, J. P., Jr. & Cofer, C. N. (1943), Mediated Generalization and the Interpretation of Verbal Behavior: II. Experimental Study of Certain Homophone and Synonym Gradients. *Journal of Experimental Psychology*, 32:168-175.
Funkenstein, D. H., King, S. H. & Drolette, M. (1954), The Direction of Anger During a Laboratory Stress-Inducing Situation. *Psychosomatic Medicine*, 16:404-413.
Gibson, E. J. (1961), Association and Differentiation in Perceptual Learning. Paper presented at meeting of Society for Research in Child Development. State College, Pennsylvania, March.
Goldberg, I. (1952), Schizophrenic Children with Reading Disabilities. *Quarterly Journal of Child Behavior*, 4:273-280.
Goldfarb, W. (1955), Emotional and Intellectual Consequences of Psychologic Deprivation in Infancy: A Reevaluation. *Psychopathology of Childhood*, Hoch, P. H. & Zubin, J. (Eds.), pp. 105-119. New York: Grune and Stratton.
Goodstein, L. D. (1958a), Functional Speech Disorders and Personality: A Survey of the Research. *Journal of Speech and Hearing Research*, 1:359-376.
——(1958b), Functional Speech Disorders and Personality: Methodological and Theoretical Considerations. *Journal of Speech and Hearing Research*, 1:377-382.
Goss, A. E. & Moylan, M. C. (1958), Conceptual Block Sorting as a Function of Amount of Discriminative Learning. *Journal of Genetic Psychology*, 93:191-198.
Harris, A. J. (1960), A Critical Reaction to *The Nature of Reading Disability* (Smith, D. E. P. & Carrigan, P. M., Eds. New York: Harcourt, Brace). *Journal of Developmental Reading*, 3:238-249.
Harris, I. D. (1961), *Emotional Blocks to Learning*. Glencoe, Ill.: Free Press.
Heidbreder, E. (1958), Woodworth and Whorf on the Role of Language in Thinking. *Current Psychological Issues*, Seward, G. S. & Seward, J. P. (Eds.). New York: Holt, Rinehart and Winston.
Hilgard, E. R. (1951), The Role of Learning in Perception. *Perception: An Approach to Personality*, Blake, R. R. & Ramsey, G. V. (Eds.), pp. 95-120. New York: Ronald Press.
Hockett, C. F. (1950), Age Grading and Linguistic Change. *Language*, 26:449-457.
Irwin, O. C. (1947), Infant Speech: Consonantal Sounds According to Place of Articulation. *Journal of Speech Disorders*, 12:402-404.
——(1960), Infant Speech: Effect of Systematic Reading of Stories. *Journal of Speech and Hearing Research*, 3:187-190.

AFFECTIVE ASPECTS OF LANGUAGE LEARNING 341

Jakobson, R. & Halle, M. (1956), *Fundamentals of Language*. The Hague: Mouton.
Kawi, A. A. & Pasamanick, B. (1959), Prenatal and Paranatal Factors in the Development of Childhood Reading Disorders. *Monograph of the Society for Research in Child Development*, 24:1-80.
Kendler, H. H. & Kendler, T. S. (1961), Effect of Verbalization on Reversal Shifts in Children. *Science*, 134:1619-1620.
Korzybski, A. (1951), The Role of Language in the Perceptual Processes. *Perception: An Approach to Personality*, Blake, R. R. & Ramsey, G. V. (Eds.), pp. 170-205. New York: Ronald Press.
Kunst, M. S. (1949), *Supplementary Education Monograph*. Staff of University of Chicago Reading Clinic.
Lenneberg, E. H. (1953), Cognition in Ethnolinguistics. *Language*, 29:463-471.
Lewis, M. M. (1959), *How Children Learn to Speak*. New York: Basic Books.
Liberman, A. M. (1957), Some Results of Research on Speech Perception. *Journal of Acoustical Society of America*, 29:117-123. Reprinted: Saporta, S. (Ed.), *Psycholinguistics: A Book of Readings*. New York: Holt, Rinehart and Winston, 1961.
Luria, A. R. (1959), The Directive Function of Speech in Development and Dissolution. *Word*, 15 (part I):341-352.
—— & Yudovich, F. I. (1959), *Speech and the Development of Mental Processes in the Child* (Trans. by Kovasc, O. & Simon, J.). London: Staples.
McCarthy, D. (1930), *Language Development of the Preschool Child*. Minneapolis: University of Minnesota Press. (Currently available in Xerox reproduction, University Microfilms, Ann Arbor, Michigan.)
——(1947), The Psychologist Looks at the Teaching of English. *Independent School Bulletin, Series of 1946-1947*, 5:3-11.
——(1949), Personality and Learning. *Education for the Preservation of Democracy. American Council on Education Studies, Series I*, 35:93-96.
——(1952a), Language and Personality Development. *Reading Teacher*, 6:28-36.
——(1952b), Factors that Influence Language Growth: Home Influences. *Elementary English*, 29:421-428, 440.
——(1954a), Language Disorders and Parent-Child Relationships. *Journal of Speech and Hearing Disorders*, 19:514-523.
——(1954b), Identifying and Helping Children with Language Disabilities. *Frontiers of Elementary Education, I*, Glennon, V. J. (Ed.), pp. 25-36. Syracuse University Press.
——(1954c), Language Development in Children. *Manual of Child Psychology*, Carmichael, L. (Ed.), pp. 492-630. New York: Wiley, second edition.
——(1956), Language in the Child's Total Development. *Language Arts in the Catholic Elementary School*, Sr. M. R. Langdon (Ed.), pp. 16-41. Washington, D. C.: Catholic University of America Press.
Meerloo, J. von (1952), *Conversation and Communication: A Psychological Inquiry into Language and Human Relations*. New York: International Universities Press.
Menyuk, P. (1963), Syntactic Structures in the Language of Children. *Child Development*, 34:407-422.
Miller, G. A. & Nicely, P. E. (1955), An Analysis of Perceptual Confusions Among Some English Consonants. *Journal of Acoustical Society of America*, 27:338-352. Reprinted: Saporta, S. (Ed.), *Psycholinguistics: A Book of Readings*. New York: Holt, Rinehart and Winston, 1961.

Milner, E. (1951), A Study of the Relationships Between Reading Readiness in Grade One School Children and Patterns of Parent-Child Interaction. *Child Development*, 22:95-112.

Moncur, J. P. (1951), Environmental Factors Differentiating Stuttering Children from Non-stuttering Children. *Speech Monograph*, 18:312-325.

Mowrer, O. H. (1958), Hearing and Speaking: An Analysis of Language Learning. *Journal of Speech and Hearing Disorders*, 23:143-151.

Murphy, G. (1956), Affect and Perceptual Learning. *Psychological Review*, 63:1-15.

Myklebust, H. R. (1957), Aphasia in Children: Chapter 3, Language Development and Language Pathology; Chapter 4, Diagnosis and Training. *Handbook of Speech Pathology*, Travis, L. E. (Ed.), pp. 503-530. New York: Appleton-Century-Crofts.

Natchez, G. (1959), *Personality Patterns and Oral Reading*. New York: New York University Press.

Nesbit, F. F. (1955), *Language, Meaning and Reality: A Study of Symbolism*. New York: Exposition Press.

Norman, R. D. & Daley, M. F. (1959), The Comparative Personality Adjustment of Superior and Inferior Readers. *Journal of Educational Psychology*, 50:31-36.

Peckarsky, A. (1952), Maternal Attitudes Towards Children with Psychogenically Delayed Speech. Unpublished doctoral dissertation, New York University.

Pitman, J. (1963), The Future of the Teaching of Reading. *Proceedings of the Twenty-eighth Educational Conference of the Educational Record Bureau.*

Pyles, M. K. (1932), Verbalization as a Factor in Learning. *Child Development*, 3:108-113.

Reiss, B. F. (1946), Genetic Changes in Semantic Conditioning. *Journal of Experimental Psychology*, 36:143-152.

Rheingold, H. & Bayley, N. (1959), The Later Effects of an Experimental Modification of Mothering. *Child Development*, 30:363-372.

——, Gewirtz, J. L. & Ross, H. W. (1959), Social Conditioning of Vocalizations in the Infant. *Journal of Comparative and Physiological Psychology*, 52:68-73.

Sayler, H. K. (1949), The Effect of Maturation upon Defective Articulation in Grades Seven Through Twelve. *Journal of Speech and Hearing Disorders*, 14:202-207.

Sears, R. R. (1957), Identification as a Form of Behavior Development. *The Concept of Development*, Harris, D. B. (Ed.), pp. 149-161. Minneapolis: University of Minnesota Press.

Shakow, D. (1959), Research in Child Development: A Case Illustration of the Psychologist's Dilemma. *American Journal of Orthopsychiatry*, 29:45-59.

Sheldon, W. D. & Carrillo, L. (1952), Relation of Parents, Home and Certain Developmental Characteristics to Children's Reading Ability. *Elementary School Journal*, 52:262-270.

Silverman, J. S., Fite, M. & Mosher, M. M. (1959), Clinical Findings in Reading Disability Children—Special Cases of Intellectual Inhibition. *American Journal of Orthopsychiatry*, 29:298-314.

Smith, D. E. P. & Carrigan, P. M. (1959), *The Nature of Reading Disability*. New York: Harcourt, Brace.

Soffietti, J. P. (1953), Why Children Fail to Read: A Linguistic Analysis. *Harvard Educational Review*, 25:63-84.

Spache, G. (1957), Personality Patterns of Retarded Readers. *Journal of Educational Research*, 50:461-469.

Spitz, R. A. (1945), Hospitalism: An Inquiry into the Genesis of Psychiatric Conditions in Early Childhood. *The Psychoanalytic Study of the Child*, 1:53-74. New York: International Universities Press.

——(1959), *A Genetic Field Theory of Ego Formation: Its Implications for Pathology.* New York: International Universities Press.

—— & Wolf, K. M. (1946), Anaclitic Depression; An Inquiry into the Genesis of Psychiatric Conditions in Early Childhood. *The Psychoanalytic Study of the Child*, 2:313-342. New York: International Universities Press.

Spriestersbach, D. C. & Curtis, J. F. (1951), Misarticulation and Discrimination of Speech Sounds. *Quarterly Journal of Speech*, 37:483-491.

Wagenheim, L. (1960), First Memories of "Accidents" and Reading Difficulties. *American Journal of Orthopsychiatry*, 30:191-195.

Walsh, A. M. (1956), *Self-Concepts of Bright Boys With Learning Difficulties.* New York: Bureau of Publications, Teachers College, Columbia University.

Whorf, B. L. (1956), *Language, Thought and Reality.* New York: Wiley.

Winitz, H. & Irwin, O. C. (1958), Syllabic and Phonetic Structure of Infants' Early Words. *Journal of Speech and Hearing Research*, 1:250-256.

Wood, K. S. (1946), Parental Maladjustment and Functional Articulatory Defects in Children. *Journal of Speech Disorders*, 11:255-275.

Wood, N. E. (1959), *Language Disorders in Children.* Chicago: National Society for Crippled Children and Adults.

——(1960), Language Development and Disorders: A Compendium of Lectures. *Monograph of the Society for Research in Child Development.*

Woodworth, R. S. (1947), Reinforcement of Perception. *American Journal of Psychology*, 60:119-124.

Wyatt, G. (1958a), Mother-Child Relationships and Stuttering in Children. Doctoral dissertation, Boston University. (University Microfilms, Ann Arbor, Michigan.)

——(1958b), A Developmental Crisis Theory of Stuttering. *Language and Speech*, 1:250-264.

——(1960), Unpublished Report of Research Project, United States Public Health M-2667A, presented before New York Society for Speech and Voice Therapy.

—— & Herzan, H. M. (1962), Therapy with Stuttering Children and Their Mothers. *American Journal of Orthopsychiatry*, 34:645-659.

Yedinack, J. G. (1949), A Study of the Linguistic Functioning of Children with Articulation and Reading Disabilities. *Journal of Genetic Psychology*, 74:23-59.

CHAPTER 13

Formation of the Concept
of "Self" and Development of
Sex Identification

JOSEF ERNEST GARAI

I. FORMATION OF THE SELF-CONCEPT

DEFINITION OF "SELF"

Every individual has a definite concept of himself. This concept may be more or less realistic depending on the degree of accordance with the evaluations of other people. We may define the self-concept as the set of inferences a person makes about himself on the basis of his experience.

By the beginning of the third year of his life the child has acquired a rudimentary concept of "self." Experimental evidence of the development of the self-concept is almost entirely lacking, as it is extremely difficult to design suitable studies on the preverbal level and during the early stages of verbal behavior. But it is possible to draw certain inferences from clinical observations of children's behavior which furnish a number of clues to the understanding of this development.

ABSENCE OF SELF-DIFFERENTIATION

The newborn child has no background of experiences that might enable him to make inferences about himself. He seems to begin life in a world without objects, a world devoid of persons and things, of space, time, and causality. He lacks the feeling of separateness from his environment and the awareness of boundaries between himself and the outside world. For adults, the mother's nipple yielding milk, her supporting arm, hand, and

344

body, her loving face, and her happy prattle are distinctly recognizable stimuli. But for the newborn baby, all these exist only as a general atmosphere of warm comfort and pleasure from which he derives a pervasive feeling of satisfaction. What appears to his mother as the baby's hunger, his discomfort, his emptiness or loneliness, exist for the baby only as boundless misery and intolerable frustration of urgent wants. He is unable to understand why he feels so miserable and what it is that he wants. When his misery is alleviated and his wants are satisfied through his mother's nurturance, his distress gives way to comfort and pleasure. Yet he cannot in the least realize what is being done for him, what he himself does, or even that there are people around him who minister to his needs or that he has a separate existence. The adult's perception of the world as a reality which is clearly delineated as to time, space, and causality of events and integrated into a stable, permanent framework of experience has been slowly created as the result of a long and elaborate learning process. Out of a welter of conflicting impressions and confusing stimuli and experiences, the mind slowly structures an integrated unit of stable relationships. This apparent firmness and permanence of the external world are in part the projections of our own firm, enduring personality organization.

In the course of the first two years of his life the child passes through several stages of progressive differentiation which result in the acquisition of an elementary self-concept. During the first few weeks of his existence the human infant is incapable of distinguishing between himself and his mother. This is due to the lack of functional boundaries. He merely feels shifts in position and changes in movement whose source he cannot clearly detect or visualize. He lives in a kind of magical world where he experiences tremendous changes in stimulation throughout his waking life with hardly any effort of his own. He feels that he and his mother form a unit of action and he comes to believe, without knowing why or how, that the sudden shifts in movement with concomitant changes of sounds and light effects are just things that occur to him. Whenever he is moved about, turned over, diapered, carried around, or taken out of doors, he perceives the infinite variety of onrushing stimuli as things that happen and, as he matures a little further, as things that he accomplishes through his own effort. He experiences being carried around or lifted up by his mother as his own magical moving about. His own joy during the feeding situation is felt as a global joy shared with his mother and, if his mother reacts with anger to his rage, he experiences a still heightened feeling of boundless rage. The sharing of all these sensations and feelings with his mother is defined as *primary identification* by Cameron (1963).

ESTABLISHMENT OF BOUNDARIES BETWEEN EXTERNAL AND INTERNAL REALITY

In the process of the maturation of his sensory and nervous apparatus, the little infant slowly gains a realization of the existence of certain boundaries. It is most likely that the first feelings of separateness are experienced during the ingestion of food. His mouth is his most mature organ at birth; it is highly sensitive. Sucking movements are initiated which are directed toward the external environment from which he must derive the nourishment to fill the void in his stomach. The first focusing toward the outside—the mother's nipple—occurs as the first goal-directed action intended to manipulate the environment for the gratification of basic drives. Furthermore, the mouth provides the child with his first experience of bodily pleasure; sucking tends to persist as a purely pleasurable activity after the satisfaction of physiological needs. The mouth serves two opposing functions, namely the admission of suitable foodstuffs and the exclusion of unwanted matter. Therefore it constitutes the basis for an early discrimination between *external reality*, that which can be taken in or denied admission, and *internal reality*, that which is always present, namely the organs that make up the mouth. As the tongue is also admirably suited to explore the texture, firmness, brittleness, and taste of solids and the flavor of liquids, the infant gets its first taste or test of reality through the manipulation of his tongue.

ORAL DISCRIMINATION

At first, the child turns his mouth toward any object at random. Anything that approaches or touches his face is seized with the lips and, if he can hold it, it is sucked. While sucking is at first haphazard and uncoordinated, it becomes more and more discriminating with increasing experience. The child will increasingly reject those objects which fail to yield milk. This discrimination between objects that yield milk and those that fail to yield milk is the first act of choice. In this primitive form of discrimination the child begins to be dimly aware of the fact that choices can be made between pleasurable and nonpleasurable objects and that only the former satisfy his needs. The possibility of choice conveys an awakening awareness of the manipulability of the external world.

DEVELOPMENT OF IMAGERY AS A RESULT OF DELAYED GRATIFICATION

Another decisive factor in the emergence of the ability to distinguish between the internal and the external world is the experience of a delay in immediate gratification which intervenes between the arousal of a drive and its satisfaction on various occasions. The struggle of the child to direct his movements toward the nipple begins in the first week after birth. For the infant who has not yet developed any concept of time the delay may frequently seem interminable. A strong element of frustration is introduced into the act of nursing as the child feels the intensity of the hunger drive. Postponement of immediate gratification and the necessity to learn to wait for the fulfillment of basic needs are instrumental in the creation of a certain basic consciousness of the fact that the source of gratification is not an automatic part of the mother-child symbiosis. The baby realizes that the satisfying action is brought to him from the outside.

During the time of delay it is likely that the food source, the nipple and the flow of milk from it, can be imagined by the child. This "imagery" keeps the child eagerly attuned to his goal. It helps him to endure the delay for a little while and provides him with an imagined anticipation of the satisfaction. This ability to visualize a future act of gratification appears to be the first step toward goal setting in the more advanced stages of later life. It enables the little baby to imagine in his mind the future gratification which he will experience as a result of obtaining the nipple.

Cameron (1963) states that the child is able to incorporate the nipple temporarily and the mother's milk permanently. Both possession through incorporation of external objects and loss of possession of objects are already experienced by the infant at this early stage. He loses the nipple when the mother takes it away, the milk through swallowing, or food by spitting out or vomiting. According to psychoanalytic theory, these early experiences of incorporation and loss play significant roles in the development of oral imagery and in later unconscious fantasies and symptom formations concerning incorporation and loss of parental traits. They are mechanisms which facilitate the process of sex identification. Symbolization can thus be traced back to the preverbal stage of the first appearance of oral imagery, and such fantasies as devouring and being devoured appear to stem from this stage, too.

COORDINATION OF VISUAL AND MANUAL DISCRIMINATION

While the mouth appears to be the first center of perception, the eyes, ears, and hands develop as the child's next perceptual foci. In the beginning, each of these functions independently of all the others; coordination and integration into combined perceptual patterns are lacking. The visual system matures slowly and develops later than the oral system. What the infant sees is not manipulated or brought to his mouth at first. He stares at his legs, feet, arms, and hands in surprise, as if they were strange objects emerging out of a void and disappearing from his view again. Any object that moves out of his perceptual field is regarded as nonexisting and the child loses interest in it. While eye and ear coordination appears to be fairly mature at birth, as indicated by the turning of his head toward the source of sounds, eye-hand coordination develops very slowly. Furthermore, pursuit movements of his eyes emerge only during the second month when he learns to fixate his eyes upon a moving object and to hold it in focus by moving with it. A little later, the eyes learn to converge upon an object to bring it into clear focus. By the third month the eyes can focus and converge upon objects and follow their course by enlisting head movements to accompany them. Thus the child's realm of experience expands in space.

With the attainment of the ability to utilize the combined aid of all the senses in an increasingly well-coordinated manner, the child begins to explore the various parts of his body through touching, scratching, fingering, and various other types of manipulation of his legs, feet, arms, head, etc. His awareness of their interrelated functions sharpens. He learns to distinguish not only the parts of his own body, but also the body parts of his mother and other persons in his environment. He learns to recognize and distinguish the faces of the people approaching him by their different features, facial expressions, and the attitudes conveyed by them, and he begins to discern familiar faces as distinct from the faces of strangers. His prolonged exploration of his body leads to the realization of a distinct "body feel" and he becomes increasingly conscious of the fact that his own body is different from the bodies of other people and the objects in his environment.

DISCRIMINATION OF PEOPLE

Another experience which appears to contribute substantially to the child's acquisition of a self-concept stems from his interaction with the significant adults in his environment. These adults meet certain of his actions with approval and others with disapproval. Some manifestations of his behavior displease his mother and she conveys her displeasure to her child through her attitudes, the tone of her voice, and facial expressions of annoyance such as frowning, or threatening gestures. On the other hand, the child soon learns that certain actions or expressions of feelings on his part are rewarded by his mother's show of delight and approval. In general, he becomes increasingly sensitive to the moods and attitudes of his parents and other persons in his environment such as siblings, relatives, servants, etc. If he feels that his mother loves him and that she has a basically warm and accepting attitude toward him, feelings of trust and confidence will develop in the course of time, whereas a rejecting attitude on the part of his mother will arouse fear, anger, rebellion, or submission with underlying hostility in the child. He will then feel insecure, unloved, and generally confront the world and other people with suspicion and distrust. At any rate, in the total situation the child learns to adapt his behavior to the expectations of his environment so as to be rewarded by praise and acceptance and to avoid punishment and rejection. Intent upon gaining and keeping his mother's approval and loving acceptance, he learns to give up or repress certain disapproved desires or attitudes and to accept certain limits which his mother sets on the free expression of his feelings and the immediate or full satisfaction of his drives.

POSITIVE AND NEGATIVE SELF-CONCEPT

While this learning process is painful and accompanied by many setbacks and the establishment of ego defenses, it nevertheless enables the child to gain valuable insights into the nature of interpersonal relations. He discovers that he is a separate and distinct individual to whom other people respond in different ways and that he, in turn, can react differently to them. The way in which other people in his environment evaluate him will greatly affect the type of self-concept he will construct. The child who meets with basic approval and genuine love from his mother is likely to build up an image of himself as an accepted, trustworthy, and competent person; he develops a positive self-concept. On the other hand, the child who feels rejected and disapproved of by his mother (or his parents) will come to look upon himself as an incompetent person who is unworthy of being loved; he will develop a negative self-concept. In a review of relevant experimental studies, Wylie (1961) states that their findings suggest that children's self-concepts are similar to the view of themselves which they attribute to their parents and that a child's level of self-regard is associated with the parents' reported level of regard for him. These studies also furnish some evidence to suggest that children see the like-sex parent's self-concept (as contrasted to the opposite-sex parent's self-concept) as being somewhat more like their own self-concept. This "looking-glass concept" as described by Cooley (1902) has evolved through the incorporation of the evaluation of one's person by significant others into one's own image of oneself. In this manner oral, visual, auditory, and manual incorporation are complemented by the incorporation of society's (i.e., the parents' and, later on, the peer group's) evaluation of the individual's personality.

THE ROLE OF LANGUAGE IN THE CLARIFICATION OF THE "SELF"

A very important role in the acquisition of the self-concept must be ascribed to the increasingly effective functioning of language. With the adoption of conventional speech, the child's world undergoes tremendous expansion in scope and manipulability. He is able to communicate his thoughts, ideas, and feelings to others and to learn from them how they categorize and interpret the experiences of the external and the internal worlds in accordance with certain commonly agreed-upon rules and concepts. Although a rudimentary self-concept has been established by the end of the first year of life even before the acquisition of language, it is extremely doubtful whether any clear-cut self-concept can ever evolve on the nonverbal level. A fairly basic clarification of his self-concept is achieved by the child when he finally refers to his own person as "I", "me," or "myself." A more realistic body-concept is acquired by the child observing his image in the mirror, an experience which is likely to have a profound effect upon the little child who, for the first time in his life, is confronted with the appearance of his own body as it is seen by other people.

THE ROLE OF SELF IN THE UNDERSTANDING OF EXTERNAL AND INTERNAL REALITY

The ability to understand one's own mirror image and to be aware of the impression one is likely to make upon others as a result of one's physical appearance seems to be peculiar to human beings. Animals are unable to recognize their own images in the mirror. Experiments with monkeys have shown that they are indifferent to their own mirror images or that they get greatly annoyed at the reflection of "another monkey" in the mirror. The observation of the cat chasing its own tail leads us to the conclusion that a cat has no other concept of its own body than that aroused by sensory impulses conveyed to the brain in response to external or internal stimulation. With the ability to form a self-concept, man has become the only animal that can make himself, i.e., his own person, the object of his own thought, perception, reflection, and imagination. Just as he is able to internalize the objects and experiences of the external world into his internal world of thoughts and imagination, he can externalize his own self, that is to say, as it were, step outside of his own existence or self and look upon himself and his own actions through the eyes of another person. He gains the advantage of imagining himself in his relationship to the environment in various situations which are as yet unreal and hypothetical, remembering himself as playing certain roles in the past, and imagining himself enacting similar or different roles in the future. The imaginary dissociation in thought of his person from his body-bound present existence enables man to engage in long-range planning to gain a more efficient control and mastery of the external environment, on one hand, and to explore the internal world of his own aspirations, drives, emotions, and impulses, to attain greater control over his unconscious urges, and to utilize them for constructive rather than destructive purposes, on the other hand. The self as the role of the generalized other in G. H. Mead's definition enables man to picture himself performing a large variety of roles in his imagination. It creates the foundation for heightened flexibility and versatility in the assumption of various roles in later life (1934).

OTHER ASPECTS OF THE "SELF"

Self-awareness, self-criticism, and self-consciousness are some aspects of the self-concept that have been invaluable aids in man's struggle to change

352   JOSEF ERNEST GARAI

his environment to adapt it to his needs. Mere mechanistic explanations of human behavior which leave out the concept of "self" as a presumably metaphysical construct which has no operational validity whatever have been compelled to replace it by all kinds of makeshift constructs which were needed to explain human motivation. Admittedly, the scientific investigation of the self-concept has encountered a host of difficulties owing to the complexity of the various factors involved in it. This has been pointed out by Wylie (1961) in her review of the literature on the self-concept. But she also expresses the hope that with more refined techniques of investigation and better theoretical constructs which can be operationally defined, this problem may yet find a satisfactory solution.

PERSISTENCE OF PRESELF COGNITIVE ORIENTATION

We must keep in mind the fact that the acquisition of the self-concept is by no means clear-cut in the sequence of its developmental stages. While the child develops a concept of his own self as a separate entity, full self-awareness is reached relatively late, and immature attitudes of confusion of the internal with the external world persist and come to the fore sporadically. For several years, the child continues to have difficulty in properly locating processes that go on "within his own mind" and in keeping them separate from external processes. Thus Piaget (1954) notes that if the child is asked, "Where is the dream when you dream?" he will say that it is "in the room" or "beside the bed." Asked by Piaget where the name of the sun is located, children usually answered that it was very high in the sky. Conversely, they attributed to words qualities signified by the objects or events. Thus the word "elephant" was declared to be a very strong word in comparison to "mouse." The child, of course, also projects human attributes onto various animals and inanimate objects. He may believe, for example, that if a pin is poked into a tree, the tree feels it, or that it hurts a rock to be broken by a hammer. He assumes that all persons are like himself, that animals are like humans, and that inanimate objects are alive. He may even identify himself with material things, identifying himself with the broken doll, with the cut flower, or with the eaten animal. If a match is burning and becomes smaller and smaller the child may believe that the match feels this painfully and that a corresponding thing might happen to himself.

This confusion of the self with the nonself may persist on the unconscious level throughout life as its return in dreams shows. But on the conscious level a more realistic concept of the self is progressively emerging. Having achieved a basic understanding of himself as a separate person, a distinct "self," the little child begins to examine what he can do with this fascinating newly acquired self. He begins to engage in role-playing activities, in "make-believe" games by means of which he tries out all kinds of different "selves" and roles which he sees enacted in his more or less immediate vicinity. The little girl makes believe that she is a mother and attempts to copy faithfully the washing, diapering, nursing, and dressing of her little doll as she has seen her mother perform these functions. Little boys visualize themselves more frequently in aggressive roles such as policemen, cowboys, Indians, firemen, astronauts, bus drivers, and captains of boats. Language is extremely helpful in these games as it supplies verbal cues for the internalization of these roles. It ought to be remembered that this role playing is not an exact copying of observed activities. The little child acts out these roles while putting his own stamp or interpretation on their meaning, and not infrequently unconscious desires and unfulfilled wishes tend to find expression in the way in which the role is enacted. Thus a little girl whose mother had established a rule that she could never have more than one piece of cake at one meal was observed playing "giving a party." After she lined up her dolls around the little table, she offered the cake to them in the following way: she placed three little pieces of cake on each plate, saying: "Help yourself to as much cake as you like. This is a party." Her unconscious wish to have more than one piece of cake at a time became clearly evident in this party game.

INTERACTION BETWEEN REAL SELF AND IDEAL SELF

There is no doubt that an individual's self-concept is greatly affected by his conscious and unconscious needs. Each person constructs an "ideal self" which incorporates all those personality traits that are regarded as desirable and essential for the attainment of his goals and the maintenance of his self-esteem. This ideal self refers to the kind of person he would like to be. If the "real self" can be defined as the kind of person he considers himself to be at present, it must be assumed that there is a discrepancy between the real self and the ideal self in normal people and, to a lesser extent, in neurotics, while psychotics generally mistake the ideal or imaginary self for the real self. Nevertheless, even normal people exhibit a tendency to exclude unfavorable traits from the real self and to incorporate favorable traits similar to those of the ideal self into it. This is partly due to the need to establish a well-integrated self-concept which does not contain too many contradictory traits.

Some theories of personality claim that adjustment and mental health can best be measured by the degree to which an individual has a realistic concept of himself. Experimentally, the correlation between a person's own evaluation of his personality traits and the evaluations by other people who know him well such as parents, teachers, siblings, husband, wife, or co-workers is considered to constitute a measure of the adequacy of one's self-concept. The higher the correlation, the more realistic is the person's self-concept. It seems to be well established that an unrealistic self-concept impairs an individual's reality testing and that it may contribute to the etiology of neuroses and psychoses. Therefore some schools of psychotherapy define the attainment of a more realistic self-concept, which includes the acceptance of undesirable as well as desirable traits and unconscious motives, as the ultimate goal of therapy.

FURTHER DEVELOPMENT OF THE SELF-CONCEPT

The self-concept undergoes further development during childhood and adolescence and probably also in adulthood. In these stages of growth the following factors appear to play a decisive role: (1) parent-child interaction; (2) social interaction; (3) peer-group interaction concerning role and status; (4) sexual identification and sex-role performance; (5) religious affiliation; (6) ethnic and racial belongingness; (7) experiences of success and failure; and (8) traumatic experiences leading to a change in life style.

SUMMARY

Summarizing our findings, we may state that the child passes through a number of progressive stages of differentiation. At first he has no knowledge of the object world and of his own separateness. He and the world are one undifferentiated mass of impressions and experiences. The first primitive differentiation occurs through mouthing by which incorporation of external objects occurs. Rudimentary concepts of form and space may be formed during the exploration of objects by means of the mouth and the tongue. Experiences of possession through oral incorporation of foods and liquids and experiences of loss through swallowing, vomiting, or spitting out further aid the baby in distinguishing external from internal events. The experience of delay of immediate gratification inherent in the feeding situation establishes a vague notion of the concept of time. It leads to the development of imagery and fantasy in which future gratification is visualized "pictorially." The beginnings of thought and cognition are thus provoked by the delay that at times intervenes between drive arousal and drive satisfaction.

Through the maturation of the eyes, which learn to focus upon and to pursue a moving object upon which they are now able to converge, spatial differentiation is extended to objects outside the child's body. With the establishment of eye-hand coordination, the mastery over these objects begins to be possible. Objects can be seen, taken, explored, and manipulated. Manipulation is now extended to the child's own body parts and slowly he relates bodily sensations to them. He begins to realize that his legs, arms, and head are separate and different from the body parts of other people. A concept of his own body develops, although it is as yet very vague and indefinite. At the same time the child begins to distinguish other persons in his environment by recognizing their distinct voices, appearances, and facial features. He comes to respond to them in different ways in accordance with his own experiences of their being either friendly and accepting or hostile and rejecting. The evaluations of his person by other people are incorporated into his own image of himself and he regards himself accordingly as either loved and accepted or unloved and rejected, as competent and secure or as incompetent and insecure, as trusted or as untrustworthy. Furthermore, he has learned by now that there are men and women, and, from the attitudes of his parents, he has received a certain impression of their expectations concerning his sexual role. The boy learns what behavior is rewarded and accepted in boys, and the girl acquires an understanding of the female sex-role.

Perception of his image in the mirror provides the child with visual cues to aid him in understanding and integrating his body concept as part of his self-concept. The acquisition of language further clarifies the separateness of his existence through the application of such terms as "I," "me," and "myself." Through make-believe games as role-learning activities the self-concept expands to include a larger variety of traits assimilated from other roles. By imagining himself in various roles and anticipating future role enactments, the child establishes more clearly defined life goals. With the emergence of the self, human beings acquire distinct capacities which are not available to subhuman species. On one hand, the external environment can be explored, mastered, and changed through man's imagining himself in various roles and enacting them successfully. On the other hand, the self-concept enables man to look at his own individual existence as seen through the eyes of other people and to explore his own conscious and unconscious drives and motives. Without having a "self" man could never learn to understand himself. He can change his internal world as well as the external world. An immense extension of the realm of internal and external experience is achieved through the emergence of the "self," and human existence becomes amenable to constant change and development.

The ideal self is to be distinguished from the real self, the former representing the type of person an individual would like to be, and the latter designating the person as he actually considers himself to be. Most people attempt to assimilate traits from the ideal self into the real self but they are aware of the discrepancies. The tendency to retain a well-integrated image of oneself leads the person to eliminate contradictory traits from both his real self and his ideal self. The attitudes, values, standards, and reactions of our parents, relatives, friends, peers, members of our religious, ethnic, and racial groups, as well as our experiences of failure and success in interpersonal and work relationships all contribute their share to the development of our specific real and ideal selves. A person who is able to evaluate his assets and liabilities realistically and in accordance with the evaluations of other people who know him well has a realistic self-concept. Mental health can be defined by the degree to which a person's self-concept is realistic. An unrealistic self-concept may lead to an unrealistic evaluation of the environment and one's own role in it and thereby be conducive to the development of personality disorders such as psychosis and neurosis. Psychotherapy aims at the development of a realistic self-concept which enables a person to accept his assets and liabilities and to become aware of his unconscious motives.

II. DEVELOPMENT OF SEX IDENTIFICATION AND SEX-ROLE PREFERENCE

UNIVERSALITY OF SEX-ROLE DIFFERENTIATION

In all known societies some degree of sex-role differentiation does exist. After a comparative study of sex-role differentiation in 224 societies, Murdock (1937) concluded that men tend to engage in such activities as the catching of sea mammals, lumbering, hunting, fishing, and trapping, whereas women tend to specialize in more sedentary but equally important tasks such as grinding grain, cooking, preserving meat and fish, and gathering fruit and vegetables. In a comparative study of 110 societies, Barry, Bacon, and Child (1957) found that large sex-role differences were associated with (1) large family groups with a high level of cooperation among their members and (2) an economy that places importance on physical strength and the motor skills requiring physical strength. The isolated nuclear family consisting solely of the parents and the children allows for a small degree of sex-role differentiation. In the contemporary American highly mechanized society with its small, nuclear family the strength of the male becomes less important as many functions formerly fulfilled by males and females are taken over by machines or transferred to services and institutions outside the home. In our society a convergence of the sex roles is gradually taking place. An increasing overlap between things and activities formerly considered "exclusively masculine" or "exclusively feminine" has been observed by several researchers (Brown, 1958b; M. Mead, 1949; G. H. Seward, 1956). Cultural differences in role differentiation are great, with certain societies rigidly structuring every aspect of sex-role behavior and others permitting a large variety of roles and activities to both sexes.

EARLY STAGES OF SEX-ROLE DIFFERENTIATION

Most children have learned to think of themselves as boys or as girls different from members of the other sex. Evidence suggests that between two-thirds and three-fourths of children by the age of 3 are able to make this distinction (Gesell et al., 1940, 1943; Seward, 1946, 1956). Sex-role differentiation appears to proceed gradually, beginning sometime during the second year of life and becoming definitely established by the age of 3 (Hartley, Frank, and Goldenson, 1952). At the age of 5 most children are capable of clearly discriminating the more obvious biological cues of maleness and femaleness and psychological cues of masculinity and femininity (Brown, 1956a; Fauls and Smith, 1956; Low, 1957; Rabban, 1950). Individual differences in the clarity of perception of these cues are great.

As identification involves the adoption of the personality traits, values, norms, and attitudes of the identification model (the parent or parent substitute) by the identifying person (the boy or girl), it is also affected by the child's perception of these characteristics of the father or mother. Children do not copy their parents exactly, but put their own stamp upon their imitation of parental roles. They enact the male or female role in accordance with their own interpretation of the meaning of the behavior they attempt to copy. As we have seen, children are conditioned at an early age to recognize and adopt their sex roles. The learning of the appropriate sex role is one of the most significant stages in the development of the little child. Identification is achieved when the child feels safe, secure, and satisfied in his emerging sexual identity. What are the prerequisites for the development of successful sex identification?

What Cameron (1963) calls primary identification of the child with the mother is, as we have seen in our discussion of the self-concept, the stage in which the child experiences himself as part of his mother and the general environment without any awareness of separateness. Throughout this time his mother serves as a temporary or substitute self in performing all those actions for her child which he is as yet too immature to perform himself. In the course of sharing an infinite variety of repeated experiences with his mother, the child develops a confident expectation that his needs will be met as they arise, including the need for multiple stimulation. This helps him to form the *basic trust* which may determine his emotional health and the richness and adequacy of his future relations with other people. The mother's dependability in fulfilling her child's needs creates an atmosphere of confidence and a protective environment in which the child can slowly mature and develop the skills needed to acquire increasing competence in mastering the internal and the external pressures impinging upon him. She protects him from excessive external stimulation, on one hand, and from internal stress, relieving pain and discomfort, on the other. The mother's protection also aims at channeling his emotional drives. She endeavors to minimize the accumulation of feelings of frustration and serves as a shield against his own excessive anxiety, teaching him to avoid harm from threatening external stimulation as well as from his own excessive anger or exertion. Adequate mothering is an indispensable prerequisite for the child's future ability to develop normal sex identification. If the child fails to obtain this support through warm, protective, and loving mothering, he will suffer from more or less severe emotional deprivation in later life which will interfere with his attempts to form warm, secure, and loving relationships with other people and, in many instances, this inability will lead to neurosis or even psychosis (Cameron, 1963).

Some dim awareness of separateness from his mother seems to develop toward the end of the first year in the child's life. But during the second year of life the child gradually learns to distinguish the faces and differential reactions of those people with whom he comes in close contact. His father's deep voice may sound different from his mother's high-pitched way of speaking. He discovers that some people have much hair on their heads while others have little. Perhaps his father engages in more vigorous games and exercises with him than his mother, throwing him high up in the air and yet catching him securely to prevent his falling. All these differences in appearance and in response to him convey impressions of basic sex differences between father and mother or brother and sister. Their different clothes furnish further clues for sex discrimination. Genitals and breasts appear to be recognized later than clothing and hair as sex-differentiating cues. Using a sample of 149 boys and 117 girls aged 3 to 9, Katcher (1955) found that in a projective paired comparison picture test the following sex clues were most easily differentiated in this order: (1) clothing, (2) hair, (3) genitals, and (4) breasts. Younger girls excelled boys in discriminating both the boys' and the girls' genital cues, and upper-class girls excelled lower-class girls in identification of boys' genitals. Apart from the recognition of differences in pitch of voice which has not yet been experimentally verified, clothing and hair seem to constitute the first major sex cues observed by the child.

Certain sex differences appear so early in life or are so universally reported from a large variety of widely differing cultures that the question arises whether they are innate. As a group, boys are physically stronger, heavier, and more active than girls at birth (Gates and Goodwin, 1936). As a result of their greater activity drive, boys develop a greater need for protein consumption and oxygen in the second year of life and retain it throughout childhood and adulthood (Beal, 1961). Boys seem to be more aggressive and to prefer physically exerting games, while girls tend to exhibit greater submissiveness and to engage in sedentary and less strenuous games (Levin and Sears, 1956; Siegel, 1956, 1958; Walters, Pierce, and Dahms, 1957). Various studies have found that girls manifest a greater interest in people than do boys, whereas boys tend to focus their main attention on the objects in their environment and their manipulation (Goodenough, 1957; Rose and Stavrianos, 1943). Girls draw more persons and mention persons more frequently in their verbalizations than do boys. Throughout life, this strong interest in people and social relationships continues to affect the female's attitude toward her environment, and she seems to have difficulty in dissociating objects and events from the people involved in them. On the other hand, interest in objects may have led to the development of the male's ability to dissociate the objective world from the people living in it and to develop abstract thinking to the point where he has acquired a superior capacity for exploring the world of matter and achieving its subjugation to his control. Recent studies have also shown that females tend to be more dependent, in their perception of the environment, on the surrounding perceptual field, while men appear to have standards of judgment of visual stimuli which are relatively less dependent on the environment (Witkin, 1949a, b, 1959). Women appear to be always aware of stimulation occurring around them, while men tend to be more able to forget the surroundings. There is some evidence that this difference appears early in life, although more studies are needed. Most researchers ascribe a greater influence to the role of cultural factors in socialization and sex typing than to the effect of biological factors. Nevertheless, the question remains whether the finally achieved sex-role differentiation reflects modeling of the environment into certain prescribed sex-role patterns alone, or whether it results in part also from constant reinforcement of certain hereditary sex differences.

PERSONAL IDENTIFICATION AND SEX-ROLE PREFERENCE

Freud made a distinction between love object and object of identification. In his view of normal psychosexual development, a postinfantile child cannot love and identify with the same person at the same time. According to Freud's theory, the original source of gratification and therefore the first love object for both sexes is the mother. In the transition from infancy to childhood, the boy need not change his love object, which remains the mother, while the girl is required to make a shift from the mother to the father as a necessary precondition for the normal development of feminine identification. Therefore, Freud postulated, the girl experiences greater difficulty in making a feminine identification than does the boy in achieving masculine identification. He has already learned how to love "women" while she has still to learn how to love "men." Mowrer (1953) proposed a revision of Freud's view. He suggests that the original relationship between infant and mother consists in identification rather than in love. Normal development would thus necessitate a shift in identification object on the part of the boy and not on the part of the girl. Brown (1956a, 1957) and Lynn (1959, 1961) support this theory, which implies that the girl has an initial advantage over the boy in moving toward identification with the sex role appropriate for her. Lynn (1959) thinks that a failure by the boy to make this shift during infancy may either severely impair or altogether prevent the attainment of adequate masculine identification in later life.

Love, identification, and sex-role preference are three processes which appear to interact so intricately as to make a clear understanding of their functions extremely difficult. In efforts to clarify the respective contributions of these factors, Brown (1958b) and Slater (1961) have recently developed theoretical approaches that attempt to explain their interaction. Following their suggestions, we will differentiate between Personal Identification and Sex-Role Preference. They correspond to the terms Identification and Preference suggested by Brown and Personal Identification and Positional Identification introduced by Slater. As we have pointed out earlier, Personal Identification involves the adoption of personality traits, values, norms, and attitudes of the identification model by the identifying person. It is the basic process in which a child, at first involuntarily, and later consciously, learns to think, feel, and act like a member of one sex in contrast to members of the other sex. Sex-Role Preference refers to the tendency to adopt the sex role of one's own sex in preference to that of the other because this role is considered to be more attractive and desirable.

In normal development, Personal Identification and Sex-Role Preference form a single, integrative process directed toward the assumption of the personality traits and the sexual role characteristic of members of one's own sex. It implies like-sex Personal Identification with cross-sex Sex-Role

Preference; for instance, a girl may identify with the feminine role and prefer to select a male as her love object. If Personal Identification is sought with a member of the opposite sex or Sex-Role Preference for members of the same sex, conflicts or deviations from the normal development occur. Like-sex Personal Identification with like-sex Sex-Role Preference may lead to homosexual behavior with enaction of the like-sex role; for example, a girl may identify with the feminine role, but prefer another girl for her sex partner whom she wants to play the masculine role while she herself enacts the feminine sex-role in their relations. Her partner would thus be likely to exhibit the opposite pattern, namely cross-sex Personal Identification combined with like-sex Sex-Role Preference, feeling and acting like a man in the relationship with the other woman. This Personal Identification with members of the opposite sex is defined as Inversion, which, according to Brown (1958a), differs from other types of homosexual behavior in so far as the invert actually feels, thinks, and acts in all respects like a member of the opposite sex in his interpersonal relationships. As Inversion implies a reversal of normal Personal Identification, it appears to be more difficult to cure by means of psychotherapy than homosexual behavior in which Personal Identification with a member of one's own sex has been established while a member of the same sex is regarded as a more attractive sex object.

DYNAMICS OF PERSONAL IDENTIFICATION AND SEX-ROLE PREFERENCE

Slater (1961) presents the following explanation of the difference between Personal Identification and Sex-Role Preference, which he calls Positional Identification:

> Personal Identification would be shown by a child who says: "I want to be like you. If I were, I would have you and your virtues with me all the time, and I would love myself as much as I love you. To achieve this, I will incorporate your qualities and your values and ideals. I will view and judge myself through your eyes." A child would manifest Positional Identification [Sex-Role Preference] in the following words: "I wish I were in your shoes. If I were, I would not be in the unpleasant position I am in now. If I wish hard enough and act like you do, I may after all achieve your more advantageous status." This situational improvement is one of two kinds: (a) "I would be strong and powerful rather than weak and helpless, menacing rather than menaced, punishing rather than punished," (b) "Mother (Father) would love me rather than you" [p. 113].

Of course, these latter two wishes spring from unconscious fantasies. The wish to be as powerful and strong as the authoritative parent is an example of the well-known defense mechanism of "identification with the aggressor," whereas the desire to replace the same-sex parent in order to become the love object of the parent of the other sex, i. e., to replace the father and to become the mother's sole lover, constitutes an example of the oedipal wish. In both cases the child does not seek any genuine Personal Identification with the like-sex parent; all he wants is to gain the same position of power and authority as that parent enjoys.

In Personal Identification a wide range of the characteristics of the model will be adopted, but with substantial modifications, since, as Sanford (1955) states, the individual "puts his own stamp" on them. In Sex-Role Preference the person will adopt only a few of the model's characteristics, namely those which symbolize the model's desired position. Slater (1961) has suggested a plausible hypothesis concerning the differential development of the two types of identification. According to this theory, Personal Identification will tend to be brought about by a general atmosphere of parental warmth, acceptance, and supportiveness, while Positional Identification (Sex-Role Preference) is more likely to result from the absence of these qualities in the parents or from an unaccepting or punitive and authoritarian family climate. A number of empirical studies have found evidence of such effects of differences in family atmosphere. Several investigators report a high correlation between gratifying parental behavior and Personal Identification (Child, 1954; Emmerich, 1959, 1962; Gray and Klaus, 1956; Heinicke, 1953; Payne and Mussen, 1956; P. Sears, 1953; Slater, 1955; Stoke, 1950). On the other hand, a negative correlation was found to exist between parental punitiveness and Personal Identification in several studies (Child, 1954; Heinicke, 1953; Sanford, 1955; Stoke, 1950). Normal Personal Identification with one's own sex appears to require the availability of a family atmosphere of parental warmth, love, acceptance, nurturance, and supportiveness which allows for a sufficient degree of permissiveness and freedom to experiment and provides opportunities for the development of initiative and independence within a secure and protective setting.

It is most likely that the experiences of the child during the anal stage, when he must learn to exercise sphincter and bladder control, affect both his Personal Identification and his Sex-Role Preference. As the latter is based upon the need to incorporate the power aspects of the sex role, toilet training probably affects this type of identification to a greater extent than it does Personal Identification. Should tensions develop between the mother and the child as a result of too strict insistence on the performance of elimination processes, the toilet training may develop into a power struggle between the mother and the child. The latter may become aware of the newly acquired power stemming from his ability either to withhold his stool altogether or to refuse to retain any stool at all. Such psychological withholding or overgiving is a subtle means of controlling the environment which seems to make excessive demands at a time when the child is not yet ready to fulfill them. Too strict and punitive toilet training may arouse the wish to "identify with the aggressor" in order to achieve her powerful status and thereby lead to the development of compulsive traits in conjunction with latent or overt homosexuality. Furthermore, a number of studies of normal as well as neurotic children suggest that emotional ambivalence is experienced by every child during the phase of self-assertion and sphincter control. Love and hate for the same person are still intermingled and unresolved. On one hand, the child seems to derive pleasurable erotic sensations from anal stimulation and the exercising of his bowel functions. On the other hand, his anger is frequently aroused as a result of the frustration experienced by the necessity to be subjected to so much parental control while he feels assertive and powerful in the performance of his bodily functions. This conflict between feelings of power and helplessness, love and hate, may result in sadomasochistic pleasure and anger. The sadistic pleasure is usually regarded as a fusion of erotic and aggressive drives. It plays an important role in the above-mentioned etiology of sex-role Inversion and homosexuality.

SEX-ROLE PREFERENCE IN CHILDREN AND ADULTS

As the male role is considered to be the more powerful, prestigeful, and rewarding of the two sex roles, girls and women generally seem to derive less satisfaction from like-sex Personal Identification than boys and men. This is borne out by the findings of a large number of relevant studies. From the age of 3 on, boys express a stronger preference for the male role than girls for the female role, with about one-third of all girls expressing preference for male roles while only 3 to 5% of all boys want to play female roles (Fortune, 1946; Gallup, 1955; Hartley, Frank, and Goldenson, 1952; Rosenberg and Sutton-Smith, 1960). At a very early age boys and girls begin to engage in different types of games. Boys prefer to engage in active, vigorous, and strenuous play activities which involve muscular dexterity and skill, and, later on, this tendency finds an outlet in organized and competitive games. From the earliest age on, girls prefer play which is more conservative, sedentary, and restrained in the range of action (Anastasi, 1958). But in a recent study Rosenberg and Sutton-Smith (1960) found that a check list of games yielded 18 items differentiating boys from girls and 40 items differentiating girls from boys in games. The check lists were administered to a sample of children in first through eighth grades in five midwestern townships. A comparison of these findings with the results of a similar study by Terman 25 years earlier (Terman and Miles, 1936) shows that girls nowadays evince a greater interest in male games and activities than was formerly the case. On the other hand, boys' roles appear to have become concentrated upon a narrower range of activities than before.

That women, as a group, are generally less satisfied with their sex role than men, is borne out by several studies. To such questions as: "Have you sometimes wished you were of the opposite sex?" or "If you could be born over again, would you rather be a man or a woman?" or "Have you ever wished that you belonged to the opposite sex?" only between 2½ and 4% of adult men compared to 20 to 31% of adult women recall consciously having been aware of the desire to be of the opposite sex (Fortune, 1946; Gallup, 1955; Terman and Miles, 1936). In Puerto Rico only 33% of a group of adult female students stated that they would prefer to be female if they "could come to life again after death," while 93% of male students wanted to be reborn as males again (Sanchez-Hidalgo, 1952). In a recent survey of several hundred Ohio State University students, 91% of the men and 66% of the women students expressed a preference for having a male rather than a female child, with combined scores indicating 75% of all students preferring boys and only 25% girls.

The woman's awareness of the lower esteem in which the female role is held may, in certain cases, undermine her self-respect and lower her self-esteem. On the other hand, women are generally permitted a greater freedom in role assumption than men. They can adopt an increasingly large variety of "masculine" roles and occupations without being exposed to ridicule or social ostracism, whereas men run such risks when they invade traditionally "feminine" fields of activity. Girls can wear masculine attire such as shirts and trousers with little or no social disapproval, but boys cannot wear skirts or dresses without being ostracized as "transvestites" and exposed to severe social censure and even legal punishment. Many girls are given masculinized names such as Jackie, Billie, Jo, Roberta, Pauline, while few boys are given feminized names. Girls may play with any or all of the toys typically associated with boys, such as cars, trucks, guns, erector sets, etc., but boys are discouraged from playing with toys that are considered feminine, such as dolls, dishes, diapers, sewing materials, etc. (Brown, 1958b; Goethals, 1953). Boys are generally more aware of sex-appropriate behavior than girls and most fathers insist that their sons look and talk as befits a man (Rabban, 1950). The question arises whether the greater satisfaction with their sex role expressed verbally by so many men reflects the greater risk of social disapproval for the preference of the opposite-sex role encountered by men just as the openly voiced dissatisfaction of women may be due to the greater latitude offered by society to women for the assumption of male roles.

Freud explains the widespread preference for the masculine role by pointing out the anatomical difference between males and females, the effect of which is assumed to make the boy proud of his masculine status (of possessing a penis) and the girl dissatisfied with hers and attempting to emulate the boy's status (penis envy). Adler, on the other hand, emphasized the sociocultural advantages accruing from the greater prestige and numerous privileges accorded to the male role. Women who envy men's superior power and status begin to seek to acquire masculine status. They are engaged in a "masculine protest." There is no doubt that our culture still ascribes greater power and prestige to the male role. The appeal of advertising is directed toward the arousal of the power drive of the male, males are paid higher wages than females for performing similar work, and males are promoted to leadership positions in government, industry, and education in preference to equally endowed or even better qualified females. With the achievement of greater equality and interchangeability of roles, a re-evaluation of the desirability of the male and the female sex roles will be necessary.

CONFLICTS BETWEEN PERSONAL IDENTIFICATION AND SEX-ROLE PREFERENCE

In view of the fact that many girls show an early preference for the masculine role, one might expect to find conflict or confusion in their sex-role development. While girls are destined to fulfill feminine functions in adulthood, they frequently attempt to emulate the masculine role either by choice or by being induced to do so in the course of attending schools geared to prepare students for masculine roles rather than feminine ones. Role conflicts often arise which tend to produce ambivalence and a lack of clarity about the feminine role (Brown, 1958b; M. Mead, 1949; G. H. Seward, 1956).

As pointed out earlier, boys must shift from identification with the mother to identification with the father. This may lead to difficulties, as the contact with the paternal role is frequently minimal and boys cannot form a clear concept of it. P. Sears (1953) reports that 6-year-old boys have not identified with their fathers as well as girls have with their mothers. From extensive observation of preschool children, Hartley, Frank, and Goldenson (1952) came to the conclusion that few boys seem to be able or willing to picture themselves as "future fathers."

The overexposure of the boy to the feminine model increases his difficulty in normal masculine identification. Most elementary-school teachers and all nursery-school teachers are women, and the boy is forced to look for identification models in his peers or in models derived from mass media of communication such as television, radio, books, and comics. Nevertheless, there appears to be some evidence that the availability of a strong, warm, loving, and decisive father enables the boy to establish a secure identification with the masculine role. The amount of time which this father spends with his son seems to be less important than the degree to which the child learns to respect, admire, love, and emulate him in his contacts with him.

MATERNAL AND PATERNAL IDENTIFICATION

Many researchers have proceeded under the assumption that parental identification occurs on an all-or-none basis, i. e., identification with the mother will automatically preclude identification with the father and vice versa. But several studies in which maternal and paternal identifications were measured independently in the same subjects have shown that they are strongly and positively related (Slater, 1955, 1961). If maternal and paternal identifications take place consecutively, the former may facilitate the latter. That maternal identification should take precedence is a conclusion to be drawn from the greater contact between mother and child during the early years and the amount of time the father is absent from the home. Some researchers have found that identification with the father seems to be dependent upon the mother's attitude toward the father (Bandura and Walters, 1959; Helper, 1955; P. Sears, 1953; R. R. Sears, Maccoby, and Levin, 1957). If the mother approves of the father as a model for her son, boys tend to copy the male role and to achieve masculine identification. On the other hand, P. Sears (1953) found that 5-year-old boys who adopted the mother's role most strongly in doll play had mothers who, while warm and affectionate, were critical of their husbands. Bandura and Walters (1959) interpret the effect of spousal relations on the offspring's adoption of sex-appropriate behavior as follows:

> One would expect a child to learn more rapidly to copy a model with high prestige than a model with low prestige, since the imitation of a highly regarded person is likely to be more rewarding. If the mother and father have a good deal of affection for each other, imitation of parental models would be facilitated. The mother's attitude and feelings toward the father may be particularly influential in the development of the masculine-role identification of a male child. If the mother loves and admires her husband, she is likely to welcome the boy's imitation of the father's behavior and attitudes. The boy's father-identification will therefore be rewarded not only by his father but by his mother as well. On the other hand, if the parents have little affection for each other, the boy will be less motivated to identify with the father. Moreover, such a situation places the boy in a dilemma. If he tries to emulate his father, he is apt to lose his mother's approval and acceptance [p. 257].

The mother's attitude toward her husband also affects the Sex-Role Preference of her daughter. If the mother is critical or hostile to the father, she may convince her daughter that men are to be feared or despised. The girl may then adopt a hostile and unaccepting attitude toward males in general and become totally unable to tolerate or comprehend masculine attitudes. While her orientation will be decidedly or even aggressively or exaggeratedly "feminine," she will lack the normal spontaneity and seductiveness which result from an adequate paternal relationship and which attest to a satisfactory heterosexual adjustment. She may become incapable of loving a man.

As maternal identification occurs early in life, it seems to be more dependent on the quality of the mother-child relationship than on the father's attitude toward the mother. The child's greater dependence on his mother and his more frequent contact with her do not provide him with sufficient opportunities to take the father's attitude into account while establishing maternal identification. The father's influence may become more important in the later stages of childhood and in adolescence when attitudes toward the opposite sex are re-evaluated and more firmly established. If the father is hostile to the mother, boys may then adopt an antagonistic attitude toward women in general.

The primacy of maternal identification is consistent with the generally accepted idea that the most serious psychological disorders such as schizophrenia involve a profound disturbance in the mother-child relationship, with the etiological role of the father being less significant (Bateson et al., 1956; Fromm-Reichmann, 1948; Rosen, 1953; Tietze, 1949). Maternal identification seems to be basic in the early stages of life, while paternal identification becomes more significant with issues involved in the later stages of development such as the oedipal situation. A failure of adequate paternal identification is probably most strongly associated, for both sexes, with neurotic disturbances in later life. Adequate sexual adjustment cannot take place unless the child of either sex develops an understanding and appreciation for masculine as well as for feminine attitudes, interests, and characteristics. This will occur in so far as the father is warm and affectionate and provides an alternative source of emotional support for the child, as shown by the findings of a number of relevant studies (Emmerich, 1959, 1961, 1962; Payne and Mussen, 1956; Slater, 1961). It will not occur if the father is too harsh, withdrawn, and ineffectual to provide such support.

THE EFFECT OF PATERNAL ATTITUDES ON IDENTIFICATION

What role does the child's perception of his father play in the development of identification? Kagan and Lemkin (1960) found that boys and girls aged 3 to 9 consistently saw fathers as more fear arousing, more competent, and more punitive than mothers, and mothers as "nicer" and more likely to give presents. Boys and girls chose the same-sex parent as the model they wished to imitate and the parent they liked best, and indicated the opposite-sex parent as the one that kissed most. Emmerich made sev-

370   JOSEF ERNEST GARAI

eral studies (1959, 1961, 1962) to clarify the relationship between the power dimension and parental identification. He found that, in the discrimination of parent roles, there was a much greater consensus on the power dimension than on the dimension of attitudinal direction. Adults were seen as having high power and children as possessing little power, and with increasing age there was an increasing tendency to discriminate male but not female age roles by power. The father's sex role was seen as more powerful than the mother's sex role. Girls discriminated sex roles by assigning positive actions to the girl and negative actions to the boy, whereas boys tended to discriminate the positiveness or negativeness of actions more objectively with reference to the specific interaction situation. In another study Emmerich (1959) found mothers to be generally more nurturant and less restrictive than fathers. Parents exerted more power toward their same-sex than toward their opposite-sex children.

Throughout the western world it is traditional to conceive of the father's role as primarily controlling and the mother's as primarily nurturing (Winch, 1962). Mussen and Distler (1960) report that kindergarten boys identify more strongly with their fathers when the latter are both controlling and nurturant than when they carry out either of these two functions alone. Furthermore, boys high in masculinity experience a more permissive, easygoing family climate, in which the parents regulate their children's behavior by means of love-oriented techniques rather than by harsh discipline, than do their less masculine peers. Hoffman (1960) reports that children of both sexes tend to show assertive and aggressive behavior when the father is the primary disciplinarian. She observed that maternal affection makes a boy feel loved but paternal affection gives him confidence.

In a perceptual problem-solving task, Witkin's Embedded Figure Test, Bieri (1958) investigated the relationship between parental identification and acceptance of authority as measured by the Acceptance of Authority Test, which is highly correlated with the F-Scale that determines authoritarian and fascistic tendencies. He found that evidently the power dimension is a better criterion for success in this test with boys, whereas paternal identification was indicative of better performance with girls. Boys who were low in Acceptance of Authority and identified with the mother performed significantly better than boys who were high in Acceptance of Authority and identified with the mother. Maternal identification appears to be greatly affected by the way in which the child accepts his mother's authority. Those children who accept maternal authority to a high degree may be the overprotected children who overidentify with their mothers and rely upon them rather than on their own resources to solve their problems for them. On the other hand, those children who identify lovingly with their mothers on a more equal footing without being compelled to submit to excessive maternal control are apparently permitted to make their own decisions and to gain greater independence and emotional maturity to solve their problems by themselves.

THE EFFECT OF PARENTAL ATTITUDES ON PERSONAL IDENTIFICATION

A review of the literature on sex identification makes one aware of the necessity to integrate the widely scattered findings into a coherent theory of the development of identification. Such a theory is developed here, while its tentativeness is borne in mind.

The successful establishment of Personal Identification may be defined as a necessary prerequisite for the attainment of emotional maturity and independence. The mother who overprotects the child and attempts to prevent him from gaining independence and emotional maturity permits him only one type of "identification," which we may designate as dependent identification or defensive identification. Such a mother regards the world as dangerous and threatening and people as untrustworthy and hostile. She constantly admonishes her child to avoid situations which she interprets as perilous or menacing and thereby intensifies his feelings of helplessness and dependency. His only refuge lies in seeking his mother's help and protection to survive among all those enemies lurking in an inhospitable world. As his own powerlessness is overemphasized, his self-concept is bound to become that of a weak, helpless, and dependent child who is too frightened to tackle any obstacle or to attempt to solve any problem on his own. Since this type of dependent identification, from the very onset, is directed toward defensive evasion, withdrawal from reality, and encapsulation into a protective shell of narrowly circumscribed activities, it fails to provide the firm emotional security which is based on confidence and trust. It supplies the child with a false feeling of security as long as he can count upon his mother's nurturance; feelings of utter helplessness and panic seize him whenever he fears he will be deprived of this maternal support. In so far as this dependent identification prevents the child from gaining independence and emotional security, it must be regarded as a failure to achieve genuine Personal Identification.

On the other hand, the mother who encourages her child to gain independence step by step and reinforces his attempts to prove his growing mastery over the environment by providing him with suitable opportunities for exploration, experimentation, manipulation of objects, contacts with other children and adults, and a variety of new experiences is inspired by quite a different philosophy of life. She regards the world as an exciting and challenging place where there are unlimited opportunities for novel experiences and the learning of various modes of adaptation. While she creates a protective atmosphere in which the child learns to deal efficiently with his internal and external world, his abilities and emotions, she conveys to him in many ways her trust in his own growing independence and his ability to learn to perform certain tasks and functions for himself. Encouraged by her confidence, this child will attack any new situation with great zeal, regarding it as an opportunity to prove to his mother that he needs her support less and less as he is learning to rely increasingly upon his own resources. From this experience he gains a strong ego and a firm feeling of emotional security which is based upon the respect he has for himself as a reflection of his mother's high esteem of him. He is not afraid of meeting new people, making friends, and showing a trust in them which reflects his mother's confidence in him. If this mother could verbalize her feelings, she might perhaps say: "Go ahead, my child, and test your mettle. As your mother, I will watch that you do not tackle any tasks that might overtax your strength and abilities or expose you to serious dangers. But I will also demand from you that you try to the best of your ability to tackle problems and to undergo experiences from which you can learn how to dispense with my aid and assistance in the future. The more you develop new skills and the more you grow to become your own self, the more deeply will I love and respect you." This type of identification may be called instrumental identification or independent identification. The attainment of independent identification is an indispensable precondition for the establishment of secure Personal Identification, particularly with boys. As dependency is regarded as a trait which is more acceptable or even desirable in women, dependent identification appears to play a role in feminine Personal Identification. This point will be clarified in our discussion of dependency later on.

While dependent identification seems to be based primarily on feelings of fear and the need to replace feelings of powerlessness by gaining power through enlisting the mother's help, it fails to lead to the development of basic trust and a belief in the power of love and acceptance. Dependent identification is, so to say, fear motivated and power oriented. In contrast, independent identification appears to be rooted in feelings of trust and confidence and a belief in the goodwill of other people and the manipulability of the environment by dint of one's own effort. It leads to the development of a mature give-and-take type of love rather than the clinging and exploitative type of "love" characteristic of the overprotected infant. The dependent identification corresponds to Slater's Positional Identification which we have called Sex-Role Preference, as both are based on a belief in the superiority of fear and power. Slater's Personal Identification parallels independent identification which stems from a firm belief in the superior power of trust, love, and understanding.

Personal Identification implies a strong wish to become equal in all respects to the identifying model, which is seen as embodying all the desirable qualities and character traits which the identifier wants to possess. It is based upon love and admiration and implies an adoption of the total personality pattern of the model as perceived by the child. Sex-Role Preference, however, implies a desire to gain the privileged position of the model through the adoption of those types of behavior which seem to be necessary for the attainment of the power status of the model. The child selects for imitation only those traits of the model which appear to lead to the attainment of the power reserved for members of the preferred sex. According to certain theories, Personal Identification tends to result from a general climate of parental warmth and supportiveness, whereas Sex-Role Preference may be a consequence of an unaccepting or punitive and authoritarian family atmosphere.

The view that the power motive and the love motive are mutually exclusive underlies the above-mentioned classification. Such a dichotomy seems to oversimplify the dynamics of identification with the parents. It is more likely that both motives interact in various combinations and that we are rarely able to encounter "pure love" uncontaminated by power motives or "pure power striving" unaffected by feelings of love. Redefining Slater's terms, we may say that Personal Identification is based on a greater emphasis on love and trust than on power and fear, while Sex-Role Preference follows the opposite course. If Sex-Role Preference were always based upon power orientation, it would follow that no heterosexual relationship could ever be established on love rather than on power seeking. Therefore, a revision of Slater's theory is required. A distinction ought to be made between two different types of Sex-Role Preference, namely: (1) Love-oriented Sex-Role Preference which combines a strong same-sex Personal Identification imparting a feeling of full acceptance of and security in one's own sexual role with a sufficiently strong cross-sex identification to be able to accept the complementary sex role as one that is based upon love, warmth, and respect rather than on fear and domination. This love-oriented Sex-Role Preference forms the basis for the mature individual to establish a close, warm, and mutually satisfactory relationship with a member of the opposite sex in later life; (2) Power-oriented Sex-Role Preference which is likely to arise from a weak or deficient same-sex Personal Identification resulting in feelings of inadequacy and insecurity in the performance of one's own sexual role and a similarly deficient and weak cross-sex identification which prevents a clear conception of the complementary sex role. Feelings of insecurity tend to be repressed and compensatory mechanisms may be employed to gain relief from the anxiety connected with this basic lack of security. The threatened individual tends to seek security by concentrating upon the power aspects of sex roles. Only the power-conferring attributes of the sex roles are internalized, and all relationships develop into power struggles with the male attempting to dominate and subjugate the female and the female attempting to act similarly or in the complementary role toward the male. As persons with weak egos can gain power by submission and "suffering" rather than by overassertiveness, sadomasochistic relationships frequently result from power-oriented Sex-Role Preference.

Recent studies by R. R. Sears (1963) have shown that the power role is more strongly integrated in the Personal Identification of the male, while the dependency role is one of the characteristic components of the Personal Identification of the female in our society. Sears found that dependency seems to be encouraged in girls, whereas boys are encouraged to give up dependent behavior and to replace it with independence as they grow up. Mothers who are permissive about their daughters' masturbation, social sex play, open about answering sex questions, and accepting of dependency behavior such as touching and holding, being near, receiving reassurance, and positive attention-getting, achieve appropriate sex typing. Dependency, sociability, and verbal responsiveness to the mother are various types of behavior which the child uses to get positive attention, and the mother's intimacy and permissiveness encourages such positive attention-getting in daughters as sex-appropriate. When similar dependency behavior is manifested by boys, however, Sears found it to be associated with coldness and slackness of standards in the mother and a rejection of intimacy by the father. The dependency supplications of such boys are, as it were, efforts to overcome indifference and neglect. They seem to be reactions to some kind of insecurity that stems from withdrawal or withholding of parental affection. In other words, girls who are clinging and dependent have warm, permissive, and reassuring mothers, while boys who are overdependent and clinging have cold mothers who do not bother to set firm limits of discipline and fathers who do not permit their sons to feel close to them and to identify with them. Dependency behavior is generally regarded as progressive in girls but as regressive in boys.

Sears also studied negative attention-getting behavior, i.e., the attempt to gain attention by engaging in aggressive, destructive, or forbidden activities. It was found to predominate among children whose mothers are sexually permissive and whose parents infantilize them by overprotection. The boys have a history of weaning and toilet-training difficulties and a current disaffection for the father, while the girls are masculinized by their close relation to the father (cross-sex Personal Identification). Negative attention-getting in girls is therefore more likely to be due to a strong identification with the father, whose aggressive traits are adopted in their masculinized behavior, while in boys it is the result of an affectional overattachment to the sexually permissive mother, combined with a resentment of the father who is seen as interfering in the boy's affectional relationship with his mother. According to Freudian theory, it would be the result of an unresolved oedipal conflict.

If the child's early dependency upon his mother is consistently rewarded, his identification will develop, whereas the mother's failure to respond satisfactorily and consistently to her child's basic needs prevents the establishment of early dependency as a basis for future identification. In order to achieve a satisfactory same-sex Personal Identification, it is indispensable to acquire a thorough understanding of the role of the opposite sex as a prerequisite for the future establishment of a warm cross-sex relationship. Therefore, a certain amount of cross-sex Personal Identification must take place to complete the same-sex Personal Identification. It is necessary for the identifier to be able to identify with the feelings, emotions, and attitudes of members of the opposite sex. This ability to accept the complementary role was described by G. H. Mead (1934) as "taking the role of the generalized other." There is little doubt that it is easier for the boy to achieve cross-sex identification with his mother than for the girl with her father. As the boy's first dependency is upon the mother, he learns to establish his first identification with her. If his father fails to provide a suitable identification model, the boy will be handicapped in his striving to achieve normal Personal Identification and will have to look for substitute models among relatives, playmates, and siblings to establish his male identification. Same-sex Personal Identification is more easily achieved by the girl, as her first identification model is her mother. Since she is more dependent upon the mother than the boy over a long period of time, the mother's attitude toward the father appears to be the most influential factor in her cross-sex Personal Identification. As we have seen, if the mother approves of the father, and respects and admires him, the girl will establish adequate cross-sex identification. Should the mother be hostile and critical toward the father, the girl will be unable to learn to identify with the male role in any suitable fashion and cross-sex identification fails to take place. To what extent the actual behavior of a warm, loving, and accepting father toward his daughter counteracts the stereotype of father as a "bad man" is still unknown and a problem to be investigated by future research. The current evidence supports the conclusion that the mother's view of the father's character tends to be accepted by her daughter as correct, and a stereotype of the father and men in general is established which tends to exclude contrary evidence from actual experience with father as irrelevant. Boys may more easily rebel against the mother's evaluation of the father and achieve masculine identification despite the mother's hostility toward the father. In general, it may be assumed that a close, warm, and friendly relationship between the parents facilitates same-sex as well as cross-sex Personal Identification of sons and daughters alike.

The optimal condition for the development of adequate same-sex and cross-sex Personal Identification in girls appears to consist in the availability of a warm, permissive mother who accepts her daughter's dependency and conveys her attitude toward the father as one of respect, love, and acceptance to the daughter. If the father is actually warm, loving, and strong, identification is further encouraged. For the boy, optimal conditions require the presence of a warm, loving, permissive, and protective mother who is, however, not overprotective or excessively seductive and who encourages his need for independence in learning to cope with his environment within fairly wide but safe limits; the father, in this case, is required to be perceived by the son as carrying out the controlling function effectively, i. e., as being quick, active, firm, secure, and decisive (Mussen and Distler, 1960). A father who is both controlling and nurturant, exhibiting warmth, love, and understanding tenderness besides firmness and decisiveness, is ideally suited to provide the appropriate climate for the development of adequate same-sex Personal Identification, as shown in a study of kindergarten boys (Hess, Wright, and Tuska, 1961).

The importance of sibling relationships for the development of identification has generally been underemphasized or altogether neglected in the literature. The number, sex, and ordinal position of the siblings appear to be significant factors in the learning of sex roles. Those children who have siblings of the opposite sex will have additional models for the learning of the characteristic behavior of members of the other sex and will therefore be able to establish cross-sex identification more easily. On the other hand, same-sex siblings provide opportunities for stronger same-sex Personal Identification. In a series of studies Koch (1944, 1954, 1955, 1956a, b, c, 1960) found that cross-sex siblings have more traits of the opposite sex than same-sex siblings, confirming the hypothesis that the presence of siblings of the opposite sex in a family facilitates the understanding of the complementary sex-role. Furthermore, the older girl with a younger brother was found to have more masculine traits than the older girl with a younger sister, while the boy with an older sister was substantially more feminine than the boy with an older brother. In general, cross-sex siblings tend to assimilate traits of the opposite sex and these traits are more pronounced in the younger of the two siblings. Apparently, the greater status which an older sibling derives as a result of his higher ordinal position in the family hierarchy enables him to become an additional model for the younger sibling. Thus, for instance, the younger girl who has an older brother can obtain a comprehension of the male role from observation of her brother as well as from watching her father. What remains to be investigated is the hypothesis that the learning of a characteristic sex role may be more adequate if two or more models are available to the child than if there is only one conspicuous model. We have good reason to assume that children who are exposed to other children in a nursery school or day-care center may be able to achieve a more adequate and more realistic Personal Identification than those who stay home with their mothers until school age. The role of playmates in the kindergarten or nursery school may be similar to that of siblings in the family in so far as it provides additional opportunities and models for identification.

Those stages in the development of the child in which he prefers the company of members of his own sex are probably important in the establishment of same-sex Personal Identification, too. Between 2 and 4 years and, later on, in the prepubertal stage (9 to 13 years), such peer-group identification becomes crucial for the child and the insistence of the group on only sex-appropriate behavior reinforces the child's tendency to identify strongly as a member of his own sex. In so far as cross-sex identification is consciously rejected at these stages, certain obstacles are placed in the way of adequate cross-sex identification. Adolescence rearouses previous stages of insecurity in identification, and the awareness of strong sexual urges frequently leads to new identification problems whose solution is made all the more difficult by the environment, which imposes taboos and provides a bewildering array of conflicting standards in an age of changing sex mores. If no fairly secure same-sex Personal Identification has been achieved prior to adolescence, these additional pressures are likely to lead to serious emotional disturbances and personality maladjustment.

PSYCHOANALYTIC THEORY OF IDENTIFICATION

In the preoedipal phase of development, children imitate their parents. Both boys and girls imitate the mother at first, but the boy soon turns toward his father as a model for role imitation. Innate sex-drive patterns appear under favorable circumstances during the preoedipal phase when boys frequently declare their intention to marry their mothers and girls act seductively toward their fathers. Parents usually reciprocate with sex-appropriate behavior and, if they are normal, encourage expressions of love in an increasingly mature manner in the form of sublimated, openly expressed affection. The child also learns to internalize the parents' value system and develops a superego which incorporates the parents' and society's moral and ethical values. If the parents act seductively toward their children, they may arouse jealousy and frustration and, if they convey strict, rigid, and overmoralistic superego attitudes, the child's normal progress toward identification is obstructed.

The oedipal phase. Sometime during the third or fourth year of life the child seems to lose the autonomy he has gained and falls deeply in love with his parent of the opposite sex. At the same time he develops intense jealousy toward the other parent as an unwelcome competitor. If the child is not too frightened or inhibited, he or she may express quite openly and spontaneously the intention of marrying the parent of the opposite sex when he or she grows up. According to psychoanalytic theory, this grand illusion is necessary to prepare little boys to grow into men who can love women and little girls to become women who can love men. It establishes the necessary cross-sex identification for understanding and empathizing with the role of the opposite sex. Of course, the child will eventually have to abandon the wish to marry his parent. But, in the course of this oedipal fantasy and the struggles resulting from it, a rudimentary understanding of sex roles and anatomical differences is acquired.

The oedipal boy develops intense pride in his clearly visible genital, the penis, and an intermittent urge to use it aggressively and to exhibit it. This pride, the sexual feelings he entertains for his mother, and the jealousy he feels toward his father seem to arouse intense anxiety, which manifests itself in a vague fear that he may lose that which he so highly values, namely his penis. This fear is defined as *castration anxiety*. While identifying with his father and admiring him for his strength and power, he also fears retaliation from him for competing with him for the love and "possession" of the mother. When he realizes that girls lack a penis, his fantasy may interpret this fact as her having lost or been robbed of a penis. He fears that a similar fate may befall him, as the penis is the center of his sexual feelings, his aggressive urges, and his hostile fantasies. Realizing that his father is powerful, that he loves his mother and has sex relations with her, the child feels angry jealousy and sullen resentment against this powerful rival for the mother's love. His sadistic fantasies of seeing father destroyed, maimed, emasculated, or dead alternate with masochistic fantasies of being maimed, emasculated, or even killed by the jealous father. Thus castration anxiety appears to be due to the guilt the boy feels for attempting to oust his father and to replace him in the role as the mother's sole lover.

The oedipal girl has a more complex and difficult situation to cope with than the oedipal boy. As she has no visible genital, she at first believes that all people are constructed like herself until she finds out that little boys possess penises. Then she feels cheated and deprived of any suitable means to give expression to her rapidly developing feelings of sexuality. Most little girls blame their mothers for having denied them a penis and they turn away from the formerly so deeply loved mother toward the father, from whom they can get what they desire. The girl falls deeply in love with her father and hopes to get her mother out of the way, while female castration anxiety appears in the form of penis envy. In her fantasy she imagines herself growing a penis or robbing her little brother of his. She also develops an intense fear of retaliation, which arises from her fantasies of getting rid of her mother or having her go away and die. She is certain that she could look after her father far better than her mother does. On the other hand, because of her imperfect knowledge of sexual functions, she has vague fears that her body may be penetrated and injured because of her feminine desires.

But in many ways, the little girl identifies with her mother. She admires her femininity which has been successful in winning and keeping her father. In spite of all the hatred she feels toward her mother as an unpleasant competitor for the father's love, she has also retained some of the deep love which she enjoyed so long as her mother's child. She is still dependent on her mother's aid and guidance in many areas of everyday life, especially since the father is away most of the time during the day. This affection for her mother increases her guilt over the hatred and contempt she feels.

Resolution of the oedipal conflict. Children finally reach a stage where they slowly start to realize that the grand illusion of replacing the same-sex parent in the love of the opposite-sex parent must be relinquished. After a long and intense struggle, the boy is finally compelled to acknowledge the fact that he is physically incapable of being his mother's husband at that time, and that his mother does not in the least share his desire for their marriage when he grows up. Similarly, the girl finally realizes that she is incapable of having babies, that her father does not want her as his wife, and that he will not wait for her until she grows up. During this prolonged and painful learning process, anger and hate are aroused as a result of the frustration of such intense longings. These feelings are directed not only against the same-sex parent who has always been a powerful competitor, but also against the opposite-sex parent who, by the rejection of the child's love, is now seen as rejecting him or her altogether.

If the parents are kind, loving, and understanding, yet firm and consistent in emphasizing the reality of the situation, the child will be able to control his anger, hate, and resentment, and resolve the conflict. He must learn to modify his identification with the one parent and his love for the other, so as to bring them both in line with what is possible. The boy must give up his childish hope of ever having his mother to himself, the girl of ever becoming her father's wife. Love for the opposite-sex parent must now exclude the sexual aspects. Such identification and object love are the affectional bonds which emotionally mature parents offer their children. They imply a sublimation of sexual feelings. To be successful in the oedipal struggle a child must realign his sexual and aggressive drives, fuse them to form more realistic fantasies, and develop a defensive organization which utilizes enough but not too much repression. He must internalize the aspects of his parents which he needs, the biosocial roles and the reciprocal roles necessary for new ego and superego identifications. These will come particularly from the parent who is experienced as more frustrating. A kind of sorting out occurs which is similar to that found in the process of normal mourning for a lost dear person. The mourner takes in the image of the lost one and makes it part of himself. Sometimes he adopts some of the leading personality characteristics of the person he mourns, and occasionally he even seems to look like the mourned one. In doing this, the mourner repeats the process by which he resolved his oedipal tragedy in childhood. When the mourning process is completed, the mourner is usually a more sober and sometimes a sadder person than before; but he is ready and able to resume normal and satisfactory relationships with other people (Cameron, 1963).

The psychoanalytic interpretation concentrates upon the unconscious motives and processes which are supposed to underlie the development of identification. Without entering into a discussion of the merits or demerits of psychoanalytic theory, it must be stated that it has opened up an approach to the study of identification processes which appears to be fruitful.

SEX-ROLE CONVERGENCE IN CULTURES WITH ADVANCED TECHNOLOGY

While more and more women enter fields traditionally regarded as the exclusive domains of men, men also tend increasingly to participate in the performance of "feminine" tasks such as doing the dishes and cleaning house. Families interact as egalitarian units where the members often interchange their roles in accordance with newly emerging necessities. Thus, for instance, it is only fair to assume that in a family in which both husband and wife hold full-time jobs, the household chores should be shared by both spouses. There is no doubt that many children see their parents sometimes fulfilling complementary sex-roles. This must have a more or less profound effect on Personal Identification. Brown (1958b), M. Mead (1949), and G. H. Seward (1956) have pointed out that this greater flexibility in sex-role learning makes for increased interfamily variability and, hence, increasing cultural diversity. With more advanced college education, this trend is more and more accepted as a salutary phenomenon.

Psychological tests have shown that males who tend to model themselves after the traditional stereotype of the male role, which incorporates physical aggressiveness, vulgarity, heavy drinking and smoking as well as boastfulness, daring, and bragging are in reality persons who are extremely insecure and weak in their masculine identification. A male who is secure and stable in his masculine identification is able to incorporate many traits into his personality make-up which are traditionally regarded as "typically feminine." Thus, for instance, the male who has a strong masculine identification exhibits a greater amount of tenderness, consideration for other people, and acceptance of weaknesses in himself and others than the insecure male who conceals his inadequate identification by putting up a hypermasculine front. With our increased knowledge of these relationships, a re-evaluation of our traditional definitions of masculinity and femininity becomes necessary. This may hasten the approach of the day when the "real man" will be able to admit to tender, kind, and nurturant feelings without being called a "sissy" and the "real woman" no longer be ashamed to reflect strength of character, firmness, and intelligence which need not be concealed in the presence of men.

SUMMARY

Differentiation of sex roles is universal. It tends to be less strict in societies which are technologically highly advanced. In these societies sex roles become increasingly interchangeable. Children are aware of the existence of sex differences early in life, as by the age of 3 most children speak of themselves as boys or girls and differentiate definite roles ascribed to either sex.

If the mother is a warm and affectionate person who manages to establish an atmosphere of protection, security, and opportunity for increasing independent exploration of the environment, the child learns to depend on her and a relationship of basic trust is established. This stage of Primary Identification is an indispensable prerequisite for future personality growth and the attainment of adequate identification. Failure to profit from such an atmosphere is likely to lead to defective identification or lack of identification in later life. Sex differences in response to parental treatment appear early in life, with boys tending to be more aggressive, energetic, interested in objects and their manipulation, and girls showing a greater inclination toward dependency, less strenuous and sedentary activities, and a stronger interest in people.

Personal Identification involves the adoption of personality traits, values, norms, and attitudes of the identification model by the child. He learns to think, feel, and act exactly as he perceives a member of his own sex to think, feel, and act. Sex-Role Preference refers to the tendency to adopt the sex role of one's own sex in preference to that of the other as this role is considered to be more attractive and desirable. In normal development, Personal Identification and Sex-Role Preference form a single, integrative process. A person comes to identify with the personality traits of members of his own sex and learns to prefer to establish loving relationships with a member of the opposite sex. If Personal Identification is sought with a member of the opposite sex, or a member of the same sex becomes the preferred sex object, homosexuality or inversion may develop as deviations from normal identification.

Identification is developed through imitation of the model with whom identification is sought. In order to establish normal identification, it is necessary to gain an empathic understanding not only of one's own sex role but also of the role of the other sex. Therefore the child attempts at times to imitate the role of the opposite sex. While in Personal Identification the model's total personality pattern is adopted, although not without the child's modifying it in accordance with his specific needs and perceptions, in Sex-Role Preference only those traits of the model are selected for imitation and adoption which symbolize the model's power status. According to some theories, Personal Identification is based primarily upon feelings of love, respect, and admiration, while Sex-Role Preference incorporates the power aspects of the model and attempts to achieve the model's powerful station in life.

There is evidence that girls and women derive less satisfaction from the performance of the female role than men from carrying out the male role. The latter is seen as more powerful and rewarding. On the other hand, in our contemporary American society, women are allowed a greater flexibility in the choice of sexual roles than men, who are restricted to a relatively narrow range of traditional "men's" roles.

Both boys and girls identify first with the female role, which they experience as the crucial role as a result of the mother's handling and nurturance. Boys must shift to identification with their fathers. In view of the unimportant roles many fathers seem to play in our society and owing to the fact that fathers are frequently absent from home, boys may lack contact with a suitable identification model. This may lead to the search for other identification models, such as older brothers or schoolmates or available relatives. Maternal and paternal identification, rather than being mutually exclusive, seem to be positively related. Once adequate identification has been established with the mother, the boy finds it easy to shift his identification to the father, provided the mother has a positive attitude toward him. Similarly, the girl will be able to establish the cross-sex identification which will enable her to enter into a satisfactory heterosexual relationship later on. Fathers who are both controlling and nurturant present better identification models for boys than fathers who are either controlling (firm, strong, and decisive) or nurturant (warm, supportive, and understanding). Fathers who are weak, ineffective, and distant may seriously impede the masculine identification of their sons.

A happy and satisfying relationship between the spouses provides the most suitable atmosphere for the development of normal identification in the children. Mothers ought to protect their children from harmful stimulation and external dangers without cutting them off from access to novel situations. While being warm, supportive and nurturant, the mother must not be overanxious and insecure in her own identification. Independence striving ought to be encouraged, especially in boys, whereas in girls a certain dependency appears to be part of normal identification. If the mother is mainly motivated by fear and power drive, the child will be unable to establish adequate Personal Identification. He will tend to see the world as a hostile place and resort to the erection of ego defenses and an excessive emphasis upon power striving and power motives. Distrust and suspicion are likely to develop to an extreme degree and interpersonal relationships to lack in trust and confidence. The mother who is able to instill a basic love of life and trust in people as well as respect for men prepares her child well for the attainment of normal sex identification.

According to psychoanalytic theory, the child must relinquish his infantile wish to become the sole love and sex object of the parent of the opposite sex. The resolution of the oedipal struggle is achieved when the child has learned to act in all ways in the manner in which he sees his same-sex parent act, and to admire and cherish the opposite-sex parent after he has sublimated his sexual feelings toward her (or she toward him).

If identification is firmly established, a greater adoption of traits of the opposite sex is frequently achieved and regarded as desirable. The man who feels secure in his masculine identification is inclined to regard the presence of "feminine" personality traits in himself as an advantage rather than a drawback. With increased technological advancement, a greater convergence of sex roles seems to be inevitable.

BIBLIOGRAPHY

Anastasi, A. (1958), *Differential Psychology*. New York: Macmillan, third edition.
Bandura, A. & Walters, R. H. (1959), *Adolescent Aggression: A Study of the Influence of Child-Training Practices and Family Inter-Relationships*. New York: Ronald Press.
Barry, H., Bacon, M. K. & Child, I. L. (1957), A Cross-Cultural Survey of Some Sex Differences in Socialization. *Journal of Abnormal and Social Psychology*, 55:327-332.

Bateson, G., Jackson, D. D., Haley, J. & Weakland, J. (1956), Toward a Theory of Schizophrenia. *Behavioral Science*, 1:251-264.

Beal, V. (1961), Dietary Intake Through Infancy and Childhood. *American Journal of Public Health and the Nation's Health*, 51:1107-1118.

Bieri, J. (1958), Acceptance of Authority and Parental Identification. *Journal of Personality*, 27:74-86.

Brown, D. G. (1956a), Sex-Role Preference in Young Children. *Psychological Monographs: General and Applied*, 70(14).

——(1956b), *The It Scale for Children*. Grand Forks, North Dakota: Psychological Tests Specialists.

——(1957), Masculinity-Femininity Development in Children. *Journal of Consulting Psychology*, 21:197-202.

——(1958a), Inversion and Homosexuality. *American Journal of Orthopsychiatry*, 28:424-429.

——(1958b), Sex-Role Development in a Changing Culture. *Psychological Bulletin*, 55:232-242.

Cameron, N. (1963), *Personality Development and Psychopathology: A Dynamic Approach*. Boston: Houghton Mifflin.

Child, I. L. (1954), Socialization. *Handbook of Social Psychology*, Lindzey, G. (Ed.), 2:655-692. Cambridge: Addison-Wesley.

Cooley, C. H. (1902), *Human Nature and the Social Order*. New York: Scribner.

Dinitz, S., Dynes, R. R. & Clarke, A. C. (1954), Preference for Male or Female Children: Traditional or Affectional. *Marriage and Family Living*, 16:128-130.

Emmerich, W. (1959), Parental Identification in Young Children. *Genetic Psychology Monographs*, 60:257-308.

——(1961), Family Role Concepts of Children Ages Six to Ten. *Child Development*, 32:609-624.

——(1962), Variations in the Parent Role as a Function of the Parent's Sex and the Child's Sex and Age. *Merrill-Palmer Quarterly*, 8:3-11.

Fauls, L. B. & Smith, W. D. (1956), Sex-Role Learning of Five-Year-Olds. *Journal of Genetic Psychology*, 89:105-117.

Fortune Survey (1946), *Fortune*, August.

Fromm-Reichmann, F. (1948), Notes on the Development of Treatment of Schizophrenics by Psychoanalytic Psychotherapy. *Psychiatry*, 11:263-273.

Gallup, G. (1955), Gallup Poll. Princeton: Audience Research Incorporated, June.

Gates, H. A. and Goodwin, J. D. (1936), The Twelve-Day-Old Baby. *Human Biology* 8:433-450.

Gesell, A., Halverson, H. M., Thomson, H., Ilg, F. L., Castner, B. M., Ames, L. B. & Amatruda, C. S. (1940), *The First Five Years of Life: The Preschool Years*. New York: Harper.

——, Ilg, F. L., Learned, J. & Ames, L. B. (1943), *Infant and Child in the Culture of Today: The Guidance of Development in Home and Nursery School*. New York: Harper.

Goethals, G. (1953), *The Relationship Between Family Esteem Patterns and Measures of Guilt, Identification, and Aggression in a Group of Four-Year-Old Children*. Unpublished doctoral dissertation, Harvard University.

Goodenough, E. W. (1957), Interest in Persons as an Aspect of Sex Differences in the Early Years. *Genetic Psychology Monographs*, 55:287-323.

Gray, S. W. & Klaus, R. (1956), The Assessment of Parental Identification. *Genetic Psychology Monographs*, 54:87-114.

Hartley, R. E., Frank, L. K. & Goldenson, R. M. (1952), *Understanding Children's Play*. New York: Columbia University Press.

Heinicke, C. M. (1953), *Some Antecedents and Correlates of Fear in Young Boys*. Unpublished doctoral dissertation, Harvard University.

Helper, M. M. (1955), Learning Theory and the Self-Concept. *Journal of Abnormal and Social Psychology*, 51:184-194.

Hess, R. D., Wright, B. & Tuska, S. A. (1961), Identificatory Origins of the Self Among Fathers. *American Psychologist*, 16:349.

Hoffman, L. W. (1960), *The Father's Role in the Family and the Child's Peer-Group Adjustment*. Paper read at American Psychological Association, Chicago, September.

Hurlock, E. B. (1953), *Developmental Psychology*. New York: McGraw-Hill.

Kagan, J. & Lemkin, J. (1960), The Child's Differential Perception of Parental Attributes. *Journal of Abnormal and Social Psychology*, 61:440-447.

Katcher, A. (1955), The Discrimination of Sex Differences by Young Children. *Journal of Genetic Psychology*, 82:131-143.

Koch, H. L. (1944), A Study of Some Factors Conditioning the Social Distance Between the Sexes. *Journal of Social Psychology*, 20:79-107.

——(1954), The Relation of 'Primary Mental Abilities' in Five- and Six-Year Olds to Sex of Child and Characteristics of His Sibling. *Child Development*, 25:205-223.

——(1955), Some Personality Correlates of Sex, Sibling Position and Sex of Sibling Among Five- and Six-Year-Old Children. *Genetic Psychology Monographs*, 52:3-50.

——(1956a), Attitudes of Young Children Toward Their Peers as Related to Certain Characteristics of Their Siblings. *Psychological Monographs: General and Applied*, 70.

——(1956b), Children's Work Attitudes and Sibling Characteristics. *Child Development*, 27:289-310.

——(1956c), Sissiness and Tomboyishness in Relation to Sibling Characteristics. *Journal of Genetic Psychology*, 88:231-244.

——(1960), The Relation of Certain Formal Attributes of Siblings to Attitudes Held Toward Each Other and Toward Their Parents. *Social Research for Child Development*, 25:5-124.

Levin, H. & Sears, R. R. (1956), Identification with Parents as a Determinant of Doll Play Aggression. *Child Development*, 27:135-153.

Low, W. B. (1957), *Sex of the Examiner in Relation to Sex-Role Preferences in Kindergarten Children*. Unpublished master's thesis, University of Denver.

Lynn, D. B. (1959), A Note on Sex Differences in the Development of Masculine and Feminine Identification. *Psychological Review*, 66:126-135.

——(1961), Sex Differences in Identification Development. *Sociometry*, 24:372-383.

Mead, G. H. (1934), *Mind, Self and Society*. Chicago: University of Chicago Press.

Mead, M. (1949), *Male and Female*. New York: Morrow.

Mowrer, O. H. (1953), *Psychotherapy: Theory and Research*. New York: Ronald Press.

Murdock, G. P. (1937), Comparative Data on the Division of Labor by Sex. *Social Forces*, 15:551-553.

Mussen, P. & Distler, L. (1960), Child Rearing Antecedents of Masculine Identification in Kindergarten Boys. *Child Development*, 31:89-100.

Payne, D. E. & Mussen, P. H. (1956), Parent-Child Relations and Father Identification Among Adolescent Boys. *Journal of Abnormal and Social Psychology*, 52:358-362.

Piaget, J. (1954), *The Construction of Reality in the Child*. New York: Basic Books.

Rabban, M. (1950), Sex-Role Identification in Young Children in Two Diverse Social Groups. *Genetic Psychology Monographs*, 42:81-158.

Rose, A. A. & Stavrianos, B. K. (1943), Sex Differences in the Perceptual Attitudes of Children. *Journal of Psychology*, 16:129-143.

Rosen, J. N. (1953), *Direct Analysis*. New York: Grune and Stratton.

Rosenberg, B. G. & Sutton-Smith, B. (1960), A Revised Conception of Masculine-Feminine Differences in Play Activities. *Journal of Genetic Psychology*, 96:165-170.

Sanchez-Hidalgo, E. (1952), The Feeling of Inferiority in the Puerto Rican Female. *Rev. Asoc. Maestros, P. R.*, 11:170-171, 190.

Sanford, R. N. (1955), The Dynamics of Identification. *Psychological Review*, 62:106-118.

Sears, P. (1953), Child-Rearing Factors Related to Playing of Sex-Typed Roles. *American Psychologist*, 8:431 (abstract).

Sears, R. R. (1963), Dependency Motivation. *Nebraska Symposium on Motivation*. Lincoln: University of Nebraska Press.

——, Maccoby, E. E. & Levin, H. (1957), *Patterns of Child Rearing*. Evanston, Illinois: Row, Peterson.

Seward, G. H. (1946), *Sex and the Social Order*. New York: McGraw-Hill.

——(1956), *Psychotherapy and Culture Conflict*. New York: Ronald Press.

Seward, J. P. (1954), Learning Theory and Identification. *Journal of Genetic Psychology*, 84:201-210.

Siegel, A. E. (1956), Film-Mediated Fantasy Aggression and Strength of Aggressive Drive. *Child Development*, 27:365-378.

——(1958), The Influence of Violence in the Mass Media Upon Children's Role Expectations. *Child Development*, 29:35-56.

Slater, P. E. (1955), *Psychological Factors in Role Specialization*. Unpublished doctoral dissertation, Harvard University.

——(1961), Toward a Dualistic Theory of Identification. *Merrill-Palmer Quarterly*, 7:113-126.

Stoke, S. M. (1950), An Inquiry into the Concept of Identification. *Journal of Genetic Psychology*, 76:163-189.

Terman, L. M. & Miles, C. C. (1936), *Sex and Personality: Studies in Masculinity and Femininity*. New York: McGraw-Hill.

Tietze, T. (1949), A Study of Schizophrenic Patients. *Psychiatry*, 12:55-65.

Walters, J., Pierce, D. & Dahms, L. (1957), Affectional and Aggressive Behavior of Preschool Children. *Child Development*, 28:15-26.

Winch, R. F. (1962), *Identification and its Familiar Determinants*. Indianapolis: Bobbs-Merrill.

Witkin, H. (1949a), The Nature and Importance of Individual Differences in Perception. *Journal of Personality*, 18:145-170.

——(1949b), Sex Differences in Perception. *Transactions of the New York Academy of Science*, Series 11, 12, 1:22-26.

——(1959), The Perception of the Upright. *Scientific American*, 200:50-70.

Wylie, R. C. (1961), *The Self Concept*. Lincoln: University of Nebraska Press.

PART VI

Cognitive Aspects of Perception

Traditionally, perception and cognition were considered to be separate and distinct facets of the total person. The sensory and perceptual processes served the function of receiving the data from the external environment. The cognitive processes were utilized for thinking, learning, and problem solving. It is now obvious, however, that normal perception is a greater or lesser function of cognitive inferences based upon knowledge about a perceived object, person, or situation.

In Chapter 14, which provides a theoretical framework for the relationship between perception and cognition, Vernon presents a discussion of the modification of percepts in children by cognitive processes and experience.

In Chapter 15, Lovell reviews the literature concerning the development of such concepts as number, mass, time, volume, weight, and velocity in children, and points out how these concepts, once developed, then structure the way in which persons perceive their world.

In Chapter 16, Goldstone and Goldfarb review the literature and then offer experimental data on the development of the perception of time. Additionally they point up the complex interrelationships of the biochemical, sensory, and cognitive variables influencing time perception.

In Chapter 17, Kagan presents a new experimental analysis of two behavioral dispositions which appear to be basic to perceptual-cognitive functioning.

In view of the known relationships between perception and cognition, the primary goal for future research should be the determination of the variables influencing the relationships and then comprehensive experimentation upon the nature and direction of the influence exerted.

CHAPTER 14

Perception in Relation to Cognition

M. D. VERNON

I

It has been customary for psychologists to allocate sensory perception and other cognitive processes such as learning and thinking to different categories, and to discuss them more or less in isolation from each other. There may be a certain justification for this procedure for adults, whose perceptual processes are well developed and stabilized, and therefore not often in need of modification through learning and reasoning. But even for adults the author has argued that perception of everyday life situations is to a considerable extent a function of cognitive inference from schematized knowledge about the nature of the situation perceived (Vernon, 1957). However, there is little doubt that the percepts of children, even if initially a function of the immediate sensory data and of innate perceptual tendencies such as those postulated by the gestalt psychologists, are modified and adapted in the light of acquired information by thought processes and by learning through experience.

Yet, unfortunately, little experimental study has been devoted to the development of perception and understanding of the environment. Extensive studies have been made of reflex and conditioned responses to isolated sensory stimuli, of the perception of simple shapes, and of the formation of concepts of shape, number, etc. But to adapt appropriately to the environment the child requires much more than the capacity to perceive and react to such relatively isolated and abstract stimuli. Most important of all, he must acquire some understanding of the nature of objects in the environment, recognizing and identifying them from their appearance and behavior, knowing what they can do and what he can do with them. Such an understanding implies a considerable amount of knowledge which must be acquired by experience and remembered afterwards; acquisition is therefore dependent upon the cognitive processes of learning and memory, supplemented increasingly by reasoning about the physical environment and the forces which operate in it. If this knowledge were stored in a random and heterogeneous manner, it could not be utilized rapidly and effectively. Thus it has been postulated (Piaget, 1952, 1955; Vernon, 1955) that perceptions and memories of perceptions and of reactions to them become coordinated in "schemes" with which similar memories are organized, together with the relevant knowledge which has been acquired in relation to these percepts. Whenever a perceptual situation is encountered, especially one difficult to perceive or understand, it will be referred to the relevant scheme. Thus the perceiver is enabled to elucidate the situation, recognize its significant features, and react appropriately. In general, the more frequently a particular situation has been encountered, the greater the expectation of its recurrence, and the easier and more rapid the operation of the appropriate scheme and the recognition and subsequent reaction.

Thus the processes of perceptual learning and of the development of schemes are vital to the young child if he is to be able to adapt himself to his environment. Certain perceptions may be innate, for instance, of light and shade, color and form; certain types of perceptual response may develop through maturation alone, for instance, the specific response of smiling at a smiling human face (Spitz and Wolf, 1946; Ambrose, 1961), and the recoil from a sudden drop in the ground (Walk and Gibson, 1961). But it cannot be supposed that there is an innate capacity to perceive, comprehend, and utilize all the objects which confront the child; such knowledge must be learned. Though in recent years there has been considerable study and discussion of perceptual learning, these have been devoted largely to the perceptual learning of adults, in whom it tends to be relatively specific to the particular situations presented. But children must acquire general and organized knowledge about the nature of the environment as a whole. They must also develop the capacity to attend and select, and to perceive rapidly and accurately, dependent in part on maturation but also assisted by learning. This learning, it may be supposed, is guided and reinforced by the consequences of actions stimulated by perception. That is to say, if children find that actions based upon what they have perceived are successful, then the perceptions are stabilized in that form; but if not, they are repeated and corrected.

Understandably, it is less easy to obtain accurate evidence about the actual perceptual experience of children than to study their overt behavior. Thus the nature of their perceptions must be inferred from their spontaneous actions or from their responses to perceptual material. In infants, we must utilize mainly inferences from spontaneous behavior, and for these we are largely dependent upon the work of Piaget. It must be noted, however, that it is difficult to validate these inferences. Thus our knowledge of the nature of perception in infancy is both incomplete and to some extent speculative. Even when, with rather older children, it is possible to introduce experimental techniques of study, the children's reactions may be affected by other than cognitive factors, for instance, motivational states. Verbal reports of what has been perceived afford additional data from the age of about a year and upwards, but again are not wholly reliable until later childhood.

However, in spite of these difficulties it is worth considering the data which have been obtained concerning the manner in which children's perceptions develop as they gain increasing facility and increasing knowledge. There appear to be two main characteristics of perception in infancy and early childhood: in the first place, it is vague and diffuse, lacking in accurate observation of detail and selection of what to us seem to be the significant aspects of the situation; and second, the child is relatively unable to make inferences from his immediate sensory perceptions of the nature of objects and of the environment because he lacks the knowledge to guide him. These two characteristics are interdependent: there is a close relationship between the inability to perceive accurately and discriminatively and to direct attention appropriately (as suggested by Piaget, 1961), on the one hand, and the partial and incomplete knowledge which the child has obtained of his environment on the other hand. Thus it may be that inability to direct attention appropriately to the significant features of the environment is caused at least in part by an incapacity to understand the nature of the situation and to perceive its significant features.

394 M. D. VERNON

II

It appears from the observations made by Piaget of the development of his three children in infancy that some understanding of the nature of solid objects and of their location in space emerges toward the end of the first year of life. This is preceded, however, by the coordination of simple sensory data into sensorimotor "schemata" (Piaget, 1952), since the infant cannot begin to realize the nature of objects until he can combine together the visual impressions of their shape and the tactile and kinesthetic impressions obtained by touching and handling them. The first stage of coordination is attained when the infant reaches for, grasps, and handles objects toward which his gaze has been directed (Gesell et al., 1949; Piaget, 1952); this occurs at about the third to the fourth month. Whereas at first these actions seem to appear when something chances to touch his hand, at 5 to 6 months the infant deliberately reaches for near objects which attract his attention, and examines and manipulates them. Especially if the object is new and unfamiliar, he uses a variety of actions to discover its nature; he feels it, explores its contour, balances it, strikes it, and hits it against other things. If it is slippery and slips from his hand, he picks it up again. He also turns it round in space and views it from different angles. In this way he learns that the same object in different spatial positions may produce different visual impressions, but that its identity is maintained whatever its spatial orientation. This is not fully grasped until the latter part of the first year. Before the age of 7 to 8 months the infant does not recognize and reach for his bottle when it is presented to him with the nipple turned away from him (Piaget, 1955), but thereafter he reaches or cries for it even if only a small part of it is visible to him.

Perhaps the most important stage in understanding the nature of objects is the realization of their continuous and permanent existence. At 6 to 7 months an infant may look for something which he has just dropped, but only for a short time while he continues to want to play with it. Or he may cry for it as he sees it disappearing. But at 8 to 9 months he may deliberately search for something which is no longer in view. Whereas before this a hidden object may seem to have vanished altogether, thereafter he conceives of its continuing existence, and tries to find it, although not necessarily in the right place. Indeed, there seems to be a tendency to conceive of objects as associated with particular spatial surroundings, and this stage may continue for some time. Thus one child, who had been playing with her sister downstairs, subsequently went upstairs to look for her in the bedroom in which she had earlier been lying ill (Piaget, 1955). However, there can be little doubt that from the age of about a year the child realizes and remembers the existence of particular objects, and may ask for them when he wants them.

How does the young child identify objects? By the mental age of 2 years he is expected to be able to identify four out of the six objects presented to him in the Terman-Merrill test (Terman and Merrill, 1937), namely, a button, a thimble, a miniature toy cat, an engine, and a spoon. Presumably, therefore, he may be able to identify the actual objects, not in miniature, at an earlier age. Since he can identify objects in any spatial orientation, it seems unlikely that identification is based upon any single isolated visual cue. What is most probable is that young children at first perceive the more immediately obvious and noticeable characteristics, including outline shape, and that these percepts are coordinated to form a general impression which is remembered. It is doubtful to what extent shape alone functions in identification; possibly it is more important in some cases than in others, as for instance the spherical shape of a ball. We know from the findings of Gellermann (1933) that even children of 2 years can distinguish and remember simple shapes such as those of a triangle and a cross. (It should be noted that this is something more than discrimination between shapes, which Ling [1941] showed to begin at 6 months.) But Werner (1948) quotes Knoblauch (1934) as finding that subnormal children of 5 to 7 years (presumably equivalent in ability to much younger normal children) matched shapes on the basis of blackness and solidity rather than on shape characteristics such as circularity and angularity. This seems to suggest that younger children may not notice shape characteristics as such unless forced to do so by the experimental conditions. Indeed, O'Connor and Hermelin (1963) found that imbecile adults of a mental age of about 5 years were less able than were normal children of the same mental age to recognize previously presented shapes visually, but in touch recognition the imbeciles were superior to the normal children. One must infer, therefore, that the visual perception of shape was the more highly developed capacity.

Again, in identifying ordinary objects, children may be influenced by the activities of the objects, and particularly by their movements, which

seem to attract attention readily. Thus such things as animals may well
be characterized and identified by their movements. At an early age children become interested in the use and function of objects. Piaget (1952)
noted that infants of 10 to 11 months were constantly trying to find what
they could do with objects, letting them fall, throwing them, sliding them
along, floating them on water. This indicates that the child was beginning to link his perceptions of objects with his actions in relation to them,
and their practical significance to him.

III

During his second year the child's perceptions and memories of particular single objects are supplemented and to some extent superseded by
the development of concepts, in which the salient characteristics of similar objects are schematized into categories, each of which can be designated by a name. From this period onward, verbalization plays an increasingly important part in many perceptions. At first, however, names
may be used for single objects only. Thus Liublinskaya (1957) noted
that at 12 to 14 months the word "cup" might be used for a small pink
cup, but not for a large white one. Welch (1940) tried to teach children
of 12 to 26 months to give the names chair, ball, etc., as class names to
groups of different examples of these objects. Though the children
learned to apply the names appropriately to several of the objects, they
could not use them as class names for whole groups.

But at about the same time the child often begins to use names for classes of objects quite spontaneously, though often incorrectly. Thus the
name "dog" may be given to a variety of animals, and the name "auntie"
to a number of different adult females. Brown (1958) has pointed out
that in fact children tend to use the names which they most commonly
hear uttered by adults. Sometimes these refer to single objects, sometimes
to classes of objects. It is only gradually that children learn to apply the
names correctly, either to single objects or to classes, as the case may be.

However, there seems little doubt that the child also has to learn gradually to differentiate the significant aspects of objects and then to generalize them, classifying them according to the correct schematic categories. It appears likely that in general some form of multiple classification
takes place at first, in terms of a number of what appear to the child to

be related characteristics of appearance and behavior. Thus Reichard et al. (1944) found that with the Goldstein test of sorting objects into groups, children aged 4 to 5 years tended to sort in an idiosyncratic manner into categories based upon incidental and nonessential likenesses which seemed obvious to them but not to other people. Up to 8 and 9 years they sorted according to the function and use of the objects, and only after that by means of abstract generalization. It seems probable, therefore, that although schematic classification of objects and situations is of great value to the child in enabling him to identify and react appropriately to new and unfamiliar objects by assimilating them to already existent categories, the categories he employs may be of his own construction, and, from the adult point of view, quite illogical and unsystematic. Again, children may attach too much weight to particular cues, and too little to a balanced representation of all the significant features. Thus Vurpillot and Brault (1959) found that children of 5 to 6 years paid relatively more attention to single identifying cues in viewing miniature objects, whereas older children were more concerned with all the principal characteristics of the objects.

Although during their second and third years children may give incorrect names to the objects they perceive, there is evidence to show that the use of language is of considerable value to them in assisting correct identification. Luria and Yudovich (1959) studied a pair of twins of 5 years, who, although they could communicate with each other, could neither utter nor understand normal speech. They could identify objects only in terms of their practical use, that is to say, by finding out what could be done with them, but they did not understand what they were from verbal descriptions. Nor could they group similar objects together. Liublinskaya (1957) found that normal children of 1 to 2 1/2 years could identify and recognize a butterfly by the pattern of stripes on its wings only when it was labeled with the word "Stripes." Cantor (1955) showed that children of 3 to 5 years could recognize faces more correctly when they had learned to attach names to them than when they had merely been shown them. O'Connor and Hermelin (1961) found that imbeciles of mental ages of 4 to 6 years were better able to recognize pictures of real objects from among others when the names of the former had previously been spoken to them than when they had seen the pictures without naming them. It appeared that the naming had impressed the pictures on their minds. Another illustration of the value of naming was given by Werner (1948) with two boys, aged 4 and 6 years, who were building with different-shaped bricks. One boy kept a store of the bricks and handed them to the other to do the building; in order to facilitate this procedure, they invented an elaborate system of names, "Big Miller," "Little Miller," etc., for the different shapes of brick.

IV

We have already noted that the perceptions of younger children generally tend to be relatively global and diffuse, and that they do not perceive detail accurately. As they grow older, they are better able to analyze perceptual material and differentiate its parts, and subsequently to reorganize these percepts in such a manner as to select and emphasize the relevant aspects of the situation, and to ignore the relatively unimportant. This differentiation and reorganization undoubtedly depend in part on the cognitive structuring of experience, and the ability to think out what is important and what irrelevant. Thus Ames et al. (1953) found that children of 2 years tended to perceive the Rorschach inkblots as wholes, naming them as if they actually represented objects rather than being vaguely similar in form. But after 3 years of age the children began to perceive the major details within the whole, and to attempt some organization of them. However, there was still a good deal of pure invention, and accurate appreciation of form did not appear until a later age.

There have been many studies of the perception of simple and complex forms which have indicated that children may perceive shapes as such before they are able to grasp their interrelations. This is apparent in studies of the Bender Visual Motor Gestalt Test (Bender, 1938), and also in the study of Gesell and Ames (1946). In the latter, children were given a figure to copy which consisted of two crosses contained in a rectangle. The "Union Jack" is shown in Figure 1. They reproduced the crosses separately before they could combine them.

The gradual development of perceptual organization is also illustrated by children's responses to pictures (Vernon, 1940; Amen, 1941). The youngest children tend to enumerate the people and objects depicted in a complex picture, slightly older children to describe their overt activities. Still later, some interpretation is given of the meanings of the ac-

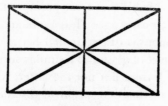

FIGURE 1

tivities, and last of all the feelings and intentions of the people in the pictures are mentioned. There is some disagreement about the ages at which these types of response appear. But at least until 5 years there is a strong tendency to introduce irrelevant and unimportant details. The younger children, according to Amen, tended to concentrate on one particular part of the picture, that which they found the most interesting even if it was not actually the most important, and to ignore the rest.

Piaget (1961) discussed the manner in which direct and immediate perception of shape is extended and corrected by perceptual activity, in which the exploration and comparison of all aspects of complex figures continue until their relation is accurately perceived and fully understood. Children up to the age of 5 and 6 years, when shown complex figures such as the visual illusions, tend to let their eyes wander at random over the whole field of view (even outside the figure), or else to remain fixated on particular salient points of the figures, ignoring the remainder. Thus they perceive many illusions, such as the Müller-Lyer, to a greater extent than do older children and adults who, given time to do so, compare the parts of the figure systematically with each other and thus to some extent dispel the illusion. They apply their intelligence in directing their perceptual activities, reorganizing their percepts in accordance with cognitive schemes based upon general ideas about the nature of form and its relation to its spatial surroundings.

V

The influence of cognitive processes is apparent in the development of perception not only of objects and forms, but also of their surroundings and their disposition in space, including distance from the observer and from each other. It is probable that some perception of distance of objects from the self begins at an early age. Thus Walk and Gibson (1961) found that infants at 6 to 7 months discriminated between a checkered surface immediately below a sheet of glass and a similar surface 4 feet below; they would crawl across the former but not the latter. Although there is some doubt about the basis of this perception of distance, it seems clear that it was immediate and direct, without cognitive inference.

Nevertheless even in the first year of life infants, according to Piaget (1955), begin to develop spatial schemata. In early infancy there may be different sensorimotor "spaces": a "mouth space" for what the infant can suck and chew; a "visual space" for things followed by the eyes; a "tactile space" for things he can touch and grasp. As he realizes that the objects located in these "spaces" are the same, the infant coordinates the separate "spaces" into a single spatial schema. The next important development is the realization that objects moving about in space retain their identity although the sizes of the images they project on the retina grow smaller or larger as the objects recede from him or advance toward him. Thus the child develops an appreciation of size constancy with near objects. Judgment of distance is checked and refined, first by the movements of reaching and grasping, later, when the child is able to crawl and walk, by movement of the whole body. During the second year, the child begins to show interest in the spatial relations of objects to each other, for instance, by throwing them and searching for the different positions in which they have fallen. Topological relations, of inside and outside, above and below, are also of great interest to him. Gradually he learns to visualize spatial relations, so that at about 1 1/2 years, for instance, he can envisage how to reach an object the direct path to which is blocked; thus he runs immediately to the further side of the sofa to retrieve a ball which has rolled underneath it. However, this perception of space relations operates almost entirely with near objects. The child's verbalized ideas about space become increasingly exact at about 2 1/2 to 3 years, and he becomes interested in far distances also at 3 to 3 1/2 years (Ames and Learned, 1948). But even then he is not at all clear about the fact that far distant objects may really be much larger than they appear. Thus Piaget (1951) noted that a child of 5 years seemed to think that a distant lake and houses actually became much larger as he approached them.

We know that in adult perception of space and judgment of distance many different types of data are utilized, particularly when the primary binocular data afforded by disparity of the retinal images and convergent eye movements are lacking. Adults can judge the distances of objects in monocular vision, and beyond the distance at which binocular cues are functional; the infant may not. Adults can utilize cues given by the gradual diminution of size in linear perspective, and of brightness, color, and surface detail in aerial perspective. They are able to coordinate these data and make fairly accurate judgments of distance even in quite difficult circumstances. Children are less adept. Thus Denis-Prinzhorn (1960) required children of 5 to 7 years to bisect the distance between two objects, one at a distance of 34 cm, the other at 200 cm. She found that, whereas adults could perform this task with fair accuracy, the children consistently underestimated the further half. This she attributed to a tendency in younger children to underestimate the expansion of far distant space by comparison with nearer space. So also Lambercier (1946a) showed that they underestimate the size of further objects by comparison with nearer objects. The greater the distance, the greater the underestimation (Zeigler and Leibowitz, 1957). Also in making such size judgments children are less well able than are adults to utilize cues to distance given by a series of objects spaced out between the near and the far one (Lambercier, 1946b).

Older children and adults may also use their spatial schemata to enable them to perceive three-dimensionality indirectly, in pictures. But Hudson (1960) found that children of 6 years tended to perceive outline drawings and even a photograph showing distance effects as flat, whereas children of 12 years perceived the three-dimensionality. However, this seems to have been to a considerable extent a result of their education, since culturally isolated adult laborers who had received little education also tended to see the drawings as flat.

We noted that children begin at an early age to perceive in a rather vague manner the relative positions and distances of objects in space. However, it is some time before they are able to visualize these and conceive such relations correctly. This fact was demonstrated in an experiment by Piaget and Inhelder (1956), in which they showed children a model layout consisting of a miniature landscape with a road, a stream, two houses, trees, and a small hill. There was an identical model rotated through 180° alongside it. A doll was placed in various positions in the first model, and the children were asked to place another doll in the same position in the rotated model. At 3 to 4 years they put it in a similar position of proximity to a single object near a house or in a field but without any regard to its exact spatial relation with the model as a whole; at 4 years, some regard was paid to position relative to two or three features of the model. At 5 to 5 1/2 years, the children seemed to realize that the second model had been rotated, but were uncertain about the effects of this and often needed several attempts before placing the doll correctly. Only at about 7 years and upwards could they grasp the nature of the whole spatial layout and visualize exactly where to place the doll. In further experiments children were required to arrange a number of objects on a board in positions corresponding to those of similar objects in a model layout. This they were unable to do with any sort of accuracy before about 7 years, and trial-and-error procedures persisted until a later age.

Both in these tasks and in another similar one, it was clear that children had considerable difficulty in envisaging any aspect of certain objects or groups of objects other than that which they perceived at that moment. Although the child acquires in infancy a knowledge of the changes in shape of objects which he rotates in his hands, apparently he is much slower to understand the similar phenomenon which occurs when his orientation to a large object or a group of objects is changed. Thus Piaget (1951) reported that a child of 4 1/2 years thought that a mountain had really changed its shape when he saw it from a new place. Again, Piaget and Inhelder (1956) presented to children a model of a group of mountains, and a collection of pictures painted in the same colors as the model, showing it from different aspects. The children were asked to select the picture which represented what the mountains would look like when seen from different viewpoints. Children of 4 to 6 1/2 years always selected the same picture, that which showed the mountains from the point of view from which they themselves were looking. At a later age, they began to realize that there are other and different aspects, but these were not accurately judged until the age of about 9 years.

Although it is perhaps not possible to determine from these data the extent to which direct spatial perception in ordinary life depends on the development of coordinated spatial schemata, it does seem probable that they play an increasingly important part, especially in circumstances in which the perceptual data are to some extent diminished. That judgments of distance can be improved even in adult life was shown by E. J. Gibson et al. (1955), who taught adults to make absolute judgments of long distances by dividing these up into halves, quarters, etc., and estimating each length separately. This highly intellectualized procedure enabled them to judge quite different absolute distances better, though it had no effect on their accuracy in comparing distances. It seems probable that in somewhat the same way children learn to make more accurate absolute judgments, by themselves moving to and fro across them; or with long distances, by traveling over them.

VI

We noted that one of the characteristics of the global perception of young children was the failure to isolate the parts within the whole, and objects from their surroundings. This remains apparent in the immediate perception even of adults, as in the case of visual illusions. But through the cognitive processes of perceptual activity they may correct and refine their immediate perceptions, and thus obtain a more veridical understanding of the nature of the environment. This is particularly apparent in judgments of movement and of the speed of movement. Even adults are likely to make mistaken judgments, and, for instance, to perceive larger and brighter objects as moving more slowly than smaller and dimmer ones; or movement as being more rapid across a heterogeneous than across a homogeneous background (Brown, 1931). But they may correct these judgments through their knowledge that speed is a function solely of the distance moved in a given time. The young child, however, depends on his immediate perceptions, and does not correct judgments in this way. According to Piaget (1946), he tends to say that the speed of movement of an object is greater than that of another only if he perceives the first to pass the second. If two objects arrive at the same point at the same moment, they are judged to be moving at the same speed no matter where they started nor what path they took. If one arrives before the other, it is judged to have moved more quickly. These errors may arise because the earliest perceptions of movement are of objects moving away from himself, which thus have a uniform starting point. But his perceptions continue to be dominated by a single aspect of the situation, the finishing point.

It requires the control of thought processes to correct and refine these early perceptions.

VII

We may conclude from this discussion that the simplest primary perceptions of sensory stimuli and of forms and their relation to their spatial surroundings are modified from infancy upward in the light of their association with other cognitive data, and in particular through the acquisition of knowledge about the nature of objects and of the environment. Thus percepts, after the first few months of life, do not exist in isolation, but are related across sensory modes; they are integrated with memories of previous similar perceptual experiences, and of reactions to these, into schematic categories of associated percepts. The categories are further refined and restructured through the development of relevant ideas by intelligent reasoning. Thus eventually the older child and adult attend to and become aware of, not so much the immediate and obvious aspects of the present situation, as those characteristics which are significant with regard to its underlying meaning, and which can be used to predict the course of action most likely to be successful for adaptation of behavior to the total situation. In the course of this development, accuracy of discrimination and rapidity of perception increase, to some extent through maturation alone, though probably also through learning. Maturation, and certainly also learning, enable the child to analyze the perceptual situation and extract its important features. But these improved capacities would be of far less value to the child if he were not constantly employed in gauging the significance to himself of the perceptual situation and in relating it to his ideas and actions.

That the ability to analyze the perceptual situation actively and differentiate its parts may show important individual differences has recently been studied by Witkin et al. (1962). These authors demonstrated that such differences may exist in children from 8 years upward; indeed, they consider that the differences may appear even earlier in life, though this has not yet been established. The analytical capacity, which they term "field independence," appears in the performance of various perceptual tasks in which the person has to differentiate certain aspects of the field and make judgments of them, ignoring any interference from the remainder of the field; and also in a high degree of structuring in the

Rorschach inkblot responses. It is correlated with performance on the WISC Picture Completion, Object Assembly, and Block Design tests, but not with any of the WISC verbal tests. However, this lack of relationship may be due to the fact that adequate tests of differentiation and analysis of verbal material were not utilized. "Field independence" seems to arise notably in children of independent personality, who are sufficiently self-reliant to treat their social and physical environment objectively, to understand its essential nature, and to utilize it actively and effectively for the satisfaction of their needs. It may have a constitutional basis, but is also considerably affected by the personality of the mother and her manner of bringing up her children. We may therefore conclude that the capacity to apply the cognitive processes generally in an active appraisal and understanding of the nature of the environment is a fundamental personality characteristic of great importance in the perceptual development of children.

BIBLIOGRAPHY

Ambrose, J. A. (1961), The Development of the Smiling Response in Early Infancy. *Determinants of Infant Behaviour*, Foss, B. M. (Ed.). London: Methuen.

Amen, E. A. (1941), Individual Differences in Apperceptive Reaction: A Study of the Response of Pre-School Children to Pictures. *Genetic Psychology Monographs*, 23:319.

Ames, L. B. et al. (1953), Development of Perception in the Young Child as Observed in Response to the Rorschach Test Blots. *Journal of Genetic Psychology*, 82:183.

—— & Learned, J. (1948), The Development of Verbalized Space in the Young Child. *Journal of Genetic Psychology*, 72:63.

Bender, L. (1938), *A Visual Motor Gestalt Test and Its Clinical Use*. New York: American Orthopsychiatric Association.

Brown, J. F. (1931), The Visual Perception of Velocity. *Psychol. Forschung*, 14:199.

Brown, R. (1958), How Shall a Thing be Called? *Psychological Review*, 65:14.

Cantor, G. N. (1955), Effects of Three Types of Pre-Training on Discrimination Learning in Pre-School Children. *Journal of Experimental Psychology*, 49:339.

Denis-Prinzhorn, M. (1960), Perception des Distances et Constance des Grandeurs (étude génétique). *Archives de Psychologie*, 37:181.

Gellermann, L. W. (1933), Form Discrimination in Chimpanzees and Two-Year Old Children. *Journal of Genetic Psychology*, 42:3.

Gesell, A. & Ames, L. B. (1946), The Development of Directionality in Drawing. *Journal of Genetic Psychology*, 68:45.

——, Ilg, F. L. & Bullis, G. E. (1949), *Vision: Its Development in Infant and Child*. New York: Harper.

Gibson, E. J. et al. (1955), The Effect of Prior Training with a Scale of Distance on Absolute and Relative Judgments of Distance over Ground. *Journal of Experimental Psychology*, 50:97.

Hudson, W. (1960), Pictorial Depth Perception in Sub-Cultural Groups in Africa. *Journal of Social Psychology*, 52:183.

Knoblauch, E. (1934), Vergleichende Untersuchungen zur Optischen Auffassung hochgradig schwachsinniger und normaler Kinder. *Zeitschrift Angew. Psychol.*, 47

Lambercier, M. (1946a), La Constance des Grandeurs en Comparaisons Sériales. *Archives de Psychologie*, 31:78.

——(1946b), Le Configuration en Profondeur dans la Constance des Grandeurs. *Archives de Psychologie*, 31:287.

Ling, B. C. (1941), Form Discrimination as a Learning Cue in Infants. *Comparative Psychological Monographs*, 17 (2).

Liublinskaya, A. A. (1957), The Development of Children's Speech and Thought. *Psychology in the Soviet Union*, Simon, B. (Ed.). London: Routledge and Kegan Paul.

Luria, A. R. & Yudovich, F. I. (1959), *Speech and the Development of Mental Processes in the Child*. London: Staples.

O'Connor, R. & Hermelin, B. (1961), Like and Cross Modality Recognition in Subnormal Children. *Quarterly Journal of Experimental Psychology*, 13:48.

—— & —— (1963), *Speech and Thought in Severe Subnormality*. London: Pergamon.

Piaget, J. (1946), *Les Notions de Mouvement et de la Vitesse chez l'Enfant*. Paris: Presses Universitaires de France.

——(1951), *Play, Dreams and Imitation in Childhood*. London: Heinemann.

——(1952), *The Origins of Intelligence in Children*. New York: International Universities Press.

——(1955), *The Child's Construction of Reality*. London: Routledge and Kegan Paul.

——(1961), *Les Mécanismes Perceptifs*. Paris: Presses Universitaires de France.

—— & Inhelder, B. (1956), *The Child's Conception of Space*. London: Routledge and Kegan Paul.

Reichard, S. et al. (1944), The Development of Concept Formation in Children. *American Journal of Orthopsychiatry*, 14:156.

Spitz, R. A. & Wolf, K. M. (1946), The Smiling Response: A Contribution to the Ontogenesis of Social Relations. *Genetic Psychology Monographs*, 34:57.

Terman, L. M. & Merrill, M. A. (1937), *Measuring Intelligence*. London: Harrap.

Vernon, M. D. (1940), The Relation of Cognition and Phantasy in Children. *British Journal of Psychology*, 30:273.

——(1955), The Functions of Schemata in Perceiving. *Psychological Review*, 62:180.

——(1957), Cognitive Inferences in Perceptual Activity. *British Journal of Psychology*, 48:35.

Vurpillot, E. & Brault, H. (1959), Étude Expérimentale sur la Formation des Schèmes Empiriques. *L'Année Psychologique*, 59:381.

Walk, R. D. & Gibson, E. J. (1961), A Comparative and Analytical Study of Visual Depth Perception. *Psychological Monographs*, 75(15).

Welch, L. (1940), The Genetic Development of the Associational Structures of Abstract Thinking. *Journal of Genetic Psychology*, 56:175.

Werner, H. (1948), *Comparative Psychology of Mental Development*. New York: International Universities Press, second edition.

Witkin, H. A. et al. (1962), *Psychological Differentiation: Studies of Development*. New York: Wiley.

Zeigler, H. P. & Leibowitz, H. (1957), Apparent Visual Size as a Function of Distance for Children and Adults. *American Journal of Psychology*, 70:106.

CHAPTER 15

The Development of
Scientific Concepts

KENNETH LOVELL

Intelligence is only one aspect of the general biological adaptation of the organism to its environment. In other words, what we humans call intelligence is but one aspect of the over-all adaptation of the individual to his physical, cultural, and social milieu. This is, of course, a central assertion in the theory of Piaget, and is accepted by the writer as there now seems to be much evidence to support this point of view.

From these premises, it would appear that all mathematical and scientific concepts are mental constructions. They originate in the mind of man. As a result of the interaction of the growing human organism with his environment, he elaborates certain concepts, and develops certain forms of thinking that are internally consistent—i.e., logical thought— and that maximize his chances of making his environment meaningful or significant, and of predicting within it. So he constructs the concepts of number, time, volume, and so forth. Man thus looks at the universe through templates that he himself constructs. However poor these may be, without them he would make no sense of his environment at all. Bronowski (1961) echoed a similar point of view when he wrote, "The theories of science are simply maps constructed by the minds of scientists to enable them to make sense of the physical world." Hence the great mental constructs of class, relation, number, length, weight, speed, etc., have their origin in the child-environment interaction, as the organism

407

strives constantly to adapt to its environment and to make it significant. It is, of course, quite true that today the school and the cultural milieu generally aid or retard the child in his attempts to elaborate these concepts, but at some time in the past, men had for the first time to construct these ideas for himself.

The writer has explained elsewhere (Lovell, 1962) that children's concepts do not usually develop suddenly into their final form. Indeed, concepts tend to widen and deepen throughout life, as long as brain and mind remain active and provided that prejudice does not interfere. It should also be noted that both children and adults may develop a concept good enough for working purposes in everyday life—and in the case of the adult, good enough for his professional or technical life—and yet be unable to give a good verbal definition of the concept. On the other hand, teachers and parents in particular are often deceived about the limits of a child's understanding because he can use the appropriate word and yet have little or no idea of the related concept. Generally speaking, three broad stages can be recognized in the development of scientific concepts. First, there is the vague level of ordinary everyday thinking about related events and data; this is the level of general ideas. Second, the concept can be considered at the level of definition, for example, the dictionary definition. Third, the concept becomes highly organized and structured.

It must be stressed that in Piaget's view, action is the basis of thought. He is not, of course, the first to make this point. Children's actions first have to build up systems of mental operations (i.e., actions performed in the mind), and when these become coordinated with one another, children can begin to interpret the physical world. So at one and the same time we have developing an outward adaptation to reality, and a build-up of inner psychic organization that parallels, as it were, the external situation. This is, perhaps, why mathematics gives us our best predictions about events within the matter-energy system.

Piaget is at pains to make clear that experience by itself, i.e., mere environmental stimulation, cannot bring about an increase in mental coordinations. These come into being by the child's actions and perceptions bringing about a reorganization of the psychic structure to give increased adaptation to the new situation, although maturation plays some part. Experience, of course, plays a supporting role in that it is child-environment interaction over the years that builds up a psychic organization at all, and the potential for restructuring it. Further, experience plays a role in that a culture produces certain conceptual frameworks which it values more than others, and so gives the child more opportunities to elaborate the relevant concepts (e.g., mathematical and scientific ones). But children do not learn from immediate experience in the sense of mere observations, or signal input, until there is a build-up of a mental structure that can either appreciate the significance of that experience or be reorganized by it.

NUMBER

THE PROBLEM OF THE BASIS OF THE NATURAL NUMBERS

It is not my intention to open this section with an elaborate discussion of whether the natural numbers have an intuitive or a logical basis. I have discussed this elsewhere (Lovell, 1962, Ch. 2) in simple language; for more advanced treatments of this topic the reader must refer to appropriate texts that deal with the foundations of mathematics. It is sufficient to say that despite the range and power of modern mathematics, the concept of the natural numbers on which the whole edifice rests remains something of a mystery.

The natural numbers are an abstract concept, although there is no doubt that as a concept it is an easier one to attain than the concepts of other numbers (e.g., negative integers or complex numbers). Man's mind has in some way, after examining the phenomena of his environment, derived from it the concept of the natural numbers; the concepts of the other numbers were not constructed out of immediate reality. But how man performs this abstraction, and the exact nature of what it is his mind constructs, is not well understood.

One of the difficulties is that we do not understand the mystery of man's strange faculty for perceiving analogies and formulating categories, and to explain this we coin words like "intuition." There are people who think that at some stage in the development of the normal child, the concept of the natural numbers comes to him as a result of some primitive intuition. From making up and seeing groups of 2, 3, or 4 objects, the child recognizes the inherent twoness, threeness, etc., in number. Actions and perceptions are thus prerequisites in the attainment of the concept of number. Eventually the child can recognize (as the English philosopher

Bertrand Russell long since reminded us) the quality of "twoness" both in a brace of pheasants and in 2 days. When the child comes up against examples of "twoness," "threeness," etc., and is able to exercise a judgment on the related data, he has attained the concept of the natural numbers. While 1, 2, 3, and 4 have their origin in action and group impression, and are the names for these groups, the higher numbers are a substitute in a conceptual way for groups that cannot be known by simultaneous apprehension.

But there are others who think that the child must have a grasp of certain logical concepts before he can understand number. Bertrand Russell, A. N. Whitehead, and Jean Piaget are among these people, although the views of Piaget are somewhat different from those of the other two. It is, however, the views of Piaget that we shall consider, since so many experimental studies on the growth of the concept of number have been based on them. In essence, his thesis is that the child must have available the concepts of *class* and *relation* before the concept of number can be available to him. The concept of class arises out of the child's activities in which he classifies objects; the concept of relation results from his ordering activities. Thus in Piaget's view, the number system results from a fusion of classification and ordering, for the idea of the number 6, say, depends upon the child's grouping in his mind 6 objects to form a class (all of whose elements are equivalent), and upon placing 6 between 5 and 7, that is, in relation.

Dienes (1959) makes a clear distinction between the two points of view that have been sketched above. He distinguishes between *constructive* and *analytic* thinking (cf. Bruner, 1960, pp. 57-58). In the former the person gets an intuition of something not fully understood; this vague perception urges him on to constructive or creative effort to confirm the intuition by logical argument. Concepts are thus built out of some broad general picture without the child's being aware of all possible relationships. In analytic thinking, however, there is an awareness of all possible logical relationships so that concepts are formulated explicitly and exactly before they are used. Dienes' view is that constructive thinking develops before analytic thinking in most people, although both are required in mathematical and scientific studies.

It is not my intention to discuss methods used in helping children to form the concept of number. The various methods that depend on visual perception, the environmental approach, structured materials, etc., have been dealt with by Lovell (1962) and in more detail by Williams (1961, 1963). Instead I will consider some of the experimental evidence which deals with the growth of this concept.

PIAGET'S EXPERIMENTAL STUDIES OF THE GROWTH OF THE CONCEPT OF NUMBER

In the study of the growth of the concept of number, as in the case of the growth of so many other concepts, the world is much indebted to Piaget. It is not, of course, proposed that what the Geneva school has said needs no qualification, but it is true that Piaget and his associates have shed great light on the difficulties the child has in arriving at concepts that educated adults take for granted. The Geneva school starts from the position that the concept of number is not based on images, or the mere ability to use symbols verbally, but on the formation and systemization in the mind of two operations: classification and seriation. Abstraction arises through the child's coming to appreciate the significance of the transformations that take place as he classifies objects, puts them in order of size; also as objects are rearranged to form first one perceptual structure, then another, and so forth. Thus the concepts and the ability to maneuver them in the mind are built from actions involving concrete material, but are independent of the actual materials used. Logical thought must come prior to an understanding of number. What takes place, as Piaget's work shows, is that children's own actions build up a psychic organization, by means of which events in the physical world can be interpreted. When this psychic organization is functioning and in clear control the child behaves quite differently from the way in which he did before. What had baffled him a few months earlier is now self-evident; apparent contradictions and absurdities at which he had not turned a hair can now be explained.

The experiments of the type involving the growth of the concept of number used by Piaget (1952) will be only briefly mentioned here as they are now well known. First a description of the chief "cardinal number" experiments:

(a) Children were asked to match various sets of objects with other sets that would go with them, e.g., eggcups and eggs, vases and flowers. If the child could do this, the experimenter then spread out or closed up one or other of the sets (e.g., the flowers might be bunched), so that the elements of the set (e.g., the eggs) no longer extended over the same area. The child was asked each time: "Are there still the same number?"

(b) The subjects had to put out counters equal in number to a random group or pattern of counters, to a closed figure, or to a row.

(c) Two equal lots of sweets were arranged; first as 4 each to be eaten in the morning and afternoon of that day; then as 1 for the morning and 7 for the afternoon of the next day. The children were asked if they would eat the same number of sweets on each day.

(d) After the subjects had seen a set of, say, 5 red flowers matched to 5 vases, and then the 5 vases matched to another set of 5 blue flowers, they were asked if there were as many red as blue flowers, and if two of the sets were equal to twice the third set.

Three stages of development were observed in the replies of the children. At stage 1 ("global" stage) number could not be conserved. Pupils at this level of development might say that there were fewer flowers when they were bunched together, or that there were more eggs when they were spread out. In experiment (b) they made a rough total guess or tried to copy the figure, and got the number correct only when the figure was a simple and familiar one, such as a square with a counter in the middle. In the experiments involving the sweets, they thought that more would be eaten on the second day as "Seven is such a lot"; while they had no idea of the equivalence of sets. Normal children remain at this stage to about 5 years of age.

Stage 2 is a transitional stage and is found between 5 and 6+ years of age ("intuitive" stage). The child may give correct answers when the eggs or flowers are not too closely bunched or too greatly spread out in (a). In experiment (b) he may be able to reproduce the original pattern correctly, but if the pattern is spread out or otherwise changed, he cannot sustain equivalence. He may also be firm about the equality of one set of flowers in experiment (d), and also of the other set of flowers and the vases, but may be very doubtful about the equality of the two sets of flowers to one another, or may even deny it. However, he may think of checking up by direct matching and so come to the correct answer by trial and error.

But at stage 3 there is a change in the child's responses. This occurs by 7-8 years of age. Logical thought is now available to the child; logical necessity demands that he give the correct answer, and because of this he will stand firm in his replies. He can now shuttle to and fro in his mind between one set of conditions and another, reversibility and compensation are now available to him, and his thinking is becoming divorced from his perceptions. Thus for Piaget his thinking is now at the "concrete operational" stage and he can "think" in relation to real situations. Moreover, Piaget maintains that for the child to be able to establish correspondence in a variety of situations he must have attained the ability to form the concept of a class, from which it follows that the latter ability underpins the development of the concept of number.

But for Piaget another mental operation (i.e., action performed in the mind) is necessary before the concept can be formed. This is the ability to arrange a series of items according to their differences. Up to about 5 years of age the child is unable to make a series of, say, sticks of increasing length; between 5 and 6+ he can put the sticks in order by trial and error, but if a stick is omitted he has difficulty in inserting it into the correct position in the series. It seems that the child is as yet unable to decompose the series in his mind. But from 7 years of age onward the child has reached the stage of operational thinking, so that he can now take the shortest stick, then the next in length, and so on, *knowing* that he will obtain a series of sticks of increasing length. He can now pass through the series of sticks mentally, and in both directions.

For Piaget, when the child is at the third stage and can set up a series, he can find the cardinal number of the class (say 8) coming before the number defined by its ordinal position (9th). If, for example, the sticks mentioned above are "stairs," he can indicate how many "stairs" a doll has climbed when he has reached a certain step on the "staircase." Thus he is said to understand the ordinal and cardinal meanings of number at the same time.

FURTHER EXPERIMENTS RELATING TO THE GROWTH OF THE CONCEPT OF NUMBER

A number of workers have carried out experiments similar to those of Piaget, sometimes using an elaboration of his technique. Hyde (1959), had a multiracial group of Arab, English, Indian, and Somali children in Aden match a number of dolls with a number of toy tin baths. The dolls were taken out and grouped in various ways yielding different perceptual configurations and the child was asked if the number of dolls and baths remained the same. In general, Hyde confirmed the stages given by Piaget. She also noted that all the children at the first two stages could count beyond 6, thus confirming Piaget's view that ability to count is no guarantee that the child has a stable number concept. Hyde also used two experiments to test the growth of the ability to seriate. First, there were a number of sticks out of which the child had to make a "staircase," putting each stick in its "right place." Second, she used 10 cardboard strips each 1-inch wide; the first was 1-inch long and the height of each succeeding strip increased by 1 inch. The subject had to make a staircase from the strips, and by counting along the bottom edge of the strips and getting the position of a given strip (ordinal number), the child could tell—at the third stage—how many of the smallest strips could be made from the given strip (cardinal number). Beard (1957) also carried out similar experiments.

The upshot of these studies was that the stages proposed by Piaget were broadly confirmed, although the studies did not necessarily support the view that children arrive at the cardinal and ordinal aspects of number at the same time. Hyde makes it clear that in her study a number of children who could say how many of the smallest strips were needed to make a bigger one failed to put the strips into correct serial order.

Many other workers have also shown that a child can be at the concrete operational stage of thinking in one test, but not in another. Dodwell (1960, 1961) gave a number of Piaget's tests to 250 Canadian primary-school children between 5 and 8 years old and found the three stages of cognitive development described by Piaget. But there were variations in the type of response from one test situation to another for a given child. Intelligence as measured by a standard group intelligence test was significantly correlated with number concept attainment, as one might well expect, and the correlation coefficient of between .4 and .5 was of the same magnitude as has so often been found in studies involving measured intelligence and concept attainment on Piaget's tests. Williams (1958), using tests of cardination and ordination, also found that some children were clearly at the concrete operational stage on some tests but at a preoperational stage on others; some pupils could appreciate ordinal positions but not cardinal positions. Mannix (1960) likewise showed that educationally subnormal special-school children[1] are not always at the same stage from test to test.

It is not easy to say why the performance of some children varies from test to test. Perhaps some of the test situations are more novel than others, and pupils need time to accommodate to them. Or, to put it rather differently, perhaps logical operations plus sheer experience of that type of situation (familiarity) bring certainty and the correct answer. Perhaps Dodwell (1960, 1961) is correct when he suggests that the variability in stages is a function of learned responses to particular situations without complete assimilation, i.e., a function of learning without adequate response generalization.

We must now turn to the question of the possible linkage between the ability to pass the Piaget type of tests and to make progress in school arithmetic; Hood (1962) has provided useful information on this point. He gave 8 experiments of the type devised by Piaget to 126 children aged 4.9 to 8.7 years in English infant schools. Included in the experiments were: conservation of liquids, equivalence of two sets, invariance of sets, the construction of a series, and the problem of ordinal correspondence. He also got the teachers to rate their pupils on the progress they were making in number, using the following scale:

Grade 1. No number ability of any kind: the child may be able to count but he cannot put out 5 or more objects from a group, or do a simple sum even with counters.

Grade 2. Can put out 5 or more objects from a group.

Grade 3. Child can do simple addition and subtraction with or without counters, orally or in writing.

Grade 4. Child can do simple problems presented verbally or in writing, and also has the skills of grade 2; in short, he can use number with apparently some understanding.

Grade 5. Any combination of number skills beyond that point.

Hood reports that 60% of the children totally or predominantly at stage 1 or 2 in the 8 experiments were at grade 1 or 2 in their arithmetic performance; and 85% of those at stage 1 or 2 were at grades 1, 2, and 3 in arithmetic. On the other hand, 12% of the pupils totally or predominantly at stage 3 in the 8 experiments were only at grade 2 in their per-

---

[1] These are the least able of the English school-educable children. About 0.8% of the school population is found in such schools, their ages ranging from about 8 to 15-16 years.

formance in arithmetic, and 25% of those at stage 3 were at grade 1, 2, or 3 in arithmetic. Clearly, unless one is consistently at the concrete operational stage of thinking on the Piaget type of test, it is almost certain that progress in number work will be poor or limited. At the same time, however, consistent performance at stage 3 on the Piaget type of test does not ensure progress in number; 12% of such pupils had made virtually no progress at all, and a further 13% had made but limited progress. I have also found that older backward children can give correct responses to Piaget's tests and yet make no progress or very limited progress in understanding number.

It is not easy to explain why this is so. Perhaps logical thought is a necessary but not a sufficient condition for number operations. There is no doubt that the ability to pass Piaget's tests develops *pari passu* with the ability to understand number in the majority of 7- to 8-year-olds. Indeed, at this age the ability to perform logical addition, logical multiplication, visual seriation, and the multiplication of asymmetrical transitive relations all develop at around the same time (Lovell, 1962), so there is no doubt of the great increase in the ability of the child to perform logical operations by 8 years of age. Yet the tests devised by Piaget to test the child's concept of number may not in fact do so completely. The tests involve qualitative logic; number and number operations involve a quantitative logic or mathematics. Although we know that mathematics and qualitative logic are closely linked, the exact relationship between them is not known. Indeed, in modern thought, logic is now often regarded as a branch of mathematics with mathematics a higher-order skill than qualitative logic. It is common experience that many people can maintain a good level of logical argument when dealing with qualitative data, yet have been unable to make much progress in mathematics.

Wohlwill (1960) proposes, as a result of an experimental study, that children might pass through three stages in achieving a well-developed number concept. First, a number is responded to wholly on a perceptual basis in the sense that a group of two blue circles can be matched with a group of two blue circles. Second, there is an increase in the extent to which individual numbers can be responded to conceptually. Thus a group of three triangles can be matched with a group of three squares, circles, or dots even when the latter group are of different color from the triangles. Visual perceptual cues are now becoming eliminated. Third, the relationships between numbers begin to be conceptualized. A small group is then conserved in spite of any change in the spatial rearrangement of its elements; there is also a clear grasp of the relationship between the small group and the new group when one element is added or taken away. Wohlwill points out that it seems that mastery of the verbal labels "one," "two," etc., to indicate the numbers 1, 2, etc., plays an important part in passage from the first to the second stage. Likewise the ability to count seems to be of help to the child in moving from the second to the third stage. But an essential requirement here is the ability of the child to conceptualize the relationships between numbers. This crucial issue is the one that we still know too little about.

Wohlwill and Lowe (1962) have provided useful evidence on the effect of selected, systematically manipulated learning experiences believed to be important in the growth of the conservation of number. They studied 72 children with a mean chronological age of 5 years 10 months from predominantly lower-middle-class schools in Worcester, Massachusetts. This age group was selected as one at which most children would still show lack of number conservation, yet would be old enough to be able, potentially, to profit from learning experience. The 72 subjects were divided into 4 groups of 18 according to a predetermined order, the 4 subgroups being closely matched in mean age.

All the subjects first took a verbal pretest of conservation. In essence, the child was presented with 2 rows of counters. There were various changes in the layout of the counters in one of the rows, and each child was questioned about conservation of number. The whole group then undertook a nonverbal pretest of conservation. Each child was presented with a row of 6, 7, or 8 stars mounted on scissorlike slats so that the number of stars could be kept constant but the length of the row quickly altered. The subject had to count the stars and find a "prize" behind a window marked 6, 7, or 8. He could only count on the first trial with each number; he then had to find the correct window on subsequent trials on the basis of the knowledge gained on the first trial and in face of the perceptual changes in the row of the stars. Following these tests each subgroup undertook one of the training programs outlined below, using the apparatus just described:

(a) *Reinforced practice.* If the child was incorrect when selecting the window, he was told to count the stars so as to find out the window he should have chosen. In theory he should learn that if the perceptual dimensions of a set are changed in this situation, its number remains the same.

(b) *Addition and subtraction*. This was similar to the pretest conservation trials, except that on two thirds of the trials, following the subject's initial response after counting, the experimenter either added or subtracted a star before changing the length. By the cumulative effect of adding or subtracting one of the elements, the child might be led to *infer* conservation as the result of a change involving neither addition nor subtraction.

(c) *Dissociation*. The length of the row varied from one trial to the next over a range of four times the smallest length. The subject was asked to count the stars and open the correct window. Each number of stars appeared equally often at each of the different settings of length. This procedure ought to eradicate the influence of an irrelevant but highly visible cue.

(d) *Control*. The conditions were as in (c) above except that the length of the row remained fixed at its maximum length.

All the subjects were then given, as posttests, the original verbal and nonverbal tests of conservation. On the nonverbal test there was an improvement in the number of correct responses from the pre- to the posttest, but the improvement for each of the subgroups was about the same so it was not possible to attribute the improvement to any specific learning situation. None of the procedures was effective in improving the scores on the verbal test demanding conservation. Indeed, it looks as if the nonverbal learning situation favored the development of an essentially empirical rule, such as, "the correct number stays the same after the experimenter lengthens or shortens the row." There was no evidence of logical necessity at work.

It seems, then, that specific experience is not very effective unless the child's thinking is nearly ready for it, i.e., until his psychic organization can be restructured by that experience. Using Piagetian terms, *accommodative* modifications in central processes of the brain take place only when the child encounters circumstances which so match his *assimilated* schemata that he is motivated by them and can cope with them (cf. my introductory comments on the value of experience per se). This problem will be referred to again in connection with Smedslund's work in the section dealing with the growth of the concept of weight.

It should be noted, however, that teachers who believe in what are often called environmental methods of teaching young children would expect to find such negative results from training experiences of the type provided by Wohlwill and Lowe. In the view of such teachers, children are much more likely to come, spontaneously, to an understanding of number in meaningful situations that have personal significance for them (cf. Lovell, 1962, Ch. 4). Thus Churchill (1958) claims an increased understanding of number concepts in young children who had experience of Piaget types of test situations embodied in games that had significance and provided enjoyment.

SUBSTANCE

By the word "substance" is meant "amount of matter," "quantity of matter," or "amount of material," and this section will deal with the growth of the concept of conservation of substance.

Piaget (1953, 1955) has indicated that awareness of the permanence of objects is achieved from the age of 18 months onward in normal children. By that age or soon after, the child has built up a picture of his world as consisting of a number of objects that continue to exist even when they pass from his gaze. The child's play in the home or nursery school is of great value in helping him to understand that he has a certain quantity of, say, sand in a bucket, a tin, or in his hands. During the preschool period he may use words without really understanding their significance, but later he comes to understand that he has "more" or "less" than his friend, or that they may both have the "same." He learns that if he takes water out of a bucket he has "less" in it, and if he adds sand to the heap he has "more." When he has "more" the amount is, usually, visibly larger, and when he has "less," the amount is visibly smaller. But the young child may well say that he has "more" or "less" than he had before if he changes the shape of his heap of sand merely because his visual perceptions are different.

In the previous section it was made clear that logical or internally consistent thinking is not available to the young child. It develops as the young child builds up an inner psychic organization that can account for outward reality. It develops as a function of an internal process which is greatly dependent on activity, so that logical thought is not derived from particular properties of the external world but from the subject placing into relationship, or seeing the significance of, his own activities. Logical thought seems to be aided by opportunities to bring out latent contradictions in a situation, for these may precipitate the process of inner organization.

EXPERIMENTAL STUDIES OF THE GROWTH OF THE CONCEPT OF THE CONSERVATION OF SUBSTANCE

Piaget, as we noted earlier, has repeatedly shown that between 4 and 7 years of age a child's thinking is largely influenced by his perceptions. The autonomous central processes of the nervous system are not yet able to continue, as it were, without immediate signal input. The child thus acts and predicts in terms of previous expectations so that if a body looks larger there must be more substance in it. If a 5- or 6-year-old is shown two balls of plasticine that he recognizes as containing the same amounts, and one is then rolled out to form a sausage, he may well claim that the sausage contains more plasticine "because it is longer." Or he may say that the sausage has less plasticine in it "because it is thinner." When he is a little older the child may claim conservation under some conditions, or at one moment, but will lose the idea under slightly different conditions. But from 7 to 8 onward, according to Piaget, the child comes to the situation with logical thought available to him. The mental operations of reversibility and compensation are now available to the child, and he realizes their interdependence, before they are actually called for, whereas earlier, at the stage of intuitive thinking, they are discovered after the event, if at all (cf. Piaget and Inhelder, 1962).

In a follow-up study by Lovell and Ogilvie (1960), all the children in an English junior school were tested, using the experiment in which one of two equal balls of plasticine was deformed to the shape of a sausage. There were 322 children, whose ages ranged from 7+ to 11+ years. In the youngest class more than one third could conserve substance in the face of very substantial perceptual changes, while in the second class 68%, in the third class 74%, and in the top class 86% could do so. The main reasons given by the conservers were: (a) Reversibility. The child said in effect, "They were the same before." (b) Coordination of relations. The response was of the type, "It's longer but it's thinner." (c) The child said in effect that nothing was "added to" or "taken from" when the ball was rolled into a sausage. In the older children the percentage of replies under (a) and (b) increased and the percentage under (c) decreased. Many of the nonconservers replied "it's more because it's longer" or some variations of this.

Hyde (1959) also repeated this experiment, and obtained similar results from her multiracial population in Aden. Likewise Elkind (1961b), using clay balls, found that by 8-9 years of age three quarters of his sample had a satisfactory grasp of the conservation of substance.

In another typical experiment devised by Piaget, two identical vessels, A and B, are filled to the same height with a colored liquid. Young children of 4 and 5 years of age will agree that the amounts of liquids in the two vessels are the same. This experiment can also be carried out using discontinuous quantities (e.g., beads) in which the subject counts the same number of objects into each of the vessels A and B and agrees that there is the same number of objects in each to begin with. However—to revert to the liquid—if the liquid in vessel A is left alone, but the liquid in B is poured into vessels C and D (identical in size and shape to A and B) so that the amounts of liquid in C and D are the same, the 5- and 6-year-olds deny that the amount of liquid in C and D together is the same as the amount in A. They may notice that there are two vessels and so they say that there is more in C and D than in A, or they notice that the level of liquid is lower and so there is less. Even at 6 to 7 years of age perceptions may decide thought in some experimental situations. For example, in the situation just described above the child may agree to conservation of substance. But if the liquid in B is poured into a wide shallow vessel E, or into a very tall narrow vessel F, so that perceptual differences become very great, then conservation may well be lost again and the child will deny that the amounts of liquid in A and E, or in A and F, are the same. However, from 7 to 8 years of age onward the child has logical thought available to him. He realizes the logical necessity of his answers. With the logical concept of an inverse operation at his disposal, the size or shape of the vessels into which the liquid from vessel B is poured do not put him off; or he may employ the logical concept of compensation or displacement of parts, realizing that what has been lost in one dimension has been gained in another.

A number of studies relating to the conservation of liquids have been carried out, e.g., Hyde (1959) and Beard (1957). Once again the stages in the growth of the concept of conservation of substance were broadly confirmed. But it must be carefully noted that the conception of conservation is not available in all media at the same time. Thus Beard found that among 60 6- to 7-year-olds she tested, some who were nonconservers when comparing balls of plasticine could conserve when water was poured from one vessel to a number of smaller ones. Lovell and Ogilvie (1960) also reported that one third of those who were nonconservers in the plasticine experiment did conserve the amount of rubber in a rubber band when it was stretched. Similarly Elkind (1961a) reported that some materials are easier to compare than others, while Smedslund (1961e) maintained that conservation of continuous quantities is rarely acquired before the conservation of discontinuous quantities.

A very interesting study is that reported by Price-Williams (1961). He worked among illiterate bush children of the Tiv tribe in Central Nigeria, and tested them on the question of conservation using both continuous quantities (earth) and discontinuous quantities (nuts). The results show that the progression of the idea of conservation followed that found in European and other Western children, although there was some doubt about the actual age at which the concept is attained in these children on account of the difficulty of obtaining their ages. Price-Williams also pointed out that conservation was attained more readily for discontinuous quantities (nuts) than for continuous quantities (earth), just as Elkind found liquids more difficult to compare than beads, and Smedslund found conservation of plasticine rarely acquired before conservation of cardboard strips.

The stages in the growth of the concept of conservation of substance proposed by Piaget have been broadly confirmed by a number of workers. Piaget and Inhelder (1959) have shown, and it has been confirmed in considerable measure by Lovell, Mitchell, and Everett (1962), that there is a great increase in the growth of logical structures between 7 and 8 years of age. With these tool structures available to him, the child can elaborate an increasing number of concepts bearing on the physical world of which conservation of substance is but one. But note that this concept is not available to the same child in all situations at once. There are differences in difficulty between continuous quantities, also between continuous and discontinuous quantities for some children. Eventually the logical apparatus is able to operate regardless of the media.

It is possible that inability to conserve substance under spatial changes affects the lives of some children, and some of the least able adults. For example, Lovell and Ogilvie (1960) report that some children were prepared to pay more money for a piece of toffee in one shape than in another. How far or how often children and less able adults are deceived by their perceptions and exploited by unscrupulous adults is unknown. Lovell and Ogilvie also point out the considerable verbal confusion found in children up to about 9 years of age. They frequently confuse such terms as *longer, fatter, shorter, bigger, thicker, smaller*. Two examples taken from the replies of 8-year-old children are:

"It'll get right long and smaller and smaller." By *smaller* it is assumed that the child meant *thinner*.

"It gets thinner and bigger, it doesn't get fat though." By *bigger* it is assumed that he meant *longer*.

The experimenter can read into the child's remarks what he thinks the child meant, but can never be sure that he understands the child correctly.

One further point made by Lovell and Ogilvie (1960, Table 5) must also be noted. They have shown that many nonconservers were clearly aware at the end of the experiment of the equality of the balls at the beginning of the experiment, yet they could draw no conclusion from it. There was an apparent facility to return in thought to the starting point, yet these pupils were unable to appreciate its significance. It thus appears that reversibility of thought is a necessary but not sufficient condition for conservation, and when the concept is fully available, thinking in relation to the concept must have the full properties of the mathematical group.

WEIGHT

The concept of "weight" is based on the experimental fact that all bodies released in a vacuum at the same place on the earth's surface fall with the same acceleration (g), and each therefore has a downward force (mg) acting on it (m being its mass). This force is known as the *weight* of the body. The weight of a body is thus not the same thing as the amount of matter it contains, for the weight of the body will be more at the bottom of a coal mine than at the top of a mountain, although the quantity of matter in it will be the same. This change in weight can be demonstrated by means of a spring balance.

In his preschool days the young child hears adults using words such as "heavy" and "light." But it is not until he has picked up objects and by means of his muscle sense felt the gravitational pull—he does not of course know it as such—that he can have any idea of the meanings of words associated with weight. Thus when attempting to help young children develop a concept of weight, "picking up" of objects or "carrying loads on the back" must come before the use of scales. The child needs much experience of comparing weights using his own muscles.

EXPERIMENTAL STUDIES OF THE GROWTH OF THE CONCEPT OF CONSERVATION OF WEIGHT

Piaget (1961) has proposed that children below a certain age are unable to understand that the weight of a given body is the same regardless of its shape. In a typical experiment carried out by Piaget and his students, a ball of clay was taken and either rolled out to form a "sausage" or cut up into sections. Each child was then asked if the sausage, or the pieces taken together, weighed as much as the original ball. It is claimed that children go through three stages, as in the case of the growth of the conservation of substance. First, they deny conservation ("It is lighter because it is thin now," or "It is heavier because there are more pieces"). Second, there is a transitional stage in which the conservation of weight is agreed to under some conditions, or at one moment, but lost again under slightly different conditions. Third, the child feels the logical necessity of conservation and will support it by argument, this last stage coming usually by 9 to 10 years of age.

Lovell and Ogilvie (1961a) essentially repeated the experiment described above. Two balls of plasticine (R1 and R2) were used. The smaller one (R1) was perceptibly heavier as it was weighted with lead shot. The subjects had first to find out which was the heavier ball using their hands on the scales provided. The larger ball (R2) was then rolled out to form a sausage and each child was questioned about the weight of the sausage and the ball (R1) under these changed conditions. The percentages of children in the first, second, third, and fourth classes of an English junior school (ages 7+ to 11+ years) who were conservers of weight under the conditions of the experiment were, respectively, 4, 36, 48, and 74. The answers given were much as Piaget suggests, and it seems that he is correct in stating that the conservation of weight comes later than the concept of substance. In the children studied by Lovell and Ogilvie, conservation was attained by three quarters of the age group roughly a year later in the case of weight than in the case of substance, while Smedslund (1961a), working with 5- to 7-year-old children, found that among those who could conserve, the conservation of substance invariably preceded that of weight.

Elkind (1961b), using an experiment similar to that reported by Piaget, also found that 75% of his subjects at 9 to 10 years of age were able to conserve weight. The mean IQ (Kuhlmann-Anderson) of his sample was 109, whereas that of the population studied by Lovell and Ogilvie was close to 100 and was drawn from less favored socioeconomic conditions. Furth (1964), however, claims 90% success for 8-year-olds in a nonverbal situation involving conservation of weight. Whether this discrepancy in age between Furth's and other workers' findings is due to the fact that language was not involved and subjects had to make a nonverbal response to signify conservation is not known. It could have been due to the fact that he used only 10 8-year-olds (together with 6-year-olds and deaf children) drawn from a lower-middle-class population.

Very interesting are the results of Goodnow (1962). She studied, among other problems, the growth of the conservation of weight in children aged 10, 11, 12, and 13 years of age in Hong Kong, drawn from extremely varied socioeconomic backgrounds. In her population were Europeans, Chinese from high-ranking Anglo-Chinese schools, Chinese schoolboys of low socioeconomic status, and Chinese schoolboys of low socioeconomic status and "semischooling." She found that schooling, milieu, and socioeconomic status had far less effect on the conservation tasks than had been anticipated, although the groups were far apart on Raven's Progressive Matrices Test. Over-all, however, the replication of the Geneva results was fairly good.

It is thus fair to say that the tests of conservation of weight devised by Piaget have been repeated by other workers and similar results have been obtained. However, as Lovell and Ogilvie have demonstrated, these tests do not tell the whole story. In the course of their study it became apparent that many children who were nonconservers of weight believed that if a lump of plasticine became fatter it became heavier, if it became thinner it became lighter, and that rolling it made it heavier for some pupils and lighter for others.

Having discovered this, Lovell and Ogilvie put further questions to 114 out of the 184 pupils who conserved weight on Piaget's tests of conservation. The questions were of the type:

"What happens to the weight of this one (R_2) if I squeeze it down to the weight of this one (R_1)?"

"What happens to the weight of this ball if I leave it in my cupboard for a time?" "If it gets harder does it get heavier?" Or "Does it get lighter?"

Nearly 70% of the 114 conservers (on Piaget's criteria) believed that weight was linked with hardness, although individuals did not think this equally true of all substances. The percentage of children who thought that the weight of a piece of butter remained the same regardless of hardness was far higher than the percentage of pupils who thought that the weight of a piece of clay remained constant regardless of hardness. The child has much experience of the weight of butter from shopping, and notices it getting harder and softer in the house from changes of temperature, yet although the child frequently plays with plasticine and clay he rarely considers their weight.

The growth of the concept of the conservation of weight is a complicated process. Piaget's conservers seem to be those who exclude "rolling out" or "cutting up" as factors causing weight changes. The journey toward the state where the child considers weight as a concept linked only with amount of substance is a long and tortuous one. The child must learn that hardening, aging, cooling, rolling, squeezing, etc., will not change its weight if the amount of substance is conserved, and, until he has done this, he will not conserve weight in the widest sense. Logical operations may well be available to the child, he may well feel some logical necessity for giving a certain answer, yet he may give a different and incorrect reply because he *believes* that some process the piece of plasticine undergoes may change its weight.

There is no doubt that some of the experiments described here can be, in themselves, learning situations for the child, and it may be that the type of experiments outlined could be undertaken by grade-school children to help them to understand that weight depends only upon the amount of material, at least for practical purposes.

It seems likely that the conservation of substance arises earlier than that of weight partly because it is under immediate visual perception and weight is not, and partly because there are no complicating issues such as hardening, for, in real life, harder objects are usually heavier than softer objects of comparable size. Thus it may be easier for logical operations to operate in relation to substance than in relation to weight. Furthermore, the now known difficulty of the grade-school child in considering the effect of one variable while holding constant the others may help to explain why these other complicating influences are eliminated but slowly. Prolonged and varied experience of the physical world enables logical operations to be made more manifest.

The work of Smedslund (1961a, b, c, d, e) is important from the point of view of whether one can speed up the growth of the conservation of weight in children. He worked with 5- to 7-year-olds in kindergarten schools in Oslo. All were tested for conservation of weight and then divided into three groups reckoned as equal from the point of view of conservation. The first group was presented with a number of pairs of objects, one pair at a time. One member of each pair was deformed, and the child asked if it weighed more, the same, or less than before. After each answer the child placed the deformed object in the balance and checked his prediction. No comment was made, but the immediate weighing of each object provided direct external reinforcement of conservation of weight over deformation. In the case of the second group, a piece of plasticine was added *or* taken away from one of the members of each pair (both of which were the same weight to begin with). The piece stuck on was clearly visible, and a piece taken off was left in full view. The object on which the addition or subtraction had been made was weighed immediately. This provided direct reinforcement of the operations of addition and subtraction. The third group had no training but took the post-tests of conservation of weight along with the other two groups. There was a tendency for the experimental groups to improve more than the control group, but the differences were not significant. It appears that direct training using external reinforcement is not particularly effective in speeding up the growth of conservation.

In another experiment Smedslund (1961b) tested the assumption that if conservation results from a reorganization of the psychic structure it should be practically impossible to extinguish it since it reflects an "inner necessity." A number of 5- to 7-year-old children were given a pretest of conservation of weight. Subjects who showed no traces of conservation of weight were given two training sessions exactly as described above. In the post-test 11 subjects gave correct answers, and these, together with 13 subjects who had already shown complete conservation of weight in the pretest, took part in the extinction trials. This extinction of conservation was attempted by cheating the subjects. One of each member of a pair of objects of the same weight was deformed and a piece of plasticine inconspicuously taken away. The objects were placed on the balance and the lack of conservation noted.

None of the subjects who had acquired conservation during the training sessions showed any resistance to extinction. They rapidly switched back to nonconservation and referred to the perceptual appearance of objects, e.g., "The ball weighs more because it is fatter." These children had learned an empirical rule. But the other pupils, who had acquired the idea of conservation spontaneously or "normally," were more likely to resist and say "You must have lost some on the floor." This experiment, in Smedslund's view, suggests that direct reinforcement does little to help the growth of the conception of conservation.

In further papers, Smedslund (1961c, d, e), dealing mainly with conservation of substance, produced experimental evidence that belief in conservation does not seem to be acquired from the observations of an empirical law, or by external reinforcement. Rather, when a child is repeatedly confronted with situations where the addition/subtraction and deformation schemata come into contact, sometimes one schema is activated more strongly than the other and the weaker one inhibited. At other times both are activated to the same extent and cognitive conflict may occur. When the child encounters circumstances that so match his assimilated schemata that he is motivated by them and can cope with them, then accommodative modifications in central processes take place. The child then provides his solution to the conflict, and it is this reorganization of psychic structure to cope with the conflicting situation that gives stable conservation. Smedslund is convinced that transition from nonconservation to conservation may be induced in situations without external reinforcement. A variety of complex problems presented to the child starts some kind of internal reorganization resulting in sudden "insights." It is at this point that we need greater knowledge of the cognitive processes involved.

VOLUME

The word *volume* may be defined as the *amount of space*. There are three aspects of the concept of volume that must be discussed. First, there is internal volume, for instance, the space inside of a box or cupboard. Second, there is the amount of "occupied" space, for instance, the amount of space taken up by a box, block, or ball. Third, there is displacement volume, the amount of space taken up by an object when it is inserted in a liquid, so that there is an equal volume of water displaced and a corresponding rise in the level of the liquid. All these aspects of the concept must be available to the child before volume is properly understood.

EXPERIMENTAL STUDIES OF THE GROWTH OF THE CONCEPT OF VOLUME
I have already discussed how the growth of the conservation of substance and weight may be studied using plasticine balls. But the Geneva school has maintained that even when the child can conserve the quantity and weight of plasticine when its shape is changed, he will still claim that the substance has expanded or contracted. If a ball of plasticine is immersed in water after having been elongated into a "sausage," he is likely to say, in his own words, that the "sausage" will take up "more space" or "less space." It is not until the age of 12 that the volume of the plasticine is conserved.

Elkind (1961b) replicated this experiment in essence, by just rolling a ball into a sausage, with children in classes from kindergarten to sixth grade. The percentage of correct responses fell well below the figure of 75 even at 11 years of age. In another investigation Elkind (1961c) studied 469 junior and senior high-school pupils drawn from lower-middle-class families. In this experiment the pupils were asked questions about the volume of a piece of clay when it was deformed into a "sausage." They had not only to predict the correct answers but also to justify them. He found that only some 47% of his subjects had an abstract concept of volume. However, since these pupils had to write their answers in books, the results are not strictly comparable with those obtained by pupils who are questioned individually.

Goodnow (1962) studied children in Hong Kong drawn from varied scholastic backgrounds and cultural milieus (see section on Weight). After the subjects had agreed on the equality of two balls of clay, one was inserted in each of two identical jugs which contained water to the same height. The children also agreed that the water rose by the same amount in each jug. One ball was then deformed into a pancake and each child was asked, "If I put the two pieces into the water again, would they push the water up the same or would one push it up higher than the other?" Up to about the age of 12 years the Europeans responded no better than the other groups; thereafter differences in schooling and milieu did seem to favor the Europeans.

In another recent publication Piaget, Inhelder, and Szeminska (1960) have described further experiments that throw light on the growth of the concept of volume. For example, children were shown a solid block representing a house. It had a base 3 cm x 3 cm and was 4 cm high. Other cardboard bases were provided measuring, say, 1 cm x 3 cm, 2 cm x 2 cm, 3 cm x 4 cm, etc., and the subjects were instructed to build another "house" with "just as much room" (i.e., of the same volume) on one or more of the pieces of cardboard. The new "house" had, of course, to have its base confined to the piece of cardboard, and each of the new houses had to be built from 1 cm x 1 cm cubes. In a variation of this experiment the child was asked to build his "house" alongside the model provided. Piaget et al. maintain that the younger children frequently built walls around the original model; they tried to reproduce, not the solid object, but the volume of that object in so far as it consisted of so much empty space bounded by surfaces. This type of response is most important for Piaget's theory; it suggests that the child first thinks of volume in terms of boundary surfaces rather than of space occupied. That is, the child's first concepts involve concepts of topology, and Euclidean characteristics will not be grasped until later.

In another experiment, 36 unit cubes were built into a block measuring 3 cm x 3 cm x 4 cm on the bottom of a vessel containing water. The child noted the extent to which the water rose and he was then questioned whether the water would rise to the same extent if the unit cubes were rearranged as, say, 6 cm x 6 cm x 1 cm. This experiment enabled the tester to study the growth of internal volume, volume as "occupied" space, and complementary or displacement volume.

Piaget, Inhelder, and Szeminska maintain from their experimental evidence that up to 6-6½ years of age there is no understanding at all of conservation of volume. The "house" constructed by the child was usually the same height as the model regardless of the fact that its base was smaller. In other words, the child could pay attention to only one dimension. There was some improvement on this between 6 and 7 years, and between 7 and 8 or 9 years clear progress was made. For example, the subject was then often successful in copying two of the three dimensions of the block, although this was done by inspection and he did not measure the model to get the exact number of unit cubes used until toward the end of this period. Moreover, he could understand the conservation of interior volume, but there was no understanding of "occupied" space in that he did not appreciate that the unit cubes, when rearranged, took up the same space as before. It was not until 11 to 12 years of age that the child realized that the dimensions of the "house" and the block must be the same if their volumes were to be equal. Now, too, he could understand that volume occupied was the same as interior volume, and because of this displacement volume was conserved.

Lunzer (1960) replicated the experiment involving the rearrangement of cubes under water. Many of the stages proposed by Piaget et al. were confirmed, others were not. He did not find that for a period some young children think of volume in terms of what is surrounded by boundary surfaces. Nor did he find that the ideas of infinity and continuity were of great significance to the testees, although in Piaget's view these ideas must be prior to the child's coming to understand "occupied" volume, and prior to the child's discovering the method of calculating volume as a function of length, breadth, and height. Lunzer thinks that the operation of multiplying three linear measurements together to calculate the volume of a cuboid comes through teaching and does not occur spontaneously. He further casts doubt on Piaget's assumption of the priority of concepts of topology over Euclidean concepts in young children, as Lovell (1959) did in another connection.

Lovell and Ogilvie (1961a) have shown that there are other influences affecting the growth of physical volume in junior-school children. In a study of 191 English children aged 7+ to 11+ years involving the growth of their understanding of internal volume, volume occupied, and complementary volume, they found:

(a) Nearly 70% of first- and second-year pupils, and over 90% of third- and fourth-year pupils conserved the internal volume of a block made up of 12 cubes when the blocks were rearranged. It seems that the fact that the cubes were hard and could not be deformed (as in the case of clay) aided conservation. It is not known if there would have been so high a proportion of conservers had there been a greater number of cubes.

(b) When cubes were rearranged in a can of one-gallon capacity, 40% of the first-year pupils and over 80% of the fourth-year pupils conserved "occupied" volume.

(c) Displacement volume is not necessarily understood as soon as is "occupied volume." In this study some 75% of the fourth-year pupils conserved displacement volume when the cubes were rearranged.

(d) Younger children often think that the amount of water displaced from a full can by a cube depends upon the capacity of the can; some children think none would be displaced from a large can. Likewise many children think that a heavier cube will displace more water than a lighter cube, or that the amount displaced depends on whether the cube is suspended or lies on the bottom of the can. These irrelevant factors are only slowly eliminated with age.

The study of Lovell and Ogilvie showed that in the first three years of the junior school only 13 out of 136 pupils had a well-developed concept of physical volume in all its varied aspects. In the fourth year the figure was 21 out of 55. There is no doubt that Piaget et al. are correct in maintaining that the concept of volume does not develop, on the average, until about 12 years of age or more. An understanding of physical volume in a generalized sense is not available to the child until the end of grade school, due, no doubt, to the fact that many irrelevant variables have to be eliminated. The grade-school child finds it very difficult, if not impossible, to consider the effect of one variable while holding the others constant. This is a cognitive skill that develops from 12 years of age onward.

TIME

The nature of time was a subject of speculation among Greek philosophers. Later, Augustine, the Bishop of Hippo, wrote in his *Confessions*,

"For what is time? Who can readily and briefly explain this?" Coming closer to our own age, the philosopher Kant considered that all knowledge begins with experience, although he did not regard the concepts of time and space as being derived in this way. Time in Kant's view was a necessary condition of our ability to experience the physical world and as such it was (with space) an innate, a priori notion, embedded in the mind and independent of experience. His point of view has been increasingly criticized since the late 19th century, and today, time and space must be regarded as mental constructs that have to be learned (cf. Whitrow, 1961).

Time can be regarded as the abstract of all possible sequences and, as we shall see, it takes some years for the child to make the abstraction and elaborate the concept, although his vocabulary of time words may be greatly in advance of his understanding. But when the necessary abstraction is made the child can coordinate, in his mind, instants and intervals, although he is not conscious of this coordination as such.

TIME PERCEPTION

It is now realized that the relationship between percepts and concepts is a very complex one. In ways little understood, perception and action lead to concepts, and this is as true of the concepts of time as of any other concept. E. G. Boring (1936) has suggested that time perception has five bases. In his view the child: (a) gets some perception of succession, or how stimuli follow one another, as, for example, when he runs his fingers over the teeth of a comb at different rates; (b) acquires some perception of continuity, as when he notes some action continuing until it stops, e.g., a slowly moving wheel; (c) obtains some idea of temporal length from the differing perceptions involved in, say, the playing of a long and a short musical note; (d) learns to respond to the environmental signals of the "present," such as the feelings of hunger associated with an empty stomach, or a pain; (e) acquires the ability to perceive patterns of successive stimuli; this ability to feel rhythm, and to respond rhythmically, may have a physiological basis.

PRIMITIVE AND EARLY CHILDHOOD CONCEPTS OF TIME

In developed countries it has long been the practice to use the category

of astronomical time. But as Sorokin and Merton (1937) point out, social phenomena have been adopted as a frame of reference in some societies, these often being fixed by the rhythm of collective life. Thus the
inhabitants of Madagascar used to speak of doing something "in the fry-
ing of a locust" (i.e., a moment) or "in a rice-cooking" (about half an
hour). Again, it seems that some peoples have only a limited linear scale
of time at their disposal. For example, Evans-Pritchard (1940) points
out that the Nuer people have words for this year, last year, and the year
before. But they have no word equivalent to "time" in Western languages,
and historical time, in the sense of a sequence of outstanding events of
significance to a tribe, goes back probably no more than 50 years. In such
cultures the remote past remains indissolubly intertwined with mythology.

The words used in other primitive societies to express time reflect no
more than the main events in an individual's day. When working with
cattle the main events in the day might divide it into time divisions such
as *watering time, milking time.* Or the year might be arranged in terms
of important events, e.g., *planting time, harvest time.* Primitive man
uses, as it were, moments of time embedded in a continuum of action.

In the case of the young child, too, time is marked off by isolated and
distinct actions and happenings which are frequently accompanied by
strong feelings. At first, time is mixed up with impressions of duration
arising out of the earliest attempts at the coordination of retroactions
and anticipations, which in turn are linked with expectation, effort, desire, failure, success, and satisfaction. Thus, according to Werner (1957),
when a 2-year-old uses the words "all done," satisfaction is expressed
about some activity just completed. Likewise when he uses the word
"bath," he indicates a wish in which the time element of the near future
is implied. Time is again embedded in a series of events—in a continuum
in which time and space are not yet differentiated.

Slowly, over the years, the adult concept of time is constructed and
elaborated. Exactly how this is done we do not know. But when this happens the child can put the events in which he is personally involved into
closer and closer relationship with events in the external world. Time is
then the abstract of all possible sequences; it becomes universal and the
same for everyone, and the sequence of a child's life is then inserted, as
a lived sequence, into a whole series of events which constitute the history of his environment.

STUDIES INVOLVING SOME ASPECTS OF THE CONCEPT OF TIME

Although we are primarily concerned with the growth of the concept of time in a scientific sense, we must also note in passing what may be called the emergent experience of temporality, of things in flux and change, of a gradual reaching out into future and past; also of the acquisition of a time vocabulary and the growth of understanding of clock and calendar.

To about the age of 5, time and space are confounded in the child's mind; time tends to be tied to certain objects or events. But from that age onward, the ordering of events into earlier or later begins to emerge so that the past is structured into a succession of events. It must be stressed, however, that the learning of time words precedes the child's grasp of time relationships and his verbalizations are a very unsafe guide to his understanding. Ames (1946) found that the understanding of time words and their use came in a fairly uniform sequence which was roughly the same for all children, although the age at which a particular child could understand or use a specific term varied. Thus children (in the U.S.A.) were able to use the terms *morning* and *afternoon* by 4 years of age, knew what day it was by about 5 years, and could tell the time by 7 years of age. Note, however, that is was found that the child could use terms like *wintertime* and *lunchtime* before the word *time* itself. Such studies suggest that a vocabulary of time words is built up by association. Thus when it is light it is *day*, when it is snowing it is *winter*, and when the corn is cut it is *autumn*. While it is of the greatest importance for the over-all development of the child that he learn the correct use of these words, these associations do not ensure that he has much understanding of time.

Springer (1952) studied 89 children aged 4 to 6 years who were attending a kindergarten. They had received no school instruction in the tasks set although they had had incidental experiences and informal instruction in the home. The following general sequence of development emerged: (a) to such a question as "What time do you have lunch?" he replies at first with a descriptive term like, "Afternoon"; or he describes a sequence of events, "After lunch I sleep and then go home." Next an unreasonable time is given; then a reasonable but inaccurate time; and finally accurate time; (b) the child can tell the clock first by whole hours, then by halves, and finally by quarters; (c) he can set the hands of a clock to whole hours, half hours, and quarter hours; (d) he can explain why a clock has two hands.

It must be noted that the children studied by Springer came from above-average socioeconomic groups; in children from less favored backgrounds the sequence may be delayed.

One of the early pioneering studies of the growth of the child's understanding of time was that of Oakden and Sturt (1922). Much of their study was replicated and mainly confirmed by Bradley (1948) some 25 years later. Sturt's (1925) work showed that although most children at 6 years of age realized that it was the same day of the week all over a small nearby town, only some 86% of the 10-year-olds realized that it was the same day in all English towns. Both studies presented children with the following type of problem: Columbus lived in 1492; (a) Would your mother be alive then? (b) Would your grandmother? Both researches showed that (a) is not understood by 75% of children before 7 years and (b) is not understood by the same proportion of pupils before 9 years. It seems that children's time perspective below the age of 9 is very shallow, becoming nebulous beyond the span of a generation or so. Bradley suggests that by 6 years of age time can be related to personal experience, e.g., morning, afternoon, and the child's own age. By 8 years there is increasing understanding of the week and of the time words used in the calendar, the tendency being for growth to occur outward, i.e., week, month, year. Beyond that age there is a gradual extension of an understanding of time in relation to both space and duration; e.g., time elsewhere, and time since the holidays.

Many researches in this field have been exclusively concerned with the child's ability to handle conventional time units or his ability to tell the time. As we have seen already, conventional time units can be handled at the purely verbal level by the young child without any understanding of the concept of time, while telling the time, although a very important social asset, involves no more than dial reading. Other studies have dealt with the passage of time in relation to changing events. One such study, in a verbal abstract setting, was quoted by Fraisse (1957). Michaud asked over 1500 children between 5 and 10 years of age questions of the type: "What happens to time when one puts the clock forward in spring, jumping suddenly from 11 P.M. to midnight?"; also "Does this make you older?" These questions are more difficult for the child than those in which he has to show his understanding of time in relation to events taking place before him, and it is to the latter type of task that we now turn, for this shows the elaboration of the concept of time in its scientific sense.

THE EXPERIMENTAL STUDY OF THE GROWTH OF THE CONCEPT OF TIME

Piaget (1946a) used simple experimental situations in which actions were sometimes performed in front of children, or they had to engage in some action themselves. As we have already said, time and space form a whole for the child at first, and some of the experiments used by Piaget forced the child to differentiate between them. Seven experiments of the type originated by Piaget will be very briefly mentioned here, as these have been reported by the writer (Lovell and Slater, 1960).

1. A container of water had an outlet tube with a control valve; the tube past the valve divided into two branches forming an upside-down Y. The flow of water in each tube was the same, and because of the valve the water both started and stopped in each branch at the same time. Two empty glasses of different widths were placed under the two outlets, and the water flowed until the narrower glass was full, the wider glass remaining only partly full. Lovell and Slater carried out this and the other experiments with 10 children of each age from 5 to 9 years in English primary schools. These children were picked by their teachers as being average or above average in attainment at each age level. It was not until 9 years of age that 7 out of the 10 children admitted that the water flowed into both vessels for the same length of time. Among the younger groups most pupils thought that the water flowed into the narrower vessel for a longer period.

2. Two colored dolls raced across a table. Both started together and stopped together, but the red doll started from behind the yellow doll and finished up in advance of it. Although two thirds of even the 5-year-olds admitted that the dolls started at the same time, it was not until 7 years that almost all understood that the dolls did not travel the same distance, while even at 9 years only about half of the responses were correct to the questions "Did the dolls run for the same time?"; "Why?" There was a decrease with age in the number who thought that the yellow doll took more time.

3. Water was siphoned from a short, wide vessel into a tall, narrow one, both vessels having the same volume. The wide vessel was full at the beginning of the experiment. It was not until 9 years of age that 7 out of

10 children understood that the water flowed out of the wide vessel for the same time that it flowed into the tall narrow one. Younger children thought that water flowed into the tall, narrow vessel for a longer period than it flowed out of the short, wide vessel.

From these three experiments it was found that an accurate perception of simultaneity came before an understanding of the equality of synchronous intervals. Indeed, the ability to make the necessary coordination of instants and intervals was not generally shown before 9 years of age. Previously one aspect of the situation was centered on at the expense of other aspects, although it must be made clear that the actual apparatus used, or the experimental situation, affected the child's replies to some extent.

Experiments 4 and 5 dealt with the growth of the understanding of age. This necessarily demands the sequential ordering of events. In Experiment 4 the subjects were shown a picture of a walnut tree and an elm tree, the pictures being on separate cards. The walnut tree had many spreading branches but was short; the elm tree was tall and had few branches. Although one could not tell the age of the trees from the photographs, most of the younger children claimed that the elm tree was older because it was taller. Not until 8 years of age did the number of children giving this response drop to 3 out of 10.

In Experiment 5 the subjects were shown 6 pictures of an apple tree and 5 pictures of a pear tree, in various stages of growth. The fifth picture of the pear tree showed a taller tree than the sixth picture of the apple tree. The children were told that the apple tree was planted 1 year before the pear tree, and they were asked which was the older tree this year (i.e., at the last picture). At 5 years of age 9 out of the 10 children said the pear tree was older and nobody selected the apple tree, whereas at 8 years of age, 10 selected the apple tree and no one the pear tree. Piaget was undoubtedly correct in maintaining that young children judge age by size, and it is not until events can be ordered in sequence, and happenings and intervals coordinated, that age becomes independent of immediate visual perception.

Experiment 6 asked the child to compare the time spent with eyes closed and arms folded with a period of equal duration (1 minute) spent looking at a picture book; Experiment 7 asked him to compare the time spent drawing lines rapidly, with a period of equal duration (1 minute) spent drawing lines carefully and slowly using a ruler. Although the youngest tended to think that the period spent sitting unoccupied was longer than that spent looking at the book, and also that the period spent drawing lines rapidly was longer than that spent drawing them slowly and carefully, there was a clear improvement with age in the ability to recognize that two intervals may be of the same duration no matter how they are spent. Thus as children get older they can increasingly differentiate between objective and subjective time, and in both of these experiments half of the age group was able to do so by 9 years.

The work of Lovell and Slater suggests that the concept of time is available to the majority of children by 9 years of age, rather than 8 years of age as suggested by Piaget. Further, Lovell's work suggests that in educationally subnormal pupils the concept of time is still developing between 12 and 15 years of age and that many of these children will leave school with a poorly developed concept of time.

VELOCITY

In this section the words velocity and speed are used interchangeably, and the problem of vector and secular quantities is ignored.

Listening to the chatter of young children leads one to believe that their first ideas of the words *faster* and *slower* are built up by association. Thus if one car passes another the 3- or 4-year-old hears his father say that the overtaking car is going *faster*. If a child's friend passes him in a race he knows that he is running *slower* than his friend because he has heard other people say so. For the young child the words *faster* and *slower* denote the movement of one of the objects when there is a change of relative position. He does not attach the same significance to these words that the high-school pupil does, namely that of a distance-time relationship. He cannot understand the word *speed* as the older person does, for as yet he has no concept of time. But he may well use the words *faster, slower,* or *speed*, and once again show us that he can use words in a correct context and yet deceive us about his actual degree of understanding.

EXPERIMENTAL STUDIES OF THE GROWTH OF THE CONCEPT OF VELOCITY
It is to Piaget (1946b) that we owe a great debt for devising many ingenious experiments that can be used for studying the growth of children's understanding of movement and velocity. He has told us that he was asked by Einstein in 1928 if a child's first ideas of velocity included

an understanding of it as a function of distance traveled and time, or whether his ideas were more intuitive and primitive. Piaget and his students thereafter devised many experiments that have thrown light on this question.

Lovell, Kellett, and Moorhouse (1962) have repeated a number of experiments of the same general type with English children. Ten children from each of the age groups 5 to 10 inclusive were selected by their teachers as being representative of English primary-school children except that very slow learners were omitted. The experiments and the results are now briefly discussed.

1. (a) A toy railway engine (blue, for example) set off from a point behind that of a second engine (red), and both, starting at the same time, arrived together at the final point so that the blue engine caught up with the red.

(b) The colors of the engines were changed to prevent any carry-over effect, and the engines then ran as before except that the first engine (starting further away) did not quite catch up to the second before both stopped at the same instant.

(c) After changing the colors of the engines again, the experiment was carried out a third time. On this occasion the first engine (starting further away) clearly overtook the second before both stopped simultaneously.

After each experiment the child was asked which engine had traveled faster and why he thought this was so. In the third experiment (but not in the first two) no fewer than 17 out of the 20 5- and 6-year-olds gave the correct answer, although only 4 could logically justify their decision. Similarly, 38 out of 40 educationally subnormal special-school children aged between 10 and 15 years gave the correct answer to Experiment 1(c) but only 6 could justify it. Here indeed is strong evidence that the child up to 6 years at least (and to 15 in the least able of the educable children) thinks of faster and slower in terms of a change in relative positions. This probably arises partly because of the manner in which the child first gets some understanding of words connected with speed, and partly because the idea of position, or order in space, seems easier to grasp than the concept of intervals on the time continuum.

2. (a) Two cars moved along concentric circles of different diameters, the cars always keeping the same relative position.

(b) Between two points A and B there were two paths. One was straight, the other went from A to B via a third point C that was well away from the direct path AB. Two cars left A at the same time, one traveled along the straight path, the other went from A to B via C. They arrived at B simultaneously.

(c) A car ran along a straight line AB and another car along a "wavy" line CD. The ends A and C were in alignment, as were the ends B and D.

(d) A toy railway engine passed through each of two tunnels PX and QY, tunnel PX being nearly 40% longer than QY, and the ends X and Y being in alignment. The engines entered ends P and Q together, and stopped simultaneously with their fronts just emerging from the ends X and Y.

In each of these four experiments the child was carefully questioned about whether both cars or trains traveled at the same speed. The results were consistent and unequivocal; it was not until 9 years of age that three quarters of the age group could give the correct response and justify it logically.

Before Experiment 2 (b) was carried out as described above, the apparatus was considered by the child in the following situation. He was told that cars would leave A for B at the same time, one traveling by each road and both traveling at the same speed. The question which each child had to answer was "Will the two cars arrive at B at the same time?" No fewer than 24 of the 30 5-, 6-, and 7-year-olds gave a correct answer to this question and justified it by such responses as "This car will arrive first because the road is shorter." Yet only 4 of those same 30 children could answer the questions posed in Experiment 2 (c) correctly. Hence Piaget's view is clearly confirmed that young children are limited to affirming that, at equal speeds, the journey recognized to be longer will take more time. A child's correct forecast that a longer distance takes more time than a shorter one, at equal speeds, is no guarantee that he has a concept of speed in the sense of distance per unit time.

THE GROWTH OF THE CONCEPT OF RELATIVE VELOCITY

To study the growth of the concept of relative velocity the following apparatus was used. A wooden frame supported an endless ribbon that could be moved across the child's field of view; a handle allowed the speed of the ribbon to be regulated and kept constant. Attached to the ribbon were 6 cardboard cyclists, the distances between the cyclists being equal. Parallel to this ribbon (and between the ribbon and the child) a taut string carried a small figure representing an observer who counted the bicycles as they passed him. The observer could be moved at various speeds either in the same direction as the cyclists or in the opposite direction.

By a carefully thought out technique (based on the work of Piaget) it was possible to show that roughly three quarters of the 10-year-olds understood relative speed and could give an excellent interpretation of the relativity of speeds.

Over-all, it can be said that the concept of velocity arises in ordinary English primary-school children by 9 years of age, a year later than the age suggested by Piaget for children in Geneva. Relative velocity was found to be understood by the majority of English 10-year-olds compared with an average age of 9 years 10 months suggested by Piaget. The performance of educationally subnormal special-school children was scarcely equal to that of the 7- to 8-year-olds when the whole range of experiments was considered. It seems that even at the age of school-leaving in Great Britain, the majority of these children have a very limited understanding of speed in the sense of distance per unit time.

BIBLIOGRAPHY

Ames, L. B. (1946), The Development of the Sense of Time in the Young Child. *Journal of Genetic Psychology*, 68:97-125.

Beard, R. (1957), *An Investigation of Concept Formation Among Infant School Children*. Unpublished doctoral dissertation, University of London Library.

Boring, E. G. (1936), Temporal Perception and Operationism. *American Journal of Psychology*, 48:519-522.

Bradley, N. D. (1948), The Growth of the Knowledge of Time in Children of School Age. *British Journal of Psychology*, 38:67-78.

Bronowski, J. (1961), *Science and Human Values*. London: Hutchinson.

Bruner, J. S. (1960), *The Process of Education*. Cambridge: Harvard University Press.

Churchill, E. M. (1958), The Number Concepts of the Young Child. *Researches and Studies*, 17:34-49, 18:28-46. University of Leeds Institute of Education.

Dienes, C. (1959), The Growth of Mathematical Concepts in Children Through Experience. *Educational Research*, 2:9-28.

Dodwell, P. C. (1960), Children's Understanding of Number and Related Concepts. *Canadian Journal of Psychology*, 14:191-205.

——(1961), Children's Understanding of Number Concepts. *Canadian Journal of Psychology*, 15:29-36.

Elkind, D. (1961a), The Development of Quantitative Thinking: A Systematic Replication of Piaget's Studies. *Journal of Genetic Psychology*, 98:37-46.

DEVELOPMENT OF SCIENTIFIC CONCEPTS 443

——(1961b), Children's Discovery of the Conservation of Mass, Weight and Volume: Piaget Replication Study II. *Journal of Genetic Psychology*, 98:219-227.
——(1961c), Quantity Conceptions in Junior and Senior High School Students. *Child Development*, 32:551-560.
Evans-Pritchard, E. E. (1940), *The Nuer*. Oxford: Oxford University Press.
Fraisse, P. (1957), *Psychologie du Temps*. Paris: Presses Universitaires de France.
Furth, H. G. (1964), Conservation of Weight in Deaf and Hearing Children. *Child Development*, 35:143-150.
Goodnow, J. J. (1962), *A Test of Milieu Effects with Some of Piaget's Tasks*. Unpublished Memoranda, George Washington University.
Hood, H. B. (1962), An Experimental Study of Piaget's Theory of the Development of Number in Children. *British Journal of Psychology*, 53:273-286.
Hyde, D. M. (1959), *An Investigation of Piaget's Theories of the Development of the Concept of Number*. Unpublished doctoral dissertation, University of London.
Lovell, K. (1959), A Follow-up Study of Some Aspects of the Work of Piaget and Inhelder on the Child's Conception of Space. *British Journal of Educational Psychology*, 29:104-117.
——(1961a), A Study of the Conservation of Weight in the Junior School Child. *British Journal of Educational Psychology*, 31:138-144.
——(1961b), The Growth of the Concept of Volume in Junior School Children. *Journal of Child Psychology and Psychiatry*, 2:118-126.
——(1962), *The Growth of Basic Mathematical and Scientific Concepts in Children*. New York: Philosophical Library.
——, Kellett, V. L. & Moorhouse, E. (1962), The Growth of the Concept of Speed: A Comparative Study. *Journal of Child Psychology and Psychiatry*, 3:101-110.
——, Mitchell, B. & Everett, I. R. (1962), An Experimental Study of the Growth of Some Logical Structures. *British Journal of Psychology*, 53:175-188.
—— & Ogilvie, E. (1960), A Study of the Conservation of Substance in the Junior School Child. *British Journal of Educational Psychology*, 30:109-118.
—— & Slater, A. (1960), The Growth of the Concept of Time: A Comparative Study. *Journal of Child Psychology and Psychiatry*, 1:179-190.
Lunzer, E. R. (1960), Some Points of Piagetian Theory in the Light of Experimental Criticism. *Journal of Child Psychology and Psychiatry*, 1:191-202.
Mannix, J. B. (1960), The Number Concepts of a Group of E. S. N. Children. *British Journal of Educational Psychology*, 30:180-181.
Oakden, E. C. & Sturt, M. (1922), The Development of the Knowledge of Time in Children. *British Journal of Psychology*, 12:309-336.
Piaget, J. (1946a), *Le développement de la Notion de Temps chez l'Enfant*. Paris: Presses Universitaires de France.
——(1946b), *Les Notions de Mouvement et de Vitesse chez l'Enfant*. Paris: Presses Universitaires de France.
——(1952), *The Child's Conception of Number*. London: Routledge and Kegan Paul.
——(1953), *The Origin of Intelligence in the Child*. London: Routledge and Kegan Paul.
——(1955), *The Child's Construction of Reality*. London: Routledge and Kegan Paul.
——(1961), *Les Mécanismes Perceptifs*. Paris: Presses Universitaires de France.
—— & Inhelder, B. (1959), *La Genèse des Structures Logiques Elémentaires*. Neuchâtel: Delachaux and Niestlé.

—— & —— (1962), *Le Développement des Quantités chez l'Enfant.* Neuchâtel: Delachaux and Niestlé, second edition.
——, —— & Szeminska, A. (1960), *The Child's Conception of Geometry.* London: Routledge and Kegan Paul.
Price-Williams, D. R. (1961), A Study Concerning Concepts of Conservation of Quantities among Primitive Children. *Acta Psychologica,* 18:297-305.
Smedslund, J. (1961a), The Acquisition of Conservation of Substance and Weight in Children—II. *Scandinavian Journal of Psychology,* 2:71-84.
——(1961b), The Acquisition of Conservation of Substance and Weight in Children—III. *Scandinavian Journal of Psychology,* 2:85-92.
——(1961c), The Acquisition of Conservation of Substance and Weight in Children—IV. *Scandinavian Journal of Psychology,* 2:153-155.
—— (1961d), The Acquisition of Conservation of Substance and Weight in Children—V. *Scandinavian Journal of Psychology,* 2:156-160.
——(1961e), The Acquisition of the Conservation of Substance and Weight in Children— VI. *Scandinavian Journal of Psychology,* 2:203-210.
Sorokin, P. A. & Merton, R. K. (1937), Social Time. *American Journal of Sociology,* 42:615- 629.
Springer, D. (1952), Development in Young Children of an Understanding of Time and the Clock. *Journal of Genetic Psychology,* 80:83-96.
Sturt, M. (1925), *The Psychology of Time.* London: Routledge.
Werner, H. (1957), *Comparative Psychology of Mental Development.* New York: International Universities Press, revised edition.
Whitrow, G. J. (1961), *The Natural Philosophy of Time.* London: Nelson.
Williams, A. A. (1958), Number Readiness. *Educational Review,* 11:31-45.
Williams, J. D. (1961, 1963), Teaching Arithmetic by Concrete Analogy. *Educational Research,* 3:112-125, 163-192; 5:120-131.
Wohlwill, J. F. (1960), A Study of the Development of the Number Concept by Scalogram Analysis. *Journal of Genetic Psychology,* 97:345-377.
—— & Lowe, R. C. (1962), Experimental Analysis of the Development of the Concept of Number. *Child Development,* 33:153-167.

CHAPTER 16

The Perception of Time by Children

"... you'd only have to whisper a hint to time, and round goes the clock
in a twinkling!"
—*Lewis Carroll*

SANFORD GOLDSTONE

JOYCE LEVIS GOLDFARB

Human perception is the aspect of behavior that involves the mysterious
translation of sensory information into conceptual experience. Energetic
configurations of an outside world assault the receptors of various sense
modalities; after a short trip centrally these inexplicit neural messages
dramatically emerge as auditory, visual, tactual, olfactory, gustatory, and
kinesthetic images which are alleged to represent the essence of the stimulus characteristics in the form of ideas, and which provide the basis for
thinking. These perceptions begin life as little more than meaningless
energies with stimulus potential only because man's nervous system is endowed with specific stimulus-defining characteristics. It is the organism
that selects or rejects an input as a stimulus, and it is the organism that
gives the stimulus dimensions, properties, and attributes. After a stimulus
has become a stimulus through acceptance and reception, it proceeds
through a rapid but complex process that leads to the emergence of a
perceptual experience. This perception is a conceptual designation of
the integration of all attributes of the stimulus, the stimulus context, the

Supported by Grant MH 01121 from the United States Public Health Service. The
experiments were conducted at St. John's School, Houston, Texas, and the authors would
like to acknowledge the cooperation of the headmaster, staff, parents, and students.

residual effects of previous encounters with similar stimuli, and the state of the organism (Helson, 1947, 1959, 1964). A person perceives a configuration or organization stabilized by constancies and adapted within the frame of reference of a stimulus context and conceptual remnants of past experience. The perception is thus a remarkable artistic creation far removed from the simple, meaningless signal that reached a receptor, and this perception reflects the nature of the organism; it is relevant to the nature of the outside world only to the extent that it permits prediction and survival (Goldstone, 1962). The consensual predictive aspects of perception permit man the luxury of projecting a *reality* beyond the point of reception and portray the image of an outside world as if that were the way it looked, sounded, felt, tasted, or smelled. Radiant energy beyond the visible spectral band and vibrations beyond the auditory frequency are not part of the perceptual world and are excluded from most people's reality. Although it has been shown (Black and Bevan, 1960; Goldstone, Goldfarb, Strong, and Russell, 1962) that signal intensities below detection influence the judgment of supraliminal intensities, these weak stimuli are not accepted as perceptions. It is clear that perceptions depend upon what the perceiver is capable of doing to or with the stimulus, and that the perception tells us more about the nature of the organism than about the mysterious agent from the outside world that acted as a trigger.

A stimulus is a stimulus because it is capable of acting upon the organism to produce a change or a response; it becomes a perception with quality when the organism can define it conceptually as, for example, a light or sound. When a person perceives visual or auditory form, he is in fact seeing or hearing the prepotent characteristics of his species and to a limited extent his own uniqueness within the framework of these characteristics. There is nothing blue about a 450 mμ light, and indeed it is not light at all; *blue light* is a perceptual response reflecting a complex translation of radiant energy at a specific point along the spectral band.

So it is with time, one of the most complex perceptual abstractions derived from a sensory attribute. Man's nervous system is endowed with the capacity to resolve stimuli into the temporal properties of succession and duration, and man's perceptual capacities have permitted him to harness this basic attribute into conceptual and communicable experiences. The temporal properties of the world are viewed as realities, but, like *blue light,* they are perceptual abstractions endowed to stimuli by the characteristics of man. The remarkable ability of people to behave as delicate, accurate, and precise timepieces and their capacity to adapt to and act upon the temporal properties of their environment represents one of the most fundamental gifts bestowed upon the human species, a gift whose importance has been acknowledged but taken for granted; a gift that is part of every human function but has been neglected in man's attempt to learn about his nature through the methods of science. While it has been noted that the perception of time is related to man's intelligence (Terman, 1916), personality (Baer, Waukasch, and Goldstone, 1963), and social status and competence (Goldstone, Boardman, Lhamon, Fason, and Jernigan, 1963), relatively little is known about this perceptual process; while it is recognized that this essentially human capacity to perceive time directly is one of the first mental functions to be impaired by psychopathology (Lhamon, Goldstone, and Goldfarb, in press), intoxication (Bromberg, 1934; Goldstone, Boardman, and Lhamon, 1958a), and metabolic dysfunction (Kleber, Lhamon, and Goldstone, 1963), the works of the human clock remain a mystery; while parents, educators, and child psychologists repeatedly observe stages in the developmental process toward the growth of the young timepiece, very little work has been accomplished regarding time perception by children. Weber (1933) surveyed the area more than 30 years ago and observed that the questionnaire method may provide valuable information about the development of temporal concepts but that further understanding of time perception required the more precise methods of the psychological laboratory. However, in a recent review of experimental methods of studying perception in children, Gibson and Olum (1960) listed only three references to laboratory investigations of the development of time perception (Fraisse and Orsini, 1958; Fraisse and Vautrey, 1952; Smythe and Goldstone, 1957). It is likely that the neglect of an area of study that represented a primary subject for investigation by the pioneers of psychological research (Nichols, 1891; Vierordt, 1868) was due to the scarcity of effective methods and theories as well as to the difficulty in developing timing devices of the accuracy and precision necessary to compete with the human clock. Fortunately there is evidence to suggest that these limitations have been partially corrected and there is renewed activity in the experimental psychology of time perception (Fraisse, 1963; Frankenhaeuser, 1959; Lhamon, Goldstone, and Goldfarb, in press; Wallace and Rabin, 1960).

Anecdotal reports, phenomenological accounts, and literary descriptions by naturalistic observers, philosophers, and psychoanalysts provide the antecedent raw materials for systematic scientific study but cannot replace tedious laboratory dissection and synthesis of the human timepiece. The scientific study of time perception requires the exploitation of the methods of psychophysics with its attention directed toward control of the stimulus and response conditions within this field of study. While it is acknowledged that one might approach the problem of time perception from a variety of points of view, this presentation will focus upon psychophysical methodology as a neglected but available and fruitful point of departure. Indeed, it is likely that the sensory attributes and the perceptual process can be explored best with the rigorous procedures provided by the psychophysical tradition but rarely used in developmental psychology.

If the present chapter were entitled "The *Conception* of Time by Children" the authors would encounter little difficulty filling these pages with agreements and disagreements concerning the developmental aspects of the use and understanding of temporal language. Much has been written about concept formation, use, and comprehension from the standpoint of growth and development, but perception has been forgotten. Somewhere along the line people interested in time and children lost the stimulus and the conditions of stimulation and focused attention upon the concept or linguistic unit as if it could be separated from the perceptual process. An adequate understanding of the development of temporal conceptual behavior requires the study of time perception which in turn demands attention to stimulus conditions in the psychophysical tradition. In this exposition we will discuss the temporal nature of life with particular attention to the developmental aspects of time perception, and will survey available knowledge regarding children's time concepts and perception. Two experiments will be reported in detail to demonstrate the kind of data that can be obtained from psychophysical studies with children, and to highlight the feasibility of, and in fact the necessity for, such research in the quest for knowledge about the perception of time by children.

THE TEMPORAL NATURE OF LIFE

Life exists within a medium of successive moments, and all creatures on earth must adjust to the temporal properties of their surroundings for the sake of survival. There is no escape from time, and organisms are variously constituted to meet their inevitable struggle with sequence and order, interval and duration. Most must accept a fate of passive enslavement, but the human species is committed to exploit its equipment in eternal combat to master time and gain control of its destiny. The capacity of people to harness time and calibrate their temporal nature with social units permits them access through the cobblestones of history onto the superhighways of the future. All mechanical timepieces are extensions of the remarkably sensitive and delicate human clock whose temporal resources have been dedicated to the development of the complex social transactions which define the essence of humanity.

Man's perceptual world is a temporal world; his reality is a temporal reality. All perceptions are immediately and automatically translated within the temporal contexts of succession and duration, and assigned a place in the diary of personal and social history. Although no perception is without a temporal component, it is the capacity of people to perceive time directly as a quality with a measurable and communicable magnitude that separates them from other creatures. It is this taken-for-granted capacity to resolve sensory information into the abstract temporal, perceptual units of experience that provides the basis for linguistic frames of reference and logical systems, both of which represent the raw materials for the conceptual developments that uniquely describe the human species. All animals can resolve inputs to the senses in terms of succession and duration; they can adapt passively to time with a prepotent present and a simple past and future. Only man has an elaborately organized and systematized world of time which can be perceived and communicated directly. This taming of the merciless savage, *time,* into a refined and useful social being has enabled the human partially to liberate himself from the bondage of mortality. Language and reason, history and education, theology and philosophy, science and technology, and the arts are the spoils of man's limited but profound victories over *time.*

But a child is not born with a language and a history; if anything, he is less capable and more helpless than other infant animals. At birth, the human clock is little more than a biological metronome regulating the basic instinctual rhythms.

The complex capacity to conceive, perceive, and communicate the temporal properties of the stimulating world develops slowly. At first, the child lives in a *now* existence dominated by momentary needs and discomforts. His personal timepiece is a rudimentary device calibrated with the rhythmic biological patterns built into the species. At the outset, a child's heartbeat, respiration, and sucking reflect native periodicities. Sleep and feeding schedules emerge as the first biological temporal events with social significance. The timing of these behaviors always involves other people, and at this point in development the parent is at the mercy of the infant's clock. The temporal helplessness of children is gradually modified through conditioned schedules permitting limited delay and postponement. When there is a quiescent period between stimulation-arousal and gratification-response, the infant has shown a primitive, unformulated past and future. However, this type of scheduling provides no mastery over time. Early conditional behavior is a complex adaptation to the temporal world and is no less automatic than the simpler biological periods. Time becomes uniquely human when the child employs temporal concepts or abstractions to perceive directly the stimulus dimensions of succession and duration. It is only when the young human can conceptualize a communicable, linguistic *before, now,* and *after* that he has shown instrumental temporal behavior rather than passive temporal adaptation. The child has actively placed events into a simple calendar and is able to activate self-determined schedules. The conceptual appreciation of temporal relations and its translation into perceptual behavior is refined further into meaningful and communicable units of magnitude. Temporal perceptions not only identify stimuli as consuming moments within the framework of a specified order; they also require the scaling of an amount of time in relation to a personal or social yardstick. The child must proceed from natural rhythms to conditional temporal adaptation to direct perception of the quality and quantity of time in order to realize his potential as a human calendar and clock.

THE PAST: A REVIEW

Although there has been considerable interest in the formation and development of the human calendar and clock, little effort has been directed toward the study of the *perception* of time by children. The first psychological laboratories emphasized psychophysical aspects of temporal judgment using adult subjects to test the Weber-Fechner function within the domain of time. Except for occasional references to musical ability and rhythm (Bolton, 1894; Squire, 1901; Swindle, 1913), temporal language development (Decroly and Degand, 1913), delayed responses (Hunter, 1912), and time estimation (Gilbert, 1894; Yerkes and Urban, 1906), very little work can be found concerning time and children prior to 1920. The recognition of the relationship between time conception and the maturation of intellectual functioning (Terman, 1916) was responsible for initiating research in the development of time concepts and attempts to designate growth stages in the use and comprehension of temporal language and conventional time scales.

This review will summarize anecdotal and experimental studies of the development of time concepts, and the few investigations of children's temporal perception and estimation. Although the studies of time conception focused attention upon language, meaning, and comprehension independent of stimulus conditions, this area of investigation represents a necessary antecedent for perceptual research which integrates the stimulus context with the conceptual response circumstances.

CHILDREN'S CONCEPTIONS OF TIME

The development, formation, use, and comprehension of temporal concepts has received considerable attention from psychologists and educators. Research has emerged from four separate areas of interest. First, the maturation and development of the capacity to perform temporal conceptual operations; second, the maturation and development of the use and comprehension of temporal language; third, the relationship between temporal conceptualization and intelligence; fourth, the relationship between temporal conceptualization and personality. Although these four areas are related, they require different methodology and provide information that can be compared across age levels using different observational procedures.

THE MATURATION AND DEVELOPMENT OF THE CAPACITY TO PERFORM TEMPORAL CONCEPTUAL OPERATIONS

The reader must depend upon Piaget (1954, 1955) for detailed observations and an analysis in depth of the development of a child's temporal field and the growth of temporal conceptual operations. In *The Construction of Reality in the Child,* Piaget (1954) employs observations of prelanguage children to provide an analysis of sensorimotor temporal operations. At this level of intellectual growth, Piaget describes the unfolding of several stages from infancy through language development and the use of time concepts. Initially, the infant performs automatic sequential movements in an egocentric practical series without regard for the ordering of external events. Within months the child is capable of perceiving a subjective series where he deals with relations among perceptions using himself as the center of the universe. At this stage objects in the perceptual field are limited by personal action and there is no series independent of the child; he is able to perceive a sequence of external events when he has participated in the activities. Objective time begins with the capacity to arrange external events in temporal sequence but at first this kind of behavior is subordinate to the employment of a subjective series. By the end of the first year of life, the child's time is able to transcend the duration of personal activity, and can be perceived in relation to things themselves, providing a serially ordered chain of events.

In attempting to show how reality unfolds for the child, Piaget discusses the development of object concepts, the spatial field, causality, and the temporal field, in that order. It is his contention that complex temporal relations cannot be understood without initial attention to objects, space, and causality; the temporal field cannot be separated from these categories. Prelanguage sensorimotor stages are particularly dependent upon stimulus conditions, and since they involve seriation without conceptualization, the child of less than one year is primarily isolated in the present. However, at this point in development the child shows the beginnings of representative series which involve the conceptual ordering of events after the disappearance of the perceptual events. This conceptual, representative series is contiguous with language development and provides the necessary temporal operations for historical sequences, a predictable future, and the rational integration of memories which depends upon causal thinking.

Piaget (1955) completed his analysis by exploring temporal operations beyond the sensorimotor level with ingenious techniques that required children older than 2 years to expose their recently acquired conceptual skills. Two additional stages were reported: first, an intermediate "pre-operative" phase between 2 and 7 years, in which the child gradually increases his ability to perform the analogues of sensorimotor acts on a conceptual level; second, at 8 years the child begins to employ concrete temporal operations. Piaget shows how children relate time, space, and speed so that at 4 to 6 years "faster" means "more time," while at 8, when the child can conceptualize time directly, this does not occur.

Two temporal systems must be identified and integrated before the 8-year-old can conceptualize time concretely and directly. First, succession or seriation, which requires the ordering of before and after; second, duration, which requires an estimate of magnitude.

Although time is given in every perception, temporal conceptual operations emerge slowly, from the sensorimotor to the simple representative levels that involve a before-after seriation and a more-less duration, to a coordination of these systems and a quantification through the use of temporal units. The interested reader is urged to refer to the original sources (Piaget, 1954, 1955) for a complete account of the analysis, observational data, and methodology.

THE MATURATION AND DEVELOPMENT OF THE USE AND COMPREHENSION OF TEMPORAL LANGUAGE

Educators and psychologists have shown considerable interest in the problem of designating the growth stages of children's expression and understanding of time concepts and temporal relations. The capacity to represent the ordinal and extensive characteristics of events with temporal linguistic units reflects specific developmental levels, and is basic in educational planning. The teaching of historical matters requires children to order events correctly in terms of a communicable, conventional calendar, and to comprehend relative duration within this positional system. The student must integrate the temporal properties of succession and duration in order to conceptualize historical information with maximum comprehension.

Anecdotal reports that describe observations of the temporal, conceptual behavior of children, structured interviews, and questionnaire techniques have provided basic and consistent developmental information.

Case studies and observations (Bromberg, 1938; Court, 1920; Decroly and Degand, 1913; Gesell and Ilg, 1943; Lewis, 1937; Schecter, Symonds, and Bernstein, 1954) have suggested a slow, predictable development of the use and comprehension of time language and relations. This gradual development proceeds from personal to conventional references, and from specific to general concepts. The emergence of expressions concerning past and future relations follows a pervasive temporal, conceptual concern with the present. Court's (1920) case report of a bright child indicated a dominant *present* before 2 years; concepts of the past reached back no more than a few days. Gradual development of temporal concepts and an expanding past and future were observed from 2 to 5 years. Temporal concepts at the preschool level are primarily related to the personal aspects of *before* and *after* with reference to simple schedules and appropriate tenses in linguistic intercourse. Although preschool children may ask questions that relate to seasons and days, they are not capable of employing or comprehending calendar and clock concepts (Bromberg, 1938; Lewis, 1937; Schecter, Symonds, and Bernstein, 1954).

Psychometric methods and questionnaire procedures were particularly valuable in producing data about school-age children, and although the items varied from study to study the general findings may be compared. Probst (1931) was concerned with the amount and types of temporal knowledge possessed by children immediately prior to elementary school. Questions involved general temporal concepts related to everyday personal experiences and abstract references to conventional time schemes. While these children were able to cope with personal and seasonal questions, they were less able to identify time in terms of the standard clock. Boys were slightly superior to girls in temporal knowledge, and performance was related to social class and parental occupation.

Ames (1946) combined observational procedures and standard questioning to depict the development of time concepts in children from 18 months to 8 years. This thorough investigation provides the best available data concerning the emergence of concepts of the past, present, and future, age, time of day, calendar units, and the relationship between representations of duration and order. In connection with the levels of temporal conceptualization, the child first responds appropriately to a time word; next he uses it in spontaneous conversation; and finally he is able to answer questions dealing with the concept. Thus, he responds to "soon" as a time concept at 18 months by waiting; he uses the phrase at 24 months; and at 42 months he can answer a question with the concept. Children's time concepts proceed from the specific to the general, or from the concrete to the abstract, with a gradual reduction in the frequency of inaccurate tenses and inappropriate temporal expressions. Ames (1946) noted that considerable individual differences appear within any level of age and intelligence in children's use and comprehension of time concepts. Many have an excellent picture of their temporal world and employ effectively time words from a very early age; others never seem to attain a clear understanding of time concepts and are only vaguely oriented in this sphere. These individual differences emphasize varying rates of maturation that may produce a permanent handicap in terms of intellectual efficiency and social adjustment. In spite of these important individual differences, Ames observed systematic and consistent patterns of growth and maturation. Words indicating the present appear first, followed by representations of the future and finally those indicating the past. Thus, *today* at 24 months precedes the *tomorrow* of 30 months which in turn precedes the *yesterday* of 36 months. Mastery of the time concepts necessary for comprehensive orientation does not appear all at once, but involves several levels of attainment. First the child can respond by waiting, then he uses the word, and then he can correctly answer questions dealing with the concept. Children report the time at which an event occurred in terms of a specific activity before they give an actual clock time. Similarly individual time words are used spontaneously in relation to a specific context before they are generalized. Words which imply duration and not just order usually appear no sooner than 36 months. As regards general conventional divisions of time, the child discriminates morning from afternoon at 4 years, but does not communicate about clock time until about age 7. This 7-year-old has reached an important level from the standpoint of readiness to employ other conventional time concepts such as the knowledge of months and seasons, and by 8 he can conceptualize the year and the day of the month. The days of the week are named correctly by 5 and the months unfold several years later. This study indicated that children can correctly identify bedtime at 5, while suppertime, time of awakening, schooltime and the onset of afternoon are identified at about 6 years. Children can designate their age by 3, the time of their next birthday by 4, and how old they will be next by 5. A detailed developmental schedule is available in the original reference (Ames, 1946).

Oakden and Sturt (1922) executed the most comprehensive study of the knowledge of conventional time concepts by school children from an educational point of view. These writers were particularly concerned with comprehension, since the purpose of their study was educational. The inquiries focused upon methods of history teaching and the age at which certain aspects of history might be initiated in a profitable fashion. Tests were constructed that provided data about children's understanding of the time words and symbols used in daily life; the power to conceptualize a time scheme extending into the past and the future, and the ability to use the dates through which the scheme is represented; the knowledge of the attributes of specific epochs in the time scheme and the ability to order these periods successively; the temporal operations used by children in dealing with historical data; the relative importance of temporal concepts in comparison with other matters of experience. The results of this investigation produced the following conclusions about the growth of children's knowledge of conventional time concepts and time relations: (1) This growth is a slow process which begins before school age. The most important period seems to be about age 11 when there is a rapid improvement in all types of time knowledge. (2) Children learn first the meaning of time words in ordinary use. (3) Marks of time are closely connected with personal activities and concrete experiences. (4) Development beyond ordinary time words to an understanding of chronology and the arrangement of historical epochs represents a major and difficult step. (5) Temporal details appear to play a less important part in children's thoughts than do those of space.

These conclusions had practical implications for the teaching of history. Oakden and Sturt suggest that up to age 11 conventional names of time periods have little meaning unless they are concretely explained in relation to aspects of the child's own experiences. When a week or 20-year period is presented, it should be connected with the life of the child and his family; the clock units of seconds, minutes, and hours should be related to the duration of specific school activities, sports, and games. It is difficult for the child under 11 years to conceive of a vivid past and a continuous history.

Other investigations of children's time concepts verified the slow, gradual, and systematic growth described by Ames (1946) and Oakden and Sturt (1922), and emphasized the difference between the use and comprehension of time concepts, and the need for educational planning in terms of this temporal, conceptual development (Bradley, 1947; Farrell, 1950; Friedman, 1944a, b; Friedman and Marti, 1945; Harrison, 1934; Pistor, 1939; Springer, 1951, 1952).

THE RELATIONSHIP BETWEEN TEMPORAL CONCEPTUALIZATION AND INTELLIGENCE

Any mental function that develops in a systematic fashion according to a consistent schedule and involves varying levels of conceptual and logical complexity is likely to find its way into our intelligence tests. It is not surprising that the rate and level of temporal conceptualization is used to reflect general intellectual growth, and that mental retardation is accompanied by a deficiency in this area.

The first research that concerned itself with the development of time concepts was carried out to place questions about time at the appropriate age levels within intelligence tests. It is interesting to note that much of the research already cited did little more than verify the earlier remarks of workers in the field of intelligence. In discussing the Binet test item at age 6 that required the child to place himself correctly in the afternoon or morning, Terman (1916) commented as follows:

> It is interesting to follow the child's development with regard to orientation in time. This development proceeds much more slowly than we are wont to assume. Certain distinctions with regard to space, as up and down, come much earlier. As Binet remarks, schools sometimes try to teach the events of national history to children whose time orientation is so rudimentary that they do not even know morning from afternoon! [p. 187].

This same test expected 9-year-olds to report the day of the week, the month, the day of the month, and the year, and Terman continued:

> It seems that practically all children in civilized countries have ample opportunity to learn the divisions of the year, month, and week, and to become oriented with respect to these divisions. Special instruction is doubtless capable of hastening time orientation to a certain degree, but not greatly. Binet tells of a French école maternelle attended by children 4 to 6 years of age, where instruction was given daily in regard to the date, and yet not a single one of the children was able to pass this test. This is a beautiful illustration of the futility of precocious teaching. In spite of well-meant instruction,

it is not until the age of 8 or 9 years that children have enough comprehension of time periods, and sufficient interest in them, to keep
very close track of the date [pp. 234-235].

The most frequently used intelligence tests continue to include items
requiring temporal conceptualization (Terman and Merrill, 1960;
Wechsler, 1949).

Buck's (1946) *Time Appreciation Test* provided a tool for rapid
screening of intelligence through responses to questions about immediate
orientation, holidays, and the definition of time phrases and relations.
Engle and Hamlett (1950, 1952) demonstrated a high correlation between intelligence measures obtained from the Stanford-Binet and Time
Appreciation Tests, and a high test-retest reliability for the Time Appreciation Test. The same writers (Engle and Hamlett, 1954) developed
a simpler device for the severely retarded, emphasizing simple practical
problems about time involving the use of the calendar and clock. Scores
for adults with a mean M.A. of 7.7 were equivalent to those of normal
children with a C.A. between 8.0 and 9.0. Research has clearly established
a relationship between intellectual level and the capacity to use and comprehend time concepts (Brower and Brower, 1947; Farrell, 1950). Gothberg (1949) studied the development of time concepts in retarded children and found a high correlation between performance and M.A. The
retarded child has little conception of sequence, relativity, or historical
time, and cannot comprehend beyond his own activities. The temporal
training of the retarded should be concrete, employing the child's experiences. Pichot (1949) discovered a continued faster spontaneous psychomotor rhythm accompanying mental retardation, and a slowing of this
tempo in normal children with maturation.

THE RELATIONSHIP BETWEEN TEMPORAL CONCEPTUALIZATION AND PERSONALITY

Although it seems reasonable to assume that personal and social characteristics and adjustments are related to individual and group concepts of
time, very little work has been accomplished in this important but complex area of investigation. There is a respectable body of information
available on the disturbances of time concepts accompanying mental disorders (Lhamon, Goldstone, and Goldfarb, in press), and a slowly increasing number of references on the relationship between personality
factors and temporal conceptualization.

Work to date on time concepts and personality in children has been limited to a few recent studies on time perspective and aspects of personal and social behavior. Children are asked to project a span of time, and its total duration as well as its past and future perspective are measured in terms of conventional time units. Thus, a child's story may require a few minutes or many years to complete the details of the theme; the story can be anchored in the present, or may travel back into the past or forward into the future.

Studies have suggested a shorter time span by children in the lower socioeconomic groups (LeShan, 1952) and among delinquents (Barndt and Johnson, 1955; Davids, Kidder, and Reich, 1962; Siegman, 1961). It has been shown that inhibition and control measures are related to time perspective. Children who are most able to inhibit a previously learned association by providing a new, spontaneous association extended their time span into the more distant future (Levine, Spivack, Fuschillo, and Tavernier, 1959), and delinquents exhibited a significant positive correlation between future time perspective scores and performance on a motor impulse control task (Siegman, 1961). One would expect less projection into the past and future by deprived children, emotionally disturbed children, and those who have demonstrated an inability to postpone gratification and inhibit established responses. However, these experimental findings reflect subtle personality factors, and since they are not replicated consistently, others have questioned their generality (Davids and Parenti, 1958; Ellis, Ellis, Mandel, Schaeffer, Sommer, and Sommer, 1955; Greene and Roberts, 1961).

The relationship between personality development, adjustment, and social factors on the one hand, and the growth of time conception on the other will be an important problem for future study. It is probable that disordered growth of temporal conceptualization will be reflected in adjustment handicaps and related disturbances in personality development and social behavior (Ames, 1946; LeShan, 1952). Although experiments have produced inconsistent results, these efforts have revealed a promising, important, and difficult avenue of investigation.

THE ESTIMATION AND PERCEPTION OF TIME BY CHILDREN

The development of temporal concepts provides the representative basis for the direct perception of the quality, *time*. However, the organism may be viewed as a meter that not only identifies time nominally, but acts as a precision instrument that can scale the ordinal and interval characteristics of time using communicable units of magnitude. People are able, indeed are required, to live in a measured temporal world, and they must estimate magnitude through the use of their native organic equipment, or mechanical extensions of this equipment. In many instances the limits of accuracy and reliability of the human calendar and clock are adequate for social adaptation. An excursion into the recent past brings us into contact with historical periods within which the human race survived and developed without today's necessary complex timepieces. Man needed little more than gross biological and environmental recurring periodicities such as hunger and fatigue, day-night, and seasons for his social, communicable units of time. However, the human timepiece is a delicate, flexible device that responds and adapts to external and internal conditions. Elaborate social yardsticks and measuring devices based upon reliable astronomical periods are required to compete with the need for increased accuracy and precision of temporal estimation.

When the human estimates duration using conventional units of magnitude, he is estimating the extensive characteristics of *something*; a *something* with an identifiable onset and termination that binds an amount of time. This *something* may begin and end with discrete identifiable stimuli or may involve conceptual representations of stimuli from the past. It is obvious that the onset of a duration which involves days, weeks, months, years, or centuries is a concept reflecting the estimator's personal past encounters with a specific stimulus context or an available, communicable point of onset provided by a historical culture. However, the onset of a duration which involves seconds or small parts of seconds is also in the past and is a conceptual residual of previous stimulation. All estimation of duration involves a conceptual representation of onset and termination of a stimulus context; all time estimation may be viewed as time perception. Distinctions between estimation and perception based upon whether the person is perceiving a short stimulating *present* or estimating a longer symbolic *past* and *future* (Fraisse, 1963) are useful only from the standpoint of methodology of investigation. The present writers prefer to consider all time estimations as perceptions with details of the past, and present, or onset and termination specifiable in quantitative stimulus terms; the conditions of stimulation are responsible for the position of the quantitative response within the framework of a conventional yardstick (Helson, 1959, 1964).

What of the growth of this human perceptual, temporal meter? What factors influence children's magnitude judgments of time? Scattered references concerning the perception and estimation of time by children extend back more than 50 years. For convenience the work may be divided into two categories according to the method of presenting the stimulus context that defined the duration to be perceived and estimated. One group of studies focused upon the global estimation of durations filled with various activities; particular attention was paid to the effect of the general conditions of activity under which the estimate was provided. Investigators in this area were not concerned with the careful control of stimulating conditions and the specific effects of these conditions upon the estimation response. The second approach involved the use of classical psychophysical methods and increased control over the stimulus characteristics.

THE EFFECT OF VARIOUS ACTIVITIES UPON THE ESTIMATION OF TIME BY CHILDREN

Yerkes and Urban (1906) had subjects estimate durations of 18 to 108 seconds under conditions of idleness, reading, writing, and accurate estimating. Although the conditions of the temporal filling influenced estimation, no differences due to age were found within the narrow range of 17 to 23 years.

Axel (1924) went further into the effects of different fillings upon estimation of time and how these estimates are influenced by age. Activities were selected that could be arranged in order of level of complexity from simple to complicated mental functions. Children of 9 to 14 years and young adults estimated time under the following conditions: (1) a vacant interval; (2) the simple motor task of tapping a pencil; (3) the sensorimotor task of number cancellation; (4) the complex mental tasks of verbal analogies and number series completion. Axel found that males underestimate time for all fillings while females overestimate time for the simple estimation, motor, and sensorimotor tasks but underestimate for the complex mental functions; in all instances females overestimated more than males. In general, higher levels of behavior accompanied greater underestimations of duration. The effect of age upon estimations of 9- to 14-year-olds depends upon the level of behavior; the higher the level of activity, the greater the tendency for equality of accuracy of judgment among the ages. Younger children overestimated more than older children and adults, particularly on the simple tasks.

PSYCHOPHYSICAL STUDIES OF TIME PERCEPTION BY CHILDREN

Use of the precise methods of psychophysics has provided valuable knowledge about the perception of time by adults (Woodrow, 1951) and holds considerable promise for studies with children (Weber, 1933). This approach has the advantage of providing information about the development of temporal perception through the gamut of procedural circumstances and stimulus arrangements provided by the psychophysical methods. The maturation and growth of the capacity to perceive time can be measured precisely under the simpler metering conditions required by the methods of comparison and reproduction, or the more complex conceptual conditions required by the method of absolute judgment and category scaling; subjects can be studied within the open-ended conditions of a method of limits or they can be bound by the restrictions of the constant method. The psychophysical approach to perception also permits determination of specific effects of stimulus characteristics such as sense mode, intensity, and patterning upon the perception of time, and allows scientific study of subtle but basic order effects that reflect the integration of past experience with present conditions. Finally, psychophysical methodology provides the quantitative data, and adaptation-level theory (Helson, 1959, 1964), the scientific schema for pooling all of the cogent details within a time-perception experiment.

Although Gilbert (1894) initiated psychophysical research on children's time perception early in the history of experimental psychology, very little work followed upon his efforts. Using the method of reproduction, Gilbert had 6- to 17-year-olds duplicate a 2-second auditory signal. Children of 6 and 7 showed the greatest error, with a sudden increase in accuracy at 10 which continued through age 17. Boys were more accurate than girls at all ages.

Gilliland and Humphreys (1943) compared the judgments of vacant intervals bound by auditory inputs provided by 11-year-olds and college students using the methods of estimation, production, and reproduction and a geometric series of durations ranging from 9 to 180 seconds. It was found that children were less accurate than adults for all three methods, but the errors were smaller for children and adults when the subjects were allowed to count actively in determining their estimates. Reproduction was found to be easier than estimation or production, an expected finding since the conceptual process involves immediate memory for reproduction and remote memory for the other procedures. In general, adults were 15 to 18% accurate for all intervals and all methods. However, the children's success indicates a considerable level of development of the capacity to perceive duration and estimate time by age 11.

Using a comparison procedure, Fraisse and Vautrey (1952) required 5-year-olds to determine which of two toy cyclists moving at variable speeds took more time to run courses of different lengths. While 88% of the replies were correct when the speed and the times of arrival and departure were the same, only 17% reported that the durations were the same when one moved twice as fast and twice as far as the other. At this age children cannot perceive the quality of duration directly. They equate time with amount of action, effort, speed, and distance. Time measurement is not possible and time as time is not perceived.

With an adjustment-reproduction technique, Fraisse and Orsini (1958) had 6-, 8-, and 10-year-olds turn off a sound when it had lasted as long as a previously experienced 30-second input. Colored lights informed the children when their reproductions were too short, correct, or too long. Accuracy increased with age and all levels improved with knowledge of results. The youngest tended to overestimate while the 10-year-olds underestimated.

Smythe and Goldstone (1957) used a modified method of limits procedure and obtained absolute judgments of auditory durations by 6- to 14-year-olds and adults who judged ascending and descending series of stimuli as *more* or *less* than their concept of a clock second. An indifference point was obtained that defined the accuracy of judgment, and a variability measure reflected the children's precision and stability. These measures were obtained before and after the subject was given a demonstration of the correct 1-second auditory duration and told to use this information as a standard when rendering future judgments. Slightly more than half of the 6- and 7-year-olds were able to complete the task, and no testing failures occurred beyond age 9. The ability to make absolute judgments of time appeared related to the capacity to use and understand conventional time concepts, and to tell time. The results demonstrated that 6- and 7-year-olds have not reached a developmental level necessary for reliable temporal, perceptual measurement. These age levels involved the largest number of testing failures, the greatest intrasubject variability, and an inability to profit from information about the correct value of the conceptual standard. There was a sudden growth spurt at age 8, when almost all children could take the test, had less variable judgments, and could improve with information. Children of all ages overestimated the value of a clock second; they identified a shorter auditory duration as equivalent to the concept of a clock second. Younger children overestimated to a greater extent than did older children and adults, conforming to the results of Axel (1924) and Fraisse and Orsini (1958). Intrasubject variability continued to decrease with age through age 14, and superior IQ 14-year-olds were less variable than average IQ children of the same age, indicating that the stabilization of this temporal concept of magnitude is a slow, continuing process that is dependent upon intelligence.

This study showed that the use of psychophysical methodology represents a fruitful approach to the investigation of human development. The measure of central tendency that quantitatively defines the conventional time standard, one clock second, and the measure of intrasubject response variability that reflects the precision of temporal judgment provides valuable growth data on the perception of time within a specific experimental context. In this instance, these measures indicate that within a method of limits in an auditory input situation, the capacity to render absolute judgments of time based upon a short, social clock unit emerges at age 8 and matures slowly through adolescence. It is further suggested that under these conditions children who cannot make perceptual estimates without help are unable or not ready to learn from demonstration. This approach can be extended to employ other psychophysical methods, sense modes, response requirements, and stimulus characteristics and patterns.

Another study which shows the relevance of these psychophysical details in considering time-perception results employed the same population described above but with the method of production, not passive perceptual estimation, defining the concept of one clock second. Goldstone, Boardman, and Lhamon (1958b) had 6- to 14-year-olds and adults produce seconds by counting to 30 aloud and silently at the rate of one count a second. Only one 6-year-old failed to complete this procedure. The size of the produced second was smaller for the 6- and 7-year groups than for all other age groups, with a sudden increase in accuracy at age 8 which appeared for the silent and aloud conditions and which was maintained for all older groups; the second produced by counting aloud was longer than that produced silently for the 8-year through adult age levels.

Comparison of these results with those obtained from passive estimation of auditory durations (Smythe and Goldstone, 1957) revealed differences in temporal perceptual estimation due to method. The median estimates of a second obtained by counting to the self from age 8 through adulthood were remarkably accurate, ranging from .92 to 1.06 seconds; the median estimates obtained by counting aloud ranged from 1.06 to 1.25 seconds. On the other hand, the median passive perceptual estimates of a clock second ranged from .38 to .58 seconds, revealing less accuracy and considerable overestimation with this method. These two studies

> . . . demonstrated considerable accuracy of individuals from 8 through young adulthood in designating their concept of a standard clock unit—the second, by counting . . . Presumably the basic mechanism in a counting procedure involves kinesthetic cues and we might assume that the learning of this short standard unit of time is at least in part muscular. Passive estimation of seconds provided through auditory stimuli when no motor production was involved resulted in a much shorter subjective second. It is suggested that at about age 8, kinesthetic cues become associated with standard temporal concepts providing part of the mechanism for temporal conceptualization and calibrated experienced duration. This cut-off point at 8 . . . suggests this age as the approximate level of maturation which would permit temporal learning, and calibrated temporal experience. Further evidence of a kinesthetic base for learned temporal units was suggested by the younger children's difficulty in counting to themselves. It was necessary for many of them to violate instructions and make manifest muscle movements. It was as though these temporal concepts were in the process of being learned and needed kinesthetic accompaniment . . . If this formulation is valid, we must presume that our 6- and 7-year old subjects had not as yet established a stable relationship between a standard duration and a muscle cue . . . It would be of interest to investigate the role of visual and tactile experience on temporal learning and appreciation [Goldstone, Boardman, and Lhamon, 1958b, p. 189].

The following section reports in detail extensions of these two studies (Goldstone, Boardman, and Lhamon, 1958b; Smythe and Goldstone, 1957) using two sense modes, audition and vision, another psychophysical procedure, the method of constant stimuli, and two levels of category-scaling complexity. The authors hope that the reader will bear with this change of pace from the narrative to the technical.

THE PRESENT: AN EXPERIMENTAL-PSYCHOPHYSICAL APPROACH TO THE STUDY OF TIME PERCEPTION OF CHILDREN

SENSORY DIFFERENTIATION AND CROSS-MODAL TRANSFER EFFECTS IN THE DEVELOPMENT OF TIME PERCEPTION

The present experiment explored the development of an auditory-visual difference in time perception (Goldstone, Boardman, and Lhamon, 1959) and studied the effects of previous experience by children with one mode upon subsequent judgments with the alternate sense. The issues of sensory differentiation and integration are basic in developmental psychology. Perceptual growth involves successive levels of complexity with regard to the organization of the senses and ultimate conceptual translation. The child becomes progressively more able to separate information to the different senses as well as integrate, pool, or transfer experience or learning from one sense to another. The auditory and visual percept *dog* should involve a similar conceptual experience; the auditory and visual second, minute, or hour should also be similar. However, similar does not mean identical; the senses are not the same. Although most perceptions involve conceptualization based upon multisensory inputs, it is reasonable to assume differences among the senses in dealing with an equivalent concept, and it is probable that these differences are functional. Children listen with comprehension before they are able to read; they can speak with meaning before they write. Auditory perception usually precedes visual within a given conceptual dimension. This order of perceptual development is characteristic of our species, and it is likely that auditory perceptual precedence will be found in all complex areas of conceptual growth. One should expect children to begin making temporal estimates of auditory durations before they can judge visual durations; they should show greater auditory to visual transfer effects than from visual to auditory. Any auditory-visual difference in time judgment that is characteristic of the human species should be observed at the point of maturation and emergence of the capacity to perceive directly the durational property of sensory inputs.

A series of recent experiments with adults demonstrated a stable inter-sensory difference in temporal perception. Sounds are judged longer than lights regardless of psychophysical method, stimulus properties such as hue, pitch, and intensity, size of and distance from the light source, and number of response categories; this difference has been obtained under various background anchor conditions, within several ranges of durations, and with different internal temporal standards and patterns of stimulation (Behar and Bevan, 1960, 1961; Goldstone, Boardman, and Lhamon, 1959; Goldstone and Goldfarb, 1963, 1964; Goldstone, Jernigan, Lhamon, and Boardman, 1959). There is no doubt that the mode of input is a relevant variable in time-perception research.

The writers will report in detail upon a two-part experiment that considered the development of human time perception in relation to this sense mode difference, and cross-modal transfer effects. This investigation involved the study of children's absolute judgments of lights and sounds using the social, temporal concept of one clock second as the standard; subjects judged auditory and visual inputs as *more* or *less* than their concept of a second. Intersensory differences and cross-sensory transfer effects were studied with measures of each subject's indifference point and judgment variability. Methods were employed that permitted the derivation of the amount of auditory and visual clock time judged by the child as equivalent to the concept of one second, and variability or relative consistency in rendering such estimates. In addition to exploring sense-mode factors, it was possible to obtain information about other issues pertaining to the development of time perception. (1) At what age does the capacity to render absolute judgments of temporal magnitude mature? Piaget (1954, 1955) suggested that the conceptualization of the temporal properties of the world directly through an integration of succession and duration emerges at age 8. (2) Is psychophysical method a relevant factor in determining the progress of the growth of time perception? This experiment employed the method of constant stimuli to study the perception of a second, while comparable developmental studies of the same temporal standard used the methods of production and limits (Goldstone, Boardman, and Lhamon, 1958b; Smythe and Goldstone, 1957. (3) Do younger children show a general tendency to overestimate the duration of sensory inputs as suggested by Axel (1924), Smythe and Goldstone (1957), and Fraisse and Orsini (1958)? (4) Are there sex differences in perception in relation to the general capacity to render absolute judgments, in relation to age of development, or in relation to specific sense modes, sense-mode differentiation or sense-mode integration? The older studies suggested that the time perception of boys developed faster than that of girls, and females overestimated more than males (Axel, 1924; Gilbert, 1894; Gulliksen, 1927; MacDougall, 1904; Probst, 1931; Yerkes and Urban, 1906). However, the negative results of more recent studies (Farrell, 1950; Friedman, 1944a, b; Friedman and Marti, 1945; Gilliland and Humphreys, 1943; Smythe and Goldstone, 1957) suggest that the male-female difference may have been a product of historical, cultural factors.

With regard to mode of input, this experiment considered the following questions: (1) Are there auditory-visual differences due to developmental factors in the accuracy and variability of children's time perception? (2) Is the basic auditory-visual difference in time perception that finds adults estimating sounds as longer than lights a function of age? If this intersensory difference is discovered at the point of the emergence of the capacity to render time judgments involving both senses, it is probable that this phenomenon is a characteristic of the species. (3) Is there any differential effect due to age upon cross-modal transfer of the effects of previous perceptual experiences with one mode upon subsequent judgments with the other mode? It is predicted that there will be more auditory-to-visual than visual-to-auditory transfer, and that this sound-to-light pooling will be the greatest at the youngest ages.

The experiment involved two parts. In Part I the children and adults judged lights and sounds using a two-category, simple response scale; in Part II subjects were required to judge along a more complex 9-category response scale. The more complex scaling procedure provides more extensive and detailed measures and an index of variability; the simpler procedure provides a single score and no variability measure. However, the simpler, two-category method permitted testing at an earlier age, and the investigators had the opportunity to observe aspects of the development of magnitude scaling.

General procedure. Children and adult subjects within various age groups made single-stimuli judgments of lights and sounds; the auditory and visual durations were judged as *more* or *less* than the subjects' concept of one clock second using either a 2- or 9-category response scale. All subjects judged separate blocks of auditory and visual inputs alternately within experimental designs that counterbalanced sense-mode order.

An electronic timer controlled auditory and visual durations with a reliable and accurate range of .01 to 9.99 sec. An audio-oscillator and headphones provided a tone of 1000 cps at 94 db (re .0002 dyne/cm^2). Heavy foam-rubber cups of the headphones attenuated some of the ambient noise. A fluorescent system illuminated a 1-inch opal glass circular target mounted 43 inches from the subjects' eyes with a blue-white light of 6.3 apparent foot candles.

The method of single stimuli was used with a series of 7 durations (D_{1-7}) from .15 to 1.95 sec. and a step interval of .30 sec. Seventy durations were randomized with each series stimulus appearing 10 times. Each subject judged a block of 70 auditory (M_1) or visual (M_2) durations and then was studied with the alternate sense. Half of the subjects in each age group received an auditory followed by visual order (O_1); the other half received a visual followed by auditory (O_2). These two orders permitted the study of the perseverative effect of one sense mode upon subsequent judgments with the alternate mode, thus providing a measure of sensory integration or transfer at different age levels. This procedure also provides the vehicle for determining whether there is a greater cross-modal transfer effect of audition on vision, or vision on audition.

Subjects were 189 students of St. John's School, Houston, Texas, ranging in age from 6 years, 2 months to 13 years, 6 months, and 40 adults, all but one of whom were mothers of children at the same school. This private school has high academic standards and carefully selects students who are good scholastic risks. These children come from educationally oriented homes and represent a higher intellectual level than found in the general population; the mean group test IQ of all children studied was 123.

Procedure Part I: 2-category response scale. One hundred and thirty-one subjects were tested in order to obtain 120 complete records; each subject was required to complete both the auditory (M_1) and visual (M_2) tasks. Six age groups (A_{1-6}) of 20 subjects each were subdivided into equal O_1 and O_2 groups; 10 subjects in each age group received the M_1 followed by M_2 order (O_1) and 10 received the M_2 followed by M_1 order (O_2). The characteristics of A_{1-6} are presented in Table 1.

TABLE 1

Characteristics of Subjects in Each of the Six Age (A_{1-6}) Groups for Part I

	Age Range (Months)	Mean Age (Months)	Sex M	F	Grade Level Range	I.Q. Range	Mean I.Q.
A_1	74–86	80.1	10	10	1–2	107–153	121
A_2	87–94	89.8	10	10	1–2	110–134	124
A_3	102–114	108.7	10	10	3–4	110–133	120
A_4	126–138	133.1	10	10	5–6	109–136	123
A_5	150–162	155.1	10	10	7–8	100–131	123
A_6	324–636	444.6	0	20	13–20		

All subjects in Part I were required to judge each auditory and visual duration as *more* or *less* than their concept of one clock second in accordance with the following instructions.

We are interested in how people tell time. You know what a clock second is, don't you? Well, I am going to let you listen to (see) a lot of sounds (lights), and your job is to match each sound (light) with your idea of a clock second and then tell me if the sound (light) you hear (see) is more or less than one clock second. Listen to (Look at) each sound (light) and tell me whether it is more or less than one clock second.

The percentages of reports *less* for each of the 7 durations for each sense mode were plotted on arithmetic probability paper and a straight line visually fitted. The Second Estimation Point (SEP), or duration each subject reported *more* or *less* than one clock second 50% of the time, was derived from these plots. An auditory and visual SEP was obtained for each subject. Nine of 19 children in A_1 were unable to complete the O_2 condition, while 2 of 12 children in A_2 were unable to complete O_2; no testing failures were obtained with O_1. The mean IQ of the A_1 and A_2 testing failures was 117.

SEP data were examined with an analysis of variance; age (A) and sense-mode order (O) were between-subjects factors, and sense mode (M) was the within-subjects factor.

Procedure Part II: *9-category response scale.* One hundred subjects were divided into 5 age groups (A$_{1-5}$). As in Part I, each age group contained 20 subjects equally subdivided into the same O$_1$ and O$_2$ conditions. The characteristics of A$_{1-5}$ are presented in Table 2.

TABLE 2

Characteristics of Subjects in Each of the Five Age (A$_{1-5}$) Groups
for Part II

	Age Range (Months)	Mean Age (Months)	Sex M	F	Grade Level Range	I.Q. Range	Mean I.Q.
A$_1$	87–100	93.5	10	10	2	107–140	127
A$_2$	102–114	108.5	10	10	3–4	114–140	122
A$_3$	126–138	132.8	10	10	5–6	113–136	123
A$_4$	150–161	155.3	10	10	7–8	115–144	127
A$_5$	252–600	475.2	0	20	12–17		

The subjects in Part II were required to judge the auditory and visual durations as more or less than their concept of one clock second using a more complex 9-category response scale in accordance with the following instructions.

We are interested in how people tell time. You know what a clock second is, don't you? Well, I am going to let you hear (see) many sounds (lights), and your job is to tell me how much more or less than a clock second each sound (light) is. In front of you is a card with the numbers 1 through 9, and each number tells you how much more or less than a clock second you think the sound (light) is. You will say *1* if you think the sound (light) is very much less than a clock second; *2* if it is much less; *3* if it is less; *4* if it is slightly less; *5* if it is equal to or the same as a clock second; *6* if it is slightly more; *7* if it is more; *8* if it is much more; *9* if it is very much more than a clock second. You listen to (look at) each sound (light) and put it into one of these numbers according to how you think it matches a clock second. The words are just there to help you make up your mind. You may use them, but I would prefer that you use the numbers instead of the words. Now remember to match each sound (light) with a clock second and tell me how much more or less the sound (light) is in numbers or words.

The subject's average category response for each of the seven durations was obtained for audition (M_1) and vision (M_2). In addition, each subject's precision of judgment was studied by obtaining the variance (s^2) for the 10 judgments of each of the 7 durations for M_1 and M_2; this measure of each subject's judgmental precision or consistency was designated *intrasubject response variance* (IRV). Average category response and IRV measures were treated with trend tests based upon analysis of variance procedures; age (A) and sense-mode order (O) were between-subjects factors, and sense mode (M) and the series durations (D) were the within-subjects factors. No testing failures were obtained in this experiment.

Table 3 summarizes the experimental conditions and the alphabetic coding which will be carried through this report.

TABLE 3

Summary of Treatments, Groups, and Measures and Their
Alphabetic Codings

Mode.........................	M:	Audition, M_1; Vision, M_2
Sense Mode Order...............	O:	O_1, M_1–M_2; O_2, M_2–M_1
Series Durations................	D:	D_{1-7}, .15, .45, .75, 1.05, 1.35, 1.65, 1.95 sec.
Age...........................	A:	Part I, A_{1-6} (See Table 1)
		Part II, A_{1-5} (See Table 2)
Second Estimation Point...........	SEP:	Part I
Intrasubject Response Variance.....	IRV:	Part II

Results Part I: 2-category. Table 4 shows the summary of the analysis of variance of the SEP measures and Table 5 provides the Mean SEP values for each age group and both sense modes. Since there was no significant order effect, O_1 and O_2 were combined on Table 5.

The significant effect of M ($F_{1/108}=82.3481$, $P<.001$) and the mean SEP values show that more visual than auditory clock time was required to reach temporal conceptual equivalence for all age groups; auditory durations were judged longer than visual across ages. These results clearly demonstrate the existence of the auditory-visual difference in time judgment at the onset of a child's ability to make single-stimuli judgments of duration in terms of a temporal concept. All children below grade 1 and younger than A_1 were unable to compare auditory or visual durations with their concept of a clock second through the use of a 2-category judgment scale.

TABLE 4

Analysis of Variance of the Second Estimation Point (SEP)
Measures

Source	df	MS	F
Between Subjects			
Age (A)	5	.3486	2.7733 *
Order (O)	1	.0792	.6301
A × O	5	.1448	1.1519
Error (b)	108	.1257	
Within Subjects			
Mode (M)	1	2.2234	82.3481 **
A × M	5	.0134	.4962
O × M	1	.0331	1.2259
A × O × M	5	.0504	1.8666
Error (w)	108	.0270	

* P < .025
** P < .001

TABLE 5

Mean Second Estimation Point (SEP) Measures in Seconds for the
Auditory (M_1) and Visual (M_2) Judgments of Each Age (A) Group

	A_1	A_2	A_3	A_4	A_5	A_6
Auditory (M_1)	.71	.65	.62	.76	.88	.88
Visual (M_2)	.94	.89	.84	.95	1.02	1.04

The significant effect of A ($F_5/_{108}$=2.7733, P<.025) indicates that the
younger children identified shorter auditory and visual durations with
their concept of one clock second. The auditory and visual SEPs of A_5
and A_6 were significantly larger than those of A_1, A_2, and A_3; A_4 was not
significantly different from the younger children or older children and
adults. Younger children overestimate both auditory and visual durations
of a clock second compared to the judgments of older children and adults,
as suggested by Axel (1924), Smythe and Goldstone (1957), and Fraisse
and Orsini (1958). Inspection of Table 5 suggests that this developmental
change occurs between A_3 and A_4 or between ages 9 and 11 years and is
stabilized by age 13 years.

Examination of the testing failures with A_1 and A_2 provides interesting
information regarding a differential cross-modal transfer effect. While

no A_1 or A_2 subject who received the auditory test first (O_1) failed to complete the task with either mode, 9 subjects in A_1 and 2 in A_2 failed with either vision or both modes when the visual task came first (O_2). It is likely that this demonstrates the primacy of the auditory mode in temporal judgment, and further suggests a greater cross-modal transfer effect from audition to vision than from vision to audition. Apparently the ability to make auditory temporal judgments emerges first, and prior experience with this mode facilitates subsequent visual judgments; initial testing with the visual mode results in more failures and occasionally impairs auditory performance.

Results Part II: 9-*category*. Table 6 shows the summary of the analysis of variance of average category responses for each duration (D) for both sense modes (M) for all age groups (A); Figure 1 provides the *Mean*

TABLE 6

Analysis of Variance of Average Category Responses: Part II

Source	df	MS	F
Between Subjects			
Age (A)	4	28.72	2.04
Order (O)	1	3.37	.24
A × O	4	5.69	.40
Error (b)	90	14.10	
Within Subjects			
Durations (D)	6	706.61	1054.64 ***
Mode (M)	1	133.61	63.02 ***
M × D	6	2.64	14.66 ***
A × D	24	1.28	1.91 **
A × M	4	5.27	2.48 *
A × M × D	24	.16	.88
O × D	6	.10	.14
O × M	1	7.13	3.36
O × M × D	6	.19	1.05
A × O × D	24	.40	.59
A × O × M	4	4.71	2.22
A × O × M × D	24	.16	.88
Error₁ (w)	540	.67	
Error₂ (w)	90	2.12	
Error₃ (w)	540	.18	

*** P < .001
** P < .01
* P < .05

Average Category Response-Durations plots for each age group and both sense modes. Since there was no significant order effect, O_1 and O_2 were combined for each A in Figure 1.

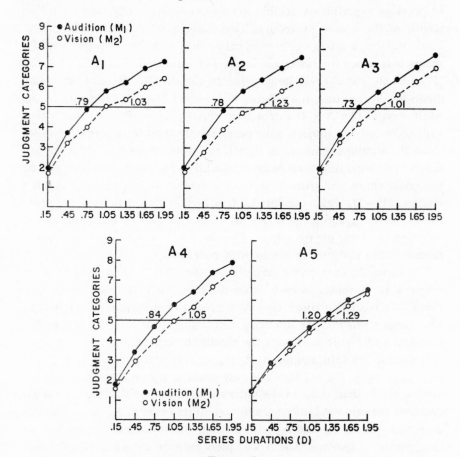

FIGURE 1

Auditory (M_1) and visual (M_2) stimulus-response plots for all age (A_{1-5}) groups combined over sense-mode order (O). Each point represents the mean *average category response* by the group for each duration (D_{1-7}). Projection of judgment category 5 (i.e., equal to one second) provides a reference point for each M_1 and M_2 curve.

The visual curves appear to the right of the auditory curves for all age groups resulting in the significant M ($F_1/_{90}=63.02$, P<.001); the M x D interaction ($F_6/_{540}=14.66$, P<.001) shows that the M_1 and M_2 curves begin close together and progressively diverge. This end effect was obtained in previous experiments (Goldstone and Goldfarb, 1964) and is characteristic of the scaling procedure. This experiment verified the auditory-visual difference across age groups using more complex response requirements that raised the lower age limit. The significant A x M interaction ($F_4/_{90}=2.48$, P<.05) was largely due to the shift of the auditory judgments for A_5 resulting in a reduced but evident M_1—M_2 difference in the adult group. The A x D interaction ($F_{24}/_{540}=1.91$, P<.01) shows that with increased age subjects gave progressively smaller category responses along the stimulus series; as in Part I, the children overestimated the auditory and visual durations more than adults. This more sensitive scaling procedure shows the greatest M_1—M_2 difference for A_1 and A_2, and the smallest M_1—M_2 difference for A_5. It is further shown that the auditory curves are remarkably stable for all children's groups but shift in the direction of visual for the adults. This suggests a modification of sensory primacy from audition to vision with development.

The intrasubject response variance measure (IRV) obtained from each subject's 10 responses to each series duration for each sense mode provided data regarding consistency or precision of judgment in relation to age. Table 7 provides the summary of the analysis of variance of the IRV measures and Figure 2 displays the significant interactions.

It is clear from the significant A ($F_4/_{90}=11.6772$, P<.001) and A x D ($F_{24}/_{540}=1.8913$, P<.01) that the judgments of the younger children are more variable than those of the older children and adults. Figure 2 demonstrates the profound difference in variability between A_1 and A_2 on the one hand and A_3, A_4, and A_5 on the other; the adult group provided the most precise judgments. The A x D plots indicate the smallest difference due to age with the shortest durations, an expected result in view of the greater psychophysical distance at the low end of the stimulus continuum and the usual anchoring of responses at the initial stimulus with this scaling procedure. The remarkable sensitivity of the IRV measure to age indicates the importance of neglected measures of variability in determining concept stability and response consistency with various developmental levels.

The significant M ($F_1/_{90}=4.9409$, P<.05) and M x D ($F_6/_{540}=6.0618$,

TABLE 7

Analysis of Variance of Intrasubject Response-Variance (IRV)
Measures: Part II

Source	df	MS	F
Between Subjects			
Age (A)	4	97.9170	11.6772 ***
Order (O)	1	9.2308	1.1008
A × O	4	19.1704	2.2861
Error (b)	90	8.3853	
Within Subjects			
Durations (D)	6	21.8168	25.0767 ***
Mode (M)	1	8.0681	4.9409 *
M × D	6	3.8905	6.0618 ***
A × D	24	1.6455	1.8913 **
A × M	4	1.8382	1.1257
A × M × D	24	1.1775	1.8346 **
O × D	6	.4243	.4877
O × M	1	13.2737	8.1289 **
O × M × D	6	.4287	.6679
A × O × D	24	1.2777	1.4686
A × O × M	4	.3317	.2031
A × O × M × D	24	.4186	.6522
Error₁ (w)	540	.8700	
Error₂ (w)	90	1.6329	
Error₃ (w)	540	.6418	

*** P < .001
** P < .01
* P < .05

$P < .001$) indicates that visual judgments are more variable than auditory and that this intersensory difference is independent of age. The M x D plots in Figure 2 show that the increased variability of visual judgments was obtained for the longer durations where discrimination is more complex because of decreased psychophysical distance between stimuli.

Perhaps the most interesting finding in this study of the variability of time perception is built into the significant O x M ($F_{1/90} = 8.1289$, $P < .01$). Inspection of the O x M plots shows that there was an obvious cross-modal transfer effect from audition to vision for the O_1 condition; previous experience with auditory judgments reduces the variability of later visual estimates. When vision came first (O_2) the variability of the judgment of

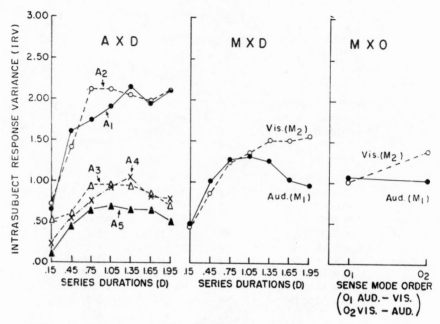

FIGURE 2

Mean *intrasubject response variance* (IRV) display for significant interactions; the higher the point on the ordinate, the greater the variability. Panel 1 shows the combined IRV-durations (D_{1-7}) plots for each age (A_{1-5}) group; panel 2 shows the combined IRV durations (D_{1-7}) for each sense mode (M_{1-2}); panel 3 shows the combined IRV-order (O_{1-2}) plots for each sense mode (M_{1-2}).

lights was greater than when visual judgments had the benefit of previous experience with an auditory series (O_1). Further, an encounter with a visual task *did not* reduce the variability of later auditory judgments; auditory estimates were equally precise for O_1 and O_2, while visual estimates were more precise for O_1. These results suggest a cross-modal transfer effect from audition to vision, while no such transfer was obtained from vision to audition. This verifies the finding in Part I that suggested the primacy of audition in the development of temporal judgment; it is probable that antecedent temporal experience and learning with the auditory mode facilitates the development of visual temporal perceptual processes.

The significant A x M x D interaction ($F_{24/540} = 1.8346$, P<.01) simply reflects the fact that the greatest variability among the youngest groups (A_1 and A_2) was obtained for visual judgments of the longest durations. This again suggests greater difficulty with the visual mode and the primacy of audition.

Although the exploration of sex differences was not a major intent of these studies, separate analyses of variance were performed on A_{1-5} for Part I, and A_{1-4} for Part II which included this factor. The results of these analyses indicated no significant difference between boys and girls in regard to the relative overestimation or underestimation of duration as reported in older studies (Axel, 1924; Gilbert, 1894; Gulliksen, 1927; MacDougall, 1904; Probst, 1931; Yerkes and Urban, 1906); there was no significant effect of sex upon the SEP and average category response measures. However, a curious sex difference in regard to variability of judgment was obtained in Part II. Analysis of the IRV measure revealed no sex difference with auditory judgments, but a much greater variability of visual judgments by girls. This greater instability of visual temporal judgment by females represents a provocative finding, and the question whether this sex difference is characteristic of adults remains open for study.

A final point worthy of mention is the fact that 11 of the 20 children in A_1 used the verbal categories to report their magnitude judgments while all subjects in A_2—A_5 used numerical scaling. Thus bright children of 6½ to 7½ years were shown to have stabilized their capacity to make 2-category, *greater-than—less-than* absolute judgments, and at about age 8 children begin to use more complex yardsticks, progressing from concrete verbal designations to a more abstract numerical scaling system. By age 9 the capacity to employ numbers within a continuous, fixed interval scale appears to be established.

DISCUSSION

This experiment clearly demonstrated a fundamental intersensory difference in the perception of time that exists in children as well as adults; sounds are judged longer than lights. These results suggest that this auditory-visual difference is present at the point of emergence of the capacity to perceive duration magnitude and is, in fact, greater for children than adults; it is probable that this phenomenon is characteristic of the species.

It is indicated further that auditory time perception appears before visual and provides at least a partial basis for the development of visual temporal perception. Sense mode factors must be considered in time perception research.

The studies regarding the perception of the concept of one second (Goldstone, Boardman, and Lhamon, 1958b; Smythe and Goldstone, 1957) which include the present experiment indicate rudimentary and partially successful attempts at magnitude estimation between ages 6½ and 7½; almost half of the children at this age are unable to provide accurate perceptions of durations and are very variable in their judgments. However, at age 8 children are capable of conventional time judgments with progressively decreasing variability. In considering absolute estimates without an exteroceptive standard, and using the ability to complete a procedure for a given age level as the criterion for success, the method of production was easiest, with the constant method and the method of limits following in that order. The method of production which used kinesthetic cues and feedback (Goldstone, Boardman, and Lhamon, 1958b) was the most accurate; the open-ended, complex method of limits was the least accurate (Smythe and Goldstone, 1957), with the constant method reported here in the middle. It is suggested that the most effective approach to teaching the magnitude of conventional clock units should employ a multisensory context emphasizing auditory durations and proprioceptive feedback first, and then transfer to visual stimulation. Classroom rhythm activities which employ the auditory and muscle senses might initiate temporal learning, followed by sports and games which would include the visual mode. The writers feel that it is not worthwhile to attempt such learning before age 7; between 7 and 8, children begin to respond readily to temporal teaching and begin the long, slow process of developing their capacity for the accurate and precise appreciation, perception, and comprehension of time.

Younger children overestimate time to a greater extent than older children and adults. Since this finding is independent of sense mode, and response requirements, as well as psychophysical method and other contextual or procedural factors (Axel, 1924; Smythe and Goldstone, 1957; Fraisse and Orsini, 1958), it may be considered a general statement regarding time perception by children.

The present study did not find sex differences in the accuracy of time perception. It is possible that the consistent finding of greater overestimation by females in older studies reflects attitudinal and role factors of a sociocultural origin. However, in this study girls were more variable than boys in visual time perceptions, a finding that cannot be interpreted without verification and further exploration.

Finally, the capacity to perceive time at the young ages depends in part upon the complexity of response requirements. With the fixed constant method and auditory durations used in this experiment, the 6½-year-old bright children were capable of rendering 2-category, more-less judgments. However, the more complex, 9-category procedure could not be accomplished much before age 8. From an educational point of view, initial teaching should focus upon a simple *greater-than—less-than* procedure, gradually approaching the standard unit, and finally requiring more refined numerical scales after age 9.

THE FUTURE

The past indicates considerable recognition by psychologists and educators of temporal conceptual behavior as a basic mental function worthy of independent investigation as an aspect of human development. With an eye upon the practical problems of temporal teaching involving conventional time scales and history, and the measurement of intelligence, research has been focused upon the designation of growth stages in temporal conceptualization. More recently attention has turned to the relationship between the development of aspects of time conception on the one hand, and personality and psychopathology on the other.

Psychophysical studies with adults have been particularly concerned with the importance of methodological factors in determining the outcome of research in time perception. No single measure of temporal perception reflects a general *time sense* and all measures must be interpreted in terms of specific stimulus characteristics, psychophysical methods, and response requirements. Knowledge of the differential effects of these factors upon the time perception of adults represents a major task of laboratory workers in this field; knowledge of the differential effects of these factors in relation to age levels and growth represents a major task of the developmental psychologist who studies children's time perception. Although there is an accumulating body of information about the psychophysics of adult temporal judgment, little has been done to explore sys-

482 SANFORD GOLDSTONE AND JOYCE LEVIS GOLDFARB

tematically the effects of age in relation to the conditions of stimulation and response. These factors must be considered in the study of children's time perception.

The present efforts to study the perception of time of children seem to be accompanying a growing awareness of the complexity of human temporal behavior. Experiments such as the one reported here highlight the importance of combining the conceptual-cognitive and the sensory-psychophysical in any systematic exploration of time perception. Much basic and practical information is available, for the taking, through the application of basic psychophysical methodology and the adaptation-level schema (Helson, 1959) to developmental research in temporal behavior.

The future will require tedious but fruitful investigation of additional stimulus and response circumstances relevant to the growth of time perception. Other psychophysical procedures may provide a scientific entrance into the temporal world of younger children. The methods of reproduction, comparison, fractionation, and adjustment will yield knowledge about the development of the perception of time under these specific conditions; work with varied stimulus patterns, different ranges of durations, and intramodal or cross-modal anchors is basic in the eventual understanding of the growth of the human calendar and clock. This understanding should be of considerable value to the educator who is responsible for teaching the use and comprehension of abstract time scales; this understanding should be of even greater value to the psychopathologist who is constantly confronted with the inadequately developed clocks of the personality disorders and mental deficiencies, or the profoundly slowed, speeded, or capricious timers that rule the psychoses, intoxications, and brain syndromes of adults and children.

These views emerged from a decade of research into the workings of the developing child-clock and the developed adult-clock. The writers began with an optimistic view of the human timer as a simple hourglass. The hourglass was soon replaced by the picture of a clock of matchless complexity involving the interaction of many timing systems, each of which had to be dissected and synthesized in relation to the others. After studying the time perceptions of almost 10,000 people including healthy children and adults, mentally ill persons, and subjects influenced by drugs and metabolic changes, using various stimulus arrangements, stimulus characteristics, and response requirements, it became evident that we were working with a biological clock with biochemical and physiological systems, and a psychological clock with sensory and conceptual systems. Each experiment increased the scope and complexity of the area, creating mysteries at a much more rapid rate than solutions. However, to the extent that these new mysteries are amenable to solution within the laboratory, the outlook is encouraging and exciting. Instruments, methods, and theoretical frameworks are readily available that should permit continued progress toward the understanding of the perception of time of children.

. . . *and* the temporal world of children must be a beautiful place within which to live. This world is lost to all but a few gifted and fortunate adults who have provided us with an allegorical glimpse into the magic of a child's *time* through the eyes of Alice, Pinocchio, Wendy, and Tyltyl and Mytyl.

" . . . the face of the clock winks its eyes and smiles genially while the door that contains the pendulum opens and releases the Hours, which, holding one another by the hand and laughing merrily, begin to dance to the sound of delicious music."—Maurice Maeterlinck

BIBLIOGRAPHY

Ames, L. B. (1946), The Development of the Sense of Time in the Young Child. *Journal of Genetic Psychology*, 68:97-125.

Axel, R. (1924), Estimation of Time. *Archives of Psychology*, 74:1-77.

Baer, P. E., Waukasch, D. C. & Goldstone, S. (1963), Time Judgment and Level of Aspiration. *Perceptual and Motor Skills*, 16:648.

Barndt, R. J. & Johnson, D. M. (1955), Time Orientation in Delinquents. *Journal of Abnormal and Social Psychology*, 51:343-345.

Behar, I. & Bevan, W. (1960), Analysis of the Prime Psychophysical Judgment. *Perceptual and Motor Skills*, 10:82.

—— & —— (1961), The Perceived Duration of Auditory and Visual Intervals: Cross-Modal Comparison and Interaction. *American Journal of Psychology*, 74:17-26.

Black, R. W. & Bevan, W. (1960), The Effect of Subliminal Shock upon the Judged Intensity of Weak Shock. *American Journal of Psychology*, 73:262-267.

Bolton, T. L. (1894), Rhythm. *American Journal of Psychology*, 6:145-238.

Bradley, N. C. (1947), The Growth of the Knowledge of Time in Children of School-Age. *British Journal of Psychology*, 38:67-78.

Bromberg, W. (1934), Marihuana Intoxication. *American Journal of Psychiatry*, 91:303-330.

——(1938), The Meaning of Time for Children. *American Journal of Orthopsychiatry*, 8:142-147.

Brower, J. F. & Brower, D. (1947), The Relation Between Temporal Judgment and Social Competence in the Feebleminded. *American Journal of Mental Deficiency*, 51:619-623.

Buck, J. N. (1946), The Time Appreciation Test. *Journal of Applied Psychology*, 30:388-398.

Court, S. R. A. (1920), Numbers, Time and Space in the First Five Years of a Child's Life. *Pedagogic Seminary*, 27:71-89.

Davids, A., Kidder, C. & Reich, M. (1962), Time Orientation in Male and Female Juvenile Delinquents. *Journal of Abnormal and Social Psychology*, 64:239-240.

—— & Parenti, A. N. (1958), Time Orientation and Interpersonal Relations of Emotionally Disturbed and Normal Children. *Journal of Abnormal and Social Psychology*, 57:299-305.

Decroly, O. & Degand, J. (1913), Observations Relatives au Développement de la Notion du Temps chez une Petite Fille. *Arch. de Psychol.*, 13:113-161.

Ellis, L. M., Ellis, R., Mandel, E. D., Schaeffer, M. S., Sommer, G. & Sommer, G. (1955), Time Orientation and Social Class: An Experimental Supplement. *Journal of Abnormal and Social Psychology*, 51:146-147.

Engle, T. L. & Hamlett, I. C. (1950), The Use of the Time Appreciation Test as a Screening or Supplementary Test for Mentally Deficient Patients. *American Journal of Mental Deficiency*, 54:521-524.

—— & —— (1952), Constancy of the Intelligence Quotient with Mentally Deficient Patients as Measured by the Time Appreciation Test. *American Journal of Mental Deficiency*, 56:775-776.

—— & —— (1954), Comparison of Mental Defectives and Normal Children in Ability to Handle Clock and Calendar Situations. *American Journal of Mental Deficiency*, 58:655-658.

Farrell, M. (1950), *Understanding of Time Relations of Five-, Six-, and Seven-Year-Old Children of High Intelligence Quotient*. Unpublished doctoral dissertation, New York University.

Fraisse, P. (1963), *The Psychology of Time*. New York: Harper and Row.

—— & Orsini, F. (1958), Etude Expérimentale des Conduites Temporelles. III. Etude Genétique de l'Estimation de la Durée. *Année Psychol.*, 58:1-6.

—— & Vautrey, P. (1952), La Perception de l'Espace, de la Vitesse et du Temps chez l'Enfant de cinq ans. II. Le Temps. *Enfance*, 5:102-119.

Frankenhaeuser, M. (1959), *Estimation of Time*. Stockholm: Almqvist and Wiksell.

Friedman, K. C. (1944a), Time Concepts of Elementary-School Children. *Elementary School Journal*, 44:337-342.

——(1944b), Time Concepts of Junior and Senior High School Pupils and of Adults. *School Review*, 52:233-238.

—— & Marti, V. A. (1945), A Time Comprehension Test. *Journal of Educational Research*, 39:62-68.

Gesell, A. & Ilg, F. L. (1943), *Infant and Child in the Culture of Today*. New York: Harper.

Gibson, E. J. & Olum, V. (1960), Experimental Methods of Studying Perception in Children. *Child Development*, Mussen, P. H. (Ed.). New York: Wiley.

Gilbert, J. A. (1894), Researches on the Mental and Physical Development of School-Children. *Studies from the Yale Psychology Laboratories*, 2:40-100.

Gilliland, A. R. & Humphreys, D. W. (1943), Age, Sex, Method, and Interval as Variables in Time Estimation. *Journal of Genetic Psychology*, 63:123-130.

Goldstone, S. (1962), Psychophysics, Reality, and Hallucinations. *Hallucinations*, West, L. J. (Ed.). New York: Grune and Stratton.

——, Boardman, W. K. & Lhamon, W. T. (1958a), Effect of Quinal Barbitone, Dextro-Amphetamine, and Placebo on Apparent Duration. *British Journal of Psychology*, 49:324-328.

——, —— & ——(1958b), Kinesthetic Cues in the Development of Time Concepts. *Journal of Genetic Psychology*, 93:185-190.

——, —— & ——(1959), Intersensory Comparisons of Temporal Judgments. *Journal of Experimental Psychology*, 57:243-248.

——, ——, ——, Fason, F. L. & Jernigan, C. (1963), Sociometric Status and Apparent Duration. *Journal of Social Psychology*, 61:303-310.

—— & Goldfarb, J. L. (1963), Judgment of Filled and Unfilled Durations: Intersensory Factors. *Perceptual and Motor Skills*, 17:763-774.

—— & ——(1964), Auditory and Visual Time Judgment. *Journal of General Psychology*, 70:369-387.

——, ——, Strong, J. & Russell, J. (1962), Replication: Effect of Subliminal Shock upon Judged Intensity of Weak Shock. *Perceptual and Motor Skills*, 14:222.

——, Jernigan, C., Lhamon, W. T. & Boardman, W. K. (1959), A Further Note on Intersensory Differences in Temporal Judgment. *Perceptual and Motor Skills*, 9:252.

Gothberg, L. C. (1949), The Mentally Defective Child's Understanding of Time. *American Journal of Mental Deficiency*, 53:441-455.

Greene, J. E. & Roberts, A. H. (1961), Time Orientation and Social Class: A Correction. *Journal of Abnormal and Social Psychology*, 62:141.

Gulliksen, H. (1927), The Influence of Occupation Upon the Perception of Time. *Journal of Experimental Psychology*, 10:52-59.

Harrison, M. L. (1934), The Nature and Development of Concepts of Time Among Young Children. *Elementary School Journal*, 34:507-514.

Helson, H. (1947), Adaptation-Level as a Frame of Reference for Prediction of Psychophysical Data. *American Journal of Psychology*, 60:1-29.

——(1959), Adaptation-Level Theory. *Psychology: A Study of a Science*, Vol. 1. Koch, S. (Ed.). New York: McGraw-Hill.

——(1964), Current Trends and Issues in Adaptation-Level Theory. *American Psychologist*, 19:26-38.

Hunter, W. S. (1912), The Delayed Reaction in Animals and Children. *Behavior Monographs*, 2:1-86.

Kleber, R. J., Lhamon, W. T. & Goldstone, S. (1963), Hyperthermia, Hyperthyroidism and Time Judgment. *Journal of Comparative and Physiological Psychology*, 56:362-365.

LeShan, L. L. (1952), Time Orientation and Social Class. *Journal of Abnormal and Social Psychology*, 47:589-592.

Levine, M., Spivack, G., Fuschillo, J. & Tavernier, A. (1959), Intelligence and Measures of Inhibition and Time Sense. *Journal of Clinical Psychology*, 15:224-226.

Lewis, M. M. (1937), The Beginning of Reference to Past and Future in a Child's Speech. *British Journal of Educational Psychology*, 7:39-56.

Lhamon, W. T., Goldstone, S. & Goldfarb, J. L. (in press), The Psychopathology of Time

Judgment. *The Psychopathology of Perception,* Hoch, P. H. & Zubin, J. (Eds.). New York: Grune and Stratton.

MacDougall, R. (1904), Sex Differences in the Sense of Time. *Science,* 19:707-708.

Nichols, H. (1891), The Psychology of Time. *American Journal of Psychology,* 4:60-112.

Oakden, E. C. & Sturt, M. (1922), The Development of the Knowledge of Time in Children. *British Journal of Psychology,* 12:309-336.

Piaget, J. (1954), *The Construction of Reality in the Child.* New York: Basic Books.

——(1955), The Development of Time Concepts in the Child. *Psychopathology of Childhood,* Hoch, P. H. & Zubin, J. (Eds.). New York: Grune & Stratton.

Pichot, P. (1949), The Effect of Rhythm and Functional Music on Mental Defectives. *Mental Health,* 9:6-10.

Pistor, F. (1939), Measuring the Time Concepts of Children. *Journal of Educational Research,* 33:293-300.

Probst, C. A. (1931), A General Information Test for Kindergarten Children. *Child Development,* 2:81-95.

Schecter, D. E., Symonds, M. & Bernstein, I. (1954), Development of the Concept of Time in Children. *Journal of Nervous and Mental Disease,* 121:301-310.

Siegman, A. W. (1961), The Relationship Between Future Time Perspective, Time Estimation, and Impulse Control in a Group of Young Offenders and in a Control Group. *Journal of Consulting Psychology,* 25:470-475.

Smythe, E. J. & Goldstone, S. (1957), The Time Sense: A Normative, Genetic Study of the Development of Time Perception. *Perceptual and Motor Skills,* 7:49-59.

Springer, D. V. (1951), Development of Concepts Related to the Clock as Shown in Young Children's Drawings. *Journal of Genetic Psychology,* 79:47-54.

——(1952), Development in Young Children of an Understanding of Time and the Clock. *Journal of Genetic Psychology,* 80:83-96.

Squire, C. R. (1901), A Genetic Study of Rhythm. *American Journal of Psychology,* 12:492-589.

Swindle, P. F. (1913), On the Inheritance of Rhythm. *American Journal of Psychology,* 24:180-203.

Terman, L. M. (1916), *The Measurement of Intelligence.* New York: Houghton Mifflin.

—— & Merrill, M. A. (1960), *Stanford-Binet Intelligence Scale.* Boston: Houghton Mifflin.

Vierordt, K. (1868), *Der Zeitsinn nach Versuchen.* Tübingen: H. Laupp.

Wallace, M. & Rabin, A. I. (1960), Temporal Experience. *Psychological Bulletin,* 57:213-236.

Weber, A. O. (1933), Estimation of Time. *Psychological Bulletin,* 30:233-252.

Wechsler, D. (1949), *Wechsler Intelligence Scale for Children (Manual).* New York: Psychological Corporation.

Woodrow, H. (1951), Time Perception. *Handbook of Experimental Psychology,* Stevens, S. (Ed.). New York: Wiley.

Yerkes, R. M. & Urban, F. M. (1906), Time-Estimation in its Relations to Sex, Age, and Physiological Rhythms. *Harvard Psychological Studies,* 2:405-430.

CHAPTER 17

Developmental Studies in Reflection and Analysis

JEROME KAGAN

The varied and murky phenomena implied by the word cognition range from the unrestrained racing of images and words to the more orderly, goal-directed sequence of mediated steps that are activated by the desire to solve a problem or acquire a new cognitive structure. This chapter restricts itself to the latter domain of cognitive events, specifically to the processes of stimulus classification and hypothesis selection. Three sequential operations typically occur when a person is confronted with a problem—an initial categorization of the relevant information, storage of the coded categorization, and, finally, the imposing of transformations (formal algorithms or mediational elaborations) upon the encoded data. The nature of the categorization, transformation, or elaborative mediation is governed, of course, by the nature of the problem. Students of cognitive development have generally assumed that the striking differences among the intellectual products of children of different ages or among children of the same age were attributable primarily to differences in the availability of vocabulary, possession of deductive or inductive rules, and mediational diversity. In essence, the superior intellectual performance of older, in comparison to younger, children has been ascribed to the

This research was supported in part by Grant M-4464 from the National Institute of Mental Health, United States Public Health Service.

greater knowledge repertoire of the older children. This supposition is intuitively attractive and empirically verified. It is not surprising, therefore, that psychologists have not seriously entertained the possibility that other factors may contribute to age and individual differences in the form and quality of cognitive products. Specifically, there has been a tendency to ignore the relevance of differences in two aspects of information processing—differences in the degree of stimulus analysis that precedes initial coding, and the degree of reflection attendant upon classification and hypothesis selection. It now appears that children and adults have clear preference hierarchies with respect to these two variables. The empirical work described in this essay is an inquiry into the significance of these two variables that are so intimately involved in the initial classification phase of problem solving, the phase during which external information is given its first symbolic coding, and the best possible solution sequence is selected.

To preview the heart of the chapter, we have discerned two stable dimensions upon which children and adults are distributed. The first is called reflection-impulsivity and describes the degree to which the child reflects upon alternative classifications of a stimulus or alternative solution hypotheses in situations in which many response possibilities (i.e., classifications or solution hypotheses) are available simultaneously. In these situations some children have a fast conceptual tempo; they impulsively report the first classification that occurs to them or carry out the first solution sequence that appears appropriate. The reflective children, on the other hand, characteristically delay before reporting a classification or carrying out a solution hypothesis. They actively consider the alternatives available to them and compare their validity. The reflective child behaves as if he cared that his first response be as close to correct as possible.

The reader is urged to withhold any premature tendency to stereotype the reflective child as excessively cautious or frightened, and the impulsive child as daring, divergent, or creative. The evidence to be presented does not allow such a glib evaluative template to be placed upon this class of behavior. We enjoin the reader to be reflective, and to withhold evaluation of the "goodness" of this predisposition until all the evidence has been considered.

A second dimension, called visual analysis, describes the child's tendency to analyze complex stimuli into their component parts. Some children fractionate a stimulus into small subunits; others label and react to a larger stimulus chunk. Analysis is relatively independent of reflection, and each of these variables contributes variance to a variety of cognitive products.

HISTORY

This line of inquiry was originally stimulated by an observation that piqued our curiosity because it did not agree with contemporary ideas concerning modal classification and conceptualization habits among normal subjects. Specifically, we found that when adult subjects were asked to select, from a large array of human figures, "a group of figures that went together on some conceptual basis," a sizable number grouped these paper figures on the basis of a shared objective element that was a component part of the total stimulus (e.g., "These three men go together because *they have no hair*," or "These people are all *holding an object in their hands*"). We called this class of concepts *analytic* because the basis for the grouping always involved a differentiated component of a set of diverse stimuli. What was more surprising, however, were the behavioral characteristics of the men who preferred this class of concepts to the more popular conceptual categories of abstract-inferential or thematic. The men who preferred analytic concepts were behaviorally more independent, more concerned with intellectual mastery, slightly more intelligent, more desirous of social recognition, and displayed more spontaneous sudomotor activity at rest than men who did not report many analytic concepts (Kagan, Moss, and Sigel, 1963). This cluster of attributes elicited cognitive dissonance, for we would have thought that ambitious, bright, independent men would prefer elegant, abstract concepts (i.e., happy soldiers, poverty-stricken people, creative artists) to the more stimulus-bound concepts classified as analytic.

Most of the work during the last four years has involved school-age children and has attempted to amplify our understanding of the significance of the analytic conceptual response, and to discover its immediate and historical antecedents. The results indicate that spontaneous analytic concepts are the product of the joint action of the two more fundamental variables of reflection and visual analysis.

There is, at present, more information on the stability and significance of the reflection-impulsivity dimension than there is on the variable of visual analysis. The data are persuasive in indicating that the child's tendency to reflect on alternative responses (in situations where several alternatives are available simultaneously) generalizes across varied problem situations, and shows remarkable intraindividual stability over periods ranging from 2 to 20 months. The operational definition of the reflection variable is response time in problem situations in which the subject is presented with a standard stimulus and an array containing the standard and 5 to 10 highly similar variants. The child is required to select the one stimulus in the array that is identical to the standard. There is typically a negative correlation between response time and number of errors (i.e., incorrect selections) in these problem situations. Children who delay before offering their first answer make fewer errors. The adjective "reflective" is most descriptive of the child who has long response times and few errors.

REFLECTION AND ANALYSIS: MEASUREMENT AND DEVELOPMENTAL CHANGES

This section describes the test situations used most frequently with children to assess the reflection and analysis variables, and the relations among the major variables derived from these tests.

Conceptual Style Test (CST). This test consists of 30 stimuli, each illustrating line drawings of three familiar objects. The child is asked to select two pictures that are alike in some way and to state the reason for his grouping. The items were constructed so that an analytic concept (i.e., a concept based on similarity in an objective element that was a differentiated component of only two of the stimuli) competed with an inferential-abstract or thematic concept. The analytic concept typically was a less obvious conceptual association to the stimulus card than an inferential or thematic concept. The two major variables derived from this test were the number of analytic concepts and the average response time to concept selection. Figure 1 illustrates 8 stimuli from this test.

The most common analytic concept to the watch-man-ruler item was, "The watch and ruler have numbers"; to the zebra-shirt-striped-shirt item, "These two have stripes"; to the house-match-pipe item, "The house and

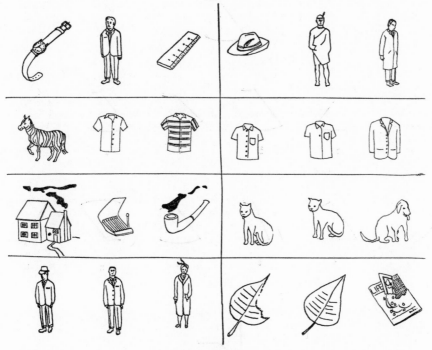

FIGURE 1

Sample Items from CST

pipe have smoke coming from them." These concepts were called analytic because the numbers, stripes, and smoke were objective, differentiated components of the total stimulus.

Delayed Recall of Designs (DRT). In this test a simple design was presented for 5 seconds. This standard was then removed, and after 15 seconds an array of 8, 9, or 10 stimuli was presented. The S selected the one design that was identical to the standard. The major variables derived were number of errors (a secondary distinction was made between major and minor errors), and average response time. Figure 2 illustrates two sample items.[1]

Matching Familiar Figures (MFF). This task was basically similar to

---

[1] These stimuli were designed originally by Eleanor J. Gibson and her colleagues at Cornell University and have been used by the Cornell group in a research project on reading.

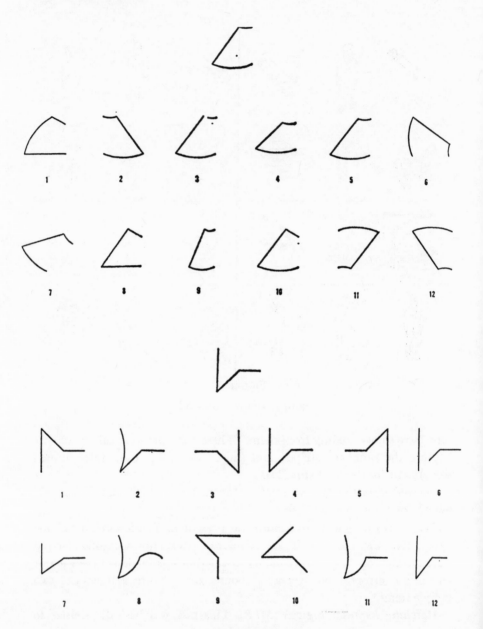

FIGURE 2

Sample Items from DRT

the DRT, but illustrated familiar objects rather than geometric designs and, unlike DRT, contained no memory requirement. The S was shown a picture (the standard) and 6 similar stimuli, only one of which was identical to the standard. The S selected the one stimulus that was identical to the standard. The standard and variations were always available to the subject. The major variables scored were number of errors, and average response time to first selection. Figure 3 illustrates two sample items.

Haptic-Visual Matching (HVM). In this task, the child first explored with his fingers a wooden form (approximately 3 inches square) to which he had no visual access. He was allowed an unlimited time to explore the form, and when he withdrew his hands, he was presented with a visual array of 5 stimuli, one of which illustrated the form he had explored haptically. The 20-item test contained geometric forms as well as familiar objects and yielded three variables: errors, response time, and palpation time (i.e., time S devoted to tactual exploration of the wooden form). Figure 4 illustrates two sample items.

Visual Analysis. This task assessed the degree to which the child attached a new label to component parts of a visual stimulus while associating the new label with the whole stimulus pattern. This task was regarded as a measure of a visually analytic attitude. The stimuli were designs that contained three distinct components: background, figural form, and element. The background component was a repetitive pattern; the figural component referred to the shape into which the discrete elements fell. That is, the elements were small, discrete geometric forms that traced out the figural pattern. Figure 5 illustrates a sample item.

The design in the upper left corner of the illustration was the stimulus to which the child associated a nonsense syllable. The semicircles were the background components, the triangles were the element components, and the "staircase" pattern was the figural component.

In the administration of this task, the child first learned 4 different nonsense syllables to each of 4 different complex designs. When the child reached criterion (8 consecutive correct trials) he was given a response-transfer task. In this transfer task he was shown separate illustrations of the background, element, and figural components, each without any perceptual support from the other two aspects of the original design. Thus, with reference to Figure 5, the child would be shown the semicircles, the

FIGURE 3

Sample Items from MFF

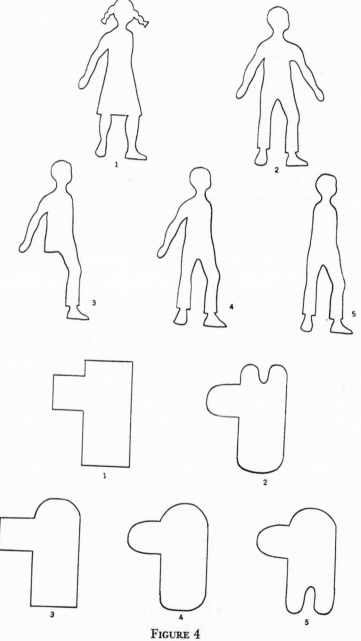

FIGURE 4

Sample Items from HVM

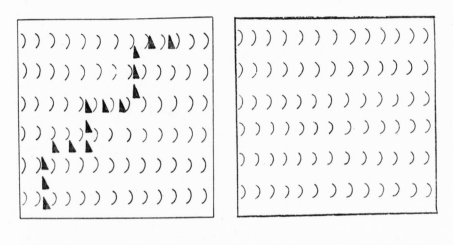

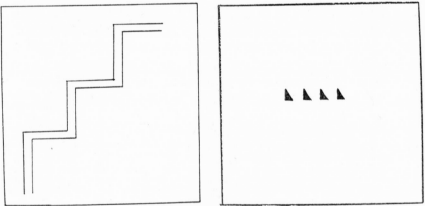

FIGURE 5

Sample Items from Visual Analysis Task

triangles, or the "staircase" and asked to apply the correct nonsense syllable. The transfer task contained two illustrations of each of the 3 components for each of the 4 designs (24 items in all). During the transfer
series the 4 nonsense syllables, which were printed on cards, were always
available to the child to insure that incorrect labeling of the separate components would not be due to forgetting of the newly acquired labels. After a short recess, a second set of 4 different designs was presented, and
the child was asked to perform a similar task. The major variables de-

rived from these tasks were number of ground, figural, and element components labeled correctly on each task.

The five tests described above have been administered to children in grades 1-4 from a variety of schools (a minimum of 50 boys and 50 girls at each grade level). Figures 6, 7, and 8 illustrate the changes in errors, response time, and level of visual analysis over these four grades.

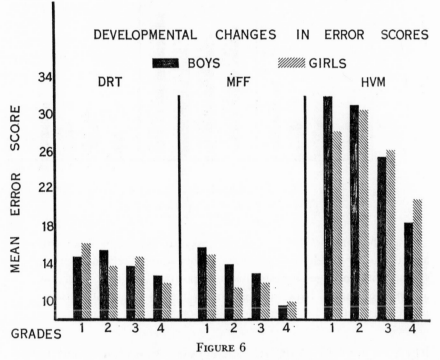

FIGURE 6

Developmental Changes in Error Scores

The developmental trends indicate that, with age, there is a linear increase in analytic concepts on the CST; a decrease in errors and an increase in response time on DRT, MFF, and HVM. The visual-analysis data are more complex, but provocative. There is a marked increase, with age, in correct labeling of the figural component, accompanied by poorer recognition of the background components. Moreover, with age, boys have higher recognition scores for ground and element components than do girls, suggesting that the boys are visually more analytic.

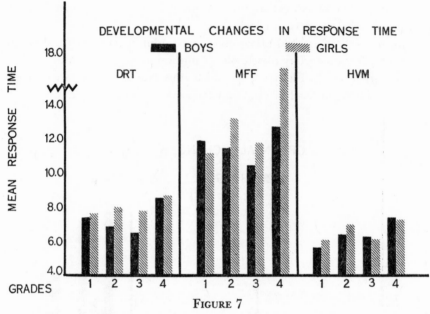

FIGURE 7

Developmental Changes in Response Time

Since the DRT, MFF, and HVM tasks are easier for older children, and the older children make fewer errors, the correlation between response time and age suggests that a disposition favoring reflection over alternative solution hypotheses grows stronger as the child matures. Supplementary data from other studies support this conclusion.

RELATIONSHIPS AMONG RESPONSE TIME, RECOGNITION ERRORS, AND VERBAL ABILITY

The three perceptual recognition tasks (DRT, MFF, and HVM) were similar in their psychological requirements, and all yielded the two variables of recognition errors and response time. In almost every sample studied there has been a negative relationship between frequency of recognition errors and average response time (i.e., the latency between presentation of the array of alternatives and the child's first selection), the coefficients typically ranging between —.30 and —.60. There was also a negative, but lower, relation between recognition errors and verbal ability

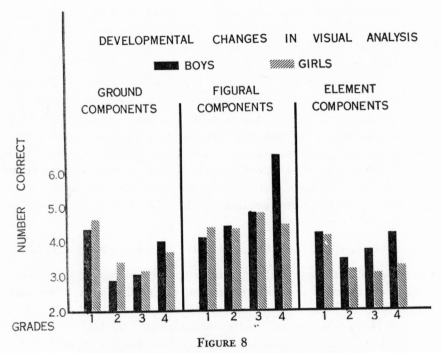

FIGURE 8

Developmental Changes in Visual Analysis

(mean score on three verbal subtests of the WISC: vocabulary, information, and similarities). The relation between errors and verbal ability was typically lower for boys than for girls. Response time to these tasks, however, was independent of verbal ability, the correlations typically falling below .20. Thus, the reflection-impulsivity dimension appeared to be relatively orthogonal to the traditional construct of verbal intelligence. The moderate relation between recognition errors and verbal skills, in girls especially, suggests that the basic cognitive processes implied by the phrase "high verbal intelligence" (e.g., richer verbal resources, greater self-confidence, problem-solving skills, stronger motivation to perform with competence) have some relevance for accuracy in perceptual recognition tasks among school-age children. Multiple correlation coefficients with recognition errors as the criterion and verbal ability and response time as the two predictors have yielded coefficients in the seventies.

There was remarkable consistency of recognition-error scores across the three tasks (coefficients typically ranged from .30 to .60 for different groups), and even higher intertask consistency for response times across the three tasks. Moreover, average response time on one task (DRT, for example) predicted not only response time but also errors on a second recognition task (MFF or HVM). Finally, both recognition errors and response time on DRT were highly stable over short (9 weeks) and long (17 months) periods. In sum, response time appears to be a critical conceptual variable; it shows generality over tasks, stability over time, and is relatively independent of verbal skills. The occurrence of recognition errors is a more complex variable, for it is related both to response time and to the multiple factors associated with verbal skills.

PSYCHOLOGICAL CORRELATES OF ANALYTIC CONCEPTS

Numerous studies early in the research attempted to explore the psychological correlates of analytic concepts on the CST (Kagan, Moss, and Sigel, 1963; Lee, Kagan, and Rabson, 1963; Kagan et al., in press). The early work on reflective and analytic attitudes used the CST because we were not yet aware of the role of the more fundamental variables of response time and visual analysis. We realized only recently that the production of analytic concepts is a joint function of these two variables. Analytic concepts are most likely to occur when the child pauses to consider alternative conceptual groupings on the CST and has a penchant for analyzing visual stimuli into smaller components. This section summarizes some salient characteristics of children who report a large number of analytic concepts, a response disposition that involves the reflection-impulsivity dimension.

It will be recalled that the frequency of analytic concepts increased with age and this disposition showed stability over a one-year period (r ranged from .47 to .73).

An impressionistically consistent cluster of characteristics was possessed by 7- to 10-year-old boys who reported many analytic concepts. These boys were less distractible in the classroom, less likely to display task-irrelevant gross motor behavior on the playground or in a restrictive laboratory setting, and less likely to report many incorrect solutions. They were more likely to become involved in sedentary tasks requiring long periods of concentration, more likely to prefer intellectual vocations that required motoric passivity (e.g., scientist, writer), and typically produced more complete drawings of objects. One of the most objective demonstrations of the relationship between motoric restlessness and analytic attitude was contained in the positive association between analytic concepts and regular, nonvariable respiratory rhythms during episodes of rest and episodes when the boy was attending to simple visual or auditory stimuli (Kagan and Rosman, in press). Moreover, boys with many analytic concepts demonstrated greater cardiac deceleration when asked to attend to external stimuli. Cardiac deceleration and regular respiration rates have been shown to be reliable indexes of the degree to which a person invests attention in external stimuli (Lacey, 1959). It appears, therefore, that young boys who prefer analytic concepts are more capable of sustained attention to visual inputs than less analytic youngsters.

Analytic concepts were positively associated with long response times to the CST and DRT and with correct labeling of the element components in the visual analysis task, but negatively related to recognition errors on the DRT. Moreover, children who produced large numbers of analytic concepts, in contrast to those with few concepts, manifested earlier acquisition (in a standard concept-formation task) of concepts requiring visual analysis. Examples of such concepts are "objects with a missing leg," and "objects with a black band around them." However, the analytic child did not show easier acquisition of concepts that did not require visual analysis (Lee, Kagan, and Rabson, 1963). Finally, there was a moderate relationship, among girls, between rejection of traditional sex-role interests and analytic concepts. There was no such relationship among boys.

Study of all the data gathered so far suggests the following interpretation of analytic concepts on the CST. To almost every item on the CST the most obvious way of grouping two pictures involves a thematic relation between the pair (see Figure 1). For example, the compelling associational tendency to the item illustrating a wrist watch, a man, and a ruler is to link the watch and the man functionally (e.g., the man wears the watch). The prepotent association to the house with smoke coming from the chimney, the matches, and the pipe is a functional link between the matches and pipe. If the child is to produce an analytic concept he must suppress these initially strong, culturally popular associations, and reflect on alternative groupings. He must display response uncertainty. If, in addition to the tendency to reflect over alternative responses, he also has a disposition favoring visual analysis, he is likely to produce an analytic concept. The capacity to delay in the service of reflection, together with a predisposition to visual analysis, appear to be the critical determinants of analytic concepts.

PSYCHOLOGICAL CORRELATES OF RECOGNITION ERRORS AND RESPONSE TIME

The early work with the CST led quickly to an appreciation of the variable of reflection in problems presenting multiple-answer possibilities. This realization prompted the investigations with the DRT, and later with the MFF and HVM tasks. It was noted earlier that recognition errors and response time on DRT were highly stable over time and were correlated with errors and response time on the MFF and HVM. Recognition errors and response times differ in their patterns of relations in several respects. First, response time was typically orthogonal to verbal ability for both sexes, whereas error scores usually had a low but significant negative correlation with verbal skills. Moreover, visual-analysis scores (i.e., correct labeling of figure and element components) were negatively related to recognition errors, but not to response time. Finally, response time usually manifested more consistent intertask generality and greater stability over time than the error scores. In one elaborate study, the average response time to 108 tachistoscopic exposures (6 different pictures) was positively related to response time on MFF (average $r = .40$). We have coined the phrase "conceptual tempo" to describe the connotative meaning we assign to the reflection variable. Some children consistently spew out the first reasonable hypothesis that occurs to them without pausing to reflect on its probable validity. Their strategy of problem solving has a shotgun character; the child fires a fusillade of answers in the hope that one will be correct, or, perhaps, because he needs immediate feedback from the environment to inform him of the quality of his performance. This child contrasts with one who characteristically pauses to consider the differential validity of several hypotheses. This child behaves as if he had a strong desire to be as correct as possible on his first attempt, and he is able to tolerate the ambiguity and tension inherent

in the period of silence that is an inevitable concomitant of response selection. Two qualifications are in order. These general statements about
the significance of long response times apply only to those problem situations in which all the alternatives are available simultaneously (either
in visual form as in the DRT, or as mental images).[2] These conclusions
do not apply to problems for which the child has no immediate solution
hypothesis (e.g., What is the cube root of 810?), or to situations in which
the child is so afraid of failure that he is reluctant to offer any answer.
We believe that our test situations minimize the latter possibility, but
are exploring ways of detecting the excessively fearful child who may
show long response times. We are currently working on a method to detect two small groups of subjects for whom the above generalizations
about response times may not always apply. There is, on the one hand, a
small group of bright subjects who can have relatively fast response times
on easy tasks (like DRT) but make few errors. These children do not
have fast response time on the MFF because this task is more difficult
than the DRT. It is crucial to use tasks that are of optimum difficulty for
each age level to guarantee that fast response times typically lead to high
error scores. A second anomalous group, also small, contains children
whose long response times result from extreme fear. These children may
have high error scores, for they are not reflecting upon alternative possibilities during the long delay. They fail to respond quickly because they
have no idea what to say and are afraid of offering any answer. It is likely
that elimination of children who show both excessively long response
times and high error scores will permit us to understand with greater clarity the antecedents of the reflection variable.

When recognition errors or response time on DRT or MFF were used
as indexes of the reflection-impulsivity dimension, an impressionistically
consistent set of relationships to other behaviors emerged. Impulsive children (i.e., high errors and fast response times) showed a marked increase
in errors of commission on a serial learning task (i.e., reporting words
not originally present on the list) after being told that their performance
on the serial learning task was inadequate. The more impulsive the child
prior to the learning task, the greater his increase in errors of commis-

---

[2] The assumption that response time is a sensitive index of response uncertainty was
well demonstrated in a recent study by Morin and Forrin (1963).

sion following this threat. A detailed summary of the study appears later.

There is much similarity between recognition errors on DRT, HVM, or MFF, and orthographic errors in reading. One might expect these two classes of errors to be related in young children learning to read. In a recently completed study of 130 first-grade children we found a strong positive relationship between errors in recognizing three-letter words (i. e., big, dog, cat, nap) and errors on DRT, MFF, or HVM. However, there was a minimal relationship between the accuracy of recognition of single letters and errors on DRT, MFF, or HVM. To illustrate, the correlation for 65 boys between HVM errors and word errors was .47 (p < .001); the correlation with single-letter errors was only .19. It appears that the tendency to read *log* for *dog, cat* for *pat*, or *eat* for *ear* is related to a disposition toward impulsive selection of hypotheses, even when the child has mastered the individual graphemes of his language.

It should be noted, finally, that recognition errors and response times are not influenced appreciably by the degree of acceptance or warmth displayed by an examiner. A carefully controlled experiment in which examiner rapport was manipulated (warm vs. impersonal, cold approach to the child) did not allow rejection of the null hypothesis (Kagan et al. in press).

THE SIGNIFICANCE OF VISUAL ANALYSIS

Systematic work on visual analysis has only recently begun, and less information is available on the significance of this variable. As noted earlier, there is a developmental shift in preferred perceptual focus. First-grade children initially recognize the solitary background components with greater accuracy than second-, third-, or fourth-grade children. The older children are more accurate in recognizing the solitary figural components. Second, accurate recognition of the element components was associated with early recognition of tachistoscopically presented scenes that contained incongruous elements. This is a reasonable association, for a disposition toward visual analysis should facilitate early recognition of pictures that contain one or two incongruous elements (e.g., person in a woman's dress smoking a pipe; living room with a tree). Finally, recognition of figural and element components was associated with low error scores on DRT, MFF, and HVM, and with analytic concepts on CST.

But these visual-analysis variables were orthogonal to response times and verbal skills.

A LONGITUDINAL STUDY OF REFLECTION-IMPULSIVITY

In order to communicate an appreciation for the details of this work, we shall summarize the major results from one continuing investigation that has followed a group of 60 boys and 53 girls for close to two years. Each child has been seen on six separate occasions. The children were seen first in the fall of 1961 when they were in grades 2 and 3 of a local public school, and were seen last in the spring of 1963, 20 months later, when they were in grades 3 and 4. The group consisted of 30 younger and 30 older boys; 28 younger and 25 older girls. Descriptions of the tests administered during each session, together with a rationale for their inclusion, appear below.

SESSION 1 (FALL OF 1961)
Design Recall Test: First administration (DRT I). The DRT was administered in the manner described earlier with mean response time and major and minor errors as the major variables coded. A major error was a selection of a variant that differed in orientation or in a basic component from the standard. In Figure 2, top design, Variants 1, 2, 3, 6, 7, 8, 10, 11, and 12 were major errors. A minor error was a selection of a variant that differed from the standard only in proportion. Variants 4 and 9 were minor errors. As might be expected, minor errors were more frequent than major errors.

Conceptual Style Test (CST). The CST was administered as described earlier, and the number of analytic concepts was the major variable coded.

SESSION 2 (WINTER OF 1961)
Design Recall Test: Second administration (DRT II). The DRT was administered as before (the order of the items was altered) and the variables scored were the same as above. The interval between the two administrations was 9 weeks.

SESSION 3 (SPRING OF 1962)
Tachistoscopic recognition task. Each S was seen for two one-hour sessions during which line drawings of incongruous objects or scenes were

presented tachistoscopically. The rationale for this kind of test session rested on the supposition that evidence for the reflection-impulsivity dimension would appear not only when the child had to choose among objectively present alternatives (as in DRT), but also when he had to select a response from a set of response alternatives that he had generated mentally. In order to maximize the effect of a reflective attitude, the pictures were constructed to contain incongruous elements, for reasons that follow. At the initially fast tachistoscopic exposures (18 milliseconds) the child could discern neither the exact nature of the stimulus nor the incongruities within the stimulus. His initial interpretation would be governed by the salient aspects of the external stimulus. With increasing exposure, however, the child would soon be forced to acknowledge the incongruous information. He would have to reconsider his earlier hypotheses, and accommodate to the incongruous aspects of the stimulus. It was anticipated that some children would reflect on the validity of their previous interpretations when they recognized the incongruity. Others were expected to describe the stimulus impulsively, giving minimal thought to the logical relation of their response to earlier interpretations or to the credibility of the interpretation about to be reported. The major prediction was that reflective children would show consistently longer response times in reporting their interpretations of the pictures.

Procedure. Each child (from grades 1 and 2) was seen for two one-hour sessions separated by one day. The child was first dark-adapted, and the examiner explained that he wanted to see how good the child's eyes were. Initially, the child was shown three simple stimuli (a cross, a triangle, and an E) in an ascending exposure series in order to determine his general visual acuity and to acclimate him to the apparatus.[3] If any child did not recognize these three designs at exposures of 175 milliseconds, he was discarded from the study. Three children were eliminated for this reason. Following the three practice items, the child was told that he would "see pictures that may seem silly to you" and was shown two incongruous pictures (a girl with rabbit ears, and a boy in a football uniform swinging at a football with a baseball bat) to insure that he had a set to expect pictures with incongruous elements. Three test items were

---

[3] The apparatus was a three-field electronic tachistoscope, using mercury-argon lamps, built by Charles J. Hlad, Jr., and designed by Charles W. Snyder of the Menninger Foundation.

then administered with a 5-minute recess after each item. When the child returned the next day he was shown a second set of 3 test pictures. The initial exposure for each of the 6 test pictures was 18 milliseconds, and each stimulus was presented for a minimum of 18 and a maximum of 30 exposures, the last exposure at 3 full seconds. For each exposure, response time (i.e., time from exposure of the stimulus to S's first significant verbalization) to the nearest 0.5 seconds was recorded by an observer. The reliability of this time score was obtained in sessions during which two observers independently recorded response times. The reliability coefficient (product-moment correlation) was .93.

The 3 test pictures in the first session were (1) a bird with a plane's fuselage, (2) a living room (couch, lamps, table) with a tree in the center of the room, and (3) a chicken's body with a pig's head. The 3 pictures on the second day were (1) a sweater with a book for the center, (2) a dog jumping on a boy, and (3) a person in a woman's dress with a man's head smoking a pipe.

SESSION 4 (FALL OF 1962)

Matching Familiar Figures (MFF). The MFF was administered in the manner described earlier; response time and errors were the major variables coded.

Visual Analysis. The visual-analysis task was administered as described earlier. The major variables coded were ground, figure, and element components correct.

SESSION 5 (WINTER OF 1962)

Design Recall Test: Third administration (DRT III). The DRT was administered the same way as described earlier; the interval between the first and the third administrations was 17 months.

Wechsler Intelligence Scale for Children: Verbal subscales. The similarities and information subtests of the WISC were administered to all children; the vocabulary scale had been administered one year earlier.

Serial learning. Each S was administered a serial-learning task with a threat imposed in the middle of the task. The major variable of interest in the present context was the occurrence of errors of commission (i.e., reporting words not present on the list). The expectation was that impulsive children would be more likely than reflective ones to offer errors of commission, hereafter called intrusion errors, throughout the serial-learning procedure, and especially following threat.

Procedure. Each child was asked to learn 4 different lists of familiar words, each list containing 12 items. He was given two trials with each list, the words presented in reverse order on the second trial. The lists were read by a male voice delivered by a tape recorder. The words on lists 1 and 4 were presented at the rate of one per second; the words on lists 2 and 3 were read at a rate of one item every 4 seconds. The major experimental variable was a threatening communication, administered after the two trials of the second list, informing the child that his performance was inadequate. The examiner said, "You are not remembering enough words. You should be remembering more, most children can remember more than you. If you can't do better you will not get the prize I showed you earlier. I will give you another chance to win the prize. Try and do better."

Lists 3 and 4 were then presented. The variable of primary concern was number of intrusion errors (i.e., reporting words not present on the list).

SESSION 6 (SPRING OF 1963)
Haptic-Visual Matching (HVM). Each child was administered the HVM as described earlier. The major variables were palpation time, response time, and errors to the 20 test items.

RESULTS
Stability of DRT performance. The first set of results summarizes the stability of errors and response time on DRT over the three administrations. Four correlations were computed for each bivariate comparison (i.e., there were 4 grade-sex groups; younger and older boys, younger and older girls). Table 1 contains the correlations between major, minor, and total errors, and mean response time on DRT I or II with the comparable variables on DRT III. It is to be noted that the relationship between performance on DRT I and II (these tests were separated by 9 weeks) was high. For major errors the correlations were .60 and .44 for boys; .56 and .84 for girls; for minor errors the correlations were .43 and .55 for boys; .28 and .59 for girls; for mean response time, .75 and .51 for boys; .54 and .71 for girls.

TABLE 1

Relation Between DRT Performances Over a 17-Month Interval

DRT III: Major Errors

	Boys		Girls	
	Grade 3	Grade 4	Grade 3	Grade 4
DRT I: Major errors	59 ****	36 **	56 ***	76 ****
Minor errors	62 ****	16	48 ***	65 ****
Total errors	54 ***	38 **	49 ***	65 ****
Response time	−27	−08	−29	51 ***
DRT III: Minor Errors				
DRT I: Major errors	10	−12	25	67 ****
Minor errors	25	24	52 **	69 ****
Total errors	12	03	28	66 ****
Response time	−24	10	02	−41 **
DRT III: Major Errors				
DRT II: Major errors	20	69 ****	41 **	74 ****
Minor errors	64 ****	38 **	36	56 ***
Total errors	46 ***	58 ***	47 ***	54 ***
Response time	−29	−17	−65 ****	−42 **
DRT III: Minor Errors				
DRT II: Major errors	12	11	07	72 ****
Minor errors	39 **	46 ***	25	46 **
Total errors	27	26	27	50 ***
Response time	−19	−10	−17	−40 **
DRT III: Total Errors				
DRT I: Major errors	47 ***	26	54 ***	76 ****
Minor errors	56 ****	24	61 ****	69 ****
Total errors	45 **	34	49 ***	68 ****
Response time	−30	−02	−20	−50 ***
DRT III: Response Time				
DRT I: Major errors	−32	25	−09	−31
Minor errors	−26	−14	−20	−31
Total errors	−25	17	−08	−32
Response time	33	38 **	23	68 ****
DRT III: Total Errors				
DRT II: Major errors	20	64 ****	33	76 ****
Minor errors	64 ****	52 ***	38 **	55 ***
Total errors	45 **	61 ****	48 ***	55 ***
Response time	−29	−19	−56 ***	−43 **
DRT III: Response Time				
DRT II: Major errors	−24	06	−15	−27
Minor errors	−48 ***	−17	−13	−41 **
Total errors	−45 **	02	−18	−36
Response time	20	41 **	69 ****	63 ****

** p < .05; two tails
*** p < .01; two tails
**** p < .001; two tails

The results indicate remarkable stability for these variables over three administrations. Total errors on DRT I and DRT II were each positively correlated with total errors on DRT III. The coefficients ranged from .34 to .68, with 7 of the 8 coefficients significant at the .05 level or better. Major errors manifested slightly better stability than minor errors.

Response time also displayed excellent stability, the relation being better for girls than for boys, and best for grade-4 girls ($r = .68$ for DRT I and .63 for DRT II; $p < .001$). As expected, there were strong negative relationships between response time and errors on each test. It is important to note, however, that response time on DRT I or DRT II was related to major errors on DRT III (average $r = -.30$, $p < .01$; $-.40$, $p < .001$ respectively). Thus, not only were errors and response time each stable over periods of 12 and 17 months, but fast response times on the early tests predicted high error scores on DRT III over one year later. This circle of relations increases our confidence in the enduring quality of a reflective or impulsive conceptual tempo.

Relations among variables from the 6 sessions. The tests administered over the 20-month interval yielded a number of variables, 15 of which were intercorrelated for this presentation. The variables from DRT II and III and visual analysis task II were not included in this analysis. The 15 variables studied were:

1. CST: Number of analytic responses.
2-4. DRT I: Major errors, minor errors, and mean response time.
5. Mean response time for trials 1-18 across 6 tachistoscopically presented scenes.
6-7. MFF: Errors and mean response time.
8-10. Visual analysis task I: Ground, figural, and element components correct.
11. Serial learning: Mean number of intrusion errors across 4 lists.
12-14. HVM: Mean palpation time, mean response time, and total errors.
15. WISC: Mean scale score for vocabulary, information, and similarities subtests.

Table 2 contains the intercorrelations among these 15 variables for the 4 grade-sex groups.

TABLE 2

Intercorrelations among Conceptual Variables (Older Ss)

	1	2	3	4	5	6	7	8	9	10	11	12	13	14	15
1. CST: Analytic response	—	-44	02	32	-03	-04	-05	16	08	10	-33	00	00	-23	30
2. DRT I: Major errors	-32	—	08	-11	28	-02	31	-26	01	-21	14	17	22	05	-38
3. DRT I: Minor errors	-29	68	—	-21	05	08	09	12	02	06	40	07	-04	09	-21
4. DRT I: Response time	16	-51	-49	—	04	-41	42	-23	-08	-07	-25	07	38	-07	08
5. Tachistoscopic response time	46	-29	-17	17	—	04	07	12	12	06	07	19	23	-27	-01
6. MFF: Errors	-18	35	59	-43	-48	—	-65	05	-06	-25	40	-16	-37	31	10
7. MFF: Response time	30	-33	-34	56	40	-60	—	-09	-12	09	-22	21	47	-14	-13
8. Visual analysis: Ground correct	04	-21	-07	14	08	-06	05	—	59	44	-04	19	-07	-15	09
9. Visual analysis: Figure correct	29	-28	-18	-03	40	-14	13	37	—	53	-12	-04	-34	-20	05
10. Visual analysis: Element correct	45	-41	-11	12	27	-11	36	00	30	—	26	-11	-18	-13	-06
11. Serial learning: Intrusion errors	-23	54	37	-61	-37	26	-43	-19	-14	-12	—	24	-03	31	-10
12. HVM: Palpation time	02	-18	-09	24	31	-17	58	-10	-07	18	-50	—	60	-24	12
13. HVM: Response time	20	-34	-23	59	39	-34	79	-20	-07	29	-56	82	—	-13	-01
14. HVM: Errors	-20	57	46	-35	-57	49	-49	-02	-05	-23	55	-68	-67	—	-43
15. WISC: Verbal skills	06	-47	-37	07	34	-40	-03	21	30	17	01	-07	-10	-43	—

Older boys to right and above diagonal (N = 30)
Older girls to left and below diagonal (N = 25)
For N = 30, r of .35 necessary for p < .05; two tailed
            r of .45 necessary for p < .01; two tailed
For N = 25, r of .39 necessary for p < .05; two tailed
            r of .50 necessary for p < .01; two tailed

TABLE 2 (Continued)

Intercorrelations among Conceptual Variables (Younger Ss)

	1	2	3	4	5	6	7	8	9	10	11	12	13	14	15
1. CST: Analytic response	—	-26	-17	-05	13	-28	-04	-23	01	44	-16	06	-02	-29	23
2. DRT I: Major errors	-52	—	78	-39	-44	59	-50	-08	-36	-35	53	-08	-33	37	-28
3. DRT I: Minor errors	-36	78	—	-29	-32	45	-42	-15	-21	-21	60	05	-13	28	-19
4. DRT I: Response time	47	-43	-46	—	14	-15	26	-01	13	05	00	19	30	-05	03
5. Tachistoscopic response time	08	-02	17	15	—	-58	64	-15	06	27	-39	21	36	-31	60
6. MFF: Errors	-21	09	-09	00	-25	—	-66	08	-28	-39	46	-39	-41	39	-53
7. MFF: Response time	29	-27	-21	48	40	-47	—	-10	29	17	-21	56	65	-43	36
8. Visual analysis: Ground correct	-24	-25	-20	-11	-32	26	-15	—	30	13	-09	-35	-25	02	-39
9. Visual analysis: Figure correct	-02	-15	-04	02	45	-19	45	29	—	49	-26	10	08	-18	-14
10. Visual analysis: Element correct	-13	02	06	-09	-32	-13	-13	13	-35	—	-07	-04	-07	-23	16
11. Serial learning: Intrusion errors	-34	33	15	-27	-03	-18	04	-25	-10	23	—	23	00	14	-35
12. HVM: Palpation time	19	-33	-15	38	43	-37	52	-02	11	-04	00	—	77	-45	35
13. HVM: Response time	37	-30	-13	35	24	-43	41	-26	-05	-09	04	75	—	-46	40
14. HVM: Errors	-53	39	-15	-31	-19	49	-38	-08	-29	03	20	-62	-62	—	-46
15. WISC: Verbal skills	34	-44	-43	14	06	-28	22	14	14	09	-08	33	24	-35	—

Younger boys to right and above diagonal (N = 30)
Younger girls to left and below diagonal (N = 28)
For N = 30, r of .35 necessary for p < .05; two tailed
         r of .45 necessary for p < .01; two tailed
For N = 28, r of .37 necessary for p < .05; two tailed
         r of .47 necessary for p < .01; two tailed

The data indicate remarkable intertask consistency for response time and errors over this 20-month period. The generality and stability of these variables are illustrated by the correlations between major errors on DRT I and errors on HVM administered nearly 2 years later ($r = .37$, .05 for boys; .39 and .57 for girls; $p < .05$ for 3 of the 4 groups). Response time showed comparable continuity for the correlations relating response time on DRT and HVM were .30, .38, .35, .59 ($p < .05$ for 3 of the 4 groups).

As usual, there was greater intertask generality for response time than for error scores. The correlations among the 3 major response-time variables (DRT, MFF, and HVM) for each of the 4 groups ranged from .26 to .79 with a median coefficient of .45, and 10 of the 12 coefficients significant at $p < .05$ or better. Moreover, the relation between response times and verbal ability was low (r ranged from $-.13$ to $+ .40$ with a median coefficient of $+.08$). The generality of errors was also high; the intercorrelations among error scores ranged from $-.02$ to $+ .59$, with a median coefficient of $+.38$ and 7 of the 12 coefficients significant at $p < .05$ or better. As with DRT, the generality of a reflective versus impulsive conceptual tempo was supported by the relationship between response time on one task and errors on a second task. For example, MFF response time predicted DRT major errors ($r = -.50$, .31, $-.27$, $-.33$), and HVM errors ($r = -.43$, $-.14$, $-.38$, $-.49$). Similarly, response time on HVM predicted errors on MFF ($r = -.41$, $-.37$, $-.43$, $-.34$).

Recognition errors on DRT, MFF, and HVM were moderately related to verbal ability (r ranged from $-.53$ to $+.10$ with a median coefficient of $-.42$, and 9 of the 12 coefficients significant at $p < .05$ or better). As expected, there was a consistently high negative relationship between response time and errors for each recognition task. The coefficients ranged from $-.13$ to $-.67$, with a median r of $-.49$, and 10 of the 12 coefficients significant at .05 or better. Recognition errors appear to be a joint function of response time and verbal skills, and multiple correlation coefficients were computed using MFF errors as the criterion and response time and verbal skills as predictors. The multiple coefficients were higher than each of the individual coefficients for the younger boys and older girls (r in the .70's), but were not higher than the response-time correlation alone for the older boys and younger girls.

For HVM, palpation time was as good a predictor of errors as response time, and these two measures were highly related (r = .75, .60, .75, .82). Children who spent a long time in tactual exploration of the wooden form also delayed a long time before selecting one of the visual alternatives.

The tendency to reflect over interpretations of the tachistoscopic scenes was also related to reflection on the 3 major tasks. The average response time to all 6 incongruous pictures was used in the analysis because there were high positive correlations among the response times to all 6 pictures. The average of the 15 correlations across the 6 pictures was .56. The mean response time for all 6 pictures for trials 1-18 was put into standard score form and correlated with the other conceptual variables. The best relationship held for response time to MFF (average r = .40, p < .001). Long response times to the tachistoscopic scenes were also correlated with long response times on HVM (average r = .31; p < .01). The correlations with DRT response time were lower, but in the expected direction. Response time to the tachistoscopic scenes was, as might be expected, negatively related to MFF errors (average r = −.34; p < .01) and HVM errors (average r = −.37; p < .001).

The moderately positive relation between verbal skills and tachistoscopic response time for younger boys and older girls was somewhat of a surprise on two counts. First, the magnitude of the relation was higher than normal, for response times were typically orthogonal to verbal resources. Second, one might assume that verbal resources would facilitate rapid conceptualizations of the tachistoscopically presented stimuli, whereas an inadequate vocabulary would be associated with a more halting performance. One tentative interpretation of this relation is that the verbally precocious child may generate more response possibilities, and, if he has a penchant for reflection, will require more time to select the most reasonable description. In the DRT, MFF, or HVM, by contrast, all the response possibilities are given and equal for all children. Verbal facility is not a factor in hypothesis generation in these tasks. This interpretation is supported by the fact that the positive association between tachistoscopic response time and verbal skills held only for the younger boys and older girls, groups for whom there was a low to moderate relation between verbal skills and reflection, but did not hold for the older boys and younger girls, groups for whom indexes of reflection and verbal resources were independent.

One implication of this discussion is that older children, in contrast to third-graders, should generate more hypotheses to the tachistoscopic exposures. Since reflection appears to increase with age (see Figure 7), older subjects should pause to consider the response possibilities they have generated and should have longer tachistoscopic response times. This prediction is based on the two assumptions that variety of hypothesis generation and a reflective disposition increase with age.

Response-time data on 40 subjects in the eighth grade (age 13 to 14) support the above prediction. Twenty boys and 20 girls were tested individually in the same tachistoscopic recognition task used with the younger group. The only difference in procedure was that the older subjects were seen for one 90-minute session rather than for two shorter sessions. The procedure and stimuli were identical in all other respects, except that the examiner and timekeeper were different from those used with the younger subjects, and had no idea of the average response times produced by the younger children.

The average response time for these older subjects was generally about 0.5 seconds longer than the times for the younger children. The differences between the older and younger subjects were significant for pictures 2, 3, 5, and 6 (p < .05 for each). When the mean response time across all 6 pictures was computed, the difference between the older and younger subjects bordered on statistical significance (p = .08). The longer response times for the older subjects violate the naïve assumption that greater verbal facility and more sophisticated problem-solving techniques should be associated with faster conceptualizations of the incongruous stimuli. Rather, these data are persuasive in suggesting that reflection over alternative hypotheses is a disposition that gains strength as the child develops. Reflection in the service of hypothesis evaluation may be a critical disposition to assess in investigations of mental processes. Group-administered tests of mental ability typically do not obtain response-time information, and it seems likely that such test procedures neglect a significant component of intellectual functioning. The claim that factor-analytic investigations of group-administered tests can yield the fundamental components of intellect may be unwarranted, for a reflective attitude cannot easily emerge as a factor if response-time variables are not in the original correlation matrix.

Relation between intrusion errors and conceptual variables. The distribution of intrusion errors on each of the four lists was skewed toward low scores. Each distribution was divided at the median for each group separately, and phi coefficients assessed the consistency of intrusion errors across all 4 lists. There was moderate interlist consistency and intrusion errors were generally independent of verbal ability; the average correlation between verbal skills and intrusion errors was -.05 for boys and +.05 for girls. Since the relationships between intrusion errors and other conceptual variables were similar for each of the 4 lists, the mean number of intrusion errors across all 4 lists was computed. This variable yielded better relationships with the reflection-impulsivity dimension and appears as Variable 11 in Table 2. Intrusion errors were positively associated with major errors on DRT (average $r = .40$; $p < .001$) and with MFF errors (average $r = .25$; $p < .05$), but negatively related to DRT response time (average $r = -.30$; $p < .01$) and MFF response time (average $r = -.21$; $p < .05$). The data suggest that the reporting of words not present on the original list was characteristic of the child whose performance on DRT or MFF we have called impulsive. This finding is reasonable, for it is assumed that impulsive children fail to reflect upon the probable accuracy of their verbal products and they would fail to ask themselves whether a word they were about to report had been presented. The minimal relation between intrusion errors and verbal skills supports the postulated independence of reflection-impulsivity and verbal resources.

The change in intrusion errors following the threat was also related to reflection-impulsivity. In this analysis the number of intrusion errors on trial 1 of list 3 was subtracted from the number of intrusion errors on trial 1 of list 2 (a constant of 10 was added to avoid negative scores). Large increases in intrusion errors following threat were characteristic of those children who were impulsive on the DRT a year earlier. The average correlations between errors or response time on the first administration of the DRT and amount of increase in intrusion errors were .23 ($p < .05$) and $-.26$ ($p < .01$) respectively. The more impulsive the child (as measured by DRT response time), the greater his tendency to manifest an increase in intrusion errors following a threat to his intellectual competence. Since frequency of intrusion errors *prior to threat* was associated with impulsive performance on the DRT, it appears that the threat made the impulsive children more impulsive. It should be noted that there was no relation between impulsivity on the DRT and change in recall score following threat (average $r = -.15$). Impulsive children, therefore, did not perform poorly with respect to the specific task required of them (i.e., remember words). The threat affected not the quality of their performance, as defined by the examiner, but influenced their preferred strategy of problem solution.

The significance of visual analysis. The tendency to recognize the element components on the first transfer task was positively related to analytic concepts on the CST (average $r = .22$; $p < .05$), and negatively related to DRT major errors (average $r = -.23$; $p < .05$). Accurate recognition of the elements, however, was independent of response time on DRT or MFF, and of verbal skills (average $r = .00$, $.13$, and $.09$ respectively).

Visual analysis and reflection-impulsivity appear to be independent determinants of the more complex variables of recognition errors and analytic concepts. To illustrate, the multiple correlation coefficient with DRT errors as the criterion and response time and element components as predictors yielded multiple correlations of $.52$ for younger boys (in contrast to coefficients of $-.39$ and $-.35$ relating the individual predictors with criterion), and $.62$ for older girls (in contrast to correlations of $-.41$ and $-.51$ for the individual predictors).

Both the response-time and visual-analysis scores were independent of verbal facility, and these data argue strongly for the postulation of two fundamental conceptual response dispositions that exert a major influence on tasks involving perceptual discriminations. Much of the child's academic activity in grades 1-4 involves accurate perceptual classifications. The child must discriminate *bag* from *bug, ear* from *eat* when he is learning to read. The second- and third-grader must note the difference between *99* and *69*, between *71* and *17*, between *x* and $+$. It is not unreasonable to conclude that, aside from the acknowledged role of verbal skills, the child's positions on the reflection and visual-analysis dimensions are of considerable relevance for the mastery of basic language and numerical skills in the early school years.

DISCUSSION AND SUMMARY

The accumulated evidence from a dozen investigations of children in the first four grades is remarkably univocal in its message. Reflection over alternative solution possibilities and visual analysis are fundamental cognitive dispositions that are independent of each other and of the richness of the child's language repertoire. Moreover, each of these dimensions influences the occurrence of the more complex cognitive products of analytic conceptual groupings (on CST) and recognition errors (on DRT, MFF, or HVM). The complementary role of visual analysis and reflection in predicting infrequent recognition errors is reasonable, for in order to select the correct variant on the first attempt one must analyze each stimulus into its components, inhibit the immediate reporting of initial hypotheses, and evaluate alternative solution possibilities. A reflective disposition displays a stability over time and a generality across tasks that is unusual for psychological attributes, and tempts one to conclude that this response tendency must be a basic component of the individual's behavioral organization.

The points of contact between these two dispositions and basic theory and research in intellectual processes are not yet clear. Witkin and his colleagues (1962) have been concerned with the dimension of field independence and have used performance on the Embedded Figures and Spatial Orientation Tests as the operational indexes of this variable. We have found no strong relation between reflection and solution time on Witkin's version of the Embedded Figures Test (Kagan et al., in press). But reflective children offer far fewer incorrect solution hypotheses prior to achieving solution. We have not assessed the relation between visual analysis and field independence, but expect it to be moderately positive.

Basic theory in intellectual development has been concerned mainly with the growth of mediational systems and the acquisition of operations (or transformation rules) that allow more complex deductive and inductive reasoning. Both European and American investigators have been fascinated by the behavior of cognitive structures, how they are born, grow, and die. They have been indifferent to those processes that mark the beginning and end of a problem-solving sequence, namely, the initial processing of external information and the characteristics of the response classes involved in the overt reporting of a completed cognitive product. The growing interest in information processing in both adult and child should amplify our understanding of these aspects of mental activity.

ANTECEDENTS OF REFLECTION-IMPULSIVITY

A search for the historical and immediate antecedents of a reflective versus impulsive attitude should consider at least three possibilities, none of which is mutually exclusive of the others. These three are constitutional predispositions, involvement in the task, and anxiety over task competence. There is some evidence favoring the idea that excessive motor restlessness and distractibility at age 8 have their anlage in congenital deficit resulting from minimal and subtle brain damage during the perinatal or early postnatal period. Since the extremely impulsive boys in our studies were also excessively restless and distractible, it is possible that these children suffered subtle cerebral damage early in life. It is possible, of course, that biological variables, unrelated to central nervous system deficit, predispose some infants and preschool children to hyperactivity and impulsive reactions. Schaefer and Bayley (1963) have found that extremely active 1-year-old infants were minimally attentive to intellectual problems at 5 and 6 years of age. The Fels longitudinal study has yielded similar results. Ratings of hyperkinesis during ages 3 to 6 were inversely correlated with ratings of involvement in intellectual activity during adolescence and adulthood (Kagan and Moss, 1962). Moreover, ratings of hyperactivity during ages 4 through 8 were negatively related to analytic concepts among 10-year-old boys (Kagan et al. in press). This relationship suggests that signs prognostic of the development of an impulsive conceptual attitude may be manifest early in development.

In sum, there are tantalizing scraps of evidence from several laboratories that lend some credibility to the idea that children who are extremely active during the opening years of development are more likely to be conceptually impulsive during the school years than those who are motorically more quiescent. We are now conducting an intensive longitudinal study of a group of infants who were seen first at 8 weeks of age and who are 13 months old at the time of this writing. Preliminary analyses indicate marked stability of the attributes of *motor activity and duration of sustained attention to external stimuli* over this 48-week period, with the activity and attention variables inversely correlated with each other.

A second class of factors that might influence reflection deals with the degree of involvement in the task. A child with high standards of performance should be more likely to reflect on alternative hypotheses and more likely to want his first answer to be correct than a child who is minimally concerned with the quality of his performance. We have found that girls who rejected traditional feminine interests were more reflective than girls with traditional feminine standards. There is a positive relation, among girls, between degree of rejection of sex-typed activities and involvement in intellectual mastery (Kagan and Moss, 1962), and this relation furnishes indirect evidence for the proposition that reflective girls may have been more highly involved in our tasks.

A final hypothesis deals with the child's anxiety over his ability to perform adequately in tasks like DRT or MFF. Let us assume that most children have a desire to do well on these tests and to convince the examiner that they are able to perform adequately. Let us look closely at the psychology of the interpersonal situation the moment the examiner presents the problem to the child. The child who is anxious about his ability to perform adequately should be less able to tolerate the period of silence that must occur if he is to reflect over various hypotheses. He may fear that his failure to respond immediately will be interpreted as an indication of his inadequacy and he may be predisposed to offer an answer quickly. The confident child, on the other hand, should be more able to tolerate the delay between presentation of the problem and the offering of a solution. The fact that children show increased response times with age suggests that reflection gains strength with development. It is difficult to determine, however, whether this increased penchant for reflection is the product of greater confidence, a stronger need to avoid reporting incorrect answers, the ability to generate more solution possibilities, or, perhaps, variables we have not yet recognized.

Our current belief, held with only moderate confidence, is that a child's position on the reflection-impulsivity dimension can be the result of either constitutional or experiential factors, with the former most relevant for children at the extreme end of the impulsivity continuum.

METHODOLOGICAL IMPLICATIONS
Responses to all psychological tests are, first of all, cognitive responses. The interpretation of an inkblot, the telling of a story to a TAT picture, or the selection of an answer on a multiple-choice test all involve the selection of one best response from a set of alternatives. The reflection-impulsivity dimension should affect the manner in which external information is classified and organized, and the content and form of the final response. It is reasonable to expect that production of motivational content variables on selected "personality tests" (e.g., aggressive or sexual imagery to inkblots or pictures) may be the partial result of tendencies

toward impulsivity or reflection. For example, there is a marked association between the production of inkblot imagery that would be coded as aggressive or sexual in content and the production of a response containing movement components. Movement responses characteristically require longer response times than nonmovement responses and typically require analysis of a component of the total stimulus. It is likely, therefore, that reflective children will produce more movement responses and, by so doing, also report a percept that has motivational content. It is reasonable to defend the idea that a penchant for reflection is one critical determinant of an "aggressive" inkblot interpretation.

A second implication for method concerns certain factor-analytic approaches to understanding intellectual functioning. Group-administered tests of mental abilities do not obtain response-time data and, therefore, cannot evaluate the reflection-impulsivity variable. If this disposition is as critical as these data suggest, it is unwarranted to assume that one can discover the basic factors of mental activity through factor analysis of these scores.

IMPLICATIONS FOR PROBLEM SOLVING

A second set of implications concerns problem-solving efficiency and the gradual establishing of permanent attitudes toward problem solving. In problems with alternate routes to solution, reflection and evaluation of the validity of solution sequences are critical for eventual success. The child who does not reflect upon the probable validity of alternative-solution sequences is likely to follow through on the first idea that occurs to him. This strategy is more likely to end up in failure than one which involves reflection. The impulsive child who reaches a cul-de-sac in a problem-solving sequence, and recognizes that he has not solved the problem, is likely to become more anxious than he was initially. As a result of the increased anxiety his selection of a second solution path is likely to be impaired and the probability of success attenuated. This maladaptive cycle may become entrenched with time, and after 4 or 5 years of experiencing the sequence: problem $\longrightarrow$ impulsive selection of invalid solution $\longrightarrow$ failure $\longrightarrow$ anxiety $\longrightarrow$ selection of second solution $\longrightarrow$ failure, etc., the child may gradually withdraw from problem situations, and apathy and hostility may become characteristic reactions toward intellectual situations.

We do not wish to paint the reflective child as necessarily the better or brighter child. It is likely that efficient learning and creative problem solving will occasionally be facilitated by a reflective approach, occasionally by an impulsive approach. Indeed, a recent study (Lee, Kagan, and Rabson, 1963) demonstrated this last point clearly. Some of the academic contents children must master require reflection and analysis, for instance, mathematics and the physical sciences. But maximal productiveness and mastery of principles in aspects of the arts, social studies, and humanities may be hampered by an excessively reflective orientation. New pedagogical procedures should acknowledge this interaction between the preferred strategy of the learner and the material to be acquired and tailor the presentation of materials to the psychological requirements of the task and the cognitive predispositions of the learner.

BIBLIOGRAPHY

Kagan, J. & Moss, H. A. (1962), *Birth to Maturity: A Study in Psychological Development.* New York: John Wiley.

——, —— & Sigel, I. E. (1963), Psychological Significance of Styles of Conceptualization in Basic Cognitive Processes in Children. *Monographs of the Society for Research in Child Development,* Wright, J. C. & Kagan, J. (Eds.), 28(2).

—— & Rosman, B. L. (in press), Autonomic Correlates of Attention and an Analytic Attitude. *Journal of Experimental Child Psychology.*

——, ——, Day, D., Albert, J. & Phillips, W. (in press), Information Processing in the Child. *Psychological Monographs.*

Lacey, J. I. (1959), Psychophysiological Approaches to the Evaluation of Psychotherapeutic Process and Outcome. *Research in Psycho-Therapy,* Rubenstein, E. A. & Parloff, M. B. (Eds.), pp. 160-208. Washington, D. C.: National Publishing Company.

Lee, C. L., Kagan, J. & Rabson, A. (1963), The Influence of a Preference for Analytic Categorization upon Concept Acquisition. *Child Development,* 34:433-442.

Morin, R. E. & Forrin, B. (1963), Response Equivocation and Reaction Time. *Journal of Experimental Psychology,* 66:30-36.

Schaefer, E. A. & Bayley, N. (1963), Maternal Behavior, Child Behavior, and Their Intercorrelations from Infancy Through Adolescence. *Monographs of the Society for Research in Child Development,* 28(3).

Witkin, H. A., Dyk, R. B., Faterson, H. F., Goodenough, D. R. & Karp, S. A. (1962), *Psychological Differentiation.* New York: John Wiley.

Indices

Name Index

Subject Index

546 SUBJECT INDEX